The Adolescent

The Adolescent
Development, Relationships, and Culture

third edition

F. Philip Rice
University of Maine

Allyn and Bacon, Inc.
Boston   London   Sydney   Toronto

Managing Editor: Steve Mathews
Cover Designer: Christy Rosso

Library of Congress Cataloging in Publication Data

Rice, F Philip.
    The Adolescent.

    Includes bibliographies and index.
    1. Youth—United States.   2. Adolescent psychology.   3. United States—Social conditions.
I. Title.
HQ796.R543   1981   305.2'4   80–23420
ISBN 0–205–07303–4

Printed in the United States of America.

10 9 8 7 6 5 4 3 2 1   85 84 83 82 81

3-1303-00050-1610

Credits, chapter opening photos: pp. 3, 45, 101, 165, 280, 357, 481, 505—Margaret Thompson; p. 27—Bobbi Carey; pp. 79, 249, 427, 532—Talbot Lovering; p. 124—Carol Palmer/The Picture Cube; p. 197—Owen Franken/Stock, Boston; p. 217—Frank Siteman/The Picture Cube; p. 306—Melissa Shook/The Picture Cube; p. 322—Judy Herzl/The Picture Cube; p. 382—George Bellerose/Stock, Boston; p. 404—Ellis Herwig/Stock, Boston; p. 447—Jeff Albertson/Stock, Boston; p. 551—Jean-Claude LeJeune/Stock, Boston.

To
David and Linda Rice

CONTENTS

PREFACE

Every effort has been expended to make this book on adolescence comprehensive, well-grounded in research, and relevant to today's youths, with an interdisciplinary orientation.

This book is unique in a number of ways. It covers a very broad scope of subjects: the adolescent in contemporary society, theories of adolescence, and the physical, emotional, social, familial, moral, educational, vocational, and ethnic aspects of adolescent development and behavior. Its orientation is eclectic, with the strengths, weaknesses, and contributions of each of the various views presented being discussed. It is both theoretical and experiential, presenting most of the major theories about the adolescent's development and behavior, as well as much of the contemporary research which illuminates what is actually happening. For this third edition, every chapter has been revised and updated with hundreds of new research studies and references.

The book discusses not only adolescent development and behavior, but also group life and culture. While the emphasis is on adolescent psychology, relevant material from sociology, anthropology, and education helps to place the American adolescent in a social perspective to gain a better understanding of his or her total life and culture. Sociological material includes such subjects as subcultural societies, music, dress, argot, and group life in and out of school. Low socioeconomic status adolescents, black adolescents, American Indian youths, and Spanish American adolescents are also discussed to show some of the cultural differences of selected minority youths.

The Adolescent includes relevant topics such as drug abuse; emotional disturbance and maladjustment; changing sexual roles, values, and behavior; early marriage; cohabitation and trial marriage; education and school; religion and today's youths; adolescents and their families; and the present employment and money situation. Finally, the book is outlined and presented in a logical style for easy use. Each chapter has an introduction as well as conclusions which contain the author's comments and evaluation of the ideas presented. New materials for use in teaching and study include case studies, selected readings, discussion questions, suggestions for interviewing adolescents, suggestions for panel discussions, topics for term papers, suggestions for biographical anecdotes, and an extensive bibliography for each chapter. The material is well-illustrated with figures and tables.

I would like to acknowledge the special help of the following professors who have offered valuable guidance in writing this book: Robert L. Hohn, University of Kansas; Nora Newcombe, Pennsylvania State University; and John A. Williamson, North Texas State University. Special thanks go also to Steve Mathews and Abbe Levine of the editorial staff of Allyn and Bacon, and to my wife, Irma Ann Rice, for her hours of proofreading.

It is my hope that professors and students alike will find that this book measures up to my expectations of it.

Adolescence

CHAPTER 1

Images of the Adolescent

Outline

Contemporary Western society is ambivalent in its attitudes and feelings toward adolescents. Adolescents are admired, praised, and almost worshiped; they are criticized, belittled, and rejected. The purpose of this chapter is to look at both the positive and negative feelings and to see what effect they have on youths, on adults, and on the relationships between the generations. A look backward to the Roaring Twenties will reveal that attitudes and relationships haven't changed much. Adults were as critical in those days as they are today. Youths were both rebellious and conformist, moral and immoral, just as they are today.

A Positive Perspective

The observer does not have to look far to discover that Western society is youth oriented and youth worshiping. The phenomenon shows itself in many ways. First, adults do all they can to be youthful and to remain young because old age is feared and youthfulness admired. Beauty and cosmetic industries have made billions of dollars by encouraging this emulation of agelessness.

Second, much of what parents do is for their young. Thousands of parents make daily sacrifices for their children. The numerous benefits heaped upon children are evident. Many mothers say: "I would give my life for my children." This feeling does not apply to all parents, but it applies to enough to be proof positive that today's adults care about their young people.

Third, most adults say that the majority of youth today are "pretty good kids." This point of view can be fairly well substantiated. The majority of studies that focus on normal adolescents agree that the majority are not problems, not in turmoil, not deeply disturbed, not at the mercy of their impulses, not resistant to parental values, not politically active, and not rebellious. (1, p. 37) In a 1977 Gallup poll, 95 percent of parents said they got along with their teenagers either very well or fairly well. Only 4 percent said they did not get along at all well. (21, p. 1238) Sometimes this positive view is carried to an overidealized extreme; parents who refuse to believe their children are ever at fault or ever capable of doing wrong tend to attack any friend, teacher, or town official who tries to tell them otherwise. Despite this overidealization most youths are not problems—to themselves or their communities. Misconceptions are formed by focusing only on the addicted, delinquent, and disturbed or on the social rebels who are in fact a minority.

Finally, although most youths today are not activist rebels like those of the late 1960s and early 1970s, youthful idealism is still much in evidence. Adolescents are much concerned about social issues such as juvenile crime, drug abuse, inflation, the energy crisis, unemployment, women's liberation, materialism and impersonalism in society, pollution, and the environment. (24, 29) They also show genuine concern for the underdog, indicated by their frequent political alliance with blacks or the poor. (48, p. 109) They will give generously and work hard to help the starving overseas or will come to the defense of convicted criminals if they feel their cause is just. (42, p. 122) Clergy and other caring adults applaud youths who adopt an antimaterialistic philosophy and who join the "love" generation to find more meaningful relationships than those between their parents at home or between business elements in a highly competitive society. (27) They encourage youths' reexamination of the values, goals, and philosophies of Western culture* in the search for greater simplicity and meaning in life. These adults emphasize that parents ought not to be critical of their young for hating corruption, injustice, or superficial values. Although they are a little awed by youths who will work for months to keep a wilderness area from being ruined by developers, value-oriented adults tell parents to admire their young and admit that their activities are more worthwhile than swallowing goldfish or seeing how many kids can crowd themselves into a telephone booth. (45)

This concern of young people for the problems of the world and their desire to do something about them is expressed in the song "Waking Up," by Michael Murphey.

Is that the morning light I see
Shining in on you and me
We must be waking up
It's been so long since this old world has seen daybreak

Think we're awake this time
We don't want to sleep through our whole lives
We don't want to lose this world in the night
So come on let's work until we get this world right

Come on let's wake up now. (38)†

However, the youths of every generation who actually become involved in work to alleviate social problems are a minority. A Gallup poll conducted in 1977 asked: "Do you yourself happen to be involved in any charity or social service activities, such as helping the poor, the sick, or the elderly?" (21, p. 1176) Only 16 percent of young adults eighteen to twenty-nine years of age answered yes, yet many of these same youths would be among the first to defend verbally the poor, the sick, or the elderly. As always, it is easier to talk about social problems than to do something about them.

Negative Stereotypes

Contemporary feeling toward adolescents includes open resentment. (11) From some of the publicity young people receive, it appears that Western society not only mistrusts its youths, it also dislikes them. Society depicts them as rebellious, unappreciative, immoral, ill-mannered, untidy, irresponsible, lazy children who are more interested in having a good time than in growing up, and whose

---

* Culture may be defined as the sum total of the ways of living.

† Michael Murphey, "Waking Up." Copyright © 1972 by Mystery Music, Inc. BMI. Used by permission.

chief delights are sexual indulgence and attending rock concerts to smoke pot and listen to shocking music. (3, 16, 18, 22)

As a result, many adults, convinced that today's youths are all problem children, deeply resent anyone who happens to be young. Nowhere are these negative attitudes more evident than in the treatment of the underprivileged. Thousands of these youths are denied services, benefits, and help that they need to improve their education and their lives, yet they are the first to be criticized for being unemployed and idle. They also are usually the first to be harassed by law enforcement officers, who personify the public resentment toward them.

Part of the problem is that all adolescents are grouped together and described with stereotyped labels, regardless of the fact that they are as diverse in personality and behavior as adults are. Today's adolescents have been negatively stereotyped as pampered and spoiled, irresponsible, hedonistic, immoral, cynical, and rebellious and rude.

PAMPERED AND SPOILED

According to one stereotype today's adolescents are pampered and spoiled, the offspring of a misled, permissive generation. Some parents, unwilling to take all the blame, have in turn blamed Dr. Benjamin Spock for selling them that book on child care.(49)

In the introduction to their book *Teen-Age Tyranny*, Grace and Fred Hechinger wrote:

> We are not writing this book to declare war on teen-agers or to put the clock back to the days when children were supposed to be seen but not heard. . . .
> What worries us is not the greater freedom of youth but rather the abdication of the rights and privileges of adults for the convenience of the immature. We believe teen-age should be regarded as a phase of human development, with both pleasant and unpleasant side effects, rather than as either an achievement or a disease. The pages which follow, therefore, are not intended as a declaration of war but as an honest attempt to make "the teens" once again a transition period to full man- or womanhood rather than a tribal "subculture"; a temporary condition to be terminated with normal speed, rather than to be artificially induced and prolonged like the life of a hot house plant, a time of growth to be treated with understanding and even indulgence but not with unlimited license. (26, p. ix)

In the pages that follow in their book, it is evident, despite the disclaimer, that the Hechingers are attacking youths who are so overindulged that they are not given a chance to grow as responsible adults. The authors try hard to assign the blame to society and parents, but fundamentally they have accepted the assumption that young people are spoiled and pampered.

The majority of adults don't feel this way. In a 1977 Gallup poll, over half of all parents surveyed felt their discipline was about right, with only about one-third feeling they had not been strict enough. (21, p. 1238) Some youths, on the other hand, feel adults should be stricter. One fifteen-year-old boy in a Chicago high school complained that teachers "just don't enforce strict enough rules." (40, p. 49) "I still don't know my multiplication tables," another girl claimed. "If teachers had buckled down at some point and told me I had to do it, learn them, I would have done it by now." (40, p. 49) The need for parental guidance is echoed by a thirteen-year-old girl who considers her parents the most important factor in her life because: "they teach me things I need to know and give me love. They guide me and tell me to do the right thing." (40, p. 55).

It must be acknowledged that some youths are spoiled. On the other hand, there are also thousands who are deprived of even the necessities of life and whose parents are too authoritarian and strict, imposing hardships and rules without much thought to their adolescents' needs. (40, p. 55)

IRRESPONSIBLE

Adolescents are also accused of being irresponsible and lazy.

"What are you doing?"
"Nothing."
"What would you like to do?"
"Nothing."

Arlo Guthrie reflects this stereotype of idle, irresponsible youth in his ballad "The Motorcycle Song."

I don't want a pickle,
Just want to ride on my motorsickle;
And I don't want a tickle,
'Cause I'd rather ride on my motorsickle.
And I don't want to die,
Just want to ride on my motorcy. (25)*

One reason for the charge of laziness is that some youths have rejected the Protestant ethic—the sacredness of work and thrift, the sinfulness of sloth—that has contributed to the establishment of a wealthy and materialistic culture. (4, p. 249) It is ironic that adolescents who reject materialism are accused of laziness and suspect motives. The young man who complains, "All my old man thinks about is making money," and who refuses to sacrifice the time, the energy, or his life to make money as his father did is not considered idealistic or motivated by higher values; rather, he has a lack of drive and ambition. A generation of parents who pulled themselves up by their bootstraps during a depression has been confronted by a generation of consuming youths, many of whom have known only affluence and material comfort, but who are learning the meaning of leisure. It is frustrating for these adults, raised on sweat, competition, and financial ambition, to see the young enjoying leisure. To them, today's adolescents are the forerunners of a lazy, worthless generation seeking to establish a workless society.

Only a small percentage of adolescents, however, deny the value of work. When asked about their attitudes toward work, 82 percent of black adolescent males said that everybody has to work, and 94 percent said that, for men, a good job is important. (47, p. 297) In another nationwide survey, only a little over a third of young women were willing to settle for marriage and children without a career. (44)

Most adolescents who aren't working want to, but can't find jobs. In the words of a seventeen-year-old black from Providence, Rhode Island:

* Arlo Guthrie, "The Motorcycle Song." © 1967, 1969 by Appleseed Music Inc. All Rights Reserved. Used by permission.

Only thing we don't have is the thing we need the most: jobs. Ain't no job for us over here. Not a one, man, and I know too, because I been looking for three years, and I ain't all that old. (29, p. 44)

HEDONISTIC

Today's adolescents have been labeled the hedonistic generation. As one father expressed it: "All my son is interested in is having fun; in girls, parties, and pot. I don't know if he will ever settle down and grow up." Youths of the 1960s may have been interested in social protest and altruistic causes, but attitudes today are reminiscent of the party days of the 1950s, when high school boys were obsessed with "scoring" and cars, and girls with curlers and catching a mate. The movies *Grease* and *American Graffiti* are prime examples of the prevalent nostalgia. The current emphasis is on fun and fitness: youths dangle from hang gliders, disco half the night, learn karate, and jog; thousands have taken up tennis.

Again, there is a tendency to accuse every generation of hedonism. The poet Edna St. Vincent Millay expressed the hedonism of yesterday's youths:

My candle burns at both ends;
It will not last the night;
But ah, my foes, and oh, my friends—
It gives a lovely light. (34)*

IMMORAL

Parents as well as the public at large commonly stereotype adolescents as immoral. To most adults, the term *immoral* connotes sexual misbehavior. As one junior high school boy (age thirteen, grade seven) put it: "Every time I show an interest in a girl my parents start worrying that I'll get her pregnant." It is clear that today's youths are more liberal in their sexual values, especially in values related to premarital sexual intercourse. (See Chapter 13.) But according to Yankelovich's nationwide study of American youths aged sixteen to twenty-five, almost two out of three believed extramarital sexual relations were wrong. (53, p. 93) Almost 90 percent still held love and friendship as very important values, and there had been an increase (to about 60 percent) in a four-year period of those who believed that doing things for others was very important. (53, p. 93) These trends indicate more sexual permissiveness, but no change in a number of other humanistic values.

CYNICAL

There is evidence that a portion of American youths have grown cynical, especially in their attitudes toward their country and its leaders. It is not that today's youths are anti-American; rather, some have lost faith in their leaders and in the ideals on which the United States was founded. Youths see corruption and graft at all levels of government, politicians making and breaking promises as though truth were inconsequential, and national heroes involved in sex scandals. As a

---

* From *Collected Poems*, Harper & Row. Copyright 1922, 1950 by Edna St. Vincent Millay. Reprinted by permission.

result, there has been a noticeable decline in patriotism among adolescents. (53) In spite of the decline, however, a 1977 replication of the Lynds' 1924 survey of adolescent attitude in Middletown, U.S.A., revealed that three out of four Middletown high school students believed the United States is unquestionably the best country in the world. (8) Only about half, however, accepted the slogan "my country, right or wrong" as a categorical imperative. (8, p. 13)

REBELLIOUS

Above all, youths are stereotyped as rebellious. (48, p. 103) They won't mind their parents; they won't accept without question the school program they are offered; they don't want to become a part of the establishment. The more they resist integration into adult folkways (whether in business or in traditional marriage), the more they are considered problems. Those who accept the world that has been handed to them, or who scheme and struggle, along with the silent majority, to uphold the prevailing values and practices, are considered models of decorous industry. Meanwhile, however, some behave in ways that frighten adults into fearing they never will become an integral part of American life.

When objective evidence is considered, it is not clear that this rebellious stereotype is accurate. One small-scale study of undergraduate students at a midwestern university showed that only 25 percent could be described as highly rebellious. (20) Fifty-five percent of the sample showed no signs of rebelliousness at all. (20, p. 231) Even the high rebelliousness was not of a dramatic, delinquent, law-breaking nature. It could be described as deliberate and open defiance, but quiet. The same study revealed that today's society is more accepting of a wider range of behavior in youths, allowing more to "do their own thing" than was the case ten or twenty years ago. Because their behavior is more accepted, fewer adolescents feel the need to rebel. The two examples that follow are typical of today's more relaxed parental attitudes.

Several subjects reported that they had used marijuana with the knowledge of their parents. . . . The parents did not seem to be particularly surprised or concerned. (20, p. 233)

One subject reported that she was living with a fellow in their own apartment. Her parents were fully aware of the situation and offered no resistance or objection. (20, p. 233)

Why the Resentment?

When it exists, the reasons for resentment against youth are varied, complex, and both psychological and sociological. (30) Psychologically, adolescents provoke fear, jealousy, resentment, and a host of other negative emotions in adults. First, *they remind adults of things adults would rather forget.* (See Chapter 14.) The father who tended to be a sissy when young panics at the thought of a teenage son with long hair who likes music; a mother who conceived her daughter out of wedlock tries to protect her daughter from the same mistake and becomes too restrictive, suspicious, and rigid; the mother who was a wallflower tries to push her daughter into popularity; the father who never succeeded in business is anxious above all for his son to be successful. Whenever a teenager reflects a parental weakness, parents become more anxious, fearful, and critical in their efforts to prevent what has happened to them from happening to their child.

Second, *adolescents present a threat to the ego, security, and status of adults.* (51, p. 28) No adult wants some "young whippersnapper" to show that he or she is as smart or capable as the adult. Older workers deeply resent young apprentices who think they know it all and who may threaten their position, statuses, and jobs. The young woman who is prettier, better trained, or more efficient is deeply resented by older women in a business environment, especially if they already feel insecure in their positions. Adults don't like to have their positions challenged, their ideas questioned, or their egos deflated, so they develop defense

"I Was Young Once"

"But I'll Never Be Young Again"

Figure 1–1.   Reprinted from P. Farrow, "The Presymposial State," *The Andover Review* 5 (Spring 1978): 34, 35. Copyright © by The Trustees of Phillips Academy. Used by permission.

mechanisms and strategies to keep adolescents in their place. One defense is to react with bitter attacks, to blame the other person—especially if that person is young. (15)

Third, *jealousy and envy may be reason enough for hostility.* No matter how competent or mature adults are, they can never regain the premium attribute of adolescence: youth. Fear of aging has so pervaded our culture that adults often end up envying their adolescents. Nowhere is this better exemplified than in styles of fashion or dance. Youths are style setters. If the change in style is radical, they are at first severely criticized by adults. This makes youths happy, so they cling to their styles to show their independence. Gradually the new styles are accepted by adults, then imitated and adopted by those who seek to be young. When this happens, youths reject the styles as outdated and adopt new ones. No matter what they do, adults are never accepted as youths. They may criticize, then emulate, but they can never duplicate. So they are sometimes isolated, and this makes them jealous and resentful.

Fourth, *adults are fearful of losing control of adolescents, not just for the ego satisfaction of the adult, but also for the protection of the young and the status quo.* The more youths rebel, the more fearful adults become. Every adult brings more experience to any situation than does a young person. The experiences of the past have made them more realistic and probably more cautious. Adolescents are less wise, less experienced, and more daring; these qualities can frighten the adult. Many adults have already lost so much control that they have little to say about the behavior of their adolescents. Other adults need to relinquish more control, gradually, so that adolescents can develop as autonomous adults. One writer feels that the misuse of power by adults is a primary cause of adolescent rebellion, irresponsibility, or dependency.

Many adults are overly occupied with policing children. . . . Such adults may use their extra power to hide from themselves the fact that they may be too full of their own importance and too self-righteous. . . . Such adults may be expecting a child to show unquestioning conformity to their behavior and beliefs or to otherwise surrender . . . uniqueness. (19, p. 518)

The role of adults is not to police adolescents but to guide them into being self-controlling adults.

Forced Segregation, Rebellion, and Warfare

One result of the resentment toward adolescents is that many are deliberately excluded from adult society. These youths are forced to establish a segregated subculture (often not really different from adult culture) and to rebel against the establishment in order to be listened to. (See Chapter 10 for a full discussion of this alienation.) (6, p. 257; 13)

In his book *Youth and the Social Order*, Musgrove reports a survey of the opinions of two hundred adults to discover their attitude toward the early entry of adolescents into adult life. He found an overwhelming rejection of the idea, and a general agreement that adolescents should inhabit a segregated and virtually autonomous, nonadult social sphere. Adults sought to define a separate population (of adolescents) and to isolate them from the world of the mature. (39, p. 13) As a result the period of adolescence is prolonged and the time delayed when youths can take their place in the adult world. (42, p. 29; 43)

James Coleman says that "our adolescents today are cut off, probably more than ever before, from the adult society." (10, p. 9) In another book he summarizes the effect of this subculture on adult-youth relationships and on education.

Adolescents have their own little society, with special symbols and language, special interests and activities. . . . Such a situation invites trouble. It encourages leadership that asserts itself against the adult demands. It encourages a disdain for those who exert effort to meet adult demands. It encourages a status system among adolescents. . . . In sum, it effectively impedes education, keeping the effort expended on learning at a minimum. (91, p. 12)

Many times youths exhibit a desire for dialogue with those over thirty but are rejected. The student council of a local university issued an invitation to the faculty to participate in its deliberations, but was refused open admission to the faculty meetings of one of the colleges. (37, p. 56) If youths remain segregated and rebel against their isolation and rejection, it is sometimes not by choice but by necessity. A deep longing to relate arises from enforced segregation.

Furthermore, adults have become so indoctrinated by the idea of adolescence as a period of acute disequilibrium, storm, and stress (33, p. 94; 52) that they are convinced that a conflict of generations is inevitable if not in progress already. The situation sometimes reaches the point at which parents respond to their children as though they were embodiments of negative ideas instead of real people.

As a result of this negative emphasis, youths have become more self-conscious. Criticized and rejected on account of their youth, they gradually assume a defensive, hostile posture to protect themselves from attacks by adults.

Figure 1–2.   Reprinted from P. Farrow, "The Presymposial State," *The Andover Review* 5 (Spring 1978): 37. Copyright © by The Trustees of Phillips Academy. Used by permission.

(33, p. 17) Why should teenagers have to apologize for being young or be defensive about their position in Western culture? The wonder is that adolescents have not returned in equal measure the hostility that adults direct at them. For the most part they are kindly disposed to their seniors, value their opinions, and aim to be cooperative with them. (39, p. 11)

Adolescents in a Previous Era: The Roaring Twenties

The reader might ask if the present situation is unique. Or has there always been adult-youth conflict and tension? One way to find an answer is to take a look at adult-adolescent relationships in former times. The 1920s have been selected because of several parallels to current times.

FLAMING YOUTH

In describing adult views of youths in the 1920s in *Wild Kids*, F. R. Donovan uses an expression that was then very much in vogue: *flaming youth*. Headlines read: "The Revolt of Youth," "Is Modern Youth Going to the Devil?" and "They Are Hell Bent." A suspected increase in juvenile delinquency brought such headlines as: "80% of Crimes Committed by Boys." (The Children's Bureau subsequently reported some slight increase during World War I, but an overall decrease for the period 1913–1923 and in some cases a reduction for 1924 and 1925.) (14, pp. 188, 189) Although there was much talk of juvenile delinquency, most of the concern was with immorality and defiance of authority rather than with crime. Juveniles were said to have adopted a horrifying moral code of their own based on promiscuous sex, excessive drinking, indecent dress for the girls (the flapper dresses and short skirts), and lewd dancing (like the Charleston). The little hussies also painted their faces and puffed daringly on cigarettes. (14, p. 192) *Century Magazine* printed an article in 1921 that read in part:

It seems that the young people have taken the bit between their teeth and are running wild. They are wholly contemptuous of the traditional controls and show no disposition to impose a speed limit upon themselves. Fond parents, maiden aunts, all the amateur censors of morals are at their wits' ends. They are shouting voluminous warnings after the runaways, but the pace only gets hotter. And the end is not in sight. . . .

The elders of today are convinced that never before have the established* and responsible members of society had to remonstrate against so many anarchic notions and such alarming behavior. No age, they say, has had on its hands such a problem of reckless and rebellious youth. (12)

Characteristically, the youths of that day also talked back in their own defense. College kids in particular were adept at throwing the ball back to their elders.

I would like to observe that the older generation had certainly pretty much ruined this world before passing it on to us. They give us this Thing, knocked to pieces, leaky, red-hot, threatening to blow up; and then they are surprised that we don't accept it with the same attitude of pretty, decorous enthusiasm with which they

* Author's note. Maybe *establishment* is not a new word.

received it 'way back in the eighteen-nineties, nicely painted, smoothly running, practically foolproof. . . . (14, p. 195)

SEX MAGAZINES AND MOVIES

Nearly as much trash was written and sold in the twenties as today. There was a bumper crop of sex magazines, confession magazines, and lurid motion picture magazines. A leading pulp magazine of the day, *Telling Tales,* featured these four stories: "Indolent Kisses," "Primitive Love," "Watch Your Step-Ins," and "Innocents Astray." The movies were doing a booming business with sex films. Clara Bow was the "It" girl. If you had "It" (sex appeal), you were in. If you did not have "It," you were out.

Psychologist Dorothy Bromley reflected the feelings of many adults of the twenties when she wrote in her study, *Youth and Sex:*

The movies' direct influence on the new sex mores . . . is generally known. . . . For young men and girls who have not yet had time to discover the comparative scale of values which life offers, the lush sensuality of these shows, night after night, may be very disturbing. The movies have taken off the bed-room doors for young people and turned life into a French peep-show. (7, p. 198)

Perhaps she had just as much basis for complaint as adults do today. Some of the movie titles were: *Sinners in Silk, Women Who Give, The Price She Paid, Queen of Sin, Rouged Lips,* and *Name the Man—a Story of Betrayed Womanhood.* A movie entitled *Flaming Youth* was advertised as offering "neckers, petters, white kisses, red kisses, pleasure mad daughters, sensation craving mothers. . . . the truth, bold, naked, sensational." (14, p. 199)

The success of such sex exploitation movies prompted the office of Postmaster General Hayes under President Harding to promulgate a movie code that made it mandatory for every movie to have a moral ending. As a result movies continued to show all kinds of violence, crime, and sexual misconduct so long as virtue triumphed in the end.

STYLES OF CLOTHING AND DANCE

Apparently, adults were also having trouble with youthful styles and fashions. The president of the University of Florida declared: "The rolled hose and short skirts are born of the Devil and his angels and are carrying the present and future generations to chaos and destruction." (14, p. 202) As a result of the short skirts, one thousand clergymen were asked what they felt the standards were for moral dress. A special committee designed a "moral gown" with hemlines 7½ inches from the floor. (It was endorsed by ministers of fifteen denominations.) A number of state legislators proposed fines and imprisonment and laws to make short skirts illegal. None of these proposals worked: the brazen flapper continued to flaunt her kneecaps and she won her freedom. (The revolt was over when adult mothers, following their daughters, started exposing their adult calves.)

There was a great deal of criticism of the dancing of the twenties, which was called by some "a syncopated embrace." It was performed to the primitive strains of the saxophone rather than the romantic melodies of the violin. The *Catholic Telegraph* said: "The music is sensuous, the embracing of the partners—the female only half dressed—is absolutely indecent." (14, p. 204)

PROBLEM SOCIAL BEHAVIORS

Parents were concerned about the social behavior of their youths. Petting parties had replaced the "spooning" of the previous generation. Boys and girls petted openly between and after dances, retiring to dark corners, lawns, or parks. One study revealed that half of all youths believed that nine out of every ten boys and girls of high school age had petting parties. (14, p. 204)

The use of contraceptives by youths of the twenties was a major scandal. Even the best hotels provided a slot machine in men's washrooms that sold contraceptive devices for a quarter.

Youthful drinking was another controversial aspect of adolescent behavior during the Roaring Twenties. Prohibition started with the Volstead Act on January 16, 1920. For a few years, drinking among young people declined. Then the speakeasy came into being. Many were expensive; the most famous, the Stork Club, catered chiefly to boys from the Ivy League colleges, to whom the proprietor sent cards of admission. Roadhouses opened everywhere and were hangouts for prostitutes. Rebellious youths everywhere carried the hip flask filled with liquor stolen from papa's bootleg liquor cabinet. One judge complained that "no petting party, no roadhouse toot, no joy ride from the prying eye of Main Street, is complete unless the boys carry flasks." (14, p. 213)

DEMISE OF FLAMING YOUTH

Gradually the reverberations from the antics of "flaming youth" subsided. (The depression probably eliminated some excesses: it was too expensive to party all the time.) H. L. Mencken, a cynic and liberal of his day, wrote a discourse in 1931 on the demise of flaming youth.

The moral divagations of the youth of today do not differ three percent from those of the youth of yesterday. When I was a youngster . . . with Victoria in full blast upon her throne, great numbers of boys were diligent lushers, just as they are now: the only difference I can make out is that they drank beer . . . whereas they now have to put up with bootleg gin, which often makes them sick. . . . There was necking too. . . . In case the business goes farther than mere necking there is some ground, of course, for sociologists to intervene, but I doubt that it goes further today any oftener than it did yesterday. . . . (14, p. 214)

Conclusions

This description of life in the Roaring Twenties shows that adult-youth feelings and relationships haven't changed much in the United States in the last fifty years. Adults still moan about their young people, who still go their own way, defending themselves as they must.

What about today's adolescent? Are they as idealistic, moral, conforming, and responsible as some say? Or do they fit the stereotypes: are they pampered and spoiled, irresponsible, hedonistic, immoral, cynical, and rebellious? Actually both views, though conflicting, are valid. The fact that adults are not unanimous in their views of today's adolescents indicates that not all young people are alike, any more than all adults are alike. Adolescents hate to be stereotypes just as anyone else does. They resent adults who classify them all as delinquent, irresponsible, or anything else. Such stereotyping is not only unfair but also untrue.

First of all, adolescents are individuals, as uniquely different as other members of society. Second, each adult who describes today's young people is different; each has his or her own prejudices, hang-ups, and limited vision. (46) One adult may use the word *lazy* to describe an adolescent who refuses to spend all his waking hours making money; another may say this adolescent has a true sense of values. The conclusion reached depends upon the point of view and sense of values of the adults making the judgment.

In writing a book on adolescents, the author has to keep in mind the wide variations in individual adolescents, as well as age, ethnic, class, and other group differences. The author also has to remember the various viewpoints and theories on adolescents that have proved useful in developing a more complete understanding. For this reason, this book rejects any one theory of adolescence as the whole truth. Instead it presents various views, which together form a kaleidoscopic picture, sometimes contradictory, but I hope always in focus, with the aid of the vast amount of research on adolescence that is available. In reading this book, the student is urged also to keep a very open mind to receive a variety of new images, new ideas, and new feelings about adolescents: their development, relationships, and culture. (14, p. 188)

Selected Readings

ADOLESCENCE IN PREVIOUS ERAS

COLONIAL AMERICA.   The puritan ethic of colonial America emphasized the importance of children's obeying their parents. The goal of discipline was to break the child's will and to force children to submit to their superiors. The following rules for proper behavior were derived from English guides and were first reprinted in the colonies in 1715. Moody's version appeared in Boston in 1772. (35)

THE GOOD MANNERS CHECKLIST

Eleazar Moody*

When at Home

1. Make a bow always when you come home, and be immediately uncovered. (remove headgear)
2. Be never covered at home, especially before thy parents or strangers.
3. Never sit in the presence of thy parents without bidding, tho' no stranger be present.
4. If thou passest by thy parents, and any place where thou seest them, when either by themselves or with company, bow towards them.
5. If thou art going to speak to thy parents, and see them engaged in discourse with company, draw back and leave thy business until afterwards; but if thou must speak, be sure to whisper.

* From Eleazar Moody, *The School of Good Manners, Composed for the Help of Parents in Teaching Their Children How to Carry It in Their Places During Their Minority* (Boston, 1772). Reprinted in *Children and Youth in America: A Documentary History*, Vol. I: *1600–1865*, ed. Robert H. Bremner et al. (Cambridge, Mass.: Harvard University Press, 1970), pp. 33–34.

6. Never speak to thy parents without some title of respect, viz., Sir, Madam, etc.

7. Approach near thy parents at no time without a bow.

8. Dispute not, nor delay to obey thy parents' commands.

9. Go not out of doors without thy parents' leave, and return within the time by them limited.

10. Come not into the room where thy parents are with strangers, unless thou art called, and then decently; and at bidding go out; or if strangers come in while thou art with them, it is manners with a bow to withdraw.

11. Use respectful and courteous but not insulting or domineering carriage or language toward the servants.

12. Quarrel not nor contend with thy brethren or sisters, but live in love, peace, and unity.

13. Grumble not nor be discontented at anything thy parents appoint, speak, or do.

14. Bear with meekness and patience, and without murmuring or sullenness, thy parents' reproofs or corrections: Nay, tho' it should so happen that they be causeless or undeserved.

In Their Discourse

1. Among superiors speak not till thou art spoken to, and bid to speak.

2. Hold not thine hand, nor anything else, before thy mouth when thou speakest.

3. Come not over-near to the person thou speakest to.

4. If thy superior speak to thee while thou sittest, stand up before thou givest any answer.

5. Sit not down till thy superior bid thee.

6. Speak neither very loud, nor too low.

7. Speak clear, not stammering, stumbling, nor drawling.

8. Answer not one that is speaking to thee until he hath done.

9. Loll not when thou art speaking to a superior or spoken to by him.

10. Speak not without Sir, or some other title of respect.

11. Strive not with superiors in argument or discourse; but easily submit thine opinion to their assertions.

12. If thy superior speak anything wherein thou knowest he is mistaken, correct not nor contradict him, nor grin at the hearing of it; but pass over the error without notice or interruption.

13. Mention not frivolous or little things among grave persons or superiors.

14. If thy superior drawl or hesitate in his words, pretend not to help him out, or to prompt him.

15. Come not too near two that are whispering or speaking in secret, much less may'st thou ask about what they confer.

16. When thy parent or master speaks to any person, speak not thou, nor hearken to them.

17. If thy superior be relating a story, say not, "I have heard it before," but attend to it as though it were altogether new. Seem not to question the truth of it. If he tell it not right, snigger not, nor endeavor to help him out, or add to his relation.

18. If any immodest or obscene thing be spoken in thy hearing, smile not, but settle thy countenance as though thou did'st not hear it.

19. Boast not in discourse of thine own wit or doings.

20. Beware thou utter not anything hard to be believed.

21. Interrupt not anyone that speaks, though thou be his familiar.

22. Coming into company, whilst any topic is discoursed on, ask not what was the preceding talk but hearken to the remainder.

23. Speaking of any distant person, it is rude and unmannerly to point at him.

24. Laugh not in or at thy own story, wit, or jest.

25. Use not any contemptuous or reproachful language to any person, though very mean or inferior.

26. Be not over-earnest in talking to justify and avouch thy own savings.

27. Let thy words be modest about those things which only concern thee.

28. Repeat not over again the words of a superior that asketh thee a question or talketh to thee.

In spite of the efforts of adults to control completely their children's behavior, the naturally high spirits and mischievousness of the young resulted in some "unseemly" behavior. The following letter to the editor might have been written today instead of in 1723. (28)

March 11, 1723

TO OLD JANUS THE COURANTEER
SIR,

The extraordinary disturbance made at Mr. Gatchell's Dancing School in Hanover Street [Boston] may be thought worth taking notice of in your paper. On Thursday the 28th of February, a company of young lads who were denied admittance, after firing several volleys of oaths and curses, threatening to kill Mr. Gatchell and using abundance of obscene discourse not fit to be mentioned, they fell upon the glass windows, shattered them all to pieces, and broke one of the iron bars. On Monday night last, ten of them were brought before a Justice of the Peace, who was obliged to remove from his house to the Town-house, by reason of the great concourse of people. The lads owned they were there, but denied the fact. However, several witnesses being sworn against them, they were bound over to answer it at the sessions. 'Tis now grown too common for our children and youth to swear and curse in the streets, and to abuse with foul language, not only one another but their superiors. And this growing wickedness is certainly in great measure owing to the many servants brought from other countries, who seldom fail of ruining most of the children in the families where they live. But I leave others to propose a method for preventing or punishing these enormities and remain, Sir,

YOUR HUMBLE SERVANT, etc.

Nineteenth-century industrial America. The way of life prescribed for young people in the nineteenth century was based on the ethic of thrift and unrelenting work. As a consequence, the transition from childhood to adulthood was brief and early compared with that of today. The Harvard student body was made up largely of boys aged fourteen and fifteen. Marriage by eighteen was the rule rather than the exception for young women. A British traveler comments on the early maturity of American youth during the middle of the nineteenth century and on the materialistic philosophy by which they lived. (23)

BORN MIDDLE-AGED

Thomas C. Grattan

All Business

. . . Children soon go from the nursery to the schoolhouse. If they are boys they run through their boyhood with marvelous rapidity. As soon as they can read they begin to study the public papers. About the same period they are turned loose into the streets, and they struggle into newsrooms, election-wardrooms, places of business, markets, caucuses, etc. They walk in political processions, with miniature banners and small music. They enter at once into public life. They, in fact, do almost everything which is unbecoming to their early years and very little, and that very imperfectly, which would give a grace to them. Their sports . . . are mere caricatures of the sports of England, and absolutely painful to one who remembers the animation of the old world, whose greatest blessing is its spirit of long-enduring youth.

A "Boston boy" is a melancholy picture of prematurity. It might be almost said that every man is born middle-aged in that and every other great city of the Union. The principal business of life seems to be to grow old as fast as possible. The boy, the youth, the young man are only anxious to hurry on to the gravity and the care of "the vale of tears." There is a velocity in their movements, as though the hill they mount were a mere molehill, and that their downward course commenced before the youth of other countries had gained a third of the upward path. The toils of life— the destiny of the poorer classes in Europe—form the free choice of the rich man of America, always excepting the indolent Southern planters.

The boys are sent to college at fourteen. They leave it with their degrees at about seventeen. They are then launched at once into life, either as merchants or attorneys' clerks, medical students or adventurers in the Western states of the Union, or in foreign countries. The interval between their leaving school and commencing their business career offers no occupation to give either gracefulness or strength to body or mind. Athletic games and the bolder field sports being unknown, nothing being done that we do—I mean, alas! that we used to do—at home, all that is left is chewing, smoking, drinking, driving hired horses in wretched gigs with a cruel velocity, or trotting on jaded and hard-mounted hacks, at a speed that makes humanity shudder, and with an awkwardness that turns our pity for the one animal into contempt for the other. I doubt if there exists an American gentleman who could take a horse over a three-foot rail in England or an Irish potato trench. Yet they constantly talk of such or such a one being "a good rider."

Young men made up of such materials as I describe are not young men at all. . . . Their chief ambition is to grow bald or gray. They are thought nothing of till that consummation happens. They think nothing of themselves. They know that till they become rich they have no influence; and there is nothing more absurd than those meetings called "Young Men's Conventions." They are a mockery. No act of theirs can be valid, for their title is a false one. The class I treat of feels this. They as soon as possible plunge into the cares of the world. They follow business like drudges, and politics with fierce ardor. They marry. They renounce partygoing. They give up all pretension in dress. They cannot force wrinkles and crow's-feet on their faces, but they assume and soon acquire a pursed-up, keen, and haggard look. Their air, manners, and conversation are alike contracted. They have no breadth, either of shoulders, information, or ambition. Their physical powers are subdued, and their mental capability cribbed into narrow limits. There is constant activity going on in one small portion of the brain; all the rest is stagnant. The money-making faculty alone is cultivated. They are incapable of acquiring general knowledge on a broad or liberal scale. All is confined to trade, finance, law, and small, local, provincial information. Art, science, literature are nearly dead letters to them. But the foregoing opinions must be taken like all those given wholesale and on general concerns, with the usual "grain of salt," in this case a very large one.

Before the Civil War, most Americans lived on farms where life was hard. Almost all work was done by hand. The young had to help along with adults, and the day was long. John Muir, a naturalist and writer, describes his boyhood on the farm. (36)

FROM SUNUP TO SUNDOWN

*John Muir**

The summer work, on the contrary, was deadly heavy, especially harvesting and corn-hoeing. All the ground had to be hoed over for the first few years, before father bought cultivators or small weedcovering plows, and we were not allowed a moment's rest. The hoes had to be kept working up and down as steadily as if they were moved by machinery. Plowing for winter wheat was comparatively easy, when we walked barefooted in the furrows, while the fine autumn tints kindled in the woods and the hillsides were covered with golden pumpkins.

In summer the chores were grinding scythes, feeding the animals, chopping stove-wood, and carrying water up the hill from the spring on the edge of the meadow, etc. Then breakfast, and to the harvest or hayfield. I was foolishly ambitious to be first in mowing and cradling, and by the time I was sixteen led all the hired men. An hour was allowed at noon for dinner and more chores. We stayed in the field until dark, then supper, and still more chores, family worship, and to bed, making altogether a hard, sweaty day of about sixteen or seventeen hours. Think of that, ye blessed eight-hour-day laborers!

In winter father came to the foot of the stairs and called us at six o'clock to feed the horses and cattle, grind axes, bring in wood, and do any other chores required, then breakfast, and out to work in the mealy, frosty snow by daybreak, chopping, fencing, etc. So in general our winter work was about as restless and trying as that of the long-day summer. No matter what the weather, there was always something to do. During heavy rains or snowstorms we worked in the barn, shelling corn, fanning wheat, thrashing with the flail, making axe-handles or ox-yokes, mending things, or sprouting and sorting potatoes in the cellar.

No pains were taken to diminish or in any way soften the natural hardships of this pioneer farm life, nor did any of the Europeans seem to know how to find reasonable ease and comfort if they would. The very best oak and hickory fuel was embarrassingly abundant and cost nothing but cutting and common sense; but instead of hauling great heart-cheering loads of it for wide, open, all-welcoming, climate-changing, beauty-making, Godlike ingle-fires, it was hauled with weary heartbreaking industry into fences and waste places to get it out of the way of the plow, and out of the way of doing good. The only fire for the whole house was the kitchen stove, with a firebox about eighteen inches long and eight inches wide and deep,—scant space for three or four small sticks, around which in hard zero weather all the family of ten persons shivered, and beneath which in the morning we found our socks and coarse, soggy boots frozen solid. We were not allowed to start even this despicable little fire in its black box to thaw them. No, we had to squeeze our throbbing, aching, chilblained feet into them, causing greater pain than toothache, and hurry out to chores. Fortunately the miserable chilblain pain began to abate as soon as the temperature of our feet approached the freezing point, enabling us in spite of hard work and hard frost to enjoy the winter beauty,—the wonderful radiance of the snow when it was starry with crystals, and the dawns and the sunsets and white noons, and the cheery, enlivening company of the brave chickadees and nuthatches.

The Industrial Revolution, with its need for cheap labor combined with the puritan gospel of work, provided a perfect rationale for exploitation of the young. Working conditions were unregulated and it was not unusual for girls to work in textile mills for twelve or fourteen hours a day. They usually stayed in boardinghouses in town to be close to their work. The following excerpt describes a visit to the textile mills of New England. (41)

A NEW KIND OF FEUDALISM

We have lately visited the cities of Lowell [Massachusetts] and Manchester, New Hampshire, and have had an opportunity of examining the factory system more closely than before. We had distrusted the accounts, which we had heard from persons engaged in the labor reform, now beginning to agitate New England; we could scarcely credit the statements made in relation to the exhausting nature of the labor in the mills, and to the manner in which the young women, the operatives, lived in their boarding houses, six sleeping in a room, poorly ventilated.

We went through many of the mills, talked particularly to a large number of the operatives, and ate at their boarding houses, on purpose to ascertain by personal inspection the facts of the case. We assure our readers that very little information is possessed, and no correct judgments formed, by the public at large, of our factory system, which is the first germ of the industrial or commercial feudalism that is to spread over our land. . . .

In Lowell live between seven and eight thousand young women, who are generally daughters of farmers of the different states of New England; some of them are members of families that were rich the generation before. . . .

The operatives work thirteen hours a day in the summer time, and from daylight to dark in the winter. At half past four in the morning the factory bell rings, and at five the girls must be in the mills. A clerk, placed as a watch, observes those who are a few minutes behind the time, and effectual means are taken to stimulate to punctuality. This is the morning commencement of the industrial discipline (should we not rather say industrial tyranny?), which is established in these associations of this moral and Christian community. At seven the girls are allowed thirty minutes for breakfast, and at noon thirty minutes more for dinner, except during the first quarter of the year, when the time is extended to forty-five minutes. But within this time they must hurry to their boarding houses and return to the factory, and that through the hot sun, or the rain and cold. A meal eaten under such circumstances must be quite unfavorable to digestion and health, as any medical man will inform us. At seven o'clock in the evening the factory bell sounds the close of the day's work.

Thus thirteen hours per day of close attention and monotonous labor are exacted from the young women in these manufactories. . . . So fatigued—we should say, exhausted and worn out, but we wish to speak of the system in the simplest language —are numbers of the girls, that they go to bed soon after their evening meal, and endeavor by a comparatively long sleep to relieve their weakened frames for the toils of the coming day. When capital has got thirteen hours of labor daily out of a being, it can get nothing more. It would be a poor speculation in an industrial point of view to own the operative; for the trouble and expense of providing for times of sickness and old age would more than counterbalance the difference between the price of wages and the expense of board and clothing. The far greater number of fortunes accumulated by the North in comparison with the South shows that hireling labor is more profitable for capital than slave labor.

Now let us examine the nature of the labor itself and the conditions under which it is performed. Enter with us into the large rooms, when the looms are at work. The largest that we saw is in the Amoskeag Mills at Manchester. It is 400 feet long and about 70 broad; there are 500 looms and 21,000 spindles in it. The din and clatter of these 500 looms under full operation struck us on first entering as something frightful and infernal, for it seemed such an atrocious violation of one of the faculties of the human soul, the sense of hearing. After a while we became somewhat inured to it, and by speaking quite close to the ear of an operative and quite loud, we could hold a conversation and make the inquiries we wished.

The girls attend upon an average three looms; many attend four, but this requires a very active person and the most unremitting care. However, a great many do it. Attention to two is as much as should be demanded of an operative. This gives us some idea of the application required during the thirteen hours of daily labor. The atmosphere of such a room cannot of course be pure; on the contrary it is charged with cotton filaments and dust, which, we are told, are very injurious to the lungs. On entering the room, although the day was warm, we remarked that the windows were down; we asked the reason, and a young woman answered very naively, and without seeming to be in the least aware that this privation of fresh air was anything else than perfectly natural, that "when the wind blew, the threads did not work so well." After we had been in the room for fifteen or twenty minutes, we found ourselves, as did the persons who accompanied us, in quite a perspiration, produced by a certain moisture which we observed in the air, as well as by the heat. . . .

The young women sleep upon an average six in a room, three beds to a room. There is no privacy, no retirement here; it is almost impossible to read or write alone, as the parlor is full and so many sleep in the same chamber. A young woman remarked to us, that if she had a letter to write, she did it on the head of a bandbox, sitting on a trunk, as there was not space for a table. So live and toil the young women of our country in the boarding houses and manufactories which the rich and influential of our land have built for them.

Students of every generation find social evils and causes to protest against. If these causes are antiestablishment, society finds ways to punish its youth for their radicalism. During the early nineteenth century, students protested against slavery and spearheaded the abolition movement. The following excerpt describes student involvement in the effort to abolish slavery. One result of the efforts described was the student founding of Oberlin Institute (later a college) in Ohio and of other schools. (31)

THE STUDENT ABOLITION MOVEMENT

Harriet Martineau

The students of Lane Seminary, near Cincinnati, of which Dr. Beecher is the president, became interested in the subject [abolition] three or four years ago, and formed themselves into an Abolition Society, debating the question and taking in newspapers. This was prohibited by the tutors but persevered in by the young men, who conceived that this was a matter with which the professors had no right to meddle. Banishment was decreed, and all submitted to expulsion but fourteen. Of course, each of the dispersed young men became the nucleus of an Abolition Society and gained influence by persecution. It was necessary for them to provide means to finish their education.

One of them, Amos Dresser, [moved about] (as is usual in the sparsely peopled West), traveling in a gig and selling Scott's Bible to raise money for his educational purposes. He reached Nashville in Tennessee and there fell under suspicion of abolition treason, his baggage being searched and a whole abolition newspaper and a part of another being found among the packing-stuff of his Bibles. There was also an unsubstantiated rumor of his having been seen conversing with slaves.

He was brought to trial by the Committee of Vigilance, seven elders of the Presbyterian Church at Nashville being among his judges. After much debate as to whether he should be hanged, or flogged with more or fewer lashes, he was condemned to receive twenty lashes with a cowhide in the marketplace of Nashville. He was immediately conducted there, made to kneel down on the flint pavement, and punished according to his sentence, the mayor of Nashville presiding and the public executioner being the agent. He was warned to leave the city within twenty-four hours, but was told by some charitable person who had the bravery to take him in, wash his stripes, and furnish him with a disguise that it would not be safe to remain so long. He stole away immediately, in his dreadful condition, on foot, and when his story was authenticated had heard nothing of his horse, gig, and Bibles, which he values at three hundred dollars. . . .

The other young men found educational and other assistance immediately, and a set of noble institutions has grown out of their persecution. There were professors ready to help them, and a gentleman gave them a farm in Ohio on which to begin a manual-labor college called the Oberlin Institute. It is on a most liberal plan, young women who wish to become qualified for "Christian teaching" being admitted and there being no prejudice of color. They have a sprinkling both of Indians and Negroes. They do all the farm and house work and as much study besides as is good for them. Some of the young women are already fair Hebrew and Greek scholars. In a little while the estate was so crowded and the new applications were so overpowering that they were glad to accept the gift of another farm. When I left the country, within three years from their commencement, they had either four or five flourishing institutions in Ohio and Michigan while the Lane Seminary drags on feebly with its array of tutors and dearth of pupils.

THE JITTERBUG ERA. Every adult generation criticizes its young for their music. Today's parents criticize their adolescents for rock music and for their desire to attend rock concerts, forgetting that they loved to go to big-band concerts to hear jazz and swing during the jitterbug era. The following excerpt from *The New York Times* in 1943 describes the gathering to hear Harry James, the new big-band idol and trumpeter, in concert at New York. (5)

GATHERING OF THE HEPCATS

*Meyer Berger**

The peculiar behavior of jitterbugs, chiefly but not entirely adolescents, who have swarmed to the Paramount Theater [in New York City] to sigh and all but swoon over the trumpeting of the band leader Harry James, continued yesterday to the disgust and amazement of police and puzzled adult passersby.

Yesterday, as on Tuesday, lines formed outside the theater in the predawn hours. Some of the boys and girls were there at four o'clock in the morning. By 9 A.M. the line reached westward to Eighth Avenue and doubled back on itself along its entire length to Seventh. Thirty patrolmen . . . and three mounted policemen rode herd on the jitterbugs. The children were good-natured and never disorderly, but their tenseness and their strange yearning for "hot music" bewildered the police.

Most of the jitterbugs wore the strange garb affected by the breed. Some were no more than twelve or thirteen years old, which is under legal age for admission to a theater without adult escort. The police cut some 75 minors out of line and sent them home. A police sergeant estimated that some 7500 children were in line by 9 o'clock. The figure included those who were admitted at 7:30 A.M., which is one hour ahead of regular opening time. During this period, when the jitterbugs are in full swing, the theater gives seven shows a day instead of five.

The children all seemed clean, bright-faced, and alert, but they also seemed inarticulate when they were asked what brought in such swarms to hear a trumpeter.

"You can't really tell what it is," the consensus seemed to be. "It's only that shivers run down your spine when that trumpet gets hot."

In the line, questioning developed, were children from fairly remote communities in New Jersey and Westchester County. Some had written to the theater a week in advance to learn what time each show went on. Many brought their lunch or lived on chocolate bars in order to stay through three, four, or five shows.

. . . *A clean blond youth* [20 years old], who is a machinist's helper, confided that he had sacrificed eleven hours' work at 75 cents an hour in order to sit all day listening to the jitterbug music. [Another boy] . . . , wearing the most extreme cut

* Meyer Berger, "Jitterbugs Again Swarm to See Their 'Hot Music' Idol in Person," *The New York Times*, April 23, 1943. Copyright © 1943 by The New York Times Company. Reprinted by permission.

and rig of the jitterbug—the porkpie hat, the fingertip coat, and the tight-bottomed trousers, said he had begged his boss in a Harlem . . . grocery store to let him off for the day. He lost five dollars in salary but said it was worth it.

. . . Children who had sat through several performances on Tuesday waited all day at the stage door for a glimpse of Harry James, who is a rather ordinary-looking chap, . . . but their god of the moment.

"We just want to see him, maybe shake his hand," one of the girl devotees told reporters simply. "He's wonderful."

This seemed to be the general attitude. It was carried one degree further by a girl who stood in silent worship before the trumpeter's picture in the lobby. . . .

Inside the theater observers noted the adolescents in a semihypnotic state when James appeared on stage bathed in a mystic blue light. Girls whispered his name, shifted restlessly in their seats, clasped their hands tightly.

When children in the audience were asked why they were so moved at sight of Mr. James and by the sounds from his trumpet, they seemed puzzled. To them the answer was simple.

"He gets you," they'd say, "but you feel it more when you're up close in the front rows. It does something to your blood. If you were a hepcat, you'd understand."

The music from the trumpet seemed quite ordinary, no different from any blare and bray of the usual jazz band, but this apparently was due to some defect in the adult makeup. The children could not understand why adults were unmoved by it.

At some points in the program the entire audience clapped hands or stamped with their feet in strange beat, following the trumpet's and the saxophones' rhythm. They swayed or bobbed in their seats and you could hear the children nearby breathe, "Come on, Harry," an appeal to the trumpeter.

Discussion Questions

1. Evaluate the validity of the statement: "Today's adolescents have been labeled the hedonistic generation."

2. Compare the rules of etiquette in "The Good Manners Checklist" with rules parents establish for their adolescents today. Which system do you feel is better for the adolescent?

3. Why are adults of every generation critical of their youths?

4. Do you believe today's youths are spoiled? Why? Why not? How do you feel the situation could be made better?

5. Comment on the life of youths in the nineteenth century as revealed in the passages that describe life in the rural United States and in the factories of New England. How did adolescent life then compare to now? Were there any advantages to this type of life over the lives of adolescents today?

6. Why do some youths say: "Never trust anyone over thirty?"

7. Do adolescents want dialogue with the older generation? Do adults want dialogue with them?

Suggestions for Interviews

1. *In-Class:* Bring in a group of parents of adolescents to act as a panel and have class members ask them questions concerning their feelings about youths today and their personal reactions to them.

2. *Out-of-Class:* Ask a number of adults individually how they feel about today's youths. Do they like them? What do they like or not like about them? How do young people today differ from those of previous generations?

Bibliography

1. Adelson, J. "Adolescence and the Generation Gap." *Psychology Today*, February 1979, pp. 33ff.

2. Bachman, J. G. *Youth Look at National Problems: A Special Report from the Youth in Transition Project.* Ann Arbor: Institute for Social Research, University of Michigan, 1971.

3. Barr, R. D. "Today's Youth: Cluttered Values and Troubled Dreams." In *Values and Youth.* Edited by R. D. Barr. Washington, D.C.: National Council for the Social Studies, 1971, pp. 11–25.

4. Bengston, V. L., and Starr, J. M. "Contract and Consensus: A Generational Analysis of Youth in the 1970s." In *Youth: The Seventy-fourth Yearbook of the National Society for the Study of Education,* Part I. Edited by R. J. Havighurst and P. H. Dreyer. Chicago: University of Chicago Press, 1975, pp. 224–266.

5. Berger, M. "Jitterbugs Again Swarm to See Their 'Hot Music' Idol in Person." *The New York Times,* 23 April 1943, p. 19. Copyright © 1943 by The New York Times Company. Reprinted by permission.

6. Braungart, R. G. "Youth and Social Movements." In *Adolescence in the Life Cycle.* Edited by S. G. Dragastin and G. H. Elder, Jr. New York: John Wiley and Sons, 1975, pp. 255–289.

7. Bromley, Dorothy. "Youth and Sex." In F. R. Donovan. *Wild Kids.* Harrisburg, Pa.: Stackpole Co., 1967.

8. Caplow, T., and Bahr, H. M. "Half a Century of Change in Adolescent Attitudes: Replication of a Middletown Survey by the Lynds." *Public Opinion Quarterly* 43 (Spring 1979): 1–17.

9. Coleman, J. S. *Adolescents and the Schools.* New York: Basic Books, Inc., 1965.

10. ———. *The Adolescent Society.* New York: Free Press, 1961.

11. Conger, J. J. "A World They Never Knew: The Family and Social Change." *Daedalus* (Fall 1971): 1105–1134.

12. Davis, Katherine. "Adolescence and the Social Structures." *Annals of the American Academy of Political and Social Science,* 263 (1944): 1–168.

13. Denisoff, R. S., and Peterson, R. A. *The Sounds of Social Change.* Chicago: Rand McNally, 1972.

14. Donovan, F. R. *Wild Kids.* Harrisburg, Pa.: Stackpole Co., 1967.

15. Drinkwater, D. J. "The Problems of Jocasta: A Theory of Adult Culpability." *Adolescence* 6 (1972): 77–94.

16. Drane, J. *A New American Reformation.* New York: Philosophical Library, 1973.

17. Farrow, P. "The Presymposial State." *Andover Review,* 5 (Spring 1978): 14–37.

18. Feigelson, N. *The Underground Revolution.* New York: Funk and Wagnalls, 1970.

19. Flasher, J. "Adultism." *Adolescence* 13 (1978): 517–523.

20. Frankel, J., and Dullaert, J. "Is Adolescent Rebellion Universal?" *Adolescence* 12 (1977): 227–236.

21. Gallup, G. H. *The Gallup Poll: Public Opinion Survey, 1976–1977,* Vol. 2. Wilmington, Del.: Scholarly Resources, 1978.

22. Gerzon, M. *The Whole World Is Watching.* New York: Paperback Library, 1970.

23. Grattan, T. C. *Civilized America,* vol. 2. London: Bradbury and Evans, 1859, pp. 314–320.

24. Grey Marketing and Research Department. "A Strategic Study for Communication Programs in Alcohol and Highway Safety." No. 10300 BR 606 Washington, D.C.: Office of Pedestrian and Driver Programs, National Highway Traffic Safety Administration, U.S. Department of Transportation, November, 1974.

25. Guthrie, Arlo. "The Motorcycle Song." Appleseed Music, Inc., 1967, 1969.

26. Hechinger, G., and Hechinger, F. *Teen-Age Tyranny.* Greenwich, Conn.: Fawcett Publications, 1963.

27. Keniston, K. *Youth and Dissent: The Rise of the New Opposition.* New York: Harcourt Brace Jovanovich, 1971.

28. "A Letter to the Editor," *The New England Courant,* 11 March, 1723.

29. "Listening to a Brain Rotting." *Psychology Today* (February 1979): 44.

30. Lorenz, D. "The Enmity between Generations and Its Probable Ethological Causes." *Psychoanalytic Review* 57 (1970): 333–377.

31. Martineau, H. *Society in America.* New York and London: Sanders and Otley, 1837, pp. 371–373.

32. Matteson, D. R. *Adolescence Today.* Homewood, Ill.: Dorsey Press, 1975.

33. Mays, J. B. *The Young Pretenders.* 2d ed. New York: Schocken Books, 1965.

34. Millay, Edna St. Vincent. *Collected Lyrics of Edna St. Vincent Millay.* New York: Harper and Row, 1939.

35. Moody, Eleazar. *The School of Good Manners, Composed for the Help of Parents in Teaching Their Children How to Carry It in Their Places During Their Minority.* Boston, 1772, pp. 17–19. Reprinted in *Children and Youth in America: A Documentary His-*

tory, Vol. 1, 1600–1865. Edited by Robert H. Bremner et al. Cambridge, Mass.: Harvard University Press, 1970, pp. 33–34.

36. Muir, John. *The Story of My Boyhood and Youth*. Boston: Houghton Mifflin Co., 1923. pp. 201–205. Copyright renewed 1941 by Wanda Muir Hanna. Reprinted by permission.

37. Muro, J. J. *Youth: New Perspective and Old Dimensions*. Columbus, Ohio: Charles E. Merrill Publishing Co., 1973.

38. Murphey, Michael. "Waking Up." Mystery Music, Inc. BMI. © 1972.

39. Musgrove, F. *Youth and the Social Order*. Bloomington: Indiana University Press, 1965.

40. "A New Generation." *U.S. News & World Report*, 6 September 1976, pp. 45–61.

41. "A New Kind of Feudalism." *The Harbinger*, 14 November 1836.

42. Panel on Youth. President's Science Advisory Committee. *Youth: Transition to Adulthood*. Chicago: University of Chicago Press, 1974.

43. Philips, I., and Szurek, S. A. "Conformity, Rebellion, and Learning: Confrontation of Youth with Society." *American Journal of Orthopsychiatry* 40 (1970): 463–472.

44. Roper Organization. "Sex . . . Marriage . . . Divorce: What Women Think Today." *U.S. News & World Report*, 21 October 1974, p. 107.

45. Sampson, E. E., and Korn, H. A., eds. *Student Activism and Dissent: Alternative for Social Change*. San Francisco: Jossey-Bass, 1970.

46. Scammon, R., and Wattenberg, B. J. *The Real Majority*. New York: Coward McCann, 1970.

47. Schab, F. "Work Ethic of Gifted Black Adolescents." *Journal of Youth and Adolescence* 7 (September 1978): 295–299.

48. Shapiro, S. H. "Vicissitudes of Adolescence." In *Behavior Pathology of Childhood and Adolescence*. Edited by S. L. Copell. New York: Basic Books, 1973, pp. 93–117.

49. Spock, Dr. Benjamin. "Don't Blame Me." *Look Magazine*, 26 January 1971.

50. Wattenberg, W. W. *The Adolescent Years*. 2d ed. New York: Harcourt Brace Jovanovich, 1973.

51. Weiner, I. B. *Psychological Disturbance in Adolescence*. New York: John Wiley, 1970.

52. Yankelovich, D. *The New Morality. A Profile of American Youth in the 70's*. New York: McGraw Hill, 1974.

CHAPTER 2

Elements of Society:
Their Influence on the Adolescent

Outline

The society in which adolescents grow up has an important influence on their development, relationships, adjustments, and problems. The expectations of the society mold their personalities, influence their roles, and guide their futures. Social conditions help create or solve their problems or influence the adjustments they must make in solving them. The structure and functions of the society either help them fulfill their needs or create new problems by stimulating further tension and frustration. Because adolescents are social beings who are part of a larger society, there is a need to understand this social order and some of the ways it influences them.

A truly comprehensive examination of the many facets of American society and the numerous ways they influence adolescents would require volumes. Instead, discussion is confined to six important influences on today's adolescents: population characteristics, technological and social change, urbanization, affluence, mass communication, and social and emotional stress. Other influences, such as the family, peers, the school, and churches, will be discussed in later chapters.

Population Characteristics

THE BABY BOOM

The sheer size of today's population of adolescents is significant. After 1925 the birthrate reached a maximum in 1947 and remained relatively high for the

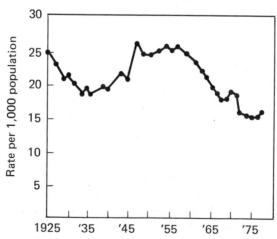

Figure 2–1. Birthrates: 1925 to 1977. (Adapted from U.S. Bureau of the Census, Department of Commerce, *Statistical Abstract of the United States, 1978* [Washington, D.C.: U.S. Government Printing Office, 1978], p. 59.)

Table 2–1.   Size of population aged 14–24 and percent change per decade.

Year	Size (Millions)	Percent Change
1900	16.5	+16
1910	20.0	+21
1920	20.8	+ 4
1930	24.8	+20
1940	26.3	+ 6
1950	24.2	− 8
1960	26.7	+10
1970	40.5	+52
1980	44.8	+11
1990	41.1	− 8

From U.S. Bureau of the Census, *U.S. Census of Population, 1960: General Population Characteristics, United States Summary*, Final Report PC(1)–1B (Washington, D.C.: U.S. Government Printing Office, 1961), Table 47; and U.S. Bureau of the Census, *Current Population Reports*, Series P-25, No. 470, "Projections of the Population of the United States, by Age and Sex: 1970 to 2020" (Washington, D.C.: U.S. Government Printing Office, 1971), Table 2, Series D.

next fifteen years. (41, 49) Today's huge population of adolescents is the result. (See Figure 2–1.) In terms of total numbers, there was a greater increase (13.8 million) in the population aged 14–24 during the one decade of the 1960s than in the rest of the century altogether. As indicated in Table 2–1, the relative rise in the past decade was an unparalleled 52 percent. (37, p. 47) The total number aged 14–24 continued to rise until 1980, after which it began to decline. (22, p. 127) Figure 2–2 shows the trend from 1900 to 1990. (48, 47)

Not only are total numbers significant, but also the proportion of young people to older people in the population. Since 1920 the proportion of youth aged 14–24 in relation to the population aged 25–64 reached a new high in 1970 and remained high until 1980, after which the ratio declined sharply. Figure 2–2 shows the trend from 1900 to 1990.

IMPLICATIONS

The high ratio of youths to adults means there are more young people to be socialized by fewer adults, and fewer to support the large number of dependents. An increasing number of social and educational services for youths are needed. And because of their large numbers, youths constitute a sizeable power segment of the population.

One immediate effect on adolescents has been economic. *Society has had difficulty absorbing such large numbers of youths into the labor force.* (12) During the decade 1960–1970, the total number of youths aged 16–24 increased 46 percent, but the total number employed increased only 36 percent. (37, p. 50) For adolescent males the figures are even more striking. The number of males in the 16–19 age group increased 44 percent from 1960 to 1970, but the number employed increased by only 11 percent (37, p. 50) This means that the proportion

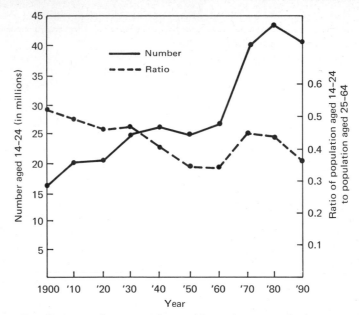

Figure 2-2.   Population aged 14–24 and ratio of population aged 14–24 to population
aged 25–64, 1900–1990. (Adapted from U.S. Bureau of the Census, *U.S. Census of
Population, 1960: General Population Characteristics, United States Summary,*
Final Report PC(1)–1B [Washington, D.C.: U.S. Government Printing Office,
1961], Table 47; and U.S. Bureau of the Census, *Current Population Reports,*
Series P-25, No. 470, "Projections of the Population of the United States, by Age
and Sex: 1970 to 2020" [Washington, D.C.: U.S. Government Printing Office,
1971], Table 2, Series D.)

of adolescent males in the labor force declined considerably, and that millions
of youths who wanted to work could not find jobs. The excessive leisure and
idleness that resulted were partly responsible for the increase in a host of other
social problems such as delinquency, drug abuse, and racial unrest.

This situation has been somewhat alleviated as the baby-boom youths have
moved into adulthood. The number of young job seekers is declining, and unemployment among youths has decreased. (18) Nevertheless, there remain jobless about one-third of nonwhite teenagers and one-sixth of white teenagers aged
16–19 in the labor force. (35)

Because of youths' inability to find employment, *the schools bore the brunt
of the population explosion.* Table 2–2 shows the increase in enrollment at the
Austin campus of the University of Texas. In 1940 enrollment was 11,000; in
1950, 14,000; and in 1960, 19,000. Most institutions could accommodate this
gradual increase. But from 1960 to 1970 enrollment jumped from 19,000 to
39,000 students—a rate of change that would challenge any school. (51, p. 23) In
1979 the enrollment leveled off at 43,000 students and is expected to decline.
The same trends have occurred in many other schools. (20, p. 2)

At the very time college enrollments were exploding, so were the disturbing social and political events of the sixties: the assassination of John F. Kennedy
and the murder of Martin Luther King; the racial confrontations in Mississippi

Table 2–2.   Student enrollment at University of Texas at Austin.

School Year	Student Enrollment
1940–1941	11,000
1950–1951	14,000
1960–1961	19,000
1970–1971	39,000
1978–1979	43,000

and Alabama; the bloody race riots in Harlem, Watts, and Newark; the war in Vietnam; student protests beginning at Berkeley and culminating in the Kent State tragedy in 1970. The rise of a powerful and idealistic political force of young people, then, occurred at the very time of maximum social and political upheaval. *Youth became a powerful political force, partly because of the sheer weight of their numbers.* Even if only one-fourth of the students participated in demonstrations (as one Gallup poll showed in May, 1969), thousands would have been involved. (7, p. 249)

The greater the number of adolescents in any society, the more the society tends to focus attention on them. Any age group that is a minority gets little attention. Adolescents, however, are not a minority. (22, p. 4) *One result is a youth-oriented, youth-dominated culture.* Moller writes:

In any community, the presence of a large number of adolescents and young adults influences the temper of life; and the greater the proportion of young people the greater the likelihood of cultural and political change. . . . The unprecedented number of young people in the world today can be isolated as one of the crucial reality factors conditioning political and cultural developments. (32, pp. 56, 72)

As the current generation of adolescents gets older, there will be a significant increase in the number of middle-aged Americans. By 1989 the typical U.S. citizen will be 32.5 years of age, the oldest on record. (24, p. 76) Gradually we will see a shift in the focus of our culture from youth to the aged.

Technological and Social Change

NATURE OF THE CHANGE

The adolescent of today lives in a society undergoing intensive and rapid technological change. Probably no society has so revered technological innovation or placed less restraint upon it than modern American culture. Americans have such unqualified acceptance of scientific advancement that they do anything to stimulate, encourage, and speed it along. Since the turn of the century they have witnessed unprecedented advances: the introduction of electricity, radio, television, the automobile, airplane, atomic energy, rocketry, and the automation of industry. Each new invention stimulates in turn a series of additional technological changes.

In every culture, technological innovation becomes the stimulus and the motor for social change as well. Consider the automobile as a modern example.

The development of the motor car has changed patterns of work and residence, making it possible for people to live dozens of miles from their jobs. Whole patterns of family living have changed, with the family becoming more mobile and its members more separated. The automobile has made possible the regional consolidation of schools, with adolescents attending with hundreds of others from a wide geographic area. The automobile has transformed the rural United States into a sprawling complex of turnpikes and freeways. It has been instrumental in encouraging urban blight as middle class families retreat to the suburbs, leaving the minority poor to inhabit the largest cities. Thus, each new technological invention has consequences for social living. A series of technological inventions necessitates an increasing number of social adjustments.

For the most part these changes have been unplanned and unguided. Social transformations have occurred in a "free, natural way" as a haphazard result of technological progress. It is difficult to guide, predict, or alter the future directions of these changes. The growth of the megalopolis, the sprawling urban complex of cities reaching out to touch each other has obliterated the countryside and polluted the environment. Not only has the physical environment become completely altered and almost unmanageable, but the social climate has suffered as well. The faster the city grows, the more difficult it is for people to exert any control over their physical environment or their social order. Eisenberg writes:

What we have failed to recognize is that the rate of change is accelerating; the conventional indices of "progress" are insufficient to measure full costs. . . . Changes in our daily lives occur at such a pace that discontinuities rather than mere differences appear between the life experiences of the old and young. (15, p. 3)

EFFECTS OF CHANGE

These rapid technological and social changes have profound effects upon the adolescent. (30) Four of these effects will be discussed here; for additional information see Chapters 3, 10, 13, 15, 21, and 22.

The past grows increasingly distant from the present. As a result the past has less influence and hold on the adolescent, and past solutions to life's problems are not necessarily relevant. The more rapid and drastic the social changes, the more different are standards and patterns of life from those of previous years. This makes the adolescent feel that anything old is also outmoded and irrelevant, so that it ought not to be allowed to exert much influence over today's life. This is one reason today's youth are contemptuous of the past: they feel that because things were so different then, the past should hold no meaning for the present.

The future grows more remote, uncertain, and unpredictable, so the adolescent feels less secure about tomorrow. When standards, customs, mores, social structures, conditions, and functions are changing rapidly, it becomes hard to predict what things are going to be like in the years to come and more difficult to prepare for that future. The adolescent is pushed into living more in the present than in the future. "Why worry about tomorrow? I can't know what tomorrow will bring. All I can do is to live day by day." Such feelings are actually quite common among modern youths and reflect their uncertainties about tomorrow. This tendency to live in the present without concern for the future is expressed in the words of a modern ballad entitled "South Canadian River Song."

Drink life one drop at a time.
Time . . .
Flow with the Stream in your Soul.
Soul . . .
Pour your Soul in the River of Life.
Life . . .
Rush to the Ocean of God.
God . . . (33)*

The relations between the generations are weakened as the rate of social innovations increases and as the generation gap widens. (34) This lapse makes communication more difficult, and parents exercise less influence. (13) There is less continuity between generations in attitudes toward political and social issues. (36) The two generations have more trouble understanding each other. Adolescents tend to think their parents' ideas are old-fashioned, so they reject their ideas. (29, p. 53) Parents are more likely to believe their adolescents' ideas are radical, so they become critical. Disagreement and conflict come about because of change. When there is rapid change, there is more likely to be conflict and misunderstanding. (7)

Rapid change weakens the roles and functions of the family. Emotional ties are loosened by geographic mobility. Fewer interpersonal contacts result in a decrease of affective interchange—socialization and emotional and morale-building functions. As a result, the nuclear family is less able to fulfill its affective functions and disintegrates under the strain, as documented by the high divorce rate and the growing number of one-parent families. This has serious consequences for the young, as we shall see. (15, p. 4)

Cultural confusion with shifting beliefs, attitudes, values, mores, and standards results in stress, conflict, and personality disturbance in the lives of young people. In a world of pluralistic standards, changing customs, and uncertain values, it becomes difficult for adolescents to know how to live and what to believe. Uncertainty and conflict create disturbing internal stress. When everyone in a culture accepts the same ideas and values, adolescents find it easier and more secure to know and accept the status quo; but when they are confronted with changing, conflicting ideas and values, they feel forced to shift about, trying to find meaning for themselves. Those who discover ideas and values that are acceptable are fortunate. The others who do not may remain in a state of confusion and turmoil for years.

One result of change is a spiritual vacuum in which adolescents have difficulty finding identity. They ask: "Can I commit my life to anything? Is there anything in human culture today worth saving, worth committing myself to?" (30, p. xii) Among some of the young this pain comes close to being a mass

* Michael Murphey, "South Canadian River Song." Copyright © 1973 by Mystery Music, Inc. BMI. Used by permission.

neurosis: a lack of faith in self, an emptiness of spirit, a lack of order and direction. (1, p. 146) As one youth expressed it very longingly; "The answer must be out there somewhere."

Urbanization

As Americans leave the farms and move to the cities in increasing numbers, the lives of people are drastically altered. (24) For one thing, the *sheer size of the city makes personal, close human relationships more difficult.* Neighbors remain strangers, so it becomes harder for people to find meaningful relationships or emotional involvement. (5) Affectional needs may not be met; the individual feels isolated and alone in a city with millions of people. (Additional information on the social adjustments of adolescents may be found in Chapter 11.)

Paul Simon expressed the isolation and aloneness of the modern adolescent in the song entitled: "I Am a Rock."

I've built walls
A fortress deep and mighty,
That none may penetrate
I have no need of friendship;
Friendship causes pain
It's laughter and it's loving I disdain.
I am a rock,
I am an island.
And a rock can feel no pain;
And an island never cries. (24)*

There are urban high schools today with student enrollments exceeding five thousand. How can the adolescent in this educational complex find identity or any sense of belonging?

Urbanization creates impersonalization in the family also. (14) Home, school, and work may be separated by great distances. The father commutes into the city to work, leaving at dawn, returning at dusk. Adolescents ride the school bus to the consolidated high school, seldom seeing their parents during daylight hours, at least in the winter. The mother may drive a different direction to her job, her shopping, or her social gathering. It becomes harder for family members to be together or to relate to each other personally when they seldom see one another or spend much time together. (10, 16)

Urbanization also creates a host of social problems: overcrowding, poverty, slums, gangs, delinquency, and other problems that go with city life. Cities have a way of altering the lives of people, imposing stresses, strain, temptations, and problems on the children and youths growing up within their confines. Not every effect of city life is negative. Sometimes the city may offer superior educational opportunities, recreational facilities, or cultural influences. But as more and more cities become dangerous and depersonalizing, the social disadvantages of living there increasingly outweigh the advantages. (6)

---

* Paul Simon, "I Am a Rock." © 1965 Paul Simon. Used with the permission of the publisher.

Affluence

PERVASIVENESS AND CONSEQUENCES

Today's generation of youths has grown up in a time of affluence unprecedented in the history of the world. The gross national product has now reached over one trillion dollars, with the majority of youths sharing in the benefits of this prosperity and a minority, by comparison, becoming poorer than ever. Those youths who were affluent refuse to worry financially about tomorrow. Money is at hand because Dad seems to offer an ample supply. As a result this generation is probably the richest ever born. This situation has had a number of important consequences.

Today's youths constitute a huge consumers' market. Business caters directly to them; clothes, cosmetics, automobiles, records, stereos, skis, snowmobiles, motorcycles, magazines, grooming aids, sports equipment, cigarettes, and thousands of other items are given the hard sell to attract the dollars of increasing numbers of youths. (3) Youths have come to expect things when they marry; the largest single group of credit buyers, they are the "buy now, pay later" generation. Why save, why be deprived now, when a credit card will get anything desired?

A segment of the youth culture, especially at the junior high and high school levels, has become a status-conscious, prestige-seeking culture. The emphasis is

The Affluent Generation

Figure 2–3. Reprinted from P. Farrow, "The Presymposial State," *The Andover Review* 5 (Spring 1978): 30. Copyright © by The Trustees of Phillips Academy. Used by permission.

on winning the struggle for status and position. (See Chapter 9 for additional information.) And because the outcome rather than the means is the important thing, ability is often subordinated to agility. The school grading system supports this emphasis: the adolescent tries to second-guess the teacher, to "get in good with the teacher," or to cheat on exams to get the grades, rather than studying to learn. (21, p. 46)

Those families who have not been able to keep up with the struggle for money, status, and prestige seem poorer than ever. As a result their adolescents feel abandoned and rejected. Those adolescents who come from extremely poor families (and these families make up at least one-tenth of the population) are non-joiners in school activities, are seldom elected to positions of prestige, and often seek status through antisocial behavior. These youths struggle for identity and sometimes become problems, because they have to find an identity that middle class society rejects. (Chapter 22 discusses further the plight of youths of low socioeconomic status.)

A certain percentage of middle class and upper middle class youth have rebelled against the overemphasis upon materialism and seem to want the other extreme. These adolescents are more content with very few material possessions, emphasizing instead relationships with other people and with the world of nature. This is partly a reaction again "life with father," in whch Dad sought to discharge his parental responsibility with money rather than by giving of himself. (9) Such youths seek position through meaningful personal relationships. Some are experimenting with various forms of group life, emphasizing love and togetherness in their relationships. (See Chapter 16.) Others have joined the activists who are openly fighting against what they feel are hypocritical, superficial, and false values and undesirable priorities and goals of society.

Affluence has created an opportunity for leisure for the young. This mixed blessing allows youth the opportunity to engage in social welfare work and reform, political activism, or conservation campaigns, but it also allows more opportunity for the pursuit of hedonistic pastimes or getting into mischief.

Child labor laws, originally passed for humanitarian reasons (to keep children from being exploited twelve to fifteen hours a day in sweatshops) sometimes operate against the well-being of youths. Restrictions on youth employment sometimes prevent those who want and need to work from finding gainful employment. In many states, adolescents are prevented from getting most types of employment until age sixteen, and many occupations classified as "hazardous" are closed to them until they are eighteen or twenty-one. Also because jobs for youths of all ages are sometimes scarce, thousands of young people wander the streets unemployed and become problems for themselves and society. Leisure is a problem to the dropout and slum occupant or to the unemployed or disenfranchised of any social class. (Additional information on employment of adolescents may be found in Chapter 21.)

Mass Communications

The mass media are partly responsible for creating the generation of consuming adolescents described in the section on affluence. Today's child has been surrounded, as no generation before, by messages on signs, billboards, in newspapers, magazines, radio, and television, urging the purchase of the newest antiperspirant, breakfast food, or shaving cream.

The mass media have also created an age of instant news: television viewers share in the experiences of starving Cambodians, the bombing of a United States embassy, or the murder of a national leader. Today's youths have not just heard about killing, they have seen and reacted to it in the nightly news. They have been bombarded with sensory information that affects the realm of emotion and feeling, as well as the cognitive perception. The insistent beat of global communication not only transforms the mind, but also motivates the will and stirs the emotions to action.

As a result some youths are skeptical about what they are told. They have learned to believe what they see happening rather than naively to accept what they are told is true. They have learned to see through false promises, to distinguish thought from action, and sham, pretense, and hypocrisy from sincerity and true concern. Furthermore, many have been moved to act and sacrifice for social causes they have come to feel are worthwhile. The media have made hypocrites, squares, and finks out of the world's big shots, and hippies, protesters, and social reformers out of some of its youths.

Social and Emotional Stress

THE VIOLENT YEARS

Today's generation of adolescents, born in the 1960s, have lived during a period that has been labeled "the violent years." (9, p. 178) This means that year after year they have been exposed to physical violence and disturbances in the world around them. A list of the most traumatic social and historical events of the last twenty years supports this claim.

1961
Freedom riders begin campaign to desegregate buses.
Cuban Bay of Pigs invasion.
Berlin crisis—dread of war.

1962
Cuban missile crisis—dread of war.
Chinese troops invade India.

1963
March on Washington.
Race riots in Birmingham—bombing of a church.
John Kennedy assassinated.

1964
Race riots in Philadelphia and Harlem.
Chinese explode A-bomb.

1965
Race riots in Watts district of Los Angeles.
Marches, race riots in Selma and Montgomery, Alabama.

Dynamiting of churches in Mississippi.
Bombing of North Vietnam.
Escalation of Vietnam war—antiwar demonstrations.

1966
Founding of Black Panther and "black power" movements.
Chicago race riots.
Student "Red Guards" in China involved in bloody cultural revolution.

1967
Race riots in 75 cities—looting, burning, 43 deaths in Detroit.
Arab–Israeli war.
Beginning of three-year civil war in Nigeria, Biafra.

1968
Martin Luther King assassinated.
Robert Kennedy assassinated.
Riots at Democratic National Convention.
Communists launch large-scale attacks in South Vietnam.
My Lai massacre in Vietnam.
Protests and violence at Columbia University.

1969
Landing on the moon.
Charles Manson murders.

1970
Attack on Cambodia.
Antiwar protests on campuses throughout the country.

1971
Invasion of Laos.
Resumption of bombing of North Vietnam.
Civil war in Pakistan, establishment of Bangladesh—millions of refugees, starvation.

1972
Communists launch major offensive in South Vietnam.
Mining of North Vietnamese harbors.
Stepped-up bombing of North Vietnam.

1973
Cease-fire in Vietnam.
Arab oil embargo begins.
Investigation of Watergate.

1974
Kidnapping of Patty Hearst.
Watergate indictments—President Nixon resigns.
Turkey invades Cyprus.
Widespread economic recession.

1975
Fall of South Vietnam to communists.
Unemployment hits thirty-three year high.
Guerrilla activity and fighting in Palestine, Lebanon.
Portuguese revolt and government overthrown.
Continued violence in Belfast, Ireland.

Investigations of FBI and CIA.
Fall of Laos government to communists.

1976
Continued bombings in Ireland.
War in Angola.
Syrian troops attack Palestinians in Lebanon to force a settlement in civil war—
    murder of U.S. ambassador.
Antibusing violence in Boston.
Political violence in Argentina.
Earthquake in China kills up to one million people.
Drought in Europe.

1977
Condemned murderer Gary Gilmore executed by firing squad.
China has worst drought since 1949.
Zambia declares war on Rhodesia.
"Son of Sam" suspect arraigned in New York City on six counts of murder.
Heavy fighting in Lebanon.
Racial violence and repression in South Africa.

1978
Air India Boeing 747 explodes killing 213 persons. Air collision kills 144 over
    San Diego.
Raging winter blizzard in North America.
Earthquake kills 25,000 in Iran.
San Francisco Mayor Moscone and superior assassinated.
Tanker Amoco Cadiz hits reef, spills record 1.6 million barrels of oil.
Vietnamese fighting in Cambodia.
Guerrilla attacks and fighting in Lebanon.
South African guerrillas fight in Angola.
Riots, martial law across Iran.
Ethiopian troops fight rebels.
Riots, demonstrations, strikes in Spain.
Italian terrorists kidnap and murder Italian Prime Minister Moro and 5 bodyguards in
    Rome.
Afghanistan President Daoud is killed.
Bolivian military seizes power.
Honduras military junta deposes chief of state.
Portuguese government falls.
Movies *Jaws* and *Star Wars* attract all-time record audiences.

A careful examination of these events suggests that today's adolescents have been living in a world characterized by Alvin Toffler as *future shock.* (46) Event has piled upon event to produce a state of trauma and unrest. Every generation has felt the shock of history, but probably not as deeply as today's youths, whose exposure has been continuous and worldwide. (51) Often this exposure has been direct and personal. One preteenager in Washington, D.C., says she sometimes walks in streets where she sees "blood everywhere." She wishes the United States were cleaner and that there were no killings or fightings.

From a psychological point of view, stress creates upset and insecurity; continued stress can result in disturbed behavior. Not all behavior of adolescents is disturbed, nor do all youths have emotional problems, but the widespread increase of mental illness, alcoholism, drug abuse, vandalism, and various forms of "acting-out" behavior among youths indicates that many do have psychological problems. Surveys show an increase in adolescent suicides, death by homicide, and overall anxiety and withdrawal behavior. (4) One of the most popular programs among youths of a local church has been a short course in death and dying. It seems certain that this increasing interest reflects anxiety. Psychiatrist Miller suggests that social stresses are partly responsible for adolescent problems. (31, p. 110)

The Spartans exposed their young to physical stress in order to toughen their society. This was a conscious decision, but eventually so much was demanded that by killing its young the society destroyed itself. Social stress applied to youth may produce similar effects in the Western world. Because of this it is very difficult for parents and other adults to know how much an adolescent's behavior is a function of family interaction and how much depends on stress in society-at-large. . . . This has been called a permissive society. . . . Society might more appropriately be considered confused and anxiety-ridden. (31, p. 123)

Miller goes on to suggest that young people need release from the tension created by these social pressures, primarily through goal-directed, constructive outlets. (31, p. 124) If constructive outlets are not provided, youths react with rage and anger, or with withdrawal. Some express their rage through vandalism or heated protest. Others withdraw and become cop-outs. In both cases the causes are the same: too much exposure to too much stress over too long a time.

Whether or not it is a unique attitude, today's youths find it hard to accept reassurances of a secure future. It is not surprising that they sometimes participate in meaningless and sometimes destructive violence against public institutions and buildings or in drug parties that turn off everyday sights and sounds to let in a psychedelic happening. Such self-destructive behavior is symbolic of a sense of uselessness and despair.

FAMILY DISORGANIZATION

Part of adolescents' emotional stress arises not from society, but from within their own families. The United States now has the highest divorce rate of any country. According to 1980 figures, about 33 percent of American marriages end in divorce. (19) Nearly two out of three of these divorces involve couples with children. (44, p. 1) The high divorce and separation rate, plus a rise in out-of-wedlock births, means that almost one-half of all children born in 1977 will spend a considerable amount of time living with one parent. (20, 50) There is also evidence that if parents remarry, living with stepparents is a more difficult adjustment for some adolescents than living with one divorced parent who does not remarry. (8, 13, 29)

This statement must be interpreted cautiously, however. Coming from a broken home has differential effects on adolescents. The effect of divorce can be positive if it ends turmoil and upset in the family. (11) Some adolescents whose parents had been divorced reported that parental conflict and tension beforehand was more stressful than the divorce itself. (27) These adolescents reported fear of physical violence, social embarrassment because of parental strife, upset over financial hardships because of separations, and anxiety and confusion because of successive separations and reconciliations of parents. (27) In such cases divorce came almost as a relief from years of strife. This is why, in some cases, children from happy but broken homes make better personality adjustments than those from unhappy but unbroken homes. (26, 41)

The overall effect of divorce depends upon the conditions of the divorce and on events before and after it. When there is little fighting between parents during and after the divorce, when the separation is amicable and when the children have free access to both parents and a lot of support from parents, siblings, and friends, upset is kept to a minimum. The situation is different in a bitterly fought divorce involving disputes over property, alimony, child custody, and other matters. (3, 40) Children are particularly affected if parents try to get them to take sides or exploit them as pawns, scapegoats, go-betweens, spies, informers, manipulators, and allies in punishing the other parent. (43) Postdivorce conflicts that go on for years increase adolescents' anxiety. Observers report an increase in adolescent irritability and aggressiveness, and a wide range of behavior disorders, neurotic conflicts, and psychotic breakdowns. (43) Sorosky reports:

Behavior problems include an abrupt decline in academic performance, aggressive acting-out at home and school, drug abuse, truancy, running away, sexual acting-out and group delinquent behavior. Neurotic conflicts include anxiety reactions, separation fears with school phobia, obsessive-compulsive symptoms with pervasive guilt, depersonalization experiences and psychophysiologic reactions, especially eating disorders. The stress of divorce can also be instrumental in precipitating a schizophrenic reaction. (44, p. 126)

One study of 5,376 juveniles showed that children of divorced parents were more than twice as likely to be charged with offenses as would be expected from their number in the population. (8) Other research, however, casts some doubt on the claim that the divorce of parents is a cause of delinquency. (23) There are simply too many variables to single out divorce as the reason. We know only that, other things being equal, a happy, unbroken home is better for adolescents than a happy, broken home, and that both are better than an unhappy, unbroken home, or an unhappy, broken home. When there is upset in the family of the adolescent, whether the parents divorce or remain unhappily married, the effect is disturbing. This is one reason why so many youths seek love and companionship and human warmth and intimacy with others outside their own family.

Conclusions

In summary, how have these elements of contemporary American society affected the adolescent?

1. The large number of adolescents resulting from the postwar baby boom has created problems for society in socializing them, educating them, and finding employment for them. Large numbers of youths mean that society has become a youth-oriented, youth-dominated culture, with young people constituting a powerful political force for change.

2. Because rapid technological and social changes have made the past less relevant and the future less secure, the present takes on major importance. Rapid

change also has made communication between generations more difficult, causing cultural confusion and personality conflict for the adolescent who is trying to find acceptable values and beliefs in a pluralistic society.

3. Urbanization and bigness make meaningful personal relationships more difficult. Because these relationships are important to adolescents, they are creating alternate life styles in order to find meaning. The city also creates a host of social, economic, and political problems that complicate the task of growing up.

4. Affluence has contributed, on the one hand, to the emergence of a generation of consuming, credit-buying, status-conscious youths and, on the other hand, to resentment among low income youths. At the same time, other adolescents have rebelled against the materialism of their culture and have returned to a simpler, more "natural" existence out of a sense of rebellion, despair, and longing. Both affluence and poverty have resulted in unemployment and increased leisure for adolescents, some of whom engage in worthwhile social action; others have not yet learned to use free time constructively.

5. Mass communication has been partly responsible for the hard sell. Instant news has had a maturing, sobering, sometimes upsetting effect upon today's youths, some of whom have become socially aware of the whole world.

6. Social violence and family disorganization have created emotional stress and insecurity which sometimes are manifested in disturbed behavior.

The next chapter will consider the whole period of adolescence, with special emphasis on the constructive, positive tasks young people face.

Discussion Questions

1. What have been the most important social changes during the years you have been growing up? (Consider important changes in customs, manners, mores, values, ethics, attitudes, habit systems, and activities in your personal life and in social groups, organizations, and institutions.) How have these changes affected your life?

2. Is there a generation gap between you and your parents or other adults you know? In what ways is there, or is there not? When a gap exists, how can it be closed?

3. Are your human needs for love, affection, companionship, and intimacy being met? Why? Why not?

4. Adolescents accuse adults of being materialistic, but aren't youths just as materialistic as their parents? What are some of the evidences of materialism in adolescent culture?

5. In what ways have television, radio, and movies, and other mass media influenced (1) your outlook on life and on society and (2) your own personality and emotional security?

6. What are the greatest stresses on the lives of adolescents today?

Term Papers

1. *Newspaper Report.* Keep a record of the headlines of newspaper articles for two weeks and summarize your findings and your reactions. How does the daily newspaper affect your life?

2. *Write a term paper on the subject:* "Youths' Search for Intimacy in Meaningful Personal Relations."

Bibliography

1. Adams, G. R., and Looft, W. R. "Cultural Change: Education and Youth." *Adolescence* 12 (Summer 1977): 137–150.

2. Alexander, S. J. "Protecting the Child's Rights in Custody Cases." *Family Coordinator* 26 (October 1977): 377–382.

3. *The American Almanac for 1972.* The Statistical Abstract of the United States. 92d ed. New York: Grosset & Dunlap, 1972.

4. "American Youth: Unhappy Days." *Public Interest* 51 (Spring 1978): 150–152.

5. Anthony, E. J., and Benedek, T., eds. *Parenthood: Its Psychology and Psychopathology.* Boston: Little, Brown, and Co., 1970, pp. 307–324.

6. Bachman, J. G. *Youth Look at National Problems: A Special Report from the Youth in Transition Project.* Ann Arbor: Institute for Social Research, University of Michigan, 1971.

7. Bengston, V. L., and Starr, J. M. "Contrast and Consensus: A Generational Analysis of Youth in the 1970s." In *Youth.* The Seventy-fourth Yearbook of the National Society for the Study of Education, Part 1. Edited by R. J. Havighurst and P. H. Dreyer. Chicago: University of Chicago Press, 1975, pp. 224–266.

8. Bowerman, C. E., and Irish, D. P. "Some Relationships of Stepchildren to Their Parents." In *Love Marriage Family.* Edited by H. E. Lasswell and T. E. Lasswell. Glenview, Ill.: Scott, Foresman and Co., 1973.

9. Bressler, L., and Bressler, M. *Youth in American Life.* Boston: Houghton Mifflin Co., 1972.

10. Bronfenbrenner, U. *Two Worlds of Childhood: U.S. and U.S.S.R.* New York: Russell Sage Foundation, 1970.

11. Chilton, R. J., and Markle, G. E. "Family Disruption, Delinquent Conduct and the Effect of Subclassification." *American Sociological Review* 33 (1972): 93–99.

12. Collins, G. "The Good News About 1984." *Psychology Today* (January 1979): 34–48.

13. Conger, J. J. "A World They Never Knew: The Family and Social Change." *Daedalus* (Fall 1971): 1105–1134.

14. Cooper, D. *Death of the Family.* New York: Pantheon Books, 1970.

15. Eisenberg, L. "Questions of Value." *Andover Review* 5 (Spring 1978): 2–12.

16. Elder, G. H. "Adult Control in Family and School: Public Opinion in Historical and Comparative Perspective." *Youth and Society,* September 1971, pp. 5–34.

17. Erikson, E. H. "Reflections on the Dissent of Youth." *International Journal of Psychoanalysis* 51 (1970): 11.

18. "Forecast of Experts: Prosperity in the Eighties." *U.S. News & World Report,* 12 February 1979, pp. 51–52.

19. Glick, P. C. "A Demographer Looks at American Families." *Journal of Marriage and the Family* 37 (1975): 15–26.

20. ———. "Future American Families." *Cofo Memo* 2 (Summer/Fall 1979): 2–5.

21. Group for the Advancement of Psychiatry. *Normal Adolescence.* New York: Charles Scribner's Sons, 1968.

22. Havighurst, R. J. "Youth in Social Institutions." In *Youth.* The Seventy-Fourth Yearbook of the National Society for the Study of Education, Part I. Edited by R. J. Havighurst and P. H. Dreyer. Chicago: University of Chicago Press, 1975, pp. 115–144.

23. Hennessey, M. et al. "Broken Homes and Middle Class Delinquency." *Criminology* 15 (February 1978): 505–528.

24. "How Population Shifts are Changing America." *U.S. News & World Report* 5 March 1979, pp. 76–78.

25. Kraemer, H. V., ed. *Youth and Culture: A Human Development Approach.* Monterey, Calif.: Brooks/Cole Publishing Co., 1974.

26. Landis, J. T. "A Comparison of Children from Divorced and Nondivorced Unhappy Marriages." *Family Life Coordinator* 11 (1970): 61–65.

27. Luepnitz, D. A. "Which Aspects of Divorce Affect Children?" *The Family Coordinator* 28 (January 1979): 79–85.

28. Mayer, L. A. "New Questions about the U.S. Population." *Fortune,* February 1971, pp. 82–85. (Source: U.S. Bureau of the Census, 1970)

29. Mead, Margaret. "Anomalies in American Post-divorce Relationships." *Divorce and After.* Edited by P. Bohannon. Garden City, N.Y.: Doubleday and Co., 1970, pp. 107–125.

30. ———. *Culture and Commitment: A Study of the Generation Gap.* Garden City, N.Y.: Doubleday and Co., 1970.

31. Miller, D. *Adolescence: Psychology, Psychopathology, and Psychotherapy.* New York: Jason Aronson, 1974.

32. Moller, H. "Youth as a Force in the Modern World." In *Youth and Culture: A Human Development Approach.* Edited by H. V. Kraemer. Monterey, Calif.: Brooks/Cole Publishing Co., 1974, pp. 56–80.

33. Murphey, Michael. "South Canadian River Song." Copyright © 1973 by Mystery Music, Inc.

34. Muuss, M. "Is There Really a Generation Gap?" *Adolescence* 6 (1971): 197–206.

35. "A New Generation: A Profile of America's Young People." *U.S. News & World Report* 6 September 1976, pp. 46–47.

36. Niemi, R. G., et al. "The Similarity of Political Values of Parents and College-Age Youths." *Public Opinion Quarterly* 42 (Winter 1978): 503–520.

37. Panel on Youth. President's Science Advisory Committee. *Youth: Transition to Adulthood.* Chicago: University of Chicago Press, 1974.

38. Rice, F. P. *Stepparenting.* New York: Condor Publishing Co., 1978.

39. Rubin, Z. "Seeking a Cure for Loneliness." *Psychology Today* (October 1979): 82–90.

40. Sabalis, R. F., and Ayers, G. W. "Emotional Aspects of Divorce and Their Effects on the Legal Process." *Family Coordinator* 26 (October 1977): 391–394.

41. Shideler, M. M. "An Amicable Divorce." *Christian Century*, May 5, 1971.

42. Simon, Paul. "I Am a Rock." © 1965 by Paul Simon.

43. "Sloppier Contraception, Not More Wanted Births, Caused 1950s Baby Boom, NFS Researcher Says." *Family Planning Perspectives* 10 (November/December 1978): 369.

44. Sorosky, A. D. "The Psychological Effects of Divorce in Adolescents." *Adolescence* 12 (Spring 1977): 123–136.

45. "Task Force Report: Divorce and Divorce Reform." Minneapolis National Council on Family Relations, October 1973. Mimeographed.

46. Toffler, Alvin. *Future Shock.* New York: Random House, 1970.

47. U.S. Bureau of the Census. Department of Commerce. *U.S. Census of Population, 1960: General Population Characteristics, United States Summary.* Final Report PC(1)-1B. Washington, D.C.: U.S. Government Printing Office, 1961. Table 47.

48. ———. "Projection of the Population of the United States, by Age and Sex: 1970 to 2020." *Current Population Reports,* Series P-25, No. 470. Washington, D.C.: U.S. Government Printing Office, 1971. Table 2, Series D.

49. ———. *Statistical Abstract of the United States: 1973.* Washington, D.C.: U.S. Government Printing Office, 1973.

50. "U.S. Family Is Changing." *Family Planning Perspectives* 10 (January/February 1978): 33–34.

51. White, R. B. "Adolescent Identity Crisis." In *Current Issues in Adolescent Psychiatry.* Edited by J. C. Schoolar. New York: Brunner/Mazel, 1973, pp. 19–33.

CHAPTER 3

The Period of Adolescence

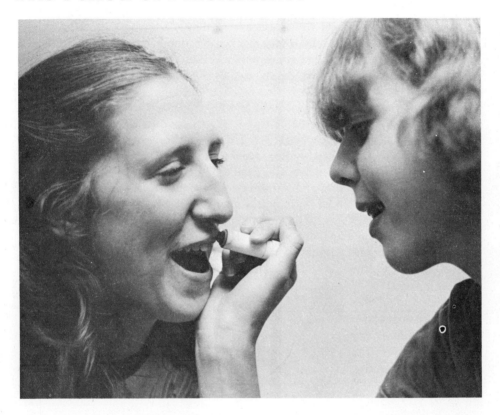

Outline

Defining Terms
Biological Views of Adolescence
Psychoanalytical Views of Adolescence
Sociopsychoanalytical Views of Adolescence
Sociological Views of Adolescence
Anthropological Views of Adolescence
A Psychosocial View of Adolescence
Conclusions
Topics for Term Papers
Bibliography

The important task of this chapter is to answer the question: What is adolescence? The answer may be found in one of a number of ways: by trying to define adolescence and related concepts such as maturity, puberty, pubescence, teenager, and juvenile. This method is used as the chapter begins with some brief definitions.

Another way to answer the question is to approach it from various points of view: from the studies of the biologist, psychiatrist, psychologist, sociologist, anthropologist, and social psychologist. This chapter presents the views of a few representative and influential writers from each of these disciplines, specifically, the following: biological views—G. Stanley Hall and Arnold Gesell; psychoanalytical views—Sigmund and Anna Freud; sociopsychoanalytical views—Erik Erikson and James Marcia; sociological views—Allison Davis and Albert Bandura and Richard H. Walters; anthropological views—Margaret Mead and Ruth Benedict; a psychosocial view—Robert Havighurst. By understanding various viewpoints, the reader will gain a truer, more complete picture of the numerous aspects of adolescence. (41)

Defining Terms

The word *adolescence* comes from the Latin verb *adolescere*, which means "to grow" or "to grow to maturity." It is defined as a period of growth between childhood and adulthood. But there is general disagreement about when it begins and ends, especially because the period has been prolonged in Western culture. (84, 96) For most people, adolescence is only an intermediate state between being a child and being an adult. (59) The transition from one stage to the other is gradual and uncertain: the beginning and the end are somewhat blurred, and the time span is not the same for every person, but most adolescents eventually become mature adults. In this sense, adolescence is likened to a bridge between childhood and adulthood over which individuals must pass before they are to take their places as mature, responsible, creative adults. One of the most perceptive definitions of adolescence has been given by Sieg:

Adolescence is the period of development in human beings that begins when the individual feels that adult privileges are due him which are not accorded him, and that ends when the full power and social status of the adult are accorded to the individual by his society. (93, p. 338)

Maturity is that age, state, or condition of life at which a person is considered fully developed physically, emotionally, socially, intellectually, and spiritually. The balance of all these characteristics is not always achieved simultaneously. A person may be mature physically but not emotionally. Conversely, there are some individuals who are intellectually quite mature but who have not attained full spiritual and moral growth. Young persons who become physically mature at age fourteen may have a lot of growing up to do before they are mature in other ways as well.

Puberty is the period during which a person reaches sexual maturity and becomes capable of begetting or bearing offspring. Puberty can be used in a fairly narrow sense to denote only that age when a person first becomes sexually capable of having children. But in a broader sense (and the sense in which it is used in this book) puberty is used to denote the several years during which physical changes relative to sexual maturation are taking place: those years during which the mature primary and secondary sexual characteristics develop. The first two years of puberty are spent in preparing the body for reproduction, and the last two years are spent in completing it. The first part of puberty overlaps childhood and adolescence, and the last part coincides with the first several years of adolescence. (55, p. 3)

Pubescence should be used synonymously with puberty to denote the whole period during which sexual maturation takes place. Literally, it means becoming hairy or downy, describing one of the important physical changes that occur during puberty. So a *pubescent* child is one who is arriving at or has arrived at puberty.

The term *teenager*, in a strict sense, means only those in the teen years: thirteen to nineteen years of age. However, because children (especially girls) sometimes mature physically before thirteen years of age, there are some discrepancies. An eleven-year-old girl may look and act like a teenager, but a fifteen-year-old boy, if not yet sexually mature, may still act and look like a child.

The word *teenager* is actually of fairly recent origin. It first appeared in the *Reader's Guide to Periodical Literature* in the 1943–1945 issue. Subsequently the term has become popular in the vocabulary of laymen. It is a word to which many youths object because of its negative emotional connotations: a hoodlum—wild, delinquent, incorrigible, and immoral. Margaret Mead objects to the term because it is too restrictive in terms of age (thirteen to nineteen years). She objects to it for emotional reasons also. There are many different types of teenagers: scholarly, intellectual teenagers; cool, swinging teenagers. The term will be avoided in this book, where the designation *adolescent* is preferred.

The word *juvenile* is generally used in a legal sense: one who is not yet considered an adult in the eyes of the law, which in most states is anyone up to eighteen years of age. The legal rights of eighteen-year-olds are confusing, however, for they vary from state to state. The Twenty-sixth Amendment gave them the right to vote, and in some areas they are called for jury duty. They may obtain credit in their own name at some stores or banks, but at others they have to obtain cosigners, even though they are legally responsible for their own debts. Many landlords still require parents to cosign leases.

Only eighteen states permit eighteen-year-olds to buy or drink alcoholic beverages. Some states use different age minimums for light wines and beer than for liquor. In Oklahoma, men must be twenty-one to buy 3.2 percent beer, whereas women there can purchase it at age eighteen. The laws are very complex and confusing. In Colorado, eighteen-year-olds can sign some contracts but not others; they can marry without parental consent; they can leave home at age sixteen, but do not attain full legal rights until age twenty-one. The net result is confusion over their identities. When do they fully become adults? Some adolescents feel they have to wait too many years to "get into the club." (63) One author suggests the law recognize an intermediate legal status between ages fifteen and eighteen when adolescents are accorded more rights than children, but fewer than those of adults. (53)

Biological Views of Adolescence

A strictly biological view of adolescence would emphasize this period as one of physical and sexual maturation during which important growth changes take place in the child's body. (91) Any biological definition would outline in detail these physical, sexual, and physiological changes; their reasons (when known); and their consequences.

This biological view would also emphasize biogenetic factors as the primary cause of any behavioral and psychological change in the adolescent. Growth and behavior are under the control of internal maturational forces, leaving little room for environmental influences. Development occurs in an almost inevitable, universal pattern, regardless of sociocultural environment.

HALL AND RECAPITULATION THEORY

One of the most influential exponents of the recapitulation theory was G. Stanley Hall (1846–1924), the first Ph.D. in psychology in the United States and the father of the child-study movement in North America. He was the first to advance a psychology of adolescence in his two-volume treatise on the subject. (48) According to Hall, during its development each human organism relives each of the stages that occurred in human evolutionary development. He outlined four major stages: *infancy* (first four years), during which the child reenacts the animal stage of development; *childhood* (five to seven), which corresponds to the cave-dwelling and hunting-fishing epoch of human history (because this is a time the child plays hide and seek, cowboys and Indians, and uses toy weapons); *youth* (eight to twelve), the preadolescent stage of development during which the child recapitulates the life of savagery, but is predisposed to learn to read, write, draw, manipulate numbers, and to learn languages, manual training, music, and other subjects through routine practice and discipline; and *puberty* (thirteen to twenty-four), the period of adolescence.

Hall described adolescence as the period corresponding to the time when the human race was in a turbulent, transitional stage, a time of great "storm and stress." Like some theorists today (54), Hall said that puberty is a time of great upset, emotional maladjustment, and instability in which the adolescent's moods oscillate between energy and indifference, gaiety and depression, or egotism and bashfulness. The end of adolescence marks a new birth in which higher, more completely human traits are born, a time corresponding to the beginning of modern civilization.

Hall's views exerted a marked influence upon the study of adolescence for many years. Because the theory held that development was controlled from within, parents were cautioned not to interfere, but to let the child pass from one stage to the other. Such a view was comforting to parents who found their children difficult at one stage; they always had the hope that the next stage would be better. One difficulty was that serious, abnormal disturbances at adolescence were sometimes accepted as normal.

Hall's view of adolescence has since been severely criticized on a number of points: (1) his biological, genetic explanation of behavior allows no room for the role of environment; (2) he felt that behavior at each stage is universal, unchangeable, and predisposed by biological drives, a tenet since refuted by cultural anthropologists; (3) he felt parents must be permissive and tolerate socially unacceptable behavior during the various stages of development; and (4) he overemphasized adolescence as an inevitable period of "storm and stress," (81, 82, 105) a point that also has been refuted by demonstrations that adolescence in some cultures is not at all stormy. Even in our culture current evidence suggests that the rate of emotional disturbance among adolescents does not differ significantly from that of the population at large. (31, p. 101) (See the section on anthropological views.) In spite of criticisms of his theory, Hall's influence is still felt in some circles today.

ARNOLD GESELL: SPIRAL GROWTH PATTERNS

Gesell (1880–1961) is known for observations of human development from birth to adolescence that he and his staff made at the Yale Clinic of Child Development and later at the Gesell Institute of Child Development. His best-known books are *Infant and Child in the Culture of Today* (44), *The First Five Years of Life* (43), *The Child from Five to Ten* (45), and *Youth: The Years from Ten to Sixteen.* (42)

Gesell was interested mainly in the behavioral manifestations of development and personality. (42, p. 32) He observed the actions and behavior of children and youths at different ages and constructed descriptive summaries of growth gradients grouped in stages and cycles of development. (77, p. 145) In his summaries he described what he felt were the norms of behavior in their chronological sequence. (77, p. 145) A few of the characteristics of adolescents from ten to sixteen years of age, as described by Gesell, are summarized below. (42)

THE TEN-YEAR-OLD. In a state of equilibrium and balance. Recognizes authority, accepts life as it comes, is confident and obedient, fond of home and friends of same sex. Joins groups and organizations, strong sense of fairness. Careless in appearance. Near end of childhood.

THE ELEVEN-YEAR-OLD. Marks dawn of adolescence, beginning of biological changes that cause psychological changes: moodiness, impulsiveness, anger, enthusiasm, negativism, quarreling with siblings, and rebellion against parents.

THE TWELVE-YEAR-OLD. Much of turbulence of eleven-year-old has disappeared. Becomes more reasonable, tolerant, positive, companionable, sociable, and enthusiastic. Trying to act grown up, be more independent of parents. Influenced more by peers, aware of appearance, wants to wear what crowd wears. Antagonism toward opposite sex fading, plays kissing games at parties.

THE THIRTEEN-YEAR-OLD. Becomes introspective, reflective, sensitive to criticism, overly conscientious, more critical of parents. Body changes affect posture, motor coordination, voice, facial expressions. Mood fluctuates from despair to self-acceptance. Fewer but closer friends.

THE FOURTEEN-YEAR-OLD. Introversion now replaced by extroversion, characterized by energy, exuberance, a degree of self-assurance, sociability, interest in own and other personalities. Bases friendships on similar interests and personality traits. Frequent identification with heroes.

THE FIFTEEN-YEAR-OLD. Large individual differences, difficult to describe. Rising spirit of independence, desire for freedom, increased tensions, and conflicts with parents and school personnel can lead to defiance, behavior problems, delinquency. Some perfectionist tendencies, beginning of self-control.

THE SIXTEEN-YEAR-OLD. Prototype of preadult: self-aware, more independent, self-confident, more balanced and integrated personality, more self-control, thoughts more oriented toward future. Cheerful, friendly, outgoing, and well-adjusted. Boy-girl companionship on a nonromantic basis.

Several explanations, implications, and criticisms need to be added for an understanding of Gesell's theory. It is essentially a biologically oriented theory, for maturation is mediated by genes and biology that determine the order of appearance of behavioral traits and developmental trends. Gesell once said of young children that there is no evidence that practice and exercise can hasten the actual appearance of activities like climbing and tower building, because the time of appearance is fundamentally determined by the ripeness of neural structures. (46, p. 114) Thus, abilities and skills appear without the influence of special training or practice.

This concept implies a sort of biological determinism that prevents teachers and parents from doing anything to influence development. Because maturation is regarded as a natural ripening process, it is assumed that time alone will solve most of the minor problems that arise in raising children. Difficulties and deviations will be outgrown, so parents are advised against emotional methods of discipline and are encouraged to combine self-regulation with developmental guidance. (42, p. 57) This means the school curriculum should be founded on a psychology of development rather than a psychology of learning, with the laws of learning reformulated in terms of the biology and physiology of development. (42, p. 298) Thus, teachers should take their cues from children, from the maturational level that determines the suitability of a particular kind of learning. For example, because fifteen-year-olds crave independence and rebel against school, many want to leave school and home and are susceptible to peer-group influences; for these Gesell suggests participation in community experiences to integrate the need for independence with growth in knowledge. (42, p. 157)

Gesell did try to allow for individual differences, accepting that each child is born unique, with his or her own "genetic factors of individual constitution and innate maturation sequences." (42, p. 22) Furthermore, Gesell accepted what he called "acculturation," the influence of the environment of the home, school, and total culture, but he emphasized that "acculturation can never transcend maturation" because maturation is of primary importance. In spite of accepting individual differences and the influence of environment on individual development, he nevertheless considered many of the principles, trends, and sequences to be universal among humans. (42, p. 22; 44, p. 41) This concept partly contradicts the findings of cultural anthropology and social and educational psychology, which emphasize significant, culturally determined individual differences.

Gesell did not see adolescence as necessarily turbulent, erratic, and troublesome, as did Hall; rather, he considered it a ripening process, a transitional period between childhood and adulthood, with many differences, reversals, and contradictions from year to year, or even within the same year. He tried to emphasize that changes are gradual and overlap from one level to the next, but his descriptions often indicate profound and sudden changes from one age to the next. Thus, twelve-year-olds enjoy a short period of interest in girls and participate in kissing games, even though they weren't at all interested at age eleven and won't be at thirteen. (42, p. 127) Gesell uses many such examples to highlight differences between the preceding and succeeding age stages. Critics have emphasized that development is more continuous than Gesell's theory admits. (77, p. 154)

Gesell did emphasize that development is not only upward, but also spiral, characterized by both upward and downward gradients that cause some repetition at different ages. Thus, freckles are evident at both sixteen and twelve; both the eleven- and fifteen-year-old are rebellious and quarrelsome, whereas the twelve- and sixteen-year-old are fairly stable. Children may develop along a particular course until they reach a certain level; then they revert to earlier forms of behavior before they are able to surpass their previous performance. Plateaus occur at both high and low points of development as children consolidate their abilities and potentials for further growth. (77, p. 149)

One of the chief criticisms of Gesell's work concerns the sample he studied. He drew his conclusions from a selected population segment in one geographic area of the United States: from boys and girls of favorable socioeconomic status, of a high to superior level of school population in New Haven, Connecticut. He contended that such a homogeneous sample would not lead to false generalizations, because he was seeking basic human sequences and directions of development that were related to biological and maturational factors common to all children. However, even when only physical factors are considered, children differ so greatly in the level and timing of growth that it is difficult to establish norms for any age level. To do so is to make parents feel that if their children do not fit the so-called norm, then something is wrong with them. Muuss points out that "lack of awareness of the difference between an average and an individual can result in much anxiety," and that "children may deviate widely from the average without being 'abnormal.'" (78, p. 146) For this reason it is difficult to accept the usefulness of the descriptions when they are applied to populations markedly different from the ones Gesell studied. Nevertheless, Gesell's books have been used by thousands of parents and exerted tremendous influence on child-rearing practices during the 1940s and 1950s. The books were considered "the child development bibles" for many students and teachers during these years.

Psychoanalytical Views of Adolescence

SIGMUND FREUD

Freud (1856–1939) was not much involved with theories on adolescence, for he considered the early years of a child's life to be the formative years. But he did deal briefly with adolescence in his *Three Essays on the Theory of Sexuality*. (39) He described adolescence as a period of sexual excitement, anxiety, and sometimes of personality disturbance. According to Freud, puberty is the culmination of a series of changes destined to give infantile sexual life its final, normal form. During the period of infancy, when the beginnings of sexual satisfaction are linked with the taking of nourishment, children employ a sexual object outside their own bodies: their mother's breasts. From this object they derive physical satisfaction, warmth, pleasure, and security. While the mother feeds her infants, she also cuddles, caresses, kisses, and rocks them. She arouses her children's sexual instincts by stimulating other erotogenic zones of their bodies. She is teaching her children to love.

Gradually children's sexual lives become autoerotic; that is, they begin to derive pleasure and satisfaction from activities that they can carry on by themselves. As they give up sucking at their mother's breasts, they find they can still derive pleasure from oral activities in which they can engage without the need of their mother. They learn to feed themselves, for example. Later, much concern and pleasure centers around anal activities and elimination. This period is followed by a developing interest in their own bodies and in the stimulation of their sex organs during the genital stage of development.

During the next stage, which Freud termed the *period of latency* (roughly from six years of age to puberty), children's sexual interests are not as intense and they continue to feel for other people who helped them and who satisfied their needs for love. Their source of pleasure gradually shifts from self to other persons. They become more interested in cultivating the friendship of others, especially those of the same sex.

At puberty this process of "object finding" is brought to completion. Along with maturation of the external and internal sexual organs comes a strong desire for resolution of the sexual tension that follows. This resolution demands a love object; therefore, Freud theorizes, adolescents are drawn to a member of the opposite sex who can resolve their tensions.

Freud stresses that the sexual aim of the adolescent is different from that of the child. The child seeks physical pleasure and psychic satisfaction through bodily contact and the stimulation of the erotogenic zones, and the pleasure derived becomes an end in itself. But at the onset of adolescence, the sexual aim changes. Now the aim is not only for erotogenic stimulation (which Freud calls *fore-pleasure*) but also for orgastic satisfaction. The sexual stimulation of the erotogenic zones of the body is no longer an end in itself, but a preparation for the greater satisfaction of orgasm in intercourse.

Fore-pleasure is thus the same pleasure that has already been produced, although on a smaller scale, by the infantile sexual instinct; end-pleasure is something new. . . . The formula for the new function of the erotogenic zones therefore: they are used to make possible, through the medium of the fore-pleasure which can be derived from them (as it was during infantile life), the production of the greater pleasure of satisfaction. (39, p. 210)

Freud also writes of the pleasure of orgasm:

This last pleasure is the highest in intensity, and its mechanism differs from that of the earlier pleasure. It is brought about entirely by discharge: it is wholly a pleasure of satisfaction and with it the tension of the libido is for the time being extinguished. (39, p. 210)

Freud emphasizes two important elements of the sexual aim at adolescence, and with these some differences between men and women. One element is physical and sensual. In men this aim consists of the desire to produce sexual products, accompanied by physical pleasure. In women the desire for physical satisfaction and the release of sexual tension is still there, but without the discharge of physical products. This desire in women is historically more repressed than in men, for the inhibitions to sexuality (shame, disgust, etc.) are developed earlier and more intensely in girls than in boys. However, there is a physical element to sexual desire in both men and women.

The second element of the sexual aim at adolescence is psychic; it is the affectionate component, which is more pronounced in females, and which is similar to the infant's expression of sexuality. In other words, the adolescent desires emotional satisfaction as well as physical release. This need for affection is especially prevalent in females, but satisfying the need is an important goal of all adolescent sexual striving. Freud would also emphasize that a normal sexual life is assured only when there is a convergence of the affectionate and the sensual currents, both being directed towards the sexual object and sexual aim. The desire for true affection and for the release of sexual tension combined are the underlying normal needs that motivate the individual to seek out a love object. (39, p. 207)

An important part of the maturing process at adolescence is the loosening of the child's emotional ties with parents. During the process of development, children's sexual impulses are directed toward their parents, with the son being drawn toward his mother and the daughter toward her father. Freud also speaks of a second oedipal situation at adolescence, when a boy may fall in love with his mother and a young girl may fall in love with her father. (37) However, a natural and socially reinforced barrier against incest restrains this expression of sexuality, so that adolescents seek to loosen their connections with their families. As they overcome and repudiate their incestuous fantasies, adolescents also complete "one of the most painful, psychical achievements of the pubertal period . . . : detachment from parental authority." (39, p. 227) This is done by withdrawing their affection from their parents and transferring it to their peers. Blos referred to this emotional loss as the "mourning of separation." (21)

Throughout his writings Freud emphasized the importance of this "non-incestuous object finding." (38) Those adolescents, especially girls, who have never repudiated their parents' authority or withdrawn their affection and who hold fast to their infantile fondness for them, become more and more emotionally disturbed. These are the girls who later in marriage lack the capacity to love their husbands. Freud says: "They make cold wives and remain sexually anaesthetic." (39, p. 227) They are still fixated at an infantile level of development and are trying to realize the ideal of asexual love in their lives that they can express without self-reproach. Even those persons who have been fortunate to avoid an incestuous fixation do not entirely escape its influence. A young man falls in love for the first time with a mature woman, or a young woman with an elderly man. Or a man looks for a mate who represents his picture of his mother. If his mother is alive, she may resent this new version of herself and meet her with hostility. If children's relationships with their parents are disturbed or the parents' marriage is unhappy, this affects their adult life later on. The ground is prepared for a predisposition to a disturbance of sexual development or to a neurotic illness. This is why adolescents' relationships with their parents are so important.

Freud assumes that object-choice during adolescence must find its way to the opposite sex. There is a need to establish heterosexual friendships as one moves away from the homosexual attachments of childhood. Freud sees no harm in sentimental friendships with others of one's own sex, provided there is no permanent inversion or reversal of the sexual role and choice of the sexual object results. (39, p. 229) Although reversal of sexual roles and sexual objects is frequent, Freud regards the reversal as a deviation from normal sexual life to be avoided if possible. (39, p. 229)

ANNA FREUD

Anna Freud (b. 1895) was more concerned with the period of adolescence than her father was and elaborated more on the process of adolescent development and the changes in the psychic structure of the child at puberty. Some of her most important ideas are summarized as follows. (35, 36)

She characterizes adolescence as a period of internal conflict, psychic disequilibrium, and erratic behavior. Adolescents are, on the one hand, egoistic, regarding themselves as the sole object of interest and the center of the universe, but, on the other hand, also capable of self-sacrifice and devotion. They form passionate love relations, only to break them off suddenly. They sometimes desire complete social involvement and group participation, at other times solitude. They oscillate between blind submission to and rebellion against authority. They are selfish and material-minded, but also full of lofty idealism. They are ascetic yet indulgent, inconsiderate of others yet touchy themselves. They oscillate between light-hearted optimism and blackest pessimism, between indefatigable enthusiasm and sluggishness and apathy. (35, p. 149)

The reasons for this conflicting behavior are the psychic disequilibrium and internal conflict that accompanies sexual maturation at puberty. (21) At puberty, the most obvious change is an increase in the instinctual drives (which have their source in the id). This is due partly to physical sexual motivation, with its accompanying interest in genitality and the flare-up of genital impulses. But the increase in instinctual drives at puberty also has a physical base not confined solely to the sexual life. Aggressive impulses are intensified, hunger becomes voracity, naughtiness sometimes erupts into criminal behavior. Oral and anal interests, long submerged, appear. Habits of cleanliness give way to dirt and disorder. Modesty and sympathy are replaced by exhibitionism and brutality. A. Freud compares this increase in instinctual forces at puberty to the similar condition of early infancy. Early infantile sexuality and rebellious aggression are "resuscitated" at puberty. (35, p. 159)

Because the impulses of the id increase at adolescence, they present a direct challenge to the individual's ego and superego. By ego Anna Freud means the sum of those mental processes that aim at safeguarding mental function. The ego is the evaluative, reasoning power of the individual. By superego A. Freud means the ego-ideal and the conscience that result from the incorporation of the social values of the same-sexed parent. Therefore, the renewed vigor of the instincts at adolescence directly challenges the reasoning abilities and the powers of conscience of the individual. The careful balance achieved between these psychic powers during latency is overthrown as open warfare breaks out between the id and superego. The ego, which previously has been able to enforce a truce, has as much trouble keeping the peace now as does a weak-willed parent when confronted by two strong-willed children who are quarreling. If the ego allies itself completely with the id, "no trace will be left of the previous character of the individual and the entrance into adult life will be marked by a riot of uninhibited gratification of instinct." (32, p. 163) If the ego sides completely with the superego, the character of the individual of the latency period will declare itself once and for all, with the id-impulses confined within the narrow limits prescribed for the child, but with the need for a constant expenditure of psychic energy on anticathexes (emotionally charged activities), defense mechanisms, and emotional sympathy to hold the id in check. A. Freud writes of the result.

Apart from the resulting crippling of the instinctual life, the fact that the victorious ego becomes rigidly fixed is permanently injurious to the individual. Ego-institutions which have resisted the onslaught of puberty without yielding generally remain throughout life inflexible, unassailable and insusceptible of the rectification which a changing reality demands. (35, p. 164)

Unless this id-ego-superego conflict is resolved at adolescence, the consequences can be emotionally devastating to the individual. A. Freud discusses how the ego employs indiscriminately all the methods of defense (in psychological terms the defense mechanisms) to win the battle. The ego represses, displaces, denies, and reverses the instincts and turns them against the self; it produces phobias and hysterical symptoms and builds anxiety by means of obsessional thinking and behavior. According to Anna Freud, the rise of asceticism and intellectualism at adolescence is a symptom of mistrust of all instinctual wishes. (See also the section on Piaget in Chapter 7.) The accentuation of neurotic symptoms and inhibitions during adolescence signals the partial success of the ego and superego, but at the expense of the individual. A. Freud does feel, however, that harmony among the id, ego, and superego is possible, and does occur finally in most normal adolescents if the superego is sufficiently developed during the latent period—but not to inhibit the instincts too much, causing extreme guilt and anxiety—and if the ego is sufficiently strong and wise to mediate the conflict. (35, p. 165)

Sociopsychoanalytical Views of Adolescence

ERIK ERIKSON: EGO IDENTITY

Erikson (b. 1902) modified Freud's theory of psychosexual development as a result of findings of modern sociopsychology and anthropology and described eight stages of human development. (28, 32, 34) In each of the eight stages, the individual has a psychosocial task to master. The confrontation with each task produces conflict, with two possible outcomes. If the conflict during that stage is successfully resolved, a positive quality is built into the personality and further development takes place. If the conflict persists or is unsatisfactorily resolved, the ego is damaged because a negative quality is incorporated into it. Therefore, according to Erikson, the overall task of the individual is to acquire a positive ego identity as he or she moves from one stage to the next. The positive solution of the task, each with its negative counterpart, is listed below for each period. (32, p. 234; 33, pp. 110–165)

1. *Infancy:* achieving trust versus mistrust. *order*
2. *Early childhood:* achieving autonomy versus shame and doubt. *Independence*
3. *Play age:* achieving initiative versus guilt. *Rules, regulations, laws*
4. *School age:* achieving industry versus inferiority. *competent*
5. *Adolescence:* achieving identity versus identity diffusion. *Self concept*
6. *Young adult:* achieving intimacy versus isolation. *Self concept - Develop relationship*
7. *Adulthood:* achieving generativity versus stagnation. *Contribution with others to life*
8. *Mature age:* achieving ego integrity versus disgust, despair. *Mental & emotional security child + posterity - fulfillment of life -*

Because this chapter is concerned only with the adolescent period, discussion will be limited to the adolescent task of establishing ego identity. Erikson emphasizes several aspects of this process.

Identity formation neither begins nor ends with adolescence. It is a lifelong process, largely unconscious to the individual. Its roots go back in childhood to the experience of mutuality between the mothering adult and mothered children. As children reach out to their first love objects, they begin to find self-realization coupled with mutual recognition. Their identity formations continue through a process of selection and assimilation of childhood identifications, which in turn depend upon parental, peer, and society's identification of them as important persons. The community both molds and gives recognition to newly emerging individuals. The child in the multiplicity of successive and tentative identifications, begins early to build up expectations of what it will be like to be older and what it will feel like to have been younger—expectations which become part of an identity as they are, step by step, verified in decisive experiences of psychosocial fittedness. (33) Thus, the process of identity formation emerges as an evolving configuration which is gradually established by successive ego syntheses and resyntheses throughout childhood. (33)

Erikson emphasizes that adolescence is a normative crisis, a normal phase of increased conflict, characterized by a fluctuation of ego strength. The experimenting individual becomes the victim of an identity consciousness that is the basis for the self-consciousness of youth. It is during this time that the individual must establish a sense of *personal identity* and avoid the dangers of *role diffusion* and *identity diffusion*. To establish identity requires individual effort in evaluating personal assets and liabilities and in learning how to use these in working to achieve a clearer concept of who one is and what one wants to be and become. Erikson feels that during adolescence there must be an integration of all converging identity elements and a resolution of conflict that he divided into seven major parts. The seven parts of the conflict are:

TEMPORAL PERSPECTIVE VERSUS TIME CONFUSION. This means gaining a sense of time and of the continuity of life so that one can coordinate the past and the future and gain some concept of how long it takes to achieve one's life plans. It means learning to estimate and allocate one's time. Research has shown that a true sense of time does not develop until relatively late in adolescence—around fifteen or sixteen. (40, p. 215)

SELF-CERTAINTY VERSUS SELF-CONSCIOUSNESS. This means developing self-confidence based upon past experiences so that one believes in oneself and feels that one has a reasonable chance of accomplishing future aims. To do this adolescents go through a period of increasing self-awareness and self-consciousness, especially in relation to their physical self-image and social relationships.

ROLE EXPERIMENTATION VERSUS ROLE FIXATION. Adolescents have an opportunity to try out the different roles they are to play in society. They can experiment with many different identities, with different personality characteristics, with a variety of ways of talking and acting, with different ideas, philosophies and goals, or with different types of relationships. Identity comes through opportunities for such experimentation. Those who have developed too much inner restraint and guilt, who have lost initiative, or who prematurely experience role fixation never really find out who they are. (34, p. 184)

APPRENTICESHIP VERSUS WORK PARALYSIS. Similarly, the adolescent has an opportunity to explore and try out different occupations before deciding on a vocation. Once entered, one's job plays a large part in determining identity. (34, p. 185) Furthermore, a negative self-image in the form of inferiority feelings can prevent one from mustering the necessary energy to succeed at school or on the job. Erikson is quite critical of the schools for the mutilation of spontaneity and the destruction of the joy of learning and the pleasure of creating. Other authors have emphasized the importance of socioeconomic and family background and of sex-role socialization in influencing achievement motivation. (40, pp. 225–241)

SEXUAL POLARIZATION VERSUS BISEXUAL CONFUSION. Adolescents continue to attempt to define what it means to be "male" and "female." Erikson feels it is important that adolescents develop a clear identification with one sex or the other as a basis for future heterosexual intimacy and as a basis for a firm identity. (34, p. 186) Furthermore, he emphasizes that for communities to function properly, men and women must be willing to assume their "proper roles"; sexual polarization, then, is necessary. (34, p. 72) Much of present-day analysis (and some criticism) of Erikson relates to his emphasis on the need for sexual polarization.

LEADERSHIP AND FOLLOWERSHIP VERSUS AUTHORITY CONFUSION. As adolescents expand their social horizons through education, work apprenticeship, social groups, and new friends and contacts, they begin to learn to take leadership responsibilities as well as how to follow others. But at the same time, they discover there are competing claims on their allegiance. The state, employer, sweetheart, parents, and friends all make demands, with the result that adolescents experience confusion in relation to authority. To whom should they listen, whom should they follow, to whom should they give their primary allegiance? Sorting out the answers requires an examination of personal values and priorities.

IDEOLOGICAL COMMITMENT VERSUS CONFUSION OF VALUES. This conflict is closely related to all the others because construction of an ideology guides other aspects of behavior. Erikson refers to this struggle as the "search for fidelity." (34, p. 235)

If the individual is able to resolve these seven conflicts, a firm identity emerges. The crisis is past when he or she no longer has to question at every moment his or her own identity, when he or she has subordinated childhood identity and found a new self-identification. (32)

Erikson acknowledges that finding an acceptable identity is much more difficult during a period of rapid social change, because the older generation is no longer able to provide adequate role models for the younger generation. Under these circumstances, adolescents may reject parental role models and turn to their peers to discover who they are. Peer example, influence, and opinion become all-important. This is why adolescents "are sometimes morbidly, often curiously, preoccupied with what they appear to be in the eyes of others. . . ." (33, p. 89) They go through a period of compulsive group conformity as a means of testing group expectations and how they themselves fit in. The peer group, the clique, and the gang help individuals find their own identities in a social context, for they provide role models and direct feedback about themselves. (77, p. 64) Adolescent clannishness and intolerance of differences in language, dress, styles, and behavior are a necessary defense against the dangers of self-diffusion that exist as long as identity has not yet been achieved. Erikson feels also that the adolescent's tendency to develop emotional crushes, infatuations, and strong love feelings for the opposite sex serves a useful developmental purpose. It becomes a means of testing one's own still undifferentiated image through the eyes of a beloved person in order to clarify self-concept and ego identity.

One interesting aspect of Erikson's theory is his concept of adolescence as a psychosocial moratorium, a societally sanctioned intermediary period between childhood and adulthood, during which the individual through free role experimentation may find a niche in some section of society. (33) Adolescence becomes a period of standing back, of analyzing, and of trying various roles without the responsibility for assuming any one role. Erikson acknowledges that the duration and intensity of adolescence vary in different societies, but that near the end of adolescence a failure to establish identity results in deep suffering for the adolescent because of a diffusion of roles. Such role diffusion may be responsible for the appearance of previously latent psychological disturbances.

Erikson comments: "Many a late adolescent, if faced with continuing diffusion, would rather be nobody or somebody bad, or indeed dead . . . than be not quite somebody." (33, p. 132) Muuss also comments:

If the adolescent fails in his search for an identity, he will experience self-doubt, role diffusion, and role confusion, and the individual may indulge in self-destructive, one-sided preoccupation or activity. He will continue to be morbidly preoccupied with what others think of him, or, even worse, he may withdraw and no longer care about himself and others. Ego diffusion and personality confusion, when they become permanent, can be found in the delinquent and in psychotic personality disorganization. (77, p. 66)*

Erikson emphasizes that whereas the identity crisis is most pronounced at adolescence, a redefinition of one's ego-identity may also take place at other periods of life: when individuals leave home, get their first job, marry, become parents, get divorced, change occupations, become unemployed, become seriously ill, are widowed or retire. The extent to which individuals are able to cope with these other changes in identity is determined partly by the success with which they have first mastered the adolescent identity crises. (43)

Since Erikson first introduced his theory, numerous research studies have validated, further clarified, or questioned his ideas (particularly those related to female subjects). (1, 2, 22, 23, 26, 50, 56, 57, 61, 62, 64, 68, 69, 79, 80, 83, 85, 86, 87, 89, 90, 95, 99, 100, 101, 102, 103, 104) For a complete summary of this research see references 22 and 23. The following are some of the highlights of this research.

Identity has many components. It includes physical, sexual, social, vocational, moral, ideological, and psychological characteristics that make up the total self. (62, 75, 79, 87, 104) Thus, individuals may be identified by their physical appearance and traits; by their gender as well as their sex roles; by their social characteristics, social relationships, and membership in groups; by their vocations and work; by their religious and political affiliations and ideologies; and by the characteristics of their psychological adjustment and extent of their personality synthesis. Identity may be described in terms of the total concept of self. It is personal because it is a sense of "I-ness," but it is also social, for it includes "we-ness," or one's collective identity. (1, p. 160)

The individual who has developed a positive ego identity is one

who is confident of his/her sexual identity, who has acquired a sense of basic trust and industry, is well-adjusted psychologically, has a more integrated personality, uses defenses in an adaptive-positive manner, and perceives physical, moral, personal, family and social self more positively. The adolescent who has achieved an identity also is more self-acceptant and more perceptive of how she/he acts. If one plots these measures on a clinical profile, it is readily evident that the high-identity adolescent appears to be a more adaptive and better-adjusted individual psychologically. (62, p. 381)

Adolescents who have a positive identity have developed a sense of being all right, of accepting themselves. (62, p. 381)

Those with low identities seem to reject their physical selves and are confused about their sexual identities and sex roles. They are less acceptant of themselves and their behavior. They perceive themselves as undesirable persons of low moral worth, and are dissatisfied with their moral values and ideologies.

The low-identity adolescent may have conflict over vocational orientation and may exhibit general anxiety or neurotic tendencies and lack of personality integration. (62, pp. 381, 382)

Some adolescents adopt negative identities, defined self-images that are contrary to the cultural values of the community.

"Failure," "good-for-nothing," "juvenile delinquent," "hood," and "greaser" are labels the adult society commonly applies to certain adolescents. In the absence of any indication of the possibilities of success or contribution to the society, the young person accepts these negative labels as his/her self-definition and proceeds to validate this identity by continuing to behave in ways that will strengthen it. (80, p. 313)

Other adolescents will behave in ways to reduce temporarily the anxiety of an uncertain or incomplete identity. Some of these "psycho-social identity defense mechanisms" are: (64, p. 504)

Escape through intense immediate experiences such as drug abuse, wild parties, rock concerts, or fast rides in cars. These emotional experiences temporarily blot out the search for identity.

Substituting temporary identities by becoming a joiner, a goof-off, a clown, a bully, a pool shark, a ladies' man.

Seeking to *strengthen* one's identity temporarily through such things as petty crime, vandalism, competitive sports, popularity contests, or short-term expedients. The person who becomes a bigot, who takes a stance against minorities, or who becomes a superpatriot seeks to build a temporary "fortress identity."

Assuring a *meaningless* identity by engaging in such fads as stuffing telephone booths, lining up dominoes, streaking, or participating in trivia contests. For some youths, a meaningless identity is better than no identity at all.

Some aspects of identity are more easily formed than others. Physical and sexual identities seem to be established earliest. (62, 104) Young adolescents are concerned with their body image before they become interested in choosing a vocation or examining their moral values and ideologies. Similarly, they must deal with their own sexual identities both before and after puberty. (62, 104) Research tends to show that adolescents achieve sexual identity before achievement in other areas. (68, 104) The low-identity adolescent seems to deny his/her physical identity and experience a sexual identity conflict, not in orienting to a masculine or feminine role per se, but in understanding his/her sexual self. High-identity females and males perceive their specific sex roles and their similarity to the same- and opposite-sex parent as well as their potential future role of wife/husband. (62, p. 382)

Vocational, ideological, and moral identities are established more slowly. These identities depend upon adolescents having reached the formal-operation stage of cognitive growth and development that enables them to explore alternative ideas and courses of action. (See the discussion on Piaget in Chapter 7.) In addition, reformulation of these identities requires a high degree of independence of thought. The exploration of occupational alternatives is the most immediate and concrete task as adolescents finish high school or enter college. (87) Religious and political ideologies are examined during late adolescence, especially the college years, but identities in these areas may be in a state of flux for years. (87)

There do seem to be some differences between males and females in identity achievement. More females than males, for example, experience a crisis in sexual identity, probably because standards for female sexual behavior are still more restrictive than those for males, even though our society is moving in the direction of a single standard. (104, p. 340) At the same time, more females than males solve this crisis and achieve sexual identity. Males less often question the sexual ideologies of their society.

In spite of the increasing emphasis on careers for women, more females than males have trouble establishing occupational identities. One reason may be that college is still more conducive to ego development in males than in females, especially in terms of making vocational decisions and preparing for an occupation. (62, p. 373) Also, at this period when female roles are in a state of flux, women are experiencing conflict in gaining a sense of confidence and worthiness as females. However, a low level of anxiety about themselves and their roles indicates that increasing numbers are solving their identity crisis. (62, p. 383) Females who have been raised by mothers who encourage independence are those most likely to find their identities apart from family living. (61; 79, p. 164) One study found that high school girls whose parents were divorced were significantly more likely to be identity achievers than were those from unbroken homes. (90, p. 324) The authors conclude:

These findings suggest that the security of the traditional family may not provide the optimal setting for the adolescent female to engage in the processes leading to identity achievement. In addition, the finding of higher identity achievement among girls from broken homes adds to the growing body of evidence that divorce does not necessarily have adverse effects on the adolescent, and, in fact, may be associated with better adjustment of the adolescent. (90, p. 324)

JAMES MARCIA

Among the many studies of Erikson's concepts, those by James Marcia have been particularly influential. (65, 66, 67, 92, 97) According to Marcia, the criteria used to establish the attainment of a mature identity are two variables, *crisis* and *commitment*, in relation to occupational choice, religion, and political ideology. "Crisis refers to the adolescent's period of engagement in choosing among meaningful alternatives; commitment refers to the degree of personal investment the individual exhibits." (65) A mature identity is achieved when the individual has experienced a crisis and has become committed to an occupation and ideology.

Marcia's research revealed four basic types of persons. (65) *Identity diffused* or *identity confused* subjects have not experienced a crisis period, nor have they made any commitment. They have not decided on an occupation nor are they much concerned about it. They are either uninterested in ideological matters or feel one outlook is as good as another, and therefore may sample them all. One author reports:

Perhaps the word which best characterizes the diffusion subject is "withdrawal." . . . The most frequent response to stress is withdrawal. Related to this is the finding that . . . diffusions have shown the lowest level of intimacy with same- and opposite-sex friends or else appeared to lack any significant social relationship. (23, p. 374)

Foreclosure subjects have not experienced a crisis, but they have made commitments to occupations and ideologies that are not the result of their own searching, but ready-made and handed down to them, frequently from parents. They become what others intend them to become, without really deciding for themselves. Foreclosure subjects are typified by youths who adopt their parents' religion, follow the vocation their parents select for them, or submerge themselves in conformity to peer groups. Such subjects score high on authoritarianism and intolerance, show a high degree of conformity and conventionality, are usually quite happy with their college education, and score very low on anxiety scales. (22, 66) When put under stress, however, they perform very poorly. Their security lies in avoiding change or stress. As Keniston writes, the "total lack of conflict during adolescence is an ominous sign that the individual's psychological maturity may not be progressing." (60, p. 364)

Moratorium subjects are involved in continual crises. They are actively searching out various alternatives but have not made any permanent commitments. As a consequence, such persons seem confused, unstable, and discontented. They are often rebellious and uncooperative, and score low on authoritarianism. Because they experience crises, they tend to be anxious. These adolescents generally have fairly permissive parents, are uncertain they have selected the right major in college, and may be unhappy with their college experience and education. Others show a high level of authority conflict, so that part of their crisis is an attempt to disengage themselves from their parents. (23, p. 373)

However, using adolescence as a period of moratorium can be an advantage. Muuss writes:

If the adolescent, while experiencing his moratorium, has sufficient opportunity to search, experiment, play the field, and try on different roles, there is a good chance that he will find himself, develop an identity, and emerge with commitments to politics, religion, and a vocational career. His final commitments are frequently less extreme than some of his tentative and exploratory commitments during the moratorium. Moratorium really is an essential prerequisite for identity achievement. (77, p. 77)*

Moratorium females score very high on measures of cognitive complexity, tolerance of ambiguity, intelligence, and social class. These high-scoring females are those who are best able to explore alternatives and to use a moratorium period in a constructive way. (85, p. 61; 86)

Research by the Watermans shows that entering college increases the number of adolescents in a state of moratorium. (99, 102, 103) This is because at college these students are more actively and thoughtfully confronted with the crisis of making an occupational commitment, and because they are stimulated to rethink their ideologies. In the Watermans' study, 80 percent of moratorium adolescents had changed their occupational plans during college. (103) By the senior year, however, there was a positive developmental shift in both the occupational

* From R. E. Muuss, *Theories of Adolescence*, 3rd ed. Copyright © Random House, Inc. Used by permission.

and ideological identity of these students. (99) A study of males at a liberal arts college showed that there was a clear, progressive developmental change, with students moving through the moratorium status to become identity achievers. A substantial majority of the identity crises experienced in college were successfully resolved. (100, p. 367) The same study showed, however, that by graduation over one-third of the seniors were still identity diffused in the area of religion and over one-half in the area of political beliefs. (100, p. 365) Similar but more comprehensive studies have shown that there were consistent increases in the successful resolution of identity, both from freshman year to senior year across subjects, and from one year to the next within subjects.

This trend did not hold as true for females as for males, however, which indicates the college environment favored male over female development in helping develop identities. This is partly explained by Toder and Marcia: "It would appear that there is still more social support for the male while he breaks away from parental values and experiments with new roles than there is for the female who can, apparently, count on less support." (97)

Identity achieved subjects have experienced a psychological moratorium, have resolved their identity crisis by carefully evaluating various alternatives and choices, and have come to conclusions and decisions on their own. They have been highly motivated to achieve, and are able to do so, not so much because of great ability as because they have attained higher levels of intrapsychic integration and social adaptation. (23, p. 373) Once an identity has been achieved, there is self-acceptance, a stable self-definition, and a commitment to a vocation, religion, and political ideology. There is harmony within oneself and an acceptance of capacities, opportunities, and limitations. There is a more realistic concept of goals and the possibility of their attainment. There is less subscription to authoritarianism and less vulnerability to anxiety. (65, 66, 67) In summary, identity achievement subjects are more advanced in their ego development. (2)

Prior to the women's movement, identity-achieved females showed less of these positive traits than did males. (47, p. 225) Identity-achieved females, for example, showed lowest in self-esteem of all the four groups studied, with foreclosure females showing the highest self-esteem. Identity-achieved females also showed considerable anxiety, indicating that they were achieving identity status through an occupation (they were also majoring in more difficult subjects), but in opposition to stereotyped, cultural expectations, and with consequent feelings of anxiety and lowered self-esteem because of perceived social stigmas. (67, 88) Studies after 1972, however, indicate this is slowly changing, with female identity achievers scoring higher in self-esteem and showing less anxiety. (56, 92) One 1974 study showed that college females reported significantly less ego diffusion than males within every age group (seventeen to twenty years). (56) It is evident that females increasingly are able to find their identity through occupations and to experience more self-satisfaction and self-esteem while doing so. (See reference 56 for a comprehensive discussion.)

Sociological Views of Adolescence

In studying adolescence, the sociologist focuses on the social environment as the determinant of adolescent development. (49) The sociologist recognizes the existence of biological and intrapersonal psychological processes, but chooses to study the interaction between the adolescent and society.

ALLISON DAVIS: SOCIALIZED ANXIETY

In *Socialization and Adolescent Personality* (29) Allison Davis (b. 1902) defines *socialization* as the process by which individuals learn and adopt the ways, ideas, beliefs, values, and norms of their culture and make them part of their personalities. Davis sees the process of maturation during adolescence as the process of becoming socialized.

According to Davis, each society defines the goals, values, and behaviors it desires of its members. Socially acceptable behavior is rewarded; unacceptable behavior is punished. Repeated punishment for unacceptable behavior induces what Davis calls "socialized anxiety," which becomes the negative motivation for socialization to take place. Once socialized anxiety has been induced in children, they seek to show behavior that minimizes it. If socialized anxiety is too strong, it can have an inhibiting or disorganizing effect. If socialized anxiety is too weak, the attainment of maturity is not likely either; therefore, it is important that a correct amount be present. (29)

Davis emphasizes that middle class and lower class cultures expect different things of their adolescents. Middle class cultures emphasize prestige, social position, success, status, and morality. These expectations give rise to more social anxiety in their adolescents than is evident in the lower class adolescent. The social anxiety that is generated in turn motivates the middle class youngster to strive even more for socially desirable goals.

Lower class cultures do not put so much emphasis on long-term goals, success, status, and a postponement of short-term pleasures like sex expression. Low socioeconomic status adolescents do not develop the kind of social anxiety that motivates them to succeed, according to middle class standards. They see no point in postponing many sexual or recreational pleasures for they do not expect to receive the rewards of a middle class culture anyhow. (29, p. 209)

Davis's views are important because they emphasize that society influences what adolescents are, what their problems are, and what they become. The sociological view alone, however, does not explain why youths from even the poorest families sometimes succeed according to middle class standards. Davis's view must be considered alongside the views of other disciplines.

ALBERT BANDURA AND RICHARD H. WALTERS: SOCIAL LEARNING THEORY

Social learning theory is concerned with the relationship between social and environmental factors and their influence on behavior. Because Bandura (b. 1925) and Walters (1918–1967) have been more concerned with the application of that theory to adolescence than have other social learning theorists, the major focus here will be on their work. Their views are outlined in four major books (5, 6, 16, 17) and in numerous articles and research studies. (4, 8, 9, 10, 11, 12, 13, 14, 15, 18)

Bandura and Walters emphasize that children learn through observing the behavior of others and by imitating this pattern. This process of observing and imitating is referred to as *modeling*. Modeling then becomes a socialization process by which habitual response patterns develop. (16, p. 23) As children grow, they imitate different models from their social environment. Young children imitate the language, gestures, mannerisms, habits, and basic attitudes and values of parents. School-age children may imitate some speech patterns or mannerisms of teachers and repeat a teacher's ideas about social or political problems in dinner conversations at home. As children grow older, entertainment heroes and peers become increasingly important as models, especially in influencing verbal expressions, hairstyles, clothing, music, food preferences, and basic social values. Imitation is important in learning such complex social behaviors as self-control, altruism, aggression, or sexual behavior, or in learning such motor skills as handwriting, driving a car, or operating a machine. Bandura showed, for example, that Guatemalan natives could learn to operate a cotton textile machine by observing the correct operation of the machine for a number of days. (7)

Bandura showed also that when children watched unusually aggressive behavior in a real-life model or a model in a film or cartoon, many of the children's responses were accurate imitations of the aggressive acts of the real-life model or the person in the film. The cartoon model elicited less precise imitation. (14) Walters found similar results among high school students, young women, and male hospital attendants. (16, 17) This research has led to much concern about the effects on children and adolescents from watching aggressive behavior on television screens: "exposure to filmed aggression heightens aggressive reactions." (14, p. 9) (See also Chapter 18.)

Bandura and Walters showed that a number of factors in the home situation contribute to effective socialization. One is early dependency of children on the parents, so that children desire approval and affection. If dependency behavior is punished or frustrated by a lack of affectional nurturance or by parental rejection, socialization is delayed or disrupted, hostility or aggressive behavior may develop, and children experience less guilt and lack the capacity to control aggressive feelings when aroused. In studies of adolescent aggression, Bandura and Walters showed that aggressive boys were less dependent on their fathers, more rejected by their fathers, and their fathers spent less time with them than did the fathers of less aggressive boys. (16)

Another home factor that contributes to socialization is the exertion of socialization pressure in the form of demands, restrictions, and limitations: in other words, discipline. The parents of less aggressive sons limited the amount of aggression they would tolerate, used more reasoning as a disciplinary method, and had higher expectations of the boys than did the parents of aggressive sons. Aggressive sons were encouraged to show aggression outside the home toward other children: to stand up for their rights, to use their fists. The fathers of aggressive boys seemed to get vicarious enjoyment from their sons' aggressive acts and were more permissive of their sons' sexual behavior. As a result, these boys had greater sexual experience than did other boys. (16)

The parents of the aggressive boys were also more punitive when the aggressive behavior was directed toward them. They used more physical discipline, isolation, deprivation of privileges, and less reasoning. The more the boys were punished physically at home for aggressive behavior, the more aggressive they became. Thus, they learned aggression by modeling the behavior of the punishing parent. Bandura writes:

> When a parent punishes his child physically for having aggressed toward peers, for example, the intended outcome of this training is that the child should refrain from hitting others. The child, however, is also learning from parental demonstration how to aggress physically. . . (13, p. 43)

The conscience development of the aggressive boys also differed from that of the less aggressive sons. The behavior of the latter was controlled by guilt and internal avoidance, whereas if the aggressive sons were inhibited at all, it was by fear of punishment rather than by guilt and internal controls. Because aggressive sons did not have as close emotional relationships with their parents, especially with fathers, their conscience development suffered.

Most social learning theorists emphasize the role of *reinforcement,* or the responses of others, in influencing future behavior. Bandura expands on this idea, speaking of *vicarious reinforcement* and *self-enforcement.* Vicarious reinforcement consists of the positive or negative consequences that one observes others experience. Observing that others are rewarded for aggressive behavior increases the possibility that the observer will also show aggression. Children who watched a movie of Rocky the Villain and saw that Rocky's aggression was rewarded were two times more likely to show aggressive behavior than a control group. When they observed Rocky being punished for aggression, they could describe the aggression but did not perform it. (15) Bandura and Perloff (13) observed that self-reinforcement was as effective as external reinforcement in influencing behavior. Once the performance of a desired response pattern, such as shooting and making baskets with a basketball, acquired a positive value, adolescents could administer their own reinforcement by producing the baskets and then feeling good afterward. Adolescents who set reasonable goal levels of performance and reach that level feel proud and satisfied internally, and become decreasingly dependent on parents, teachers, and bosses to give them rewards.

Bandura questions the stage-theory assumption that adolescence is inevitably a period of "storm and stress, tension, rebellion." (4) He feels that the description of turmoil, anxiety, sexual tensions, compulsive conformity, and acute identity crises applies to the actual behavior of only "the deviant ten percent of the adolescent population." (48) Current research tends to prove Bandura correct; data indicate that "the rate of emotional disturbance for adolescents does not differ significantly from the population at large." (31, p. 101) Bandura feels that well-adjusted youths are more numerous than is commonly assumed, and that they are the products of a warm, supportive preadolescence in which firmness and socialization pressure in childhood slowly gave way to increasingly more freedom during adolescence. According to Bandura, when marked changes occur in adolescence, they are due to sudden changes in social training, family structure, peer-group expectation, or other environmental factors, not to hormonal or other biological changes. Adolescence is not a separate stage; human development is continuous from infancy to adulthood. The same principles of learning that explain child development are applicable also to adolescent development; only the models and the environmental influences change. External stimulus conditions, rather than hidden, subconscious, internal dynamics, control normal as well as deviant behavior.

The work of social-learning theorists is of great importance in explaining human behavior. It is especially important in emphasizing that what adults do and the role models they represent are far more important in influencing adolescent behavior than what they say. Teachers and parents can best encourage human decency, altruism, moral values, and a social conscience by exhibiting these virtues themselves. (76)

Anthropological Views of Adolescence

MARGARET MEAD AND RUTH BENEDICT

Margaret Mead (1901–1978) made an empirical field study of a number of cultures, showing contrasts with our own and casting new light on the role of culture in personality development and socialization. She is best known for two books that are relevant to the study of adolescent development: *Coming of Age in Samoa* (71) and *Growing Up in New Guinea.* (72) The former is particularly important, for it is devoted entirely to adolescence.

Ruth Benedict (1887–1948) is best known for her book *Patterns Of Culture*. (20) Her theory of development is expounded from a cultural anthropological viewpoint in the article "Continuities and Discontinuities in Cultural Conditioning." (19)

The theories of these and other cultural anthropologists have been called *cultural determinism* and *cultural relativism* because anthropologists emphasize the importance of the social environment in determining the personality development of the child. And because social institutions, economic patterns, habits, mores, rituals, and religious beliefs vary from society to society, culture is relative. The kinds of influences that mold the child depend on the culture in which the child grows up. (20, 71)

The later writings of Mead (73, 74) and others have undergone some modification; they show some recognition of universal aspects of development (incest taboos, for example) and more acknowledgment of the biological role in human development. Today extreme positions are generally disregarded by both geneticists and anthropologists. They agree that a composite view that acknowledges both biogenetic factors and environmental forces comes closest to the truth.

What did Mead and Benedict have to say about adolescence?

CULTURAL CONTINUITY VERSUS DISCONTINUITY

Anthropologists challenge the basic truths of all age and stage theories of child and adolescent development. Mead discovered, for example, that Samoan children follow a relatively continuous growth pattern, with no abrupt changes from one age to the other. They are not expected to behave one way as children, another way as adolescents, and yet another way as adults. They never have to change abruptly their ways of thinking or acting; they don't have to unlearn as adults what they learned as children, so adolescence does not represent an abrupt change or transition from one pattern of behavior to another. This principle of continuity of cultural conditioning may be illustrated with three examples suggested by Benedict and Mead. (19, 71)

First, the responsible roles of children in primitive societies are contrasted with the nonresponsible roles of children in Western culture. Children in primitive societies learn responsibility quite early. Play and work often involve the same activity; for example, by "playing" with a bow and arrow, a boy learns to hunt. His adult hunting "work" is a continuation of his youthful hunting "play." In contrast, children in Western culture must assume drastically different roles as they grow up: they shift from nonresponsible play to responsible work, and must do it rather suddenly.

Second, the submissive role of children in Western culture is contrasted with the dominant role of children in primitive society. Children in Western culture must drop their childhood submission and adopt its opposite, dominance, as they become adults. Mead (71) showed that the Samoan child is not taught submission as a child and then suddenly expected to become dominant upon reaching adulthood. On the contrary, the six- or seven-year-old Samoan girl dominates her younger siblings and in turn is dominated by older ones. The older she gets, the more she dominates and disciplines others and the fewer there are to dominate her (the parents never try to dominate her). When she becomes an adult, she does not experience the dominance-submission conflict of the adolescent in Western society.

Third, the similarity of sex roles of children and adults in primitive cultures is contrasted with the dissimilar sex roles of children and adults in Western culture. Mead indicates that the Samoan girl experiences no real discontinuity of sex roles as she passes from childhood to adulthood. She has the opportunity to experiment and become familiar with sex with almost no taboos (except against incest). Therefore, by the time adulthood is reached, she is able to assume a sexual role in marriage very easily.

By contrast, in Western culture infant sexuality is denied and adolescent sexuality is repressed; sex is considered evil and dangerous. When adolescents mature sexually, they must unlearn these earlier attitudes and taboos and become sexually responsive adults.

STORM AND STRESS VERSUS CULTURAL CONDITIONING

In showing the continuity of development of children in some cultures in contrast to the discontinuity of development of children in Western culture, anthropologists and some psychologists (58) cast doubt upon the universality of ages and stages of growth of children in all cultures. Only those societies that emphasize discontinuity of behavior (one type of behavior as a child, another as an adult) are those described as "age-grade societies." (19)

Anthropologists challenge the inevitability of the storm and stress of adolescence by minimizing the disturbance of physical changes and by emphasizing the interpretation given those changes. Menstruation is a case in point. One tribe may teach that the menstruating girl is a danger to the tribe (she may scare the game or dry up the well); another tribe may consider her condition a blessing (she could increase the food supply or the priest could obtain a blessing by touching her). (24, 25, 78) A girl taught that menstruation is a positive good will react and act differently from a girl who is taught that it is a "curse." Therefore, the stress and strains of pubescent physical changes may be the result of certain cultural interpretations of those changes and not due to any inherent biological tendencies. (94)

CROSS-CULTURAL VIEWS ON PARENT-ADOLESCENT RELATIONS

Anthropologists describe many conditions in Western culture that create a generation gap, but they deny the inevitability of that gap. (74) Rapidity of social change, pluralistic value systems, and modern technology make the world appear too complex and too unpredictable to the adolescent to provide them with a stable frame of reference. Furthermore, early physiological puberty and the need for prolonged education allow many years for the development and assimilation of a peer-group culture in which adolescent values, customs, and mores may be in conflict with those in the adult world. (98) Mead feels that close family ties should be loosened to give adolescents more freedom to make their own choices and live their own lives. By requiring less conformity and less dependency and by tolerating individual differences within the family, Mead feels that adolescent-parent conflict and tension can be minimized. (71, p. 141) Also, Mead feels that youths can be accepted into adult society at younger ages. Gainful employment, even part time, would promote greater financial independence. Parenthood should be postponed, but not necessarily sex or marriage. (See also the section on Mead's two-stage marriage proposal in Chapter 16.) Adolescents should be given a greater voice in the social and political life of the community. These measures would eliminate some of the discontinuities of cultural conditioning of children growing up in Western society and would allow for a smoother, easier transition to adulthood.

A Psychosocial View of Adolescence

HAVIGHURST: DEVELOPMENTAL TASKS

In *Developmental Tasks and Education* Robert Havighurst (b. 1900) outlines what he feels are the major developmental tasks of adolescence. (51) His developmental task theory is an eclectic one combining previously developed concepts; it has been widely accepted and considered useful in discussing adolescent development and education.

Havighurst sought to develop a psychosocial theory of adolescence by combining consideration of individuals' needs with societal demands. What individuals need and society demands constitute the developmental tasks. They are the skills, knowledge, functions, and attitudes that individuals have to acquire at certain points in their lives through physical maturation, social expectations, and personal effort. Mastery of the tasks at each stage of development results in adjustment and preparation for the harder tasks ahead. Mastery of adolescent tasks results in maturity. Failure to master the adolescent tasks results in anxiety, social disapproval, and inability to function as a mature person.

According to Havighurst there is a teachable moment, a correct time for teaching any task. Some of the tasks arise out of biological changes, others from societal expectations at a given age, or the individual's motivation at certain times to do particular things. Furthermore, developmental tasks differ from culture to culture, depending on the relative importance of biological, psychological, and cultural elements in determining the tasks. If a task is determined primarily by biological factors, it may be almost universal; if determined by cultural elements, then great differences in the nature of the task may exist from culture to culture. There are significant differences in developmental tasks in the upper, middle, and lower classes in the United States.

THE EIGHT TASKS

Havighurst outlined eight major tasks during the adolescent period. (51)

1. Accepting one's physique and using the body effectively.
2. Achieving new and more mature relations with age mates of both sexes.
3. Achieving a masculine or feminine social-sex role.
4. Achieving emotional independence from parents and other adults.
5. Preparing for an economic career.
6. Preparing for marriage and family life.
7. Desiring and achieving socially responsible behavior.
8. Acquiring a set of values and an ethical system as a guide to behavior—developing an ideology.

These eight developmental tasks need to be interpreted. What did Havighurst say about them? (51, 52)

ACCEPTING ONE'S PHYSIQUE AND USING THE BODY EFFECTIVELY. One of the characteristics of adolescents is their emerging, often extreme, self-consciousness about their physical selves as they reach sexual maturity. This self-consciousness leads them to spend a great deal of time worrying about their rates of development and their physical characteristics and appearance. Some adolescents are pleased with their physiques; others are very unhappy. Both sexes worry about "inferior" traits such as crooked teeth, acne, or obesity. They wonder whether they are normal in comparison to others, or whether others consider them good-looking.

Adolescents need to accept their particular physique and the pattern of growth of their own body to understand the process of growth, to care for their body, and to learn to use the body effectively in sports and athletics, in recreation, in work, and in performing everyday tasks. (51, p. 51)

ACHIEVING NEW AND MORE MATURE RELATIONS WITH AGE MATES OF BOTH SEXES. Adolescents must move from the same-sex interests and playmates of middle childhood to establish heterosexual friendships. They need to get acquainted with both boys and girls as people and as friends and learn how to relate maturely with them in meaningful, caring ways. Becoming an adult means also learning social skills and behaviors required in group life. (51, p. 51)

ACHIEVING A MASCULINE OR FEMININE SOCIAL-SEX ROLE. What is a man? What is a woman? What are men and women supposed to look like, how are they supposed to behave, what are they supposed to be? Psychosexual social roles are established by each culture, but because masculine-feminine roles in Western culture are undergoing rapid changes, part of the maturing process for adolescents is to reexamine the changing sex roles of their culture and to decide what aspects they must adopt for themselves. Unless individuals accept their own sexuality as a male or female and have found an acceptable sex role, they will feel and be maladjusted. (51, p. 49)

ACHIEVING EMOTIONAL INDEPENDENCE FROM PARENTS AND OTHER ADULTS. Up to this time, children have depended mostly on parents for fulfillment of their emotional needs. They have sought their praise, love, and tenderness. Now they must become free from childish dependence on parents; they must develop understanding, affection, and respect without emotional dependence. Adolescents who are rebellious and in conflict with their parents and other adults need to develop a greater understanding of themselves and adults and the reasons for their conflict. (51, p. 55)

PREPARING FOR AN ECONOMIC CAREER. One of the primary goals of adolescents is to decide what they want to become, vocationally speaking, to prepare for that career, and then to become economically emancipated from parents by earning their own living. There are several aspects to these goals. One is to decide not just how they are going to make a living, but what they are going to do with their lives. Large numbers of youths have "hit the road" to live independently of parents, but have not yet found their life goals. Part of their task is to discover what they want out of life. Another aspect is to choose a career, become educated for it, and to start to work in it. This task is especially important for those who seek to organize their lives around a career in which they can invest their time and energy, grow in competence, responsibility, and income, and plan for an orderly future. (51, p. 62)

PREPARING FOR MARRIAGE AND FAMILY LIFE. Patterns of marriage and family living today are being readjusted to the changing economic, social, and religious characteristics of society. Many youths marry before completing their education or achieving economic independence. New experiments in living together and in trial marriage have developed to challenge traditional concepts. The majority of youths desire a happy marriage and parenthood as one important goal in life and need to develop the positive attitudes, social skills, emotional maturity, and necessary understanding to make marriage work. They need individual guidance and guidance through school courses in marriage and the family if their desires are to be fulfilled. (51, p. 59)

DESIRING AND ACHIEVING SOCIALLY RESPONSIBLE BEHAVIOR. This goal includes the development of a social ideology that takes into account societal values. The goal also includes participation in the adult life of the community and nation. Many adolescents are disturbed by the ethical quality of their society. Some become radical activists; others join the ranks of the uncommitted who refuse to act. These adolescents must find their place in society in a way that gives meaning to their lives and provides service to their community. (51, p. 75)

ACQUIRING A SET OF VALUES AND AN ETHICAL SYSTEM AS A GUIDE TO BEHAVIOR—DEVELOPING AN IDEOLOGY. This goal includes the development of a sociopolitico-ethical ideology and the adoption and application of meaningful values, morals, and ideals in one's personal life. Adolescents need to study and analyze societal value systems as well as their own morals and ideals in order to acquire a combination of expressive and instrumental values that maintain the positive qualities of their culture and bring beauty and love, as well as economic benefit, to people's lives. (51, p. 69)

In introducing his discussion of the developmental tasks of adolescence, Havighurst comments on the changing values of our society. He writes:

Instead of giving priority and precedence to *instrumental* activities—such as sacrificing something now for a greater future gain, working hard to make a more productive economy, studying now in preparation for future competence in an occupation—the modern society tends to favor *expressive* activities—such as enjoying the present moment without worrying about the future, spending time on activities that broaden and deepen one's experience, "doing one's thing." (51, p. 69)

Havighurst feels that many modern youths have not been able to achieve identity and therefore suffer from aimlessness and uncertainty about themselves. He says that the way most youths (especially boys) achieved identity in the first half of the twentieth century was through selecting and preparing for an occupation; work was the whole axis of life. Now, he feels, with the emphasis on expressive values, nothing has yet replaced occupational choice and preparation as the sure means of identity formation. (51, p. 69) Many adolescents, of course, would disagree; they would say that identity comes through a close, meaningful, loving relationship with another person, or persons, or through oneness with nature, or through an activist cause. What do you think?

Conclusions

Adolescence is not an abnormality, but, as the evidence shows, a period in the life cycle that presents many challenges and some stress. For most, the stress is moderate, within the bounds of normal behavior. There is some conflict with parents, but usually over domestic issues rather than fundamental values. Many young people experience degrees of anxiety and unhappiness, but these rarely constitute a crisis.

Most adolescents get on well with adults, cope with school and/or a job, and make major adjustments with a minimum of stress. They do it largely because they have a period in which to deal with issues one at a time. They spend the process of adaptation over a span of years—perhaps as many as fifteen years. Different problems, different relationship issues come into focus and are tackled at different stages, so that stress is rarely concentrated all at one time. The result is that adolescents can cope; but it takes many years to bridge the gap between childhood and adulthood. Given that some youths don't come to terms with their sexuality until age twenty or later, or find their vocational niche or the right marital partner until age twenty-five or later, one can only conclude that such important adjustments take a long time, especially in a complex industrial society such as ours. (27)

What about the various theories of adolescence? Which view or views are correct? Each view has contributed to an understanding of adolescence; each has an emphasis that is needed. Although no student of adolescent behavior today relies on Hall's recapitulation theory, many scholars would emphasize biogenetic factors as important determinants. Hereditary factors, biological drives, and physical changes exert a tremendous influence, although they are not the only factors influencing behavior. Gesell emphasized the importance of maturation in learning—an important emphasis—even though he neglected environmental contributions to personality growth. Sigmund and Anna Freud made a significant contribution in their emphasis on sexual and psychic drives and needs. The desire to satisfy sexual instincts and psychic needs for affection are both strong motivating factors in influencing ado-

[handwritten margin notes: pleasure, reality, super, socialt, moral; storm & stress]

lescent behavior. Similarly, S. Freud's explanations of the need for emotional emancipation from parents, the need to establish heterosexual friendships with peers, and the need to find a love object for emotional fulfillment are helpful in understanding adolescent-parent-peer relationships. A. Freud's explanation of the psychic disequilibrium of adolescents helps us understand the causes of their erratic behavior. Erikson's explanation of the adolescent's need for identity and the process by which the adolescent forms identity has had a marked influence on adolescent theory and research for over twenty years. Marcia has helped to clarify Erikson's view and to show how it applies to various types of adolescents. Sociologists have made an important contribution in showing the influence of society and culture in the lives of youths, in describing the process by which socialization takes place, and in pointing to the cultural differences among adolescents of different ethnic, economic, and social backgrounds. Similarly, anthropologists have made the careful student aware that there are few universal patterns of development or behavior, so that general conclusions about adolescents should be formulated to take into account the cultural vantage point from which one speaks. By making cultural comparisons, anthropologists enable the student to see some of the positive and negative elements in each culture that become a help or a hindrance to the adolescent. Havighurst's outline of the developmental tasks of adolescence are helpful to youths themselves in discovering some of the things they need to accomplish to reach adulthood. The outline is also helpful to parents, educators, and adult leaders who seek to teach and guide adolescents on their road to maturity.

One view alone gives only a partial picture, for, after all, adolescents are biological, psychological, social and cultural beings: genetically controlled organisms, and psychologically and sociologically conditioned products of the family and society of which they are a part. (30, p. 6) To understand adolescents, one must stand in many places and look from many points of view. (3, 77)

Topics for Term Papers

1. A Comparison of the Views of Adolescence of G. Stanley Hall and Arnold Gesell
2. Adolescent Sexuality according to Sigmund Freud
3. Defense Mechanisms during Adolescence according to Anna Freud
4. Ego Identity and the Choice of a Vocation according to Erikson
5. A Critique of Erikson's Views on Sex-Role Development and Polarization
6. The Effects of a Foreclosure of Identity during Adolescence (see Marcia)
7. Children and Violence: The Effects of Movies and Television (see Bandura and Walters and other research)
8. Adolescence as a Period of Storm and Stress: Pros and Cons (see A. Freud, Erikson, Mead)
9. The Causes and Consequences of Prolonged Adolescence (see Erikson, Mead, Benedict)
10. Cultural Continuity versus Discontinuity as Revealed in Parent-Child-Adolescent Relationships: Causes, Consequences, and Remedies (see Mead and Benedict)
11. The Developmental Tasks of Adolescence and Their Implications for Education (see Havighurst)

Bibliography

1. Adams, G. R. "Personal Identity Formation: A Synthesis of Cognitive and Ego Psychology." *Adolescence* 12 (Summer 1977): 151–164.

2. Adams, G. R., and Shea, J. A. "The Relationship between Identity Status, Locus of Control, and Ego Development." *Journal of Youth and Adolescence* 8 (March 1979): 81–89.

3. Alissi, A. S. "Concepts of Adolescence." *Adolescence* 7 (1972): 491–510.

4. Bandura, Albert. "The Stormy Decade: Fact or Fiction?" *Psychology in the Schools* 1 (1964): 224–231.

5. ———. *Principles of Behavior Modification.* New York: Holt, Rinehart and Winston, 1969.

6. ———. *Aggression, a Social Learning Analysis.* Englewood Cliffs, N.J.: Prentice-Hall, 1973.

7. ———. "Social Learning through Imitation." In *Nebraska Symposium on Motivation.* Edited by M. R. Jones. Lincoln: University of Nebraska Press, 1962.

8. ———. "Behavioral Modifications through Modeling Procedures." In *Research in Behavior Modification.* Edited by L. Krasner and L. Ullmann. New York: Holt, Rinehart and Winston, 1965.

9. ———. "Vicarious and Self-Reinforcement Processes." In *The Nature of Reinforcement.* Edited by R. Glaser. New York: Academic Press, 1971.

10. Bandura, Albert, and Kupers, C. J. "Transmission of Patterns of Self-Reinforcement through Modeling." *Journal of Abnormal and Social Psychology* 69:1–9, 1964.

11. Bandura, Albert, and McDonald, F. J. "Influence of Social Reinforcement and the Behavior of Models in Shaping Children's Moral Judgments." *Journal of Abnormal and Social Psychology* 67:274–281, 1963.

12. Bandura, Albert, and Mischel W. "Modification of Self-Imposed Delay of Reward through Exposure to Live and Symbolic Models." *Journal of Personality and Social Psychology* 2:698–705, 1965.

13. Bandura, Albert, and Perloff, B. "Relative Efficacy of Self-Monitored and Externally Imposed Reinforcement Systems." *Journal of Personality and Social Psychology* 7:111–116, 1967.

14. Bandura, Albert; Ross, D.; and Ross, S. A. "Invitation of Film-Mediated Aggressive Models." *Journal of Abnormal and Social Psychology* 66 (1963): 3011.

15. ———. "Vicarious Reinforcement and Imitative Learning." *Journal of Abnormal and Social Psychology* 67 (1963): 601–607.

16. Bandura, Albert, and Walters, R. H. *Adolescent Aggression.* New York: The Ronald Press, 1959.

17. ———. *Social Learning and Personality Development.* New York: Holt, Rinehart and Winston, 1963.

18. Bandura, Albert, and Whalen, C. K. "The Influence of Antecedent Reinforcement and Divergent Modeling Cues on Patterns of Self-Reward." *Journal of Personality and Social Psychology* 3 (1966): 373–383.

19. Benedict, Ruth. "Continuities and Discontinuities in Cultural Conditioning." *Psychiatry* 1 (1938): 161–167.

20. ———. *Patterns of Culture.* New York: New American Library, 1950.

21. Blos, P. "The Child Analyst Looks at the Young Adolescent." In *Twelve to Sixteen: Early Adolescence.* Edited by J. A. Kagan and Robert Coles. New York: W. W. Norton and Co., 1972.

22. Bourne, E. "The State of Research on Ego Identity: A Review and Appraisal. Part I." *Journal of Youth and Adolescence* 7 (September 1978): 223–251.

23. ———. "The State of Research on Ego Identity: A Review and Appraisal. Part II." *Journal of Youth and Adolescence* 7 (December 1978): 371–392.

24. Brown, Judith K. "Adolescent Initiation Rites among Preliterate Peoples." In *Studies in Adolescence.* 2d. ed. Edited by Robert E. Grinder. London: Macmillan Co., 1969.

25. ———. "Female Initiation Rites: A Review of the Current Literature." In *Issues In Adolescent Psychology.* Edited by Dorothy Rogers. New York: Appleton-Century-Crofts, 1969.

26. Ciaccio, N. V. "A Test of Erikson's Theory of Ego Epigenesis." *Developmental Psychology* 4 (1971): 306–311.

27. Coleman, J. C. "Current Contradictions in Adolescent Theory." *Journal of Youth and Adolescence* 7 (March 1978): 1–11.

28. Coles, Robert. *Biography of Erik Erikson.* Boston: Little, Brown and Co., 1970.

29. Davis, Allison. "Socialization and Adolescent Personality." In *Adolescence.* Yearbook of the National Society for the Study of Education, Vol. 43, Part I, 1944.

30. Dreyfus, E. A. *Adolescence: Theory and Experience.* Columbus, Ohio: Charles E. Merrill Publishing Co., 1976.

31. Ellis, E. H. "Some Problems in the Study of Adolescent Development." *Adolescence* 14 (Spring 1979): 101–109.

32. Erikson, Erik. *Childhood and Society.* New York: W. W. Norton & Co., 1950.

33. ———. *Identity and the Life Cycle.* New York: International Universities, 1959.

34. ———. *Identity: Youth and Crisis.* New York: W. W. Norton and Co., 1968.

35. Freud, Anna. *The Ego and the Mechanism of Defence.* New York: International Universities, 1946.

36. ———. *Psychoanalytic Study of*

the Child. New York: International Universities Press, 1958.

37. Freud, S. A. "Three Contributions to the Sexual Theory." *Nervous and Mental Disease Monograph Series*, No. 7, 1925.

38. ———. *A General Introduction to Psychoanalysis.* Translated by Joan Riviere. New York: Permabooks, 1953.

39. ———. "Three Essays on the Theory of Sexuality." vol. 7. London: Hogarth Press, 1953.

40. Gallatin, J. E. *Adolescence and Individuality. A Conceptual Approach to Adolescent Psychology.* New York: Harper and Row, 1975.

41. ———. "Theories of Adolescence." In *Understanding Adolescence.* 3d ed. Edited by J. F. Adams. Boston: Allyn & Bacon, 1976.

42. Gesell, Arnold, and Ames, L. B. *Youth: The Years from Ten to Sixteen.* New York: Harper and Row, 1956.

43. Gesell, Arnold et al. *The First Five Years of Life.* New York: Harper and Row, 1940.

44. Gesell, Arnold, and Ilg, F. L. *Infant and Child in the Culture of Today.* New York: Harper and Row, 1943.

45. ———. *The Child from Five to Ten.* New York: Harper and Row, 1946.

46. Gesell, Arnold, and Thompson, H. "Learning and Growth in Identical Twins: An Experimental Study by the Method of Co-Twin Control." *Genetic Psychology Monographs* 6 (1929): 1–124.

47. Guadro, C. J. *The Adolescent as Individual: Issues and Insights.* New York: Harper and Row, 1975.

48. Hall, G. Stanley. *Adolescence: Its Psychology and its Relation to Physiology, Anthropology, Sociology, Sex, Crime, Religion and Education.* 2 vols. New York: D. Appleton and Co., 1904.

49. Hall, G. Stanley, and Lindzay, G. *Theories of Personality*, 2d ed. New York: John Wiley & Sons, 1970.

50. Hauser, S. "Black and White Identity Development: Aspects and Perspectives." *Journal of Youth and Adolescence* 1 (1972): 113–130.

51. Havighurst, R. J. *Developmental Tasks and Education*, 3d ed. New York: David McKay Co., 1972.

52. ———. *Human Development and Education.* New York: Longmans, 1953.

53. Heyneman, S. P. "Continuing Issues in Adolescence: A Summary of Current Transition to Adulthood Debates." *Journal of Youth and Adolescence* 5 (December 1976): 309–323.

54. Hirsch, E. A. *The Troubled Adolescent.* New York: International Universities, 1970.

55. Hurlock, E. *Adolescent Development.* 4th ed. New York: McGraw-Hill, 1973.

56. Josselson, R. "Identity Formation in College Women." Ph.D. dissertation. University of Michigan, 1972.

57. ———. "Psychodynamic Aspects of Identity Formation in College Women." *Journal of Youth and Adolescence* 1 (1972): 3–52.

58. Kagan, J. A. "A Conception of Early Adolescence." *Daedalus* (Fall 1971): 997–1012.

59. Keniston, K. "Youth: A New Stage of Life." *The American Scholar* 39 (1970): 4.

60. ———. "The Tasks of Adolescence." In *Developmental Psychology Today.* Del Mar, Calif. CRM Books, 1971, pp. 363–384.

61. Kirsch, P. A. et al. "Ideology and Personality: Aspects of Identity Formation in Adolescents with Strong Attitudes toward Sex-Role Equalitarianism." *Journal of Youth and Adolescence* 5 (December 1976): 387–401.

62. LaVoie, J. C. "Ego Identity Formation in Middle Adolescence." *Journal of Youth and Adolescence* 5 (December 1976): 371–385.

63. "Legal Rights Still Cloudy for 18-Year-Olds." *U.S. News and World Report*, 8 March 1976, pp. 27–28.

64. Logan, R. D. "Identity Diffusion and Psycho-Social Defense Mechanisms." *Adolescence* 13 (Fall 1978): 503–507.

65. Marcia, J. E. "Development and Validation of Ego Identity Status." *Journal of Personality and Social Psychology* 3 (1966): 551–558.

66. ———. "Ego Identity Status: Relationship to Change in Self-Esteem, 'General Maladjustment,' and Authoritarianism." *Journal of Personality* 35 (1967): 118–133.

67. Marcia, J. E., and Friedman, M. L. "Ego Identity Status in College Women." *Journal of Personality* 38 (1970): 249–263.

68. Matteson, D. R. "Exploration and Commitment: Sex Differences and Methodological Problems in the Use of Identity Status Categories." *Journal of Youth and Adolescence* 6 (December 1977): 353–374.

69. McClain, E. W. "An Eriksonian Cross-Cultural Study of Adolescent Development." *Adolescence* 10 (1975): 527–541.

70. McDonald, G. W. "Parental Identification by the Adolescent: A Social Power Approach." *Journal of Marriage and the Family* 39 (November 1977): 705–719.

71. Mead, Margaret. *Coming of Age in Samoa.* New York: New American Library, 1950.

72. ———. *Growing Up in New*

Guinea. New York: New American Library, 1953.

73. ———. *Culture and Commitment: A Study of the Generation Gap.* Garden City, N.Y.: Doubleday and Co., 1970.

74. ———. "Adolescence." In *Youth and Culture: A Human Development Approach.* Edited by H. V. Kraemer, Monterey, Calif.: Brooks/Cole Publishing Co., 1974.

75. Miller, J. P. "Piaget, Kohlberg, and Erikson: Developmental Implications for Secondary Education." *Adolescence* 13 (Summer 1978): 237–250.

76. Mischel, W. *Introduction to Personality.* New York: Holt, Rinehart and Winston, 1971.

77. Muuss, R. E. *Theories of Adolescence.* 3d ed. New York: Random House, 1975.

78. ———. "Puberty Rites in Primitive and Modern Societies." *Adolescence* 5 (1970): 109–129.

79. Newman, B. M., and Newman P. R. "The Concept of Identity: Research and Theory." *Adolescence* 13 (Spring 1978): 157–166.

80. Newman, P. R., and Newman, B. M. "Identity Formation and the College Experience." *Adolescence* 13 (Summer 1978): 311–326.

81. Offer, D. *The Psychological World of the Teen-Ager: A Study of Normal Adolescent Boys.* New York: Basic Books, 1969.

82. Offer, D. et al. "A Longitudinal Study of Normal Adolescent Boys." *American Journal of Psychiatry* 126 (1970): 917–924.

83. Orlofsky, J. L. "Identity Formation, Achievement, and Fear of Success in College Men and Women." *Journal of Youth and Adolescence* 7 (March 1978): 49–62.

84. Ralston, N. C., and Thomas, P. "America's Artificial Adolescents." *Adolescence* 6 (1972): 137–142.

85. Raphael, D. "Identity Status in University Women: A Methodological Note." *Journal of Youth and Adolescence* 6 (March 1977): 57–62.

86. ———. "Identity Status in High School Females." *Adolescence* 13 (Winter 1978): 627–641.

87. ———. "Sequencing in Female Adolescents' Consideration of Occupational, Religious and Political Alternatives." *Adolescence* 14 (Spring 1979): 73–80.

88. Roessler, R. T. "Sexuality and Identity: Masculine Differentiation and Feminine Constancy." *Adolescence* 6 (1971): 187–196.

89. Rothman, K. M. "Multivariate Analysis of the Relationship of Psychosocial Crisis Variables to Ego Identity Status." *Journal of Youth and Adolescence* 7 (March 1978): 93–105.

90. St. Clair, S., and Day, H. D. "Ego Identity Status and Values among High School Females." *Journal of Youth and Adolescence* 8 (September 1979): 317–326.

91. Salzman, L. "Adolescent: Epoch or Disease?" *Adolescence* 8 (1973): 247–256.

92. Schenkel, S., and Marcia, J. E. "Attitudes toward Premarital Intercourse in Determining Ego Identity in College Women." *Journal of Personality* 40 (1972): 472–482.

93. Sieg, A. "Why Adolescence Occurs." *Adolescence* 6 (1971): 337–348.

94. Stanton, M. "The Concept of Conflict at Adolescence." *Adolescence* 19 (1974): 537–546.

95. Stark, P. A., and Traxler, A. J. "Empirical Validation of Erikson's Theory of Identity Crises in Late Adolescence." *Journal of Psychology* 86 (1974): 25–33.

96. Thornburg, H. *Development in Adolescence.* Monterey, Calif.: Brooks/Cole Publishing Co., 1975.

97. Toder, N. L., and Marcia, J. E. "Ego Identity Status and Response to Conformity Pressure in College Women." *Journal of Personality and Social Psychology* 26 (1973): 287–294.

98. Wagner, H. "Adolescent Problems Resulting from the Lengthened Educational Period." *Adolescence* 5 (1970): 339–344.

99. Waterman, A. S.; Geary, P. S.; and Waterman, C. K. "A Longitudinal Study of Changes in Ego Identity Status from the Freshman to the Senior Year at College." *Developmental Psychology* 10 (1974): 387–392.

100. Waterman, A. S., and Goldman, J. A. "A Longitudinal Study of Ego Identity Development at a Liberal Arts College." *Journal of Youth and Adolescence* 5 (December 1976): 361–369.

101. Waterman, A. S., and Waterman, C. K. "The Relationship between Ego Identity and Partner Perception on a Prisoner's Dilemma Game." *Journal of Social Psychology* 82 (1970): 117–126.

102. ———. "A Longitudinal Study of Changes in Ego Identity Status during the Freshman Year at College." *Developmental Psychology* 5 (1971): 167–173.

103. ———. "Relationship between Ego Identity Status and Subsequent Academic Behavior: A Test of the Predictive Validity of Marcia's Categorization for Identity Status." *Developmental Psychology* 6 (1972): 179.

104. Waterman, C. K., and Nevid, J. S. "Sex Differences in the Resolution of the Identity Crisis." *Journal of Youth and Adolescence* 6 (December 1977): 337–342.

105. Weiner, I. R. *Psychological Disturbance in Adolescence.* New York: John Wiley & Sons, 1970.

PART 2

Physical

Sexual Maturation and Change

Adolescence has been described as a period of sexual maturation and change. The purpose of this chapter is to discuss these sexual changes: what changes take place, when and how they occur, and some of the health concerns that arise partly as a result of these sexual changes.

The Endocrine Glands

The endocrine glands are ductless glands that secrete their biochemical substances, called *hormones* (meaning "I excite"), directly in the bloodstream. (3) The hormones bathe every cell of the body, but each also has target organs on which it acts specifically. The hormones act as an internal communication system, telling the different cells what to do, and when to act. (17, p. 185; 38)

The rate of secretion of hormones is closely controlled by a phenomenon known as *negative feedback*. When a physiologic effect of a hormone has been achieved, information is fed back to the endocrine organ to check its activity. If the endocrine organ is undersecreting, the negative feedback decreases and the gland is allowed to secrete more hormone. If there are sufficient hormones in the bloodstream, the hormones send a message to the endocrine glands to stop production. Thus the rate of secretion of a hormone is controlled by the needs of the body for the hormone. (47) Some of the hormones are secreted all the time; others are secreted intermittently in rhythmic cycles. All are secreted in minute quantities and may be measured in *micrograms* (one microgram = 1/1000 milligram) or in nanograms (one nanogram = 1/100,000 milligram). (17, p. 184)

Because of their importance in sexual maturation and growth, two of the glands of the endocrine system will be discussed here. These are the *pituitary gland* and the *gonads*, called the *ovary* in the female and the *testes* in the male.

PITUITARY GLAND

The pituitary gland is a very small gland—about one-half inch long—weighing less than half a gram and is located in the skull at the base of the brain. It consists of three lobes: anterior, intermediary, and posterior. The anterior pituitary lobe is known as the master gland of the body, for it produces several hormones that control the action of the other glands. (15, p. 119) Not all the hormones secreted by the pituitary have been identified or their actions defined, but the best-known ones and their functions are described here.

The growth hormone, referred to as HGH *(human growth hormone)* or SH *(somatotrophic hormone)*, affects the growth and shaping of the skeleton. An excess causes *giantism;* a deficiency causes *dwarfism.* (37, p. 398) Sometimes an excess is secreted after normal bone growth has ceased, causing the bones of the hands and feet to lengthen disproportionately, the jaw to grow with the lower section projecting forward, and the teeth to become widely separated. The condition is known as *acromegaly*, "big extremities." (17, p. 155)

Gonadotropic hormones are secreted by the anterior pituitary and are so named because they influence gonad functioning. (20, 21; 47, p. 61) There are three gonadotropic hormones. (26, p. 53) The *FSH (follicle-stimulating hormone)* is secreted to stimulate the growth of the Graafian follicles (which grow into mature egg cells in the ovaries) and of the seminiferous tubules in the testes (which produce sperm). The *LH (luteinizing hormone)* in the female controls the production and release of *estrogen* and of *progesterone* by the ovary. The *ICSH (interstitial cell-stimulating hormone)* in the male controls the production and release of *testosterone* by the testes. (12, p. 27) It is ICSH in the male that is responsible for stimulating spermatogenesis; without ICSH, the production of sperm does not go beyond the second cell division and second stage of growth. The chief function of ICSH, however, is to stimulate the interstitial cells of the testes in their production of the male hormone testosterone. (44)

In addition to its secretion of growth hormones and gonadotropic hormones, the pituitary secretes a lactogenic hormone, *LTH (luteotropic hormone)*, containing the hormone *prolactin*, which stimulates the secretion of milk by the mammary glands of the breast.

GONADS

The gonads, or sex glands, secrete a number of sex hormones. The *ovaries* in the female secrete a whole group known as *estrogens* (meaning "producing mad desire") that stimulate the development of female sex characteristics such as breast development, the growth of pubic hair, and the distribution of fat on the body. These hormones also maintain the normal size and function of the uterus, its tubes, and the vagina; they maintain the normal condition and function of nasal and oral mucous membranes, control the growth of breast duct tissue, influence normal uterine contractions, and develop and maintain physical and mental health in other ways. Through negative feedback to the pituitary they control the production of various pituitary hormones. Studies have also shown that estrogens influence olfactory sensitivity, which is greatest midway between menstrual periods when estrogen levels are the highest. (26, p. 55)

A second female hormone, *progesterone*, is produced in the ovaries by a new cell growth, yellow in color, under the stimulus of LH from the pituitary, following the rupture of the ovum from the ovarian follicle. When an egg cell is discharged from a follicle in ovulation, the remaining follicular cells multiply rapidly and fill the cavity. This new cell growth becomes the *corpus luteum* (yellow body), which secretes progesterone for about thirteen days following ovulation. If the ovum has not been fertilized, the corpus luteum disintegrates and the secretion of progesterone ceases until ovulation occurs again during the next cycle. If, however, the ovum is fertilized, and the corpus luteum does not degenerate, it continues to secrete progesterone and keep the *endometrium*, or uterine lining, ready to receive the fertilized egg. The corpus luteum continues to secrete progesterone for the first few months of pregnancy; after this time the *placenta* takes over the task of secreting both estrogen and progesterone for the remainder of the pregnancy. (17, p. 228; 26, p. 56)

Progesterone is an extremely important hormone. It controls the length of the menstrual cycle from ovulation until the next menstruation. It is of primary importance in preparing the uterus for pregnancy and maintaining the pregnancy itself. A proper amount of progesterone is necessary to inhibit premature uterine contractions; it is often prescribed when there is danger of spontaneous abortion. It also stimulates the mammary glands of the pregnant woman, causing enlargement of the breasts. In the nonpregnant female it keeps breast tissue firm and healthy, reduces the possibility of painful menstruation, premenstrual tension, and other gynecological problems. (26)

The *testes* in the male, under the stimulation of ICSH from the pituitary, begin the production of the androgenic hormone, *testosterone*. It is this male hormone that is responsible for the development and preservation of masculine secondary sexual characteristics, including facial and body hair, voice change, muscular and skeletal development, and for the development of the other male sex organs: the seminal vesicles, prostate gland, epididymis, penis, and scrotum. (26, p. 58)

Both the estrogens and androgens are found in both boys and girls, but in negligible amounts prior to puberty. They are produced by the adrenals and the gonads in moderately increasing amounts during childhood. As the ovaries mature, the production of ovarian estrogenic hormones increases dramatically and begins to show the cyclic variation in level during various stages of the menstrual cycle. The level of androgens in the girl's bloodstream increases only slightly. As the testes mature in the male, the production of testosterone increases dramatically, whereas the level of the estrogens in the boy's bloodstream increases only slightly. It is the ratio of the levels of the male to female hormones that is partly responsible for development of male or female characteristics. An imbalance in the natural hormonal state in a growing child can produce deviations in primary and secondary sexual characteristics and affect the development of expected masculine or feminine physical traits. A female with an excess of androgens may grow a mustache and body hair, develop masculine musculature and strength, or evidence an enlarged clitoris or other masculine characteristics. (2) Female track stars sometimes take male hormones to increase their strength and endurance. A male with an excess of estrogens may evidence decreased potency and sex drive and an enlargement of the breasts. (26, p. 59)

Maturation and Functions of Male Sex Organs

The primary male sex organs include the *testes, scrotum, epididymis, seminal vesicles, prostate glands, Cowper's glands, penis, vas deferens,* and *urethra.* They are depicted in Figure 4–1.

A number of important changes occur in these organs during adolescence. The growth of the testes and scrotum accelerates, beginning at about age 11½, becoming fairly rapid by age 13½, and slowing thereafter. These ages are averages, of course. Rapid growth may start between 9½ and 13½ years, ending

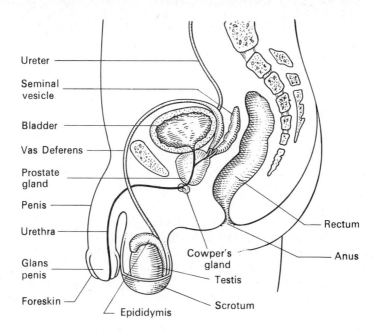

Ureter

Seminal vesicle

Bladder

Vas Deferens

Prostate gland

Penis

Urethra

Glans penis

Foreskin

Cowper's gland

Testis

Epididymis

Scrotum

Rectum

Anus

Figure 4–1.   The male reproductive system.

between ages 13 and 17. (24) During this time the testes increase 2½ times in length and about 8½ times in weight. Before puberty the epididymis is relatively large in comparison with the testes; after maturity the epididymis is only about one-ninth the size of the testes.

SPERMATOGENESIS

The most important change within the testes themselves is the development of mature sperm cell. This occurs when the FSH from the pituitary stimulates the growth of the *seminiferous tubules* (there are about 1,000 of them) that contain an increasing number of cells known as *primitive spermatogonia,* which constitute the first stage of *spermatogenesis* (the production of sperm cells). Through cell division the spermatogonia form other spermatogonia plus *spermatocytes,* each of which divides into two smaller *secondary spermatocytes.* Secondary spermatocytes appear in boys at about age twelve or thirteen (although the age varies considerably) and do not grow any further until the ICSH hormone is secreted by the pituitary, causing the spermatocytes to split again into the last primitive germinal cells, the *spermatids.* Spermatids then grow, develop, and rearrange their component parts until they finally mature into *spermatozoa,* the fully formed male sperm. The total process of spermatogenesis, from the time the primitive spermatogonium is formed until it grows into a mature sperm, is about ten days. (26, p. 72)

Following spermatogenesis the sperm migrate by contraction of the seminiferous tubules to reach the epididymis where they may remain for as long as six weeks. Sperm are then transported by ciliary action through the epididymis into the vas deferens where many are stored. There they are conducted by ciliary action through the vas deferens, eventually reaching the seminal vesicle and prostate gland where they are made more mobile by the addition of the *seminal fluid*, passing with it through the urethra and out of the penis at each ejaculation. The seminal fluid, a highly alkaline, milky fluid, keeps the sperm alive, healthy, and mobile, and serves as a vehicle for carrying the sperm out of the penis.

THE DEVELOPING PENIS

The penis doubles in both length and girth during adolescence, with the most rapid growth taking place between ages fourteen and sixteen. Genital growth usually takes 3 years to reach the adult stage, but some males complete this development in 1.8 years and others take as many as 4.7 years. (24, p. 13) In the adult male, the flaccid (limp) penis averages from 3 to 4 inches in length and slightly over 1 inch in diameter. The tumescent (erect) penis, on the average, is 5½ to 6½ inches in length and 1½ inches in diameter; sizes vary tremendously from male to male. (30, p. 66)

Adolescent boys are often concerned with the dimensions of their penis, for they associate masculinity and sexual capability with penis size. In fact the size of the flaccid penis has little to do with the size of the erect penis, for the small penis enlarges much more in proportion to its size than does the large penis. Moreover, the size of the erect penis has little to do with sexual capability, for the vagina has few nerve endings and female sexual excitation comes primarily from stimulation of the external genitalia. The degree of pleasure experienced by both the man and woman has nothing to do with the size of the male organ. (25, p. 191)

The head of the penis (*glans penis*) is covered by a loose fold of skin, the *prepuce* or *foreskin*, which is often removed surgically through circumcision for hygienic or religious reasons. Circumcision today is considered a wise health measure, since penile cancer is more common in the uncircumcised male and cervical cancer is more common in wives of uncircumcised males. Furthermore, if the prepuce is tight over the glans, a smelly cheeselike substance known as *smegma* collects, acting as a breeding ground for irritants and disease. (26, p. 68)

Erection of the penis is possible from infancy; it may be caused by tight clothing, local irritation, the need to urinate, or by manual stimulation. Freud was the first to acknowledge infant sexuality and the likelihood that the small boy may gain pleasure from masturbation. Kinsey pointed out that young children sometimes masturbate to orgasm. (18) However, ejaculation of semen does not occur prior to sexual maturity. Chapter 13 provides information on masturbation during adolescence.

THE PROSTATE GLAND

At puberty, between 10 and 11 years of age in the average boy, the prostate gland begins to increase rapidly in size. There is some evidence of prostatic secretion soon after, with ejaculation of the first semen taking place at about age 13½, but possibly as early as age 12. (26, p. 51) Ejaculation may take place even before sperm are mature.

COWPER'S GLANDS

The Cowper's glands, which also mature at this time, secrete an alkaline fluid that lubricates and neutralizes the acidity of the urethra for easy and safe passage of the semen. This fluid may be observed at the opening of the glans during sexual excitement and before ejaculation. Because the fluid contains sperm in about 25 percent of cases examined, conception is possible whenever intercourse occurs, even if the male withdraws prior to ejaculation. (26, p. 65)

NOCTURNAL EMISSIONS

One of the things that adolescent boys wonder and worry about is nocturnal emissions or the so-called wet dreams. Kinsey reported that almost 100 percent of men have erotic dreams, and about 83 percent of them have dreams that culminate in orgasm. These dreams occur most frequently among males in their teens and twenties, but about half of all married men continue to have them. (18) The incidence of nocturnal emissions is higher among college men than among those with less education. Over 99 percent of college men have sexual dreams resulting in orgasm, compared to 85 percent of those who completed only high school and 75 percent of those who completed only grade school. (18, p. 19) Nocturnal orgasms may cause anxiety; a boy who has a first orgasm nocturnally may be puzzled, confused, or guilty. One mother accused her son of wetting the bed, which made him feel very childish and ashamed. Some boys develop feelings of guilt and anxiety, because they believe they have impure thoughts and feel there must be something wrong with them to have such feelings. They should be reassured that such experiences are normal, that no harm comes from them, and that they should be accepted as a part of their sexuality.

MOOD CHANGES

There is substantial evidence that men go through cycles of mood that affect their behavior. (30, 33) One researcher found the greatest number of mood cycles in some men were between seven and twenty-three days and in others between thirty to forty-five days, with men exhibiting more cycles than women. (30) But there is no sure evidence that these cycles correspond to fluctuations in levels of the male hormone testosterone. (11) So many factors—weather, health, fatigue, time of week, social happenings—affect mood fluctuations that it is impossible to say they are based entirely upon physiological changes. One study showed some correlation between high levels of testosterone and depression, but no direct correlation between day-to-day hormone levels and mood. (11)

Maturation and Functions of Female Sex Organs

The primary internal female sex organs include the *ovaries, fallopian tubes, uterus,* and *vagina.* The external female sex organs are known collectively as the *vulva* and include the *mons veneris (mons pubis),* the *labia majora* (major or large outer lips), the *labia minora* (small inner lips), the *clitoris,* and the *vestibule* (the cleft region enclosed by the labia minora). The *hymen* is a fold of connective tissue that partly closes the vagina in the virginal female. The *Bartholin's*

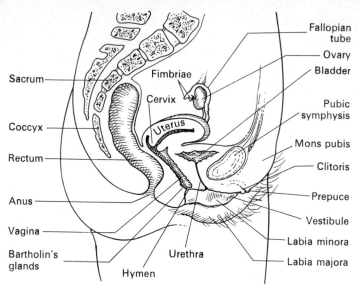

Fallopian tube
Ovary
Bladder
Pubic symphysis
Mons pubis
Clitoris
Prepuce
Vestibule
Labia minora
Labia majora

Fimbriae
Cervix
Uterus

Sacrum
Coccyx
Rectum
Anus
Vagina
Bartholin's glands
Hymen
Urethra

Figure 4–2.   The female reproductive system.

glands, situated on either side of the vaginal orifice, secrete a drop or so of fluid during sexual excitement. The female sexual organs are depicted in Figure 4–2.

VAGINAL DEVELOPMENT

The vagina matures at puberty in a number of ways. It increases in length, and its mucous lining becomes thicker, more elastic, and turns a deeper color. The Bartholin's glands begin to secrete their fluids, and the inner walls of the vagina change their secretion from the alkaline reaction of childhood to an acid reaction in adolescence.

CHANGES IN THE VULVA AND UTERUS

The labia majora, practically nonexistent in childhood, enlarge greatly, as do the labia minora and the clitoris. The clitoris becomes erectile by developing an extensive system of blood vessels. The mons veneris becomes more prominent through the development of a fatty pad. (26, p. 49)

A dramatic change also takes place in the uterus, which doubles in length, showing a straight-line increase during the period from ten to eighteen years of age. The uterus of the mature nonpregnant female is a hollow, thick-walled, muscular organ shaped like a pear, about 3 inches long, 2½ inches at the top and narrowing to a diameter of 1 inch at the cervix. (26, p. 82)

OVARIAN CHANGES

The ovaries increase greatly in size and weight. They ordinarily show a fairly steady growth from birth to about eight years of age. From eight to about the time of ovulation (twelve or thirteen years) the rate of growth accelerates somewhat, but the most rapid increase occurs after sexual maturity is reached. This is due, no doubt, to the maturation of the follicles within the ovary itself.

Every infant girl is born with about 200,000 to 400,000 follicles in each ovary. By the time puberty has been reached, this number has declined to about 10,000 in each ovary. Ordinarily, one follicle ripens into an ovum every 28 days for a period of about thirty-five years, which means that only about 455 have ripened during the woman's reproductive years. (22; 26, p. 78)

MENSTRUATION

On the average the adolescent girl begins her menstrual cycle at twelve to thirteen years of age, although she may mature considerably earlier or later (nine to eighteen years is an extreme range). *Menarche* (the onset of menstruation) usually does not occur until after maximum growth rates in height and weight have been achieved. (13) Because of superior nutrition and health care, girls start menstruating earlier today than in former generations. (3, 40, 43) One study showed that girls today reach menarche 4.5 months earlier, on the average, than did their mothers, primarily because of better nutrition. (46) Figure 4–3 shows the percentage of girls of each age, by race, that have started menstruation. (23) As the figure shows, and as substantiated by other research (43), race is not a significant factor.

Figure 4–4 illustrates the menstrual cycle. During the first half of the cycle, the pituitary secretes FSH and stimulates the growth of a follicle in one ovary.

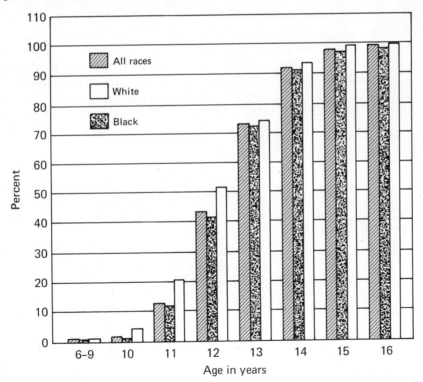

Figure 4–3. Percentage of girls whose menstrual periods have started, by race and age, in the United States. (Adapted from B. MacMahon, "Age at Menarche: United States," *Vital and Health Statistics,* Series 11, No. 133 [Washington, D.C.: U.S. Department of Health, Education and Welfare, 1974].)

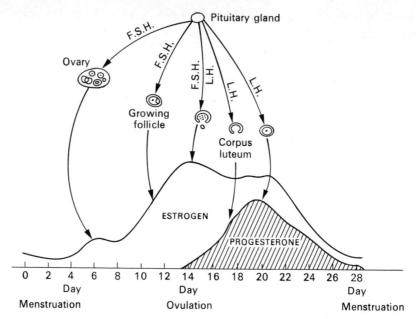

Arrows from pituitary to ovary, follicles, and corpus luteum indicate hormonal stimulation from pituitary to these organs.

Arrows from ovary and follicles to graph lines indicate estrogen secretion at the level shown on the graph at that particular stage of growth of the follicle.

Arrows from corpus luteum to graph lines indicate progesterone secretion at the level shown on the graph at that particular stage of development of the corpus luteum.

Figure 4–4.   Rise and fall of female hormone levels in the blood.

After the follicle matures into an *ovum* (mature egg cell), it erupts from the ovary (*ovulation*) and passes into the Fallopian tube. In the meantime the inner lining of the uterus (endometrium) is being built up to receive a possible fertilized egg. Following ovulation the pituitary secretes LH, stimulating the growth of the cells from which the ovum has erupted, forming the corpus luteum (the yellow body), which itself becomes an endocrine gland that secretes progesterone. During the first half of the menstrual cycle, the level of estrogen rises in the bloodstream until ovulation. When it rises, it inhibits the pituitary from secreting additional FSH to cause another follicle to mature. Following ovulation, if the egg is not fertilized, the level of estrogen slowly declines while the level of progesterone rises and then falls. Progesterone helps prepare the interior lining to receive a fertilized egg. If the egg is not fertilized, the corpus luteum dies and the production of progesterone declines, allowing the endometrium to be sloughed off in the process of *menstruation*. With the levels of estrogen and progesterone at a minimum, the negative feedback to the pituitary gland ceases and it once more begins to secrete FSH during the first half of the cycle and LH during the last half.

One of the questions adolescents ask concerns the exact time ovulation occurs. Ordinarily the time of ovulation is about two days before the midpoint of the menstrual cycle, which would be on the twelfth day of a twenty-eight-day cycle, and on the thirteenth or fourteenth day of a thirty-one-day cycle. However, there is some evidence to show that girls have become pregnant on any one day of the cycle, including during menstruation itself, and that some girls may ovulate more than once during a cycle, possibly due to the stimulus of sexual excitement itself. With the exact time of ovulation difficult to predict, there are really no completely "safe" times during the month when a girl cannot become pregnant. (26, p. 252)

A girl may menstruate *anovulatorily* (without ovulation) when her menstrual cycle begins until the ovaries mature enough to discharge mature ova, and until the endocrine glands secrete enough of their hormones to make ovulation possible. (39) The first periods may be scanty and irregular, spaced at varying intervals until a rhythm is established. (14, p. 134) It is not uncommon for the flow to last only a day or so for the first few periods. Later it may last from two to seven days with the mean usually about five days. The total amount of blood lost is not great, and averages one and a half ounces (three tablespoonsful). A normal range is from one to five ounces. Only a part of the menstrual fluid is blood. The total discharge amounts to approximately one cupful (six to eight ounces) and is composed partly of mucus and broken-down cell tissue. (26, p. 93)

MENSTRUAL PROBLEMS AND CONCERNS

Beginning menstruation can be a traumatic event for some girls who are not prepared ahead of time. One sixteen-year-old commented:

I was very frightened of the sexual changes that occurred in my body. The first change I noticed was my menstrual period. I was very frightened of the blood; I didn't know why it occurred. When I finally asked my mother, she did not really take the time to explain to me, so I didn't really know just why or how it happened. (12, p. 43)

Other girls are able to accept menstruation in a natural way because they have been taught what to expect. One girl remarked:

I was aware of the changes that were going to take place in my body before they occurred. I was not really frightened of the changes in my body because I was told a lot about it by my next door neighbor and my mother. (12, p. 42)

Still other girls look forward to maturing. Such were the feelings of one fifteen-year-old.

When I began developing I was quite fascinated, overjoyed. It was something new, a part of me. I began to realize that I was growing up and it excited me, made me very anxious. No embarrassment was involved, or shame. I took it as it came and lived the best I could, which was great. Still is. (12, p. 42)

Whether or not the adolescent girl experiences any menstrual problem will depend upon both physical and emotional factors. (28) Almost all girls experience variations of mood according to the stage of the menstrual cycle. There is a physical basis for this emotional fluctuation. Depression, hostility, anxiety, and emotional upset are more evident just before and during the menstrual period when the female hormones are at their lowest level. Feelings of joy and happiness are greatest midway between periods when the estrogen level is at its highest. (4, 19, 28, 35) However, so many environmental factors can influence mood that it is a mistake to attribute all emotional fluctuations to female hormones. The truth of the matter is that both men and women experience biological and psychological cycles that depend upon everything from the weather to personal relationships with parents, teachers, or the opposite sex. Good and bad moods cannot be predicted solely on the basis of the time of month.

The young girl's attitudes and feelings about menstruation are also very important. In Margaret Mead's studies of the women of Samoa, only one woman of the entire population understood what was meant by problems during menstruation, and she was employed by a white missionary family (31) that had conditioned her to expect problems. The implication was that negative teaching contributed to her difficulty.

Unfortunately, many girls are negatively conditioned even before menses. One study of sixth to eighth graders in white, middle and upper class schools revealed that menstruation was associated mainly with negative attitudes and expectations. Most believed that it was accompanied by physical discomforts, increased emotionality and mood changes, and disruption of activities and social life. Because some of the girls answering the questions had not yet menstruated, their responses reflected, not actual experiences, but negative cultural stereotypes and negative beliefs that they had learned from others. Their menstrual experiences were primed to become self-fulfilling prophecy. (7, p. 233)

Other researchers have demonstrated the relationship between sociopsychological factors and menstrual distress. (5) One study showed that women who have more liberal attitudes about the role of women in society experience less psychological stress that may manifest itself in menstrual difficulties. (5, p. 140) Another study demonstrated that women in therapy who were encouraged to understand and appreciate their female role reported decreased menstrual symptomatology. (5, p. 140) Warm, supportive family and peer relations also may be conducive to less stressful menstrual cycles and to fewer physical difficulties in general. (5)

Some adolescent females experience physical difficulties with their menstrual periods. These physical problems usually fall into one of four categories.

Dysmenorrhea is painful or difficult menstruation: menstrual cramps or abdominal pain, with or without other symptoms such as backache, headache, vomiting, fatigue, irritability, sensitivity of the genitals or breasts, pain in the legs, swelling of the ankles, or skin irritations such as pimples. Gray reports that about 25 percent of adolescent females have at least some periods that are so painful or difficult during any one year that they consult a doctor for relief. In addition, 11 percent have severe abdominal pain of a generalized nature during their periods, with nausea, vomiting, and digestive distress. (16) Because dysmenorrhea may have either organic or functional origins, possible physical difficulties should be investigated before emotional factors are suspected. (26, p. 439)

Menorrhagia is excessive bleeding due to physical or emotional factors. Gray reports that 12 percent of girls seek medical help because of excessively profuse bleeding. Such bleeding should be looked into because it may indicate an endocrine disturbance, systemic disease, malposition of the uterus, or severe hypertension. (16)

Amenorrhea is absence of flow. This may be due to a physical cause like an endocrine disorder, or to a change of climate, overwork, emotional excitement, and other factors. Gray reports that 9 percent of adolescent females seek medical help because of scanty or no bleeding. (16) Amenorrhea may be primary (having always occurred) or secondary (occurring in a girl who previously had normal periods). Secondary amenorrhea is common, especially in young women.

Metrorrhagia, bleeding from the uterus at times other than during a menstrual period, is not common; it demands a medical checkup to determine physical and/or emotional causes.

Many questions arise concerning exercise, bathing, or swimming during the menstrual period. Exercise is not only possible but also beneficial; doctors may even prescribe certain exercises to relieve menstrual cramps. Bathing is desirable if the water is not too cold or hot; excessively cold water will stop the menstrual flow and sometimes cause cramps. Swimming is also permissible, if chilling or excessive fatigue is avoided.

One report studied 203 high school females, ages fifteen through eighteen, from North High School in Des Moines, Iowa. (1) These adolescents consisted of two groups: 138 in the eleventh grade who had completed their compulsory swimming requirements the previous year, many of whom had discontinued regular exercise; and 65, grades nine to twelve, in a special swimming group known as the Dolphins. All the Dolphins and 62 out of 138 non-Dolphins swam during menstruation. The results of the study indicate that regular exercise contributes positively to reducing menstrual discomfort and that swimming does not increase it. Forty-seven percent of the entire group at some time had menstrual discomfort (51 percent of the non-Dolphins and 40 percent of the Dolphins). But the fact that there was less discomfort for the Dolphin group than for the non-Dolphins shows that even vigorous swimming during the menstrual cycle is not a causative factor in dysmenorrhea. (1) (See Table 4–1 for further comparisons.)

In addition, a follow-up study was done of 111 former North High School females who had been competitors in vigorous, unrestricted athletic programs

Table 4–1. Menstrual discomfort: non-Dolphins versus Dolphins.

	No.	Had Discomfort at Some Time in Association with Menstruation		Still Has Discomfort in Association with Menstruation		Has Sought Professional Advice for Menstrual Discomfort		Takes Medication for Menstrual Discomfort		Has Missed a Social or Scholastic Event Because of Menstrual Discomfort	
		Yes	No	Yes	No	Yes	No	Yes	No	Yes	No
Total No.	203	96	107	93	3	52	44	35	61	15	81
Non-Dolphins	138	70	68	67	3	40	30	29	41	10	60
Dolphins	65	26	39	26	0	12	14	6	20	5	21

Adapted from T. W. Anderson, "Swimming and Exercise during Menstruation," *Journal of Health, Physical Education, Recreation* 36 (1965): 66–68. Used by permission.

that required practice and competition during all phases of the menstrual cycle. This group included 61 national and state champions in synchronized swimming and 50 rope jumpers, tennis, and golf players. Among these 111 former competitors, 69 were married at the time of the study and had from one to four children. None of the group had experienced obstetrical or gynecological difficulties or had infertility problems. Their childbearing experiences had been normal. Thus, there was evidence that these female athletes were not obstetrically or gynecologically penalized by having previously participated in a vigorous exercise program that involved training and competition during the menstrual cycle. The author of the study concluded that parents, teachers, and school administrators should deemphasize menstruation as a debilitating aspect and allow girls who are so inclined to lead active lives during their menstrual periods. The author did not suggest forcing vigorous exercise during menstruation, but did observe that the continuation of normal professional and athletic activities during all phases of the menstrual cycle decreases the amount and intensity of menstrual discomfort. (1)

Development of Secondary Sexual Characteristics

Sexual maturation at puberty includes development not only of the reproductive organs, but also of secondary sex characteristics. (37, p. 13) These include the appearance of body hair, voice changes, the development of mature male and female body contours, and other minor changes. (45, p. 91)

The sequence of development for boys and girls is given in Table 4–2. (32) The development of some of the primary sexual characteristics is also included to give a picture of the total sequence of development (primary characteristics are marked with an asterisk). (14, p. 63; 34; 36, p. 441)

The ages provided in the table are averages: actual ages may extend several years before and after. Marshall and Tanner found that, in American girls, the height spurt may begin anywhere from 9.5 to 14.5 years of age; menarche may occur from 10 years to as late as 16.5; breast development may start as young as 8 or not until age 13. (24) In boys the height spurt may begin anywhere from 10.5 to 16 years of age; penile growth may begin at 10.5 to 14.5 and not end until 12.5 to 16.5 years of age. (24) It is evident, therefore, that although the average girl matures about two years before the average boy, the rate of development is not always consistent. An early-maturing boy may be younger than a late-maturing girl. (38) The mean age of menarche is 12.5; the mean age for first ejaculation of semen is 13.7. (34) But it is untrue to refer to these ages as the norm. The age of sexual maturity extends over such a wide range (9 to 18 years is not unusual) that any ages within the range should be considered normal.

MALES

The development of secondary sexual characteristics in boys is a gradual process. (24) The development of pubic hair starts with sparse, straight hair at the base of the penis, and then the hair gradually becomes more profuse and curled, forming an inverse triangle and spreading up to the umbilicus. Axillary hair

Table 4–2.   Sequence of development of primary* and secondary sexual characteristics.

Boys	Age Span		Girls
Beginning growth of testes, scrotum, pubic hair	11.5–13	10–11	Height spurt begins
			Slight growth of pubic hair
Some pigmentation, nodulation of breasts (later disappears)			Breasts, nipples elevated to form "bud" stage
Height spurt begins			
Beginning growth of penis			
Development of straight, pigmented pubic hair	13–16	11–14	Straight, pigmented pubic hair
Early voice changes			Some deepening of voice
Rapid growth of penis, testes, scrotum, prostate, seminal vesicles*			Rapid growth of vagina, ovaries, labia, uterus*
First ejaculation of semen*			
Kinky pubic hair			Kinky pubic hair
Age of maximum growth			Age of maximum growth
Beginning growth of axillary hair			Further enlargement, pigmentation, elevation of nipple, areola to form "primary breast"
			Menarche*
Rapid growth of axillary hair	16–18	14–16	Growth of axillary hair
Marked voice change			Filling out of breasts to form adult conformation, secondary breast stage
Growth of beard			
Indentation of frontal hair line			

usually first appears two years after the appearance of pubic hair, with the growth of the beard coming near the end of the total sequence, and the indentation of the hair line (this does not occur in girls) the final development. (39) Muscular development, widening of the shoulders and chest, and other changes in body contours continue. Usually a boy has reached 98 percent of his adult height by 17¾ years of age, plus or minus ten months. (34)

Changes in the boy's voice are due to the rapid growth of the larynx (the Adam's apple) and the lengthening of the vocal cords across it. The vocal cords nearly double in length, lowering the pitch one octave. Volume also increases and the tonal quality is more pleasant. Roughness of tone and unexpected pitch changes may last until sixteen or eighteen years of age.

Before and during the period when sexual maturation takes place, some boys suffer what has been referred to as the locker room syndrome. (41, p. 396) The boy in middle school or junior high is herded into the shower after gym where he has to undress and bathe in front of others. The range in normal developmental rates is great enough so that some boys are completely underdeveloped, while others are ahead of their classmates. The boy with little pubic or axillary hair, no noticeable beard, an underdeveloped penis, or a childlike body feels immature in front of his more fully developed friends. Those who have started to develop may become very self-conscious at their new sexual image. Involuntary erection in front of others is especially embarrassing. Boys with noticeable body odor are shunned by others, and they wonder why. Even little things become a source of embarrassment: an old pair of socks with holes, loud-colored underwear that invites negative comments. The desire to avoid critical comments leads some boys to become excessively modest or withdrawn and to retreat from the world through daydreaming. Some boys become very hostile and defensive, ready to argue or fight at the slightest provocation; others become daring show-offs, exhibiting bravado to hide their anxieties and their lack of self-confidence.

One of the most immediate results of sexual maturation is a developing preoccupation with sex. Attention becomes focused on sex, new sexual sensations, and the opposite sex. One study of graffiti on the bathroom walls of junior high schools indicated that the greatest percentage of inscriptions were sex related. The graffiti of the males were most often related to sexual activity, whereas those of females most often expressed sexual desire. (31) Adolescent boys and girls spend a lot of time thinking or dreaming about sex, reading sex-oriented literature, or talking about the opposite sex. The following feelings of one boy are quite typical.

I've been aware how growing into adulthood (physically) has changed my feelings. Sexual desires are an important aspect in my life now, and I consider such feelings when I'm involved with members of the opposite sex. It's not an overriding sensation, but it occupies my mind now. In the past, when [I was] younger, it wasn't so important. (12, p. 44)

These awakening sexual interests motivate adolescent boys to devote much time and attention to grooming and clothes, to body building and care, or to various attempts to attract the attention of girls. Some boys become preoccupied with finding girls who are sexually cooperative, available as outlets for sexual tension. Others turn their attention on themselves through masturbation. Others partially sublimate their urges through sports, work, or other constructive outlets. Quite typically, there are wide variations in the strength of the sexual drive in adolescent boys, but most have to learn how to deal with their urges in socially acceptable ways. The developing male is usually able to adjust to these sexual changes and to come to grips with his feelings and urges only gradually. But sex remains a problem for most adolescent boys until they develop satisfying relationships with girls. (See Chapter 13 on sexual behavior.)

FEMALES

Development of pubic hair in girls is similar to that of boys. On the average girls are 11.9 years of age when straight, pigmented pubic hair begins to grow first along the labia, then becomes more abundant and kinky, spreading over the mons in an inverse triangular pattern, and by late adolescence spreads to the medial surface of the thighs. (39)

Facial hair of girls appears first as a slight down on the upper lip, then spreads to the upper part of the cheeks and finally to the sides and lower border of the chin. This hair is less pigmented and of finer texture than that of men, but brunettes may have a darker, heavier down than blonds. Axillary hair grows about two years after pubic hair and is generally coarser and darker in brunettes than in blonds. Body hair, especially on the arm and legs, is the last hair to develop. Ordinarily, girls do not have noticeable hair on their chests, shoulders, or backs except in cases of glandular disturbance.

One of the most noticeable changes in girls is the development of the breasts. It takes place in three stages: (36, p. 453)

Bud stage. Elevation, enlargement, and pigmentation of the nipple and
    surrounding areola, usually starting about two and a half years before
    menarche.
Primary stage. Increase in underlying fat surrounding the nipple and areola,
    causing the areola to project in a mound above the level of the chest wall.
Secondary or mature stage. Development of mammary gland tissue—larger,
    rounder breast. Areola recedes and is incorporated in the breast itself so
    that only the papilla (nipple) protrudes. This mature stage usually comes
    after menarche. Regardless of when development starts, it usually takes
    three years before the papilla projects out from the surrounding breast.

The size and shape of breasts vary among girls of the same age. One study of girls eleven through fourteen years of age (22) showed that 38 percent had small breasts, 34 percent had medium size, and 28 percent had large ones. In shape, 20 percent were flat, 20 percent were conical, and 60 percent were round.

Adolescent girls today are very concerned about the size and shape of their breasts. Some girls who are flat chested feel very self-conscious because they are influenced by the "playboy" element in their society, which emphasizes fullness of breast as a mark of beauty and sexuality. Some adolescent girls go to the extremes of wearing padded bras, tight jerseys, or sweaters, or even getting medical help to enlarge their breasts. Such girls find advertising promises to "put inches on your bosom in only a few days" very appealing. Girls who have huge, pendulous breasts are also self-conscious when they suffer unkind remarks and incredulous stares.

Also of concern to girls are the changes that take place in body contours. The most noticeable change other than breast development is the widening and rounding of the hips. This is due to the broadening of the pelvis and the increased deposition of fat in the subcutaneous tissue of this area. These changes occur over about an eighteen-month period, usually starting at about the same time that the first breast buds appear. Whereas during this period girls are acquiring subcutaneous fat on their hips, boys seem to lose body fat across the hips at the same time. (22) Girls stop growing in height, on the average, at 16¼, plus or minus thirteen months. (34)

There is some evidence that adolescent girls become more concerned than boys about the physical changes that are taking place in their bodies. The principal reason is that our society places great emphasis on a woman's physique. Musa and Roach report that women get rewards in this society for their appearance rather than for achievements. (29) It follows, therefore, that a girl is going to be concerned about her body for it helps her to determine whether she fits in socially and what her self-concept will be. (12, p. 38) The adolescent girl's concern is with meeting cultural standards of physical appearance and obtaining the approval of friends. As a consequence, glamour and popularity become important concerns. (9, p. 110)

Skin Gland Development

At the onset of puberty, due to actions and reactions of the hormones of the body, the glands of the skin increase their activity. Three kinds of skin glands can cause problems for the adolescent.

1. *merocrine* sweat glands, distributed over most of the skin surfaces of the body.
2. *apocrine* sweat glands, located in the armpits, mammary, genital, and anal regions.
3. *sebaceous* glands, oil-producing glands of the skin.

During the adolescent years, both the merocrine and apocrine sweat glands secrete a fatty substance with a pronounced odor that becomes more noticeable, causing body odor. The sebaceous glands develop at a greater speed than the skin ducts through which they discharge their skin oils. As a result the ducts may become plugged and turn black as the oil oxidizes and dries upon exposure to the air, creating a blackhead. This in turn may become infected, causing a pimple or acne to form. (42, p. 47)

Acne can become a serious medical problem, but it is even more of a psychological problem to oversensitive adolescents concerned about their appearance. One severe case was that of Jim, who developed cystic acne at age fourteen, with pus running down the side of his face and other patches staining his shirt. From an outgoing, secure, successful boy, Jim became withdrawn and self-conscious. When he was not invited to boy-girl parties he attributed it to some serious inferiority within himself. He seldom complained, because he considered it unmanly, and he was too proud to discuss his social rebuffs. At sixteen, in grade ten, he was taken out of school for a time. He became so tired and dragged out he could not work, because his entire body became infected with bacteria from the acne. Antibiotics, bathing with antibacterial detergents, daily change of bedding and linens, and acne surgery to drain the abscesses and cysts put Jim on the road to recovery. Even severe cases of acne can be cured within a year or so. (6, p. 5)

For less severe cases, treatment from the beginning will prevent acne from becoming serious, either physically or psychologically. Adolescents need to keep their skin scrupulously clean, not with harsh soaps, but with mild, medicated soaps. One mother reported treatment with a hand steamer as being particularly effective in cleansing certain areas of skin on her son's face. However, adolescents should not be made to feel that the reasons they get acne is because they are unclean. Some keep their skin very clean, yet still have problems. Sometimes adolescents are restricted from eating certain foods, especially chocolate and fatty foods, but the role of these foods in triggering acne is not proven, and the results of dietary restrictions are often uncertain. (40) It is known, however, that victims of acne have receptors in their cells that accept the male androgens, which in turn stimulate the activity of the sebaceous glands. Some doctors counteract this activity by prescribing oral contraceptives containing female estrogens. This suppresses the overactivity of the sebaceous glands and eliminates the excess oiliness. However, such pills work on only some patients and undesirable side effects have made physicians more cautious. As a result, antiandrogen agents without the side effects of estrogens are being sought in research efforts. (40) Other drugs taken orally, particularly those containing synthetic derivatives of vitamin A, are now being used on an experimental basis with some promise of success. (8)

Acne may be aggravated by tension and emotional upset that activate the skin glands. (48) This is one reason why emotional upset may bring on acne, or why a tense adolescent may be more susceptible to acne than a calm one. In all cases, the adolescent should receive concerned, prompt treatment.

Conclusions

The physical changes that take place as primary and secondary sexual characteristics develop during adolescence. These changes are triggered and controlled by the endocrine glands, especially the pituitary gland and the sex glands, each of which secretes hormones that stimulate and regulate the total growth and motivation process.

The adolescent's emotional reactions to the changes are as important as the physical changes themselves. Until the endocrine system completes its changes and gets into balance, the adolescent may exhibit emotional instability, fluctuations of mood, extreme emotional sensitivity, temper tantrums, periods of anger or moodiness, crying spells, or periods of excessive elation. This emotionalism has a physiological basis that ought to be considered along with social and familial pressures and relationships in understanding the causes of adolescent behavior. With physical changes taking place so rapidly, it is only natural that an often exaggerated self-consciousness and a hypersensitivity to physical appearance should develop. In relation to developing sexuality, every adolescent wants to know: Am I normal? Will I be able to have a normal sex life, have children, and am I built and do I look sexually like others? Adolescents are concerned about whether their sex organs are of normal size and shape and whether their bodily physiques and builds are pleasing and acceptable to themselves and others. They also have some particular health concerns in relationship to sexual maturation. Girls become conscious of menstrual hygiene, boys of nocturnal emissions. Both boys and girls become concerned about sexual behavior and about acne. Other physical changes at adolescence, together with the adolescents' concern about their bodily images, are discussed in the next chapter.

Interviews of Adolescents

One of the ways of understanding adolescents is to ask them questions to discover attitudes, feelings, and problems. The subject of sexual maturation is well suited to the person-to-person interview technique for gaining understanding. It would be helpful to interview adolescents at different stages of growth and development, to see if there are differences among them. The interview can be taped if a permanent record is desired as a basis for writing up a report. Or the teacher can play several of the best tapes in class as a basis for discussion. Interviews should be kept anonymous with only age and gender identified.

The following are suggestions of questions to ask during the interviews.

Questions for Boys or Girls

1. At what age did you begin to mature physically?
2. Was this before or after your friends began to develop? Were there any special problems because you matured early (or late)?
3. How did you feel about maturing sexually? Glad? Embarrassed? Self-conscious? Anxious?
4. Did you understand what was happening to your body? Did your parents or teachers explain so you would understand the changes taking place?
5. Did you read anything that helped you to understand? Explain.
6. Do you feel any differently now that you are mature (maturing)? What is different? Have your interests changed? Have you noticed any difference in your attitudes?
7. What worries you the most about your physical development? Explain.
8. Do you think you're normal? Different? How?
9. Have there been any physical problems that necessitated your going to see a doctor? Explain. What happened?

Questions for Girls

1. Have you begun to menstruate? or When did you start to menstruate? Can you remember what happened? What did you do?
2. Were you prepared for it?
3. How do you feel about menstruating? Any special problems?
4. A lot of girls worry about breast development. Does this worry you? Why? Why not? Do you think there is too much emphasis on the size of a girl's breasts?
5. What do you like most about your figure? What do you like least? If you could change anything about your figure or physical appearance what would you change?

Questions for Boys

1. Sometimes boys are required to undress or dress in front of others in locker rooms at school or other places. Does this embarrass you? Why? Why not? Do you worry that others will criticize you because of your build?
2. What do you like most about your build? What do you like least?
3. Each boy develops physically at his own speed. Some boys mature early, some late. How would you rate the progress of your development now in relationship to your friends? How do you feel about this? In what ways does it affect you the most?
4. Does the size of a boy's sex organs have anything to do with whether or not he's manly? Does it affect whether or not he's sexy? Will it affect his sex adjustment in marriage?
5. Have you heard the expression *wet dream*? (Explain if the boy doesn't

understand.) Have you had one yet? (Assure the boy who hasn't that this may be perfectly normal at his age level.) How do you feel about it?

6. Do you know anyone who has very severe acne? How does that person feel about it? How does it affect him or her? What can be done about acne?

7. Do you know any fellows who have strong body odor that is really noticeable in gym? How do you feel about them? What should be done?

Bibliography

1. Anderson, Theresa W. "Swimming and Exercise During Menstruation." *Journal of Health, Physical Education, Recreation* 36 (1965): 66–68.

2. Bardwick, J. *Psychology of Women: A Study of Bio-Cultural Conflicts.* New York: Harper and Row, 1971.

3. Bojlen, K., and Bentzon, M. W. "The Influence of Climate and Nutrition on Age at Menarche: A Historical Review and a Modern Hypothesis." *Human Biology* 40 (1968): 69–85.

4. Boulford, M. E., and Bardwick, J. M. "Patterns of Affective Fluctuation in the Menstrual Cycle." *Psychosomatic Medicine* 30 (1968): 336–345.

5. Brattesani, K., and Silverthorne, C. P. "Social Psychological Factors of Menstrual Distress." *Journal of Social Psychology* 106 (October 1978): 139–140.

6. Clark, Marguerite. "Health Problems of Adolescents." *PTA Magazine* 60 (1966): 4–7, 33–34.

7. Clarke, A. E., and Ruble, D. N. "Young Adolescents' Beliefs Concerning Menstruation." *Child Development* 49 (March 1978): 231–234.

8. "Clear Skin: Possible Help for Severe Acne." *Time,* 26 February 1979, p. 59.

9. Conger, J. J. *Adolescence and Youth.* New York: Harper and Row, 1973.

10. Coussons, H. "Clinically Important Aspects of Adolescent Development: A Brief Review." *Journal of the Oklahoma State Medical Association* 65 (1972): 483.

11. Doering, C. H. et al. "A Cycle of Plasma Testosterone in the Human Male." *Journal of Clinical Endocrinology and Metabolism* 40, 1975.

12. Dreyfus, E. A. *Adolescence. Theory and Experience.* Columbus, Ohio: Charles E. Merrill Publishing Co., 1976.

13. Frisch, R., and Revelle, R. "Height and Weight at Menarche and a Hypothesis of Critical Body Weights and Adolescent Events." *Science* 169 (1970): 397–399.

14. Gallatin, J. E. *Adolescence and Individuality.* New York: Harper and Row, 1975.

15. Garrison, K. C. "Physiological Development." In *Understanding Adolescence,* 3d ed. Edited by J. F. Adams. Boston: Allyn and Bacon, 1976.

16. Gray, L. A. "Gynecology in Adolescence." Symposium on Adolescence. *Pediatric Clinics of North America* 7 (1960): 43.

17. Harrison, Richard J., and Montagna, William. *Man.* New York: Appleton-Century-Crofts, 1969.

18. Kinsey, Alfred et al. *Sexual Behavior in the Human Male.* Philadelphia: W. B. Saunders Co., 1948.

19. Kopell, B. et al. "Variations in Some Measures of Arousal During the Menstrual Cycle." *Journal of Psychosomatic Research* 13 (1969): 37–44.

20. Kulin, H. E. "The Physiology of Adolescence in Man." *Human Biology* 46 (1974): 133–143.

21. Kulin, H. E., and Reiter, E. O. "Gonadotropins during Childhood and Adolescence: A Review." *Pediatrics* 51 (1973): 260–271.

22. Lloyd, C. W. *Human Reproduction and Sexual Behavior.* Philadelphia: Lea and Febiger, 1964.

23. MacMahon, B. "Age at Menarche: United States." *Vital Health Statistics,* Series 11, No. 133. Washington, D.C.: U.S. Department of Health, Education and Welfare, 1974.

24. Marshall, W. A., and Tanner, J. M. "Variations in the Pattern of Pubertal Changes in Boys." *Archives of Diseases in Children* 45 (1970): 13.

25. Masters, W. H., and Johnson, Virginia. *Human Sexual Response.* Boston: Little, Brown and Co., 1966.

26. McCary, James. *Human Sexuality.* New York: Van Nostrand Co., 1967.

27. Mead, Margaret. *Coming of Age in Samoa.* New York: William Morrow, 1928.

28. Moos, R. H. et al. "Fluctuations in Symptoms and Moods during the Menstrual Cycle." *Journal of Psychosomatic Research* 13 (1969): 37–44.

29. Musa, K. E., and Roach, M. E. "Adolescent Appearance and Self-concept." *Adolescence* 3 (1973): 385–393.

30. Parlee, M. B. "The Rhythms in

Men's Lives." *Psychology Today* (April 1978): 82 ff.

31. Peretti, P. O. et al. "Graffiti and Adolescent Personality." *Adolescence* 12 (Spring 1977): 31–42.

32. "The Pill Loses as Acne Treatment." *Science Digest*, August 1974, p. 50.

33. Richter, C. "Periodical Phenomena in Man and Animals: Their Relations to Endocrine Mechanisms." In *Endocrinology and Human Behavior: Proceedings*. Edited by R. P. Michael. New York: Oxford University Press, 1968.

34. Schonfeld, W. A. "The Body and the Body-Image in Adolescents." In *Adolescence: Psychosocial Perspectives*. Edited by G. Caplan and S. Lebovici. New York: Basic Books, 1969.

35. Sherman, J. A. *On the Psychology of Women*. Springfield, Ill.: Charles C Thomas, 1971.

36. Smart, M. S., and Smart, R. C. *Children, Development and Relationships*. New York: Macmillan Co., 1967.

37. ———. *Adolescents. Development and Relationships*. New York: Macmillan Co., 1973.

38. Tanner, J. M. "Growth and Endocrinology of the Adolescent." In Gardner, L. J., ed., *Endocrine and Genetic Diseases of Childhood*. Philadelphia: Saunders, 1969.

39. ———. "Physical Growth." In *Carmichael's Manual of Child Psychology*, vol. 1. 3d ed. Edited by P. H. Mussen. New York: John Wiley & Sons, 1970.

40. ———. "Sequence, Tempo, and Individual Variation in Growth and Development of Boys and Girls Aged Twelve to Sixteen." *Twelve to Sixteen: Early Adolescence*. Edited by J. Kegan and Robert Coles. New York: W. W. Norton and Co., 1972.

41. Thomas, J. K. "Adolescent Endocrinology for Counselors of Adolescents." *Adolescence* 8 (1973): 395–406.

42. Thornburg, H. D. *Development in Adolescence*. Monterey, Calif.: Brooks/Cole Publishing Co., 1975.

43. Weir, J. et al. "Race and Age at Menarche." *American Journal of Obstetrics and Gynecology* 3 (1971): 594–597.

44. Winter, J. S. D., and Fairman, C. "Pituitary-Gonadal Relationships in Male Children and Adolescents." *Pediatric Research* 6 (1972): 126–135.

45. *Youth: Transition to Adulthood*. Report of the Panel on Youth of the President's Science Advisory Committee. Chicago: University of Chicago Press, 1974.

46. Zacharias, L.; Wurtman, R. J.; and Schatzoff, M. "Sexual Maturation in Contemporary American Girls." *American Journal of Obstetrics and Gynecology* 108 (1970): 833–846.

47. Zachman, M. "The Evaluation of Testicular Endocrine Functions Before and in Puberty." *Acta Endocrinology (Supplement 164)*, 3, 1972.

48. Zeller, W. W. "Adolescent Attitudes and Cutaneous Health." *Journal of School Health* 40 (1970): 115–120.

Physical Growth and the Body Image

Outline

One of the earliest and most obvious physical changes of adolescence is the growth spurt that begins in early adolescence. This growth in height is accompanied by an increase in weight and changes in body proportions. In addition, there are subtle changes in strength and endurance, in motor ability and performance, and in nutritional needs and digestion. This chapter discusses these physical changes and the adolescent's reactions and adjustments to them.

Skeletal Age

Because of the great variation in the timing and extent of physical growth during adolescence, chronological age is not a good measure for degree of maturity. A group of adolescents of the same chronological age will have a range of six years or more in maturational age. Skeletal age is a better measure of degree and rate of maturation because it is a highly accurate measure; it is unaffected by absolute age and can be determined at any point in the life span. (11) Furthermore, the developmental sequence is essentially the same for all adolescents, regardless of sex or individual variations.

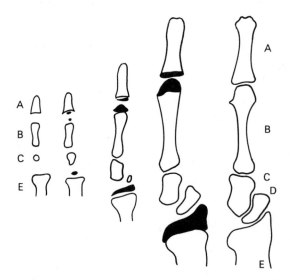

A. First phalanx
B. Metatarsal
C. Capitate (wrist bone)
D. Navicular (wrist bone)
E. Radius (larger bone in forearm)

Dark areas are the epiphyses

The last diagram shows
epiphyses fused to bone

Figure 5–1. Growth of the middle finger.

Using this method, the level of maturity is determined by taking X-ray pictures of the bones in the hands and wrist. The photographs show the degree of ossification that has taken place and provide an accurate measure of skeletal age, hence actual maturational age. Figure 5–1 shows successive stages of growth of the middle finger.

The finger and wrist of the immature child are composed of widely separated bones, joined together by cartilage. (The X ray shows only the hardened bone; the soft cartilage appears as blank spaces.) The skeleton matures as the cartilage slowly ossifies and becomes bone, filling in the spaces. In addition, an appendage called an *epiphysis* grows into a shape that fits the bone to which it becomes attached. In Figure 5–1, three epiphyses have fused with the bones, with the line of fusion still showing. Note that at maturity the long bones with their fused epiphyses are several times longer than at birth. When the bone epiphyses are fully calcified or closed, no further potential for bone growth remains and skeletal maturity is said to have been reached. (3, p. 867) Studies also show correlations between the degree of skeletal maturity and physical maturity, that is, sexual development and maturation of physiological functions. (50, p. 51) A child who is advanced in skeletal maturity also shows precocious development of secondary sexual characteristics and of physiological functions such as decrease of heart, respiratory, and metabolic rate with age.

Growth in Height and Weight

Longitudinal studies of growth in height and weight of individual children are made by measuring the same children year after year. These studies give an accurate picture of individual growth rates at different ages. The combined data provide a composite picture of growth trends in groups of children.

GROWTH TRENDS

Figure 5–2 shows the growth in height of a group of California boys and girls from ages two to eighteen. Figure 5–3 shows their increase in weight. (64, p. 203) Girls grow fastest in height and weight at approximately twelve years of age; boys grow fastest in height and weight at approximately fourteen. (See Figure 5–4) (57) Girls are usually shorter and lighter than boys during childhood. However, because they start to mature earlier, they average slightly taller than boys between twelve and fourteen and heavier than boys between the ages of ten and fourteen. Whereas girls have reached 98 percent of their adult height (at 16¼ years), boys do not reach 98 percent of their adult height until 17¾ years. (48, 57) These rates vary, and what is normal for one individual may not apply to other individuals. (35) By using skeletal age, actual height achieved, and actual age it is possible to predict with some accuracy the height a mature individual will attain. (66, p. 19)

DETERMINANTS OF HEIGHT

A number of factors are believed to be important in determining the total mature height of the individual. The most important factor is heredity. (11, 66) Tall

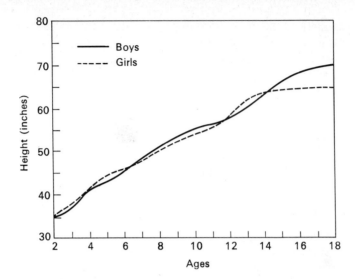

Figure 5–2.   Growth in height. (Adapted from R. D. Tuddenham and M. M. Snyder, "The Physical Growth of California Boys and Girls from Birth to Eighteen Years," *University of California Publications in Child Development* 1[1954]:203. Originally published by the University of California Press, reprinted by permission of The Regents of the University of California.)

parents tend to have tall children, short parents short children. The most important environmental factor is nutrition. (60) Children who are better nourished during the growth years become taller adults than less well-nourished persons. (24) Studies have shown that children from higher socioeconomic groups grow taller than those from poorer families. The reason is poorer nutrition, not income, job, and education as such. (37) Depression or war also can affect growth because it affects nutrition. During the last years of World War II and for several years afterward, growth retardation of children was widespread.

The age when sexual maturation begins also affects the total height finally achieved. (60) Boys and girls who are early maturers tend to be shorter as adults than those who are later maturers. (3, p. 863) Sexual maturation results in the secretion of sex hormones from the gonads; the hormones inhibit the pituitary from further production of HGH (human growth hormone). A later maturer has a longer time to grow before the sex hormones stop the pituitary from stimulating further growth. (50, p. 5)

Furthermore, the growth achieved before puberty is of greater significance to total adult height than is the growth achieved during puberty. Broverman and his staff report from their study that "the adolescent growth spurt contributes, in absolute terms, relatively little to the postadolescent skeletal dimensions, and only moderately to weight and strength." (3, pp. 865–866)

Evidence indicates that the total process of growth is speeding up; children and adolescents today experience the growth spurt earlier, grow faster, attain a greater total adult height, and attain this height earlier than did children and adolescents sixty or seventy years ago. The normal healthy girl is ½ to 1 inch

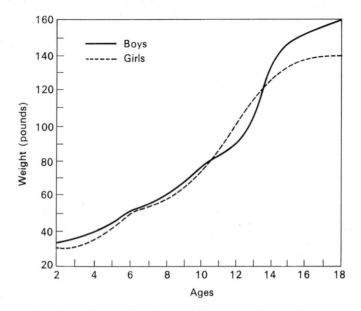

Figure 5–3.   Growth in weight. (Adapted from R. D. Tuddenham and M. M. Snyder, "The Physical Growth of California Boys and Girls from Birth to Eighteen Years," *University of California Publications in Child Development,* 1[1954]:203. Originally published by the University of California Press, reprinted by permission of The Regents of the University of California.)

taller and reaches menarche ten months earlier than her mother. (40, p. 267) Girls at the turn of the century reached their adult height at eighteen or nineteen; the average today has dropped to sixteen. (40, p. 270) Tanner reports an increase in adult height of males of 2½ to 3½ inches during the last century. (58) In 1880 they did not reach their final height until twenty-three to twenty-five years of age; today their adult height is reached at age eighteen. (58) The average height of American sailors in the War of 1812 is estimated at 5 feet, 2 inches, which explains why the decks of the U.S.S. *Constitution* did not need to be more than five feet, six inches high. (23)

Other dimensions, too, are larger today. The average male today wears a size 9 to 10B shoe; his grandfather was size 7. The seats of the famous La Scala opera house in Milan, Italy, constructed in 1776, were eighteen inches wide; today, comfortable seats need to be twenty-four inches wide. (40, p. 271) These accelerated growth patterns, referred to as the *secular trend,* are beginning to taper off, at least in the United States and some other developed countries. There is a limit to the ultimate size of human beings. (40, p. 274)

Some adolescents are dissatisfied with the height they attain. This is especially true of boys, and to a lesser extent of Oriental girls, who tend to be shorter than they would like. Figure 5–5 shows a comparison between mean and desired heights of twelfth-grade boys and girls, by race. (22, p. 139) Boys generally wanted to be taller than they were; most girls seemed content with their height. (22, p. 138)

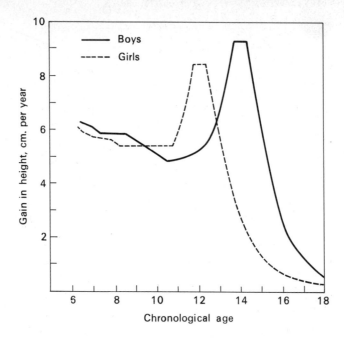

Figure 5–4. Increase in height. (Adapted from J. Tanner, *Growth at Adolescence,* 2d ed. [Springfield, Ill.: Charles C Thomas, 1962]. Used by permission of the author.)

Body Image

BODY TYPES

Three "pure" body types have been identified: *ectomorph, mesomorph,* and *endomorph.* Most people are a mixture rather than a pure type, but identifying the pure types helps considerably in any discussion of general body build. Ectomorphs are tall, long, thin, and narrow, with slender, bony, basketball-player builds. Endomorphs are at the other extreme with soft, round, thick, large, wide, heavy trunks and limbs, and wrestler builds. The mesomorphs are between these two types. They have square, strong, tough, hard bodies, well muscled, with medium-length limbs and wide shoulders. They represent the athletic type of build and participate in strenuous physical activity more frequently than the others. (56)

Body proportions of each type change as the individual grows older. Adolescents tend to grow up before they grow out, so they may be long, slim "bean poles" before they round out. Parts of their bodies grow disproportionately. Their hands, feet, and limbs grow faster than the trunks of their bodies so they may seem gangly, clumsy, and short-waisted. (61, p. 5) Parts of their faces, such as the nose or chin, may protrude from the relatively long heads until the flesh of the face fills in and the head becomes rounder. Gradually, however, the trunk lengthens, so that sitting height increases in relation to standing height. (15) The waistline drops, the shoulders widen, the hips of the female broaden, and the body takes on a more mature appearance. The muscles of the limbs develop and

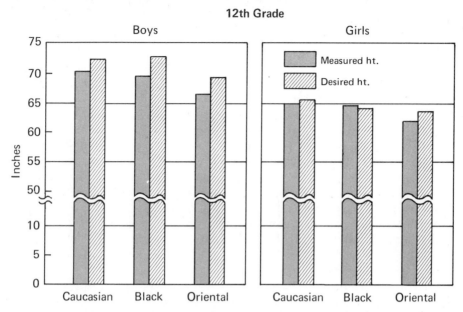

Figure 5–5. Comparison of mean and desired heights of twelfth-grade boys and girls by race. (From R. L. Huenemann et al., *Teenage Nutrition and Physique,* 1974, p. 139. Courtesy of Charles C Thomas, Publisher, Springfield, Illinois.)

flesh is added, so the hands and feet no longer seem out of proportion to the rest of the body. (59) Finally, when growth is complete, the body seems back in balance again.

OBESITY

Many adolescents worry about being overweight. Ten to 15 percent of all adolescents are truly obese, girls more than boys. (27, p. 31) Being overweight not only represents a future health hazard—obesity is related to cardiovascular disease, hypertension, joint disease, and gynecological disorders—but also affects the adolescent's social relationships, school performance, and emotional adjustment. (11, p. 246) Furthermore, if an obese teenager has a history of a weight problem and does not reduce, the odds are twenty-eight to one that she or he will become and remain a fat adult. (69)

The causes and cure of obesity are not a simple matter. Three general causes have been described. (69) One is *heredity;* because obesity tends to run in families, it has a genetic foundation for some young people. (20, p. 246) One report shows that 70 percent of overweight adolescents have one or both parents who are obese. (20, p. 246) Another cause is *stress* or *crisis.* All children gain security from oral activity. If stress is excessive while growing up, some children turn to eating as a means of relieving tension. The third cause of obesity is *development,* which arises as a disturbance in the maturation of the total personality. In this type of obesity there has been a close mutual dependency in the mother-child relationship. The mother overfeeds and the child, unwilling to give up the pleasures of infancy, continues to overeat. (83, p. 33)

Obese adolescents may have numerous psychological and social problems. These problems are usually in one of four areas. (20, p. 246)

Dependency. Some adolescents are passive, overprotected, overly dependent persons whose parents, particularly their mothers, kept them emotionally close. As a result, they never grow up as emotionally mature adults. (53, p. 83)

Sex identification. Girls may have little preparation for pubertal changes, and obese boys often show few masculine interests. They are reluctant to date or become involved in boy-girl activities, and may have trouble adjusting to the new drives and impulses puberty brings on. Their sex education is often scanty.

Peer relationships. Social relationships are sometimes poor for adolescents. These students are often loners: isolated, introverted, distant, and withdrawn, often limiting contacts to those of the same sex. They show considerable social anxiety, feelings of alienation, and a low sense of self-worth. (51)

School. Some adolescents function poorly in the academic setting: they are underachievers or have attendance problems. Interest in academic achievement is generally low because of their personal and social problems.

One study compared the personality traits of 100 obese adolescent girls with those of 65 nonobese control subjects and reported that the obese girls showed personality traits similar to those of ethnic and racial minorities: passivity, concern with status, acceptance of dominant values, withdrawal, and close ties within the group. (47, p. 39)

The image of the obese adolescent as a heavy eater is not borne out by fact. Obese girls generally have a lower intake of calories and a poorer intake of nutrients than do girls of normal build. (22, p. 59) Obese girls eat less, and less frequently. (22, p. 61) Lean girls may eat as much as or more than fat ones, but the lean girls are much more active physically. One study showed that obese adolescent girls may be inactive 60 to 70 percent of the time during a tennis game in comparison to 10 to 20 percent of inactivity among nonobese girls. (27, p. P-91) Observation of the swimming activity of adolescents in Boston revealed that the nonobese group swam for forty minutes out of each hour, while the obese group logged only seven minutes of swimming. (34, p. F-12) The problem of the obese is one not only of overeating, then, but also of underactivity. The deficiency is partly exercise, with obesity the result of an excess of calories taken in comparison to calories burned up in daily activities.

The important question is how best to help obese adolescents to lose weight. One report of the use of a group approach to help significantly overweight adolescent girls showed mixed results. (69) Ten girls aged twelve to eighteen, with an average weight of 231 pounds, started the program. Five dropped out in the initial sessions and had an average net gain of 8 pounds over a six-month period. Of the five who stayed in the program for six months, three each lost an average of over 8 pounds, but each of the other two gained an average of over 7 pounds. Like most people on diets, all five both gained and lost weight during the six-month period. It is significant that this intense behavior modification program, which developed consciousness of eating habits, tried to change them, and helped with weight reduction diets, failed to produce better results. (69) This effort illustrates how difficult it is to modify eating behavior that is already well established by adolescence. Certainly, a better approach is for parents to develop moderate eating habits in young children so they will never be faced with unacceptable obesity in adolescence.

The most successful approaches to treating obesity recognize that it is a multicausal problem. (54) Comprehensive medical examinations are necessary to elicit genetic, metabolic, environmental, and emotional factors. After reasons for obesity are diagnosed, proper medical and dietary treatments are instituted. Persons who are considerably overweight need crash diets in the beginning, carefully regulated by a knowledgeable physician, so they will lose weight fast and not get discouraged. If weight is to be kept off, however, behavorial therapy is needed. An important part of trying to change eating behavior is to require subjects to keep a food diary for a week: the time of day they eat, the kinds of foods they eat, what they're doing when they eat, their emotional state while eating, and the situations to which they're reacting by eating. Once awareness is established, specific techniques for altering eating behavior can be used. If people eat cookies, for example, eliminate the cookie jar from the house; if they eat fattening foods, never buy them in the first place; if they overeat while reading, unconscious of amounts, eliminate the reading; if they eat foods that are left out on kitchen counters, learn to put the foods away. One center tries to substitute sex for food by emphasizing the slogan: "Reach for your mate instead of a plate." (54, p. 104) If eating becomes an effort to relieve anxiety, therapy may be needed to deal with the basic emotional causes.

UNDERWEIGHT

Underweight adolescents have the opposite problem: they are burning up more calories than they are consuming. They need to conserve energy by spending more hours in bed and omitting strenuous exercise; increase the consumption of fattening foods such as cream, butter, bacon, rich desserts; and overcome a poor appetite. Good results in treating underweight adolescents have been obtained by increasing the number of hours they spend in bed. Breakfast in bed, going to bed early (as early as 8 p.m. weekdays and 10 p.m. on weekends) and eating nothing between meals in order not to decrease the appetite for the next meal all help to increase the total number of calories available to be stored as body fat.

CONCEPTS OF THE IDEAL

Being overweight or underweight is a problem because adolescents are affected profoundly by the images of ideal body builds taught by their culture. Most adolescent boys and girls would prefer to be medium types. Tall, skinny boys or girls are unhappy with themselves, as are short or fat adolescents. (6) The female endomorph is especially miserable, for Western culture overemphasizes the slim, chic, but well-proportioned feminine figure. If a girl does not have such a figure, but is short and fat instead, she is much more likely to be ignored by boys and less likely to have dates. Such social rejection is difficult to live with. (39) This means that self-esteem and self-satisfaction are closely related to acceptance and satisfaction with her physical self. (42)

The attitudes of adolescents toward ideal body concepts are a reflection of the concepts of female attractiveness emphasized by our culture and learned by children as they grow up. One study of sixty females, ages seven to nine and ten and eleven, showed that two-thirds preferred the mesomorphic silhouette and one-third preferred the ectomorphic silhouette. None chose the endomorphic build, and all the adjectives they assigned to this type were unfavorable. (52) A study of girls six, fifteen, and nineteen years old showed that they most preferred the mesomorph figure and least favored the endomorph figure. (2) A few preferred to look like the ectomorph, but none preferred the endomorph figure. (2, p. 556) Other studies provide further evidence of the social importance of physical attractiveness and of possessing an average physique. (21)

Some girls are particularly self-conscious about certain aspects of their figures: bust too large or too small; ankles, hips, or thighs too fat; protruding buttocks or stomach; nose too long, pointed, wide, or pug; chin pointed, sunken, or double; eyes bulgy, sunken, too big, the wrong shape, or crossed; teeth crooked, decayed, or missing; face homely, scarred, pimply or mole-spotted. (38, p. 19) One study showed the importance of individual body characteristics in self-ratings of physical attractiveness by female and male college students. (30, 32) The mean age of females was 19.5 years and of males 20.4 years. These ratings, given in Table 5–1, show that both females and males felt that general appearance, face, facial complexion, weight distribution, body build, and teeth were important to physical attractiveness. Females also emphasized eyes, shape of legs, hips, waist, and chest. Males were not as concerned about these features, but placed more emphasis on profile, height, neck, and shoulder width. Males and females were moderately but equally concerned about hair texture, nose, and mouth. Both were least concerned about ankles, ears, hair color, and arms. It is evident that these evaluations reflect cultural stereotypes of attractiveness.

The ideal masculine body image consists of dark hair, broad shoulders and chest, big muscles, a slim waist, and well-proportioned arms and legs. (16) Some adolescent boys, however, at least early in their development, look skinny, uncoordinated, out of proportion, and weak. Late developers are still short and childlike. Others are wide, fat, and dumpy, some with protruding breasts. Boys who deviate from the norm may be given nicknames: "slim," "beany," "broomstick," "Crisco," or "fatso." The boy with the weak-looking build may spend hours working out on barbells or in the school gym to try to improve his build. The fat adolescent who isn't able to diet successfully may withdraw from normal social contacts with girls and show marked symptoms of emotional maladjustment. So much emphasis is put on having an athletic build that the boy who is not able to conform feels extremely self-conscious and isolated.

Investigations of underweight adolescents reveal that teachers consider them lacking in physical skills and social poise, socially anxious, and somewhat withdrawn and introverted. (21) The fact that they are more involved with television viewing than others indicates that being underweight and thin causes some isolation and lack of contact with peers. (21, p. 192)

In one experimental test of body stereotyping, three groups of male adolescents were asked to view a series of pictures of men fitting the three body types already mentioned. The males scored each picture on fifteen personality traits.

Table 5–1. Mean importance of selected body characteristics for own physical attractiveness for males ($N = 70$) and females ($N = 119$).*

Body Characteristics	Female's Own Importance	Male's Own Importance
General appearance	1.3	1.5
Face	1.4	1.5
Facial complexion	1.6	1.8
Distribution of weight	1.7	2.0
Body build	1.7	1.9
Teeth	1.9	2.0
Eyes	1.9	2.4
Shape of legs	2.2	2.8
Hips	2.2	2.8
Hair texture	2.3	2.3
Waist	2.3	2.4
Chest	2.4	2.6
Nose	2.4	2.4
Mouth	2.4	2.4
Profile	2.5	2.3
Thighs	2.5	2.9
Height	2.9	2.7
Chin	3.1	2.8
Arms	3.1	3.0
Hair color	3.2	3.2
Neck	3.2	2.8
Width of shoulders	3.4	2.9
Ears	3.9	3.5
Ankles	4.1	4.2

* Respondents ranked characteristics on a scale of 1 to 5, from very important to very unimportant, respectively.

Adapted from R. M. Lerner and S. A. Karabenick, "Physical Attractiveness, Body Attitudes, and Self-Concept in Late Adolescents," *Journal of Youth and Adolescence* 3 (1974): 307–316. Used by permission.

The mesomorphic body type was associated with socially positive personality traits by all three age groups. Endomorph and ectomorph pictures were frequently associated with negative personality items. (29) Other studies confirm these findings. (31; 36, p. 129) Phrases like "unpopular" and "doesn't have many friends" are more often associated with extreme ectomorphs and endomorphs. (47, p. 37) In view of these findings, it is not surprising that boys who deviate from the mesomorphic type are dissatisfied with their bodies and wish they were different.

Physical Ability

STRENGTH AND MUSCLE FATIGUE

Boys in particular are concerned not only with height and body build, but also with strength. Muscular strength increases greatly during adolescence, but boys and girls differ in degree of muscular power as well as in the timing of develop-

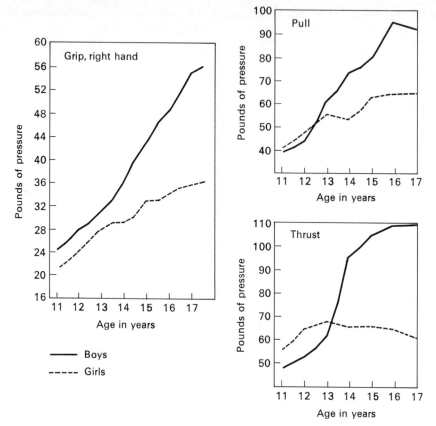

Figure 5–6.   Changes in muscular strength. (Adapted from H. E. Jones, "Motor
Performance and Growth: A Developmental Study of Static Dynamometric
Strength," *University of California Publications in Child Development,*
1[1949]:35–36. Originally published by the University of California Press,
reprinted by permission of The Regents of the University of California.)

ment. (59, 60) Jones (26) made a longitudinal study of the strength of 89 boys
and 87 girls. The strength of each child was measured every six months from ages
eleven to seventeen and a half. Three tests were conducted: (1) strength of grip,
(2) pull strength when the arms are held at shoulder level and the registering instrument grasped by both hands, and (3) thrust with the arms in the same position. The results are graphed in Figure 5–6. (26)

Jones's study found that boys are superior to girls in strength of grip at all
ages, but the most significant differences appear after the boys mature (after
13½ years of age). Between the ages of 11 and 12¾ years, girls are superior
to boys in pull and thrust strength, but boys become significantly stronger than
girls after that. After age 13, the thrust strength of girls declines, the pull strength
declines briefly, then rises slowly, but both the pull and thrust strength of the
boys increases greatly to age 16 years. The great difference in strength between
the two sexes is due to a significant difference in muscle size. (26)

Overall muscular strength may be correlated with the extent of sexual maturity. Clarke and Degutis studied 237 Caucasian boys ten, thirteen, and sixteen

years of age from the Medford, Oregon, public schools to compare various physical and motor factors with pubescent development. They discovered there was more difference in physical maturation at age thirteen than among boys of the other two age groups, and that the thirteen- and sixteen-year-old boys who were advanced in pubescent development had higher mean scores on all experimental tests included in the study with only a few exceptions. (4)

The same principle applies with girls. Jones, in the findings of the California Adolescent Growth Study, compares the strength of early- and late-maturing girls. The early maturers experienced menarche at age 11.7; the late maturers at age 14.5 years. The early maturers were stronger at all ages from 10.8 years until after age 16, at which time the late maturers caught up and sometimes even surpassed the early maturers. (26)

Muscle fatigue does not follow the same pattern. Rich studied muscle fatigue in 200 boys and girls from eight to seventeen years old and found that the older boys and girls were stronger but became fatigued more quickly, although older girls reached their fatigue level more slowly than older boys. The reason is that older boys exert more strength initially and tire more quickly. So, although boys are stronger, they are not more effective on tasks that require strength over a moderate period of time. (46)

MOTOR ABILITY AND COORDINATION

Total coordination is important to adolescents, particularly to those who are interested in athletics and sports. A number of studies have been conducted over the years to measure levels and changes in motor performance and coordination during adolescence. One of the best-known and most widely used tests has been that of Brace, who vaguely defined motor ability as "that ability which is more or less general, more or less inherent, and which permits an individual to learn motor skills easily and to become readily proficient in them." (1) The Brace test consists of twenty standardized tasks of varying difficulty. Some examples are:

- Kneeling on both knees and standing again.
- Jumping into the air and making a full turn, landing on the same spot.
- Changing from lying to sitting without raising the feet from the floor.
- Squatting on the left foot with right foot extended forward, then standing again. (1)

Numerous results from this test indicate that motor ability and coordination of boys improve continuously during adolescence, with improvement more rapid in the prepubescent and postpubescent periods than in the period just preceding that of maximum growth (age 14). (55) The scores of girls and boys on the different tests show only a slight difference until 13.8 years, when boys begin to excel in all events and to increase their superiority rapidly at each successive age level. Scores for girls show little change after the thirteenth year. (14)

Effects of Early and Late Maturation

The effect of early or late physical maturation on both the psychological and social characteristics and adjustments of boys and girls has been the subject of intensive investigation. The results of these studies are important in understanding those adolescents who differ from the norm in either the timing or the rate of their development.

EARLY-MATURING BOYS

Early-maturing boys are large for their age, stronger, more muscular, and better coordinated than late-maturing boys, so they enjoy a considerable athletic advantage. They are better able to excel in football, basketball, swimming, track, tennis, soccer, and other competitive sports. They also enjoy considerable social advantages in relation to their peers. Their superior build and athletic skills enhance their social prestige and position. They participate more frequently in extracurricular activities in high school. (42, p. 132) They are often chosen for leadership roles; their peers tend to give them greater social recognition by appointing them to school offices, committee chairmanships, and by mentioning them in the school newspaper. (18, p. 92) They tend to show more interest in girls and to be popular with them because of superior looks and more sophisticated social interests and skills. Early sexual maturation thrusts them into heterosexual relationships at an early age.

Adults, too, tend to favor early-maturing boys. Adults tend to rate them as more physically attractive, more masculine, better groomed, and more relaxed than late-maturing boys. (19, p. 167) Even more important, adults accept and treat them as more mature, able persons. (50, p. 33) The boys look older; the community therefore gives earlier recognition to their desires to assume adult roles and responsibilities. (41, p. 132) As a result they are given privileges reserved for older people. (28, p. 106) This attitude of adults has some disadvantages as well as advantages. Adults tend to expect more of them, and expect adult behavior and responsibilities. (24, p. 39) Early-maturing boys have less time to enjoy the freedom that comes with childhood. One adolescent boy remarked:

I was tall and well developed by the time I was 13 years of age. People always thought I was 5 or 6 years older than I really was. Consequently, they criticized me or made fun of me if I acted up or fooled around. "Don't be a kid, act your age," they used to tell me. My Dad expected me to help out around the place. I had to go to work when I was only 15—I lied about my age to get the job. I never seemed to have time to have fun like the rest of the kids my age.

Peskin (41) has suggested other drawbacks to early maturation. The boy has a shorter time in which to adjust to the hormonal and physiological changes of adolescence. Thus, there may be greater initial anxiety at the time of pubertal onset. Early maturers become less active, less given to exploratory behavior, more submissive, intellectually less curious, more somber, and more anxious as they are forced into a premature identity. (41)

After the shock of initial adjustments, however, early-maturing boys manifest more favorable personality characteristics. They appear to be more poised, relaxed, good-natured, unaffected, and more likely to be admired by peers than are their later-maturing counterparts. (5, p. 44) Furthermore, this pattern of success continues into adulthood. When studied up to age thirty-eight, early maturers were found to be socially more active and held leadership roles in their communities more often than did late maturers. Apparently, the healthy concept of self they developed as adolescents, from the way parents, peers, and other adults treated them, persisted into adult and enabled them to make superior adjustments. They made better impressions on others, were more willing to carry social responsibilities, were cooperative, enterprising, persistent, goal directed, sociable, warm, conforming, and somewhat overcontrolled. They were therefore more successful vocationally. (18, p. 92; 24, p. 40)

LATE-MATURING BOYS

Late-maturing boys suffer socially induced inferiority because of their delayed growth and development. (41, p. 132) A boy who has not reached puberty at age fifteen may be eight inches shorter and thirty pounds lighter than his early-maturing male friends. Accompanying this size difference are marked differences in body build, strength, motor performance and coordination, and reaction time. Because physical size and motor coordination play such an important role in social acceptance, late maturers develop negative self-perceptions and self-concepts. They have been characterized as less attractive physically, less well groomed, less popular, more affected, more restless, bossy, and rebellious against parents and as having feelings of inadequacy, rejection, and dependency. (9, p. 38) They often become self-conscious; some withdraw because of their social rejection.

In the following example, a fifteen-year-old boy, Stephen, adjusted to his late maturation by overconformity to rules on the one hand and by efforts to excel verbally and academically on the other hand. In relation to his parents he was dependent, undercontrolled, rebellious, and childish.

Stephen at fifteen was slight of build and had not as yet experienced any secondary sexual changes, such as body hair development, voice change, and the like. Always a good student, his application to his studies was far in excess of what was required and bordered on obsessional perfectionism. Indeed he had many features of the obsessive compulsive in his character structure, which had developed and continued from latency. He was punctilious, tidy, compliant, and fearful of authority. His strict regard for the rules to which he adhered with almost a legalistic fanaticism made him a questionable asset in games with his peers. As would be expected, he veered away from athletic pursuits and found success and pleasure in such activities as the debating team. All his aggressiveness and competitiveness focused on verbal, intellectual pursuits and he delighted in fault-finding and one-upping both peers and teachers. But at home, he let his guard down, as it were, and was given to temper outbursts, demanding, whining behavior, and fierce rivalry with his brother, four years younger. . . . Stephen was thus still a latency child at fifteen, with no apparent heterosexual interests; his sexuality was limited to the crude locker room vulgarity more characteristic of the eleven-year-old. (49, p. 95)

As evident in the above example, late maturers sometimes overcompensate by becoming overly dependent on others or overly eager for status and attention. At other times they try to make up for their inadequacies by belittling, attacking, or ridiculing others, or by using attention-getting devices. (18, p. 92; 62, p. 44) A typical example is the loud, daring show-off with a chip on his shoulder, ready to fight at the least provocation. The effects of these early negative social attitudes may persist into adulthood, long after physical differences and their social importance have disappeared. (67) It has been found that late-maturing boys delay adult psychological commitments such as marriage, and are less secure in their vocational status because they earn less. (41, p. 132) In extreme cases of physical retardation caused by physiological factors, androgens are sometimes administered to hasten puberty, but social retardation may continue long afterward. (33)

EARLY-MATURING GIRLS

Early maturation in girls tends to have a negative effect during their elementary school years. (7, p. 116) A girl who is already physically mature in fifth or sixth grade is at some disadvantage because she is out of phase with the majority of her classmates. She is taller, more developed sexually, and tends to feel awkward and self-conscious because she is different. For this reason she enjoys less prestige at this age than do her prepubertal friends.

By junior high school, however, the early-maturing girl comes into her own. She begins to look more like a grown-up woman, is envied by other girls for her adult looks and clothes, begins to attract the attention of older boys (which she likes), and starts dating earlier than normal. (62, p. 42) This creates some problems for her, however. Parents begin to worry because of her precocious heterosexual interests and may strive to curtail her social desires and activities. The girl may find herself emotionally unequipped to deal with sophisticated social activities and with sexual enticements. This may create stress for her, so that this period of adjustment may be one of anxiety and upset. Overall, however, by the time early-maturing girls have reached seventeen years of age, they have more positive self-concepts, score higher on total adjustment and family adjustment, and enjoy better personal relations than do later maturers (19, p. 117), although the net positive effect of early maturation does not seem to be as pronounced for girls as for boys. (18, p. 93; 50, p. 33)

LATE-MATURING GIRLS

Late-maturing girls are at a distinct social disadvantage in junior high school and high school. They look like "little girls" and resent being treated as such. They are largely bypassed and overlooked in invitations to boy-girl parties and social events. One study of adolescent girls in New York City showed that those who experienced menarche at ages fourteen to eighteen were especially late daters. (43) As a consequence, late maturing girls may be envious of their friends who are better developed. However, they are generally on a par with normal-maturing boys, and so have much in common with them as friends. However, they avoid large mixed groups of boys and girls, and their activities reflect the interests of those of younger age groups with whom they spend their time. One advantage is that late-maturing girls do not experience the sharp criticism of parents and other adults as do girls who develop early. The chief disadvantage seems to be the temporary loss of social status because of their relative physical immaturity.

Adolescent Nutrition

DIGESTION

One of the things adults notice most about adolescents is that they are constantly eating. During the period of rapid growth the adolescent needs greater quantities of food to take care of bodily requirements. The stomach increases in size and capacity in order to be able to digest these increased amounts of food. Research shows that the caloric requirement for girls may increase on the average by 25 percent from ages ten to fifteen and then decrease slightly and level off. The caloric requirement for boys may increase on the average by 90 percent from ages ten to nineteen. (25) No wonder the adolescent boy finds it almost impossible to get enough to eat!

THE IMPORTANCE OF NUTRITION

Development of proper eating habits during adolescence is extremely important to individual health. Attainment of maximum height, strength, and physical well-being depends upon the individual's eating enough body-building foods. Bone, muscle, nerve, and other tissue growth requires good nutrition. Nutritional deficiencies are related to physical and mental retardation, reduced stamina, lower resistance to infection, premenstrual tension in girls, and emotional instability. (25)

Considerable attention has been given to the importance of good nutrition to pregnant teenage girls. Pregnancy during those years, when the adolescent mother's body is still in the formative stage, creates added physiological stress for the young girl. Her body makes increased nutritional requirements both for the growth of her body and for the development and subsequent feeding of her baby. Because many of these girls become pregnant out of wedlock, get very little or no prenatal care in the early stages of pregnancy, and show a depressed emotional state before and during pregnancy, they are poor obstetrical risks; their babies may be born prematurely, have congenital defects, or lack the necessary nutrients to survive during the first days and months of life. Furthermore, these young mothers may be prone to such complications of pregnancy as toxemia (the presence of toxic substances in the blood) or eclampsia (convulsions).

NUTRITIONAL DEFICIENCIES

Most studies of nutrition during adolescence show that many adolescents have inadequate diets. Deficiencies may be summarized as follows:

1. Insufficient calcium—due primarily to an inadequate intake of milk.
2. Insufficient iron—especially true for girls.
3. Inadequate protein—usually true only of girls.
4. Insufficient vitamins, especially A and C—due primarily to lack of enough fresh vegetables and fruit in the diet.
5. Insufficient thiamine and riboflavin.

Adolescent girls have nutritional deficiencies more often than boys. (27, p. P-40) Several factors contribute to this deficit: girls eat less, and so are less likely to get the necessary nutrients; they diet more often, depriving themselves of necessary nutrients; and the additional need for some nutrients because of menstruation or pregnancy imposes special problems.

Why do so many adolescents, both boys and girls, have inadequate diets? The reasons may be summarized as follows:

They skip breakfast because of lack of time in the morning, because they would rather sleep late, and for other reasons. Skipping breakfast is also more common when: (1) family members do not get together, (2) there is no one to prepare a meal for the teenager, (3) ready-to-eat foods are not available, and (4) the feelings of the peer group are against eating breakfast. (8, p. 44) All nutritionists agree that breakfast is one of the most important meals of the day. Studies show that persons who eat a high-protein breakfast evidence increased efficiency, perspective, motor coordination, and emotional stability.

Snacks, which make up about one-fourth of the daily intake of food, do not compensate for meals missed, because the snacks are primarily fats, carbohydrates, and sugars, or because the intake from snacks is not sufficient to make up for the food missed.

Small quantities of foods are eaten, especially of fruits, vegetables, milk, cheese, and meat. Girls usually need more eggs and whole grain cereal than they eat. Also, girls who are dieting often develop nutritional deficiencies because of a low intake of food.

Inadequate knowledge of nutrition influences the development of poor nutrition practices. Many times high school boys and girls know so little about nutrition that they cannot select a well-balanced meal in a cafeteria. (27, p. 8)

Social pressures may cause poor eating habits. Adolescents who adopt bizarre eating habits often reflect the ideas of their social or cultural group. Some ethnic groups are notorious for their poor nutritional habits, regardless of the amount of money available to buy food. (65)

Troubled family relationships and personal adjustments seem to accompany poor eating habits. Adolescents from broken or troubled homes may not have parents at home to cook for them or to see that they get an adequate diet. Those with emotional problems may have nervous stomachs, ulcers, or more complex reasons for not eating properly.

FOOD FADS AMONG YOUTHS

In recent years, with the development of various countercultures, a growing number of older youths are adopting faddish dietary patterns. These patterns may be classified into three groups: *vegetarians, organic and health food advocates,* and *the followers of the Zen macrobiotic regimen.* (17, p. 12) There are vegetarians, called *vegans,* whose diet contains no animal foods whatsoever. The *lactovegetarians* eat no meat or fish but they do eat milk and cheese products. The ovolactovegetarians eat an all-vegetable diet supplemented with dairy products and eggs. The *fruitarians* subsist primarily on raw or dried fruit and nuts.

In general, nutrition research reveals that a dietary intake consisting of a variety of fruits and vegetables, whole grain cereals, nuts, legumes, and seeds appears to be nutritionally adequate, especially if eggs and milk products are included. (10, 44, 45) Researchers found no significant difference among vegans, lactovegetarians, and nonvegetarians in height, weight, protein, albumen, and globulin measurements, not in blood count or blood pressure, although pure vegetarians more closely approximated their ideal weight. Cholesterol levels, however, are higher in the nonvegetarian group. The one nutrient most often deficient in the vegan diet is vitamin B_{12}. (13)

Table 5–2.   Phases of the macrobiotic diet.

Stage	Cereals	Vege-tables	Soup	Animal	Fruits Salads	Dessert	Drinking liquid
						Percent of Total Diet	
7	100	—	—	—	—	—	Sparingly
6	90	10*	—	—	—	—	Sparingly
5	80	20	—	—	—	—	Sparingly
4	70	20	10	—	—	—	Sparingly
3	60	30	10	—	—	—	Sparingly
2	50	30	10	10	—	—	Sparingly
1	40	30	10	20	—	—	Sparingly
−1	30	30	10	20	10	—	Sparingly
−2	20	30	10	25	10	5	Sparingly
−3	10	30	10	30	15	5	Sparingly

Source: R. T. Frankle and F. K. Heusenstamm, "Food Zealotry and Youth," *American Journal of Public Health* 64 (1974): 11–18. Used by permission.

The consequences of eating organic and health foods are more difficult to determine because individual nutritional intake varies so widely. Organically grown foods are those fertilized with manure rather than chemical fertilizers, grown without application of pesticides, and processed without the use of food additives. (17, p. 13) The rationale for eating these foods has been explained in such articles as *Ramparts* magazine's "Food Pollution." (71) The organic and health food movement has grown considerably in recent years. Such universities as Yale, University of California in Los Angeles, Stony Brook, and Goddard now make health foods and packaged dried fruits and nuts available in their cafeteria lines. By November 1971, Yale's health food restaurant was serving about 10 percent of the 4800 undergraduates. (63) Brown rice was a favored food.

Sometimes health-food store employees prescribe particular diets for those with special health problems. Extravagant and often unfounded claims are made for these diets. Some harm can come from a delay in getting adequate medical care because of a reliance on the health-food retailer as a physician. (17, p. 12)

The Zen macrobiotic diet, the most rigorous of the new dietary styles, has proven extremely harmful in its effects when carried to extremes. The term *macrobiotic* means "the way of long life," but the effect of the more rigorous phases has been to shorten life, even causing death in some instances. Table 5–2 shows the various phases of the macrobiotic diet. (17) The disciplined convert is expected to move from the minus diets to diet number 7 with the promise of reaching enlightenment or Nirvana. (17, p. 5) The usual result is a deficiency of vitamins A, C, and D, of many minerals such as calcium and phosphorus, and of essential proteins. The dangers of the diet are dramatically highlighted in a review of six cases of death or near death in testimony before a Passaic County, New Jersey, grand jury.

Individuals consuming this diet for a considerable period of time could develop anemia and eventually would develop vitamin deficiencies and, if continued, irreversible tissue damage. This diet can result in death. . . . An individual consuming this diet would in a few weeks develop scurvy because of the lack of vitamin C. . . . He would develop osteoporosis . . . because of the lack of calcium in the bone structure. (70, p. 134)

Conclusions

This chapter has discussed the process of growth in height and weight, in strength, and in motor ability and coordination during adolescence. It has outlined various body types and proportions and the adolescent's concern about build and figure. The subject of nutrition during adolescence has also been summarized, because of the importance of nutrition to the figure and to individual health, and because the diet of adolescents is notoriously inadequate.

A summary of the facts of physical growth, however, does not cover either the psychological and emotional components of this growth or the adolescent's feelings about and reactions to physical changes. Adolescents who are shorter or taller than average feel "different," and their feelings may lead to self-consciousness and a sense of inferiority.

Adolescents are also very conscious of their body proportions and weight. Either obesity or being underweight is a problem to those who want to be like others their own age. Adolescents are also concerned about boy-girl differentials in rate of development. During the period between twelve and fourteen years of age, when the average girl may be taller than the average boy, boys feel embarrassed in social situations such as a junior high dance. The boys look short and immature, the girls tall and sophisticated, and many times they feel the same way.

Because there is considerable variation in the rates at which individuals mature, either very early or very late maturers need reassurance that variations in growth rates are normal, and that late maturers will soon catch up with the others. (See Chapter 4.) Boys who mature early enjoy considerable physical and social advantage over their male peers, an advantage that continues into adulthood. Late-maturing boys suffer socially induced inferiority that continues as a handicap well into the adult years.

Girls who mature early are at a disadvantage during their elementary years. Not only are they taller, heavier, and stronger than many boys their own age, but they are also advanced over other girls. However, during junior high school these disadvantages are largely overcome. Because early physical maturity and social maturity go together, these girls prefer to associate with older adolescents. They become interested in boys, dances, and dates very young, a situation that causes anxiety for their parents. However, they generally develop more positive self-concepts and make better total adjustments than do late maturers. The late maturer suffers if she is much out of phase with her friends.

Each adolescent is an individual, with his or her own pattern of growth and development. Just as each develops physically, so each should be allowed to proceed at a reasonable rate emotionally and socially. Parents or teachers who put too much pressure on the immature or who try to retard the more advanced, are not giving enough attention to their patterns of development and to the total needs of the individual.

Topics for Term Papers

1. Heredity as a Determinative Factor in Height
2. The Role of Nutrition in Determination of Ultimate Height

Bibliography

1. Brace, D. K. *Measuring Motor Ability.* New York: Barnes, 1927.

2. Brenner, D., and Hinsdale, G. "Body Build Stereotypes and Self-Identification in Three Age Groups of Females." *Adolescence* 13 (Winter 1978): 551–561.

3. Broverman, Donald M. et al. "Physique and Growth in Adolescence." *Child Development* 35 (1964): 857–870.

4. Clarke, H., and Degutis, Ernest. "Comparison of Skeletal Age and Various Physical and Motor Factors with the Pubescent Development of 10, 13, and 16 Year Old Boys." *American Association for Health, Physical Education and Recreation Research Quarterly* 33 (1962): 356–368.

5. Clausen, J. A. "The Social Meaning of Differential Physical and Sexual Maturation." In *Adolescence in the Life Cycle.* Edited by S. E. Dragastin and G. H. Elder, Jr. New York: John Wiley and Sons, 1975.

6. Clifford, E. "Body Satisfaction in Adolescence." *Percentage Motor Skills* 33 (1971): 119–125.

7. Conger, J. J. *Adolescence and Youth.* New York: Harper and Row, 1973.

8. Cooksey, E. B., and Ojemann, Ralph. "Why Do They Skip Breakfast?" *Journal of Home Economics* 55 (1963): 43–45.

9. Dreyfus, E. A. *Adolescence: Theory and Experience.* Columbus, Ohio: Charles E. Merrill Publishing Co., 1976.

10. Dwyer, J. T. et al. "The New Vegetarians." *Journal of Dietary Association* 62 (1973): 506.

11. Eichorn, D. H. "Physiological Development." In *Carmichael's Manual of Child Psychology,* vol. 1. 3d ed. Edited by P. H. Mussen. New York: John Wiley and Sons, 1970.

12. ———. "Asynchronizations in Adolescent Development." In *Adolescence in the Life Cycle.* Edited by S. E. Dragastin and E. H. Elder, Jr. New York: John Wiley and Sons, 1975.

13. Ellis, F. P. et al. "Veganism, Clinical Findings, and Investigations." *American Journal of Clinical Nutrition* 23 (1970): 249–255.

14. Espenschade, A. "Development of Motor Coordination in Boys and Girls." *American Physical Education Association Research Quarterly* 18 (1947): 30–43.

15. Eveleth, P. "Difference between Populations in Body Shape of Children and Adolescents." *American Journal of Physical Anthropology* 49 (September 1978): 373–381.

16. Feinman, S., and Gill, G. W. "Sex Differences in Physical Attractiveness Preferences." *Journal of Social Psychology* 105 (June 1978): 43–52.

17. Frankle, R. T., and Heusenstamm, F. K. "Food Zealotry and Youth." *American Journal of Public Health* 64 (1974): 11–18.

18. Grinder, R. E. *Adolescence.* New York: John Wiley and Sons, 1973.

19. Hamachek, D. E. "Development and Dynamics of the Self." In *Understanding Adolescence.* 3d ed. Edited by J. F. Adams. Boston: Allyn and Bacon, 1976.

20. Hammar, S. L. "The Obese Adolescent." *Journal of School Health* 35 (1965): 246–249.

21. Hendry, L. B., and Gullies, P. "Body Type, Body Esteem, School, and Leisure: A Study of Overweight, Average, and Underweight Adolescents." *Journal of Youth and Adolescence* 7 (June 1978): 181–195.

22. Huenemann, R. L. et al. *Teenage Nutrition and Physique.* Springfield, Ill.: Charles C Thomas, 1974.

23. Hunt, J. McV. "Has Compensatory Education Failed? Has It Been Attempted?" In *Environment, Heredity, and Intelligence.* Reprint Series No. 2 compiled from *Harvard Educational Review,* 1969, 130–152.

24. Hurlock, E. *Adolescent Development,* 4th ed. New York: McGraw-Hill Book Co., 1973.

25. Johnston, J. A. "Nutritional Problems of Adolescence." *American Medical Association Journal* 137 (1948): 1587–1588.

26. Jones, H. E. "Motor Performance and Growth: A Developmental Study of Static Dynamometric Strength." *University of California Publications in Child Development* 1 (1949): 35–36.

27. Kilander, H. Frederick. "Adolescents Fail on Food Facts." *PTA Magazine* 59 (1965): 7–8.

28. Lambert, B. G. *Adolescence: Transition from Childhood to Maturity.* Monterey, Calif.: Brooks/Cole Publishing Co., 1972.

29. Lerner, R. M. "The Development of Stereotyped Expectancies of Body Build–Behavior Relations." *Child Development* 40 (1969): 137–141.

30. Lerner, R. M., and Darabeneck, S. A. "Physical Attractiveness, Body Attitudes, and Self-Concept in Late Adolescents." *Journal of Youth Adolescence* 3 (1974): 307–316.

31. Lerner, R. M. et al. "Attitudes of High School Students and Their Parents toward Contemporary Issues." *Psychological Reports* 31 (1972): 255–258.

32. ———. "Physical Attractiveness, Physical Effectiveness, and Self-Concept in Late Adolescents." *Adolescence,* 11 (Fall 1976): 313–326.

33. Lewis, V. G. et al. "Idiopathic Pubertal Delay Beyond Age Fifteen: Psychologic Study of Twelve Boys." *Adolescence* 12 (Spring 1977): 1–11.

34. Lopez, Joanne. "Obesity A Problem: Get A Move On." *Forecast for Home Economics* 13 (1968): F–12t.

35. Marshall, W. A., and Tanner, J. M. "Variations in the Pattern of Pubertal Changes in Boys." *Archives of Diseases of Children* 45 (1970): 13.

36. Matteson, D. R. *Adolescence Today.* Homewood, Ill.: Dorsey Press, 1975.

37. Meredith, H. V. "Relation between Socio-Economic Status and Body Size in Boys 7–10 Years of Age." *American Journal of Diseases of Children* 82 (1951): 702–709.

38. Miller, D. *Adolescence: Psychology, and Psychotherapy.* New York: Jason Aronson, 1974.

39. Minahan, N. "Relationships among Self-Perceived Physical Attractiveness, Body Shape, and Personality of Teen-age Girls."

Dissertation Abstracts International 32 (1971): 1249–1250.

40. Muuss, R. E. "Adolescent Development and the Secular Trend." *Adolescence* 5 (1970): 267–284.

41. Peskin, H. "Pubertal Onset and Ego Functioning." In *The Adolescent: Physical Development, Sexuality and Pregnancy.* Edited by J. Kestenberg. New York: MSS Information Co., 1972.

42. Pomerantz, S. C. "Sex Differences in Relative Importance of Self-Esteem, Physical Self-Satisfaction, and Identity in Predicting Adolescent Satisfaction." *Journal of Youth and Adolescence* 8 (March 1979): 51–61.

43. Presser, H. B. "Age at Menarche, Socio-Sexual Behavior, and Fertility." *Social Biology* 25 (Summer 1978): 94–101.

44. Raper, N. R., and Hill, M. M. "Vegetarian Diets." *Nutritional Progress News.* U.S.D.A. July/August 1973.

45. Register, V. D., and Sonnenberg, L. M. "The Vegetarian Diet." *Journal of the American Dietary Association* 62 (1973): 257.

46. Rich, George Q. "Muscular Fatigue Curves for Boys and Girls." *American Association for Health, Physical Education, and Recreation Research Quarterly.* 31 (1960): 485–498.

47. Rogers, D. *Adolescence: A Psychological Perspective.* Monterey, Calif.: Brooks/Cole Publishing Co., 1972.

48. Schonfeld, W. A. "The Body and the Body-Image in Adolescents." In *Adolescence: Psychosocial Perspectives.* Edited by G. Caplan and S. Lebovici. New York: Basic Books, 1969.

49. Shapiro, S. H. "Vicissitudes of Adolescence." In *Behavior Pathology of Childhood and Adolescence.* Edited by S. L. Cope. New York: Basic Books, 1973.

50. Smart, M. S., and Smart, R. C. *Adolescents. Development and Relationships.* New York: Macmillan, 1973.

51. Snow, D. L., and Held, M. L. "Group Psychotherapy with Obese Adolescent Females." *Adolescence* 8 (1973): 407–414.

52. Staffieri, J. R. "Body Build and Behavioral Expectancies in Young Females." *Developmental Psychology* 6 (1972): 125–227.

53. Steele, C. I. "Obese Adolescent Girls: Some Diagnostic and Treatment Considerations." *Adolescence* 9 (1974): 81–96.

54. Stockton, W. "Conspiracy against Fatness." *Psychology Today* (October 1978): 97ff.

55. Stuart, Harold C. "Normal Growth and Development During Adolescence." *New England Journal of Medicine* 234 (1946): 666.

56. Sugerman, A. A., and Haronian, F. "Body Type and Sophistication of Body Concept." In Kestenberg, J. et al. *The Adolescent: Physical Development, Sexuality and Pregnancy.* New York: MSS Information Co., 1972.

57. Tanner, J. M. *Growth at Adolescence.* Springfield, Ill.: Charles C Thomas, 1962.

58. ———. "Earlier Maturation in Man." *Scientific American* 218 (1968): 21–27.

59. ———. "Growth of Bone, Muscle and Fat during Childhood and Adolescence." In *Growth and Development of Mammals.* Edited by G. A. Lodge. London: Butterworth, 1968.

60. ———. "Physical Growth." In *Carmichael's Manual of Child Psychology,* vol. 1. 3d ed. Edited by P. H. Mussen. New York: John Wiley and Sons, 1970.

61. ———. "Sequence, Tempo, and Individual Variation in Growth and Development of Boys and Girls Aged Twelve to Sixteen." In *Twelve to Sixteen: Early Adolescence.* Edited by Jerome Kagan and Robert Coles. New York: W. W. Norton & Co., 1972.

62. Thornburg, H. D. *Development in Adolescence.* Monterey, Calif.: Brooks/Cole Publishing Co., 1975.

63. Treaster, J. B. "Yale versus Those Mushy Vegetables." *New York Times,* November 15, 1971.

64. Tuddenham, R. D., and Snyder, M. M. "The Physical Growth of California Boys and Girls from Birth to Eighteen Years." *University of California Publications in Child Development* 1 (1954): 183–364.

65. Walter, J. P. "Some Reflections on the Economics of Nutrition: Deprived Urban Black and Mexican American Youth." *American Economist* 21 (Fall 1977): 30–34.

66. Young, H. B. "The Physiology of Adolescence." In *Modern Perspectives in Adolescent Psychiatry.* Edited by J. G. Howells. New York: Brunner/Mazel, 1971.

67. *Youth: Transition to Adulthood.* Report of the Panel on Youth of the President's Science Advisory Committee. Chicago: University of Chicago Press, 1974.

68. Zakus, G., and Solomon, M. "The Family Situations of Obese Adolescent Girls." *Adolescence* 8 (1973): 33–42.

69. Zakus, G. et al. "A Group Behavior Modification Approach to Adolescent Obesity." *Adolescence* 14 (Fall 1979): 481–490.

70. "Zen Macrobiotic Diet Hazardous: Presentment of the Passaic Grand Jury." *Public Health News* 46 (1966): 132–136.

71. Zwerdling, D. "Food Pollution." *Ramparts* 9 (1971): 31–37.

CHAPTER 6

Drug Abuse, Smoking, and Excessive Drinking

Outline

This chapter focuses on three selected health problems of adolescents: drug use, smoking, and excessive drinking. These three problems have been selected because of their frequency and their importance in the lives of adolescents. Drug use is considered by some the greatest social health problem relating to today's youths. The purpose of this section is to take a look at the total problem, and to ask and try to answer a number of questions. Which drugs are most commonly abused? Has the abuse of drugs been overestimated? Who is using drugs, and for what reasons? Why do adolescents try drugs? Where? With whom? Why do many adolescents not try or use them? Large numbers of youths smoke tobacco, even though the medical profession is now strongly allied against its use. Although drinking is usually considered a personal matter, it becomes a problem for society as well as for the individual when it is excessive. In discussing these problems, several aspects will be emphasized: the incidence of use (how many adolescents are involved, who are they, and what are they like?), the patterns of use, the reasons for use, and some ways and means of dealing with these problems.

Drug Abuse

INCREASING CONCERN

Probably no social problem involving adolescents has caused more concern in recent years than drug abuse. (81, p. 1) One reason for the concern has been a dramatic increase in the extent of drug abuse. In 1960, official government estimates placed heroin dependency at fewer than 100,000 persons in the country, but by 1980 these estimates ranged up to 500,000. (112, p. vii) The majority of these addicts were under thirty years of age. (112, p. 99) An increasing percentage —estimated at 20 percent—were female. (24) One sampling of men and women, ages seventeen to twenty-five, serving at U.S. military installations in Germany, showed that 10 percent used heroin while on duty. (38, p. 29) The increase in the use of marijuana has also been considerable. In 1971, 14 percent of youths aged twelve to seventeen and 39 percent aged eighteen to twenty-five had tried marijuana. By 1977 these figures had increased to 28 percent and 60 percent, respectively. (131) Figure 6–1 shows a breakdown by age groups. (131)

Another source of concern was the marked increase in drug-related arrests among youths. Most of the arrests were for simple possession of marijuana. As the arrest figures climbed along with the use of marijuana, public uneasiness grew, especially when the sons and daughters of prominent citizens—governors, congressmen, military officers, doctors and lawyers—began to show up on police blotters. No one seemed immune. (112, p. 19) Even the president's son, Jack Carter, received a general discharge from the U.S. Navy for smoking marijuana.

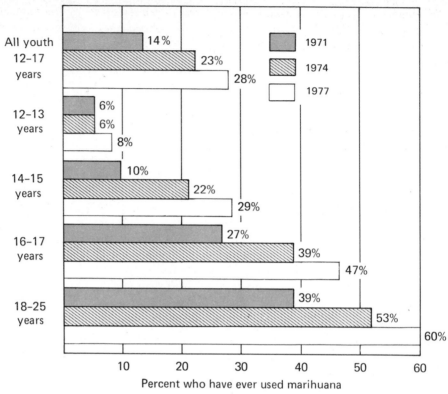

Figure 6–1. Marihuana use among youths: 1971, 1974, and 1977. (Adapted from U.S. Bureau of the Census, Department of Commerce, *Statistical Abstract of the United States, 1978* [Washington, D.C.: U.S. Government Printing Office, 1978], p. 123.)

(38, p. 29) One result was the creation of the National Commission on Marijuana and Drug Abuse. (114) The commission felt that the application of criminal penalties for simple possession of marijuana was "inappropriate" and subsequently recommended the private possession and use of marijuana should not be a criminal offense. (112, p. 20) By 1974 the federal government and all fifty states had reduced the offense for possession of marijuana from a felony to a misdemeanor. Sale of the drug continued to carry stiff penalties. (112, p. 27)

Concern over drug abuse increased in relation to some drugs and decreased in relation to others. The initial shock waves created among the adult population when marijuana use became widespread have subsided somewhat, although concern is growing again over the sharp increase in the number of habitual users. (53) Experts estimate that one in eleven high school seniors now smokes marijuana daily. (38, p. 28; 71) This heavy usage, together with a marked increase in the quality of "grass" smoked, is having negative effects on users that could not be demonstrated before, when only weak U.S. varieties were smoked at infrequent intervals. Concern over the use of narcotics, LSD, amphetamines, barbiturates, and volatile chemicals has increased, as more and more is learned about their dangers to health, their effects on individual behavior, and the social consequences of their use. (35) As a result, schools and various community organizations throughout the United States have organized themselves to combat drug abuse through programs of education, counseling, and rehabilitation.

PHYSICAL ADDICTION AND PSYCHOLOGICAL DEPENDENCY

By definition, a drug is a substance used as a medicine. As such, some drugs are used by virtually everyone. Aspirin is a very effective drug, but even aspirin is lethal if taken in excess. Drug abuse, therefore, is the use of a drug for other than a medicinal purpose or in improper quantities or administration. The problem is drug abuse, not drug use.

There is also a distinction between *drug addiction*, or *physical dependency*, and *psychological dependency*. (134) An addictive drug is one that is physically habit-forming because the body builds up a physical need for the drug, so that its sudden denial results in withdrawal symptoms. Psychological dependency is the development of a persistent, sometimes overpowering psychological need for a drug, resulting in a compulsion to take it. A well-established habit of psychological dependency may be more difficult to overcome than one involving physical dependency, especially if people become so deeply involved with a drug that they cannot function without it. Physical dependency on heroin, for example, may be broken, but individuals go back to it because of psychological dependency on it. It is a mistake, therefore, to assume that the only dangerous drugs are those that are physically addictive.

WHICH DRUGS?

The drugs most commonly abused may be grouped into a number of categories: *Narcotics, stimulants, depressants, hallucinogens, marijuana*, and *inhalants*. *Alcohol* and *nicotine* are also drugs. Because they are more widely used than any of the others, they will be discussed in separate sections of this chapter.

NARCOTICS

Narcotics include *opium* and its derivatives such as *morphine, heroin*, and *codeine*. (84) Opium is a dark, gummy substance extracted from the juice of unripe seed pods of the opium poppy. Opium is usually taken orally or sniffed—that is, it is heated and its vapor inhaled. (14, p. 1) *Morphine*, the chief active ingredient in opium, is extracted as a bitter, white powder with no odor. Each grain of opium contains about one-tenth of a grain of morphine. Morphine is used medicinally to relieve extreme pain because of its depressant effect on the central nervous system. (63, p. 23) Addicts refer to it as "M" or "monkey." It may be sniffed, but the powder is usually mixed with water and injected under the skin with a hypodermic needle ("skin popping"). For maximum effect, it is injected directly into a vein ("mainlined").

Heroin ("H," "horse," or "Harry") is produced from morphine by a simple chemical process. Like its relative, it is a white, odorless powder. If dirty needles or ingredients are used, the result may be blood poisoning or serious infections like hepatitis, a leading cause of death among addicts. Heroin is the most widely used opiate, but is more addictive than morphine because it is stronger. Traditionally, more hard-core heroin addicts come from the ghettos of large cities than from any other area. A large percentage of all heroin addicts came from New York alone. If California, Illinois, and New Jersey are added, these four states contain 78 percent of the heroin addicts in the United States. (18, p. 5-1) Street supplies are diluted ("cut") with milk sugar to squeeze out maximum profits. (63, p. 28) Heroin is also often diluted with bitter tasting quinine, to make it impossible for addicts to gauge the heroin concentration by tasting the mixture. Pure quinine injected in sufficient quantity may be a leading cause of the deaths that are attributed to a heroin overdose. (14, p. 110) Addicts often die, also, if they shoot heroin while under the influence of alcohol or barbiturates, for the combination of drugs has a double depressive effect. (14, p. 112) In all likelihood this is what happened to Janis Joplin. *Time* magazine gave this report of her death on October 19, 1970.*

The quart bottle of Southern Comfort (whiskey) that she held aloft onstage was at once a symbol of her load and a way of lightening it. As she emptied the bottle, she grew happier, more radiant, and more freaked out. . . .

Last week . . . Janis Joplin died on the lowest and saddest of notes. Returning to her Hollywood motel room after a late-night recording session and some hard drinking with friends at a nearby bar, she apparently filled a hypodermic needle with heroin and shot it into her left arm. The injection killed her. . . . (129)

Codeine is also a morphine derivative. Often used in cough syrups or to relieve mild body aches, it has the same, but milder analgesic properties as other narcotics. *Paregoric*, a liquid preparation containing an extract of opium, is used medicinally to counteract diarrhea and abdominal pain. Codeine and paregoric are often used by young people who think they are not addictive. Actually, they can be.

The synthetic opiates, *Demerol* (meperidine) and *Dolophine* (methadone), were created as chemical substitutes for the natural opiates and are used in medicine as pain relievers. They are addictive and restricted by law to medical use.

The consequences of morphine and heroin use are severe. They are the most physically addictive of all drugs. (14) Users quickly develop tolerance and physical dependence, and must therefore gradually increase the dosage. They quickly develop a psychological dependence as well. Because dependence becomes total and heroin is expensive (addicts spend from $20 to $180 daily), many users turn to crime or prostitution to support their habit. Without the drug, withdrawal symptoms begin to appear. (26) The first symptoms are running eyes and nose, yawning, sweating, dilation of the pupils of the eye, and appearance of goose pimples on the skin (from which the expression "cold turkey" originated). Within twenty-four hours addicts develop leg, back, and abdominal cramps, violent muscle spasms, vomiting, and diarrhea. The expression "kicking the habit" developed as a result of the muscle spasms during withdrawal. Bodily functions such as respiration, blood pressure, temperature, and metabolism, which have been depressed, now become hyperactive. These symptoms gradually diminish over a period of a week or more. (63, p. 28) Females who have babies while addicted deliver infants who are addicts or who are born dead from drug poisoning.

* "Blues for Janis," *Time*, 19 October 1970. Reprinted by permission from *Time, The Weekly Newsmagazine*; Copyright Time, Inc., 1970

Addiction may have other effects. Addicts usually lose their appetite for food, with consequent extreme weight loss and severe malnutrition. They neglect their health, suffer chronic fatigue, and are in a general devitalized condition. Sexual interest and activity decline; most marriages end in separation or divorce. They become accident-prone—fall frequently, drown, or may set themselves on fire if they drop off to sleep while smoking. (43) They lose the willpower to carry on daily functions and pay little attention to their appearance. Ambition, purpose, pride, and honesty disappear. Their whole life centers on getting the next "fix."

What is the prognosis of a cure of severe heroin addiction? One twelve-year study of 100 patients who were released from the U.S. hospital for addicts in Lexington, Kentucky, showed that within two years, all but ten were again addicted. (134) Three of these ten died within four years, two turned to alcohol, three had never used narcotics more than once a day, and one used drugs intermittently after discharge. Subsequent to Lexington, these 100 patients served over 350 prison terms and underwent over 200 known voluntary hospitalizations for addiction. (134) At any one time, from 10 to 25 percent of graduates from Lexington may appear to be abstinent, nonalcoholic, employed, and law-abiding. But almost all become readdicted, reimprisoned, and rehospitalized over and over again. (14, p. 71)

Because the prognosis for curing heroin addiction is so discouraging, methadone is now given as a substitute drug through medically recognized methadone maintenance programs. The drug blocks the hunger for heroin and the effects of it, with the result that the majority of addicts no longer have a constant desire to obtain blackmarket heroin. Recent studies show outstanding success with methadone maintenance. The majority of patients who are regularly given medically prescribed doses of methadone become productive citizens, returning to work or school and evidencing arrest-free behavior. (14, chapter 15.)

STIMULANTS

Cocaine ("snow") is extracted from the leaves of the South American coca plant and is available as an odorless, fluffy, white powder. (112, p. 160) It is mistakenly classified as a narcotic, and is therefore subject to the same penalties as opiates, but it is a stimulant rather than a depressant to the central nervous system. (14, p. 271) Even though it is expensive, it is becoming more widely used in the youth drug culture, as well as among more affluent groups. The percentage of persons between eighteen and twenty-five who admitted experimenting with the drug doubled between 1972 and 1977. (38, p. 28) As a result, cocaine seizures by federal agents have increased 700 percent since 1969. (112, p. 160)

The drug depresses the appetite and increases alertness. It is not effective when taken orally, so users sniff or inject it intravenously into the bloodstream. Aside from financial depletion, the main undesirable effects of "social snorting" are nervousness, irritability, and restlessness from overstimulation, sometimes extending to mild paranoia; physical exhaustion and mental confusion from insomnia; loss of weight; fatigue or depression when "coming down"; and various afflictions of the nasal mucous membranes and cartilage. (54, p. 41) Physical dependence is so slight that the physical effects of cocaine withdrawal are minor. However, cocaine addiction and taking large doses can lead to a severe psychosis while the person is still on the drug. Large doses can produce headache, cold sweat, rapid and weak pulse, hyperventilation, nausea, vertigo, tremors and convulsions, unconsciousness, and even death. (54, p. 42) Psychological dependence is severe; withdrawal is characterized by a profound depression for which cocaine itself appears to be the only remedy. The compulsion to resume cocaine is strong; once established the habit is difficult to break. (14, p. 276)

Amphetamines are stimulants and include such drugs as benzedrine, dexedrine, diphetamine, and methedrine ("speed"). They are used medically for treating obesity, mild depression, fatigue, and other conditions. The drugs are usually taken orally in the form of tablets or capsules. Because they are stimulants, they increase alertness, elevate mood, and produce a feeling of well-being. Large doses may produce a temporary rise in blood pressure, palpitations, headache, dizziness, sweating, diarrhea, pallor and dilation of the pupils, vasomotor disturbances, agitation, confusion, apprehension, or delirium. Regular amphetamine users do not develop physical dependence, for withdrawal does not produce abstinence symptoms, but users soon develop an intense psychological need to continue taking the drug and require larger doses as tolerance develops. Mental depression and fatigue are experienced after the drug has been withdrawn, so psychic dependence develops quickly because the "high" is so enticing and the "low" so depressing. (119) Patients usually need to be treated in mental hospitals, especially those who inject the drugs into their veins. Some users end up swallowing whole handfuls of tablets instead of only one or two. The outcome of this or injecting the drugs intravenously is an amphetamine psychosis. (14, p. 279) Authorities state: "The intravenous injection of large doses of amphetamines . . . is among the most disastrous forms of drug use yet devised." (14, p. 281)

One of the amphetamines, *methedrine* ("speed"), is particularly dangerous because it is commonly injected under the skin or directly into a vein, often causing rupturing of the blood vessels and death. Other hazards are infections like tetanus, syphilis, malaria, or hepatitis from dirty needles. The heavy user displays a potential for violence, paranoia, physical depletion, or bizarre behavior. Suicides are frequent during the periods of deep depression following withdrawal.

DEPRESSANTS

Barbiturates are depressants that decrease the activity of the central nervous system, usually producing sedation, intoxication, and sleep. They include drugs commonly used in sleeping pills, such as *Nembutal, Seconal, Amytal*, or *phenobarbital*. Some of these drugs—Nembutal and Seconal, for example—are short-acting, meaning the effects set in sooner and wear off sooner. Others, such as phenobarbital, are long-acting. (14, p. 245) Barbiturates are widely prescribed medicinally for insomnia, nervousness, or epilepsy. When taken as directed, in small doses, there is no evidence that the long-acting barbiturates are addictive. There is a greater chance of addiction with the short-acting drugs. (14, p. 248) All barbiturates are dangerous when abused because they develop total addiction: both physical and psychological dependence. Dosages must be increased as tolerance develops; an overdose may cause death.

Barbiturate abusers exhibit slurred speech, staggering gait, and sluggish reactions. They may be easily moved to tears or laughter, are emotionally erratic, and are frequently irritable and antagonistic. They are prone to stumble, to drop objects, and are often bruised or have cigarette burns.

When the abuser has become physically dependent, withdrawal symptoms become severe in about twenty-four hours. Increasing nervousness, headache, anxiety, muscle twitching, tremor, weakness, insomnia, nausea, and a sudden drop of blood pressure occur. Convulsions that can be fatal are an ever-present danger with barbiturate withdrawal. Delirium and hallucinations may develop. When barbiturates are taken in combination with alcohol or narcotics, the sedative effect is multiplied and can result in coma or death.

Tranquilizers such as *Miltown, Equanil, Placidyl, Librium,* and *Valium* are similar to barbiturates in their effects, for they too act upon the central nervous system. The hazards of Valium are supplied to physicians by the manufacturer, Roche Laboratories. The product information supplied reads in part:

Warnings: . . . patients receiving . . . Valium (diazepam) should be cautioned against engaging in hazardous occupations requiring complete mental alertness such as operating machinery or driving a motor vehicle. . . .

Since Valium (diazepam) has a central nervous system depressant effect, patients should be advised against the simultaneous ingestion of alcohol and other central nervous system depressant drugs. . . .

Physical and Psychological Dependence: Withdrawal symptoms (similar in character to those noted with barbiturates and alcohol) have occurred following abrupt discontinuance of diazepam (convulsions, tremor, abdominal and muscle cramps, vomiting and sweating). . . . Particularly addiction-prone individuals (such as drug addicts or alcoholics) should be under careful surveillance when receiving diazepam. . . . (135)

In short, these products, when abused, have the same dangers as barbiturates. (50) Because Valium is now the largest-selling drug in the United States (3 billion tablets were sold in 1974), and Librium is fourth (sales of more than 1 billion), there is considerable danger that some users will abuse the use of these drugs and become addicted. Until mid-1975, Valium and Librium were marketed free of federal controls. Now, however, prescriptions may be refilled only five times and may not be refilled at all after six months. (112, p. 156) In spite of these precautions, the Drug Enforcement Administration reported in 1977 that Valium was the drug most often abused by patients who had to be admitted to hospital emergency rooms for drug-related treatment. (24, p. 647) Fifty-nine percent of these patients were female; most had received their drugs through legal prescriptions. Drugs like Valium, Librium, and Darvon have been called the "opium of the masses," particularly because fully half of the most common drugs abused may be classified as tranquilizers, barbiturates, or nonbarbiturate sedatives. (24, p. 642)

Other common depressants used sometimes, but not as often abused, include bromides and sleep remedies such as Nytol. (33) When used in excess, however, they produce psychological dependence.

HALLUCINOGENS

Hallucinogens, or psychedelic drugs, include a broad range of substances that act on the central nervous system to alter perception and the state of consciousness. (1) The best known psychedelic drug is *LSD* (lysergic acid diethylamide), a syn-

Table 6–1.   Total number of 550 male users of psychedelics who used each type of drug.

Drug	Number of Males 20–30 Years of Age Who Had Used Drug
Mescaline	395
LSD	382
THC	298
Peyote	157
Psilocybin	156
PCP	108
STP	70
DMT	64
MDA	21
Others or don't know	40

Adapted from J. O'Donnell et al., *Young Men and Drugs: A Nationwide Survey*, NIDA Research Monograph 5 (Rockville, Md.: National Institute on Drug Abuse, 1976), p. 138.

thetic drug that must be prepared in a laboratory. Other hallucinogens include *peyote* and *mescaline* (derived from the peyote cactus plant), *psilocybin* (derived from a species of mushrooms), and four synthetics, *PCP* (phencyclidine), *STP* (also known as DOM—dimethoxymethylamphetamine), *DMT* (dimethyl tryptomine), and *MDA* (methylene dioxyamphetamine). DMT may also be prepared from natural plants that grow in the West Indies and parts of South America. STP and MDA also share some of the same characteristics of the amphetamines. (112, p. 161) A 1975 nationwide survey of drug usage among young men twenty to thirty years old revealed that mescaline and LSD had been used more frequently than any other psychedelic drugs. (97) Table 6–1 shows the total number of the 550 users of psychedelics who had used each specific type of drug. Note that THC, the active ingredient in marijuana, was also included in the list.

Each compound has users who claim unique effects from using a particular drug. In general, the drugs produce unpredictable results, including distortions of color, sound, time, and speed. A numbing of the senses in which colors are "heard" and sounds are "seen" is common. Some people experience "bad trips" that are intensely frightening and characterized by panic, terror, and psychosis. In one study of young, middle class male users, a majority of those who experienced a "bad trip" reported the feeling that "no one anywhere could help," that they were "no longer able to control their perceptions," or that they were afraid they had "destroyed part of themselves with the drug." (107, p. 8) Users have been driven to suicide, violence, or murder, or have been permanently hospitalized as psychotic.

LSD, or "acid," must be viewed with extreme suspicion because the drug is so powerful, its strengths are often unknown, and its effects are so unpredictable. A dose of only 50 to 200 micrograms (no larger than a pinpoint) may take the user on a "trip" for eight to sixteen hours. Hallucinations and other psychotic reactions sometimes occur days or months after the last dose, indicating possible brain damage. (18, p. 9-1; 25; 26; 87) Infants born of mothers who have taken

LSD during pregnancy have shown abnormalities of chromosomal structures. But whether LSD causes pathological chromosomal deviations and genetic defects in users is not definitely known. (31, 66) Users develop psychological, but not physical dependence.

Peyote and mescaline are milder hallucinogens than LSD (18, p. 9-2; 100), as is psilocybin. Peyote has been used for years by Navajo Indians, members of the Native American Church, as part of their religion. (9) DMT is a shorter-acting hallucinogen whose effects may come and go within the space of two hours, after a sudden and harsh onset. (63, p. 245) STP appeared on the psychedelic scene in the early spring of 1967. Doses of more than three milligrams can cause hallucinations lasting eight to ten hours. It is said to be 200 times more powerful than mescaline, but only one-tenth as potent as LSD. (120)

MARIJUANA

Marijuana (cannabis) is made from the dried leaves of the wild hemp plant. The plant is hardy and useful: it thrives in virtually every country of the world and produces a strong fiber for making cloth, canvas, and rope. The oil serves as a fast-drying paint base. For these reasons, United States farmers grew cannabis, and as late as World War II the federal government licensed production of cannabis in the South and the West. When federal law forced commercial production to cease, large fields went to weed. As a result, in 1969, a congressional investigating committee was told that in Nebraska alone, 156,000 acres of farmland were infested with marijuana "weed." (112, p. 31)

The principal active ingredient in cannabis is a chemical labeled delta-9-THC, which will be referred to here as simply THC. The THC content of cannabis varies, depending upon the variety. In recent years, new varieties have been produced containing larger and larger percentages of THC; these have more noticeable effects on users than did weaker strains. The THC content also varies with the part of the plant that is utilized. There is very little THC in the stem, roots, or seeds; the flowers and leaves contain more. *Ganja,* which comes from the flower tops and small leaves, ranges from 4 to 8 percent in THC content. *Hashish,* derived from the resin extracted from unfertilized female flowers, may have a THC content of 12 percent. *Hashish oil,* a concentration of resin, is stronger still (112, p. 32)

This variability in the THC content of different varieties of plants, and in the different parts and preparations made from them, has made it difficult for scientists to determine physical effects and psychological effects of marijuana use. Studies often yield conflicting results because of a lack of standardized procedures. What do the most up-to-date research studies show concerning marijuana?

Tolerance to cannabis, diminished response to a given repeated drug dose, has now been well substantiated. Users are able to ingest ever larger quantities without disruptive effects. (89, 123)

Physical dependency, as indicated by withdrawal symptoms, does not occur in ordinary users ingesting small or weak amounts. However, withdrawal symptoms can occur following discontinuance of high-dose chronic administration of THC. These symptoms include irritability, restlessness, decreased appetite, sleep disturbance, sweating, tremor, nausea, vomiting, and diarrhea. (123) It should be emphasized that these symptoms occur only after unusually high doses of orally administered THC under research-ward conditions. Psychological dependency may develop over a period of time and may make it difficult for chronic users to break the marijuana habit.

An increase in heart rate and reddening of the eyes are the most consistently reported physiological effects of marijuana. The heart rate increase is closely related to dosage. Marijuana use decreases exercise tolerance of those with heart disease (4, 103); therefore, use by those with already existing cardiovascular deficiencies appears unwise. (83, p. 4) However, the drug produces only minimal changes in heart function of young, healthy, subjects.

Clinical studies are beginning to point to possible harmful effects of marijuana on the lungs. (136) The smoke contains far stronger tars and irritants than do regular cigarettes; one "joint" has the equivalent of twenty cigarettes of tobacco, so heavy usage over a long period may harm the lungs. (141, p. 52) Exactly what the effect may be is not yet clear.

Because marijuana is an intoxicant, it impairs memory and concentration, alters time and space sense, impairs vision, and retards reaction time and performance abilities in manipulative and coordination tasks. (101) The more complex the task and the more acute the intoxication, the greater the degree of disruption. (26; 83, p. 5; 138) Drivers believe they are doing a good job of keeping in the correct lane when in fact they are weaving. One low-dose street joint can result in a significant decrease in driving skill; a strong dose of two joints may result in reduced performance for five to six hours. Therefore, driving under the influence of marijuana is hazardous; the degree of hazard is related to the degree of intoxication. (73) The simultaneous use of alcohol and marijuana is more dangerous than that of either substance alone. (83, p. 5)

No conclusive evidence exists yet regarding chromosomal and genetic damage produced by marijuana. (83, p. 6) Similarly, evidence is still insufficient to show that heavy usage of hashish causes brain damage. (106, 123) There is some evidence that chronic cannabis use is associated with reduced levels of the male hormone, testosterone, in the blood stream. (123) However, clear causal relationships have not been established. There is also some doubt as to the biological significance of these findings; despite suspicion that decreasing testosterone levels may lower the sperm count or produce problems of impotence in males, no studies have as yet either positively confirmed or denied the role of marijuana in this problem. (83, 91, 130, 141) Because the effects of marijuana on pregnant women and human fetuses have not been sufficiently established, most doctors strongly advise against smoking pot during pregnancy. (95)

The long-term effects of chronic cannabis usage on behavior are only partially known. It is certain, however, that the overall effect depends upon the level and length of usage. Prolonged cannabis psychosis has been reported in Eastern literature under conditions of unusually heavy use. Studies in the United States have not isolated the causative role of marijuana or detected evidence for cannabis-related psychosis. (57, 90) Foreign observers have argued that cannabis diminishes intellectual performance, motivation, and interest in work and other conventional activities. (83, p. 6) But these studies were of chronic usage of higher and stronger doses of the drug. Studies of American college student performance have generally failed to prove impaired intellectual performance, lower grade point averages, or diminished educational achievement. (83, p. 7) There is evidence that marijuana users may have more difficulty in deciding career goals and may more often drop out of college to reassess their goals. (16) But this may be due to the fact that chronic users may more often be the kind of people who reject the work ethic and competitive achievement. It is difficult, therefore, to isolate the effects that marijuana has on motivation from other factors that may exert influence. There is some evidence that marijuana administration coupled with monetary reward for work performance results in a decline in productivity with heavier marijuana consumption. (17, 101, 123)

There is more positive evidence that daily and heavy usage among young adolescents interferes with school work and performance. The so-called burn-out finds it difficult to concentrate on what is happening in the classroom, to remember his lessons, or to do homework effectively, so grades suffer. Also, some of those who are already doing poorly in school may turn to drugs. Once on drugs, they often drop out of school completely. (34)

Research is also revealing some positive and therapeutic uses of marijuana. The usefulness of cannabis in treating glaucoma by reducing internal eye pressures has been confirmed. (61) The use of THC in reducing nausea and vomiting of cancer patients receiving chemotherapy shows unusual promise. (110) Because THC dilates pulmonary air passages, its usefulness in treating asthmatics has been demonstrated. (124) Marijuana is a lung irritant, however, so use of aerosolized THC seems prudent. (83, p. 9)

In the years ahead, more important questions in relation to marijuana use will be answered. In the meantime, pressure continues from some sources to make marijuana legal. (14; 18, p. 536) Those in favor of legalization, however, are in the minority in the United States. A 1977 Gallup poll revealed that less than one-third of all persons interviewed thought that the use of marijuana should be made legal. (39, p. 1077) Among those aged eighteen to twenty-four, opinion for and against legalization was fairly evenly divided. (39, p. 1078) In 1978 the public was asked whether there should be more acceptance of marijuana usage. Three out of four surveyed said it would not be welcome. Among those aged eighteen to twenty-five, opinion was fairly evenly divided. (40, p. 191) Even among youths, therefore, there is no unanimity on the question.

INHALANTS

The solvent fumes from plastic glue, gasoline, paint thinner, and other hydrocarbons are sniffed to give an intoxicating effect. (26) Blurring of vision, ringing ears, slurred speech, and staggering are common, followed by drowsiness, stupor, and even unconsciousness for about an hour. Upon recovery, the individual usually does not recall what happened during the period of intoxication. Accidental deaths while intoxicated from glue sniffing include suffocation from a plastic bag over the head and falls from high places. (18, p. 331) Although reports of damage to the kidneys, liver, heart, blood, and nervous system from sniffing glue with a toluene base have not been completely substantiated by research evidence, their truth remains a possibility. (7; 18, p. 330; 45)

PATTERNS AND INTENSITY OF USE

The National Commission on Marihuana and Drug Abuse has identified five patterns of drug use. (35, p. 94)

Experimental use is defined as the short-term, nonpatterned trial of one or more drugs, with a maximum frequency of ten times per drug. It is motivated primarily by curiosity or by a desire to experience new feelings. (35, p. 95) Users in this category feel they are in control of their lives, rarely use any drug on a daily basis, and tend not to use drugs to escape the pressure of personal problems. (11, p. 1471)

Social-recreational use occurs in social settings among friends or acquaintances who desire to share an experience. Social and recreational use tends to vary in frequency, intensity, and duration, but not to escalate in either frequency or intensity to patterns of uncontrolled use. Users typically do not use addictive drugs like heroin; they are therefore able to exercise control over their behavior. (35, p. 96)

Circumstantial-situational use is motivated by the desire to achieve a known and anticipated effect. This would include the student who takes stimulants to stay awake or the person who takes sedatives to relieve tension and go to sleep. Paton and Kandel identify four psychological conditions that lead to illicit drug use by adolescents: a depressed mood, normlessness (not having definite values, opinions, or rules to live by), social isolation, and low self-esteem. (98, p. 190) The greatest danger from this type of use is that the person will become accustomed to drug use to solve problems and ultimately escalate to intensified use. (35, p. 96)

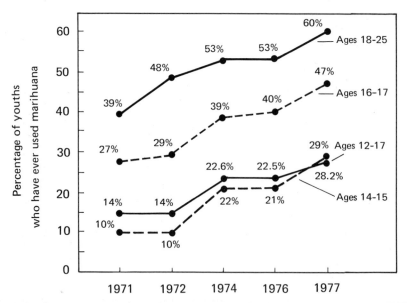

Figure 6–2. Increase in marihuana use among youths, 1971–1977. (Adapted from H. I. Abelson et al., *National Survey on Drug Abuse: 1977* [Rockville, Md.: National Institute on Drug Abuse, 1977].)

Intensified drug use is generally a long-term pattern of using drugs at least once daily to achieve relief from a persistent problem or stressful situation. Drug use becomes a customary activity of daily life, with people ordinarily remaining socially and economically integrated in the life of the community. Some change in functioning may occur depending on the frequency, intensity, and amount of use. (35, p. 97)

Compulsive drug use is use at both high frequency and high intensity of relatively long duration, producing physiological or psychological dependence, with discontinuance resulting in physiological discomfort or psychological stress. Motivation to continue comes from the physical or psychological comfort or relief obtained by using the drug. Users in this category include not only the street "junkie" or skid-row alcoholic, but also the opiate-dependent physician, the barbiturate-dependent housewife, or the alcohol-dependent businessman. (35, p. 98)

All research studies show that the most frequently used drugs in the United States are alcohol, tobacco, and marijuana, in that order. Figure 6–2 shows the increase in the use of marijuana among youths during the years 1971 through 1977. (2)

A nationwide sample of high school seniors showed the following lifetime illicit usage figures: (71)

90 percent had used alcohol.

75 percent had used cigarettes.

24.4 percent had used stimulants.

18.4 percent had used tranquilizers.

17.3 percent had used other sedatives.

15.6 percent had used hallucinogens.

14.1 percent had used cocaine.

13.0 percent had used inhalants.

12.6 percent had used opiates (other than heroin).

2.0 percent had used heroin.

These data indicate that drug use among high school seniors is not limited to alcohol, tobacco, and marijuana. (71) A number of other potentially harmful and dangerous drugs are used as well. (24, p. 640)

It is significant that youths are trying drugs at increasingly younger ages. It is not unusual for children eight to ten years old to use drugs. An elementary school official in Washington, D.C., complained that he had not been able to keep one third-grader from smoking marijuana every day at recess. (34) Threats of expulsion did not help because the child insisted he couldn't break the habit. He did refuse to share his cigarettes with classmates because, he said, "the habit is dangerous." (34, p. 31)

SOURCES OF SUPPLY

Youths report little difficulty in obtaining drugs. When they first try any drug, they usually obtain it as a gift from a friend. The one exception is heroin, which is usually purchased even the first time. (97, p. 62) Drugs that continue to be

Table 6–2.   Methods by which drugs were obtained by young men, 20–30 years of age, nationwide survey, 1974–1975.

Method by Which Drug Was Usually Obtained	Percentages of All Occasions Drugs Were Obtained						
	Mari-juana	Psyche-delics	Stimu-lants	Seda-tives	Heroin	Opiates	Cocaine
Free, as a gift	48	30	32	42	27	36	43
Bought from friend or dealer	50	69	63	46	71	41	55
From respondent's own prescription	0	0	3	8	0	15	*
From a forged prescription	0	0	1	*	0	1	*
Stole the drug	*	0	*	2	1	1	*
Grew or made own supply	1	*	*	0	0	*	*
Some other way	*	1	1	2	1	6	1

* Less than 0.5 percent.
Adapted from J. O'Donnell et al., *Young Men and Drugs: A Nationwide Survey*, NIDA
    Research Monograph 5 (Rockville, Md.: National Institute on Drug Abuse, 1976).

used are usually purchased from a friend or dealer, although friends still offer drugs as gifts on a third to a half of all the occasions when drugs are used. (97, p. 62) As can be seen by Table 6–2, stimulants, sedatives, and opiates are often obtained from a person's own prescription or from forged prescriptions. (97, p. 62) Sedatives, heroin, and other opiates are the drugs most frequently stolen, primarily because they are the most physically addictive.

Studies at the University of Maine refute the common stereotype of sinister adult drug pushers hanging around school to persuade innocent youths to try "dope." Students most commonly obtain drugs from a best friend or school classmate, or occasionally from dropouts who come on school grounds to sell drugs to students. (23)

The place where drugs are used depends somewhat on the type of drug. Marijuana, LSD, and other hallucinogens were most frequently used by University of Maine students in a social setting with one or more close friends, and less frequently with larger groups of people or with a fiancé or steady boyfriend or girlfriend. (23, p. 14) Stimulant-depressants and narcotics, however, were frequently used when the person was alone. (23, p. 14)

CORRELATIONS WITH DRUG USE AMONG MALES

A number of factors correlate with drug use. A 1975 nationwide survey of drug use among men twenty to thirty years of age showed the following correlations.

Greater percentages of blacks than whites had ever used marijuana, psychedelics, sedatives, heroin, and cocaine. Slightly greater percentages of whites than blacks had ever used alcohol or stimulants. (97, p. 15)

Residents of cities with a population of over one million showed the highest percentages of drug use, with the lowest percentage of use among those from towns with less than 2,500. For example, 70 percent of men from cities of over one million had used marijuana. The figure dropped to around 60 percent in smaller cities, and to 43 percent in places under 2,500. (97, p. 18)

Drug use tended to be higher among unemployed or part-time employees than among those working thirty or more hours per week. (97, p. 22)

The lower the educational level achieved, the higher the drug use. Drug use tended to be higher among those who attended college but dropped out than among those who were still in school. Among those remaining in college, drug use was higher among social science, fine arts, and humanities majors than among those in other major fields. (97, p. 21)

There was a definite correlation between family status and drug use. The percentage of those using drugs was lowest for married students, next lowest for men living with parents, higher for those living independently, and highest for those living with women to whom they were not married. (97, p. 22)

Men who were less conventional in terms of a variety of indicators of conventionality tended to show a higher incidence of drug usage. (97, p. viii)

Veterans, whether they served only in the United States, overseas other than Vietnam, or in Vietnam, showed no higher rates of current drug use than non-veterans. Their lifetime use of marijuana or heroin was slightly higher, however. (97, p. viii)

CORRELATIONS WITH DRUG USE AMONG MALE AND FEMALE COLLEGE STUDENTS

A study of drug use on two campuses of the University of Illinois showed some differences between men and women in drugs used. Greater percentages of females than males used prescription pain preparations and tranquilizers. Greater percentages of males than females used psychedelics. Almost an equal percentage used marijuana. (78) In relation to marital status, greater percentages of single persons used marijuana, psychedelics, cocaine, and heroin, but greater percentages of married persons used prescription pain preparations and tranquilizers. Use of amphetamines, psychedelics, and marijuana increased from the freshman to the junior year, then dropped. Use of alcohol, tobacco, and tranquilizers tended to increase between the freshman and senior years, and to remain at a permanently high level. (78) There was also a relationship between religious preference and drug use. The findings here agree with other studies in pointing to a considerably higher use of drugs among students who are Jewish or who express no religious preference than among Catholics and Protestants. (44, 51, 78) The outstanding finding in relation to race and ethnicity was the low rate of use of all types of drugs by the Chinese and Japanese. Like other studies, this one also showed a higher rate of drug use among students in liberal arts and sciences and in architecture and art, and the lowest rate for engineering students. Business administration and education students ranged somewhere in between. (51, 78, 105)

Data on living arrangements pointed to some clear relationships with drug use. The greatest exposure to drugs occurred among students living off campus in an apartment. The lowest exposure was among students living at home with parents. Somewhat greater rates of use, but still low, were exhibited by those living with spouse or in a college dorm. Fraternity or sorority house residents

Table 6–3.   Social profiles of University of Illinois undergraduate students at high
and low risk of drug use.

Social Characteristic	High Risk	Low Risk
Marital status	Single	Married
Class	Sophomore or junior	Freshman or senior
Age	19–25	17–18, or 26 and over
Religion	No preference, or "other"	Catholic or Protestant
Race-ethnicity	—	Oriental
College (major)	LAS or A & A	Engineering
Father's social status	Upper middle class	Blue collar
Living arrangements	Shared apartment	Live with parents or spouse
Dating patterns	—	Date infrequently
Grade point average	—	4.5–5.0 (highest)

Adapted from L. Levy, "Drug Use on Campus: Prevalence and Social Characteristics of
Collegiate Drug Users on Campuses of the University of Illinois," *Drug Forum* 2 (1973):
141–171. Used by permission.

were somewhere in between. (78) These findings were in accord with previous
reports. (5) It was found also that the higher the father's social status as measured
by education, income, and occupation, the higher the rate of drug use. (78)
Other studies have also pointed out the significance of peer influences. Drug
usage is significantly and substantially higher among students who admire and
identify with other drug users. (44, pp. 23, 27)

One of the questions frequently asked is whether or not drug use is related
to grade point average. In this study at the University of Illinois, the highest
scholastic achievers were low in experience with drugs, with the exception of
tranquilizers, which they used with higher frequency. This pattern did not hold
true for intermediate and low levels of achievement, however, where drug-use
patterns were more similar. (78) Table 6–3 summarizes the data from the University of Illinois study.

Among other differences between those who use drugs and those who do
not, it has been found that users of certain types of drugs tend to be less conventional in their social orientation and life style. For example, one study of
female drug users at West Virginia University showed that 75 percent of drug
users reported having sex relations with four or more partners. Thirty-eight
percent had full coitus with ten or more partners. This was in sharp contrast to
the nonusers' group, in which no one reported relations with as many as four
partners. (80, p. 195) One must not assume from this study that all drug users
are sexually promiscuous. When those who used only marijuana were analyzed
separately, it was found that these females were no more promiscuous than those
who did not use any drugs. However, among other drug users and multiple drug
users, the number of sex partners correlated more highly with drug use than did
any other factor measured. (80, p. 194)

Other research tends to emphasize that collegiate marijuana users tend to be
more sociable, more socially skilled but politically unconventional, and more impulsive, self-expressive, open-minded, nonconforming, and independent in decision making. (41, 44, 62, 93) This does not mean they are social dropouts. Their

grades may be slightly above average. But it does mean they are less interested in conformity and more interested in personal freedom and self-expression. Many use drugs because they do not feel the drugs are harmful. The highest student users of marijuana are also those who report higher levels of psychological distress. (44, p. 27) Other comparisons of undergraduate marijuana users with nonusers have found users more alienated socioculturally and more hostile toward generally accepted values, as indicated by attitudes toward law, government, marriage, and the work ethic. (74, 75) As use of marijuana spreads, however, and even conservative students use it, its popularity will be less and less associated with a counterculture. (83, p. 2)

DRUG USE IN MIDDLE SCHOOL AND HIGH SCHOOL

For a number of years, studies of drug use among adolescents have shown a steady increase in the percentage of youths using drugs. This does not mean that these increases will necessarily continue, however. One revealing study of marijuana use among male high school students in San Mateo County, California, shows the tendency for increases to level off. (10) As can be seen in Table 6–4, there has been a leveling off in this county of the percentages of students who are using marijuana. Because San Mateo County is adjacent to San Francisco, it had an earlier exposure to the counterculture movement and to associated drug use, so that the plateau in the growth of marijuana use may have already reached its limit. (83, p. 14)

A survey of drug use among 25,000 youths in elementary and high schools from a cross section of communities in Maine reveals that use will vary depending upon whether drugs have recently been introduced and their use is still on the rise, has already peaked, or is declining. (96, p. 5) This study also shows that the extent of drug usage will vary tremendously from community to community,

Table 6–4.   Percentage of marijuana use among male San Mateo County high school students.

	One or More Uses in Past Year		Ten or More Uses in Past Year		Fifty or More Uses in Past Year	
	9th grade	*12th grade*	*9th grade*	*12th grade*	*9th grade*	*12th grade*
1968	27	45	14	26	NA	NA
1969	35	50	20	34	NA	NA
1970	34	51	20	34	11	22
1971	44	59	26	43	17	32
1972	44	61	27	45	16	32
1973	51	61	32	45	20	32
1974	49	62	30	47	20	34
1975	49	64	30	45	20	31
1976	48	61	27	42	17	30
1977	48	65	27	48	16	34

Adapted from L. Blackford, *Student Drug Use Surveys: San Mateo County, California, 1968–1977,* San Mateo, Calif.: Department of Public Health and Welfare, 1977. Used by permission.

even in the same state. No appreciable difference was found in drug usage between the public and the parochial schools of Maine, but there were wide variations among schools. The study also showed that vacationing summer populations had a major impact on the extent of drug use in Maine communities. (96, p. 6)

A study of marijuana use among suburban high school students in Westchester County, New York, showed the following characteristics of those who use drugs versus those who do not: (126)

Those who liked school were less likely to use marijuana than those who disliked it.

Those who said they worked hard in school were less likely to use marijuana than those who said they did not work hard.

Those who were pleased with their teachers and/or felt that their teachers were pleased with them were less likely to use marijuana than those who did not like their teachers and/or felt their teachers did not like them.

Those who felt that doing well in school would help them get ahead in life were less likely to use marijuana than those who did not feel this way about education and who didn't care about getting ahead.

Students who aspired to become professionals (doctors, scientists, lawyers, etc.) were less likely to use marijuana than those who had no plans at all.

Those who aspired to be athletes were least likely of all students to use marijuana. Those aspiring to be artists were the most likely to use the drug. Those aspiring to be laborers or tradespeople were not as prone to use marijuana as were those of most other groups (except athletes).

The authors of the study conclude: "If members of a given system are dissatisfied with its many features, are uninvolved and uncommitted to its basic aims and expectations, they will find it easier to engage in behavior disapproved of by the system than those who are satisfied, involved, and committed to its basic aims." (126, p. 16) One study found that drug use among Mexican-American secondary students from the lower Rio Grande Valley was lower than among Anglo secondary students from Houston. (56) These data contradict the popular assumption that students from minority groups are always the greatest drug abusers.

WHY DRUGS ARE FIRST USED

Why do adolescents first use drugs? *The overwhelming majority try drugs out of curiosity, to see what they are like.* (23, p. 18; 76; 96, p. 8) Apparently this is a very strong motive for trying a drug. Adolescents have heard what different drugs do and decide to try them. For example, the hallucinogens are supposed to release a store of elaborate, rich, and colorful fantasies; marijuana will reduce ego controls and provide an experience of intoxication. If adolescents are more attracted by the promises of a drug than repelled by its potential harm, they may be led to experiment.

Another reason for trying drugs is fun or sensual pleasure. (23, p. 18; 110, p. 30) Users do it because they are seeking an exciting experience. Adolescents are growing up in a fun-oriented culture that emphasizes the need and value of having a good time. If smoking grass is fun, this becomes a strong motive for its use.

Another aspect of having fun is to experience sensual pleasure. This pleasure may be sexual, and many adolescents feel that pot makes the exploration of sex less inhibited and more delightful. (49) The pleasure motive may be in seeking an increased sensitivity of touch or taste. A marijuana party or LSD trip also may involve a period when everyone "gets the hungries" and explores as wide a variety of taste delights as is available. (110, p. 31)

Another strong motive for trying drugs is the social pressure to be like friends or to be a part of a social group. (23, p. 18; 76) Adolescents say: "Many of my friends tried it and I didn't want to be different," or "Everybody is doing it," or "My friends urged me to try it, and I didn't want them to think I was chicken." This motive is especially strong among immature adolescents who are seeking to belong to a crowd or gang. (126) Some youths gain recognition by being far more daring than others, by taking chances that others won't take. In this case, the pressure is to go beyond what others are doing to show them how much more grown-up they are.

One important motive for trying drugs is to relieve tensions, anxieties, pressures, to escape from problems, or to be able to deal with or face them. (23, p. 18; 96, p. 8) Students say:

"I needed to get away from the problems that were bugging me."
"I felt tired and depressed and needed a lift."
"I had to stay awake to study for exams."
"When I'm on grass, I have more self-confidence and can do anything."

Those who use drugs as an escape from tension, anxiety, problems, or reality, or to make up for personal inadequacies are likely to become entwined in some drug habit. (26, p. 109) These are the emotionally immature who are insecure, passive, dependent persons, who find life frustrating and anxiety provoking, who tend to withdraw from active involvement as much as possible, or who lean on others, or drugs, for help.

There are those users whose primary motive for trying a drug is to gain self-awareness, increased awareness of others, more religious insight, or to become more creative. (55, 110) The sense of increased awareness or greater creativity may be more imagined than real, but the person believes that the drug provides the awareness. There is the appeal that the drug has the potential to create a mystical experience, to give crucial insights into personality problems, emotional hang-ups, or a new vision of life in terms of loving relationships. This is an especially strong motive for using the psychedelics.

COMPULSIVE DRUG USE

The reasons for adolescents' first using drugs and for continuing to use them are sometimes different. Those who continue to use nonaddictive drugs as a means of trying to solve emotional problems become psychologically dependent upon the drugs. (18, p. 4-2) Drugs become a means of finding security, comfort, or relief. When individuals become psychologically dependent upon drugs that are also physiologically addicting—drugs such as alcohol, barbiturates, and heroin—dependence is secondarily reinforced by the desire to avoid the pain and distress of physical withdrawal. (35, p. 97)

The need to use drugs excessively originates within the families in which children grow up. (118) It has been found that adolescents who use marijuana regularly are more likely to have parents who drink excessively and/or use other psychotropic drugs; they are more likely to come from broken homes or not to live with both parents. (125, 127) Chronic users find family relationships rewarding and meaningful less often, experience parental deprivation more often, are more dissatisfied with parents, and find the family salient less often than do those who don't use marijuana at all or less often. (125, 127) The likelihood of marijuana use also increases when parental control is excessive and unfair, especially when not accompanied by warmth, or when parents show indifference and rejection. (125) Sixty-nine percent of male drug addicts in one study said they had gotten their own way at home whenever they wanted; many indicated there was "nobody around to stop me." (79, p. 9) In nearly every case, drug-addicted males had a negative relationship with their father, or no father with whom to have a relationship. (79, p. 14) This and other studies indicate that deficient socialization and inadequate parenting contribute to drug use. (76) In another study males who regularly used drugs remembered their mothers as permissive and granting a great deal of autonomy, and their fathers as less accepting, less child-centered, and more hostilely detached than nonusers, experimental users, or recreational users. (29, p. 477)

A study of public secondary school students from eighteen high schools in New York State revealed the following correlations. Students who started to use illicit drugs:

Lacked closeness to parents.
Had parents who used authoritarian control in discipline.
Had parents who used hard liquor and psychoactive drugs.
Lacked intimate ties with a best friend.
Had a history of marijuana use.
Exhibited signs of depression.
Were more often involved in delinquency than nonusers. (72, p. 29)

Another study of the family relationships of adolescent drug users in comparison to nonusers revealed that the families of users:

More often treated the adolescent as a scapegoat for family problems.
Showed inferior ability in arriving at decisions.
Evidenced fewer positive communications among members.
Allowed less freedom for open expression of opinions.
Were less cooperative with one another. (42)

Overall, the family relationships of adolescents who abused drugs were similar to those of adolescents who were emotionally disturbed. (42)

The net effect of these types of family situations is to create personality problems that cause individuals to be more likely to turn to drugs. Numerous other studies correlate drug addiction and dependency with such personality factors as a high incidence of psychotic disorders, a tendency toward schizophrenia, (85) more hysterical-obsessive personality traits, (140) high scores on psychopathic scales, (16) and efforts to protect oneself against homosexual urges. (48) An examination of 250 youths between eighteen and twenty-six, as part of a research project in the Haight-Ashbury district of San Francisco, showed that many individuals exhibited gross deficits in ego functioning. (102) They used drugs to remedy apathy, boredom, depression, and lack of capacity for intimacy. (3, p. 291) Regular drug users often show elevated hostility, (92) a preference for passive life styles, and little purpose in life. (115) Most normal adolescents experience anxieties, tensions, fears, and confusion about their identity and values, but some do not have the inner resources to master these normal difficulties. Lacking the capacity to solve these problems and unable to rely on early family relationships or current friendships for help, they turn to drugs to lessen the pain and conflict, as a substitute for meaningful human relationships. (3, p. 289)

Tobacco and Smoking

INCIDENCE

Today over half of all junior high school students and two-thirds of all senior high school students have smoked cigarettes. (35, p. 81) About one-third of senior high school students are regular smokers. (35, p. 81; 108) More than half of all youths who smoke have their first cigarette before the age of twelve; 85 percent who smoke do so before they are fifteen. (14, p. 236; 111) The incidence of cigarette smoking increases with age and reaches a peak of not quite half the youth population in the eighteen to thirty-five age bracket. (40, p. 80) Overall, there are almost as many female as male youths who smoke, but there are still greater percentages of adult males than females who do. (35, p. 47) This high incidence of cigarette smoking continues in spite of anticigarette campaigns that emphasize the dangers of smoking. One recent study showed that 99 percent of children and youths aged seven to fourteen believed that smoking can cause cancer. (111)

WHY ADOLESCENTS START SMOKING

If youths are aware of the dangers of smoking, why do they start and continue to smoke in ever increasing numbers? Typical answers of youths include:

"Because the rest of my crowd smokes."
"It makes me look big."
"To feel sophisticated."
"I was curious."
"Because I was tense and nervous."
"Because I enjoy smoking."
"Because I wasn't supposed to."

Fundamentally, these reasons are in accord with sociological and psychological explanations. *Adolescents are brainwashed from the early years of childhood by the huge advertising industry.* Cigarette smoking is identified with masculinity, independence, nature, athletic prowess, beauty, youth, intelligence, sex appeal, sociability, wealth, and the good life. Every conceivable gimmick and scheme has been used by the advertising industry to encourage smoking. The appeal is always to the emotions and to the desire for acceptability, popularity, datability, and sexual allure. The sultry woman's voice, the society setting, the back-to-nature promises, the tattooed hairy hands: all promise rewards the teen-ager seeks. (27)

Youths are also imitating their parents and other adults who smoke. There is little hope of changing teenage smoking habits unless the habits of parents and older (perhaps adult) siblings are changed. One of the primary reasons so many adolescents smoke is that they see adults smoking; they are striving to imitate adult behavior and find peer approval. (88)

Some adolescents start smoking because of peer-group pressure. This is apparent in the early years of adolescence. Those who are the first to exhibit adult habits are admired; those who do not smoke are "chicken"; those who have not learned to inhale are missing all the fun. Adoption of the smoking habit starts as an act of conformity to peers as well as to parents and advertisers.

Early smoking may be linked also to self-esteem and status needs of some youths. Often, adolescents who smoke do so as a compensatory device because they have fallen behind their age equals in school, because they do not participate in extracurricular activities, or because they are taking the less scholastically demanding course of school work. Children of lower class parents often begin smoking earlier than children of middle class parents. One study at Harvard College revealed that upwardly mobile middle class students were more likely to be smokers than upper class students. (64) There is also some evidence to suggest that male smokers are physically less masculine than nonsmokers, and that the adolescent boy starts smoking to prove his masculinity. (113)

WHY ADOLESCENTS CONTINUE TO SMOKE

Once they begin to smoke, youths continue for the same reasons that adults do.

Relief of tension. Heavy smokers tend to be overly tense and restless people.

Development of an unconscious habit. A reflex action develops that is hard to break: the action of reaching for a cigarette.

Association with sociability and pleasure. Smokers associate the activity with after-dinner coffee, conversation, a social gathering, or pleasant surroundings.

Compulsion for oral activity. This oral hypothesis states that smoking is an attempt to regain the passive pleasure of infantile nursing. One study revealed that Harvard students who found it easiest to give up smoking were those who had had the longest period of breast feeding in infancy. (86)

Physical addiction to nicotine. Numerous studies now support the con-clusion that smokers not only become psychologically dependent upon smoking, but also physically addicted. (37, 67, 77, 109) This finding is based upon several facts. First, the body develops a physical craving for nicotine that can be allevi-ated by injecting nicotine or by increasing the nicotine content of cigarettes smoked. (37)

Second, only about 2 percent of smokers are able to use cigarettes intermittently or occasionally. (109) The typical pattern of nicotine use is not only daily but hourly. According to Russell:

> The level of nicotine in the brain is crucial. . . . It is probable that nicotine is present in the brain . . . within a minute or two of beginning to smoke, but by 20–30 minutes after completing the cigarette most of this nicotine has left the brain for other organs. This is just about the period when the dependent smoker needs another cigarette. The smoking pattern of the dependent smoker who inhales a cigarette every 30 minutes of his waking life (a pack and a half per day) is such as to insure the maintenance of a high level of nicotine in his brain. (109, p. 8)

Third, withdrawal of nicotine produces withdrawal symptoms including nervousness, drowsiness, anxiety, lightheadedness, headaches, energy loss, fatigue, constipation or diarrhea, insomnia, dizziness, sweating, cramps, tremor, and palpitations. (14, p. 225; 77)

Fourth, smokers become tolerant of nicotine. Youthful smokers can tolerate only a few puffs. Gradually, they can tolerate one, then two, then three or more cigarettes. If they exceed their tolerance level, they show signs of acute anxiety. As tolerance levels rise, smokers may reach levels that would have been disastrous earlier in their smoking career. (109)

Fifth, when the supply of cigarettes is curtailed, smokers evidence unreasonable, antisocial behavior similar to that of heroin addicts. When the tobacco ration for men in Germany was cut to two packs per month after World War II, it was noted that

> the majority of habitual smokers preferred to do without food even under extreme conditions of nutrition rather than to forgo tobacco. Thus, when food rations in prisoner-of-war camps were down to 900–1,000 calories, smokers were still willing to barter their food rations for tobacco. Of 300 German civilians questioned, 256 had obtained tobacco at the black market. . . . In disregard of considerations of personal dignity, conventional decorum, and esthetic-hygienic feelings, cigarette butts were picked up out of the street dirt by people who . . . would in other circumstances have felt disgust at such contact. Smokers also condescended to beg for tobacco, but not for other things. . . .
> 80 percent of those questioned declared that it felt worse to do without nicotine than without alcohol. (16, p. 226)

Sixth, follow-up studies of smokers who have quit show a high relapse rate. At the end of forty-eight months, more than 80 percent of those who had successfully stopped were smoking again. (67) This percentage does not include those who entered smoking clinics but were not able to stop.

The conclusion is that cigarette smoking is a highly addictive habit that is most difficult to break. Once started, it is not a habit that the majority of smokers can break by an effort of the will. One answer in the future may be to offer smokers a chemically equivalent nicotine substitute. (16, p. 243)

KEEPING ADOLESCENTS FROM STARTING

The best answer is to keep adolescents from starting in the first place. A number of studies have been conducted to determine the most effective way to keep adolescents from starting to smoke and to help more of them to stop once they have started. (See Reference 29 for a complete discussion.) Some of the most important suggestions include the following proposals:

Antismoking education should avoid extreme scare tactics that attempt to frighten adolescents into stopping. It is all right to point to the facts, such as the relationship between smoking and lung cancer, respiratory illnesses, and cardiovascular disease, or the dangers of smoking during pregnancy, or while taking oral contraceptives. (52) Moderate anxiety can be especially useful in preventing adolescents from starting. But extreme scare tactics lead adolescents to deny that smoking will cause physical harm and to reject the teachings of the person who is trying to scare them. (65, p. 284) Research shows that teachers who are against smoking are more effective in antismoking education than are teachers who are neutral. (128, p. 251) Teachers need to take a stand, but not to use extremely negative approaches, especially those that exaggerate.

The primary appeal should be positive. The program should appeal to adolescents' vanity, their pride, their belief in themselves, and their sense of achievement. They should be encouraged to establish control over their own behavior.

Adolescents should be told all the facts as honestly as possible. A program should avoid half-truths and make every effort to avoid creating a credibility gap. (65, p. 285) Even when adolescents have the facts about the hazards of smoking, some start or continue to smoke anyway because of the tendency to feel: "Lung cancer or other illnesses won't happen to me." (116, 117, 128) Presenting factual information on the hazards doesn't often change behavior, but it usually has considerable influence on knowledge and attitudes. (128, p. 252)

Efforts should enlist the help of student leaders and of students themselves. An antismoking campaign at Central High School in Great Falls, Montana, was sponsored by the students' cancer club. When the campaign ended, the whole cultural climate of the high school had changed from prosmoking to antismoking and most of the students had pledged themselves not to smoke. (65, p. 287) A research study at the University of New Hampshire showed that nonsmokers suffered negative physiological and psychological symptoms from tobacco smoke pollution in public places, which suggests that schools have a responsibility to limit smoking. (116, 117) However, even students who don't smoke feel that their friends who do ought to have a place provided by the school, primarily because they feel the decision to smoke is a personal one to be regulated by the individual, not by the school. (108, p. 524)

A program should begin early, when the child is young, and continue periodically over a span of years. A recurring program is more effective than a single mass exposure. Ten percent of children in the United States are regular smokers by age twelve. (41, p. 46) Education laws in New York State require that antismoking education be started after grade eight. This is too late. Fourth or fifth grade is a better time to begin.

Students should be helped to discover and analyze their own inner, hidden, emotional, or social reasons for smoking and to deal with these problems so that the smoking crutch will not be needed.

No one teaching method can be considered best. A comparison of didactic approaches, group discussion, psychological persuasion, and a combination of all three showed that the didactic approach was most successful in changing behavior, the combination approach was best at improving knowledge, and psychological persuasion had the most effect on attitudes. (128, p. 251)

Antismoking education programs have been largely unsuccessful in changing smoking behavior among adolescents who already smoke. The percentage who now smoke is similar to the number in 1970. But if antismoking education can be given in elementary grades before students start smoking, the program can be effective in reducing the number who begin. (108)

Alcohol and Excessive Drinking

DRINKING IN HIGH SCHOOL

Studies of junior high, senior high, and college students reveal that a substantial proportion of adolescents drink. Findings from 1974 and later surveys indicate that among seventh graders, 63 percent of boys and 54 percent of girls have had a drink. (131, 132) As Figure 6–3 indicates, the proportion of youths who have ever had a drink increases each grade to 93 percent of boys and 87 percent of girls in the twelfth grade. (132, p. 7) Given that drinking is a common practice in the American life style, it is no surprise that a vast majority of adolescents have been introduced to alcohol. (133, p. 5)

It is not drinking as such, but frequent drinking that creates problems. Fifty-five percent of parents in a 1977 Gallup poll said they believed drinking to be a serious problem among youths in their communities. (39, p. 1236) The teenagers surveyed said they considered alcohol abuse to be one of the three most important problems facing their own generation. In addition, when asked why

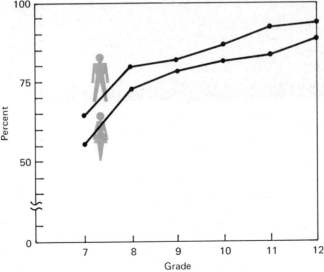

Figure 6–3.   Percentage of teenagers who have ever had a drink of wine, beer, or spirits, by school grade and sex, U.S.A., 1974. (From U.S. Department of Health, Education and Welfare, Public Health Service, *Alcohol and Health*, Second Report to the U.S. Congress, 1974 [Rockville, Md.: National Institute on Alcohol Abuse and Alcoholism, 1975], p. 8.)

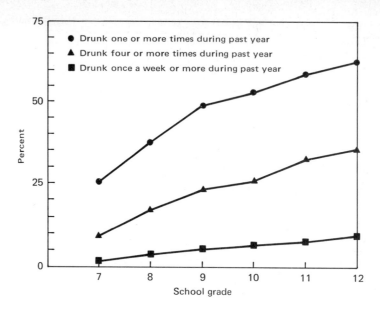

Figure 6–4. Percentage of teenage drinkers who report getting drunk or very high, by frequency and school grade, U.S.A., 1974. (From U.S. Department of Health, Education and Welfare, Public Health Service, *Alcohol and Health,* Second Report to the U.S. Congress, 1974 [Rockville, Md.: National Institute on Alcohol Abuse and Alcoholism, 1975], p. 21.)

almost half the road accidents and deaths in the United States involve drivers under the age of twenty-two, adolescents cited three main causes: drinking, reckless driving, and drugs. (39, p. 1236) In a 1978 Gallup poll, 26 percent of youths aged eighteen to twenty-four said that liquor had been a cause of trouble in their family. (40, p. 195) With problem drinking defined as getting high or tight at least once a week, (19, 21) 1974 and later surveys indicated that 5 percent of junior high and senior high students were problem drinkers. (132, p. 20) As can be seen in Figure 6–4, the proportion of students who reported getting drunk (or very high) increases with school grade, so that by twelfth grade, about 9 percent of the students reported getting drunk once a week or more. (132, p. 21) If just senior high school students are considered, a 1975 survey indicated that about 60 percent reported getting drunk at least once a month. (122) In every age group, boys drink more and more often than girls, but the use of alcohol among girls has begun to approach that of boys. (132, p. 10)

As can be seen in Figure 6–5, beer is the preferred beverage among boys of all ages, regardless of the frequency with which they drink, and among girls of all ages who drink once a week or more. Older girls who drink only once a month or more or once a year or more prefer distilled spirits to beer. (132, p. 9)

The social contexts in which adolescents drink are subject to legal restrictions. Youths drink before they can legally buy alcoholic beverages or patronize licensed premises. Most who begin to drink do so at home under parental supervision. (132, p. 16) Much of this drinking occurs on holidays and other special occasions. As youths grow older, they tend to drink more often outside the home, until the most likely drinking places are those where adults are not present. (70)

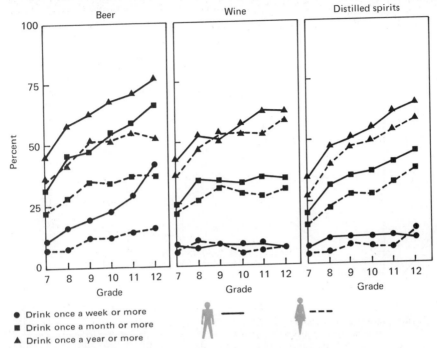

Beer   Wine   Distilled spirits

● Drink once a week or more
■ Drink once a month or more
▲ Drink once a year or more

Figure 6–5. Percentage of drinkers among teenagers, by sex, school grade, frequency of drinking, and type of beverage, U.S.A., 1974. (From U.S. Department of Health, Education and Welfare, Public Health Service, *Alcohol and Health,* Second Report to the U.S. Congress, 1974 [Rockville, Md.: National Institute on Alcohol Abuse and Alcoholism, 1975], p. 9.)

Figure 6–6 shows the age trends. As can be seen, 60 percent of seventh graders report drinking at home with their parents on special occasions; a few (22 to 36 percent) drink away from home without parental supervision. At each succeeding grade level, the proportion drinking at home tends to remain the same, but away-from-home drinking increases, so that by grade twelve, 50 percent of youths who drink do so at night in cars and 75 percent do so at teenage parties with no adults present. (132, p. 16)

The increase in drinking among junior high and senior high youths has motivated many states to reexamine their laws regulating legal drinking ages. After the Vietnam War, many states lowered the drinking age to eighteen. The argument was: "If they're old enough to fight, they're old enough to vote and to drink." (32) But authorities complained that giving eighteen-year-olds the right to purchase alcoholic beverages also made them available to their younger friends in junior and senior high school—the seniors purchased it for them. (6) As a result some states that lowered the drinking age raised it again; about half the states now outlaw the sale of spirits to anyone under twenty-one. (32)

DRINKING AFTER HIGH SCHOOL

It is clear that alcohol is the drug of choice and the primary recreational drug for adolescents and young adults, just as it has been for decades. The highest proportion of drinkers are those aged twenty-one to twenty-four, but the highest

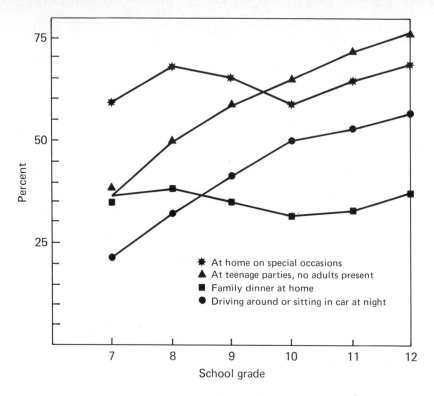

Figure 6–6.   Where adolescents usually drink, by school grade and in percent,
U.S.A., 1974. (From U.S. Department of Health, Education and Welfare, Public
Health Service, *Alcohol and Health*, Second Report to the U.S. Congress, 1974
[Rockville, Md.: National Institute on Alcohol Abuse and Alcoholism, 1975], p. 17.)

proportion of heavier drinkers are men aged eighteen to twenty and thirty-five
to thirty-nine, and among women aged twenty-one to twenty-four. See Figure
6–7 for age trends. The lowest proportion of drinkers are the oldest.

The frequency of regular drinking typically increases for both men and
women during the first three years after graduation from high school. The amount
of regular drinking among those who join the military is higher than among those
who take civilian jobs or enter college. Two separate surveys of drinking among
military personnel indicate that officers and enlisted men both get into trouble
because of drinking considerably more often than civilians of equal age. (20, 22)
Larger proportions of enlisted men were heavy and problem drinkers than were
officers. Heavy drinking and problem drinking declined with increasing age, rank,
and length of service, although enlisted men continued to drink heavily. (20, 22)

Studies of drinking in college indicate that fraternity members are more likely
than nonfraternity members to be drinkers; these data indicate that peer influences on drinking behavior are substantial. (82) It has been found also that church-
affiliated colleges, which put pressure on students not to drink, have lower
percentages of students who do drink, but that among those students who do,
excessive drinking is much more common. (132, p. 22) Furthermore, students
who violate the accepted drinking customs of their families are more apt to go

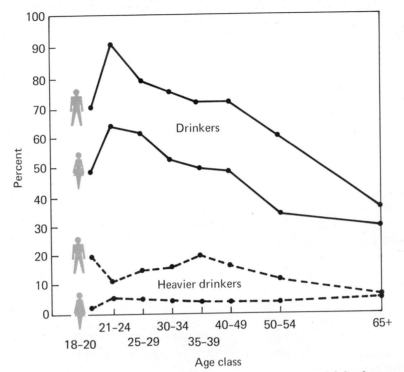

Figure 6–7.   Percentage of drinkers and "heavier" drinkers among adults, by sex and age class, U.S.A., autumn 1972. (From U.S. Department of Health, Education and Welfare, Public Health Service, *Alcohol and Health*, Second Report to the U.S. Congress, 1974 [Rockville, Md.: National Institute on Alcohol Abuse and Alcoholism, 1975], p. 11.)

further in their drinking than do students for whom drinking is acceptable behavior. (132, p. 22) Few Mormon students drink, but among those who do, 42 percent of males and 41 percent of females report social complications as a result. By contrast, only 20 percent of males and 2 percent of females among Jewish students report social complications from drinking. (121)

CORRELATIONS WITH DRINKING

These figures reflect the wide variations in drinking habits among different ethnic groups. Some groups, such as Italian-Americans and Jews, exhibit drinking habits that are well integrated into their culture. (132, p. 12) The vast majority drink, but these groups have the lowest rates of alcoholism of any groups in the United States, primarily because of the patterns of their drinking. Italian-Americans have strong sanctions against drunkenness, and the whole family usually drinks wine with meals. As a consequence, they have few alcohol-related problems, although second and later generations begin to show higher rates of heavy drinking. (69)

In contrast to these patterns, Irish-Americans have more problem drinkers than do other Americans of the same social class. They often deliberately seek to get drunk, often drink distilled spirits rather than wine, and often take five or six drinks on a single occasion. Consequently, they have very high rates of alcoholism and their adolescents follow their example.

Drinking patterns among adolescents generally follow the adult models in their communities. (11) Parents who drink or who sanction drinking are more likely to have adolescents who drink; parents who do not drink or who disapprove of drinking are more likely to have youths who do not. (8) Furthermore, chronic alcoholism is more likely to run in families. About one-third of any sample of alcoholics will have had at least one parent who was an alcoholic. (28, p. 111) Children who are exposed to drinking by their parents, however, do not necessarily grow up to be problem drinkers. The highest rates of alcoholism among adolescents are found in groups that are under pressure to refrain from drinking until age twenty-one, or in families, such as the Irish, who themselves have very high rates of alcoholism.

Drinking is also related to religious affiliation and church attendance. Jews have the lowest proportion of abstainers among the three major religions, and the lowest proportion of heavy drinkers. Catholics and liberal Protestants have a relatively high proportion of drinkers and heavy drinkers. Conservative Protestants have the largest proportion of abstainers and the lowest proportion of heavy drinkers. In a longitudinal study of drinker status in adolescence, one group of investigators reported that religiousness and frequency of church attendance were strongly related to abstinence. (68) In other studies, problem drinkers among youths score lower than nonproblem drinkers on an index of religious participation.

There are a number of other significant correlations with drinking. These may be summarized as follows:

1. The highest proportion of abstainers (62 percent) in the general population is found among people with less than an eighth-grade education. The proportion of heavier drinkers increases fairly steadily, from 6 percent of those with grammar school education to 15 percent of college graduates. (59)

2. Proportionately more people on the lower socioeconomic levels are abstainers than are those on the upper levels. Both moderate and heavier drinking increases as social class rises. (59) Alcohol use among adolescents is highest when fathers are professionals or managers. (30)

3. Youths from rural areas and small towns are more likely to be abstainers than are adolescents from cities and suburbs. The largest proportions of heavy drinkers live in urban and suburban areas; the smallest proportions of heavy drinkers live in rural communities and small towns. (59)

4. The incidence of deviant drinking among juvenile delinquents is decidedly higher than in the general adolescent populations, suggesting that overdrinking is but one class of antisocial behavior among those who are maladjusted and who have the potential for getting into trouble. (13, 68) Those who are the heaviest drinkers are those who are also most often involved in such crimes as shoplifting, breaking and entering, and auto theft. (97, p. 83)

WHY ADOLESCENTS DRINK

Adolescents drink for a number of reasons. Drinking is a widespread adult custom, so drinking by adolescents reflects their perception of the attitudes and behavior of adults in our society. Adolescents use alcohol as an integral part of adult role playing, as a "rite of passage" into the adult community.

Youths drink also because of peer group pressure and the need for peer identification, sociability, and friendship. Drinking becomes a social custom of a particular group, therefore the adolescent who wants to be a part of the group drinks too.

There are tremendous differences in drinking habits among different youthful social groups. Reister and Zucker studied the drinking habits of junior and senior high school youths in eight social subgroups in a town of 13,000 people located in the Middle Atlantic states. (104) The eight subgroups into which the authors divided the youths were:

Collegiates—doing well in college prep, actively involved in extracurricular activities.

Peripheral collegiates—have acquaintances in collegiates but not really a part.

Leathers—do not compete in academic or extracurricular programs, frequently in trouble at school, hang around town, customize their cars.

Peripheral leathers—have acquaintances in leathers but not really a part.

Average kids, or quiet ones—average academically, most not going to college, nongroup affiliated, members of small cliques, seldom date or attend parties, spend leisure with adults, at home.

True individuals or hippies—close friends not from high school, value performing arts, reject extracurricular activities as adolescent, sporadic academic work.

Intellectuals—totally involved in academics, participate in verbal extracurricular activities, excellent grades, all will attend college.

Kids who have a steady—intense relationship, spend all leisure time with steady, not leaders in organizations or academically, plan job and marriage after school.

The drinking habits of youths in each of these eight subgroups are indicated in Table 6–5. (104) As can be seen from the table, peer-group membership influenced drinking behavior. Identification with either the collegiate or leather subgroups was associated with high use of alcohol. In fact, 90 percent of the regular drinking behavior in this sample was by those in either core or peripheral membership in the collegiates or leathers. The most frequent situation for drinking was social, involving groups of adolescents. Collegiate and leather males drank primarily with male friends and secondarily with male and female peers in a party setting.

Efforts have been made also to sort out racial factors and their influence on adolescent drinking habits. Globetti made a comparative study of white and black teenage drinking in two Mississippi communities. (46) The sample included 314 white and 214 black students, male and female, grades nine to twelve, chosen at random. Globetti discovered that white and black drinking habits were quite similar, although a greater percentage of white drinkers (37 percent) were frequent users than were black drinkers (24 percent). But regardless of racial difference, if a student was a male, belonged to a higher socioeconomic level, was

Table 6–5. Social groupings and drinking behavior of junior and senior high school students in a small town in the Middle Atlantic states.

	Percentage		
Group	Regular Drinkers (High Users)	Moderate	Nondrinkers
Leathers	75	18	6
Collegiates	60	35	5
Peripheral leathers	30	54	8
Kids who have a steady	20	47	33
True individuals, hippies	20	40	40
Peripheral collegiates	15	48	36
Quiet or average kids	0	21	78
Intellectuals	0	11	88

Adapted from A. E. Reister and R. A. Zucker, "Adolescent Social Structure and Drinking Behavior," *Personnel and Guidance Journal* 47 (1968): 304–312. Copyright 1968 American Personnel and Guidance Association. Reprinted with permission.

an upperclassman, resided in a community where there was a favorable attitude toward alcohol, and had a weak identification with religion, he tended to drink. Significant, however, were the different reasons why whites and blacks drank. Whites more often tended to drink to get along in a crowd or to avoid ridicule from friends. Blacks more often drank in imitation of parents. Drinking among black youths was governed more by adults than was drinking in the white system. Drinking among white youths was not considered an appropriate activity for young people; therefore, it usually occurred outside the home without the permission or governance of adults, and was more frequent and excessive. White students usually obtained their intoxicants from illegal sources such as a bootlegger. It was obvious that they drank in spite of parents and because of peer pressure. (46)

Another major reason why some youths drink is as a means of rebellion, indicated especially in studies of adolescents who are problem drinkers. (46, 47) Such youths evidence signs of rebellion and alienation from adults and adult institutions. They drink in defiance of parental authority or of community norms and as a means of expressing hostility toward individuals who symbolize authority. (46, 47) In other words, their drinking is antinormative, indicative of their estrangement from family and community. (47, p. 155) This is why adolescents who are excessive drinkers are also more likely to commit delinquent acts than are moderate drinkers. (8, p. 577) When drinking is a means of rebellion, there is far greater likelihood that the adolescent will become a problem drinker. Occasional social drinkers seek to imitate permissible adult custom or to identify with peer groups. Problem drinkers start to drink in excess for psychological rather than social reasons. Heavy, escapist drinking is symptomatic of serious personality problems. Problem drinkers are youths with problems: often they don't get along at home or at school; they receive more failing grades, are more delinquency prone, participate less often in extracurricular activities, spend more nights out away from home, and are not as close to their parents. (47, 99)

Only a small percentage of youths are problem drinkers, but they are already evidencing the psychological imbalance that prompts them to rebel or to seek escape through alcohol.

Conclusions

Adolescents smoke, drink, or use various kinds of drugs for similar reasons. They imitate the example set by adult society in their efforts to be grown up; they are curious; they start because of social and peer-group pressure; they want fun, pleasure, or kicks; they seek to escape, to relieve tension and anxiety, or to solve problems; they desire personal enhancement, greater awareness, or a mystical experience. Those who become chronic users do so because they become physically addicted or psychologically dependent.

Young people start to drink, smoke, or use other drugs quite early: as young as eleven to thirteen years of age, with boys beginning earlier than girls. The incidence increases throughout junior and senior high school and the early years of college. This means that any programs of education and prevention need to be started early—at least by the fifth grade.

Youths who are most likely to become addicted or dependent on drugs are those with personal, emotional, social, and family problems. Addiction or dependency develops out of a desire to solve or escape these problems. This means that programs of prevention have to go beyond education to include counseling, guidance, rehabilitation, and direct help with the larger problems of which chronic drug usage is only a symptom.

If society does not want its adolescents to smoke, drink, or use other drugs, it needs to stop brainwashing them into believing that such use is synonymous with being grown-up, sexy, masculine, feminine, rich, sociable; with the good life; with having fun; with returning to the beauties of nature; or with having a pleasurable, marvelous, almost mystical experience. Drug abuse is a problem created by a society that pushes drugs onto its children and then condemns them if they become addicted.

Panel Discussion

Form a student panel to discuss the subject of drug abuse, asking four to six members of the class to serve on the panel. Numerous aspects of the subject might be emphasized in the discussion. The following ideas are only suggestions.

1. *Drug abuse in high schools they attended and in the communities in which they were brought up.* Which drugs were most often employed? Where were the drugs obtained? At what age did students begin using drugs? Were there many chronic users in their high schools? Were they any different from others? Why did they abuse drugs? What effect was drug abuse having on the lives of these adolescents? Did the school offer drug education? What type of program? With what effect? What approaches should be taken to combat drug abuse among adolescents? What should parents do if they discover their adolescent is smoking marijuana, taking dangerous drugs like LSD or speed, is hooked on heroin?

2. *Drug abuse in college.* Discuss the current situation here in college, its effects and consequences, and what, if anything, should be done about it.

3. *The use of a particular drug.* The panel may want to concentrate on an

in-depth discussion of one category of drugs, such as marijuana or hallucinogens, and on what the latest research findings say about this drug and its use.

4. *Drinking in high school or college.* Discuss the extent, drinking patterns as they exist, effects, and consequences on the lives of adolescents.

5. *How to stop smoking.* Discuss ways and means of how to quit smoking, such as smoking clinics (what they do and how they help), and smoking campaigns. The panel may want to engage in an in-depth discussion of medical research findings on the effects of smoking on the human body.

Bibliography

1. Aaronson, B., and Osmond, H. *Psychedelics: The Uses and Implications of Hallucinogenic Drugs.* Cambridge, Mass.: Schenkman Publishing Co., 1971.

2. Abelson, H. I. et al. *National Survey on Drug Abuse: 1977.* Rockville, Md.: National Institute on Drug Abuse, 1977.

3. Amini, F. et al. "Adolescent Drug Abuse: Etiological and Treatment Considerations." *Adolescence* 11 (1976): 281–299.

4. Angelico, I., and Brown, J. "Marihuana and Angina Pectoris." *New England Journal of Medicine* 191 (1974): 800.

5. Anker, J. L. et al. "Drug Usage and Related Patterns of Behavior in University Students: 1. General Survey and Marihuana Use." *Journal of the American College Health Association* 19 (1971): 178–186.

6. "As States Crack Down on Teen-Age Drinking." *U.S. News & World Report,* 18 September 1978.

7. Barman, M. L.; Sigel, N. D.; Beedle, D. B.; and Larson, R. K. "Acute and Chronic Effects of Glue Sniffing." *California Medicine* 100 (1964): 19–22.

8. Barnes, G. M. "The Development of Adolescent Drinking Behavior: An Evaluative Review of the Impact of the Socialization Process within the Family." *Adolescence* 12 (Winter 1977): 571–591.

9. Bergman, R. L. "Navajo Peyote Use: Its Apparent Safety." *American Journal of Psychiatry* 128 (December 1971): 695–699.

10. Blackford, L. *Student Drug Use Surveys: San Mateo County, California, 1968–1975.* San Mateo, Calif.: Department of Public Health and Welfare, 1975.

11. Blum, R. H. et al. *Society and Drugs. Vol. 2, College and High School Observations.* San Francisco, Jossey-Bass, 1970.

12. Braucht, G. N. "A Psychosocial Typology of Adolescent Alcohol and Drug Users." In *Proceedings of the Third Annual Alcoholism Conference of the National Institute on Alcohol Abuse and Alcoholism.* Edited by M. E. Chafetz. DHEW Pub. No. (ADM) 75–137. Washington, D.C.: U.S.

Government Printing Office, 1974, pp. 129–144.

13. Braucht, G. N. et al. "Psychosocial Correlates of Empirical Types of Multiple Drug Abusers." *Journal of Consulting and Clinical Psychology* 46 (December 1978): 1463–1475.

14. Brecher, E. M., and the Editors of *Consumer Reports* magazine. *Licit and Illicit Drugs.* Boston: Little, Brown and Co., 1972.

15. Brill, H. Q. "Personality Factors in Marijuana Use." *Archives of General Psychiatry* 24 (1972): 163–165.

16. Brill, H. Q., and Christie, R. L. "Marihuana Use and Psychosocial Adaptation: Follow-up Study of a Collegiate Population." *Archives of General Psychiatry* 31 (1974): 713–719.

17. Bruhn, P., and Maage, N. "Intellectual and Neuropsychological Functions in Young Men with Heavy and Long-Term Patterns of Drug Abuse." *American Journal of Psychiatry* 132 (1975): 397–401.

18. Bureau of Narcotics, U.S. Department of Justice. "Fact Sheets." Washington, D.C.: U.S. Government Printing Office, 1969.

19. Cahalan, D. *Problem Drinkers.* San Francisco: Jossey-Bass, 1970.

20. Cahalan, D., and Cisin, I. H. *Report of a Pilot Study of the Attitudes and Behavior of Naval Personnel Concerning Alcohol and Problem Drinking.* Conducted for the United States Navy Department Bureau of Naval Personnel. Washington, D.C.: Bureau of Social Science Research, February 1973.

21. Cahalan, D., and Room, R. *Problem Drinking among American Men.* Monograph No. 7. New Brunswick, N.J.: Rutgers Center of Alcohol Studies, 1974.

22. Cahalan, D. et al. *Drinking Practices and Problems in the U.S. Army, 1972.* Final report of a study conducted for the Deputy Chief of Staff, Personnel Headquarters, Department of the Army under contract Report Number 73-6, December 1972.

23. Center for Counseling and Psycho-

logical Services. "Survey of Drug Usage: Preliminary Report." Report no. 2. Orono, Me.: University of Maine, 1970.

24. Clayton, R. R. "The Family and Federal Drug Abuse Policies Programs: Toward Making the Invisible Family Visible." *Journal of Marriage and the Family* 41 (August 1979): 637–647.

25. Cohen, S., and Edwards, A. E. "LSD and Organic Brain Impairment." *Drug Dependence.* National Institute of Mental Health no. 2, 1969, pp. 1–4.

26. Coles, R. et al, *Drugs and Youth: Medical, Legal, and Psychiatric Facts.* New York: Liveright, 1970.

27. *The Consumers Union Report on Smoking and the Public Interest.* Mount Vernon, N.Y.: Consumers Union, 1962, pp. 188–192.

28. Cotton, N. S. "The Familial Incidence of Alcoholism." *Journal of Studies on Alcohol* 40 (January 1979): 89–116.

29. Davis, G. L., and Cross, H. J. "College Student Drug Users' Memories of Their Parents." *Adolescence* 7 (1973): 475–480.

30. DeLint, J., and Schmidt, W. "Consumption Averages and Alcoholism Prevalence: A Brief Review of Epidemiological Investigations." *British Journal of Addiction* 66 (1971): 97–107.

31. Dishatsky, N. I. et al. "LSD and Genetic Damage." *Science* 172 (1971): 431–439.

32. "The Drinking Age." *Economist,* 13 January 1979. p. 39.

33. Drug Education Advisory Committee, State of Maine Department of Education, Department of Health and Welfare. "Drug Education in Maine." [Undated report from the early 1970s].

34. "Drug Pushers Go for Even Younger Prey." *U.S. News & World Report,* 13 August 1979, p. 31.

35. *Drug Use in America: Problem in Perspective.* Second Report of the National Commission on Marihuana and Drug Abuse, March 1973. Washington, D.C.: U.S. Government Printing Office, 1973.

36. Feigelson, N. *The Underground Revolution: Hippies, Yippies, and Others.* New York: Funk and Wagnalls, 1970.

37. Firth, C. D. *Psychopharmacologia* 19 (1971): 188–192.

38. "45 Billion Yearly Drug Traffic Hits Main Street." *U.S. News & World Report,* 19 February 1979, pp. 28–30.

39. Gallup, G. H. *The Gallup Poll: Public Opinion 1977.* Wilmington, De.: Scholarly Resources, Inc., 1978.

40. ———. *The Gallup Poll: Public Opinion 1978.* Wilmington, De.: Scholarly Resources, Inc. 1979.

41. "Gallup College Drug Survey." *New York Times,* 6 February 1972.

42. Gantman, C. A. "Family Interaction Patterns among Families with Normal, Disturbed, and Drug-Abusing Adolescents." *Journal of Youth and Adolescence* 7 (December 1978): 429–440.

43. Gardner, R. "Deaths in United Kingdom Opioid Users, 1965–1969." *Lancet* (1970): 650–651.

44. Ginsberg, I. J., and Greenley, J. R. "Competing Theories of Marijuana Use: A Longitudinal Study." *Journal of Health and Social Behavior* 19 (March 1978): 22–34.

45. Glaser, H. H., and Massengale, O. N. "Glue Sniffing in Children: Deliberate Inhalation of Vaporized Plastic Cements." *Journal of the American Medical Association* 181 (1962): 300–303.

46. Globetti, G. "A Comparative Study of White and Negro Teenage Drinking in Two Mississippi Communities." *Phylon* 28 (1967): 131–138.

47. Globetti, G., and Windham, G. O. "The Social Adjustment of High School Students and the Use of Beverage Alcohol." *Sociology and Social Research* 51 (1967): 148–157.

48. Gonzalez, R. M. "Hallucinogenic Dependency during Adolescence as a Defense against Homosexual Fantasies: A Reenactment of the First Separation-Individuation Phase in the Course of Treatment." *Journal of Youth and Adolescence* 8 (March 1979): 63–71.

49. Goode, E. "Drug Use and Sexual Activity on a College Campus." *American Journal of Psychiatry* 128 (1972): 92–96.

50. Goodman, L. S., and Gilman, A., eds. *The Pharmacological Basis of Therapeutics,* 4th ed. New York: Macmillan, 1970.

51. Greenwald, B. S., and Luetgert, M. J. "A Comparison of Drug Users and Non-Users on an Urban Commuter College Campus." *International Journal of Addiction* 6 (1971): 63–78.

52. Greenwood, S. G. "Warning: Cigarette Smoking Is Dangerous to Reproductive Health." *Family Planning Perspectives* 11 (June 1979): 168–172.

53. Grinspoon, L. *Marijuana Reconsidered.* Cambridge, Mass.: Harvard University Press, 1971.

54. Grinspoon, L., and Bakalar, J. B. "A Kick from Cocaine." *Psychology Today* (March 1977): 41ff.

55. Grossman, J. C. et al. "Openness to Experience and Marijuana Use: An Initial Investigation." *Proceedings,* 79th Annual Convention, American Psychological Association (1971): 335–336.

56. Guinn, R., and Hurley, R. S. "A

Comparison of Drug Use among Houston and Lower Rio Grande Valley Secondary Students," *Adolescence* 11 (Fall 1976): 457–459.

57. Halikas, J. A. "Marihuana Use and Psychiatric Illness." In *Marijuana: Effects on Human Behavior.* Edited by L. L. Miller. New York: Academic Press, 1974.

58. Harnett, A. L. "How We Do It." *Journal of School Health* 34 (1964): 173–176.

59. Harris, L., and Associates, Inc. *Public Awareness of the National Institute on Alcohol Abuse and Alcoholism Advertising Campaign and Public Attitudes Toward Drinking and Alcohol Abuse.* Reports prepared for the National Institute on Alcohol Abuse and Alcoholism. Phase Four Report and Overall Summary, 1974.

60. Hembree, W. "Effects of Marihuana on Gonadal Function in Man." Paper presented at the Satellite Symposium on Marihuana of the Sixth International Congress of Pharmacology, Helsinki, Finland, July 26–27, 1975.

61. Hepler, R. S., and Frank, I. R. "Marihuana Smoking and Intraocular Pressure." *Journal of the American Medical Association* 217 (1971): 1392.

62. Hogan, R. et al. "Personality Correlates of Undergraduate Marijuana Use." *Journal of Consulting and Clinical Psychology* 35 (1970): 58–63.

63. Horman, R. E., and Fox, A. M., eds. *Drug Awareness.* New York: Avon Books, 1970.

64. Horn, D. "Behavioral Aspects of Cigarette Smoking." *Journal of Chronic Diseases* 16 (1963): 383–395.

65. Horowitz, M. J. "Psychological Aspects of Education Related to Smoking." *Journal of School Health* 36 (1966): 281–286.

66. Hungerford, D. A. et al. "Cytogenic Effects of LSD-25 Therapy in Man." *Journal of the American Medical Association* 206 (1968): 2287–2291.

67. Hunt, W. A., and Matazarro, J. D. "Habit Mechanisms in Smoking." In *Learning Mechanisms in Smoking.* Edited by W. A. Hunt. Chicago: Aldine, 1970.

68. Jessor, R., and Jessor, S. L. *Problem Drinking in Youth: Personality, Social, and Behavioral Antecedents and Correlates.* Institute of Behavioral Science Publication no. 144. Boulder, Colo.: University of Colorado, 1973.

69. Jessor, R. et al. "Perceived Opportunity Alienation, and Drinking Behavior among Italian and American Youth." *Journal of Personality and Social Psychology* 15 (1970): 215–222.

70. Johnston, L. *Drugs and American Youth.* Ann Arbor, Mich.: University of Michigan, Institute for Social Research, 1973.

71. Johnston, L.; "Drug Use among American High School Students, 1975–1978." Rockville, Md.: National Institute on Drug Abuse, 1978.

72. Kandel, D. B. et al. "Antecedents of Adolescent Initiation into Stages of Drug Use: A Developmental Analysis." *Journal of Youth and Adolescence* 7 (March 1978): 13–40.

73. Klonoff, H. "Effects of Marihuana on Driving in a Restricted Area and on City Streets: Driving Performance and Physiologic Changes." In *Marijuana: Effects on Human Behavior.* Edited by L. L. Miller. New York: Academic Press, 1974.

74. Knight, R. C.; Sheposh, J. P.; and Bryson, J. B. "College Student Marijuana Use and Societal Alienation." *Journal of Health and Social Behavior* 15 (1974): 28–35.

75. Kohn, P. M., and Mercer, G. W. "Drug Use, Drug-Use Attitudes, and the Authoritarianism-Rebellion Dimension." *Journal of Health and Social Behavior* 12 (1971): 125–131.

76. Levine, E. M., and Kozak, C. "Drug and Alcohol Use, Delinquency, and Vandalism among Upper Middle Class Pre- and Post-Adolescents." *Journal of Youth and Adolescence* 8 (March 1979): 91–101.

77. Levinson, B. L. et al. "Smoking Elimination by Gradual Reduction." *Behavior Therapy* 2 (1971): 477–487.

78. Levy, L. "Drug Use on Campus: Prevalence and Social Characteristics of Collegiate Drug Users on Campuses of the University of Illinois." *Drug Forum* 2 (1973): 141–171.

79. Lieberman, J. J. "The Drug Addict and the 'Cop-out' Father." *Adolescence* 9 (1974): 7–14.

80. MacDonald, A. P. et al. "College Female Drug Users." *Adolescence* 8 (1973): 189–196.

81. Macleod, A. *Growing Up in America: A Background to Contemporary Drug Abuse.* Rockville, Md.: National Institute on Drug Abuse, 1975.

82. Maddox, G. L., ed. *The Domesticated Drug: Drinking among Collegians.* New Haven, Conn.: College and University Press, 1970.

83. *Marihuana and Health.* Fifth Annual Report to the U.S. Congress From the Secretary of Health, Education and Welfare, 1975. Rockville, Md.: National Institute on Drug Abuse, 1976.

84. Maurer, D., and Vogel, V. H. *Narcotic Addiction*, 4th ed. Springfield, Ill.: Charles C. Thomas Publisher, 1973.

85. McAree, C. P. et al. "Personality Factors and Pattern of Drug Usage in College Students." *American Journal of Psychiatry* 128 (1972): 890–893.

86. McArthur, D.; Waldron, E.; and Dickenson, J. "The Psychology of Smoking." *Journal of Abnormal and Social Psychology* 56 (1958): 267–275.

87. McGlothlin, William et al. "Long-lasting Effects of LSD on Normals." *Archives of General Psychiatry* 17 (1967): 521–532.

88. McKennell, A.C. "Smoking Motivation Factors." *British Journal of Social and Clinical Psychology* 9 (1970): 8–22.

89. Mendelson, J. H. et al., eds. *The Use of Marihuana: Psychological and Physiological Inquiry*. New York: Plenum Press, 1974.

90. Meyer, R. E. "Psychiatric Consequences of Marihuana Use: The State of the Evidence." In *Marihuana and Health Hazards: Methodological Issues in Current Marihuana Research*. Edited by J. R. Tinklenberg. New York: Academic Press, 1975.

91. Miller, L., ed. *Marijuana: Effects on Human Behavior*. New York: Academic Press, 1975.

92. Mirin, S. et al. "Casual versus Heavy Use of Marijuana: A Redefinition of the Problem." *American Journal of Psychiatry* 13 (1970): 163–173.

93. Mizner, G. L. et al. "Patterns of Drug Use among College Students." *American Journal of Psychiatry* 127 (1970): 15–24.

94. Moos, R. H. et al. "College-Student Abstainers, Moderate Drinkers, and Heavy Drinkers: A Comparative Analysis." *Journal of Youth and Adolescence* 5 (December 1976): 349–360.

95. Nahas, G. G. *Keep Off the Grass*. New York: Reader's Digest Press, 1979.

96. New England Learning and Research, Inc. "A Survey of Drug Use in a Cross-Section of Maine Communities." Augusta, Me., 1970.

97. O'Connell, J. et al. *Young Men and Drugs: A Nationwide Survey*. National Institute on Drug Abuse Monograph 5. Rockville, Md.: 1976.

98. Paton, S. M., and Kandel, D. B. "Psychological Factors and Adolescent Illicit Drug Use: Ethnicity and Sex Differences." *Adolescence* 13 (Summer 1978): 187–200.

99. Pearce, J., and Garrett, H. D. "Comparison of the Drinking Behavior of Delinquent Youth versus Nondelinquent Youth in the States of Idaho and Utah." *Journal of School Health* 40 (1970): 131–135.

100. Pelner, L. "Peyote Cult, Mescaline Hallucinations, and Model Psychosis." *New York State Journal of Medicine* 67 (1967): 2838–2843.

101. Pihl, R. O., and Segal, H. "Motivation Levels and the Marihuana High." *Journal of Abnormal Psychology* 87 (April 1978): 280–285.

102. Pittel, S. M. et al. "Developmental Factors in Adolescent Drug Use: A Study of Psychedelic Drug Users." *Journal of American Academy of Child Psychology* 10 (1971): 640–660.

103. Prakash, R. et al. "Effect of Marihuana and Placebo Marihuana Smoking on Hemodynamics in Coronary Disease." *Clinical Pharmacology and Therapeutics* 18 (1975): 90–95.

104. Reister, A. E., and Zucker, R. A. "Adolescent Social Structure and Drinking Behavior." *Personnel and Guidance Journal* 47 (1968): 304–312.

105. Robbins, E. S. et al. "College Students' Drug Use." *American Journal of Psychiatry* 126 (1970): 85–93.

106. Rodin, E. A. et al. "The Marihuana-Induced 'Social High': Neurological and Electroencephalographic Concomitants." *Journal of the American Medical Association* 213 (1970): 1300–1302.

107. Rubinow, D. R., and Cancro, R. "The Bad Trip: An Epidemiological Survey of Youthful Hallucinogen Use." *Journal of Youth and Adolescence* 6 (March 1977): 1–9.

108. Rudolph, J. P., and Borland, B. L. "Factors Affecting the Incidence and Acceptance of Cigarette Smoking among High School Students." *Adolescence* 11 (Winter 1976): 519–525.

109. Russell, M. A. H. "Cigarette Smoking: Natural History of a Dependence Disorder." *British Journal of Medical Psychology* 44 (1971): 9.

110. Sallan, S. E.; Zinberg, N. E.; and Frei, D. "Antiemetic Effect of delta-9-Tetrahydrocannabinol in Patients Receiving Cancer Chemotherapy." *New England Journal of Medicine* 293 (1975): 795–797.

111. Schneider, F. W., and Vanmastrict, L. A. "Adolescent-Preadolescent Differences in Beliefs and Attitudes about Cigarette Smoking." *Journal of Psychology* 87 (1974): 71–81.

112. Schroeder, R. C. *The Politics of Drugs*. Washington, D.C.: Congressional Quarterly, 1975.

113. Seltzer, C. C. "Masculinity and Smoking." *Science* 130 (1959): 1706–1707.

114. Shafer, R. P. et al. *Marihuana: A Signal of Misunderstanding*. New York: New American Library, 1972.

115. Shean, G., and Fechlmann, F. "Purposes in Life Scores of Student Marijuana Users." *Journal of Clinical Psychology* 27 (1971): 112–113.

116. Shor, R. E., and Williams, D. C. "Normative Beliefs about Tobacco Smoking on Campus in Relation to an Exposition of the Viewpoint of the Nonsmoker's Rights Movement." *Journal of Psychology* 100 (November 1978): 261–274.

117. ———. "Reported Physiological and Psychological Symptoms of Tobacco Smoke Pollution in Nonsmoking and Smoking College Students." *Journal of Psychology* 101 (1979): 203–218.

118. Singer, A. "Mothering Practices and Heroin Addiction." *American Journal of Nursing* 74 (January 1974): 77–82.

119. Smith, D. E., and Wesson, D. R. *Uppers and Downers.* Englewood Cliffs, N.J.: Prentice-Hall, 1973.

120. Snyder, Solomon. "STP: A New Hallucinogenic Drug." *Science* 158 (1967): 669–670.

121. Straus, R., and Bacon, S. *Drinking in College.* New Haven, Conn.: Yale University Press, 1953.

122. Swift, P. "High School Drunks." *Parade Magazine,* 9 February 1975, p. 13.

123. Szara, S., and Braude, M., eds. *Pharmacology of Marihuana.* New York: Raven Press, 1976.

124. Tashkin, D. P. et al. "Effects of Smoked Marijuana in Experimentally Induced Asthma." *American Review of Respiratory Disease* 112 (1975): 377–386.

125. Tec, N. "Family and Differential Involvement with Marihuana: A Study of Suburban Teenagers." *Journal of Marriage and the Family* 32 (1970): 656–664.

126. ———. "Some Aspects of High School Status and Differential Involvement with Marihuana: A Study of Suburban Teenagers." *Adolescence* 6 (1972): 1–28.

127. ———. "Parent-Child Drug Abuse: Generational Continuity or Adolescent Deviancy." *Adolescence* 9 (1974): 351–364.

128. Thompson, E. L. "Smoking Education Programs 1960–1976." *American Journal of Public Health* 68 (March 1978): 250–257.

129. *Time,* 19 October 1970, p. 54.

130. Tinklenberg, J. R. *Marijuana and Health Hazards.* New York: Academic Press, 1975.

131. U. S. Bureau of the Census, Department of Commerce. *Statistical Abstract of the United States, 1978.* Washington, D.C.: U.S. Government Printing Office, 1978.

132. U.S. Department of Health, Education and Welfare. Public Health Service. *Alcohol and Health.* Second Special Report to the U.S. Congress, 1974. Rockville, Md.: National Institute on Alcohol Abuse and Alcoholism, 1975.

133. ———. *Alcohol and Health.* Second Special Report to the U.S. Congress. Summary and Excerpts. Rockville, Md.: National Institute on Alcohol Abuse and Alcoholism, 1975.

134. Vaillant, G. E. "A Twelve-Year Follow-Up of New York Narcotic Addicts: I. The Relation of Treatment to Outcome." *American Journal of Psychiatry* 122 (1965): 729–730.

135. Valium package insert. Nutley, N.J.: Roche Laboratories, 1971.

136. "White House Prepares War on Marijuana." *U.S. News & World Report,* 21 May 1979, p. 49.

137. Wikler, A. "Drug Dependence." *Clinical Neurology* 2 (1971): 1–53.

138. ———. "Clinical and Social Aspects of Marihuana Intoxication." *Archives of General Psychiatry* 23 (1970): 320–325.

139. Wolk, D. J. "Youth and Drugs." *Social Education* 33 (1969): 667–674.

140. Zanbey, N., and Weil, A. "A Comparison of Marijuana Users and Non-Users." *Nature* 226 (1970): 119–123.

141. Zinberg, N. E. "The War over Marijuana." *Psychology Today* (December 1976): 44ff.

PART 3

Intellectual

CHAPTER 7

Intellectual and Cognitive Growth and Change

Outline

This chapter begins with a discussion of the important subject of mental growth. What would be a typical mental growth pattern from birth through adulthood? Is there a spurt of intellectual growth at adolescence that accompanies the spurt of physical growth? What changes take place in the pattern of mental growth at adolescence? The chapter then discusses the subject of IQ variations in the individual and the relationship of such factors as anxiety, motivation, and sociocultural influences to IQ scores. The first part of the chapter ends with a discussion of growth in memory ability and vocabulary during adolescence.

The second part of the chapter deals with cognitive growth and change. Piaget's stages of cognitive development are outlined as a basis for understanding the qualitative changes in thought that take place during adolescence. Piaget's formal operational stage of thought development is discussed in detail along with the effect of this development on adolescent personality and behavior. The chapter ends with a critique of Piaget's formal operational stage on the basis of subsequent research.

Mental Growth

TYPICAL GROWTH PATTERNS

Numerous studies have been conducted to investigate mental growth from birth through adulthood. General mental growth curves have been drawn to represent the "true" course of mental development. They are actually the records of the average performances of groups of individuals on standardized general intelligence tests. Curves for separate mental abilities that enter into these general scores show varying forms, as do the mental growth curves of individuals. Thus, any general curve will not predict the growth of an individual nor how individuals of the same age vary. Individual adolescents of the same age differ widely in their mental abilities; nevertheless, it is helpful to have a general idea of the progress of growth through the years. Figure 7–1 represents an average growth pattern. In the typical curve, mental growth accelerates from birth through the early preschool and grade school years, after which it continues to rise rapidly but at a slower rate each year. During the early and late teens there is a still less rapid increase in growth, so that growth begins to peak in the midtwenties. Early studies (58) indicated that mental performance begins to drop at about the midtwenties, with the drop minimal until the forties, after which there is a steady decrease in most mental functions. More recently, however, studies on a wide range of adult populations indicate continued improvement for some adults, continued maintenance of general intellectual level for others, and rapid decline in intellectual functions for still others, particularly after age forty. (4, 58, 75)

Researchers frequently ask if there is an intellectual growth spurt at pubes-

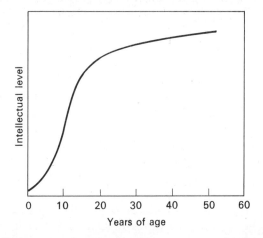

Figure 7–1.   The growth of intelligence from birth to the middle years. (From N. Bayley, "Development of Mental Abilities from Birth through 36 Years," *Roche Report: Frontiers in Hospital Psychiatry* 5[1968]:5–6, 11. W. A. Owens, Jr., "Age and Mental Abilities: A Second Adult Follow Up," *Journal of Educational Psychology* 57[1966]:311–325. Copyright 1966 by the American Psychological Association. Reprinted by permission.)

cence that accompanies the physical growth spurt. Some authors have said that intellectual growth shows a fairly steep rise in early adolescence and tapers off in middle adolescence. Generally the rate of growth does gradually decelerate as adolescence progresses. But there is no conclusive evidence that there is a prior intellectual growth spurt for all adolescents with the onset of puberty.

INDIVIDUAL IQ CHANGES

The so-called IQ (intelligence quotient) originally referred to a score on the Stanford-Binet intelligence test, obtained by applying a formula that is now no longer used. The use of the abbreviation IQ has been retained by psychologists and educators as a convenient way of referring to a score on an intelligence test. In the Wechsler Intelligence Scales and the 1972 revision of the Stanford-Binet, scores are converted into IQ by referring to tables in the test manuals. (41, 83) But to interpret a student's IQ properly, it is not enough to know his or her IQ score; one must also know which test was used and the standard deviation of that test. An IQ score of 105 on a test with a standard deviation of 5 equals an IQ score of 116 obtained on a test with a standard deviation of 16, because both scores are one standard deviation above the mean. Therefore, if a student gets an IQ score of 110 on a test with a standard deviation of 5, he or she has scored higher than a student with an IQ score of 125 obtained on a test with a standard deviation of 15, because in the first instance the student's score is two deviations above the mean, whereas in the latter instance the student's score is not quite two deviations above the mean. The Wechsler tests now use a mean of 100 and a standard deviation of 15; therefore, to find a student's IQ, the examiner multiplies the standard score (z) by 15 and then adds 100. (23, p. 688) Rather than speak of IQ as a constant number on all tests, it is proper to speak of deviation IQs, which state the scores while taking into account the standard deviations of different tests. (17, p. 447)

It used to be a truism that IQ remains constant throughout one's life. (43) Now it is recognized that the IQ of an individual may vary considerably during his or her lifetime: it may rise or fall, depending upon the intellectual environment in which the person is placed. Pinneau reanalyzed the data from the Berkeley Growth Study and converted all the scores to deviation IQs. He found that children tested at five years and at subsequent ages up to seventeen years showed median changes from 6 to 12 points, with the range of individual changes from 0 to 40 points. (66) The direction of the change is not always predictable, at least for individuals. In general, predictability of test scores varies with the length of the interval between tests and with the age at the initial test. Test-retest correlations decrease as the interval between tests increases.

Overall, it has been found that scores on IQ tests show some significant change during adolescence that may be related to sex-role stereotypes. One comparison of IQ scores at seventh grade and again at twelfth grade showed that boys experienced an average gain of 1.62 and girls an average decline of 1.33 points. Altogether, 33 percent of boys increased IQ points while 29 percent of girls decreased points. (15, p. 631) The researcher attributes the difference to acceptance of the stereotype that it isn't feminine to be smart. (15, p. 634) Only one-third of the girls whose scores declined said they had never acted stupid in order to impress boys.

In summary, it should be emphasized that although most adolescents do not show gross changes in relative IQ placement during their junior and senior high years, some do, so that an IQ measurement should not be interpreted as a fixed attribute of an individual, but rather as a score on a test at that particular time. The score may change as a result of a number of influences, creating the need for retesting over a period of years to make current judgments of the IQ of some people.

FACTORS INFLUENCING TEST RESULTS

One of the reasons for variations in IQ is that it is sometimes difficult to get valid test results. Results vary not only because intelligence may vary, but also because of factors influencing test scores. One of the most important influences is the presence of anxiety in the subjects tested. Anxious youths do not do as well on tests as those evidencing greater emotional security. (24) A prime example is that of a ten-year-old in the Boston school system who would not answer test questions and whose record subsequently contained this entry: "The child's IQ is so low she is not testable." After a young psychologist talked with the child, she was tested and achieved an IQ score of 115. (3, p. 78)

Motivation also has a marked influence on test results. An otherwise bright student, poorly motivated to do well on a test, will not measure up to his or her capacity. Furthermore, the tests are not free of cultural biases. Tests to measure IQ were originally designed to measure "innate" general intelligence apart from environmental influences. But research over a long period has shown that sociocultural factors play a significant role in the outcome of the tests. (7, 12, 76, 80, 89) The language, illustrations, examples, and abstractions are middle class, and thus are designed to measure intelligence according to middle class standards. (89) Many adolescents from low socioeconomic status families grow up in a nonverbal world, or a world where words used are so different that understanding middle class expressions on an intelligence test becomes most difficult. Adolescents do poorly, not because they are less intelligent, but because they do not comprehend language foreign to their backgrounds and experiences. Also, American Indian adolescents and others from rural areas who have been raised in an environment free from considerations of time do poorly on tests with a time limit. When allowed to do the test at their own rate, they score much higher.

Efforts to develop culturally unbiased tests have been very frustrating. The general approach has been to use language that is familiar to the particular minorities for which the test is designed. But the major problem with the tests so far developed is how to evaluate their accuracy. Most have been measured against IQ scores, which continue to reflect a cultural bias. (68, p. 34)

A more promising approach is known as SOMPA ("System of Multicultural Pluralistic Assessment"), which consists of the Wechsler IQ test, an interview in which the examiner gets the child's health history, a "sociocultural inventory" of the family's background, and an "adaptive-behavior inventory" of the child that evaluates the child's nonacademic performance in school, at home, and in the neighborhood. A complete medical exam evaluates the child's physical condition, manual dexterity, motor skill, and visual and auditory ability. The final score on SOMPA is obtained not only from the IQ test but also through the other inventories. Thus, a child who receives 68 on the Wechsler may earn an "adjusted IQ" of 89 when her or his scores on the sociocultural and the adaptive-behavior inventories are taken into account. (68, p. 34) Thus, SOMPA measures potential rather than current ability.

THE DANGERS OF LABELING

One must therefore be particularly cautious about labeling an individual "superior," "average," or "dull" on the basis of intelligence test scores, even over a period of time. This caution applies especially to black and Mexican-American children. Not only do the tests not accurately measure the learning ability of these children, but the testers may be incompetent to interpret test results, ignorant of anxieties experienced by children having language problems and insensitive to the cultural backgrounds of minority children. (15, p. 56) Yet, in some communities IQ scores determine whether children are put into classes for the mentally retarded. (3, p. 78) Once labeled "slow" or "mentally retarded," the social stigma may remain with these individuals all their lives. (14, p. 56)

Labels also have a way of becoming self-fulfilling prophecies, because youths tend to try to live up to what is expected of them. The central theme of a classic book, *Pygmalion in the Classroom*, is that "one person's expectation for another person's behavior can quite unwittingly become a more accurate prediction simply for its having been made." (69, p. vii) As an example, the authors present findings from a study in which 20 percent of the children in a classroom were randomly selected and their teachers told they would show marked academic growth during the school year. Eight months later, this group was found to have achieved much more than other children in the class even though there was no factual reason for this improvement, because the group had been selected at random. The important element was that once the teachers expected the children to show significant gains, they did so. The prophecy of high achievement became self-fulfilling when interested people related to the students as though the achievement level had already been reached.

NATURE VERSUS NURTURE

One of the major questions about intelligence is whether it is inherited from parents through genes or whether it is acquired. Which is more important, heredity or environment? The only honest answer is that both heredity and environment play a part. Of the two factors, however, the genetic factor seems to exert the greater influence. (43, 44) This conclusion is based upon several considerations.

Similarities in measured intelligence of pairs of people increase steadily as their genetic relationship increases. (56, p. 92) Studies of twins have been particularly helpful in sorting out heredity versus environmental influences, suggesting that heredity accounts for about 70 to 80 percent of the variations in intelligence. The fact that identical twins (with identical heredity) show greater intellectual similarity than fraternal twins (who have only about half their genes in common) indicates that the greater genetic similarity of identical twins is responsible for their greater similarity in ability. Even when identical twins are reared separately in completely unrelated environments, there is always a high correlation between their intelligence scores. (44) In one case of identical twins, one of whom had been deaf since early in life, the difference in IQ was only 20 points. (56, p. 89) After reviewing the literature concerning environmental effects on intelligence, Bloom (10) concludes that the maximum effect on intelligence of extreme environmental differences was about 20 points.

One must remember, however, that differences in IQ of 20 to 30 points are significant. A person with an IQ of 100 is considered average, whereas one with 70 to 80 would be considered quite dull, and one with 120 to 130 would be judged superior. (56, p. 71) Environment itself may therefore be the determining factor in whether a person is average rather than dull, or superior rather than average. Research indicates that family environment is especially important. (44) Children reared in stimulus-rich environments may show enduring superiority in intelligence capacities, whereas those reared under intellectually sterile conditions may become quite retarded in relation to what they would otherwise be capable of doing. (74)

Scholastic Aptitude

SAT

One of the most widely used tests in the United States is the SAT, or Scholastic Aptitude Test. It is an important test because it is used by a majority of colleges as one basis for admission. Over one million high school seniors took the test in 1979. The combined verbal and math scores often determine eligibility not only for admission but also for scholarships and financial aid. The Educational Testing Service, which produces the SAT, claims that, in combination with high school records, the SATs have proven to be better predictors of students' first-year performance in college than any other measurement. Nevertheless, the rumblings and protests against the use or misuse of the test grow louder. (67, p. 77)

Objections to the test arise from the claim that it measures basic abilities acquired over a student's lifetime and is thus immune to last-minute cramming and "coach-proof." But a recent study by the Federal Trade Commission's Bureau of Consumer Protection showed that special coaching can improve SAT scores by an average of 25 points out of the possible 800. (67, p. 30) More than eighty coaching schools in one nationwide chain tutored 30,000 students in a recent year, charging $275 for a ten-week course, and improved scores on the average by 25 points. The schools claim that in individual cases they can improve scores up to 100 points. Recently, the author talked to a lawyer who had wanted to raise his verbal score on the SAT before applying to law school. He studied a vocabulary of 5,000 most-used words and was able to raise his verbal score on the SAT by 60 points.

The basic question is: If coaching can raise a student's score, should the test be relied on as a basic measure of scholastic aptitude? And should admission to college depend partly on a skill gained by those who can afford a coaching course? In all fairness, the College Entrance Examination Board has long issued warnings against making admissions decisions on the basis of the SAT score alone. The ETS itself has said that an individual's score can vary plus or minus 30 to 35 points, a spread of 60 to 70 points. For these reasons some of the best schools rely equally or more on student essays, interviews, and other admission procedures. Even high marks from school may be called in to question, for they vary greatly from school to school and the standards for good grades have been declining since the late 1960s. The number of students with A averages has increased so rapidly that there are now as many straight A students as there are those with C averages. (39)

DECLINING SCORES

The SAT score averages for college-bound seniors dropped again in 1979 for the tenth straight year of decline. (19) Table 7–1 shows score averages from 1969 through 1979. The declining scores have led to increased criticism of the schools for relaxing teaching and learning standards and for not teaching the basics. Because average scores on Achievement Tests have also declined for the third straight year, there is objective evidence that students are not learning as much. Part of the blame has also been laid to changes and problems in the family, increased television viewing, and such problems as turbulence in national affairs. (73) As Table 7–1 shows, males have higher SAT scores than females. No explanation has been offered, except that this probably reflects cultural pressure on women not to be "too smart" or to get "too much education."

Table 7–1. SAT score averages for college-bound seniors, 1969–1979.

| | Verbal | | | Mathematical | | |
	Male	*Female*	*Total*	*Male*	*Female*	*Total*
1969	459	466	463	513	470	493
1970	459	461	460	509	465	488
1971	454	457	455	507	466	488
1972	454	452	453	505	461	484
1973	446	443	445	502	460	481
1974	447	442	444	501	459	480
1975	437	431	434	495	449	472
1976	433	430	431	497	446	472
1977	431	427	429	497	445	470
1978	433	425	429	494	444	468
1979	431	423	427	493	443	467

Memory and Vocabulary Development

MEMORY ABILITY

The ability to remember or to reproduce experience is fundamental to all learning and intellectual growth. Without memory, the individual cannot learn from the past and would continually have to solve problems by trial and error.

Effective memorizing requires the ability to *fixate,* to focus concerned attention on what is to be learned at the moment. Adolescents whose attention flits from one thing to another are not able to concentrate on the material studied and will therefore learn and retain little. Emotional excitement, tension, worry, and various environmental distractions interfere with the learner's ability to fixate upon study stimuli.

Memory also includes *retention,* the persistence of an experience in one's mind. Retention depends in turn upon a number of factors: the strength, length, and importance of the original experience; the lapse of time and the use made of the material subsequent to the original exposure; and the attitude, motivation, age, and intelligence level of the learner.

Memory also includes *recognition,* the ability to recall when exposed to appropriate stimuli. Much of what the individual learns may not be remembered through *spontaneous recall,* but may be recalled only in association with something else. Students are encouraged to learn through *association,* relating one thing to be learned to something with which they are already familiar, to stimulate recall.

The speed of forgetting depends partly upon the nature of the material learned. Nonsense syllables, once "learned," may be forgotten in a few days, whereas meaningful materials are retained longer and more completely. Learners also differ in their ability to learn and remember. Bright, interested, motivated learners retain more and forget less quickly than do slower learners who are uninterested and see little value in what they are supposed to be learning. The rate of forgetting is also affected by the kind of experiences subsequent to learning. Sleep retards forgetting, but interesting experiences unrelated to the learning interfere with retention. (20, pp. 175, 176)

Many studies of memory ability were done years ago when the emphasis in education was on rote memory. These studies showed that memory ability improves with age. A study of the ability of children and youths to memorize lines of poetry showed that seven-year-olds averaged 9.8 lines, eighteen-year-olds 22.4 lines. (82) A study of the ability to recall ideas from a motion picture showed that grade school children could recall only 26 percent of the ideas presented, but college students could recall 61 percent. (50) Also, the quantity of material recalled and the length of time it was remembered increased at each age from elementary school to adulthood. (50)

A more recently study was done on the effects of distraction on the recall of relevant and incidental material presented to children in grades one, three, five, and seven. (49) The central task assigned the children was to remember which picture cards had a certain background color that matched a color chip the experimenter displayed. An array of cards was first shown with the background color displayed, then turned over so the color was hidden. After a series of trials, the child was asked to recall also the incidental material, which consisted of the pictures superimposed upon each background color.

Half the subjects at each grade level were distracted, half were not. The distraction consisted of a subsidiary task. A piano tape was played with a melody of high notes interrupted periodically by single bass notes. The subjects were required to tap whenever they heard a bass note. All subjects in the age ranges tested were able to do this while carrying out the central task.

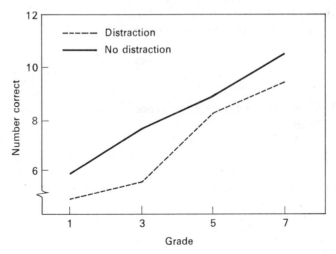

Figure 7–2.   Recall on central task. (Adapted from E. E. Maccoby and J. W. Hagen, "Effect of Distraction upon Central versus Incidental Recall: Developmental Trends," *Journal of Experimental Child Psychology* 2[1965]:280–289. Used by permission.)

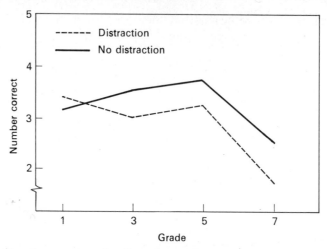

Figure 7–3. Recall on incidental task. (Adapted from E. E. Maccoby and J. W. Hagen, "Effect of Distraction upon Central versus Incidental Recall: Developmental Trends," *Journal of Experimental Child Psychology* 2[1965]: 280–289. Used by permission.)

Figures 7–2 and 7–3 show the results. Age was a significant factor in the ability of children to recall in relation to the central task. Distraction also had a significant effect upon central recall, lowering scores at all age levels, with errors rising by 26 percent. Whether distracted or not, the seventh graders did less well on incidental recall than did the younger subjects. Apparently, somewhere between the fifth and seventh grade, the children began to ignore irrelevant aspects of the task, indicating that incidental recall declined with age, while central recall increased regularly with age.

VOCABULARY DEVELOPMENT

Both the number of words understood and the number of words actually used continue to increase during adolescence. One study of the recognition vocabulary of adolescents showed the number of words understood in grade twelve to average 80,300, with a range from 36,000 to 136,500. The recognition vocabulary of college students has been estimated at 156,000 words. The actual number of words used can only be estimated. At age fourteen it may range between 8,000 and 10,000 words. By age twenty it has probably increased another 10,000 words, giving a total vocabulary of 18,000 to 20,000 words. (78, p. 540; 79, p. 78)

Equally important are changes in the way children define words as they get older. Preschool and early elementary school children define word objects by their function or appearance. A mother is "someone who takes care of you." A grandmother "has gray hair." By age nine or ten, children frequently use synonyms in defining words. This method of definition increases throughout the following years. Using demonstrations or illustrations to define words seems to decrease during adolescence, as the ability to symbolize grows. The explanation type of response grows in use until early adolescence. Additional qualitative changes in adolescent thought will be discussed in the next section.

Piaget's Stages of Development

In addition to quantitative changes in intellectual performance during adolescence, there are also qualitative changes in the adolescent's cognitive processes. The work of Piaget (60) and Inhelder and Piaget (42, 65) has been especially helpful in developing an understanding of the stages of cognitive development through which the child progresses; these stages will be reviewed briefly here as a background to understanding the changes during adolescence. (45)

Piaget divides cognitive development into four major periods. (34, p. 33)

1. *The sensorimotor stage*—from birth to about two years.
2. *The preoperational stage*—from about two to seven years.
3. *The concrete operational stage*—from about seven to eleven or twelve years.
4. *The formal operational stage*—from eleven or twelve years on.

Berzonsky provides one of the best descriptions of Piaget's four stages.

According to Piaget's theory, thought is internalized action. One initially acts overtly, i. e., one walks to the sink to get a drink of water. When one is thinking, however, the behavior is carried out covertly in one's mind, thought is thus internalized action. True directed thinking for Piaget is known as operations and involves internalized action that is reversible; i. e., one can mentally cancel out actions that have actually occurred. The type of operation that an individual is capable of using is the basis for naming the four stages. Sensorimotor operations are those carried out in action, not mentally. Concrete operations are internal actions which can be reversed but they involve actual behavior. Preoperations deal with the internalization process; they are rigid rather than reversible. Formal operations are not restricted to actual transformations of reality, they deal with abstractions which are independent of reality. (9, p. 279)

THE SENSORIMOTOR STAGE

During the *sensorimotor stage,* learning is related to the mastery of sensory-motor sequences. (32, p. 43) The infant moves from a self-centered, body-centered world to an object-centered world as the senses of vision, touch, taste, hearing, and smell bring him or her into contact with things with various properties and relationships to other objects. The child becomes intrigued with such things as picking up objects, falling backward on a pillow, blowing, and other simple motor activities. Thinking, if any, occurs as a stimulus-response connection with the physical word without mediation, although the latter part of this period marks a transition to symbolic play, imitation, and representation of objects. Elkind labels the principal cognitive task during this period the *conquest of the object.* (27)

THE PREOPERATIONAL STAGE

The *preoperational stage* is the period when language is acquired so that children can deal with their world by manipulating symbols that represent the environment, as well as through motor activity and direct interactions with the environment. Symbolic play, or *internalized imitation,* emerges. When the imitations become internalized as what Piaget calls *images,* they become the first true *signifiers,* as opposed to the *significates,* or the objects or events being imitated.

Perhaps the most important developments of this period are the increasing use of words as signifiers of things that are imitated and increasing differentiation of the signifiers from the significates. (59, p. 56) Elkind labels the principal preoperational task the *conquest of the symbol*. (27)

During this period there is evidence of *transductive reasoning* rather than *inductive* or *deductive reasoning*. Transductive reasoning occurs when the child proceeds from particular to particular, without generalization, rather than from the particular to the general (inductive), or from the general to the particular (deductive). For example, the dog Fido jumps on you because he has, and Brownie will jump on you because he is frisky like Fido, but Blackie will not jump on you because he is too big (when in fact he may). An error in judgment is made because the general concept that dogs jump on you is never developed. (46, p. 450)

At this stage children sometimes make errors of *syncretism*, trying to link ideas that are not always related. Mother had a baby last time she went to the hospital, so next time she goes to the hospital, it is mistakenly expected she will bring home another baby. Children also make startling errors because their thinking is not *reversible* (it cannot go back to the beginning, to the point of origin). For example, if children are shown two plasticene balls of equal size and are asked: "Are they the same size, or does one have more plasticene in it than the other?" they reply: "They are the same." But if, while they are watching, one ball is rolled into a sausage shape, and they are asked the same question, they reply that one (usually the sausage) has more plasticene than the other. (59, p. 61)

Preoperational thinking is also *egocentric*; that is, children have difficulty understanding why someone else cannot see something in the same way they do. (59, p. 63) They get upset, for example, when they cannot convince their mother not to wash their dirty rag doll. They gain security from it, and that is the important thing to them, whereas to their mother the important thing is that the doll is dirty. Children are also egocentric in their attitudes about other things. (37, p. 88) Space and time are focused on them: when they walk, the moon follows them. Gradually, however, children learn to conceive of a time and spatial world existing independently of themselves, and, through social interaction, to take into account the viewpoints of others. Social feedback is extremely important in developing the capacity to think about their own thinking, without which logic is impossible. (59, p. 63)

Related to all the preceding characteristics is *centering*. It refers to children's tendency to focus attention on one detail and their inability to shift attention to other aspects of a situation. (55, p. 63) For example, they may conclude there is more water in a test tube than in a glass because the tube is taller, even though they have already seen all the water poured from the tube into the glass. They ignore the smaller diameter of the tube and the demonstration of pouring. (59, p. 63) As a result of their inability to maintain more than one relationship in their thinking at a time, children make errors of judgment, give inadequate or inconsistent explanations, show a lack of logical sequence in their arguments, and a lack of comprehension of constants (for example, if they have a brother, they need to realize their brother also has a brother). There is evidence of thinking, but still an absence of operational thinking.

THE CONCRETE OPERATIONAL STAGE

During the *concrete operational stage*, children show a greater capacity for logical reasoning, though still at a very concrete level. One of the reasons they can think more logically is that they are able to arrange objects into *hierarchical classifications* and comprehend *class inclusion relationships* (the inclusion of objects in different levels of the hierarchy at the same time). This gives children the ability to understand the relations of the parts to the whole, the whole to the parts, and the parts to the parts. For example, suppose children are given a randomly organized array of blue and red squares and black and white circles. If they understand inclusion relationships, they discover there are two major collections (squares and circles) and two subtypes of each (blue vs. red squares and black vs. white circles). There is a hierarchy whose higher level is defined by shape and whose lower level is defined by color. This enables them to say that all squares are either blue or red, that there are more squares than blue squares, that there are more squares than red squares, that if you take away the red squares, the blue ones are left, and so on. (37, p. 124)

Concrete operational children are capable also of *serialization*, serial ordering. In arranging animals, such as dogs and cats, into a hierarchy of classes, they may arrange dogs and cats into separate classes, and then dogs into further subdivisions such as bulldogs and setters or into subdivisions according to color or size. They learn that different objects may be grouped by size, by alphabetical order, or by age, or that an object may simultaneously belong to more than one class. A child may be a boy, a fourth grader, an athlete, and a redhead, all at the same time. They learn that some relationships are *symmetrical* or *reciprocal* —two brothers are brothers to each other. (46, p. 452) In dealing with numbers, children learn that different combinations of numbers make the same total and that *substitutions* may be made with the same result. (46, p. 452) In dealing with liquids and solids, they learn that a change in shape does not necessarily change their volume or mass; the amount is conserved.

Piaget calls this stage the *concrete operations stage* of cognitive development because it involves concrete elements (objects, relations, or dimensions) and operations (such as addition or subtraction) and rules, or *properties*, that describe the way the operations may be performed. Elkind calls the major cognitive task of this period *mastering classes, relations,* and *quantities.* (27)

Muuss summarizes four concrete operations the child is able to perform.

1. *Combinativity.* Two or more classes may be combined into one larger, more comprehensive class of the same grouping. All men and all women equal all adults. . . . A is larger than B and B is larger than C may be combined into a new statement that A is larger than C. . . .

2. *Reversibility.* Every mathematical operation has an opposite that reverses it. Supraclasses can be taken apart, so that the effect of combining subclasses is reversed. All adults except all women equal all men. . . .

3. *Associativity.* The child whose operations are associative can reach a goal in various ways . . . but the results obtained . . . remain the same. For example, (3 plus 6) plus 4 equal 13, and 6 plus (3 plus 4) equal 13.

4. *Identity or nullifiability.* An operation that is combined with its opposite becomes nullified. Illustrations . . . are: 3 minus 3 equal 0; I drive one mile west and I drive one mile east equal I am where I started. (55, p. 189)

It is important to remember that the child's thinking is still linked to empirical reality. (62) Inhelder and Piaget write: "Concrete thought remains essentially attached to empirical reality. . . . Therefore, it attains no more than a concept of 'what is possible,' which is a simple (and not very great) extension of the empirical situation." (42, p. 250) Children have made some progress toward extending their thoughts from the actual toward the potential, (28, p. 44) but the starting point must still be the real, because concrete operational children can reason only about those things with which they have had direct personal experience. When children have to start with any hypothetical or contrary-to-fact proposition, they have difficulty. Elkind (27) also points out that one of the difficulties at this stage is that the child can deal with only two classes, relations, or quantitative dimensions at the same time. When more variables are present, the child flounders. This ability to consider more than two variables at once is achieved only during the formal operations stage that follows.

One example illustrating combinatorial logic and the capacity to deal with problems in which many factors operate at the same time is the following. There are four differently colored poker chips: red (R), blue (B), yellow (Y), and green (G). The problem: arrange them in as many different color combinations as possible. The answer—there are sixteen color combinations as follows: R;B;Y;G;RB;RY;RG;BY;BG;YG;RBY;RBG;BYG;RYG;RBYG; and none. Most adolescents can easily form all of these combinations; children cannot. It is in this sense that the combinatorial reasoning of the adolescent goes beyond the simpler syllogistic reasoning of the child. (28, p. 100)

THE FORMAL OPERATIONAL STAGE

The last stage of cognitive development, *the formal operational stage,* begins during early adolescence at eleven to twelve years of age and becomes firmly established in some people by age fifteen, with marked variations in the age of individuals. (38, 81, 88) Some adolescents and adults never reach this formal operational stage because of limited intelligence or cultural deprivation. (47) Elkind calls this final stage the *conquest of thought.* (27) During this stage, the thinking of the adolescent begins to differ radically from that of the child. (5; 42, p. 335; 63) The child has developed concrete operations and carried them out in classes, relations, or numbers; but their structure has never gone beyond the elementary level of logical "groupings" or additive and multiplicative numerical groups. He or she has never integrated them into a single, total system found in formal logic. Adolescents, however, are able to superimpose propositional logic on the logic of classes and relations. Consequently, they come to control not only *hypothetico-deductive reasoning* and experimental proof based on the variation of a single factor with the others held constant, but also a number of operational schemata that they use repeatedly in experimental and logico-mathematical thinking. (42, p. 335) In other words, formal operations adolescents are able, through *inductive reasoning*, to systematize their ideas and deal critically with their own thinking to be able to construct theories about it. Furthermore, they can test these theories logically and scientifically, considering several variables, and are able to discover truth, scientifically, through *deductive reason-*

ing. In this sense, adolescents are able to assume the role of scientist, because they have the capacity to construct and test theories. (57, p. 377)

The difference between the way children approach problems and the logical, systematic approach of adolescents is given in the following example.

E. A. Peel . . . asked children what they thought about the following event: "Only brave pilots are allowed to fly over high mountains. A fighter pilot flying over the Alps collided with an aerial cableway and cut a main cable, causing some cars to fall to the glacier below. Several people were killed." A child at the concrete-operational level answered: "I think the pilot was not very good at flying." A formal-operational child responded: "He was either not informed of the mountain railway on his route or he was flying too low. Also his flying compass may have been affected by something before or after take-off, thus setting him off course causing collision with the cable."

The concrete-operational child assumes that if there was a collision the pilot was a bad pilot; the formal-operational child considers all the possibilities that might have caused the collision. The concrete-operational child adopts the hypothesis that seems most probable or likely to him. The formal-operational child constructs all possibilities and checks them out one by one. (47, pp. 1061–1062)

One of the experiments conducted by Piaget, which led to discovering the strategies adolescents use in solving problems, involved a pendulum. (34) The selected subjects were shown a pendulum suspended by a string. The problem was to discover what factors would affect the oscillatory speed of the pendulum. The subjects were to investigate four possible effects: changing the length of the pendulum, changing its weight, releasing the pendulum from various heights, or starting the pendulum with various degrees of force. The subjects were allowed to solve the problem in any way they chose.

The adolescents showed three basic characteristics in their problem-solving behavior. First, they planned their investigations systematically. They began to test all possible causes for variation in the pendulum swings: long or short string, light or heavy weight, high or low heights, and various degrees of force of push. Second, they recorded the outcomes accurately and with little bias under the different experimental conditions. Third, they were able to draw logical conclusions.

For example, they observed that height of drop and force had no effect upon oscillatory speed. Believing that pendulum weight or length of string might be involved, they tried different combinations of weight with different combinations of string length, only to find out that whatever the weight, the oscillation speed remained the same. They discovered, however, that changing the string length did alter the oscillation speed. They were able to conclude that pendulum length alone determined the speed of oscillation. (42; 54, p. 61) Since this original experiment, the methods and result have been replicated by other researchers. (51)

Younger subjects given the same problem may come up with the right answer by trial and error, but fail to use systematic and scientific procedures or to be able to give a logical explanation of the solution. (35, p. 201) Children tend to form conclusions that seem warranted by the facts. But often these conclusions are premature and false because the child has not considered all of the important facts and is not able to reason logically about them. Even when presented with contrary evidence, the child tends to hold tenaciously to the initial hypothesis and to try to make the circumstances fit these preconceived notions. (28)

For example, Piaget (60) says that children below age twelve rarely solve this problem:

• Edith is fairer than Susan.
• Edith is darker than Lily.
• Who is the darkest of the three?

Children below age twelve give such answers as: "Edith and Susan are fair, Edith and Lily are dark; therefore, Lily is darkest, Susan is fairest, and Edith in between." Children draw wrong conclusions because they are unable to reason logically with so many possibilities. Furthermore, they get trapped by their initial hypothesis because they can't entertain other variables. However, Piaget and other researchers have found that between twelve and fourteen years of age children show a rapid increase in their ability and willingness to accept and reason with the conditions as given. Adolescents are able to solve this and other problems because they are able to understand the conditions, reason with them, try out various solutions systematically, and discard those that don't fit. Because they can reason logically and are able to consider different variables, they are able to check their conclusions to see if they are true. (26) Gallagher and Noppe conclude:

In summary, three interrelated characteristics of adolescent thought have emerged. These are: the ability to derive a proportion from two or more variables or a complex relationship; the ability to suggest mentally the possible effect of one or more variables upon another when a certain relationship is suspected among variables; and the capacity to combine and separate variables in a hypothetical-deductive framework ("if this is so, this will happen") so that a reasonable possibility is recognized before the test is made in reality. The fundamental property of adolescent thought is this reversible maneuvering between reality and possibility. (35, p. 202)

One characteristic of adolescents' thinking that these ideas suggest is an ability to be *flexible*. They can be quite versatile in their thoughts and in dealing with problems. They can devise many interpretations of an observed outcome. Because they can even anticipate many possibilities prior to an actual event, they are not surprised by unusual outcomes. They are not stuck with their preconceptions. (79, p. 70) In contrast, younger children are confused by atypical results that are inconsistent with their simple perceptions of events. (54, p. 60)

It has already been suggested that the preoperational child begins to utilize symbols. But the formal operational adolescent now begins to utilize a second symbol system: a set of symbols for symbols. (28, p. 117) For example, metaphorical speech or algebraic symbols are symbols of other words or numerical symbols. The capacity to symbolize symbols makes the adolescent's thought much more flexible than the child's. Words can now carry double or triple meanings. Cartoons can represent a complete story that would otherwise have to be explained in words. It is no accident that algebra is not taught to elementary school children or that children have difficulty understanding political cartoons or religious symbols until approximately junior high age. (28, p. 117)

Another important difference between concrete operational children and formal operations adolescents is that the latter are able to orient themselves toward what is abstract and not immediately present. They are able to escape the concrete present and think about the abstract and the possible. This facility enables them to project themselves into the future, to distinguish present reality from possibility, and to think about what might be. Not only do adolescents have the capacity to accept and understand what is given, but they also have the ability to conceive of what might be possible, of what might occur. Ross writes:

> In Piaget's outline of the formal operations, much emphasis is placed on the adolescent's increasing ability to move from the *actual* to the *possible*. That is, with the onset of the formal operations, the person is no longer limited to thinking solely in terms of the given, concrete reality. The capacity now exists to consider rather abstract alternatives to the immediate situation. (72, p. 609)

Because they can construct ideas, they have the ability to elaborate on what they receive, to generate new or different ideas and thoughts. They become inventive, imaginative, and original in their thinking, and "possibility dominates reality." (37, p. 203) "The adolescent is the person who commits himself to possibilities . . . who begins to build 'systems' or 'theories' in the largest sense of the term." (42, p. 339) This ability to project themselves into the future has many important consequences for their lives, as will be seen in the following section.

In summary, formal thinking, according to Piaget, involves two major aspects: thinking about thought (propositional logic) and distinguishing the real from the possible. These two cognitive aspects have profound effects upon the adolescent's personality and behavior.

Effects of Adolescent Thought on Personality and Behavior

IDEALISTIC REBELLION

Piaget begins his discussion of the relationship of adolescent thought to personality and behavior by stating that adolescence is that age at which the individual starts to assume adult roles. (42, p. 337) For one thing, adolescents begin to discard their childhood inferiority and subordination to adults and to consider themselves as their equals, and to judge them, with complete reciprocity, on the same plane as themselves. Because they want to be adults, they are motivated to take their places in the adult social framework, partly by participating in the ideas, ideals, and ideologies of adult society through the medium of a number of verbal symbols to which they were indifferent as children. (42, p. 341) As they become oriented to the adult world, their powers of reflective thinking enable them to evaluate what they learn. Furthermore, their ability to distinguish the possible from the real enables them to discern not only what the adult world is, but what it might be like, especially under ideal circumstances. This ability of adolescents to grasp what is and what might be makes them idealistic rebels. They compare the possible with the actual, discover that the actual is less than ideal, and become critical observers of things as they are and usually ultracritical of adults as well.

For a while, some adolescents develop the equivalent of a messianic complex. In all modesty, they attribute to themselves essential roles in the salvation of humanity. They may make a pact with God, promising to serve Him without return, but planning to play a decisive role in the cause they espouse. (62) They see themselves in a major effort to reform the world, usually in verbal discussions, but, for some, in group movements. Some adolescents get caught up in political idealism and become preoccupied with the utopian reconstruction of society. Once they discover politics, they leap exuberantly into its possibilities—into ideation, fantasy, and building brave new doctrines and worlds. Becoming aware of their newly acquired cognitive capacities, they give themselves, in excited exchange with like-minded friends, to the criticism of current institutions and the search for a more just society. (2, p. 120)

At the same time that adolescents become political idealists, they also become champions of the underdog. Shapiro (77) feels that it is adolescents' own inner turmoil that accounts for their empathic capacities for the suffering of others. By virtue of their own insecure psychological positions, they can easily identify with the weak, the poor, the oppressed, the victims of selfish society. Thus, social injustices that they perceive mirror their own internal, individual struggles. (77, p. 109) Elkind (27) feels that young adolescents rebel primarily on a verbal level, doing little to work for humanitarian causes they espouse. Only later in adolescence do young people begin to tie their ideal to appropriate actions and to be more understanding, tolerant, and helpful.

HYPOCRISY

Because of the discrepancy between what they say and what they do, adolescents are sometimes accused of hypocrisy. Elkind gives two examples to illustrate this tendency. (31) First, his son complains at great length about his brother's going into his room and taking his things. He berates his father for not punishing the culprit; yet the same boy feels no compunction about going into his father's study, using his typewriter and calculator, and playing rock music on his father's stereo without asking. (31, p. 132) Second, a group of young people were involved in a "Walk for Water" drive, in which sponsors were paying them for each mile walked. The money was for testing the water of Lake Ontario and for pollution control. Elkind describes how pleased he was that these youths were not as valueless and materialistic as they were sometimes described to be. Yet, the next day, a drive along the route the youths had walked revealed a roadside littered with McDonald wrappers and coke and beer cans. City workers had been hired to clean up the mess. The question was: Did the cost of cleaning up amount to more money than was collected? And weren't these adolescents hypocritical? On the one hand, they objected to pollution, yet they were among the chief offenders in defacing their environment. (31, p. 133)

The behavior of these adolescents was hypocritical to the extent that it revealed a discrepancy between idealism and behavior. But this assumes that they had the capacity to relate general theory to specific practice, which young adolescents are not necessarily able to do. Early adolescents have the capacity to formulate general principles such as "Thou shalt not pollute," but lack the experience to see the application of these general rules to specific practice. This is due to intellectual immaturity rather than to a defect of character. Youths believe that if they can conceive and express high moral principles, they have attained them, and that nothing concrete need be done. This attitude confuses and upsets adults, who insist that ideals have to be worked for and cannot be attained instantly. This attitude is in turn considered cynical and hypocritical by youths, who respond: "Don't trust anyone over thirty," especially those who recognize the practical difficulties involved in realizing ideals in everyday life. (31, p. 133)

PSEUDOSTUPIDITY

Elkind points out that young adolescents also often demonstrate what he calls *pseudostupidity*, the tendency to approach problems at much too complex a level, and fail, not because the tasks are difficult, but because they are too simple. For example, adolescents go shopping to find a sock, shoe, or book, but look in the least obvious places. Or they try to solve a problem by holding a number of variables in mind at the same time, but lack the capacity to assign priorities and to decide which choice is more appropriate. In other words, the ability to perform formal operations gives them the capacity to consider alternatives, but this newfound capacity is not completely under control. Thus, adolescents appear stupid because they are in fact bright, but not yet experienced. (31, p. 128)

EGOCENTRISM

Another effect of adolescents' intellectual transformation is their development of a new form of egocentrism. As adolescents develop the capacity to think about their own thoughts, they become acutely aware of themselves, their person, and ideas. As a result they become egocentric, self-conscious, and introspective. They become so concerned about themselves that they may conclude that others are equally obsessed with their appearance and behavior. "It is this belief that others are preoccupied with his appearance and behavior that constitutes the egocentrism of the adolescent." (27, p. 1029) As a result adolescents feel they are "on stage" much of the time, so that much of their energy is spent "reacting to an imaginary audience." (27, p. 1030) Elkind writes:

And, since the audience is of his own construction and privy to his own knowledge of himself, it knows just what to look for in the way of cosmetic and behavioral sensitivities. The adolescent's wish for privacy and his reluctance to reveal himself may, to some extent, be a reaction to the feeling of being under the constant critical scrutiny of other people. (27, p. 1030)

The need to react to an imaginary audience helps account for the extreme self-consciousness of adolescents. Whether in the lunchroom or on the bus going home, youths feel that they are the center of attention. Sometimes groups of adolescents react to this audience by loud and provocative behavior because they believe everyone is watching them. (31, p. 129)

Elkind also discusses what he terms *personal fable*, adolescents' beliefs in the uniqueness of their own experiences. Because of their imaginary audiences and their beliefs that they are important to so many people, they come to regard themselves as special and unique. This may be why so many adolescent girls believe that unwanted pregnancies happen only to other girls, never to them. (48, p. 64; 79, p. 1031)

Egocentrism and self-consciousness have other manifestations. On the one hand, adolescents believe everyone is looking; on the other hand, they feel totally alone, unique in a vast, uncaring universe. To be always on stage, scrutinized but rarely understood, imposes a terrific emotional strain. As a result, youths become very critical and sarcastic in their relations with others, partly as a defense against their own feelings of inferiority and as a way of making themselves look good. (29) They employ numerous psychological mechanisms to protect their frail egos. The intellectualization and newfound asceticism of college students has been explained as just such a defense mechanism. (11)

Whereas adolescents are often self-centered, they are frequently self-admiring too. Their boorishness, loudness, and faddish dress reflect what they feel others admire. The boy who stands in front of the mirror for two hours combing his hair is probably imagining the swooning reactions he will produce in his girl. Likewise, the girl applying her makeup is thinking about the admiring glances that will come her way. But when these two meet, each is concerned more with being the observed than with being the observer. Each young person is an actor to himself or herself and an audience to others. (79)

Egocentrism may also be linked to adolescents' desires for social reform and to their efforts to assume adult roles. They try not only to adapt their egos to the social environment, but also to adjust the environment to their egos. They begin to think how they might transform society. Piaget writes:

the adolescent goes through a phase in which he attributes an unlimited power to his own thoughts so that the dream of a glorious future or of transforming the world through Ideas (even if this idealism takes a materialistic form) seems to be not only fantasy but also an effective action which in itself modifies the empirical world. This is obviously a form of cognitive egocentrism. (42, p. 345)

SELF-CONCEPT

The capacity to think about themselves is also necessary in the process of developing self-concept and identity. (57, p. 373) In doing this, adolescents have to formulate a number of postulates about themselves, such as "I am physically attractive" or "I'm smart in school" or "I'm popular." These postulates are based upon a number of specifics, such as "I'm attractive because I have pretty hair, a nice figure, or the boys notice me." Because of formal operational thinking, they are able to entertain a number of simultaneous ideas, and to test each one by, for example, asking a friend: "What do you think of my hair?" or "Do you think I have ugly hair?" Gradually they begin to sort out what they feel is truth from error about themselves and to formulate total concepts of self.

DECENTERING AND A LIFE PLAN

The process of adoption of adult roles, which is directly related to cognitive development, does not stop with egocentrism. The adolescent conceives of fantastic projects that are like a sophisticated game of compensatory functions whose goals are self-assertion, imitation of adult models, and participation in circles that are actually closed. Adolescents follow paths that satisfy them for a time, but are soon abandoned as adolescents develop more cognitive objectivity and perspective. (42, p. 344) In other words, they begin to cure themselves of their idealistic crises and to return to the reality that is the beginning of adulthood. (42, p. 344) Piaget goes on to emphasize that:

the focal point of the decentering process is the entrance into the occupational world or the beginning of serious professional training. The adolescent becomes an adult when he undertakes a real job. It is then that he is transformed from an idealistic reformer into an achiever. (42, p. 346)

Piaget also refers to the importance of adolescent work in the community as a facilitator of human growth. He states that work helps the adolescent meet the storm and stress of that period. True integration into society comes automatically when the adolescent reformer attempts to put his ideas to work. (53, p. 246)

In this process, the ego is gradually decentered as the personality develops and begins to affirm a life plan and adopt a social role. Affirmation of a life plan is important also because it is an indication of autonomy, which is one requirement for being an adult. Personality formation, affirmation of a life plan, and the assumption of adult roles go together, and are in turn related to and dependent upon the transformation of the adolescent's thinking. (42, p. 350)

Critique of Piaget's Formal Operational Stage

AGE AND PERCENTAGES

Since Piaget originally formulated his concept of a formal operational stage of cognitive development, investigators have been examining various components of the formulation. One question concerns the age at which formal operational thought replaces the concrete operational stage. Recently, Piaget himself has advanced the possibility that in some circumstances the appearance of formal operations may be delayed to fifteen to twenty years of age, and "that perhaps in extremely disadvantageous conditions, such a type of thought will never really take shape." (63, p. 7) Piaget acknowledged that social environment can accelerate or delay the onset of formal operations. (64) It has been found that in fact fewer economically deprived adolescents achieve formal thought than do their more privileged counterparts, and that there is a complete absence of formal operations among the mentally retarded. (81) Ross (36, 71) has suggested that the absolute percentage of adolescents demonstrating formal operational thinking has usually been below 50 percent, and that when a larger proportion (around 60 percent) have shown formal thinking, they have been drawn from "gifted" samples (25) or from older, more academic, college students. (70)

It is important for adults, especially parents and teachers, to realize that not all adolescents are at the same stage of development. Many have not yet achieved formal operations. (53, p. 243) These youths cannot yet understand reasoning that is above their level of comprehension; to ask them to make decisions among numerous alternatives or variables that cannot be grasped simultaneously is to ask them to do the impossible. A very few youths may make the transition to formal operations by age ten or eleven, but only about 40 percent have progressed beyond concrete operations by high school graduation. (8, p. 88)

TEST CRITERIA

The measured percentages of people reaching formal operational thinking depend partially upon which criteria of formal thinking are used and the level of the tests employed. Piaget distinguishes between an easiest level (III-A) and a more advanced level (III-B). One researcher (84), using Piaget's III-A level to measure the percentage of females achieving formal operational thinking, demonstrated that 32 percent of eleven-year-old girls, 67 percent of college women, and 54 percent of adult females had reached that level. But when the more advanced III-B criteria were used in measurements, the percentages were 4 percent for girls, 23 percent for college students, and 17 percent for adults. (84, p. 364)

Although not all adolescents or adults reach the formal level, there is still a significant increase in the use of formal operational thinking during adolescence, especially between ages eleven and fifteen. (71, p. 414)

MATURATION AND INTELLIGENCE

To what extent does the maturation of the nervous system play a role in cognitive development? It is certain that maturation plays a part: the nervous system must be sufficiently developed for any real thought to take place. This is one reason why a greater percentage of older adolescents evidence formal thought than do younger adolescents. (72, 85)

In order to determine the relationship among maturation, intelligence, and cognition, Webb (86) tested very bright (IQs of 160 and above) six- to eleven-year-old children to ascertain their levels of thinking. All subjects performed the concrete operational tasks easily, indicating that they were very skilled in thinking at their developmental stage, but only four males, aged ten and older, solved the formal thought problems, indicating that regardless of high intelligence, a degree of maturation interacting with experience was necessary for movement into the next stage of cognitive development. (35, p. 216; 86)

Other research helps clarify further the relationship among development, intelligence, and cognition. Yudin (88) found that, other things being equal, individuals of high IQ are more likely to develop formal thought sooner than those of low IQ, but that it is the interaction of both age and intelligence that contributes to cognitive ability. (18) Thus, older adolescents of superior intelligence are more efficient in problem solving than are older adolescents of average intelligence or younger adolescents of superior intelligence. Younger adolescents of inferior intelligence are less efficient in problem solving than are older adolescents of inferior intelligence or younger adolescents of average intelligence. (88) Yudin concludes:

The attainment of logical operations as an integral aspect of functioning is not uniform or rigid for all adolescents. . . . Individuals of differing abilities not only achieve at different levels but they follow significantly different patterns of development in their obtaining similar, more efficient approaches to problem solving.

Development, whether accelerated or retarded, brings with it a shift in emphasis from concreteness to abstractness and a new way of dealing with facts and relations, but experience alone is not sufficient to bring about this shift. (88)

Thus, the research emphasizes that cognitive development is influenced both by the maturation of the nervous system (age) and by the level of intelligence. Not all adolescents reach formal operations, but if they do reach it, not all do so at the same age, and not all reach it to the same level for all tasks. (77, p. 44)

CULTURE AND ENVIRONMENT

Cross-cultural studies in which task results are compared across different cultures and environments have shown that formal thought is more dependent upon social experience than is sensorimotor or concrete operational thought. (16) The attainment of the first three Piagetian stages appears to be more or less universal, but full attainment of formal thinking, even in college students and adults, is far from guaranteed. (9, p. 285) Adolescents from various cultural backgrounds show considerable variability in abstract reasoning abilities. Some cultures offer more opportunities to adolescents to develop abstract thinking than others do, by providing a rich verbal environment and experiences that facilitate growth by exposure to problem-solving situations. Cultures that provide stimulating environments facilitate the acquisition of cognitive skills necessary to deal with the abstract world. Piaget has cited research to indicate, for example, that children on Martinique are slower than children in Montreal to develop cognitively. (53, p. 237)

Social institutions such as the family and school accelerate or retard the development of formal operations. Parents who encourage exchanges of thoughts, ideational explorations, academic excellence, and the attainment of ambitious educational and occupational goals are fostering cognitive growth. Schools that encourage students to acquire abstract reasoning and develop problem-solving skills enhance cognitive development. (54, p. 64)

Underdeveloped societies do not encourage advanced levels of cognitive development. One reason may be that in simple cultures there is not as great a need for formal thought. (22, 25) The degree of urbanization, (87) literacy, and the amount of education (16) also relate to formal thought development. (35) Because formal thought relies heavily upon verbal factors, a lack of linguistic skills will result in poorer performance in solving formal thought problems. (35, p. 211) However, a lack of linguistic skills does not imply an inability to solve problems as much as it implies a lack of ability to perform well on a particular cognitive test. Similarly, understanding language does not guarantee high-level thinking, even though formal thought is enhanced by verbal interchange. (33)

APTITUDE

It has been found, also, that different people have different aptitudes for solving different types of problems. For example, boys do significantly better than girls in solving conservation of volume tasks. (30, 40, 84) This must be interpreted as a matter of differential socialization and application of mental abilities, not as evidence of a difference in ability to do formal thinking. (30, p. 52) Girls, on the other hand, score much higher on tests of creative thinking. (52, 72) Formal thinking, then, is not applied with equal facility to all types of tasks. A particular student may be able to apply formal reasoning to a science task, another to a problem with semantic content, or to one involving the processing of personal information. (9, p. 284) Students who have studied the sciences may do exceptionally well on some of the Piagetian formal thought tasks. (The pendulum experiment is commonly employed in physics classes.) Gallagher and Noppe (35) write:

According to Piaget, a lawyer may be formally operational with respect to law, whereas carpenters, mechanics, or locksmiths can reason deductively about aspects of their particular trades. With this hypothesis in mind, it is possible that the persons most able to exhibit logical-mathematical reasoning while completing traditional tasks designed by Inhelder and Piaget are individuals associated with the sciences. Unfortunately, at present, there are few tasks devised to tap formal thought in specific content area. (35, p. 209)

Assuming that formal operations are manifested within the context of a particular aptitude, to get accurate measurement it will be necessary first to isolate the superior aptitude of each individual and then to present a formal task congruent with that aptitude. So far, no such individualized approach has been accomplished. (71, p. 418)

MOTIVATION AND RESPONSE

Mishra (54) urges caution in using the results of formal operations tests in predicting the scholastic behavior of adolescents. Test models describe what adolescents are capable of doing intellectually, but not necessarily what they will do in a specific situation. Fatigue, boredom, or other factors affecting motivation may prevent adolescents from displaying full cognitive performance in any given situation. Also, Piaget's models are qualitative, not quantitative, measurements. They are used to describe thought problems and do not necessarily duplicate or predict in depth the performance of adolescents.

THE ROLE OF SCHOOL AND EDUCATION

The development of abstract thinking and formal operations problem solving is encouraged in a number of ways. (21) Experimental or problematic situations can be presented that allow students opportunities to observe, analyze possibilities, and draw inferences about perceived relationships. Teachers who use authoritative approaches rather than social interchange stifle real thinking. Discussion groups, debates, question periods, problem solving sessions, and science experiments are approaches that encourage the development of formal thinking and problem solving abilities. Teachers need to be prepared to handle group discussions and stimulate interchange and feedback. (35, p. 226) Teachers must also be willing to give explicit help and encouragement and allow the necessary time for reasoning capacities to develop. Some students develop such abilities at a relatively slow pace. (4, p. 7) Piaget (61) sets forth two goals of education that incorporate this philosophy.

The principal goal of education is to create men who are capable of doing new things, not simply of repeating what other generations have done—men who are creative, inventive, and discoverers. The second goal of education is to form minds which can be critical, can verify, and not accept everything they are offered. . . . We need pupils who are active, who learn early to find out by themselves, partly by their own spontaneous activity and partly through material we set up for them; who learn early to tell what is verifiable and what is simply the first idea to come to them. (61, p. 5)

According to Elkind, several general principles of education are implicit in Piaget's image of the child. (28) The child's mind is not an empty slate. On the contrary, the child has a host of ideas about the natural and physical world, but they differ from those of adults and are expressed in a different linguistic mode. *The first prerequisite for educating children is to develop effective modes of communication with them.* (28, p. 108)

The second concept of education important for children is the need to aid them in the modification of their existing knowledge, in addition to helping them learn new material. Children are always unlearning, relearning, and acquiring new knowledge. They come to school with their own ideas of space, time, causality, quantity, and number. The purpose of education is to broaden incomplete knowledge.

Third, children are by nature knowing creatures, and the desire to know is part of their makeup. *Education need not concern itself with instilling a zest for knowledge; rather, it needs to insure that it does not dull their eagerness by overly rigid curricula that disrupt the child's own rhythm and pace of learning.* (28, p. 109) The best teacher is dedicated to the growth of both pupils and self, is curious to learn, is willing to try new things, to evaluate and be critical, and tries to instill similar values in the pupils. A true dedication to growth involves a commitment to help children find their own abilities in their own way in their own time, but it realizes that growth, like life, involves conflict, constant change, and problems. A dedication to growth involves courage to live. (28, p. 127)

Conclusions

One significant point of this chapter is that there is no set pattern of mental growth during adolescence. The rate of mental growth for the individual young person may remain the same, speed up, slow down, or accelerate and decelerate in steps. What happens to the individual will depend upon such factors as opportunities for learning experiences to which he or she is exposed.

Second, an IQ score is not something with which one is born. It is not a measure of innate intelligence, and should never be considered one, for emotional, motivational, and sociocultural factors have a dramatic influence on test scores. Furthermore, there are individual variations in IQ over a period of years, sometimes as much as 40 points. Scores should never be used to label the individual dull, average, or superior; rather, scores should be used as a general guide to the level of mental functioning (on standardized tests) at that particular time. Because many tests are biased against those from low socioeconomic status groups and different ethnic and national backgrounds, any test results from such individuals must be interpreted with extreme caution.

Third, contrary to popular opinion, the ability of adolescents to remember is superior to that of children; this ability continues to improve from childhood to adulthood. Adolescents have a greater ability to sort out irrelevant material; they are less distractible and can concentrate on material they are supposed to remember.

Fourth and most important, during adolescence (Piaget says around eleven or twelve years of age) the cognitive processes change from the concrete operational stage to the formal operational stage. That is, many adolescents develop the ability to think about thought, become capable of propositional logic, and begin to distinguish the real from the possible.

Fifth, these new cognitive abilities of adolescents have some profound effects on their behavior. As they evaluate their parents, society, and the world, they grow dissatisfied with things as they are, dream of the way things might be, and often become idealistic rebels, critical of the adult world and society around them. The idealism of younger adolescents is largely on a verbal level, for they initiate little positive action to change things. Late in adolescence, they either have begun to give up unrealistic idealism or to initiate some actions to express their ideals.

During this time, adolescents become very egocentric as they begin to look at themselves and think about their thoughts. This makes them very self-conscious, with the feeling that others are watching and observing everything they say and do. They sometimes become overly concerned with their appearance and behavior. Their egocentricism is also expressed along with their idealism in wanting to reform the world according to their own ideas and images. A developing interest in intellectualization and asceticism is but one of numerous psychological defense mechanisms adolescents use to protect their fragile egos.

Because of their ability to project themselves into the future, adolescents become concerned about the development of a life plan for themselves and how they can best adopt a social role so that they can take their places in the adult world. When they undertake a real job, they become achievers, not just dreamers, and are assuming roles as autonomous adults.

Topics for Term Papers

1. Cultural Deprivation and How It Affects Mental Growth
2. Nutritional Deficiencies and Their Effects on Mental Retardation
3. Heredity and Intelligence
4. How Environment Influences Intelligence
5. Language and Formal Operational Thinking
6. How Adolescent Thought Differs from Childhood Thought
7. Abstract Thinking of Adolescents
8. The Relationship of Logic to Formal Operational Thought
9. Contemporary Research Findings on Formal Operational Thinking
10. Formal Operational Thinking and the Scientific Method
11. Idealism during Adolescence
12. Adolescent Egocentricism
13. Correlations with Achieving Formal Operational Thinking
14. The Relationship of IQ and Formal Operational Thinking Ability
15. Formal Operational Thinking and Underdeveloped Societies and Cultures
16. Can Formal Operational Thinking be Taught?
17. Piaget's Philosophy of Education in Relation to Formal Operational Thinking

18. The Parental Role in Developing Creativity
19. Criticisms of Piaget's Formal Operational Stage of Development
20. The Practical Significance of Formal Operational Thinking

Bibliography

1. Adams, G. R. "Personal Identity Formation: A Synthesis of Cognitive and Ego Psychology." *Adolescence* 12 (Summer 1977): 151–164.

2. Adelson, J. "The Political Imagination of the Young Adolescent." In *Twelve to Sixteen: Early Adolescence.* Edited by Jerome Kagan and Robert Coles. New York: W. W. Norton & Co., 1972, pp. 106–143.

3. "Aptitude-Test Scores: Grumbling Gets Louder." *U.S. News & World Report*, 14 May 1979, pp. 76ff.

4. Arons, A. B. "Reasoning Modes and Processes Arising in Secondary and College Level Study of Natural Science, Humanities, and the Social Sciences." *Andover Review* 5 (Fall 1978): 3–8.

5. Barenboim, C. "Developmental Changes in the Interpersonal Cognitive System from Middle Childhood to Adolescence." *Child Development* 48 (December 1977): 1467–1474.

6. Baughman, E. E. "Development of Mental Abilities from Birth through 36 Years." *Roche Report: Frontiers in Hospital Psychiatry* 5 (1968): 5–6, 11.

7. ———. *Black Americans.* New York: Academic Press, 1971.

8. Bauman, R. P. "Teaching for Cognitive Development." *Andover Review* 5 (Spring 1978): 83–98.

9. Berzonsky, M. D. "Formal Reasoning in Adolescence: An Alternative View." *Adolescence* 13 (Summer 1978): 279–290.

10. Bloom, B. S. *Stability and Change in Human Characteristics.* New York: John Wiley and Sons, 1964.

11. Blos, P. *The Young Adolescent: Clinical Studies.* New York: Free Press, 1970.

12. Bodmer, W. F., and Cavalli-Sforza, L. L. "Intelligence and Race." *Scientific American* 4 (1970): 19–29.

13. Brown, W. H. "Before and After." *Andover Review* 5 (Spring 1978): 40–49.

14. Calhoun, G. "New Trends in Special Education." *Adolescence* 13 (Spring 1978): 55–58.

15. Campbell, P. B. "Adolescent Intellectual Decline." *Adolescence* 11 (Winter 1976): 629–635.

16. Carlson, J. S. "Crosscultural Piagetian Studies: What Can They Tell Us?" Paper presented at the biennial meeting of the International Society for the Study of Be-

havioral Development. Ann Arbor, Mich., 1973.

17. Cattell, R. B. *Abilities: Their Structure, Growth and Action.* Boston: Houghton Mifflin Co., 1971.

18. Cloutier, R., and Goldschmid, M. L. "Individual Differences in the Development of Formal Reasoning." *Child Development* 47 (December 1976): 1097–1102.

19. College Entrance Examination Board. *National College-Bound Seniors.* Princeton, N.J., 1979.

20. Crow, A. *Educational Psychology*, rev. ed. Totowa, N.J.: Littlefield, Adams & Co., 1972.

21. Danner, F. W., and Day, M. C. "Eliciting Formal Operations." *Child Development* 48 (December 1977): 1600–1606.

22. Dasen, P. "Cross-cultural Piagetian Research: A Summary." *Journal of Cross-Cultural Psychology* 3 (1972): 23–39.

23. DeCecco, J. P. *The Psychology of Learning and Instruction: Educational Psychology.* Englewood Cliffs, N.J.: Prentice-Hall, 1968.

24. Dowaliby, F. J., and Schumer, H. "Teacher-centered versus Student-centered Mode of College Classroom Instruction as Related to Manifest Anxiety." *Proceedings*, 79th Annual Convention, American Psychological Association 108 (1971).

25. Dulit, E. "Adolescent Thinking à la Piaget: The Formal Stage." *Journal of Youth and Adolescence* 1 (1972): 281–301.

26. Elkind, D. "Conceptual Orientation Shifts in Children and Adolescents." *Child Development* 37 (1966): 493–498.

27. ———. "Egocentrism in Adolescence." *Child Development* 38 (1967): 1025–1034.

28. ———. *Children and Adolescents: Interpretive Essays on Jean Piaget.* New York: Oxford University Press, 1970.

29. ———. "Measuring Young Minds." *Horizon* 13 (1971): 35.

30. ———. "Recent Research on Cognitive Development in Adolescence." In *Adolescence in the Life Cycle.* Edited by S. E. Dragastin and G. H. Elder, Jr. New York: John Wiley and Sons, 1975, pp. 49–61.

31. ———. "Understanding the Young Adolescent." *Adolescence* 13 (Spring 1978): 127–134.

32. Furth, H. G. *Piaget and Knowledge.*

Englewood Cliffs, N.J.: Prentice-Hall, 1969.

33. ———. "On Language and Knowing in Piaget's Developmental Theory." *Human Development* 13 (1970): 241–257.

34. ———. *Piaget for Teachers.* Englewood Cliffs, N.J.: Prentice-Hall, 1970.

35. Gallagher, J. M., and Noppe, I. C. "Cognitive Development and Learning." In *Understanding Adolescence.* 3d ed. Edited by J. F. Adams. Boston: Allyn and Bacon, 1976, pp. 199–232.

36. Gaylord-Ross, R. J. "Paired-Associate Learning and Formal Thinking in Adolescence." *Journal of Youth and Adolescence* 4 (1975): 375–382.

37. Ginsburg, H., and Opper, S. *Piaget's Theory of Intellectual Development: An Introduction.* Englewood Cliffs, N.J.: Prentice-Hall, 1969.

38. Higgins-Trenk, A., and Guithe, A. J. H. "Elusiveness of Formal Operational Thought in Adolescents." *Proceedings,* 79th Annual Convention, American Psychological Association 108 (1971).

39. "High School Grades Show Standards Drop." *Maine Sunday Telegram* 16 January 1977.

40. Hobbs, E. D. "Adolescents' Concepts of Physical Quantity." *Developmental Psychology* 9 (1973): 431.

41. Holroyd, R. G., and Bickley, J. "Comparison of the 1960 and 1972 Revisions of the Stanford Binet LM." *Journal of Youth and Adolescence* 5 (1976): 101–104.

42. Inhelder, B., and Piaget, J. *The Growth Of Logical Thinking from Childhood to Adolescence.* New York: Basic Books, 1958.

43. Jensen, A. R. "How Much Can We Boost IQ and Scholastic Achievement?" *Harvard Education Review* 39 (1969): 1–123.

44. ———. "IQ's of Identical Twins Reared Apart." *Behavior Genetics* 1 (1970): 133–148.

45. Kagan, J. A. "A Conception of Adolescence." *Daedalus* (Fall 1971): 997–1012.

46. Kennedy, W. A. *Child Psychology.* Englewood Cliffs, N.J.: Prentice-Hall, 1971.

47. Kohlberg, L., and Gilligan, C. "The Adolescent as a Philosopher: The Discovery of the Self in a Postconventional World." *Daedalus* (Fall 1971): 1051–1086.

48. Looft, W. R. "Egocentrism and Social Interaction in Adolescence." *Adolescence* 6 (1971): 487–494.

49. Maccoby, E. E., and Hagen, J. W. "Effect of Distraction upon Central versus Incidental Recall: Developmental Trends." *Journal of Experimental Child Psychology* 2 (1965): 280–289.

50. May, M. A., and Lumsdane, A. A. *Learning from Films.* New Haven, Conn.: Yale University Press, 1958.

51. Mecke, G., and Mecke, V. "The Development of Formal Thought as Shown by Explanation of the Oscillations of a Pendulum: A Replication Study." *Adolescence* 6 (1971): 219–228.

52. Milgram, R. M. "Quantity and Quality of Creative Thinking in Children and Adolescents." *Child Development* 49 (June 1978): 385–388.

53. Miller, J. P. "Piaget, Kohlberg, and Erikson: Developmental Implications for Secondary Education." *Adolescence* 13 (Summer 1978): 237–250.

54. Mishra, S. P. "Cognitive Growth in Adolescence." In *Contemporary Adolescence: Readings.* 2d ed. Edited by H. D. Thornburg. Monterey, Calif.: Brooks/Cole Publishing Co., 1975, pp. 58–64.

55. Muuss, R. E. *Theories of Adolescence.* 3d ed. New York: Random House, 1975. Used with permission.

56. Nichols, R. C. "Nature and Nurture." In *Understanding Adolescence.* 3d ed. Edited by J. F. Adams. Boston: Allyn and Bacon, 1976, pp. 84–116.

57. Okun, M. A., and Sasfy, J. H. "Adolescence, the Self-Concept, and Formal Operations." *Adolescence* 12 (Fall 1977): 373–379.

58. Owens, W. A., Jr. "Age and Mental Abilities: A Second Adult Follow-Up." *Journal of Educational Psychology* 57 (1966): 311–325.

59. Phillips, J. J., Jr. *The Origin of Intellect: Piaget's Theory.* San Francisco: W. H. Freeman and Co., 1969.

60. Piaget, J. *The Psychology of Intelligence.* London: Routledge and Kegan Paul, 1950.

61. ———. "Development and Learning." In *Piaget Rediscovered: A Report of the Conference on Cognitive Studies and Curriculum Development, March 1964.* Edited by R. E. Ripple and V. N. Rockcastle. Ithaca, N.Y.: Cornell University Press, 1964.

62. ———. *Six Psychological Studies.* Translated by A. Tenzer and D. Elkind. New York: Random House, 1967.

63. ———. "Intellectual Evolution from Adolescence to Adulthood." *Human Development* 15 (1972): 1012.

64. ———. "The Theory of Stages in Cognitive Development." In *Measurement and Piaget.* Edited by D. R. Green. New York: McGraw-Hill, 1971.

65. Piaget, J., and Inhelder, B. *The Psychology of the Child.* New York: Basic Books, 1969.

66. Pinneau, S. R. "Changes in Intelli-

gence Quotient." Boston: Houghton Mifflin Co., 1961.

67. Rice, B. "The SAT Controversy: When an Aptitude Is Coachable." *Psychology Today* (September 1979): 30ff.

68. ———. "Brave New World of Intelligence Testing." *Psychology Today* (September 1979): 27ff.

69. Rosenthal, R., and Jacobson, L. *Pygmalion in the Classroom: Teacher Expectation and Pupil's Intellectual Development.* New York: Holt, Rinehart and Winston, 1968.

70. Ross, R. J. "Some Empirical Parameters of Formal Thinking." *Journal of Youth and Adolescence* 2 (1973): 167–177.

71. ———. "The Empirical Status of the Formal Operations." *Adolescence* 9 (1974): 413–420.

72. ———. "The Development of Formal Thinking and Creativity in Adolescence." *Adolescence* 11 (Winter 1976): 609–617.

73. "SAT Scores Take Nose Dive for Tenth Straight Year." *Maine Sunday Telegram*, 9 September 1979.

74. Scarr, S., and Weinberg, R. A. "The Influence of 'Family Background' on Intellectual Attainment." *American Sociological Review* 43 (October 1978): 674–692.

75. Schaie, K. W., and Strother, C. R. "A Cross-Sequential Study of Age Changes in Cognitive Behavior." *Psychological Bulletin* 70 (1968): 671–680.

76. Scarr-Salapatek, S. "Environment, Heredity, and Intelligence: The IQ Argument." *Science* 174 (1971): 1223–1228.

77. Shapiro, S. H. "Vicissitudes of Adolescence." In *Behavior Pathology of Childhood and Adolescence.* Edited by S. L. Copel. New York: Basic Books, 1973, pp. 93–117.

78. Smart, M. S., and Smart, R. C. *Children: Development and Relationships.*

2d ed. New York: Macmillan Co., 1972.

79. ———. *Adolescents: Development and Relationships.* New York: Macmillan Co., 1973.

80. Stennet, R. G. "Relationship of Sex and Socioeconomic Status to IQ Change." *Psychology in the Schools* 6 (1969): 385–390.

81. Stephens, B. et al. "Ages at Which Piagetian Concepts Are Achieved." *Proceedings.* 79th Annual Convention, American Psychological Association 108 (1971).

82. Stroud, J. B., and Maul, R. "The Influence of Age on Learning and Retention of Poetry." *Journal of Genetic Psychology* 42 (1933): 242–250.

83. Terman, L. M., and Merrill, M. A. *Stanford Binet Intelligence Scale: Manual for the Third Revision: 1972 Norms Edition.* Boston: Houghton Mifflin Co., 1973.

84. Tomlinson-Keasey, C. "Formal Operations in Females from Eleven to Fifty-four Years of Age." *Developmental Psychology* 6 (1972): 364.

85. ———. "The Emergence of Specific Cognitive Operations during the Period of Formal Operations." Paper presented at the Annual Meeting of the Eastern Psychological Association, April 1972.

86. Webb, R. A. "Concrete and Formal Operations in Very Bright 6- to 11-year-olds." *Human Development* 17 (1974): 292–300.

87. Youniss, J., and Dean, A. "Judgment and Imaging Aspects of Operations: A Piagetian Study with Korean and Costa Rican Children." *Child Development* 45 (1974): 1020–1031.

88. Yudin, L. W. "Formal Thought in Adolescence as a Function of Intelligence." *Child Development* 37 (1966): 697–708.

89. Zach, L. "IQ Test: Does It Make Black Children Unequal?" *School Review* 78 (1970): 249–258.

PART 4

Emotional

CHAPTER 8

Self-Concept and Self-Esteem

Outline

Perhaps no aspect of adolescent psychology has received more attention over the years than the subjects of self-concept and self-esteem. (32) As early as 1890, William James devoted a whole chapter to the self in *The Principles of Psychology*. (32, 41) Carl Rogers made his 1947 address before the American Psychological Association on self-concept (70), as did Hilgard in 1949. (37) More recently, Morris Rosenberg was co-winner of the 1963 Socio-Psychological Prize given by the American Association for the Advancement of Science with his monumental study and report on *Society and the Adolescent Self-Image*. (73) The subject continues to receive more attention than probably any other topic in adoloscent psychology.

This chapter will consider and discuss the meaning of both self-concept and self-esteem and their importance and relationship to mental health, interpersonal competence and social adjustments, school progress, vocational aspirations, and delinquency. The development of a positive self-concept will be emphasized along with its relationship to maternal and paternal identification, parental interest and concern, broken homes, socioeconomic status, and birth order. The chapter concludes by considering the relative stability of self-concept during adolescence; that is, whether the adolescent's self-conception changes.

Meaning and Explanation

SELF-CONCEPT

The *self* has been defined as that part of one's personality of which one is aware. *Self-concept* may be defined as conscious, cognitive perception and evaluation by individuals of themselves; it is their thoughts and opinions about themselves. It has been called the individual's "self-hypothesized identity." Erikson refers to it as the individual's "ego identity," or the individual's self-perceived, consistent individuality. (25, 26) It begins with an awareness of uniqueness, an awareness that individuals are distinct, separate from others, people in their own right. (25) This first awareness was described by a young adolescent girl: "I was sitting in the taxi with my mother when I suddenly realized, it dawned on me, that I am I and she is she." The first step in the development of a self-concept is the recognition that one is a distinct, separate individual.

Self-concept also implies a developing awareness of *who* and *what* one is. (25, 38) It describes what individuals see when they look at themselves, in terms of their self-perceived physical characteristics, personality skills, traits, roles, and social statuses. It might be described as the system of attitudes they have about themselves. (55; 89, p. 509) It is their ego identity or personal identity, which is the sum total of their self-definitions or self-images. (1, p. 151)

Numerous writers have emphasized that a development of the sense of self is not possible until adolescents reach a formal operations stage of cognitive development. (1, 22, 24, 53, 58, 94) This stage enables them to think about themselves, to become self-conscious, to become introspective. Adolescents gather evidence that helps them evaluate themselves: Am I competent? Am I attractive to the opposite sex? Am I intelligent? Am I friendly? From this evidence they form postulates about themselves and check out their feelings and opinions through further experiences and relationships. They compare themselves with their own ideals and those of others.

Through experience (often painful . . .) the adolescent gradually becomes more specific and realistic in his self-theory; he draws parameters for his self-theory to avoid unnecessary disillusionment and to insure optimal functioning. . . . We can view adolescence not only as physical emergence, but as a unique type of cognitive emergence embracing the important function of the construction of a viable self-theory. (58, p. 378)

Whether individuals have an accurate self-concept is significant. All people are really six different selves: the people they really are, the people they think they are, the people others think they are, the people they think others think they are, the people they really want to become, and the people they think others want them to become. Self-concepts may or may not be close approximations of reality, and the self-concepts are always in the process of becoming, particularly during childhood, when they are undergoing the maximum change. A number of years ago, in a book entitled *Becoming: Basic Considerations for a Psychology of Personality*, Gordon W. Allport (3) emphasized that personality is less a finished product than a transitive process: it has some stable features, but at the same time it is undergoing change. Allport coined the word *proprium*, which he defined as "all aspects of personality that make for inward unity." This is the self or ego that has a core of personal identity that is developing in time.

Ruth Strang, of Columbia University, outlines four basic dimensions of the self. (86) First, there is the overall, basic self-concept, which is the adolescent's view of his or her personality and "perceptions of his abilities and his status and roles in the outer world." (86, p. 68)

Second, there are the individual's temporary or transitory self-concepts. (86, p. 71) These ideas of self are influenced by the mood of the moment or by a recent or continuing experience. A recent low grade on an examination may leave a temporary feeling of being stupid, a critical remark from parents may produce a temporary feeling of deflated self-worth.

Third, there are the adolescents' social selves, the selves that they think others see, which influence in turn how they see themselves. If they have the impression that others think they are dumb or socially unacceptable, they tend to think of themselves in these negative ways. Their perceptions of others' feelings color their views of themselves. Identity comes partly from an involvement of the self with others, in intimacy, love, group participation, cooperation, and competition. It evolves through social interactions, encompassing both continuity of self and identification with something beyond the self. William Carlyle states: "Show me the man who is your friend and I will know what your ideal of manhood is— and what kind of man you wish to be." (17)

A part of self-concept is the sense of social status, the position in which individuals place themselves in the social system in the present or the future. For example, adolescents from low socioeconomic status groups who see themselves as not belonging there, but as members of a higher socioeconomic class, are molding/new identities because of their higher aspirations.

Fourth, there is the ideal self, the kind of people adolescents would like to be. (86, p. 71; 92) Their aspirations may be realistic, too low, or too high. Ideal selves that are too low impede accomplishment; those that are too high may lead to frustration and self-deprecation. Realistic self-concepts lead to self-acceptance, mental health, and accomplishment of realistic goals.

SELF-ESTEEM

Having built concepts of themselves, adolescents must deal with the esteem with which they view themselves. When they perceive themselves, what value do they place on the selves they perceive? Does this appraisal lead to self-acceptance and approval, to a feeling of self-worth? If so, then they have enough self-esteem to accept and live with themselves. If people are to have self-esteem, there must be a correspondence between their concepts of self and their self ideals. (16, 18)

With the onset of puberty, most young people begin to make a thorough assessment of themselves, comparing not only their body parts but also their motor skills, intellectual abilities, talents, and social skills with those of their peers and their ideals or heroes. It is not surprising that this critical self-appraisal is accompanied by self-conscious behavior that makes adolescents vulnerable to embarrassment. (48, p. 141) As a consequence, throughout adolescence, they are preoccupied with attempting to reconcile their selves as they perceive them with their ideal selves. By late adolescence they may have managed to sort themselves out—to determine what they can most effectively be and to integrate their goals into their ideal selves. (71, p. 19)

Carl Rogers is one of the most important contemporary theorists in the development of a theoretical and practical structure of self-ideals. (70) Rogers pictures the end point of personality development as a basic congruence between the phenomenal field and experience and the conceptual structure of the self—a situation that results in freedom from internal conflict and anxiety. What individuals discover they are and what they perceive themselves to be and want to be begin to merge, and they are therefore able to accept themselves, be themselves, and live as themselves without conflict. Their self-perception and relationships with others bring self-acceptance and self-esteem. Psychological maladjustment occurs when there is a divergence between the selves they are being in relationship to others and the selves they perceive that they are or want to be. (32, p. 9)

Importance of an Adequate Self-Concept and Self-Esteem

MENTAL HEALTH

Self-esteem has been called "the survival of the soul"; it is the ingredient that gives dignity to human existence. It grows out of human interaction in which the self is considered important to someone. The ego grows through small accomplishments, praise, and success.

A definite correlation has been established between mental health and identity achievement. (59) One author describes several male students with very diffused or uncertain identities.

These people were diffused in that they seemed to have few plans or personal commitments. . . . With regard to politics, religion and sexual relationships, these individuals were also vague and sometimes had trouble dealing with the questions at all. . . . The identity diffused not only had made few commitments but were unable or unwilling to attempt to define what they wished or what they felt. "I don't know" and "I'm not very settled about that" were frequent answers. . . . In appearance these students were conventional enough, but they shared a sheepish, apprehensive look, as if they expected to be called to task by a critical voice.

The daily lives of these students tended toward disorganization. They slept more and at more irregular hours. . . . They cut class frequently, but spent the extra time alone, not talking with friends. . . . They appeared isolated and without interest in the people or activities around them. . . .

Feelings of "inferiority," "alienation," and "ambivalence" were often mentioned. . . . Of all those we interviewed, these seemed to have the lowest sense of self-esteem. They were frightened, sad people. (20, p. 32)

Individuals whose identities are weak or whose self-esteem has never sufficiently developed, manifest a number of symptoms of emotional ill health. They may evidence psychosomatic symptoms of anxiety: hand trembling, nervousness, insomnia, palpitations of the heart, pressures or pains in the head, fingernail biting, shortness of breath when not exercising or working hard, palm perspiration, sick headaches, and nightmares. (3, p. 54) They are more likely to indicate that they suffer from nervousness, loss of appetite, insomnia, and headache. Conversely, those with the highest self-esteem are much less likely to have psychosomatic symptoms. (73, pp. 149–154)

Sometimes the adolescent with a weak identity and low self-esteem tries to develop a false front or facade with which to face the world. The facade is a compensating mechanism; its aim is to overcome the feeling of worthlessness by convincing others that one is worthy: "I try to put on an act to impress people." But putting on an act is a strain. To act confident, friendly, and cheerful when one feels the opposite is a constant struggle. The anxiety that one might make a false step and let the guard slip creates considerable tension.

Another reason for anxiety is that the person with low self-esteem shows a shifting and unstable identity. Rosenberg showed that students with low self-esteem were four times as likely as those with high self-esteem to have "very unstable" self-pictures. (73, p. 152)

Adolescents with low self-esteem are overly vulnerable to criticism, rejection, or any evidence in their daily lives that testifies to their inadequacy, incompetence, or worthlessness. They may be deeply disturbed when laughed at, scolded, blamed, or when others have a poor opinion of them. The more vulnerable they feel themselves to be, the higher their anxiety levels. Such adolescents report: "Criticism hurts me terribly" or "I can't stand to have anyone laugh at me or blame me when something goes wrong." As a result they feel awkward and uneasy in social situations and avoid embarrassment whenever they can.

INTERPERSONAL COMPETENCE AND SOCIAL ADJUSTMENTS

Those with poor self-concepts are often rejected by other people. Acceptance of others, acceptance by others, and acceptance by best friends are related to self-concept scores, with highest acceptance in a group with moderate self-concept scores and lowest in a group with low self-concept scores. "Acceptance of self is positively and significantly correlated with acceptance of, and by, others." Thus, "there is a close relationship between self-acceptance and social adjust-ment." One of the signs of possible disturbance during adolescence is an inability to establish friendships or to meet new people. (4, p. 58; 27, p. 290)

Poor social adjustment, which is related to low self-concept and self-esteem, manifests itself in a number of ways. Adolescents with low self-esteem tend to be outstanding in their social invisibility. (See Chapter 11.) They aren't noticed or selected as leaders and they do not participate as often in class, club, or social activities. They don't stand up for their own rights or express their opinions on matters that concern them. (4, p. 58) These adolescents more often develop feel-ings of isolation and are more often afflicted with pangs of loneliness. One man writes: "I used to be so shy that I first went out with a woman at 21. Words cannot express how excruciatingly, how desperately lonely I was in those days." (93, p. 18) These people often feel awkward and tense in social situations, which makes it more difficult for them to communicate with others: "I am kind of hes-itant in a large group of people." "I get all quiet." "I don't like to say anything, the words just don't come out right." They desperately want others to like them, but because they are less likely to feel they have likeable qualities, they are less likely to consider themselves well-liked and respected. Because they want to be liked, they are more easily influenced and led, and usually let others make de-cisions because they lack the necessary self-confidence. One person commented: "I believe now that one of my ways of coping with shyness was to go to great lengths to be pleasing, even to the point of being submissive in thought and action." (93, p. 18) Those who submit unwillingly to others are less likely to like them, and to have faith in them. If adolescents have a fundamental contempt for themselves, they will hate and despise others, but if they trust and respect themselves, then they also will trust and respect others as members of the human race.

PROGRESS IN SCHOOL

An increasing amount of evidence supports the theory that there is a correlation between self-concept and achievement in school. Successful students feel more sense of personal worth and somewhat better about themselves. In general, the higher the grade averages, the more likely the student is to have a high level of self-acceptance. Strathe and Hash write: "A significant relationship among such things as academic achievement, school satisfaction, and self-esteem has been reported for individuals at all grade levels from primary grades through col-lege." (87, p. 185) The authors point out that there are "significant and positive correlations between self-concept and performance in the academic role," and that studies of school dropouts show that low aspirations, accomplishments, and self-esteem were already present or predictable by the start of the tenth grade. (87, p. 186) One reason is that students who have confidence in themselves have

the courage to try and are motivated to live up to what they believe about themselves. Students who have negative attitudes about themselves impose limitations on their own achievement. (64) They feel they "can't do it anyhow" or
they are "not smart enough." (32, p. 59)

This relationship between negative self-concept and school achievement begins very early. (32, p. 59) Unfavorable views of self may already be established
before children enter first grade. These children start out in school with a feeling
they aren't going to do well, and as a result, they don't. Underachievement can
begin in first grade, become more serious by third grade, and be well established
and increasingly difficult to deal with in the high school years. This has been
found to be especially true of males, who seem to exhibit a stronger relationship
between self-concept and achievement than do females. (32, p. 60)

Which comes first, a positive self-concept or high achievement? The two
factors are mutually reinforcing. A positive self-concept contributes to high
achievement, and high achievement in turn can enhance self-concept. (30, 87)
This is not necessarily true, however, for boys from minority groups. As a group,
Rosenberg found that these boys had distinctly lower grades than other boys,
although about one-fourth had better than average grades. This small group
had higher self-esteem not because of their grades but in spite of their grades,
for high grades were criticized by this minority group. (73, p. 120) Whenever an
intelligent student is underachieving, there is almost always some kind of emotional difficulty: "They are working in a vacuum, have a feeling of basic inferiority, are being rebellious, or have a fear of success." (10, p. 28) One survey of
ninth-grade girls showed that 54 percent of these girls revealed some fear of
success in relation to academic achievement. (33) They feared that others would
reject them for being too outstanding and that they would not be normal in the
eyes of their friends. In other cases, they were simply unable to accept that success could be possible for them. (33, p. 138)

In another study, females consistently underestimated their actual IQ scores
in relation to those of males, and they typically attributed higher IQs to others
than they claimed for themselves. These self-perceived intellectual limitations,
due no doubt to socially imposed prejudicial images, would certainly be a handicap to them. (39)

The attitudes of significant others—mothers, fathers, grandparents, older
siblings, special friends, teachers, or school counselors—can have an important
influence on students' academic self-concepts. In one study, 40 percent of black
high school seniors ranked above average in their academic self-concepts, and
54 percent of the remaining students ranked average. (42) These high self-
concepts were the result of the positive attitudes and support other important
persons showed toward these students. The students in this sample felt that
others had confidence in their academic abilities, so they had confidence in
themselves. (42)

VOCATIONAL ASPIRATIONS

The desire and expectation to get ahead vocationally also depend upon self-
esteem. Studies have shown that women who have a chance to have both a
career and marriage tend to have higher self-esteem than those who have become

homemakers. (9) Boys who aspire to upward mobility also show a strong sense of self-esteem, whereas downwardly mobile boys more often wish for changes in self that are so extensive that they indicate self-rejection. Both those with low and high self-esteem consider it important to get ahead, but those with low self-esteem are less likely to expect they will succeed. They are more likely to say, "I would like to get ahead in life, but I don't think I will ever get ahead as far as I would like." They less often think they possess those qualities essential for success. Rosenberg reports: "The only quality considered essential for success which low self-esteem people feel they possess as much as others is 'knowing the right people.' " (73, p. 236)

There is a difference also in the types of positions desired by low and high self-esteem adolescents. In general, those with low self-esteem want to avoid both positions in which they will be forced to exercise leadership and jobs in which others dominate them; they want to be neither power wielders nor power subjects. Avoiding leadership or supervision by others is a way of avoiding criticism or judgment. The occupational predicament of the low self-esteem person may be summarized thus: "The very thing that makes him so strongly desire success, viz., his low self-esteem, also makes him anticipate failure and very likely helps to produce failure." (73, pp. 225–239)

The relationship between self-esteem and occupational success was revealed by an examination of personality characteristics of youthful Peace Corps volunteers. (83) Volunteers who were successful had self-concepts of competence and were self-confident, dependable, and responsible; felt their own lives were important and that it mattered what they did with them; were open to experience and ready to learn; were tolerant and understanding; and were intellectually articulate in formulating their situations and problems. (83, p. 400) Those who were unsuccessful had low self-esteem; were basically dependent, leaning on others for support; had high levels of anxiety; were pessimistic and expected little of life; generally lacked energy; were suspicious of others; gave up easily when faced with setbacks; tended to drift when things went badly; were unable to accept help from others when in need; were preoccupied with physical health; were irritable over petty annoyances; were concerned with maintaining face; and tended unrealistically to minimize or to deny the difficulties they faced. (83, p. 400)

DELINQUENCY

There is also a close relationship between delinquency and self-concept. Delinquent youths tend to show lower self-esteem than do nondelinquent youths. (54, 67) Their delinquency may be over-compensation for their inadequate self-concepts. One theory is that they have low self-esteem, and so adopt deviant patterns of behavior to reduce self-rejecting feelings. (45) In other words, if their behavior begins to match their low opinions of themselves, they decrease their own self-derogation and rejection. (45) They seek to restore their self-respect by aligning themselves with deviant groups which accord them the approval denied by the rest of society. (76) Thus, an adequate self-concept protects the adolescent from delinquency; those who see themselves as "good people" or "nondelinquents" have developed an inner containment against becoming delinquent. (80)

Development of a Positive Self-Concept

A number of factors contribute to the development of a positive self-concept and high self-esteem. (11) These factors are summarized in the following paragraphs.

MATERNAL RELATIONSHIP AND IDENTIFICATION

Late adolescent girls who feel close to their mothers tend to see themselves as confident, wise, reasonable, and self-controlled. Those who feel distant from their mothers tend to perceive themselves in negative terms: as rebellious, impulsive, touchy, and tactless. (31, p. 159) These findings indicate that the degree of maternal identification influences self-concept. Both males and females who identify closely with a parental model strive to be like the model in such a way that a blending of self with the qualities of the model brings about a real likeness but not an identity. (6, 52) Erikson felt that over-identification with parents cuts off a "budding identity" by stifling the ego. (25) However, children with inadequate parental identification will also have poor ego identity. (52) Research indicates that ego identity of girls is weak with poor maternal identification and weak again with over-identification that borders on the pathological. A moderate degree of identification seems to be the most healthy.

The mothers with whom adolescent girls identify vary greatly. Mothers who believe in sex-role equality, whose concepts of ideal daughters are those who are independent, self-sufficient, and free of external control, are likely to have daughters who develop positive self-images by believing in the same principles. These are the girls who grow to become active members of the women's liberation movement, who are politically and socially gregarious, and who value personal autonomy and humanitarianism. (46)

PATERNAL RELATIONSHIP AND IDENTIFICATION

Fathers are important, too, in a girl's development. Warm, rewarding father-daughter relationships play a vital role in helping a girl to value her femininity and to move toward a positive acceptance of herself as a woman. (8, 36) The adolescent girl who values and loves her father and whose father values and loves her invariably seems more comfortable with her own femaleness and with her relationship to men. (31, p. 159) As a result she is able to make easier and more satisfactory heterosexual adjustments. The same is true for the adolescent boy. If he is identified with his father but shares mutually warm feelings with his mother, his relationships with women are more likely to be comfortable and pleasant. (31, p. 159)

Middle class fathers are considerably more likely than working class fathers to be supportive of their sons, although only somewhat more likely to be supportive of their daughters. As a result middle class boys tend to have a higher self-esteem than those from working class families, for adolescents who have a close relationship with their fathers are considerably more likely to have high self-esteem and a stable self-image than are those who describe these relationships as distant. In order to test the thesis that father-son closeness and not social class is the determining factor in self-esteem, Rosenberg controlled (by means of standardization) the theoretical father-son relationships of upper and lower class boys so they were equally close to their fathers. Under these conditions, he found that the upper class boys were slightly less likely to have self-esteem than were the lower class boys. (73, p. 45) This study emphasizes dramatically that the relationship of an adolescent boy with his father is even more important than social class in building self-esteem. Other data confirm the well-known psychoanalytic theory that boys' positive relationships with their fathers and girls' relationships with their mothers are more crucial to adequate self-concept than is membership in a social class.

PARENTAL INTEREST, CONCERN, AND DISCIPLINE

A key factor in determining whether or not parents have a positive effect in helping their adolescents build a healthy ego identity is the warmth, concern, and interest they show them. (19) The more parental care and interest there is, the more likely the adolescent is to have high self-esteem. (31) High self-esteem adolescents also report that their parents accept, understand, and like them; those with low self-esteem have parents who use psychological pressure techniques such as withdrawal of love, guilt, or self-pity to control them. Students who say their parents know most of their friends have higher self-esteem than those whose parents know only a few of their friends. Students whose parents give supportive responses to good grades and other positive behavior have higher self-esteem than those who report indifferent or critical responses. (47) Furthermore, high self-esteem adolescent boys have parents who are democratic but also less permissive than those of low self-esteem boys. (7) Their parents are strict but consistent, and they demand high standards, although they are also flexible enough to allow deviations from rules under special circumstances. (28, p. 47) There seems to be a proper combination of warmth and firm discipline. The relationship with parents appears to be characterized by good communication, strong identification, and ties of affection. (60, p. 229) Low self-esteem boys have parents who are sometimes permissive but occasionally harsh when their children go beyond the limits they will tolerate. Sometimes the parents are too restrictive or inconsistent in their discipline (31) or they are critical and rejective of their children. (32, p. 27)

BROKEN FAMILIES

What happens to the self-esteem of the growing child when a family is broken by divorce? Rosenberg found that it depends upon a number of factors. (73, p. 105) The mother's age at the time of the marital rupture is important: if the mother was very young, the negative effect upon the child was much greater than if the mother was older, because the younger mother was less able to cope with the upset of divorce. He found that the effect also depends upon the child's age at the time of the marital rupture. Young children were more adversely affected than were older children. Remarriage also poses a threat to the child's self-esteem: children in families in which the mother remarries tend to be more disturbed than children whose mother does not remarry. (21, 27) Rosenberg found similar but less negative results when a family is broken by death. Students whose mothers were relatively young when they were widowed were less likely to have high self-esteem. These students were not conspicuously poorly adjusted, but tended to be in the intermediate category. (73, p. 97)

Other research does not completely support Rosenberg's findings. Burchinal studied some eighteen hundred adolescent boys and girls in the seventh and eleventh grades from Cedar Rapids, Iowa. He compared their personality characteristics after grouping them into five family types: those from broken homes with mother only at home, with mother and stepfather, with both parents remarried, and with a father and stepmother. Burchinal reports no statistically significant differences in personality characteristics of these adolescents in any of the five family types. Also, there were no significant differences among the youths from these five family types in grades, participation in school or community activities, number of friends, or attitudes toward school. It must be emphasized that Burchinal did not measure self-esteem but did have one question relating to how well the youths thought they were liked by classmates. He found nonsignificant differences in the responses. (14)

Other studies tend to confirm Burchinal's finding. Nye compared children from intact but unhappy homes with children from broken homes and found few real personality differences. He did find, however, that adolescents from the happy broken homes showed less psychosomatic illness, less delinquent behavior, and better adjustment to parents than the youth from the intact, unhappy homes. (56) One study of high school female seniors showed that two-thirds of those who were high in ego identity (identity achievers) came from homes broken by either divorce or death. (78) These findings indicate that broken homes do not necessarily have the adverse effects on adolescents that are sometimes supposed. Another study of third-, sixth-, and eighth-grade children from intact, single-parent, and reconstituted families found no significant differences in self-concept scores of children from these different types of homes. (65) Self-concept scores were significantly lower, however, for children who reported higher levels of family conflict, regardless of family type. It was the quality and harmony of interpersonal relationships that were the important factors, not alone the type of family structure. (65)

Studies show, then, that one must be cautious in predicting the effects of divorce upon children. Some children of divorced parents undoubtedly develop a poorer self-concept and a lower-esteem, but the results are variable and the reasons are not always clear. The socioeconomic level of the homes needs to be taken into account. (69) The impact of the divorce upon the mother will vary, and her reaction will have differing effects on the children. Mothers who experience high trauma during the divorce process are more likely to report that their children are not too happy. (72) Mothers who are the happiest seem to have children with the highest self-concepts. (65)

SOCIOECONOMIC STATUS

In general, adolescents from lower socioeconomic status families have lower self-esteem than those from higher status families; membership in a disadvantaged group often has an important influence on self-concept. (13) (See Chapter 22) It is certain that one major factor in the unrest of black Americans is the quest for identity. (34) Socioeconomic status of the parents, however, by itself is not enough to produce low self-esteem children. Lower class, low income families produce high self-esteem children if the parents' self-esteem is high. This parental self-esteem depends in turn upon the prestige of the nationality or religious group, or on the self-acceptance of the members within the group. The best example is that of Jewish adolescents, who, even though they come from a religious group that does not enjoy high prestige in American society, nevertheless have far greater self-esteem than do Catholics or Protestants, probably because of the high self-esteem of the Jewish parents and the generally adequate parent-child relationship, measured by the degree of interest Jewish parents show in their children. (73, p. 51; 74, p. 99)

The degree of adolescent self-esteem, regardless of class, is partially dependent upon the group in which those youths are placed. For example, those placed in schools among those of their own kind have higher self-esteem than they do when placed in schools among those unlike themselves. If lower class youths attend higher class schools, or if middle or upper middle class adolescents attend lower class schools, both groups experience lower self-esteem than if they attend schools with others from their own social and economic class. (74, p. 97)

RACE AND NATIONALITY

The influence of dissonance on self-esteem is also felt among mixed racial groups. In general when black adolescents attend white schools, they evidence a lower self-esteem than when attending predominantly black schools. (77) Black students in segregated schools have higher self-esteem than black students in integrated schools. (5, 62) The desegregated school may have certain advantages, but enhancing self-esteem is not one of them. (74, p. 101)

Overall, there is some evidence that black youths have higher self-esteem than whites, especially when not exposed to white prejudices. (77, 81) When surrounded primarily by blacks with similar physical appearance, social class standing, family background and school performance, they rate themselves much higher in self-esteem than when surrounded by whites who rank higher in other dimensions. (81, p. 87)

Some efforts have been made to do cross-cultural comparisons of adolescents. Comparisons of Indian, American, Australian, and Irish adolescents showed that American youths had higher self-concepts and self-esteem than did the others, with Australian, Indian, and Irish adolescents following in order of declining ego strength. (2) When American, Irish, and Israeli youths were compared, Americans ranked highest, with Irish and Israeli youths lower but similar to each other. (57)

BIRTH ORDER

There is little correlation between the child's birth order in the family and his self-esteem. (88) An only child, however, is more likely to have higher self-esteem than those with siblings. Also, those who are the first of their gender to be born in their family seem to have some advantage. Thus, a first-born boy in a family of all daughters enjoys high self-esteem, as does a first-born girl in a family of all sons. (73, p. 118)

PHYSICAL HANDICAPS

As might be expected, adolescents with physical handicaps or negative body images have more difficulty developing positive self-concepts and self-esteem than do those who are physically more average. (15, 75, 84) The importance of physical attractiveness and body image has been discussed in Chapter 5. It is certain that the degree of physical attractiveness and acceptance of one's physical self are influential factors in the development of a total self-concept. (50, 61) One study showed that adolescents who thought themselves "too short" or "too heavy" showed not only lower self-concepts but also lower self-actualization, indicating that the fulfillment of their innermost potential may be greatly in-hibited by their negative sense of self-worth. (40)

Changes or Stability in Self-Concept

To what extent does self-concept change during adolescence? Self-concept gradually stabilizes, but is fairly steady during adolescence. (32) One researcher found that the self-concepts of both eighth and tenth grade high school students remained relatively stable over a two-year period. This stability was attributed to the fact that internal organization and crystallization of self-concept are achieved earlier in development. (23) Another researcher found that self-esteem is a relatively stable dimension of the self and independent of the sex role; that is, there were no sex differences in either the level or stability of self-esteem. Evalua-tion of stability were made over a six-year period: at sixth grade and again at twelfth grade. Over the six-year period, however, girls showed an increase in social orientation (interpersonal skill, social sensitivity, passivity, conformity, and in orientation to others), while boys showed an increase in personal orienta-tion (autonomy and independence). Ego integration in girls was related to social growth and adjustment; ego integration in boys was related to the development of personal, independent standards. (16) Overall, research has shown that for most adolescents, there are no sex differences per se in the level of self-esteem and that ego identity becomes more positive during the high school years. (49, 79) Other research has confirmed that identity achievement is related to the degree to which students have achieved independence from their families. (90, 91)

In spite of the relative stability of the inner core of self during adolescence, youths are extremely sensitive to the evaluations and opinions of others. A group of seventh- and eighth-grade boys was asked to perform various simple physical tasks in front of a physical development expert who showed either approval or

Table 8–1.   Percentage rating selves very favorably on each characteristic among those who care "very much" about that characteristic, by age.

Qualities	Age 8–11	Age 12–14	Age 15 or Older
Smart	26%	9%	5%
Good-looking	20%	13%	6%
Truthful or honest	54%	38%	38%
Good at sports	50%	46%	42%
Well-behaved	46%	31%	39%
Working hard in school	71%	50%	39%
Helpful	60%	46%	46%
Good at making jokes	49%	40%	46%

Adapted from R. Simmons, F. Rosenberg, and M. Rosenberg, "Disturbance in the Self-Image at Adolescence," *American Sociological Review* 38 (1973): 558. Used by permission.

disapproval. Increases in self-concept rating and in preference for directly related physical activities followed the approval treatment, and, in some cases, these changes persisted for a three-week period. Disapproval treatment was, in general, followed by an opposite effect, but this negative effect showed a tendency to return more quickly to normal than did the positive effect. The important point is that the reaction of the significant others did result in temporary changes in the self-ratings of these boys. (51)

Adolescents are extremely sensitive also to important events and changes in their lives. Adolescents who have been getting along very well but who get involved with the wrong crowd and begin to adopt their deviant behavior may show less self-respect and an increase in their own self-derogation. (44) One study of 1,917 third- to twelfth-grade pupils in Baltimore showed that the transition from elementary school to junior high school represented significant stress for many youths that affected their self-images. (82)

Table 8–1 shows the proportion of pupils at each age level who rated themselves very favorably on various characteristics they cared very much about. It is quite evident that twelve- to fourteen-year-olds rated themselves much less favorably than did eight- to eleven-year-olds. By age fifteen, self-image had become much more stable. Figure 8–1 shows the increase in low-esteem by age. The researchers raised the question: what important factors were responsible for the sharp decline in a positive self-image? By applying careful statistical controls they showed that the onset of puberty itself was not the determining factor, for twelve-year-olds in junior high school had lower self-esteem, higher self-consciousness, and greater instability of self-image than did twelve-year-olds in elementary school. When differences in race, socioeconomic class, or marks in school were considered, none of these variables were found to be determinative: the general findings held true for blacks as well as whites, middle class as well as working class respondents, and for students with high as well as low grades. Nor was age itself significant: there was virtually no difference between the self-image ratings of eleven- and twelve-year-olds in the sixth grade, or between twelve- and thirteen-year-olds in the seventh grade. The one factor that was determinative was whether the student had entered junior high school. The move from a protected elementary school, where a child had few teachers and one

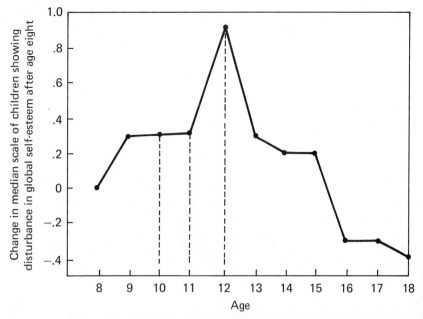

Figure 8–1. Increase in low self-esteem by age. (Adapted from R. Simmons, F. Rosenberg, and M. Rosenberg, "Disturbance in the Self-Image at Adolescence," *American Sociological Review* 38[1973]:560. Used by permission.)

set of classmates, to a much larger, more impersonal junior high, where teachers, classmates, and even classrooms were constantly shifting, was disturbing to the self-image. Similar disturbances were not found in the move from junior to senior high-school. (82)

Another study of the effect of transition from elementary school to junior high school sheds additional light on the feelings of pupils in going from one school to another. (12) A common reaction in moving into junior high school was to feel less positive about oneself, to participate less in school activities, and to feel a high degree of anonymity in the new school environment. In addition, the students moved from a relatively safe elementary school environment to a more hostile junior high school in which males, particularly, were much more likely to experience victimization such as being harassed or beaten up. (12) This study clearly illustrates that self-image can be affected, at least for a while, by disturbing events.

Educators can take into account the effect of different schools on self-concepts, and put pupils who are having difficulties into alternative schools to try to change the pupils' attitudes, behavior, and self-concepts. Transferring pupils to different schools is particularly effective with junior high school pupils, less effective at the senior high level. (87)

This also means, however, that self-image and self-esteem can be improved by helpful events. Counselors of adolescents use this principle positively to try to help youths change their self-images. One report of the work of a Massachusetts community counseling center for adolescents revealed that it was possible through psychotherapy, group activity, and therapeutic community techniques to significantly raise the self-esteem scores of about half of the troubled youths aged fourteen to twenty-three who came to the center. (68) These youths had difficulties at work, school, and with friends and parents. Eighty-one percent were using some form of drugs. Follow-up interviews showed many youths had developed more self-confidence after treatment, enabling them to drop harmful friendships and initiate new relationships. They reported better rapport with parents and improved relationships at work and school. Many showed a decrease or cessation of drug taking. (68) The important point is that the self-images and the lives of many of these adolescents were changed, with difficulty, but nevertheless with positive results.

Rathus and Ruppert (66) report good results with what they call *assertion training* of secondary and college level students who are timid and withdrawn and incapable of dealing with other students, teachers, and relatives. The youths are taught how to talk to others, to greet them, to ask questions, and to express their own feelings about things. By so doing, they are able to overcome their reputations of nonassertiveness and to change others' opinions of them. (66)

In summary, the concept of the self is not completely solidified by adolescence, although recognizable trends and traits persist. With increasing age, these recognizable traits become more stable. (63; 71, p. 25) However, self-concepts are subject to change under the influence of powerful forces. Assisting the adolescent who has a negative identity to find a mature and positive image of self is a major undertaking, but it can be done in some cases. (31, p. 151) It is certain that the change is easier during adolescence than later in adulthood.

Conclusions

Adolescents' self-concepts and self-esteems are important to their mental health, to their competence in social relationships, and to their progress in school. Self-concept and self-esteem affect vocational aspirations and success and determine whether or not adolescents may become socialized members of society. In fact, these concepts affect everything they are, try to be, or do. Adolescents with inadequate self-conception and low esteem, whose concepts of themselves are much less positive than their images of an ideal self, manifest internal conflict and anxiety. This in turn influences all their external relationships. Nothing is more crucial, therefore, than the development of an adequate self-concept.

How does this concept develop? The beginning and foundation must be within the family. If children have positive role models (their parents) with whom they can identify, they are better able to build positive identities. The parental image and the parent-child relationship are more important for ego building than is the socioeconomic status of the family. Regardless of socioeconomic status or ethnic group, high self-esteem parents are more likely to rear high self-esteem children. Other factors, such as whether children are brought up in a broken home or an intact home, or whether they are an only child, youngest child, or oldest child, are not in and of themselves the key to an adequate self-concept. The secret lies in the subtle dynamics of the parent-child interaction process: in the degree to which the parents show love, concern, and reasonable, consistent discipline. If children do not find these emotional supports in their relationships with parents, it does not mean they will automatically suffer with inadequate ego images the rest of their lives. It does mean they will have to find substitutes or supplementary relationships and activities outside the home if they are to overcome the ego handicaps that an inadequate home life has imposed upon them.

Interviews of Adolescents

One way of understanding how adolescents feel about themselves is through personal interviews with them. Students may want to select youths from different age groups, of different races, of varying socioeconomic statuses, and from both intact and broken families. The results can be summarized in a formal report, or the interviews tape recorded to play back to the class.

The selection of questions will depend upon the particular youths interviewed. The following questions are only suggestions.

1. How do you feel about yourself? Do you like yourself? Why? Why not?
2. If you were to describe yourself, what would you say?
3. In what ways do your concepts of yourself differ from your ideals of what you would most want to be like?
4. What do you like most about yourself? What do you like least?
5. Do you feel you will change much, or that your feelings about yourself will change as you get older? Why? Why not?
6. What do you believe your teachers think you are like? Why do you say that?
7. How do your parents feel about you? How do your parents' views of you affect your feelings about yourself?
8. How do your friends feel about you? What do you believe they think you are like?
9. What things have happened in your life that have most influenced how you feel about yourself?
10. How would you describe the socioeconomic level of your family? What work does your father/mother do? How have these factors influenced your self-image and the attitudes and opinions of others toward you?
11. Are your parents: divorced, separated, living together with the family? Have these factors influenced your self-esteem?

Bibliography

1. Adams, G. R. "Personal Identity Formation: A Synthesis of Cognitive and Ego Psychology." *Adolescence* 12 (Summer 1977): 151–164.

2. Agrawal, P. "A Cross-Cultural Study of Self-Image: Indian, American, Australian, and Irish Adolescents." *Journal of Youth and Adolescence* 7 (March 1978): 107–116.

3. Allport, Gordon W. *Becoming: Basic Considerations for a Psychology of Personality.* New Haven, Conn.: Yale University Press, 1950.

4. "An Expert Tells How to Cope with Shyness." *U.S. News & World Report*, 9 October 1978, pp. 58–60.

5. Bachman, J. O. "The Impact of Family Background and Intelligence on Tenth-Grade Boys." *Youth in Transition*, vol. 2. Ann Arbor, Mich.: Institute for Social Research, 1970.

6. Bandura, A. "Social Learning Theory of Identificatory Processes." In *Handbook of Socialization Theory and Research*. Edited by D. A. Gosselin. Chicago: Rand McNally, 1969, pp. 213–262.

7. Baumrind, D. "Early Socialization and Adolescent Competence." In *Adolescence in the Life Cycle*. Edited by S. E. Dragastin and G. H. Elder, Jr. New York: John Wiley and Sons, 1975, pp. 117–143.

8. Biller, H. B., and Weiss, S. D. "The Father-daughter Relationship and the Personality Development of the Female." *Journal of Genetic Psychology* 116 (1970): 79–93.

9. Birnbaum, J. L. A. "Life Patterns, Personality Style, and Self Esteem in Gifted Family Oriented and Career Committed Women." Ph.D. dissertation. University of Michigan, 1972.

10. Blaine, Graham B., Jr. "Stress and Distress and Identity Formation in College and High School." *Journal of National Association of Women Deans and Counselors* 27 (1963): 25–31.

11. Blos, P. "The Child Analyst Looks at the Young Adolescent." *Daedalus* (Fall 1971): 961–978.

12. Blyth, D. A. et al. "The Transition into Early Adolescence: A Longitudinal Comparison of Youth in Two Educational Contexts." *Sociology of Education* 51 (July 1978): 149–162.

13. Brown, N. W., and Renz, P. "Altering the Reality Self-Concept of Seventh Grade Culturally Deprived Girls in the Inner City." *Adolescence* 8 (1973): 463–474.

14. Burchinal, L. G. "Characteristics of Adolescents from Unbroken, Broken, and Reconstituted Families." *Journal of Marriage and the Family* 26 (1964): 44–51.

15. Campbell, M. M. et al. "Psychological Adjustment of Adolescents with Myelodysplasia." *Journal of Youth and Adolescence* 6 (December 1977): 397–407.

16. Carlson, Rae. "Stability and Change in the Adolescent's Self-Image." *Child Development* 36 (1965): 659–666.

17. Carlyle, W. *You're My Friend So I Brought You This Book*. Edited by John Marvin. New York: Random House, 1970.

18. Connell, D. M., and Johnson, J. E. "Relationship between Sex-Role Identification and Self-Esteem in Early Adolescents." *Developmental Psychology* 3 (1970): 268.

19. Donovan, J. M. "Identity Status and Interpersonal Style." *Journal of Youth and Adolescence* 4 (1975): 37–55.

20. ———. "Identity Status: Its Relationship to Rorschach Performance and to Daily Life Pattern." *Adolescence* 10 (1975): 29–44.

21. Duberman, L. "Step-Kin Relationships." *Journal of Marriage and the Family* 35 (1973): 283–292.

22. Elkind, D. "Recent Research on Cognitive Development in Adolescence." In *Adolescence in the Life Cycle*. Edited by S. E. Dragastin and G. H. Elder, Jr. New York: John Wiley and Sons, 1975, pp. 49–61.

23. Engle, Mary. "The Stability of the Self-Concept in Adolescence." *Journal of Abnormal and Social Psychology* 58 (1959): 211–215.

24. Enright, R. D., and Deist, S. H. "Social Perspective Taking as a Component of Identity Formation." *Adolescence* 14 (Spring 1979): 185–189.

25. Erikson, E. H. "The Problem of Ego Identity." *Journal of American Psychoanalytic Association* 4 (1956): 56–119.

26. ———. *Identity: Youth and Crisis*. New York: Norton, 1968.

27. Gallatin, J. E. *Adolescence and Individuality*. New York: Harper and Row, 1975.

28. Graybill, D. "Relationship of Maternal Child-Rearing Behaviors to Children's Self-Esteem." *Journal of Psychology* 100 (September 1978): 45–47.

29. Griffore, R. J., and Samuels, D. D. "Self-Concept of Ability and College Students' Academic Achievement." *Psychological Reports* 43 (August 1978): 37–38.

30. Hamachek, D. E. *Encounters with the Self*. New York: Holt, Rinehart and Winston, 1971.

31. ———. "Development and Dynamics of the Self." In *Understanding Adolescence*. 3d ed. Edited by J. F. Adams. Boston: Allyn and Bacon, 1976.

32. Hansen, J. C., and Maynard, P. E. *Youth: Self-Concept and Behavior*. Columbus, Ohio: Charles E. Merrill Publishing Co., 1973.

33. Harvey, A. L. "Goal-Setting as Compensation for Fear-of-Success." *Adolescence* 10 (1975): 137–142.

34. Hauser, S. T. *Black and White Identity Formation*. New York: Wiley Interscience, 1971.

35. Hensley, W. E. "Differences between Males and Females on Rosenburg Scale of Self-Esteem." *Psychological Reports* 11 (December 1977): 829–830.

36. Hetherington, E. M. "Girls without Fathers." *Psychology Today* (February 1973): 47–52.

37. Hilgard, E. R. "Human Motives and the Concept of Self." *American Psychologist* 4 (1949): 374–382.

38. Hodgson, J. W., and Fischer, J. L. "Sex Differences in Identity and Intimacy Development in College Youth." *Journal of Youth and Adolescence* 7 (December 1978): 371–392.

39. Hogan, H. W. "IQ Self-Estimates of Males and Females." *Journal of Social Psychology* 106 (October 1978): 137–138.

40. Hogan, H. W., and McWilliams, J. M. "Factors Related to Self-Actualization." *Journal of Psychology* 100 (September 1978): 117–122.

41. James, William. *The Principles of Psychology*. New York: Holt, 1890.

42. Johnsen, K. P., and Medley, M. L. "Academic Self-Concept among Black High

School Seniors: An Examination of Perceived Agreement with Selected Others." *Phylon* 39 (September 1978): 264–274.

43. Jones, F. R., and Swain, M. T. "Self-Concept and Delinquency Proneness." *Adolescence* 12 (Winter 1977): 559–569.

44. Kaplan, H. B. "Increase in Self-Rejection and Continuing/Discontinued Deviant Response." *Journal of Youth and Adolescence* 6 (March 1977): 77–87.

45. ———. "Deviant Behavior and Self-Enhancement in Adolescence." *Journal of Youth and Adolescence* 7 (September 1978): 253–277.

46. Kirsch, P. A. et al. "Ideology and Personality: Aspects of Identity Formation in Adolescents with Strong Attitudes toward Sex-Role Equalitarianism." *Journal of Youth and Adolescence* 5 (December 1976): 387–401.

47. Kokenes, B. "A Factor Analytic Study of the Coopersmith Self-Esteem Inventory." *Adolescence* 12 (Spring 1978): 149–155.

48. Lambert, E. G. et al. *Adolescence: Transition from Childhood to Maturity.* Monterey, Calif.: Brooks/Cole Publishing Co., 1972.

49. LaVoie, J. C. "Ego Identity Formation in Middle Adolescence." *Journal of Youth and Adolescence* 5 (December 1976): 371–385.

50. Lerner, R. Me. et al. "Physical Attractiveness, Physical Effectiveness, and Self-Concept in Late Adolescents." *Adolescence* 11 (Fall 1976): 314–326.

51. Ludwig, David J., and Maehr, Martin L. "Changes in Self Concept and Stated Behavioral Preferences." *Child Development* 38 (1967): 453–467.

52. Lynn, D. B. *Parental and Sex-Role Identification: A Theoretical Formulation.* Berkeley, Calif.: McCutchan, 1969.

53. Manaster, G. J. et al. "The Ideal Self and Cognitive Development in Adolescence." *Adolescence* 12 (Winter 1977): 547–558.

54. McKinney, F. et al. "Self-Concept, Delinquency, and Positive Peer Culture." *Criminology* 15 (February 1978): 529–538.

55. Mouly, G. J. *Educational Psychology.* New York: Holt, Rinehart and Winston, 1974.

56. Nye, F. I. "Child Adjustment in Broken and in Unhappy Unbroken Homes." *Marriage and Family Living* 19 (1957): 356–361.

57. Offer, D. et al. "The Self-Image of Adolescents: A Study of Four Cultures." *Journal of Youth and Adolescence* 6 (September 1977): 265–280.

58. Okum, M. A., and Sasfy, J. H. "Adolescence, the Self-Concept, and Formal Operations." *Adolescence* 12 (Fall 1977): 373–379.

59. Oshman, H., and Manosevitz, M. "The Impact of the Identity Crisis on the Adjustment of Late Adolescent Males." *Journal of Youth and Adolescence* 3 (1974): 207–216.

60. Petersen, A. C., and Kellam, S. G. "Measurement of the Psychological Well-Being of Adolescents: The Psychometric Properties and Assessment Procedures of the How I Feel." *Journal of Youth and Adolescence* 6 (September 1977): 229–247.

61. Pomerantz, S. C. "Sex Differences in the Relative Importance of Self-Esteem, Physical Self-Satisfaction, and Identity in Predicting Adolescent Satisfaction." *Journal of Youth and Adolescence* 8 (March 1979): 51–61.

62. Powell, G. J., and Fuller, M. "School Segregation and Self-Concept." Paper presented at the 47th Annual Meeting of the American Orthopsychiatric Association in San Francisco, California, March 23–26, 1970.

63. Protinsky, H. O., Jr. "Eriksonian Ego Identity in Adolescents." *Adolescence* 10 (1975): 428–432.

64. Purkey, W. W. *Self-Concept and School Achievement.* Englewood Cliffs, N.J.: Prentice-Hall, 1970.

65. Raschke, H. J., and Raschke, V. J. "Family Conflict and Children's Self-Concepts: A Comparison of Intact and Single-Parent Families." *Journal of Marriage and the Family* 41 (May 1979): 367–374.

66. Rathus, S. A., and Ruppert, C. "Assertion Training in the Secondary School and College." *Adolescence* 7 (1973): 257–264.

67. Rathus, S. A., and Siegel, L. J. "Delinquent Attitudes and Self-Esteem." *Adolescence* 8 (1973): 265–276.

68. Reinherz, H. et al. "Shared Perspectives: A Community Counseling Center for Adolescents." *Adolescence* 11 (1976): 167–179.

69. Reiss, I. L. *The Family System in America.* New York: Holt, Rinehart and Winston, 1971, pp. 297–300.

70. Rogers, C. R. *On Becoming a Person: A Therapist's View of Psychotherapy.* Boston: Houghton Mifflin Co., 1961.

71. Rogers, D. *Adolescence: A Psychological Perspective.* Monterey, Calif.: Brooks/Cole Publishing Co., 1972.

72. Rose, V. L., and Price-Bonham, S. "Divorce Adjustment: A Woman's Problem?" *Family Coordinator* 22 (1973): 291–297.

73. Rosenberg, Morris. *Society and the*

Adolescent Self-Image. Princeton, N.J.: Princeton University Press, 1965.

74. ———. "The Dissonant Context and the Adolescent Self-Concept." In *Adolescence in the Life Cycle.* Edited by S. E. Dragastin and G. H. Elder, Jr. New York: John Wiley and Sons, 1975, pp. 97–116.

75. Rosenberg, B. S., and Gaier, E. L. "The Self-Concept of the Adolescent with Learning Disabilities." *Adolescence* 12 (Winter 1977): 489–498.

76. Rosenberg, F. R., and Rosenberg, M. "Self-Esteem and Delinquency." *Journal of Youth and Adolescence* 7 (September 1978): 279–291.

77. Rosenberg, Morris, and Simmons, R. G. "Black and White Self-Esteem: The Urban School Child." American Sociological Association Monograph Series. Washington, D.C., 1972.

78. St. Clair, S., and Day, H. D. "Ego Identity Status and Values among High School Females." *Journal of Youth and Adolescence* 8 (September 1979): 317–326.

79. Schiff, E., and Koopman, E. J. "The Relationship of Women's Sex-Role Identity to Self-Esteem and Ego Development." *Journal of Psychology* 98 (March 1978): 299–305.

80. Schwartz, Michael, and Tangri, Sandra S. "A Note on Self-Concept as an Insulator against Delinquency." *American Sociological Review* 30 (1965): 922–934.

81. Simmons, R. G. et al. "Self-Esteem and Achievement of Black and White Adolescents." *Social Problems* 26 (October 1978): 86–96.

82. Simmons, R.; Rosenberg, F.; and Rosenberg, M. "Disturbance in the Self-Image at Adolescence." *American Sociological Review* 38 (1973): 553–568.

83. Smith, M. B. "Toward a Concept of the Competent Self." In *Youth and Culture: A Human-Development Approach.* Edited by

H. V. Draemer. Monterey, Calif.: Brooks/Cole Publishing Co., 1974, pp. 388–407.

84. Sobel, H. J. "Adolescent Attitudes toward Homosexuality in Relation to Self-Concept and Body Satisfaction." *Adolescence* 11 (Fall 1976): 443–453.

85. Stoner, S., and Kaiser, L. "Sex Differences in Self-Concepts of Adolescents." *Psychological Reports* 43 (1978): 305–306.

86. Strang, R. *The Adolescent Views Himself.* New York: McGraw-Hill, 1957.

87. Strathe, M., and Hash, V. "The Effect of an Alternative School in Adolescent Self-Esteem." *Adolescence* 14 (Spring 1979): 185–189.

88. Stroup, A. L., and Hunter, K. J. "Sibling Position in the Family and Personality of Offspring." *Journal of Marriage and the Family* 27 (1965): 65–68.

89. Thornburg, H. D. *Contemporary Adolescent Readings.* 2d ed. Monterey, Calif.: Brooks/Cole Publishing Co., 1975.

90. Waterman, A. S., and Waterman, C. K. "Relationship between Freshman Ego Identity Status during the Freshman Year in College, and Validity of Marcia's Categorization System for Identity Status." *Developmental Psychology* 6 (1968): 179.

91. ———. "A Longitudinal Study of Changes in Ego Identity Status during the Freshman Year in College." *Developmental Psychology* 5 (1971): 167–173.

92. Whiteside, M. "Age and Sex Differences in Self-Perception as Related to Ideal Trait Selection." *Adolescence* 11 (Winter 1976): 585–592.

93. Zimbardo, P. G. "Misunderstanding Shyness: The Counterattack." *Psychology Today* (June 1978): 17ff.

94. Zongker, C. E. "The Self-Concept of Pregnant Adolescent Girls." *Adolescence* 12 (Winter 1977): 477–488.

CHAPTER 9

Emotional Disturbances and Maladjustments

Outline

A wide variety of human emotions—joy, love, affection, fear, anxiety, anger, and hostility—are found in various degrees in all people. From one point of view the only factors distinguishing so-called normal from abnormal emotions are the degree and frequency with which these feelings are inhibited or expressed. It is common to be anxious under some circumstances, but when anxiety becomes constant and all-consuming, completely dominating a person's life, no one could say it is usual or healthy. Most people can express love and affection; when a person cannot, the condition must be considered atypical of the usual emotional response. Similarly, all people feel some anger and hostility, but when these become so intense that they result in the destruction of self or others, they become problem behavior.

This chapter is concerned with some selected emotional disturbances found in adolescents. Those selected for discussion here are:

Anxiety or depressive states—*anxiety neurosis, conversion hysteria,* and *depression.*

Phobias, obsessions and compulsions—these include a whole category of neuroses called *psychasthenia.* Special attention will be given here to *pyromania.*

Psychosomatic illnesses—symptoms may show up in many different organs or systems of the body. One particular illness will be emphasized here: *anorexia nervosa.*

Withdrawal, retreat, or escape mechanisms—adolescents can withdraw, retreat, or escape in many ways: through social isolation, dropping out school, running away from home, through overactivity of any kind, or through sleep, sex, drugs, or alcohol. Most of these forms of withdrawal are discussed in other chapters; only *schizophrenia* will be discussed here, because it is the most frequent type of psychological withdrawal and psychosis found in adolescents.

This chapter is also concerned with two particular manifestations of emotional maladjustment: *suicide* and *juvenile delinquency.* These two types of "acting out" behavior may be partially the result of emotional disturbances, but they are also frequently the result of societal, environmental, familial, and personal circumstances, relationships, and events with which adolescents have difficulty coping. In one case, their reaction is to destroy themselves. In the other case, they lash out at others through unlawful behavior.

Anxiety or Depressive States

ANXIETY NEUROSES

Anxiety as an alerting response to internal or external dangers is not an illness. But when the anxiety becomes so pervasive and tenacious that it interferes with continued functioning of the personality, it is a neurotic illness. (67, p. 78) Neurotic anxiety is far more severe than most people experience, but it can be felt in even the most routine circumstances. (8, p. 26) Adolescents suffering from anxiety neuroses tend to make an enormous catastrophe out of the smallest mishap and believe that the perceived catastrophe exists. People in this state cannot see the facts in the situation; therefore it is impossible to reason them out of their feelings. Such internal anxiety may be accompanied by feelings of inferiority, sleep disturbances, nervousness, shaking and trembling, sweating, tearfulness, somatic complaints such as respiratory or digestive disturbances, dizziness, or an increase in psychomotor activity to try to escape or cover up the fear. (59, p. 357) It may also manifest itself in behavior disturbances.

John, a boy of sixteen who had made straight A's in grade ten and D's and E's in grade eleven, was referred to a psychiatrist because he missed 120 class periods in one semester. He said, "I know my parents want me to do well and last year that was enough, but now I hassle with them all the time; particularly my mother. I want to go into a profession, but this worries me; and I can't get my head together enough to do any work." (50, p. 345)

In this case, John lost two teachers that he especially liked when he started grade eleven. He neither knew nor liked any of the new teachers to whom he was assigned. Because he was an insecure boy anyhow, this episode was enough to stimulate intense anxiety which he tried to get away from by skipping school. (50, p. 346)

CONVERSION HYSTERIA

Sometimes anxiety becomes so severe that it results in definite physical symptoms in the form of a neurosis called *conversion hysteria*. Severe symptoms may show up as temporary blindness, paralysis, or other physical disability. (67) The illness is usually the result of one or more emotionally charged life situations with which the person finds difficulty coping. The unconscious conflict produces malfunctioning of one of the special senses or of the voluntary nervous system, such as temporary blindness or paralysis. (67, p. 79)

A 13-year-old black girl was evaluated by pediatrics for lower extremity weakness and for "strange spells." The girl's spells had occurred about five times over a 4-year period. She described the spells as numbness of left side of body, difficulty in breathing, shaking of her body, and brief loss of consciousness. She also had auditory and visual hallucinations of dead family members who had advised her to be "good."
   Her family history was tragic: the mother had died after the girl was born, 4 siblings had been burned to death, the father had died of a heart attack one year before, and the grandmother had died of cancer 6 months before. The girl was living with her great aunt at the time she was being evaluated. The girl's first spell occurred after the fire that killed her siblings, with recurrences taking place at times of tragedy or when she thought about the deaths of her family. (69, p. 176)

DEPRESSION

Depression is not at all uncommon during adolescence. One study of seventh- and eighth-grade boys and girls in a school in Philadelphia revealed that one-third of the school population was experiencing moderate to severe depression, and 35 percent acknowledged current suicidal ideation. (2) The most severe depression occurred in eighth grade, especially among girls, indicating that this was a critical period of development. Students showed high correlation between difficulties in social and school adjustment and depression. Those who gave the most negative evaluations of teachers also showed the most depressive symptoms. (2, p. 306)

Usually one thinks of a depressed person as sad, in a despairing mood, melancholic, listless, with a reduction of mental activity and physical drive. (77, p. 359) The depression may be accompanied by one or more physical complaints such as gastrointestinal disturbances, with the person preoccupied with hypochondriasis. Depressed adolescents may complain frequently of fatigue, being excessively tired upon wakening in the morning after an adequate amount of sleep. (77, p. 364) They may describe feelings of emptiness, isolation, and alienation from others. They often complain of difficulty in concentrating in school. In fact, bright students who fail are frequently suffering from anxiety and/or depression. If they try to improve, without result, they may spend long hours going to the movies, watching television, or just wasting time. Depressed adolescents may show suicidal tendencies and in some cases actually attempt suicide. Some succeed.

In an effort to escape or deny their depression, adolescents may also become overactive. Sexual promiscuity, especially in females, is often a disguised attempt to avoid feelings of depression and loneliness. (77, p. 364) Continually dating, going out, and engaging in a never-ending round of social activities may be an attempt to escape depression. (65, p. 107)

Phobias, Obsessions, and Compulsions

PHOBIAS

A phobia is an excessive, uncontrolled fear that usually develops during childhood through exposure to severe, traumatic episodes that they subsequently repress in their memory. The episode passes but the phobia remains. Or a phobia may develop out of reaction to fear or guilt. *Mysophobia,* fear of dirt or contamination, may result in excessive cleanliness or constant and repeated washing; it may have originated because of fear and guilt. For example, adolescents who feel guilty about masturbation and therefore wash their hands whenever they have the urge, are symbolically eliminating the desire or the effect. (67, p. 80) Other common phobias are *acrophobia,* fear of high places; *claustrophobia,* fear of closed places; or *homilophobia,* fear that other people may find something wrong with one's appearance, attire, or demeanor.

OBSESSIONS AND COMPULSIONS

These often develop from traumatic experiences that may have been only partly suppressed. Children try to forget about a disturbance by engaging in some type of distracting behavior. For example, to relieve tension they go outdoors and concentrate on stepping on each crack in the sidewalk. The traumatic experience passes, but thereafter, each time they feel tense, they experience a compulsion to step on the cracks of the sidewalks. They have long since forgotten the incident, but the compulsion remains.

Compulsions take many forms, such as the urge to check again and again to be certain the gas is off in the stove or to see that a door is closed. The urge to steal, *kleptomania,* or the urge to engage in a series of ritualistic acts (like "knocking on wood") to ward off bad luck, fear, or to relieve anxiety are all compulsions.

One common and serious compulsion is *pyromania,* the urge to set fires. It is serious because arson is a criminal offense, yet many thousands of such fires are set each year.

Joan S. was a sophomore in college at the time she began to set fires in her dorm. The first fire was set in a room down the hall, the second—a week later—was set in a room across from hers. By this time, fire insurance personnel were deeply involved in investigating to see who was starting the fires. The next day Joan set fire to her own room, after carefully removing some of her best clothes from her closet. A lie detector test administered routinely to all dorm residents pointed to Joan as the culprit. She didn't know why she set the fires, was sorry that she did, and was referred to a psychiatrist for diagnosis and treatment.

Not all adolescents who set fires are pyromaniacs. Some become involved out of boredom and a need for excitement. Setting hay fields or empty buildings on fire in these instances becomes a means of generating a little excitement. However, true pyromaniacs act compulsively, and sometimes impulsively, out of neurotic need. Most have sexual conflicts or problems they are trying to resolve. Others suffer from acute anxiety, rejection, or conflict with parents. Some adolescents set fires as a means of attracting attention because of feelings of rejection or inferiority. Those who set fires to their own houses usually do so out of anger, resentment, or hostility toward parents or siblings who have withheld love or attention, or who have mistreated or misunderstood them. Although they have no desire really to injure anyone, their actions are nevertheless deep-seated expressions of negative emotions. Often the adolescent puts the fire out himself or herself, calls the fire station, or is the one who "discovers" the fire. (8, p. 43)

Psychosomatic Illnesses

Many types of mental illness have psychosomatic manifestations; that is, they create physical illness and symptoms without an organic cause. Hysteria, which has already been discussed, is one example. A number of psychosomatic disorders come from persistent fear or rage, even though the emotional condition is not labeled as a particular neurosis or psychosis. Asthma, hay fever, eczema, ulcers, headaches, and many other physical difficulties sometimes have an emotional origin.

The American Psychological Association has classified ten types of psychosomatic reactions according to the organs or systems of the body affected. (38, p. 148)

1. Skin reactions: some types of eczema, acne, hives.
2. Musculoskeletal reactions: backache, arthritis, rheumatism (due to functional causes).
3. Respiratory reactions: asthma, hay fever, bronchitis.
4. Cardiovascular reactions: high blood pressure, migraine headaches, palpitation of heart.

5. Blood and lymphatic reactions.

6. Gastrointestinal reactions: ulcers, colitis, constipation, hyperacidity.

7. Genitourinary reactions: menstrual disturbances, painful urination, vaginal contractions.

8. Endocrine reactions: glandular disturbances, obesity, hyperthyroidism.

9. Nervous system reactions: anxiety, fatigue, convulsions.

10. Sense organ reactions: quite varied.

ANOREXIA NERVOSA

Anorexia nervosa is a psychosomatic illness characterized by an extreme disturbance of appetite, appearing most commonly in females; all food becomes repugnant, and the person is unwilling and unable to eat, with a consequent loss of weight. Such a physical illness has emotional roots, and may become quite serious if not properly treated, with the mortality rate due to starvation as high as 10 percent. (67, p. 81)   The most common age for the onset of anorexia nervosa is fourteen to fifteen years of age. (81, p. 277)   Typically, the adolescents are stout for their age and height. They are of high intelligence, make good grades, are reserved, self-controlled, over-sensitive, very precise, conscientious, meticulous, and have an exaggerated sense of duty. (81)

The first manifestations are often precipitated by teasing with such epithets as "tubby" or "fatso." Usually the affected adolescents begin with restricted food intake, become very interested in counting calories, and eat less and less. They start hiding their food, throwing it away, inducing vomiting, and rejecting all parental efforts to get them to eat. Some even begin to cry with hunger, but restrain themselves from eating. This may be accompanied by increased activity, work, and exercise to reduce even more. (81)

By this time, they may become emaciated, cold and antagonistic toward family members, and may sever contacts with them. Eventually they have to be hospitalized for a variety of physical symptoms. The hospital stay may be long; often several months, during which they are given medication, psychotherapy, and an appropriate diet. (81) In some cases hospitalization occurs too late and the girl dies.

This illness usually originates with an intense desire to get slim, with the person becoming intensely fearful of obesity. In addition, there is often intense ambivalence, a struggle for control between mother and daughter over the latter's autonomy, fear of sexual maturation and pregnancy, distorted body image perceptions, and lack of concern about the gravity of the weight loss. (67, p. 81) The cultural premium on slimness and youth has undoubtedly given impetus to the development of the disease in vulnerable adolescents. (67, p. 82)

Withdrawal, Retreat, and Escape Mechanisms: Schizophrenia

One way of adjusting to disturbing situations is to withdraw, retreat, or escape from them. Sometimes the withdrawal is harmless and helpful: college students drop a course they don't really need in which they are doing poorly. At other times adolescents find life and circumstances so unpleasant and unbearable that they withdraw completely into an imaginary world of their own making or choosing. In its extreme form such withdrawal becomes one of the most common psychoses of adolescence: *schizophrenia.* The high-risk age for the onset of the illness begins at seventeen years. (34)

There are various degrees of withdrawal between dropping a course and schizophrenia, in which the withdrawal is only partial but nevertheless effective in providing temporary relief. Adolescents withdraw by isolating themselves from social groups, or through alcohol, drugs, or sleep. They withdraw by dropping out of school, or they seek to escape through athletics, an over-active social life, staying away from home, or promiscuous sex. Becoming preoccupied with school work to the exclusion of any close friendships or leisure-time activities is a form of escape.

The primary cause of schizophrenia in adolescents is rejection at home while growing up. Typically the children grow up in families where the father is a very weak figure. Many times the children have been unplanned and unwanted. Studies of characteristics of adolescents who become schizophrenic reveal that they tend to be social isolates, show less social interest in others, group activities, or athletics. They evidence a high degree of social incompetence, exhibit few leadership skills, and are more submissive, anxious, dependent, and careless. (34) Thus, they could be characterized as shut-in, withdrawn personality types. Many show deviant antisocial behavior such as aggression and incorrigibility.

Schizophrenic adolescents also evidence excessive dependency on parents (61) and on staff and hospital personnel during treatment. (34, p. 274) In early childhood many have had some infectious illnesses, more physical handicaps, a greater number of eating and sleeping disturbances, slower motor development and physical coordination, and delayed development of speech. (19) During early childhood, also, their degree of social isolation is quite evident. They achieve less in school and in their jobs as adults than one would expect on the basis of their intellectual levels. (30, 83)

Most of these adolescents have rejecting mothers, though the manifestations of rejection vary. Some mothers are hostile; others are over-protective. Some are perfectionists. The effect of the hostile perfectionist on the adolescent is quite damaging. Such a mother is cold, hard, severe, rigid, domineering, and ambitious.

There are various manifestations of schizophrenia. (38) The simple type is characterized by idleness, daydreaming, lack of interest in others, and shiftlessness. The adolescent seems far away in thought—"not all there." The *hebephrenic type* often acts silly, laughs or smiles without provocation, shows fleeting hallucinations and fantastic delusions, or engages in symbolic, repetitive motions. The *catatonic type* may remain muscularly rigid in one position or refuse to talk, fearful that any movement may have devastating consequences to the world. (48, p. 95) In an over-excited phase, this type may destroy property or injure others. The *paranoid type* evidences delusions of grandeur and of persecution and may have upsetting hallucinations. (38, p. 149)

Suicide

FREQUENCY

The incidence of suicide among children, especially among those under age fifteen, is rare. It is rare because children are still dependent on love objects for gratification; they have not yet completed the process of identification within themselves; thus, the thought of turning hostility toward themselves is too painful and frightening. Only as children find more self-identity can they be independent enough to commit suicide. (62)

The suicide mortality rate increases with advancing age, reaching a peak in black males and females at ages 25 to 34, in white females at ages 45 to 54, and in white males at age 65 and over. (78) Figure 9–1 shows the trends. (78) The rate per 100,000 among white males ages 15 to 24 is 19.2; among other males ages 15 to 24, 14.7; among white females ages 15 to 24, 4.9; and among black and other nonwhite females ages 15 to 24, 4.0. (79) The suicide rate among college students is about 50 percent higher than among adolescents in the general population; (51, p. 10) there may therefore be elements in the college environment conducive to suicide. (6, p. 110)

Only a small percentage of attempted suicides succeed. Estimates of the ratio of suicide attempts to fatalities vary from as high as 120:1 in children to 5:1 in adults. (15, 51, 63) Females attempt suicide much more frequently than do males, but many more males than females are successful in completing the suicide. (29; 32, p. 198; 73, p. 131) One of the reasons males more often succeed is that they

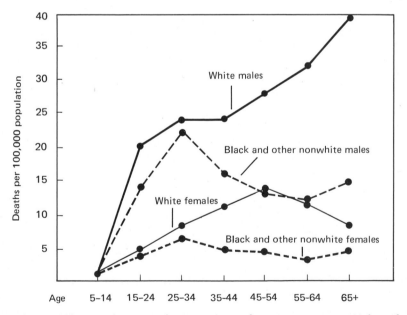

Figure 9–1. Suicide mortality rates, by sex, race, and age groups, 1976. (Adapted from U.S. Bureau of the Census, Department of Commerce, *Statistical Abstract of the United States, 1978*. [Washington, D.C.: U.S. Government Printing Office, 1978], Table 298, p. 183.)

frequently use more violent means—hanging, jumping from heights, shooting, or stabbing themselves—whereas females more often use passive and less dangerous methods, such as taking pills. Females more often make multiple threats, but less often really want to kill themselves or actually do it. (84, p. 253)

CAUSES AND MOTIVES

What are the causes of adolescents seeking to take their own lives? What are their motives? There is a variety of contributing factors.

Suicidal adolescents tend to come from disturbed family backgrounds. (15) There may have been much conflict between the parents and between the parents and children, or the parents may have manifested negative, rejecting attitudes toward the children. There may have been frequent unemployment and economic stress in the home, early parental physical or emotional deprivation, the absence or loss of one or both parents, or illness or abandonment by the father. (15, p. 1) Studies of adolescent suicide attempts in Los Angeles County, California, revealed the following:

1. Seventy-two percent had one or both natural parents absent from the home.
2. Fifty-eight percent had a parent who was married more than once.
3. Eighty-four percent of those with stepparents felt they were contending with an unwanted stepparent.
4. Sixty-two percent had both parents working (or one parent at work when there was only one parent present). (73, p. 133)

As a consequence, there is often an absence of any warm, parental figure with whom to identify and a sense of emotional and social isolation. (15, p. 2; 35) Suicide attempters often state that they do not feel close to any adult. They often have trouble communicating with significant others around them. Yacoubian states: "Dynamically, social isolation appears to be the most effective factor in distinguishing those who will kill themselves from those who will not." (87, p. 158) "There is no one to turn to when I need to talk to someone" is a typical comment. (73, p. 137)

The background of social isolation makes these adolescents particularly vulnerable to a loss of love object, which may trigger the suicide attempt. The loss of a parent in childhood makes any subsequent loss of a family member, mate, boyfriend, or girlfriend particularly hard. (51, p. 20) Yusin writes:

Suicidal behavior in adolescents is initiated by many factors. . . . One such factor may be a fantasy in which the adolescent sees himself unable to cope with his environment and destroyed by it. This fantasy may be aroused when the adolescent experiences the loss of a perceived nurturing life sustaining object and believes that his or her intrinsic worthlessness drove the object away. Therefore he or she can never replace it. The adolescent then sees himself or herself alone, at the mercy of a hostile environment. . . . The fear of this annihilation leads, in part, to the initiation of suicidal behavior. (88, p. 26)

One frequent component of suicidal tendencies is depression. This depression may follow the loss of the love object, and is characterized by mourning, crying spells, dejected mood, withdrawal of interest in the world, the inhibition of activities, lack of motivation in performing tasks, and a painful dejection.

(59, p. 364; 88, p. 20) Psychosomatic symptoms such as appetite loss, sleep disturbance, increased fatigability, or decreased sexual interest may appear. (83)

Sometimes the depression may not be readily apparent; the individual may try to cover it up with overactivity, preoccupation with trivia, or "acting out" behavior such as delinquency, use of drugs, or sexual promiscuity. (51, p. 13) In one study of thirty-four suicides at Harvard College over a twenty-five-year period, none showed profound depression just prior to killing themselves. (5, p. 154)

Stress may also stimulate suicidal attempts. Part of this stress may originate in poor home conditions that produce terrible strains. One author reports that with 29 percent of adolescent attempted suicides their childhood home situations were so bad that the Society for Prevention of Cruelty to Children had to be called in. (51, p. 13) The stress may also arise from current situations: the pressure of completing school work and getting acceptable grades, the indecision of vocational choice, the pressure to find social acceptance, conflict over sexual intimacy (especially without close emotional involvement), and the feeling of inadequacy as pressure mounts. (51, p. 19; 61) One sixteen-year-old girl who had attempted suicide revealed her feelings.

I felt up against the wall. I had another hassle with my mother, things weren't going well in school and I'd stopped using drugs two weeks before that. . . . Now pressures were piling up on me from all over the place and I didn't have any kind of escape. (3, p. 461)

Lack of investment in the future is characteristic of suicidal adolescents. They are more likely to view their futures with feelings of hopelessness, without real plans or expectations. They usually see only the discomfort and pain of the present situation. (15, p. 5)

Some suicidal adolescents have been categorized as immature personalities with poor impulse control. (15, p. 3) The combination of impulsiveness and resurgent sexual and aggressive drives, coupled with poor ego development, is illustrated in the following case.

Bob . . . was preoccupied with pleasure seeking, he had little supervision, and would be passively defiant and withdrawn when interrupted. Since age four he had been hospitalized at least once a year with head and body injuries, four of which resulted from being hit by cars. When a teacher reprimanded him for taking liberties with a girl, he hung himself with his belt in the cloakroom where the teacher had sent him. "I was sore at the teacher because of my report card the day before," he said. (87, p. 155)

Other suicidal adolescents have been shown to be highly suggestible in following the directions or examples of others. (51, p. 14) This factor of suggestibility has been borne out by studies of adolescent "suicide epidemics," and "anniversary suicides," when suicide is attempted on the anniversary date of another's death. A tragic example of suggestibility is the case in which a boy hanged himself in a way similar to a hanging in a comic book he had just read. (51, p. 15) Another example is a fourteen-year-old boy, Rocky Hensley, from Albion, Michigan, who was an avid fan of rock singer Alice Cooper. Hensley was fascinated by the mock suicide by hanging that the performer included in his stage performances. Rocky's death apparently was the result of imitating the Alice Cooper suicide act. (24) Suicidal adolescents are likely to have a history of suicide within the family and close friends who have killed themselves. (15, p. 4) Teicher (73) found that 40 percent of adolescent attempted suicides had a parent, relative, or close friend who had committed suicide. (73, p. 133)

Suicide may be a direct result of mental illness, either neuroses or psychoses. A study of a special group of sixty suicidal adolescent boys and girls, ages 11½ to 15½ years, who were admitted to the children's unit of Creedmoor State Hospital (a residential treatment center for emotionally disturbed children and adolescents), revealed that 40 percent of the adolescents had experienced hallucinations telling them to kill themselves. Another 10 percent had threatened suicide, in part because of anticipated guilt occasioned by voices directing them toward external aggression. Eighty-three percent had experienced hallucinations of some kind within the year preceding admission. Generally, the auditory hallucinations were "good" and "bad" voices telling them to do or not to do something. The younger children generally heard internal voices, whereas the adolescents generally heard the voices from some external source. The "bad" voices may have told the individual to kill himself or herself or someone else, set a fire, steal, run away, or threatened dire consequences for sexual activity. (84, p. 253)

Guilt and/or anger and hostility are important emotional components of suicide. Teicher (73) reports that 36 percent of all suicide-attempting girls in a study in southern California were in the terminal stages of a romance. Two-thirds of these girls were pregnant or believed themselves pregnant as a result of their romance. (73, p. 136) Their suicide attempts were to punish either themselves or their boyfriends. Guilt and shame over an out-of-wedlock pregnancy can be powerful motivating factors in suicides. (57, p. 120)

In such cases, suicide becomes an act of aggression, expressed inwardly at the self, in contrast to homicide, an act of aggression expressed outwardly. (43; 47, p. 105; 67, p. 84) The pregnant girl, for example, could try to get even with her boyfriend by killing herself (suicide) to make the boy feel sorry or by killing him directly (homicide). Miller writes:

Of all the aggressive acts of which people are capable, suicide is [sometimes] one of the most aggressive; it is a hostile act directed at loved ones, at society, as well as at the self. The survivors are always left wondering how they failed. (50, p. 305)

Suicide is a cry for help to get attention or sympathy, or an attempt to manipulate other people. Attempted suicide is not an effort to die, but rather a communication to others in an effort to improve one's life. As a matter of fact, desired changes in the life situation as a result of attempted suicide may be accomplished. However, many suicidal gestures made in an attempt to gain attention and sympathy or to signal for help misfire and lead to death. This often happens when a person takes an overdose of drugs such as barbiturates. (57, p. 119) Each successive attempt is more likely to succeed; every suicidal gesture must therefore be taken seriously and treated as an indication that something is wrong and needs prompt attention. Of the 1,400 people who call the San Francisco Suicide Prevention agency each month, 1 in 5 will kill himself or herself if the volunteer worker cannot talk the person out of the suicide plan. This statistic refers only to those who call; a large number of attempted suicides never tell anyone ahead of time. (6, p. 111)

Contrary to common opinion, suicide attempts in a great majority of cases are considered in advance, weighed rationally against other alternatives. The attempter may have tried other means: rebellion, running away from home, lying, stealing, or other attention-getting devices. Having tried these methods and failed, the person then turns to suicide attempts. If others are alerted in time, if they pay attention to these developments and take them seriously enough to try to remedy the situation, a death may be prevented. (73, p. 131)

Juvenile Delinquency

DEFINITIONS

The term *juvenile delinquency* refers to the violation of the law by a juvenile, in most states anyone under eighteen years of age. The legal term *juvenile delinquent* was established for young lawbreakers to avoid the disgrace and stigma of being classified in legal records as criminals and to separate underage people and treat them differently from adult criminals. Most are tried in juvenile courts where the intent is to rehabilitate them.

A young person may be labeled a delinquent for breaking any of a number of laws, ranging from murder or armed robbery to running away from home or truancy from school. Because laws are inconsistent, a particular action may be labeled delinquent in one community but not in another. Furthermore, law enforcement officials differ in the method and extent of enforcement. In some communities, the police may only talk to adolescents who are accused of minor crimes; in others the police refer youths to their parents; in still others, they may arrest them and refer them to juvenile court. As with adults, many crimes adolescents commit are never discovered, (26, p. 101) or if discovered, are not reported or prosecuted. (42) Most statistics, therefore, understate the extent of juvenile crime.

INCIDENCE

Statistics on juvenile delinquency include either the numbers of *persons* arrested, the number of *court cases* handled, or the number of *offenses* committed. Obviously, one adolescent may commit more than one offense. (75, p. 333) As seen in Figure 9–2, the number of juvenile court cases leveled off after a number of years of rapid increase, but has begun to increase again. (78, 80) Any increase must be considered in terms of the juvenile population, ages ten to seventeen, which has also increased. In 1971 the ratio of juvenile court cases to the population ten to seventeen years old was 34.1; in 1972 it was 33.6; in 1973, it was 34.2.(80) During that period the proportion of ten- to seventeen-year-olds who were delinquent was fairly constant. (25, p. 56) In 1974, however, it increased to 37.5, and to 39.9 in 1975.

Of all persons arrested in 1977, 24 percent were juveniles—under age eighteen; an additional 32 percent were ages eighteen to twenty-four. Figure 9–3 shows the percentages. This means that 56 percent of all arrests during 1977 were of people under age twenty-five. As seen in Figure 9–4, the incidence of

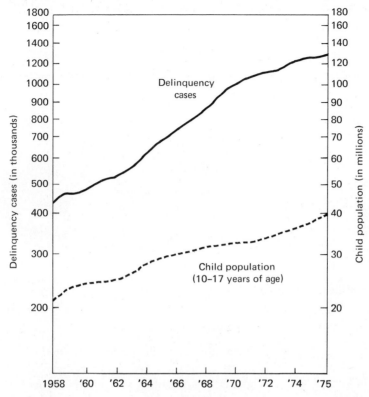

Figure 9–2.   Trends in juvenile court cases handled and in child population, ages
10–17, 1957–1975. (Adapted from U.S. Office of Human Development and U.S.
Office of Youth Development, *Juvenile Court Statistics Annual.* [Washington,
D.C.: U.S. Government Printing Office, 1970 and 1973]. Beginning 1974, The
National Center for Juvenile Justice, Pittsburgh, Pa. Unpublished data.)

delinquency among males under age eighteen is over three and one-half times
that among females of the same age. (78)

TYPES OF CRIME

As shown in Tables 9–1 and 9–2, the largest single category of crimes committed
by both male and female juvenile offenders is crimes against property, primarily
theft of some kind. (78) This type of crime (marked by an asterisk in Tables 9–1
and 9–2) continues to increase. So-called victimless crimes, which include primarily violations of narcotic drug laws or liquor laws, drunkenness, driving while
intoxicated, gambling, prostitution or commercial vice, carrying or possessing
illegal weapons, and such things as disorderly conduct or vagrancy constitute the
second largest category of crimes committed by juveniles. The total number of
these crimes (marked with a *V* in Tables 9–1 and 9–2) has increased; they con-
stituted a larger percentage of total crimes committed by juveniles in 1977 than
in 1970. Crimes against people, including assault, rape, murder, manslaughter,
sex offenses other than rape or prostitution, and offenses against family or
children (marked with a *P* in Tables 9–1 and 9–2) increased both in absolute

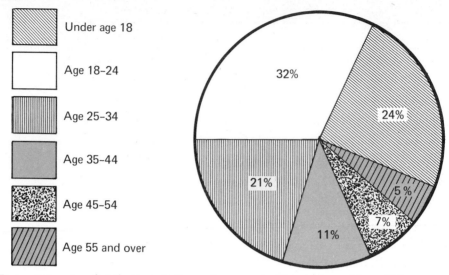

Figure 9–3. Age distribution of all people arrested, 1977. (Adapted from U.S. Bureau of the Census, Department of Commerce, *Statistical Abstract of the United States, 1978* [Washington, D.C.: U.S. Government Printing Office, 1978], Table 305.)

number and in relation to the total number of all crimes committed between 1970 and 1977. All other miscellaneous crimes are grouped together and labeled *A*. The census bureau groups eight crimes together as "serious crimes" and gives totals for them (see Table 9–1); these crimes include larceny, burglary, motor vehicle theft, robbery, aggravated assault, forcible rape, murder, and manslaughter by negligence. Table 9–3 shows that from 1970 to 1977 this group of crimes

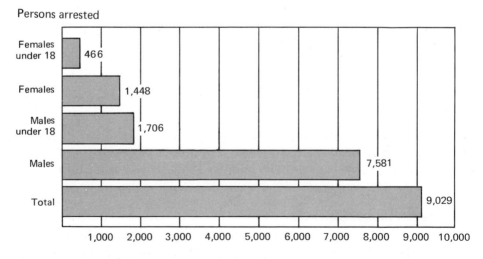

Figure 9–4. People arrested, by sex and age, 1977. (Adapted from the U.S. Bureau of the Census, Department of Commerce, *Statistical Abstract of the United States, 1978.* [Washington, D.C.: U.S. Government Printing Office, 1978].)

Table 9–1.   Number of arrests, by type of crime, sex, and age, 1977.

Offense	Males under 18	Females under 18
Serious crimes		
* Larceny	213,700	86,800
* Burglary—breaking and entering	145,300	9,300
* Motor vehicle theft	42,800	4,300
* Robbery	22,000	1,700
P Aggravated assault	20,100	3,600
P Forcible rape	2,700	—
P Murder	1,000	100
P Manslaughter by negligence	200	less than 50
Subtotal	447,800	106,000
All other		
V Drug abuse violations	73,100	14,500
V Disorderly conduct	66,300	15,800
V Liquor laws	59,200	16,900
P Other assaults	43,800	11,800
V Drunkenness	26,900	4,400
* Stolen property	21,300	2,000
V Weapon (carrying, possession)	14,500	1,000
V Driving while intoxicated	11,300	1,200
P Sex offenses (except rape and prostitution)	6,900	900
* Forgery and counterfeiting	3,900	1,600
V Vagrancy	3,100	800
* Fraud	2,800	1,100
P Offenses against family and children	1,100	700
V Gambling	1,500	less than 50
V Prostitution and commercial vice	800	1,700
* Embezzlement	500	100
A All other offenses except traffic	307,000	40,800
Total, all crimes	1,091,800	314,500

* = Crimes against property; P = crimes against other persons; V = victimless crimes.
Adapted from U.S. Bureau of the Census, Department of Commerce. *Statistical Abstract of the United States, 1978* (Washington, D.C.: U.S. Government Printing Office, 1978), Table 306.

increased faster than any other: 3 percent for males under eighteen and 17 percent for females under eighteen. (78) These increases can be compared to decreases in all other types of crimes for males, and only slight increases for female juveniles. (78, Table 306) The rapid increase in the more violent and serious crimes has caused considerable concern among authorities. The only category of serious crime committed by juvenile males that showed a decline between 1970 and 1977 was motor vehicle theft. However, motor vehicle theft by females increased drastically during the same period. (78, Table 306)

CAUSES OF DELINQUENCY

Concern about the problem of delinquency has motivated considerable investigation and research efforts to try to find its causes. In general, the causes may be grouped into three major categories: *sociological factors* include influential elements in our society and culture; *psychological factors* include the influences of

Table 9–2.   Percentage of types of crimes committed by delinquent males and females under age 18, 1970 and 1977.

Type of Crime	Delinquent Males under 18		Delinquent Females under 18	
	1970	1977	1970	1977
* Crimes against property (primary theft)	38%	41%	29%	34%
P Crimes against other persons	6%	7%	5%	5%
V Victimless crimes	23%	24%	17%	18%
A All other offenses except traffic	33%	28%	49%	43%

Note: P = Assault, rape, murder, manslaughter, sex offenses (other than rape and prostitution) against family, children; V = Drugs, alcohol, gambling, prostitution, weapons, driving, disorderly conduct, vagrancy.
Adapted from U.S. Bureau of the Census, Dept. of Commerce. *Statistical Abstract of the United States, 1978* (Washington, D.C.: U.S. Government Printing Office, 1978), Table 306.

interpersonal relationships and personality components; *biological factors* include the effects of organic and physical elements.

Sociological factors in delinquency. The most important sociological factors that have been investigated in relation to juvenile delinquency are the following:

• Socioeconomic status and class
• Affluence, hedonism, and cultural values
• Peer-group involvement and influences
• Neighborhood and community influences
• Social and cultural change, disorganization, and unrest
• School performance
• Family background

Socioeconomic status and class have been found to be less important in relation to juvenile delinquency than was once thought. (39; 74, p. 400) Traditionally, delinquency was thought to be a by-product of poverty and low socioeconomic

Table 9–3.   Increases in "serious" crimes and "all other" crimes committed by persons under age 18, 1970 and 1977.

Type of Crime	Total Male Arrests		% Change	Total Female Arrests		% Increase
	1970	1977		1970	1977	
Serious Crime*	435,171	447,800	3%+	88,506	106,000	17%
All Other Crime	1,133,092	1,091,800	4%−	311,039	314,500	1%

* Serious crime includes larceny, burglary, motor vehicle theft, robbery, aggravated assault, forcible rape, murder, manslaughter by negligence.
Adapted from U.S. Bureau of the Census, Department of Commerce, *Statistical Abstract of the United States, 1978* (Washington, D.C.: U.S. Government Printing Office, 1978), Table 306.

status. (44, p. 164) Juvenile males became delinquent as a form of protest against female-dominated homes and as a method of asserting their manliness. Violence, aggressiveness, and daring were not only accepted but admired. They were the way lower class males proved their manhood. Juvenile females became delinquent out of frustration. Their romantic ideals never quite matched the reality of their lives. They were exposed to middle class goals and ideals in terms of marriage, parenthood, and female vocations, but were unable to achieve any of these because of the incongruity between their aspirations and their opportunities. Thus, delinquency was an act of despair, a defiant reaction against their inability to succeed in a class system that is middle class oriented.

Recent studies show, however, that juvenile delinquency is becoming more evenly distributed through all socioeconomic status levels. (26; 39; 42; 75, p. 346) In fact there is as great an incidence of some forms of delinquency among adolescents of the middle class as among those of other classes. (18, 39) The big difference is that middle class adolescents who commit delinquent offenses are less often arrested and charged with them than are their lower class counterparts. (18, 53) The son or daughter from a well-to-do family is let off with a warning, while those from poorer families are arrested and punished. (26)

Affluence and hedonistic values and life styles among modern youths are conducive to delinquent patterns of behavior. (17, 76) Today's youths, especially those of the middle class, have access to cars, alcoholic beverages, drugs, and pocket money. They are involved in a whirl of social activities: dating, dances, sports events, partying, rock concerts, driving around, parking, and hanging out at their favorite meeting places. Their interests and attitudes lend themselves to late hours, getting into mischief, and involvement in vandalism or delinquent acts. Thus, delinquency among contemporary adolescents is a by-product of participation in the legitimate youth culture. (53, 66)

As a result, *peer-group involvement* becomes a significant influence in delinquency. Those adolescents who have a high degree of peer orientation are also more likely to have a high level of delinquency involvement. (53) Table 9–4 illustrates the relationship. Data were obtained from 284 male sophomores enrolled in schools in a county in the Pacific Northwest. (53) These data show that adolescents who spend more of their time hanging around with friends are more likely to become involved in delinquent social behavior. (75, p. 356) The types

Table 9–4. Percentage of delinquency involvement by levels of peer orientation among middle class boys, in a county in the Pacific Northwest.

Delinquency involvement	Peer Orientation		
	Low	Medium	High
Low	70%	34%	13%
Medium	21%	38%	23%
High	8%	28%	63%
Number	52	32	30

Table 1 from "A Reassessment of Middle-Class Delinquency," by Kenneth A. Polk, is reprinted from *Youth and Society*, Vol. 2, No. 3 (March 1971) pp. 333–354, by permission of the publisher, Sage Publications, Inc.

of friends adolescents associate with are extremely important; both males and females whose friends are delinquent are more likely themselves to report high delinquency. (27)

Various *neighborhood and community influences* are also important. Most larger communities can identify areas in which delinquency rates are higher than in other neighborhoods. Not all adolescents growing up in these areas become delinquent, but a larger than average percentage do because of the influence and pressures of the cultural milieu in which they live. (14, p. 534)

Today's adolescents are also living in a period of *rapid cultural change, disorganization, and unrest,* which tends to increase delinquency rates. (See Chapter 2.) Values that once were commonly accepted are now questioned. Social institutions such as the family that once offered security and protection may exert an upsetting influence instead. The specter of social, economic, and political unrest stimulates anxieties and rebellion. It has been shown that the children of immigrants, who have to adjust to drastic cultural changes in moving from one country to another, have twice the delinquency rates of native-born children. (14, p. 533)

School performance also is an important factor in delinquency. (20, 54) A lack of school success—poor grades, classroom misconduct, and an inability to adjust to the school program and to get along with administrators and teachers —are all associated with delinquency. (27; 44, p. 166; 53, 68) Senna (64) suggests that youths who do not conform to expectations in the academic setting are soon labeled as troublemakers. The negative attitudes of school personnel stimulate additional misbehavior. Absenteeism increases as do hedonistic activities such as alcohol and marijuana use. These activities in turn prevent students who become "high" in school from performing academically. Senna (64) also found that delinquents tend to have poorer study habits, to fail more courses, and to receive lower grades that nondelinquents, and that classroom misconduct is most strongly correlated with crimes against property (theft and vandalism). Youths who do not respect the property and integrity of others outside the classroom are also those who argue with teachers and cheat in the classroom. (64, p. 492)

Family background has an important influence on adolescent development and adjustment and hence on social conduct. Broken homes and strained family relationships both have been associated with delinquent behavior. (10, 31) Father absence in particular seems to have a negative effect upon males. (66) Lambert writes:

Perhaps the most influential factor is that many broken homes tend to be matriarchal in structure, thereby failing to provide the male adolescent with a suitable masculine figure with whom to identify. As a result, he develops conflict over his sexual role and an obsessive concern with his masculinity, and his delinquent acts often function as a means of resolving this sexual role conflict. (44, p. 164)

A recent study of 5,376 juveniles showed that children from broken homes were more than twice as likely to be charged with offenses as would be expected by their number in the population. (10)

PSYCHOLOGICAL FACTORS IN DELINQUENCY. It is quite obvious that broken homes can be a contributing factor to delinquency. But broken homes in and of them-

selves are no worse than, and sometimes not as detrimental as, intact but unhappy, disturbed family relationships. Usually studies of delinquency compare
the rates for adolescents from broken homes with those from intact homes, many
of which are fairly happy. However, if comparisons are made between adolescents
from broken homes with adolescents from intact but unhappy homes, the results
are fairly similar.

Adolescents' relationships with their fathers are particularly important. A
study of ninety female delinquents from Georgia and eighty-five female delinquents from Oklahoma showed that the girls were not close to their fathers and
that their fathers were neither very interested in them, loving, kind, nor understanding. (46) These delinquent adolescent girls perceived their fathers as cold,
rejecting, and uninvolved. Discipline was either nonexistent or excessive and inconsistent. (46, pp. 475–481) Other studies of both male and female delinquents
show that their fathers are more neglectful, punitive, cold, mistrusting, and rejecting than fathers of nondelinquents. (4, 12, 27, 58, 70) There is also a higher
incidence of alcoholism and/or criminality in the families of adolescents who
become delinquent than of those who do not become delinquent. (45) In a comparison of the mothers and fathers of delinquents, the fathers emerge as the
more damaging of the parents. (4, 46)

There have been efforts also to determine whether certain *personality factors*
predispose the adolescent to delinquency. Is there such a thing as a criminal
type? No one personality type can be associated with delinquency, but it is known
that those who become delinquent are more likely to be socially assertive, defiant,
ambivalent to authority, resentful, hostile, suspicious, destructive, impulsive,
and lacking in self-control. (1) They consistently exhibit a low self-esteem or
negative self-image. (27, 36) They view themselves as "lazy," "bad," or "dumb."
Their delinquency appears as a defense against their feelings of inferiority, rejection, and frustration. (14, p. 535; 27; 83) In some cases, delinquency is a
symptom of deeper neuroses, an outgrowth of fears, anxieties, or hostilities. (55)
In other instances, it occurs in basically emotionally healthy adolescents who
have been handled incorrectly, misdirected, misled, or suffered temporary traumatic experiences. (55, p. 197) In some cases, delinquency is the result of poor
socialization that results in the adolescents not developing proper impulse controls. (55, p. 197) Thus, the psychodynamics of delinquents' behavior are different, even though the results of that behavior lead to similar trouble.

BIOLOGICAL FACTORS IN DELINQUENCY. Most delinquency has environmental
causes, but in some cases organic or biological factors may be directly or indirectly influential. It has been found, for example, that some juvenile delinquents
show evidence of a maturational lag in the development of the frontal lobe system
of the brain, which can result in neurophysiological dysfunction and in delinquent
behavior. (55) Ponitus (56) suggests that about 15 to 20 percent of juvenile delinquents evidence this neurophysiological dysfunction. It is not so much that
their cognitive function is impaired; rather, they cannot act on the basis of the
knowledge they have. (56, p. 290)

Genetic studies also have uncovered a variety of chromosomal aberrations.
One of these involves the presence of an extra Y chromosome in the male so that

he has an XYY combination. This has been associated with increased height; above average aggressiveness; impulsiveness; explosive, undisciplined behavior; and a greater than expected incidence of criminality. (52) One of the most publicized cases associated with this chromosome pattern involved a man who murdered eight nurses in Chicago. (11) However, most male criminals do not have this chromosomal pattern.

Sheppard (68) believes that at least 25 percent of delinquency can be blamed on organic causes. He cites the case of a fifteen-year-old girl who was suffering from too much insulin in her blood, keeping her blood sugar count too low. She was restless, jumpy, and fidgety, unable to think or act rationally. Proper medication and diet soon corrected the difficulty. (68, p. 24) Sheppard cites other examples of delinquency due to a hearing impairment, hyperactivity from hyperthyroidism, or abnormal brain wave patterns. (68, p. 26) In all cases, therefore, it is wise to check out chemical and medical reasons for behavioral problems before assuming the difficulties are completely environmental or psychological.

JUVENILE STREET GANGS

Adolescents join street gangs for a number of reasons. Members highlight the benefits of street gang membership as companionship, protection, excitement, and heterosexual contacts. (22, p. 600) One factor that predisposes youths to gang membership is poor family relationships. If emotional and social needs of adolescents are not met through interpersonal relationships in the family, youths turn to the gang to fulfill status needs that would otherwise go unmet. (22, p. 601) Friedman's study of street gangs in Philadelphia showed that gang members had poor mother-son relationships, and of the over 60 percent who had fathers or father substitutes at home, large numbers reported shouting at, cursing, or striking their fathers. (22) Parental defiance was the single most important correlate of gang membership.

The problem with gang membership is that members are forced to commit illegal acts, especially violent ones, that many would never do if acting on their own. Street gangs hold nearly absolute control over the behavior of individuals. Table 9–5 compares street gang members and nonmembers in Philadelphia in terms of gang coercion to commit antisocial and illegal acts. As can be seen, gangs forced both members and nonmembers to engage in antisocial and illegal acts, but significantly more gang members than nonmembers were forced to cause trouble in the neighborhood, verbally abuse police, get drunk, fight, get or hide a weapon, stab or injure someone with a weapon, shoot at someone with a gun, steal, fight at school, skip homework, stay away from school, break up parties, destroy public property, and mark or spray paint on walls. (23, p. 529) The violent nature of these gangs is revealed in the fact that 44 percent of members were forced to fight, 22 percent were forced to stab or injure someone, and 25 percent were forced to shoot at someone. (23, p. 529) Thus, the gangs held life-and-death power over others and were a direct challenge to the authority of the family, community, police, the school, and the individual himself. Members were forced to submit to the gang's decisions or face more personally destructive consequences. (23, p. 532) In such instances, the only way to deal with the problem of

Table 9–5.   Percentage of gang coercion of street gang members and nonmembers to commit antisocial and illegal acts.

Item	% Gang	% Nongang
Stay out all night long	17	16
Cause trouble in neighborhood	21	13
Call police names	22	14
Get drunk	32	16
Bother grownups	15	10
Fight	44	21
Get a weapon or hide a weapon	29	12
Stab someone or injure someone with a weapon	22	10
Shoot at someone	25	9
Take heroin, scag, or smack	7	8
Have sex with a girl	38	14
Have sex with other guys	4	3
Steal	27	13
Fight at school	38	18
Skip homework	25	9
Take pot, grass, reefers, hash, or marijuana	20	15
Stay away from school	24	13
"Shake down" other guys	24	33
Take speed or meth or methedrine	7	6
Break up parties	26	9
Destroy public property	20	12
Mark or spray paint on walls	30	15

Adapted from C. J. Friedman et al. "Juvenile Street Gangs: The Victimization of Youth," *Adolescence* 11 (1976): 527–533. Used by permission.

delinquency is to dismantle or redirect the criminal activities of the street gangs. (41)

THE JUVENILE JUSTICE SYSTEM

The statutes and customs of each state determine the process for handling juvenile delinquents. Although this process varies from state to state, each system consists of four separate entities: the police, the juvenile court, the correctional system, and private community programs. (16, p. 110)

THE POLICE. The first contact any adolescent has with the juvenile justice system is the local police department. Charged with maintaining and enforcing the law, the police perform the function of screening cases that may go before the court. When offenses are discovered, the police may take any one of several actions: (1) ignore the offenses; (2) let the juvenile go with a warning; (3) report the problem to parents; (4) refer the case to the school, a welfare agency, clinic, counseling or guidance center, or family society; (5) take the juvenile into custody for questioning, to be held or reprimanded by a juvenile officer; or

(6) after investigation, arrest the juvenile and turn the matter over to a juvenile court. If arrested and waiting trial, the juvenile may be released with or without bail or kept in a special detention center awaiting deposition of his or her case. If special juvenile facilities are not available, juvenile offenders are sometimes kept in jail with adult offenders.

One problem is that in the beginning of the process the matter is left entirely to police discretion. They must enforce the law, but they do so differentially. An individual officer may arrest adolescents who come from the wrong section of town or have the wrong color skin or wild hair, but may let other adolescents go who come from well-to-do-families or are neatly dressed. Many officers enjoy harassing any one who is an adolescent or a "hippie type" kid. Some officers are far harder on juveniles than are other officers. Also, parents who are able to afford lawyers ensure that their youths will be treated more fairly before the law. One of the reasons adolescents become bitter toward the police is because of unfair and differential treatment or harassment. (16, p. 111)

Some communities hire juvenile officers who are specialists in dealing with youths. Such officers go far beyond law enforcement functions and strive to assist adolescents and their families in solving problems. Some large cities have separate juvenile bureaus with five basic functions:

1. The discovery of delinquents, potential delinquents, and conditions contributing to delinquency.
2. The investigation of cases of juveniles who are delinquents or involved as accessories by association with adult criminals.
3. The protection of juveniles.
4. The disposition of juvenile cases.
5. The prevention of juvenile delinquency.

Police in many communities now go far beyond law enforcement, from sponsoring boys' clubs to offering drug education programs or safety education in local schools. Police in Richmond, California, wanting to do something to placate riotous youths, arranged to meet and talk with hostile black youths who had been on the rampage for several nights. The sessions grew in attendance, various other discussion groups were organized, and relationships improved as meaningful dialogue and mutual understanding developed. (25, p. 313)

THE JUVENILE COURT. As a last resort, the juvenile court is asked to make the disposition of a case. But procedures vary from state to state. How "fatherly" should the judge be? Cases are often dealt with informally in private hearings. The "trial" consists of private talks in the judge's chambers. But without any formal trial what happens in such cases depends completely on the inclinations of the judge. Plea bargaining between lawyers is common so that in this instance the attorneys decide the case.

The most important juvenile court case to reach the United States Supreme Court was of a fifteen-year-old boy, Gerald Gault, on probation, who was accused along with a friend of calling a neighbor and using indecent language. Gerald stated that he had called the number and handed the phone to his friend. He was taken into custody by the sheriff; his parents were not notified their son was arrested nor of the hearing the following morning. There was no sworn testimony, no transcript, nor record of the proceedings. As a result of the hearing, Gerald was committed to the state industrial school until age twenty-one—a six-year sentence. In reviewing the case, the Supreme Court insisted that due process of law had been violated, and that if Gault had been an adult, he would have received a fine of five to fifty dollars or less than two months' imprisonment. (16, p. 112)

At the present time, the best juvenile court systems hire judges with special qualifications for juvenile court work, who understand not only the law but also child psychology and social problems. A variety of medical, psychological, and social services are available along with adequate foster family and institutional care, and recreational services and facilities. A qualified probation staff with limited case loads and plans for constructive efforts works under state supervision. Detention of juveniles is kept at a minimum—if possible, outside of jails and police stations. An adequate record system is maintained and safeguarded against indiscriminate public inspection. (16, p. 113)

THE CORRECTIONAL SYSTEM. The majority of juvenile offenders brought to court, especially those charged for the first time, are placed on probation, given suspended sentences, and/or ordered to get help from the proper medical, psychological, or social service agency or personnel. The purpose of the court is not just to punish, but also to ensure proper treatment and rehabilitation of the delinquent. Thus, the judge often must make quick decisions regarding the best treatment.

The backbone of the correctional procedure is the *probation system*, whereby the juvenile is placed under the care of a probation officer to whom she or he must report and who strives to regulate and guide his or her conduct. For the system to work, however, the delinquent has to have a clear understanding of probation requirements and of the punishments for violating probation. Stumphauzer (72) tells of one teenage child molester who understood that while on probation he was "to stay out of trouble" and "mind his grandmother" or he "would get into more trouble." But when asked which behaviors were permitted, which were not, and what "minding his grandmother" meant, he did not know. He wasn't even sure what would happen if he molested another child. Only after consultation was it made clear that if he molested another child he would be taken out of his home and placed in juvenile hall. He also was given some *positive* behaviors to perform (be in by 9:00 on week nights), which would be rewarded (being able to stay out until 11:00 on one weekend night) if he obeyed. (72, p. 22) Probation based entirely on threat of punishment is poor rehabilitation. Programs that focus on positive behavior and positive reinforcement are more helpful. Studies show that juvenile offenders placed on probation have lower rearrest rates and generally better records than those detained in juvenile facilities. (16, p. 114)

Most juvenile correction systems include *detention centers* of one kind or another. Most of these are reception and diagnostic centers where juveniles are placed under temporary restraint awaiting a hearing, or if hearings have already been held, they are placed in the center for further diagnosis and evaluation before more permanent action is taken. (13, p. 44) About one-third of adolescents in detention centers are not even delinquents. (78, Table 326) They are juveniles in need of supervision (JINS) who are wards of the court because their parents can't, won't, or shouldn't care for them. Some of the parents are ill or deceased, others have neglected, rejected, or abused them to the point where they have been taken out of the home. Others are youths who have run away from home. Many are awaiting disposition by the court.

Detention centers have many critics. Dreyfus writes:

> The most talked about institution, and certainly one of the biggest failures is the system of juvenile detention and juvenile court. In Los Angeles, the immediate detention facility is juvenile hall. As any youth who has been there will tell you, juvenile hall is no place for juveniles. I have been there when the facility was so overcrowded that bare mattresses were placed on the floor to accommodate the large number of persons held there. Due to the overcrowding, sexual psychopaths and narcotics peddlers were sleeping side by side with juveniles arrested for curfew violations. The officers in charge were often harsh and unsympathetic, and occasionally dangerous. When my friend Art was arrested for drunk driving, the officers attempted to place him in Men's Central Jail, even though Art was only seventeen. Although Art's father was present, he was not allowed to see or speak to his son, or intervene to prevent the illegal action. When Art resisted, one of the officers grabbed him by the throat and threw him to the ground. Apparently, Art is not the only juvenile to have such experiences when taken into custody. (16, p. 105)

The correctional system also includes *training schools, ranches, forestry camps, and farms.* About three-fourths of the juveniles in public custody are held in these types of facilities. (79) (These do not include the juveniles in jail, in privately operated facilities, foster homes, facilities exclusively for drug abusers, homes for dependent or neglected children, or federal correctional facilities.) Figure 9–5 shows the numbers held in each type of facility. Most authorities feel that in their traditional forms such training schools and correctional institutions do not correct or rehabilitate. (72) While youths are being punished, "rehabilitated," or "corrected," they are exposed to hundreds of other delinquents who spend their time running their own behavior modification program to shape additional antisocial and delinquent behavior. The influence is therefore negative, not positive. The system has been improved greatly by what has been called *token economy,* which places the emphasis on a "24-hour positive learning environment." In this system, students earn points for good behavior, with points convertible to money that can be used to purchase goods or privileges. Money can be spent for room rental, fines for misconduct, in the commissary or snack bar, or for recreation. The Robert F. Kennedy Youth Center (KYC) in Morgantown, West Virginia, classifies students as "trainees," "apprentices," and "honor students." (37) They earn points for academic accomplishments and school work, for proper social behavior, for doing chores or other jobs, or for social development. Under this system students make great gains in academic achievement, on-the-job training, or in eliminating assaultive, disruptive, and antisocial behavior. (86)

One of the criticisms of correctional institutions for youthful offenders is that once the juveniles are released to the community, they often come under

Type of facility

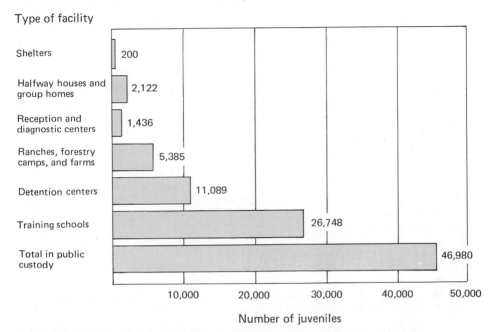

Figure 9–5. Total number of juveniles in public custody in each type of facility. (Adapted from U.S. Law Enforcement Assistance Administration, "Children in Custody: Advance Report on the Juvenile Detention and Correctional Facility Census of 1974, 1975, and 1977." Unpublished data.)

the same influences and face some of the same problems that were responsible for their getting into trouble in the first place. One suggestion has been to use *halfway houses* and *group homes* where youths could live, going from there to school or to work. This way, some control can be maintained until they have learned self-direction (72, p. 48) Halfway houses and group homes are also used in lieu of other types of facilities, especially for runaways or dislocated adolescents, or for emotionally or socially troubled youths. (7, 21) Youths are given food, shelter, and clothing as needed, opportunities for recreation, transportation to and from school or other activities, occupational therapy and vocational guidance, on-the-job training opportunities, and individual and group counseling. Referrals are also made to help adolescents get proper treatment and services. (21, p. 231)

Sending adolescents to *prison* is the worst way to rehabilitate them. An advertisement for the National Council on Crime and Delinquency in *Time* magazine, June 15, 1970 shows a boy with a gun in his hand and the caption: "Prison isn't a waste of time, a lot of kids come out learning a trade." Goshen (28) estimates that only 10 to 20 percent of a prison population are sociopaths who prefer antisocial behavior, have no regard for the interests of others, show little or no remorse, are untreatable, and for whom prison may be justified. (28, p. 167) Goshen feels that perhaps 70 to 80 percent of adolescents in prison were put there for relatively minor offenses. (28, p. 168) They tend to be passive, dependent youths who are easily bullied, try to maintain friendships with others, and then get into trouble trying to model their behavior after the group's expectations. They have had no adequate adult male models with whom they could have had significant relationships. They are often school dropouts, unemployed, and without plans for the future. Left with no reasonable course of action they engage in random activities with the wrong gang that eventually get them into trouble with the law. Once they have a prison record, their chances of finding a useful life are jeopardized. (28, p. 169)

When sent to prison they learn that guards are arbitrary and unfair in the way they mete out punishment. One prisoner may be denied the privilege of one movie for a given offense while another may be placed in solitary for ten days. They learn that fear, bribery, cheating, and sadism are ways of dealing with problems. When they compare their lot to that of the guards, they notice the complete lack of work activity of the guards and conclude it does not pay to work. In addition, many timid souls are harassed and bullied by fellow prisoners who may use them for any number of things including homosexual activities. If adolescents were not antagonistic toward authority and the system upon arrival in prison, they soon become so. They grow to hate the prison and vow never to return, not by becoming law abiding, but by never again being caught. Prison provides a model of criminal behavior, unleashes the revenge of society, guards, and prisoners on other prisoners, and stimulates each inmate to want to get out to seek his own vengeance. Goshen writes: "Vengeance has never in the entire history of human civilization been shown to be an effective means of inducing a change, but only a means of perpetuating a vicious cycle of hostility." (28, p. 185) The result is that two-thirds to three-fourths of those committed to prison are repeaters. (28, p. 181)

Counseling and therapy both individually and in groups are also important parts of any comprehensive program of treatment and correction of juvenile offenders. Individual therapy on a one-to-one basis is time consuming with too few professionals and too many delinquents, but is effective in some instances. (72, p. 19) Group therapy is commonly employed either on an outpatient basis with juveniles attending by order of the court (40, p. 198) or as part of the program of a correctional center or school. (49) Some therapists feel that group therapy reaches a juvenile sooner than individual therapy because the delinquent feels less anxious and defensive in the group situation. (49, p. 251) Group therapy is sometimes offered to both juvenile offenders and their parents, when it becomes similar to other types of family therapy. (71)

PRIVATE, COMMUNITY PROGRAMS. Private, community programs established to treat delinquency have taken many forms. Communities have established drug abuse centers, rap centers, coffee houses, youth centers, boys' or girls' clubs, big brother or big sister programs, and youth employment agencies. One program called *Project Uplift* in Lee County, Alabama, brought together numerous agencies and programs in a comprehensive youth services system to try to prevent delinquency and to rehabilitate offenders. (33) In one year the number of juveniles processed by the Lee County Juvenile Court was reduced by 20 percent. (33, p. 259) The success of the program indicates that youths and their families can best be served by institutions and agencies cooperating in planning and executing programs. (33, p. 260)

Conclusions

Anyone who believes that adolescence is a carefree, happy time of life for all people has not been confronted with the extent of emotional disturbance and maladjustment that exists. The majority of youths go through periods of emotional upset they must work out before they can find greater security, self-esteem, stability, and competency. Some youths are able to solve their problems and make mature adjustments. Others become so disturbed that they need professional help. Some become so upset that they attempt to take their own lives by committing suicide. Others act out their frustrations, anger, and hostility by engaging in delinquent acts. Sensitive, understanding parents and leaders will watch for signs of difficulties and, if they can't help adolescents themselves, will assist them in finding adequate counseling help, for the longer problems persist, the more difficult it is to deal with them. Ideally, troubled adolescents should have received help in early and middle childhood, when the foundations of difficulties were being laid. However, adolescence is not too late for help, at least for most youths. Therefore, adults should do everything possible to see that these young people get the help they need before they end up as mental patients, suicide victims, or criminals. Sometimes a small investment of concern and interest at the right time is all that is needed to help youths through difficult periods.

Topics for Term Papers

1. Why Some Adolescents Want to Take Their Own Lives
2. Suicide Prevention
3. The Work of Suicide Prevention Agencies
4. Phobias—Their Causes and Cure
5. Symptoms of Emotional Disturbance in Adolescents
6. The Depressed Adolescent
7. Kleptomania
8. Arson as a Psychological Problem and Criminal Act
9. Allergies as Psychosomatic Illnesses
10. Enuresis (Bedwetting) in Adolescents
11. Adolescent Schizophrenia
12. Juvenile Delinquency and Minority Groups
13. Juvenile Delinquency among Puerto Ricans
14. Juvenile Delinquency and Chinese-American Culture
15. The Juvenile Court: Its Role in Crime Prevention
16. Delinquency among Juvenile Females
17. Vandalism and the Adolescent
18. Why the Increase in Violent Crimes among Youths?
19. Crime and Adolescent Unemployment
20. Middle Class Values and Culture and Their Contributions to Delinquency
21. Peer Groups, Pressures, and Delinquency
22. How to Raise a Child to Be a Delinquent
23. Parents as Causal Influences in Adolescent Delinquency
24. The System of Juvenile Justice
25. Punishment as a Deterrent to Crime
26. State Training Schools for Delinquents
27. The Probation System in Treating Delinquents
28. Counseling Delinquent Adolescents
29. Group Therapy with Delinquents
30. Big Brother and Big Sister Programs for Delinquents

Bibliography

1. Ahlstrom, W. M., and Havighurst, R. J. *400 Losers*. San Francisco: Jossey-Bass, 1971.

2. Albert, N., and Beck, A. T. "Incidence of Depression in Early Adolescence: A Preliminary Study." *Journal of Youth and Adolescence* 4 (1975): 301–307.

3. Babow, I., and Kridle, R. "Problems and Encounters of a Suicidal Adolescent Girl." *Adolescence* 7 (1972): 459–478.

4. Biller, H. B., and Meredith, D. *Father Power*. New York: Anchor Press, 1975.

5. Blaine, G. B., Jr. "The Emotionally Ill Adolescent." In *The Adolescent: His Search for Understanding*. Edited by W. W. Bier. New York: Fordham University Press, 1963, pp. 152–158.

6. ———. *Youth and the Hazards of Affluence*. New York: Harper and Row, 1966, pp. 109–113.

7. Blakeney, R. N. "The Evaluation of the Operation of an Adolescent Halfway House: An Organizational Effectiveness View." *Adolescence* 11 (1976): 217–227.

8. Cain, A. H. *Young People and Neurosis*. New York: John Day Company, 1970.

9. Carter, R. M. "Delinquency in the Upper and Middle Classes." In *Youth, Crime, and Society*. Edited by J. A. Gazell and G. T. Gitchoff. Boston: Holbrook Press, 1973.

10. Chilton, R. J., and Markle, G. E. "Family Disruption, Delinquent Conduct and the Effect of Subclassification." *American Sociological Review* 37 (1972): 93–99.

11. "Chromosomes and Crime." *Time*, 3 May 1968, p. 41.

12. Cloninger, C. R., and Guze, S. B. "Female Criminals: Their Personal, Familial, and Social Backgrounds." *Archives of General Psychology* 23 (1970): 554–558.

13. Compton, R. C. "Diagnostic Evaluation of Committed Delinquents." In *Youth in Trouble*. Edited by B. L. Kratoville. San Rafael, Calif.: Academic Therapy Publications, 1974, pp. 44–56.

14. Conger, J. J. *Adolescence and Youth*. New York: Harper and Row, 1973.

15. Corder, B. F. et al. "A Study of Social and Psychological Characteristics of Adolescent Suicide Attempters in an Urban, Disadvantaged Area." *Adolescence* 9 (1974): 1–6.

16. Dreyfus, E. A. *Adolescence: Theory and Experience*. Columbus, Ohio: Charles E. Merrill Publishing Co., 1976.

17. England, R. W., Jr. "A Theory of Middle Class Juvenile Delinquency." In *Youth, Crime, and Society*. Edited by J. A. Gazell and G. T. Gitchoff. Boston: Holbrook Press, 1973, pp. 217–227.

18. Erickson, M. L. "Group Violation, Socioeconomic Status and Official Delinquency." *Social Forces* 52 (1973): 41–52.

19. Fish, B., and Hagin, R. "Visual-Motor Disorders in Infants at Risk for Schizophrenia." *Archives of General Psychiatry* 27 (1972): 594–598.

20. Frease, D. E. "The Schools, Self-Concept, and Juvenile Delinquency." *British Journal of Criminology* (1972).

21. Frede, M., and Holland, T. A. "Assessment of the Adequacy of the Services Provided by a Halfway House for Adolescents." *Adolescence* 11 (1976): 228–233.

22. Friedman, C. J. et al. "A Profile of Juvenile Street Gang Members." *Adolescence* 10 (1975): 563–607.

23. ———. "Juvenile Gangs: The Victimization of Youth." *Adolescence* 11 (1976): 527–533.

24. Garner, H. G. "An Adolescent Suicide, the Mass Media, and the Educator." *Adolescence* 10 (1975): 241–246.

25. Gazell, J. A., and Gitchoff, G. T., eds. *Youth, Crime, and Society*. Boston: Holbrook Press, 1973.

26. Gold, M. *Delinquent Behavior in an American City*. Monterey, Calif.: Brooks/Cole Publishing Co., 1970.

27. Gold, M., and Mann, D. "Delinquency as Defense." *American Journal of Orthopsychiatry* 42 (1972): 463–479.

28. Goshen, C. E. "The Characterology of Adolescent Offenders and the Management of Prisons." *Adolescence* 6 (1971): 167–186.

29. Gould, R. E. "Suicidal Problems in Children and Adolescents." *Journal of Psychotherapy* 19 (1965): 228–246.

30. Grinder, R. R., and Holzman, P. S. "Schizophrenic Pathology in Young Adults: A Clinical Study." *Archives of General Psychiatry* 28 (1973): 168–175.

31. Harris, J. R. "A Participant Observer Study: The Everyday Life of a Group of Delinquent Boys." *Adolescence* 9 (1974): 31–48.

32. Henderson, A. S. et al. "Epidemiological Aspects of Adolescent Psychiatry." In *Modern Perspectives in Adolescent Psychiatry*. Edited by J. G. Howells. New York: Brunner/Mazel, 1971.

33. Hodson, N. G. et al. "Project Uplift: A Coordinated Youth Services System." *Family Coordinator* 25 (1976): 255–260.

34. Holzman, P. S., and Grinker, R. R.,

Sr. "Schizophrenia in Adolescence." *Journal of Youth and Adolescence* 3 (1974): 267–279.

35. Jacobs, J. *Adolescent Suicide*. New York: John Wiley and Sons, 1971.

36. Jenson, G. F. "Delinquency and Adolescent Self-Conceptions: A Study of the Person Relevance of Infraction." *Social Problems* 20 (1972): 84–102.

37. Karacki, L., and Levinson, R. B. "A Token Economy in a Correctional Institution for Youthful Offenders. *Howard Journal of Penology and Crime Prevention* 13 (1970): 20–30.

39. Keezer, W. S. *Mental Health and Human Behavior*, 3d ed. Dubuque, Iowa: Wm. C. Brown Co., 1971.

39. Kelly, D. H., and Pink, W. T. "Status Origins, Youth Rebellion, and Delinquency: A Reexamination of the Class Issue." *Journal of Youth and Adolescence* 4 (1975): 339–347.

40. Kimsey, L. R. "Some Observations on the Psychodynamics of Juvenile Delinquents." *Adolescence* 5 (1970): 197–206.

41. Klein, M. W. *Street Gangs and Street Workers*. Englewood Cliffs, N.J.: Prentice-Hall, 1971.

42. Kratcoski, P. C., and Kratcoski, J. E. "Changing Patterns in the Delinquent Activities of Boys and Girls: A Self-Reported Delinquency Analysis." *Adolescence* 10 (1975): 83–91.

43. Kreider, D. G., and Motto, J. A. "Parent-Child Role Reversal and Suicidal States in Adolescence." *Adolescence* 9 (1970): 365–370.

44. Lambert, B. G. et al. *Adolescence: Transition from Childhood to Maturity*. Monterey, Calif.: Brooks/Cole Publishing Co., 1972.

45. Landau, B. "The Adolescent Female Offender: Our Dilemma." *Canadian Journal of Criminology and Corrections* 17 (1975): 146–153.

46. Lang, D.; Pampenfuhs, R.; and Walter, J. "Delinquent Females' Perceptions of Their Fathers." *Family Coordinator* 25 (1976): 475–481.

47. Lester, D. "Attempted Suicide and Body Image." In *The Adolescent: Physical Development, Sexuality and Pregnancy*. New York: MSS Information, 1972, pp. 105–108.

48. Lidz, T. "Schizophrenia Thinking." *Journal of Youth and Adolescence* 3 (1974): 95–98.

49. Lievano, J. "Group Psychotherapy with Adolescents in an Industrial School for Delinquent Boys." *Adolescence* 5 (1970): 231–252.

50. Miller, D. *Adolescence: Psychology, Psychopathology, and Psychotherapy*. New York: Jason Aronson, 1974.

51. Miller, J. P. "Suicide and Adolescence." *Adolescence* 10 (1975): 11–24.

52. Polani, P. "Chromosome Phenotypes—Sex Chromosomes." In *Congenital Malformations*. Edited by F. C. Fraser and V. A. McKuisick, New York: Excerpta Medica, 1970.

53. Polk, K. A. "A Reassessment of Middle-Class Delinquency." *Youth and Society* 2 (1971): 333–354.

54. Polk, K., and Schafer, W. O. *Schools and Delinquency*. Englewood Cliffs, N.J.: Prentice-Hall, 1972.

55. Ponitus, A. A., and Ruttiger, K. F. "Frontal Lobe System Maturational Lag in Juvenile Delinquents Shown in Narratives Test." *Adolescence* 11 (1976): 509–518.

56. Ponitus, A. A. "Neurological Aspects in Some Types of Delinquency, Especially among Juveniles." *Adolescence* 7 (1972): 289–308.

57. Ralston, N. C., and Thomas, G. P. *The Adolescent: Case Studies for Analysis*. New York: Chandler Publishing, 1974.

58. Reige, M. G. "Parental Affection and Juvenile Delinquency in Girls." *British Journal of Criminology* 12 (1972): 55–73.

59. Reynolds, D. J. "Adjustment and Maladjustment." In *Understanding Adolescence*. 3d ed. Edited by J. F. Adams. Boston: Allyn and Bacon, 1976, pp. 334–368.

60. Rodneck, E. H., and Goldstein, M. J. "A Research Strategy for Studying Risks for Schizophrenia during Adolescence and Early Childhood." Paper presented at Conference on Risk Research, Dorado Beach, Puerto Rico, 1972.

61. Ross, M. "Suicide among College Students." *American Journal of Psychiatry* 126 (1969): 220–225.

62. Schecter, M. P. "On Recognition and Treatment of Suicide in Children." In *Clues to Suicide*. New York: McGraw-Hill, 1957.

63. Schneidman, E., and Swenson, D. "Suicide among Youth." *Bulletin of Suicidology*, Supplement, December 1969.

64. Senna, J. et al. "Delinquent Behavior and Academic Investment among Suburban Youth." *Adolescence* 9 (1974): 481–494.

65. Shapiro, S. H. "Vicissitudes of Adolescence." In *Behavior Pathology of Childhood and Adolescence*. Edited by S. L. Copel. New York: Basic Books, 1973, pp. 93–117.

66. Shanley, F. J. "Middle-Class Delinquency as a Social Problem." In *Youth,*

Crime, and Society. Edited by J. A. Gazell and G. T. Gitchoff. Boston: Holbrook Press, 1973, pp. 298–312.

67. Shenker, I. R., and Schildkrout, M. "Physical and Emotional Health of Youth." In *Youth: The Seventy-fourth Yearbook of the National Society for the Study of Education,* Part I. Edited by R. J. Havighurst and P. H. Dreyer. Chicago, Ill.: University of Chicago Press, 1975.

68. Sheppard, B. J. "Making the Case for Behavior as an Expression of Physiological Condition." In *Youth in Trouble.* Edited by B. L. Kratoville. San Rafael, Calif.: Academy Therapy Publications, 1974.

69. Simonds, J. F. "Hallucinations in Nonpsychotic Children and Adolescents." *Journal of Youth and Adolescence* 4 (1975): 171–182.

70. Smith, R. M. "The Impact of Fathers on Delinquent Males." Ph.D. dissertation, Oklahoma State University, 1974.

71. Steininger, E. H., and Leppel, L. "Group Therapy for Reluctant Juvenile Probationers and Their Parents." *Adolescence* 5 (1970): 67–77.

72. Stumphauzer, J. S. "Modifying Delinquent Behavior: Beginnings and Current Practices." *Adolescence* 11 (1976): 13–28.

73. Teicher, J. D. "A Solution to the Chronic Problem of Living: Adolescent Attempted Suicide." In *Current Issues in Adolescent Psychiatry.* Edited by J. C. Schoolar. New York: Brunner/Mazel, 1973, pp. 129–147.

74. Thornburg, H. D. *Contemporary Adolescence: Readings.* 2d ed. Monterey, Calif.: Brooks/Cole Publishing Co., 1975.

75. ———. *Development in Adolescence.* Monterey, Calif.: Brooks/Cole Publishing Co., 1975.

76. Toby, J. "Affluence and Adolescent Crime." In *Youth, Crime, and Society.* Edited by J. A. Gazell and G. T. Gitchoff. Boston: Holbrook Press, 1973, pp. 228–259.

77. Toolan, J. M. "Depression in Adolescents." in *Modern Perspectives in Adolescent Psychiatry,* vol. 4. Edited by J. G. Howells. New York: Brunner/Mazel, 1973, pp. 358–380.

78. U.S. Bureau of the Census, Department of Commerce. *Statistical Abstract of the United States, 1978.* Washington, D.C.: U.S. Government Printing Office, 1978.

79. U.S. Law Enforcement Assistance Administration. *Children in Custody: A Report on the Juvenile Detention and Correctional Facility Census of 1972–1973.* Washington, D.C.: Superintendent of Documents, 1976.

80. U.S. Office of Human Development and U.S. Office of Youth Development. *Juvenile Court Statistics Annual.* Washington, D.C.: U.S. Government Printing Office, 1970 and 1973.

81. Ushakov, G. K. "Anorexia Nervosa," In *Modern Perspectives in Adolescent Psychiatry.* Edited by J. G. Howells. New York: Brunner/Mazel, 1971, pp. 274–289.

82. Watt, N. F. et al. "Social Adjustment and Behavior of Children Hospitalized for Schizophrenia as Adults." *American Journal of Orthopsychiatry* 40 (1970): 637–657.

83. Weiner, T. *Psychological Disturbance in Adolescence.* New York: John Wiley and Sons, 1970.

84. Winn, C. "Adolescent Suicidal Behavior and Hallucinations." In *Adolescence: Psychosocial Perspectives.* Edited by G. Caplan and S. Lebovici. New York: Basic Books, 1969, pp. 252–263.

85. *World Book Encyclopedia,* s.v. "Juvenile Delinquency." Volume 11. Chicago: Field Enterprises Educational Corporation, 1974.

86. Wotkiewicz, H. "Operant Strategies with Delinquents at Kennedy Youth Center." Unpublished manuscript, West Virginia University, 1972.

87. Yacoubian, J. H., and Lourie, R. S. "Suicide and Attempted Suicide in Children and Adolescents." In *Pathology of Childhood and Adolescence.* Edited by S. L. Copel. New York: Basic Books, 1973, pp. 149–165.

88. Yusin, A. S. "Attempted Suicide in an Adolescent: The Resolution of an Anxiety State." *Adolescence* 8 (1973): 17–28.

PART 5

Social

CHAPTER 10

Adolescent Society, Culture, and Subculture

Outline

A careful sociological analysis of adolescents as an identifiable segment of the population ought to make a distinction between adolescent society and adolescent culture. *Adolescent society* refers to the structural arrangements of subgroups within an adolescent social system; according to Havighurst it refers to the "organized network of relationships and association among adolescents." (38, p. 59) *Adolescent culture* is the sum of the ways of living of adolescents; it refers to the "body of norms, values, attitudes and practices recognized and shared by members of the adolescent society as appropriate guides to action." (38, p. 60) Adolescent society refers to the interrelationships of adolescents within their social systems; their culture describes the way they think, behave, and live.

This chapter is concerned both with adolescent society and with adolescent culture. It focuses on both formal and informal adolescent societies, but especially on the formal in-school groups and subsystems. Factors that influence the adolescent's social position in a formal group are outlined and discussed, along with the subculture that exists at the high school and college levels. The chapter concludes with a discussion of two important material aspects of adolescent culture; clothing and automobiles; and two nonmaterial aspects of adolescent culture: music and language.

Culture and Society

Adolescent society is not one single, comprehensive, monolithic structure that includes all young people. (33, 74) When Coleman writes about *Adolescent Society* (10) he confines his study almost entirely to relationships among students in ten different high schools in northern Illinois. Smith's study, *American Youth Culture* (85), is limited to those youths who are "American, white, urban, middle-class, and post-pubertal, not yet filling adult roles." (85, p. 4) Havighurst's *Growing Up in River City* (38) describes a group in sixth grade in Quincy, Illinois, and follows them until they are twenty years old, whether or not they graduated from high school and went on to college. Gordon's book, *The Social System of the High School* (31), is limited in scope to the student body of Ferguson, Missouri. Each of the authors of these studies correctly and cautiously avoids generalizing beyond the data about adolescent societies. Coleman is as careful in describing the differences among his ten high school student bodies as he is in noting similarities.

Furthermore, the society of adolescents is itself only vaguely structured. It exists without any formal, written codification and without traditions of organizational patterns. Individuals move into and out of the system within a few short years, contributing to structural instability. Each local group of adolescents is provincial, with few ties beyond school membership and the local gang and clique. Although there are nationwide youth organizations, fan clubs, or competitive athletic events, most adolescent societies are primarily local, variably replicated in community after community.

The same cautions should be applied to adolescent culture. One cannot speak of United States adolescent culture as though it were a body of beliefs, values, and practices uniformly espoused by all youths throughout the country. Just as there are regional, ethnic, and class versions of the national adult culture, so there are variations in expression of adolescent culture among differing segments of the population. Adolescent culture is not homogeneous; the popular image of adolescent culture usually refers to urban, middle class youth. Actually there may be important deviations from this pattern. A more accurate description would convey that there are numerous versions of teenage culture expressed by various segments of American youth who share some common elements of a general middle class youth culture, but who participate selectively and in varying degrees in the activities of the organized adolescent society.

But before adolescent society or culture can be analyzed, an important question needs to be answered: Are adolescent society and culture unique and different from those of the adult world?

The Adolescent Subculture

According to one point of view, adolescent subculture emphasizes conformity in the peer group and values that are contrary to adult values. (30; 49, p. 194; 77, p. 149) This subculture exists primarily in the high school, where it constitutes a "small society, one that has most of its important interactions within itself, and maintains only a few threads of connection with the outside adult society." (10, p. 3) This happens because children are set apart in schools, where they take on more and more extracurricular activities for longer periods of training. Segregated from the adult world, they develop subcultures with their own language, styles, and, most importantly, with value systems that may differ from those of adults. (10, p. 3) Coleman, one of the principal exponents of the view, observes that societal changes

have taken not only job-training out of the parents' hands, but have quite effectively taken away the whole adolescent himself. . . . The adolescent is dumped into a society of his peers, a society whose habitats are the halls and classrooms of the school, the teen-age canteens of the corner drug store, the automobile, and numerous other gathering places. (10, p. 4)

As a result the adolescent lives in a segregated society and establishes a subculture that meets with peer, but not adult, approval. (68)

An opposite point of view is that adolescents reflect adult values, beliefs, and practices; the theory of an adolescent subculture, segregated and different from adult culture, a myth. (90) This view is substantiated by a number of recent studies. Weinstock and Lerner (94) reviewed a series of studies on the generation gap and concluded that there was no strong evidence for major discrepancies in attitudes between today's adolescent and parental generations. (94) An analysis of the parent-peer orientations of 9,056 adolescents in grades seven through twelve throughout North Carolina and Ohio revealed that "parents were clearly more important as reference sources than were friends." (16, p. 488) A national survey of 3,522 youths ages sixteen to twenty-five, reported by Yankelovich, revealed that 75 percent of noncollege and 68 percent of the college population accepted the same kind of conditional life style as their parents or society offered them. (96, p. 92) Two other researchers compared parent versus adolescent political views over an eight-year period and found that the generations were moving closer together rather than apart. (46) In another study, only 4 percent of parents felt an increase in alienation during adolescence, and only 5 percent of the young people themselves reported actual rejection of parents. (78) One investigator found that when there was conflict between generations, it usually centered on mundane, day-to-day issues such as noisiness, tidiness, punctuality, and living under the same roof, rather than on fundamental values such as honesty, perseverance, and concern for others. (12)

From this point of view, the cultural norms shared by teenagers in the United States are not very different from those shared by adult Americans. (14, 96) (Were it otherwise, the indoctrinational efforts of parents, teachers, preachers, and others would constitute a pretty sorry record; and the theory of learning by imitation would be totally—instead of only partially—discredited.) This same idea is reflected in Jessie Bernard's preface to a special edition of the *Annals of the American Academy of Political and Social Science* on the subject of "Teen-Age Culture."

Even 19 million individual rebellious adolescents do not add up to an army or even a resistance movement. They add up—as so many of the articles in this volume indicate—to bearers of a conservative, traditional culture, which far from rejecting adult values, pays them the supreme compliment of imitating or borrowing them and adapting them to its own needs. Teenage culture, even in its contrapuntal forms, is an adaptation, or prototype or caricature of adult culture." (6, p. ii)

A FALSE DICHOTOMY

The more studies that are conducted and the more closely these are analyzed, however, the more evident it becomes that adolescents choose to follow neither parents nor friends exclusively. (20, 69) The study by Yankelovich already cited showed that 61 percent of noncollege and 68 percent of college youths said they identified with their family on political views, but a similar percentage also said they identified with the political views of people of their generation. (96, p. 126) One explanation is that in many instances parents and friends are quite alike, so that the peer group serves to reinforce rather than violate parental values. (11; 19, p. 64) Adolescents tend to choose friends who are like themselves; thus there may be "considerable overlap between the values of parents and peers because of commonalities in their backgrounds—social, economic, religious, educational, even geographic." (15, p. 291)

Also, there are considerable differences among adolescents depending upon their age and year in school, sex, socioeconomic status, and educational level. The younger adolescents are, the more likely they are to conform to parental values and mores, and less likely to be influenced by peers. (25; 84, p. 129) Girls ages

Table 10–1.   Percent of orientation of 409 respondents, by grade level.

Orientation	Grade Level				Total
	6	8	10	12	
Parent	62	36	15	14	30
Ambivalent	33	37	50	49	43
Peer	5	27	35	37	27

From H. H. Floyd, Jr., and D. R. South, "Dilemma of Youth: The Choice of Parents or Peers
as a Frame of Reference for Behavior," *Journal of Marriage and the Family* 34 (1972):
630. Used by permission.

twelve to fifteen have been found to be significantly more parent oriented than
peer oriented, with younger girls giving mothers first place, fathers second,
and friends third. (70, p. 594) With increasing age, however, peer influence increases and parental influence declines. Parental influence has been found to
be greatest at the sixth-grade level and least at the twelfth-grade level. (28)
Table 10–1 shows the percent of orientation by grade level in a study of 409
students in grades six, eight, and ten, and twelve in a public school system in a
small southern community. (28) At the college level, freshmen show less disagreement with parents on certain social problems than do juniors or seniors.
(45, p. 849) Apparently increasing age and education widens the gap between
parents and adolescents. College itself sems to have a liberalizing effect upon
students. (22) It has also been found that adolescents with the highest IQs are
more likely to be peer oriented than those with less intelligence. (70, p. 594)

Sex is also a significant variable in the degree of parent-peer orientation.
Males tend to show more disagreement with parents than do females, but females who do disagree with parents, tend to do so at younger ages, reflecting the
earlier maturational age of the females. (22, 39) As might be expected, males
more closely identify with fathers, (58) females with mothers.

There are also socioeconomic status differences in parent-peer orientation.
College-educated youths tend to disagree with their parents more often than do
noncollege young people, especially if the parents have less education than their
offspring. (39, 88) This seems to be a reasonable conclusion since college students with working class family origins would likely experience greater social
change on campus than would their middle class counterparts. (39, p. 850)

Whether adolescents are more parent or peer oriented will depend partially
on the degree of emotional closeness between parents and their youths: that is,
on the *affect* relationship. Youths who have a close emotional attachment to
parents will more likely be parent oriented than will adolescents who are hostile
toward parents or who reject them. To put it another way, the quality of adolescent-adult interaction is inversely related to peer-group involvement. (22, p.
631; 36, p. 333) This finding is illustrated in Figure 10–1, which shows the variations of parental influence according to parent-adolescent affect and according
to grade level and sex. (55) As can be seen, adolescents who experience a high
degree of satisfaction in relation to their parents (high parent-adolescent affect)

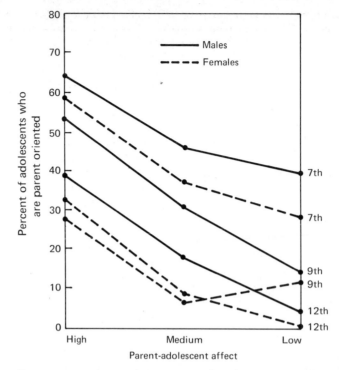

Figure 10–1. Parent priority by grade level, parent-adolescent affect, and sex. (Figure 1 from "The Relative Influence of Parent-Adolescent Affect in Predicting the Salience Hierarchy Among Youth," by Lyle E. Larson, is reprinted from *Pacific Sociological Review*, Vol. 15, No. 1 (January 1972) pp. 83–102 by permission of the publisher, Sage Publications, Inc.)

also have a high degree of parent orientation. The lower the level of parent-adolescent affect, the lower the orientation toward parents. (55) It is evident from this graph that seventh graders are more parent oriented than twelfth graders. This study shows also that when both males and females are satisfied with parental relationships, males at any one grade level are more parent oriented than females. Males, however, are usually less parent oriented than females, because the parent-adolescent male affect is usually lower than the parent-adolescent female affect. (55)

Other research has revealed that individual adolescents differ markedly in their parent and peer orientations. (56) Also, it has been shown that those who are strongly peer oriented are often unsatisfied and anxious about it. (13) They "are not 'socialized' enough to the values of the adult world to seek approval by displaying the 'proper' behavior and attitudes, but neither are they so independent of such values as to feel content with their present adjustment." (13, p. 552) They become overly dependent upon the peer group and conform to socially undesirable peer subcultures by necessity rather than by choice. This "necessity" is created in families in which the parents establish a climate of "passive neglect," thereby pushing the children from the home and forcing them to seek approval and affection elsewhere. (13)

The peer-oriented child is more a product of disregard than of the attractiveness of the peer group. . . . The vacuum left by the withdrawal of parents and adults from the lives of children is filled with an undesired—and possibly *undesirable*— substitute of an age-segregated peer group. (8, p. 96)

DISTINCTIVE SOCIAL RELATIONSHIPS AND CULTURE

It is nevertheless useful to recognize as distinctive a system of social relation- ships in which adolescents engage, not in the sense that it is the only world to which they are responsive, but in the sense that it is a society over which adults exercise only partial control. Most modern teenagers are *both* typically confused adolescents in the adult world and relatively self-assured and status- conscious members of their peer groups—depending on the set of interactions being analyzed.

These same conclusions might be reached with respect to other aspects of adolescent culture. Adolescents reflect many adult values and norms, but certain aspects of their lives are distinguishable from American adult culture because in these areas adolescents can exercise some control and make their own de- cisions. (19, p. 64; 49, p. 196) Such matters as styles of dress, tastes in music, language, popular movie and recording stars, use of the automobile, dating customs and practices, and behavior at youth hangouts or at sporting events are properly adolescent subcultural, for they may even sometimes run counter to adult preferences. (15, 71) It is therefore proper and possible to point to cer- tain aspects of adolescent culture that are identifiable as separate, because they are developed and practiced predominantly by adolescents, sometimes in contra- diction to adult norms. (1) Furthermore, the farther along adolescents are in school, the more likely they are to listen to peers rather than to parents in matters pertaining to social judgments. Figure 10–2 shows the frequency with which ado- lescents mentioned parents, other adults and peers as competent referents in matters pertaining to making social judgments. (97, p. 248)

Two especially notable areas of adolescent-adult disagreement today are drugs and sexual behavior. (4, 72) The primary reason adolescents and adults disagree in these matters is that cultural change has been so rapid and so great that youthful behavior *is* different from adult values. Take the attitude toward the smoking of marijuana, for example. In 1977 only 7 percent of adults age thirty-five and over had ever used marijuana, in contrast to 60 percent of youths age eighteen to twenty-five. (91, p. 123) This wide difference between adolescent and adult behavior indicates that youthful marijuana smoking is subcultural. Furthermore, those adolescents who are the most peer oriented are most likely to be users; those who are most parent oriented are less likely to use it. Table 10–2 shows the relationship between frequency of marijuana use and the degree of parent-peer orientation among students at a large southwestern university.

Similarly, several recent attitude surveys have revealed that the sexual at- titudes of both high school and college students are considerably more liberal than those of adults; these youthful values may therefore be regarded as sub- cultural. (26, 58, 59)

Thus, whether or not a youthful subculture exists depends upon what par-

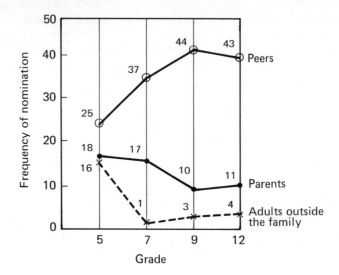

Figure 10–2. Frequency of reference group nominations for social items, as a function of grade level. (From J. W. Young and L. R. Ferguson, "Developmental Changes through Adolescence in the Spontaneous Nominations of Reference Groups as a Function of Decision Content," *Journal of Youth and Adolescence* 8[June 1979]:239–252. Used by permission.)

ticular areas of concern one is examining. Overall, youth culture reflects adult culture. In specific areas, however, youth culture is a distinct subculture.

Also, youths' views are changing very rapidly. Their views on the role of women in society is an example: in 1967, 67 percent of males and nearly half of females agreed that "the activities of married women are best confined to the home and family"; by 1976, however, less than 30 percent of all college freshmen agreed. (3, p. 53) This growing liberalism has been demonstrated by a steadily increasing interest among women in such fields as business, law, and medicine.

Rapid change is also quite evident in youths' views on raising children. The percentage of freshmen who feel that raising a family is an important goal in life has fallen from 71 percent to 57 percent over the past ten years. (3) Three

Table 10–2. Relationship of parent-peer orientation and frequency of marijuana use.

	Frequency of Marijuana Use				
Orientation	Never	Past user	Occasional	Regular	(N)
Parent	66%	19%	9%	7%	(351)
Neither	41%	28%	12%	19%	(58)
Peer	22%	22%	23%	33%	(352)
(N)	(336)	(159)	(117)	(149)	(761)

Data Source: L. H. Stone, A. C. Miranne, and G. J. Ellis, "Parent-Peer Influence as a Predictor of Marijuana Use," *Adolescence* 14 (Spring 1979): 119. Used by permission.

out of four youths, however, still say that having a good marriage is an extremely important goal in life. (4)

Thus, the more rapid the social change, the more likely that youth's views become different than those of their parents. In this sense, certain aspects of adolescent life become subcultural—at least for a while.

Formal and Informal Adolescent Societies

Like adult social structures, adolescent societies may be divided into two groups: formal and informal.

FORMAL SOCIETIES

Formal adolescent societies include primarily groups of in-school youth. Linkages with peers are determined by whether adolescents are enrolled in school, which school they are enrolled in, and which student organizations they join. They are identified with their particular school, team, and teachers. There are also out-of-school church or youth groups, but for the most part only in-school youths participate in these activities also. Therefore, any formal, well-defined social system to which adolescents belong is invariably related to in-school youth. Hollingshead, in his study *Elmtown's Youth and Elmstown Revisited*, reported that only 1 percent of school withdrawers belonged to "adolescent associations" and only 5 percent had identifiable ties with any organized nonfamily groups. (40)

INFORMAL SOCIETIES

Informal adolescent societies generally describe those loosely structured groups of out-of-school youth who get together socially, but who have little opportunity to participate in a formally structured network of social relationships. (93, p. 204) These youths are too scattered and too involved in trying to find their places in adult society to be characterized as a separate adolescent society. One exception might be the adolescent street gang, which may exist as a sub-society all its own. (93, p. 206)

This does not mean that all adolescents who remain in school are actively participating members of the organized adolescent society. Some adolescents remain in school, but are really excluded from school life. Those who finally drop out of school have poor attendance records and rarely hold school office or have been active in school affairs. (38, p. 62) There are some who are socially outside "the society," even though they may still be physically in it.

Age-Grade Societies

Adolescent societies are not only in-school, but also age-grade societies. Adolescents are identified with a certain grade or class in school. This identification allows them to take certain courses, participate in certain school-sponsored activities (for which being a freshman or a senior is a prerequisite for eligibility), or give or attend parent-permitted parties (for one's classmates). Freshmen compete with sophomores in sports or other events. Coleman emphasizes the importance of class membership in influencing friendship associations. "Among pairs of friends, the one item that the two members had in common far more often than any other—including religion, father's occupation, father's education, common leisure interests, grades in school, and others—was class in school." (10, p. 76)

In-School Subsystems

In-school adolescent societies also may be divided into distinct subsystems in which adolescents participate and in which they are assigned status positions. Furthermore, a particular student may be simultaneously involved in more than one of three distinct subsystems. (31, p. viii)

THE FORMAL, ACADEMIC SUBSYSTEM

The student is involved in a formal, academic subsystem shaped by the school administration, faculty, curriculum, textbooks, classrooms, grades, rules, and regulations. (31, p. viii) In this system seniors outrank freshmen, and the honor roll student outranks the D student, but the degree varies from school to school. In some schools, being an exceptionally good student academically may place one in a lower status group. However, whether getting good grades has a positive value or not will depend upon the social group of which a student is a part. One reason for underachievement is negative peer pressure against studies. (68, p. 411)

THE SEMIFORMAL, ACTIVITIES SUBSYSTEM

The student may be involved in a semiformal, activities subsystem, which includes all sponsored organizations and activities such as athletics, drama, and departmental clubs. In his study of the social systems in the high school at Ferguson, Missouri, where the high school population was only 576, Gordon found fifty independent formal school organizations that could be subdivided further into ninety subgroups, ranging from varsity basketball to the knitting club. Each group had a definite prestige ranking in the eyes of the students, which conveyed a certain status rating to its members. Each group had specific offices, with the result that the individual's status was partly determined by which of these offices he or she held. Gordon found 464 offices ranging all the way from star quarterback to news reporter. The amount of prestige that any position added depended upon its rank within each respective group and the prestige standing of the group in relation to all other groups. (31, p. 51)

Educators are not completely in agreement about the value of extracurricular activities and organizations in preparing the student for adult life. Students who participate in extracurricular high school activities have been found to be those most involved in adult voluntary organizations and most politically active fifteen years after graduation. (36) Apparently, participation in high school has taught these persons how to take part in the political and organizational life of the community. Participation in extracurricular activities has no direct effect on adult occupation, income, and socioeconomic achievement, but the effects are mediated indirectly through educational attainment: those who achieve the most educationally are those who are also the participators in school activities. (36, p. 487)

FRIENDSHIP SUBSYSTEM   *not sponsored by adults chosen by themselves*

The student may be involved in an informal network of friendship subsystems that operate primarily within the boundaries of the school world. (84, p. 131) Gordon found that not only were friendship choices directed overwhelmingly to other students in the same school, but 84 percent of these choices were directed to members of the same grade and sex group. (31, pp. 80–90)

Of the three subsystems, membership in the informal friendship system is most important in the eyes of other students. This is the only subsystem unencumbered by adult sponsorship. This is the adolescent's world, and the status an individual enjoys in this world is of major importance. Status in the academic and activities subsystems is coveted, but primarily for the prestige, acceptance, and standing it gives one within the network of informal peer groupings. (48) Gordon found that "the dominant orientation to action was to accept those roles which would establish a prestige position in the *informal organization*." (31, p. 22)

The students themselves attached prestige rankings to being a member of one clique rather than another. Various descriptive titles conveyed the general reputation, central values, and activities shared by the group, such as "leading crowd," "athletic crowd," "dirty dozen," "sexy six," and "beer drinkers." (31, p. 106) Gordon worked out an elaborate scheme for reporting the ranked position of individual students in each of the three spheres. (31, Appendix A) His scheme was correctly based on the assumption that the adolescent's general social status within the student body appears to be a function of his or her combined rankings within each of the several subsystems. Furthermore, a student who scores high or low in one system is likely to hold a similar position within the others, but because the important system from the student's viewpoint is the informal one, it is more determinative of behavior than the other two.

Social Class and Status

Evidence continues to mount that an individual's ready acceptance by and active involvement in adolescent society are influenced by socioeconomic background. (See Chapters 11 and 22.) Social leadership scores of children in middle class schools are higher than those of children in working class schools, and the average scores for aggressive and withdrawn maladjustment are lower in middle class than in working class schools. (38, p. 30) Higher social class students are far more often involved in attending athletic events, dances, plays, and musical activities than are those from the lower classes. Furthermore, those youths who identify themselves with organized youth groups such as Boy Scouts, Girl Scouts, and church youth fellowship groups are preponderantly from middle class rather than lower class homes. (37, 38, p. 30) It is obvious that adolescent society, like adult society, is run by those of middle and upper class socioeconomic status, who cultivate friendships, who participate in activities and projects, and whose experiences prepare them for positions of leadership.

This does not mean that every individual from low socioeconomic status families is a social reject. Chapter 8 emphasizes that the youngster who has been given high self-esteem, even though from a poor home, will adjust more easily than another poor youngster with low-esteem. Furthermore, there are variations in what students themselves report to be a relevant criterion for being in the leading crowd. In general, they feel that coming from the right family or neighborhood or having money is less valued than personality, reputation, athletic skills, or good looks. (10, p. 70; 54, p. 71) Nevertheless, students whose fathers are college graduates (one clue to middle class status) are far more likely than students whose fathers have only grade school education to be identified as members of the leading crowd, to be chosen as friends, and to be viewed as people whom one would "like to be like." (93, p. 34) Therefore, even though lower class youths are present in greater numbers, particularly at the junior high school level, adolescent society continues to be dominated by middle class youths.

Identifying Adolescent Subcultures

Another way to understand adolescent societies is by studying subcultures within those societies.

HIGH SCHOOL SUBCULTURES

There are at least three identifiable subcultures within the average American high school. (9, 15)

The *fun subculture* comprises extracurricular activities: athletic events, school dances, selection of a football queen, informal clubs, and the general concern for school spirit.

The *academic subculture* is involved with the formal and traditional aspects of the learning process. Students in this group are concerned with intellectual pursuits, attaining knowledge, achievement, and making the honor role. In some schools these students are rejected socially, especially if they also manifest undesirable personality traits; other students may refer to them as "grinds," "creeps," "drags," "finks." In recent years, however, students have become more and more aware of the emphasis upon academic achievement in the high schools and have been more willing to be identified with those getting good grades. The "bookworm" is a social isolate who is still scorned. The very bright student who gets A's without studying is admired and envied, especially if she or he also participates in the extracurricular and athletic activities of the school.

Ramsey reports on one study with 200 adolescents to determine their criteria for social acceptability. The following types of high school students are ranked in decreasing order of acceptability:

1. Brilliant nonstudious athlete
2. Average nonstudious athlete
3. Average studious athlete
4. Brilliant studious athlete
5. Brilliant nonstudious nonathlete
6. Average nonstudious nonathlete
7. Average studious nonathlete
8. Brilliant studious nonathlete.(75, p. 56)

It is obvious that participation in athletics is one important criterion for social acceptability in the average high school, and that most students place athletic achievement ahead of academic excellence. However, students who make very poor grades are often social rejects also, particularly if they manifest undesirable personality traits and do not participate in extracurricular school functions. Grinder summarizes this subtle relationship among educational achievement, athletic participation, and prestige.

There is a complex relationship between youth culture participation and educational aspirations. Interaction with peers and school achievement seems to produce a curvilinear relationship. Moderate interaction is positively related to school success, but neither extensive nor infrequent participation correlates with academic orientation. Adolescents and adults alike give high priority to athletic competition. Athletic contests enable young people to share collective goals and develop a strong, positive, identification with the high school. They seem to recognize that scholastic achievement is more important to their future than athletics; however, the tremendous prestige accorded to athletics sometimes diverts their attention from academic matters. For most youths, athletic participation is positively related to academic achievement, and athletics already has an important place in high school. The problem is one of balance. . . . (34, p. 480)

As students go on through college, athletes begin to discover tangible benefits to participation. Not only do they enjoy financial benefits and a superior social status while in college, but also they are more socially mobile and achieve superior economic levels and business success when they get out. An investigation of adult males who had played football at Notre Dame revealed that "first team football players experienced greater income mobility in later life than second team and reserve players, and first team ballplayers were over-represented as top ranking executives in their companies. (Thirty-four percent were top executives.)" (79, p. 65) The authors conclude:

The fame the first team athletes receive gives them entree to high paying positions which demand people with celebrity status. . . .

It might also be argued, however, that the interpersonal skills and character traits which make successful athletes are precisely those which make successful entrepreneurs.

Whether the income and business success for first team athletes is the result of their celebrity status or their ability to thrive in highly competitive situations is a question worthy of further research. (79, p. 65)

This success was achieved despite the fact that fewer ball players earned graduate degrees than did other students.

The *delinquent subculture* consists of those who are in active, open rebellion against the school's educational and social activities. They reject the rules of the school system and flaunt authority. Cohen subdivides this group into *greasers* and *hippies*. (9) The greasers are interested in cars, drinking, and fights and emphasize hedonism, toughness, and an early adoption of adult privileges usually denied adolescents. The hippies are also in rebellion, rejecting the legitimacy of the adult world and serious planning or preparation for adulthood. (9, p. 500)

COLLEGIATE SUBCULTURES

Similar classifications of collegiate subcultures have been made in order to reach a better understanding of the college student's world. Four separate classifications have been identified. (8, 32)

The *collegiate subculture* is the college world of football, Greek letter societies (sororities and fraternities), cars, drinking, dates, and card parties, with
courses and professors in the background. Students in this subculture are not
hostile to college, but avoid its academic demands, preferring instead to turn
college into a country club. It is a characteristically middle and upper middle
class group, for it requires money and leisure to pursue the strenuous schedule
of social activities.

The *vocational subculture* prevails in urban colleges and universities attended
by children of lower middle class families. Many of these students are married
and putting themselves through school. "They buy their education somewhat as
one buys groceries"; (96, p. 11) since they are customers in a diploma market.
The symbol of their subculture is the student placement office. There is some
indication that an increasing number of middle and upper middle class students
are now becoming interested in the vocational aspects of college, for they are
attending college as a means of professional advancement and preparation.

The *academic subculture* has learning, knowledge, and ideas as central values.
"The distributive qualities of this group are (a) they are seriously involved in
their course work beyond the minimum required for passing and graduation and
(b) they identify themselves with their college and its faculty." (8, p. 2)

The *nonconformist subculture* includes the intellectual, radical, alienated,
bohemian student, often classified as a "hippie" type. This is a more difficult
group to identify because it is essentially nonconformist and includes a wide
variety of types of students. It may include the violent, radical, anarchist pro-
tester; the scholarly, intellectual, but social rebel; the deviant, long-haired, but
peaceful, isolate. When students' intellectual, political, social, and cultural norms
are at odds with their teachers, parents, and school, they form their own nonconformist cultures.

That's me!

College culture has changed drastically in the years since World War II.
After World War II, returning veterans dismissed the previously dominant collegiate subculture as childish and worked to make college a stepping-stone to
better jobs and careers. Following the Soviet Union's launching of Sputnik in
1957, the need for highly trained U.S. scientists, technicians, and scholars shifted
emphasis to the academic subculture. During the 1960s, civil rights, war, ecology,
and other social concerns became of major interest, with many students participating in what adults characterized as the nonconformist, radical subculture.
Today, the trend is toward a middle-of-the-road position. (22, p. 133) Rapidly
rising tuition costs have stimulated students to want to get their money's worth,
with the result that most seem more serious about their education and careers
than the radical campus spokesmen of the late 1960s. (75, p. 56) Since 1971 there
has been a steady decline in political liberalism. (22) There are fewer causes and
fewer rebels, leaving students freer to concentrate on their own lives and on
personal fulfillment. (4, p. 79) They are more interested in "finding steady work,"
in "being successful," or in "having strong friendships." For the most part, they
desire conventional marriages; the majority consider it "very likely" that they
will stay married to the same person for life. (4, p. 84)

On campus, the once-fading images of fraternities and sororities have been
restored, with the Greek societies taking on new members and new life, some on

a coeducational basis. Fraternal organizations are meeting a real need among students for closer, more personal relationships in universities that have grown so large and impersonal that students get lost in the shuffle. (29, p. 46)

Material Concerns of Adolescent Culture

Another way to understand adolescent culture is to examine the material artifacts that youths buy or make and use in their daily lives. Two groups—adolescent clothing and automobiles—have been selected for discussion because they are so important in the adolescent's life.

CLOTHING

One of the most noticeable aspects of adolescent culture is the adolescent's preoccupation with clothing, hair styles, and grooming. (See also Chapter 5.) Adults, reflecting on this preoccupation, accuse adolescents of being rebellious nonconformists, or, at the other extreme, of being superficial in their values. Sociologists and social psychologists point out that neither accusation is true. Adolescents are conformists, especially when it comes to clothing and appearance within their own peer groups. (61) And, rather than showing superficiality because of their concern about appearance, they are actually evidencing both their need to find and express their own individual identity and their need to belong to a social group.

Clothing is an important means by which individual adolescents discover and express their identities. As adolescent boys and girls search for self-images with which they can be comfortable, they are preoccupied with experimentation with their appearance. Clothing and appearance are expressions of themselves as they strive to control their impressions on others. Clothing is a visual means of communicating to others the kind of role a person wishes to play in life. Adolescents applying for jobs, for example, endeavor to communicate by the clothes they wear the kind of people they are and the type of job they expect to obtain. (50)

Appearance also plays an important role in social interaction, for it provides a means of identification. If a boy dresses like a tough delinquent, he is likely to be treated as a delinquent, just as a schoolteacher who looks like an old maid is likely to be treated as an old maid. Clothing enables one adolescent to discover the social identity of another person and to pattern his or her behavior and responses according to what is expected. As human beings within a society develop social selves, dress and adornment are intimately linked to their interacting with one another.

Clothing is one means by which adolescents express their dependence-independence conflicts or their conformity-individuality conflicts. Clothing can be a medium of rebellion against the adult world. Adolescents who are hostile or rebellious toward their parents may express their antipathy by wearing clothes or hair styles they know their parents dislike. The more fuss the parents make, the more determined adolescents are to stick to their own styles. Nonacceptable clothing styles, deliberately chosen by adolescents, mirror their rebellion against authority. According to Evans, 58 percent of a group of 159 tenth- and twelfth-grade students from a high school in Vandalia, Missouri, indicated that the desire to be independent was the dominant motive in wanting to make their own clothing selections. (27) However, the dominant motives in selecting the styles were the desire to be recognized by others as superior or the desire to depend on and be like others. Adolescents who buy clothes to show independence (from parents especially) wear clothes that will give them recognition or acceptance in their own peer groups. (See Table 10–3.) In a study of mother-versus-peer influence in the clothing selection of seventh-grade girls, whatever influence mothers may have expected must have been indirect, for it was not evident in measured evaluations of mother-daughter associations. (51) Rather, the norms these girls used for clothing selection were derived largely from what older girls deemed appropriate. (51, p. 349)

In recent years, clothing and hair styles have been used by some youths as an expression of rebellion against particular mores and values in adult society. Adult puritanical culture emphasized that "cleanliness is next to godliness"; therefore, some express their rejection of what they perceive as a hypocritical, materialistic, godless culture, by choosing to remain unclean and unkempt. Youths of the 1960s chose various symbols of a youth culture that was predominantly antiwar and antiestablishment. Ban-the-bomb symbols; beads, flowers, and headbands; fringed leather, Indian-style jackets; granny dresses; moccasins or sandals; beards and wild hair were an expression of independence, of dissatisfaction with the status quo, and of the determination of these youths to show solidarity against the onslaughts of adult criticism and attack. Such clothing symbolized their rejection of middle class philosophy and values.

One study of the relationship between clothing styles and counterculture attitudes of undergraduate college males showed that those students with the

Table 10–3.   Importance of motivational forces determining the purchase and wearing of clothing.

Motivational Force	Purchase of Clothing		Wearing of Certain Styles	
	Order of importance	Times motivation dominated	Order of importance	Times motivation dominated
To depend on and be like others	3	12.2%	2	38.3%
To be independent of and different from others	1	58.4%	4	4.4%
To compensate for other inadequacies or social impediments	4	4.4%	3	6.3%
To be recognized as superior to others	5	0	1	49.1%
Combination of the first two	2	18.8%		

Adapted from S. Evelyn Evans, "Motivation Underlying Clothing Selection and Wearing," *Journal of Home Economics* 56 (1964): 739–743. Copyright by the American Home Economics Association, Washington, D.C. Used by permission.

most radical departure from traditional male dress customs (i.e., long hair and beard, unkempt appearance, flamboyant shirt and trouser styles and colors, and the use of such accessories as beads and fringes) also showed the most radical attitudes in relation to political philosophy, premarital sexual permissiveness, and sex-role stereotyping. They also showed more age-grade consciousness, that is, awareness of youths as a distinct social group. (81) The researchers also felt that the trend toward unisex dress was some indication of repudiation of traditional sex-role standards.

The changes we are witnessing in dress among youth, particularly the trend toward "unisex" dress, may herald a widespread change in masculine sex-role standards. This apparent change in definition of masculinity has implications for a wide range of other norms and values. . . . In each instance, those students who dressed in a "radical" fashion were found to hold attitudes which have been described by various observers as being "counter" to the dominant American culture. Dress behavior which violates basic dress "custom" appears to be related to a tendency to violate other cultural norms, and hence be indicative of a general "counterculture" outlook. (89, p. 110).

Clothing remains a basic expression of personality, life-style, and political philosophy. Researchers at Pennsylvania State University found they could predict students' social and political beliefs with 76 percent accuracy simply by observing their dress. (53, p. 431)

The large number of women adopting pants as a daily mode of dress have become a symbol of the liberation, freedom, independence, and newfound sexuality of the modern American woman. Adolescents, however, continue to favor their blue jeans, sweat shirts, or sweaters as comfortable expressions of youthfulness and informality. Regardless of the particular styles chosen, clothing behavior mirrors the personal feelings of an adolescent.

For adolescents, the most important function of clothing is to assure their identity and sense of belonging with peer groups. A number of studies have shown the relationship between adolescents' appearances and their social acceptance. (27, 35, 39, 60, 95) Those who are defined by their peers as fashionable dressers have high status; well-dressed but not fashionable students occupy the middle ground; poorly dressed students have low status. (48, p. 330) Williams and Eicher studied the relationship between appearance and social acceptance in a class of 154 ninth-grade girls in a midwestern community. When all the girls responded to an open-ended question on general acceptance of others, clothing was considered the attribute first in importance in describing the characteristics of the most popular girl. In describing the characteristics by which a new girl would be evaluated in trying to "get in" with the popular girls, the respondents mentioned clothing as second and looks as third in importance, while personality ranked first. (95, p. 459) The majority (75 percent) of the girls agreed that there were girls in the school who "were not dressed right." These girls were described as being from poor families, and their clothing was most frequently described as not "in fashion." Other girls denied having these girls as their friends. A sociogram of the entire population indicates that of the girls who "were not dressed right" 16 percent were social isolates and 35 percent were in the two lower class groups. (95, p. 461)

Table 10–4.   Self-evaluation of personal appearance as related to personal adjustment for girls, in percentages.

Personal Adjustment	Rated Self above Peers	Rated Self Same as Peers	Rated Self below Peers
Low range	39.1	22.2	62.5
Middle range	30.4	30.6	16.7
High range	30.4	47.2	20.8

Adapted from K. E. Musa and M. E. Roach, "Adolescent Appearance and Self Concept," *Adolescence* 8 (1973) : 385–394. Used by permission.

Hendricks and his associates made a similar study of the relationships between appearance and social acceptance, but with a group of senior girls. These girls also agreed that "first impressions count" and that clothing influenced a girl's popularity in high school. One girl made the following remark about a new girl: "Dress is considered first before they get to know her, personality later, and then general attitudes and beliefs." (39, p. 170) This group also was aware that some girls did not "dress right." One respondent stated: "It's nothing she should be blamed for; it's mostly her environment." (39, p. 170) But consciously or not, other girls look down on those not dressed correctly. Eighty-eight percent of the individuals chosen as best dressed were group members and few were isolates, but 35 percent of the "not dressed right" were isolates, and 27 percent were members of the lower social class group. Hamilton and Warden, in a study of 294 high school juniors from a midwestern high school, noted that "students with acceptable clothing behavior participated in more extracurricular activities and held more offices than did students with non-acceptable clothing behavior." (35, p. 790)

Adolescents who are satisfied with the way they look also have a more acceptable self-concept and make a more adequate personal adjustment. Table 10–4 shows the relationship between self-evaluation of personal appearance and the personal adjustment of eighty-three high school junior girls in a middle-sized midwestern industrial city. (67) A high percentage (62.5 percent) of those girls who rated their personal appearance below their peers also evidenced poor personal adjustment. (67, p. 390)

Preoccupations with clothing and appearance are not superficial or unimportant to youths who are concerned about peer-group acceptance. They must either conform or be rejected.

THE AUTOMOBILE

Another material aspect of adolescent culture is the automobile. One study of adolescents in the San Francisco area revealed that 40 percent of high school seniors were car owners and considerably more had access to a car. (23) The automobile has become of major importance in the life of the adolescent for a number of different reasons.

The automobile is a status symbol. Coleman reports that when boys are asked what impresses the girls the most, they rank being an athlete first, followed by being in the leading crowd, followed by having a nice car. (10, p. 46) Owning or having access to a car adds to one's prestige in the eyes of the crowd.

The type of car one owns or drives is important, and the status attached to various types changes over the years. Not long ago, to drive the family car—especially if it was a new, large, and expensive one—added greatly to prestige. Lacking a new, expensive family car, the adolescent who owned a jalopy was "in" with the crowd. Later the big car was out, and the small, fast, expensive sports car was in. Now college students are turning to the small, inexpensive compacts, primarily because, as one newscaster put it, "Americans are losing their love for their automobiles as they begin to see them as the chief polluters of the environment." The fuel shortage also has made youths more aware of gas mileage in automobile selection. Some youths have turned to motorcycles as a status symbol of the mod generation. But for the majority of youths, owning a car is still one of the most coveted symbols of status.

The automobile is a means of freedom and mobility. A car allows adolescents the opportunity to get away from home and drive to the neighboring town, to the big city, or to Florida during the spring break from school. It provides adolescents with a home away from home. If particularly devoted to it, they may spend hours in it each day, eating at drive-in restaurants, watching movies at drive-ins, talking with the gang, or making love.

The automobile is a symbol of power and masculinity. Even the names convey the message: Cougar, Mustang, Thunderbird. Gasoline puts "a tiger in your tank"; the tachometer gives a measure of the adolescent's daring and speed. The insecure boy especially finds that the automobile becomes a means of controlling an enormous amount of power and of gaining for himself a feeling of strength and virility. The larger the engine, the louder the muffler, the more the tires will scream, the faster the car will go, and the more daringly the boy drives it, the more manly he feels. Some boys become exhibitionists, primarily to impress girls. As one teenager said, "We don't drag much when the girls aren't around to watch." (37, p. 83)

For a number of youths an automobile has become a hobby. Many adolescent boys share a love for power and speed. Drag strip or stock car races are opportunities to compete in socially sanctioned ways to see who can build the fastest engine or soup up an old car. Such races provide opportunities for boys to prove themselves as men and as expert mechanics. One author reports that there are 16 hot rod magazines on the stands, with a total monthly circulation of 3 million. (37, p. 82) When one boy was asked why he was interested in drag racing, he replied:

Why do people have to collect stamps? Look, it's a hobby with us. We like cars. We build engines. We like to see how they hop up, see? And when we drive, there's a thrill. There really is. There's a thrill you can't describe. (37, p. 83)

The automobile has become a symbol of glamour and sexuality, of romantic conquest and acceptability. Madison Avenue has been quick to use not only snob appeal but also sex appeal. Advertisements imply that any man who drives a certain car will automatically fill it with beautiful girls, or that any girl who drives up in a certain car with plush upholstery will be considered as glamorous and beautiful as the model in the ad. The sensuous beauty in a low-cut evening gown or miniskirt caresses her automobile in such a fashion as to make every male watcher identify with the car—if he only had that car, maybe she would caress him too.

The automobile has become a favorite lovers' retreat. It allows for mobility, a fair degree of privacy, and even some degree of comfort and warmth, something that the local lovers lane cannot offer in the middle of winter. Kinsey reports that 41 percent of respondents who had engaged in premarital sex mentioned the automobile as a common place. (The home of either the boy or girl was mentioned as a more common place, however.) (52)

For some, the automobile has become a means of expressing hostility and anger. Psychiatrists have hypothesized that driving a powerful automobile provides an outlet for expression of frustration and hostility. Immature people who jump into their cars when frustrated and angry and go careening down the highway are unintentionally using the automobile as a convenient weapon to kill, maim, mutilate, or destroy. It has been widely publicized that hostile and explosive mental attitudes are major causes of injuries and deaths from automobiles, and that the accident-prone driver rebels against authority. The way adolescents use cars and the attitudes with which they drive are fair indications and tests of their emotional maturity. One investigator has pointed to the fact that some disturbed adolescents use the automobile as a means of committing suicide or murder, and that after such a suicide is publicized, the number of similar auto fatalities increases by almost one-third. (73) Apparently the behavior of young automobile drivers is affected by the processes of suggestion and modeling. (73, p. 1167)

Nonmaterial Aspects of Adolescent Culture

MUSIC

Music is an important part of adolescent culture. Unlike fads in clothing, trends in music are of longer duration. Rock music has endured since the early 1950s, longer than any other music fad in recent American history. It has undergone changes and reformed its outward style and presentation every two or three years, but retains its basic characteristics. Elvis Presley entered the music stage in the midfifties and probably did more than any other performer to introduce rock to American youth. His grinding, pumping presentations and new sounds caused riots in San Jose, Hartford, Atlanta, and London. Educators took a dim view of him when they found out a majority of Elvis fans had below a C average. Frank Sinatra called rock music a "rancid smelling aphrodisiac," and Samuel Cardinal Stritch compared it to "tribal rhythms." (76) The rock style flourished and received new impetus with the initial presentation of the Beatles on the "Ed Sullivan Show" in 1964. It was estimated that seventy million Americans saw and heard the program.

Since then the new music has become a synthesis: a blending of dixieland, rhythm and blues, folk music, country Western, jazz, and rock. One author best describes it as "forceful." Whether loud or soft, upbeat or slow, played on a flat-picked guitar or a plucked sitar, it is direct and candid in its sensuality, emotionalism, or chagrin. Lyrics show stark realism and shocking sophistication. Although simple-minded jingles are still performed, some songs now contain good poetry.

Since the late 1960s and early 1970s, the themes of modern music have changed. During those years, many of the songs were ballads of protest: against the war in Vietnam, against the draft and the military, against racial injustice or the bomb. Musicians like Bob Dylan, Arlo Guthrie, Joan Baez, and Judy Collins were protesting poets and troubadours against what was happening, whether in the world of nations or in the struggle against pollution. They were effective stimuli in awakening the conscience of the world and in reflecting the feelings and fears of the young.

There are still some songs that comment on everyday problems. Singers like David Bowie, Bonnie Raitt, and Frank Zappa deal with some social commentary. Stevie Wonder sings about everything from love to the problems of black people. Bob Dylan's "Slow Train" covers a wide variety of social problems: man's inflated ego, outdated laws, false leaders, nonbelievers talking in the name of religion, people starving while grain elevators burst with food. He even touches on the energy crisis: foreign oil control America's future while jeweled sheiks walk around like kings. (21)

Life in suburban America is described in Joni Mitchell's "Hissing of Summer Lawns." (65) A husband buys his wife a diamond necklace, puts her in a ranch house on a hill where she can see her neighbors' barbecues, their blue swimming pools, and hear "the hissing of summer lawns" (a reference apparently to lawn sprinklers). He also gives her a room full of Chippendale furniture that is never used and good reasons to leave him, but she stays with him with some kind of love. This is her choice: the hissing of summer lawns. (65)

One song in a somewhat lighter vein, by Paul Simon, deals with the problem of living in an apartment house where "One Man's Ceiling Is Another Man's Floor." (80) Apparently, two tenants get angry and have a fight over some things that were said. They bloody their noses and clothes and mess up the lobby floor of the building. The song admonishes "apartment house fools" to keep the house rules and to be considerate of one another because "One Man's Ceiling Is Another Man's Floor." (80)

Most of today's songs deal more with interpersonal relationships and feelings between people. One analysis of the songs of Joni Mitchell and Paul Simon from 1968 to 1975 showed that protest themes are now replaced by songs about love and the need to nurture and build gratifying relationships. (80) Personal feelings are emphasized. Simon writes about tenderness, honesty, and peace. Mitchell deals with suspicion, frustration, and going crazy. The songs reflect concern for love relationships that are permanent and stable. There is fear of depth and permanence on the one hand, but a yearning for real care and stability on the other hand. In her song "Down to You," Mitchell laments that everything is transitory: lovers and styles of clothes come and go; things that once were held true are lost or change as the days go by. (63) Her song "Trouble Child" also reflects the lack of caring relationships. While lying in a sterilized hospital room it comes as a shock to her that she really has no one on whom she can depend.

There is only a river of constantly changing faces that trickles past; she feels her humanity is being lost too. (64)

Simon, too, emphasizes the lack of permanence in human relationships. In "I Do It For Your Love," he tells about a couple who were married. They lived in a musty apartment with old pipes and cold water, so they had to drink a lot of orange juice for their colds; they bought an old rug in a junk shop with the orange and blue colors running together. Eventually there are arguments, tears, and polarization. Their love disappears. (81) Dionne Warwick's "I'll Never Love This Way Again" reflects the fear that love will not last. (92) Her lover has looked inside her fantasies and has made each one come true. She knows she can never love like that again, so she's holding on before the good has gone. If her lover should go away, she'll remember how good the love has been, but in the meantime she's holding on. (92)

At the same time that there is a longing for love, there is a fear of permanent commitment in marriage. In his song "You're Kind," Simon tells of meeting a girl who was so kind, so good, who rescued him when he was having a hard time. She introduced him to her whole neighborhood. He never had so many friends before. She was so good, so very good. She didn't mistreat him like others did. But then when he started to realize she was going to love him like that indefinitely, he became panicky and said good-bye, offering the feeble reason that he liked to sleep with the window open and she wanted it closed. (83)

Other singers also reflect this lack of permanence in human relationships. In a song entitled "Enough Is Enough—No More Tears," Barbra Streisand and Donna Summer urge their listeners when they've had enough, when the feeling is gone and they've reached the end, when there is nothing left to talk about, not to shed a tear but just to pack their man's raincoat, look him in the face, tell him they can't go on, and that they want him out the door. (88) They shouldn't think twice, but should get it over with as soon as possible.

The group Steely Dan also sings of the impermanence of marriage in the song "Haitian Divorce." (17) Two people, the Wallys, were so much in love that they embarrassed the clergyman at the wedding. In the very next line, love is dead. The couple shout and wrangle; the girl's father tells her she has to leave her husband. Without hesitation, tears, broken hearts, or remorse, they get a quick Haitian divorce. The consequences of divorce are the subject of the ballad "Sunday Father" by Barry Manilow. (62) The song is about a divorced father who has visitation privileges to see his son only once a week, on Sundays. They walk through the park, fly balloons, and wander about hand in hand. At the end of the day, which is all too short, he leaves his child by a modest home that he no longer shares with the woman inside. He longs to see his son more, but there is no way to let him know. (62)

Joan Baez, too, writes of the impermanence of love in "Love Song to a Stranger/Part II." First she met a tall, dark, Irish man with whom she slept under a burgundy quilt, but he was lost in the Irish fog. Then she remembered a boy from a monastery who wanted to be a monk. She couldn't marry him. Her next lover was a smooth-talking "son of a dog" from Tennessee. They followed one another around for over a year, but apparently he didn't want marriage so they just lived together in sin. Her final lover was a "black-eyed beauty" from Boston. Their relationship lasted two days. She is left with some of the gifts her lovers had bought: a basket of fruit, two glass finger bowls. The German wine is gone. She concludes that love is a "pain in the ass." (5)

Not all songs are without hope. Some reflect the confidence of youth that love will conquer all. A song entitled "Different Worlds" from the television series "Angie" reflects this confidence. (18) Two lovers meet who have completely different backgrounds. They are drawn together and convinced that nothing can divide them because love seeks, finds, conquers, and binds. (18)

A winsome tale about a young man who is quite shy is told in "The Diary of Horace Wimp," recorded by the Electric Light Orchestra. (24) Horace goes to work each day and is usually late. He knows he may be fired if he's late again. He's a sad person because he's never had a girl. Then one day a voice from above urges him to go out and find a wife, be a man, and he'll have a great life plan. The very next day he meets a small, pretty girl. He's shy and afraid, but very much in love. Finally he gets up enough nerve to ask her for a date to go to the café down the street. Horace can't believe it, but she says yes. The very next day he asks her to marry him, and he cries when she answers "Gladly." Two days later, we find Horace at the church, where his wife for the rest of his life comes down the aisle. (24)

Some songs reflect youths' fear of growing up. Childhood is freedom, joy, and play; adulthood is joyless, materialistic, and colorless. Almost no songs speak of fulfillment; many emphasize emptiness, pain, inadequacy, and vulnerability. The adult that emerges is aware of social problems and concerned about the next generation, but nowhere is there any emphasis on work as a vocation, as a satisfying, rewarding pursuit. It is easy to see why the counterculture is antimaterialistic and antiestablishment. The emphasis is on freedom "from" rather than on freedom "to do." (79)

Some of today's songs deal with the generation gap and youth's relationships with their parents. In his song "Mama Can't Buy You Love," Elton John talks about a girl whose parents give her everything, at least all the joy that money can buy. (47) But her mama doesn't want her, her daddy doesn't need her, and all their money can't bring her happiness and love. Elton John pleads with her to come away with him, since only he can give her love. (47)

Janis Ian is a voice that has shocked the older generation with her songs about alienation, parental influence, and sex. Her song "Janey's Blues" tells the story of an unwanted child in an affluent society. (43) Janey was an accident, a mistake, born the day after the beginning of Lent. And because she was unwanted, she is also neglected. While the mother plays on the golf course each day, Daddy is at home playing with the maid. Neither parent is taking care of Janey.

Another of Ian's songs tells the story of a girl who is robbed of her childhood by parents who push her into growing up too fast. "Hair Of Spun Gold" is the saga of life, love, and age from ages five through twenty-one. At ten the girl throws away her toys and works on getting noticed by the boys. At sixteen the girl's mother has pushed her into pregnancy. She stands at the altar to get married with her baby in her arms. Finally, later, the girl looks down on her baby and resolves that her baby will be allowed to be a child in the way she never was. She vows that her child will have a chance to laugh and to play before it's time to throw her toys away. (42)

Not all the songs of the young have a serious message or meaning. Some are simply filled with youths' exuberance for life, for love, or for nature. A sense of striving and hope for the future and youths' search for identity and meaning is expressed in Herb Alpert's recording "Rise." (31) He urges his listeners to rise, to reach for the sky, and not to let life pass them by; he speaks of the need to believe in themselves, to fly away and to find their own star and shine, the need to shine as best they can, always to reach out to understand others, and to lend a helping hand. If only they believe, they will be able to rise. (2)

Often the older generation does not listen to the music of today's youth. "Will you please turn that music down?" is the most commonly heard remark above the din and beat of the adolescent's stereo. The music is often so loud that the message never comes through. Perhaps if it did, parents would learn from it what their children are saying. (81, p. 39)

LANGUAGE

The other aspect of the nonmaterial culture of adolescents that will be discussed is language. The special language of a particular group or social class is referred to by linguists as *argot*. Each group in society has its own argot, including professional groups like lawyers or doctors, but also other groups: youth in general, or deviant groups such as drug addicts or delinquents. Each of these groups develops a language of its own that is meaningful to its members.

The meanings of slang expressions change quite rapidly, and there are variations from one section of the country to the other. It is, therefore, difficult to discuss word meanings. The following list is intended only as a representative sample of slang expressions used in the year 1977. The list was compiled by a group of high school and college youths on the East Coast.

All-night bender—all-night party
Barf—vomit, throw up
Bogus—disgusting
Book—to leave the scene, to split, cut out
Bowl—pot pipe
Brodie—spin a car 360°, also called a donut
Buzzed—high or stoned (on drugs)
Cashed—a pipe all out of pot
Check it out—investigate
C-9—cloud nine
Cracked—crazy
Crash—come out of a high
Drone—one who is boring, dull, a drag
Flick—movie
Fried—extremely high, drunk

Gross—disgusting

Heavy—very serious relation or responsibility

Hoochie—pot, grass, weed

Hunk—a gorgeous guy

Hustle—to flirt, same as scag

I hear you—I understand completely

Jock—an athlete, especially a guy who is straight

Lagger—a person who won't party, who won't do what others are doing

Loaded—state of being drunk

Pick off—to go in front of a person while driving, or skiing

Pissa—good, great, keen

Pussy whipped—when a girl has a guy wrapped around her finger

Rag—a "used," promiscuous girl, an insulting remark about a girl

Roach—stub end of a joint

Rush—something strange, surprising, amazing

Scag—hustle, flirt

Shotgun—a way of smoking pot where one person blows out the bowl of a pipe
   and another person sucks smoke from the stem.

Score—get some drugs or have sexual intercourse with a girl

Stick it—if you don't like it, go to hell, shove it

The pits—terrible, the worst of everything

Toke—take a draw off a joint

Truck—get out of there, move

Turkey—a jerk

Wicked—very

Wiped out—completely out from smoking too much pot

One study of adolescents in a surburban high school twelve miles from Boston revealed a number of cliques, each with their own language. (57) The "chewers" chewed tobacco in and out of school. They used terms like *scumbags* or *scuzbags* for women of disputed reputation. (57, p. 496) The "jocks" were those who participated in school sports. They had their own language which reflected their athletic participation. To *spike the ball* meant to slam a football down on the field after scoring a touchdown. A team member who made a mistake was a *flake*. (57, p. 497)

Another major clique was the "motorheads," who spent most of their time working on their cars. (57, p. 498) They had nicknames for every kind of car on the road.

"Toilet Odors" were Toyotas, "Farts" were Fiats, "Detroit" was a General Motors car. A Ford was called a "Found on the road dead" or a "Fix or repair daily." A GTO was called a "goat." An undesirable car was called a "shitbox" or a "Bondo." (Bondo is a plastic body filler used to fix up dents.) A car with a lot of horsepower was called a "hypo."

There were also terms used to describe the car engines. A "six pack" was a car with three two-barrel carburetors. "Dual Quads" was a car with two four-barrel carburetors. (57, p. 499)

Other terms described various activities of the motorheads. *Riding the gun* meant riding in the passenger seat; *lighting the tires* meant gunning the engine, spinning the rear tires, and causing them to burn; *pulling a chirper* meant making the tires give a loud squeaking noise. (57, p. 499)

The "fleabags" were those students who took drugs regularly; they were often referred to as "weirdos" or "jerks" and were not well liked by the other students. They used different means of smoking marijuana. One was to *shotgun* —to put a lit cigarette into one's mouth backward and blow the smoke into the mouth of one's partner. The other way was to use a "bong" pipe, consisting of tubes and water. A *roach clip* was a small tweezer to smoke a short cigarette. (57, p. 501)

Why do adolescents feel they need to have their own language? What functions does it serve? There are at least three major functions of adolescent argot:

Argot is a shorthand device designed to save elaborate explanation and time. To say "cool" is much simpler than to go into a lengthy explanation of one's reactions or feelings. The word makes a concept clear for the teenager by summing up complex and recurrent phenomena in one word.

Argot is coined to make possible a more precise reference to certain observations or experiences than the ordinary adult vocabulary would allow. To use the word *gut* for an easy course or *rap* for a discussion is to impart specific meaning to adolescent experience. It's possibly easier and more meaningful to say "I really dig him" than to try a longer explanation of why you like a boy or find him attractive.

Adolescent argot also is used as a reinforcer and maintainer of group solidarity. Adolescents who speak the language of the group reflect a desire to be a part of the group; they reflect the feelings, attitudes, and culture of the group; and they show they are in the group. Just as the background, breeding, and social status of Englishmen is associated with their language and the accent with which they speak, so adolescents' group identifications are judged and reflected by whether or not they speak a particular language. Their language reflects who and what they are and with what group they are identified.

Conclusions

In the college classroom, four questions are asked most frequently about the material in this chapter. Discussion of these questions here will serve to draw together some of the ideas already presented.

1. Is adolescent society subcultural or not? There are two conflicting views. One says that adolescent culture is merely a reflection of adult culture; the others says that adolescent society, based as it is in the peer group, is distinct, segregated, and different from adult culture.

Each view is only a partial one. There is plenty of evidence that adolescent culture, in general, is a reflection of adult culture. Research indicates that when adolescents become adults they tend to be members of the same political party, join the same church, espouse the same values, follow similar ethical principals, and adopt the same customs and manners as their parents did. (This is more true of adolescents who have received only a high school education, but, overall, it is true.)

However, certain aspects of adolescent culture are different from the adult world. Two examples are sexual values and the use of marijuana. Adolescents want their own segregated organizations and societies; they adopt their own styles of dress, dances, interests, and social customs. Theirs is in some respects a subculture within a larger culture, even though many of the differences are petty and inconsequential, and do not last. Overall, however, adolescent culture gives way to adult culture as adolescents mature.

There are some adolescents who are trying to rebel and reject as completely and permanently as possible the values and customs of the adult society. They are subcultural because they are out of the mainstream, but they constitute a minority of all youths.

2. The studies cited (Coleman, Smith, Havighurst, Gordon, and others) present the life and values of high school youths as quite superficial, with their emphasis on athletics, extracurricular clubs and organizations, clothes, and cars. Aren't adolescents today more serious-minded than these studies indicate? Aren't they less superficial, more concerned with world problems, ecology, and academics?

Some are more concerned, but they are a minority in high school, although there are many more at the college level. The extracurricular and social whirl of the typical American high school is more central to the life of the average middle class student than is the academic program or world problems. Clothes, cars, sports, and boyfriends and girlfriends are of greater interest than algebra, history, or world government.

3. Adolescents from low socioeconomic status families seem to be at a disadvantage: they are described as seldom seen in clubs, as nonjoiners, and as nonparticipants in extracurricular activities. They are followers rather than leaders and usually not among the most popular students in school. Is this really true? Although there are individual exceptions, the facts presented are correct. This does not mean such a situation should be condoned or that it is right, but it does mean that this is the way it is. Any description of adolescent society and culture must take these socioeconomic differences into account.

4. Is clothing as important to adolescents today as this chapter claims? Yes, it is, but this does not mean that wearing "nice" or expensive clothes is always important. What is important is that individual adolescents wear clothing that their social group considers appropriate and acceptable. Styles vary from group to group, but youths are still as much conformists in clothing selection as they ever were. What is different is the clothing youth consider appropriate. Proper dress now is much more casual than in previous generations.

Topics for Term Papers

The subject matter of this chapter is so varied that students have a wide variety of topics from which to choose in writing term papers. The following are only suggestions.

1. How My Parents and I Agree or Disagree on Important Values
2. The Generation Gap: Fact or Fiction?
3. The Influence of College on the Values of Youths
4. Is College Alienating Youths from their Parents and from Society?
5. Parent-Adolescent Emotional Attachments as an Influence in Parental Socialization of the Teenager

6. Parents versus Peers—Who Exerts the Greatest Influence in the Lives of Youths?

7. Youth Organizations and their Roles in Adolescent Development

8. Extracurricular Activities as a Factor in Adolescent Development

9. Snobbishness and Socioeconomic Class Discrimination in High School

10. Factors That Determine Popularity and Prestige in High School

11. Collegiate Culture Today

12. The Place of Fraternities and Sororities in College

13. Contemporary Clothing Styles of Adolescents

14. Should High School Students Be Allowed to Own Cars?

15. The Music of ———— (select a song writer or singer)

16. What Popular Music Is Saying to Today's Youths

17. The Place of Music in the Lives of Today's Adolescents

Bibliography

1. Aldridge, J. W. *In the Country of the Young.* New York: Harper and Row, 1971.

2. Alpert, H. "Rise." Copyright 1979, Almo Music Corporation and Badazz Music.

3. Astin, A. "The New Realists." *Psychology Today* (September 1977): 50ff.

4. Bachman, J. G., and Johnston, L. C. "The Freshmen, 1979." *Psychology Today* (September 1979): 79ff.

5. Baez, J. "Love Song to A Stranger/Part II." Copyright 1975, Chandos Music. ASCAP.

6. Bernard, Jessie: "Teen-age Culture: An Overview." *Annals of the American Academy of Political and Social Science* 338 (November 1961): 63–69.

7. Bronfenbrenner, U. *Two Worlds of Childhood: U.S. and U.S.S.R.* New York: Russell Sage Foundation, 1970.

8. Clark, Burton R., and Trow, Martin. "Determinants Of College Student Subculture." In "The Study of College Peer Groups: Problems and Prospects for Research." Social Science Research Council, Ann Arbor and Berkeley, 1959–1960. Mimeographed.

9. Cohen, J. "High School Subcultures and the Adult World." *Adolescence* 14 (Fall 1979): 491–502.

10. Coleman, James S. *The Adolescent Society.* New York: Free Press, 1961.

11. Coleman, J. C. "Current Contradictions in Adolescent Theory." *Journal of Youth and Adolescence* 7 (March 1978): 1–11.

12. Coleman, J. et al. "Adolescents and Their Parents: A Study of Attitudes." *Journal of Genetic Psychology* 130 (1977): 239–245.

13. Condry, J., and Siman, M. L. "Characteristics of Peer- and Adult-Oriented Children." *Journal of Marriage and the Family* 36 (1974): 543–554.

14. Conger, J. J. "A World They Never Knew: The Family and Social Change." *Daedalus* (Fall 1971).

15. ———. *Adolescence and Youth.* New York: Harper and Row, 1973.

16. Curtis, R. L., Jr. "Adolescent Orientations toward Parents and Peers: Variations by Sex, Age, and Socioeconomic Status." *Adolescence* 10 (1975): 483–494.

17. Dan, Steely. "Haitian Divorce." Copyright 1976, American Broadcasting Company.

18. "Different Worlds." Copyright 1979, Bruin Music Co.

19. Dreyfus, E. A. *Adolescence.* Columbus, Ohio: Charles E. Merrill Publishing Co., 1976.

20. Duncan, D. F. "Measuring the Generation Gap: Attitudes toward Parents and Other Adults." *Adolescence* 13 (Spring 1978): 77–81.

21. Dylan, B. "Slow Train." Copyright 1979, Special Rider Music.

22. Eitzen, D. S., and Brouillette, J. R. "The Politicization of College Students." *Adolescence* 14 (Spring 1979): 123–134.

23. Elder, G. H., Jr. "The Social Context of Youth Groups." *International Social Science Journal* 24 (1972): 280.

24. Electric Light Orchestra. "The Days of Horace Wimp." Copyright 1979, United Artists Music, Ltd. and Jet Music, Inc.

25. Emmerich, H. J. "The Influences of Parents and Peers on Choices Made by Adolescents." *Journal of Youth and Adolescence* 7 (June 1978): 175–180.

26. Eitzioni, A. "Youth Is Not a Class." *Psychology Today* (February 1978): 20ff.

27. Evans, S. Evelyn. "Motivation Underlying Clothing Selection and Wearing." *Journal of Home Economics* 56 (1964): 739–743.

28. Floyd, H. H., Jr., and South, D. R. "Dilemma of Youth: The Choice of Parents or Peers as a Frame of Reference for Behavior." *Journal of Marriage and the Family* 34 (1972): 627–634.

29. "Fraternities Bound Back, with Big Changes." *U.S. News & World Report*, 12 March 1979, p. 46.

30. Gallagher, B. J. "Attitude Differences across Three Generations: Class and Sex Components." *Adolescence* 14 (Fall 1979): 503–516.

31. Gordon, Wayne C. *The Social System of the High School*. Glencoe: Free Press, 1957.

32. Gottlieb, D., and Hodgkins, B. "College Student Subcultures: Their Structures and Characteristics in Relation to Student Attitude Change." *School Review* 71 (1963): 377–385.

33. Greenfield, N., and Finkelstein, E. L. "A Comparison of the Characteristics of Junior High School Students." *Journal of Genetic Psychology* 117 (1970): 37–50.

34. Grinder, R. E. *Adolescence*. New York: John Wiley and Sons, 1973.

35. Hamilton, Janice, and Warden, Jessie. "The Student's Role in a High School Community and his Clothing Behavior." *Journal of Home Economics* 58 (1966): 789–791.

36. Hanks, M., and Eckland, B. K. "Adult Voluntary Associations and Adolescent Socialization." *Sociological Quarterly* 19 (Summer 1978): 481–490.

37. Hanson, R. E., and Carlson, R. E. *Organizations for Children and Youth*. Englewood Cliffs, N.J.: Prentice-Hall, 1972.

38. Havighurst, Robert J. et al. *Growing Up in River City*. New York: John Wiley & Sons, 1962.

39. Hendricks, Suzanne et al. "Senior Girls' Appearance and Social Acceptance." *Journal of Home Economics* 60 (1968): 167–171.

40. Hollingshead, A. B. *Elmtown's Youth and Elmtown Revisited*. New York: John Wiley and Sons, 1975.

41. Iacovetta, R. G. "Adolescent-Adult Interaction and Peer-Group Involvement." *Adolescence* 10 (1975): 327–336.

42. Ian, Janis. "Hair of Spun Gold." Copyright 1965, Dialogue Music, Inc.

43. ———. "Janey's Blues." Copyright 1967, Dialogue Music, Inc.

44. Isenberg, P. et al. "Psychological Variables in Student Activism: The Radical Triad and Some Religious Differences." *Journal of Youth and Adolescence* 6 (March 1977): 11–24.

45. Jacobsen, R. B. et al. "An Empirical Test of the Generation Gap: A Comparative Intrafamily Study." *Journal of Marriage and the Family* 37 (1975): 841–852.

46. Jennings, M., and Niemi, R. "Continuity and Change in Political Orientations: A Longitudinal Study of Two Generations." *Journal of Youth and Adolescence* 7 (March 1978): 1–11.

47. John, E. "Mama Can't Buy You Love." Copyright 1979, Mighty Three Music.

48. Jones, S. S. "High School Social Status as a Historical Process." *Adolescence* 11 (Fall 1976): 327–333.

49. Kandel, D. B. "The Concept of Adolescent Subculture." In *Adolescents in the American High School*. Edited by R. F. Purnel. New York: Holt, Rinehart and Winston, 1970.

50. Kelley, E. et al. "Working Class Adolescents' Perceptions of the Role of Clothing in Occupational Life." *Adolescence* 9 (1974): 185–198.

51. Kernan, J. B. "Her Mother's Daughter? The Case of Clothing and Cosmetic Fashions." *Adolescence* 8 (1973): 343–350.

52. Kinsey, Alfred C. *Sexual Behavior in the Human Female*. Philadelphia: W. B. Saunders Co., 1953.

53. Kness, D., and Densmore, B. "Dress and Social-Political Beliefs of Young Male Students." *Adolescence* 11 (Fall 1976): 431–442.

54. Lambert, B. G. et al. *Adolescence: Transition from Childhood to Maturity*. Monterey, Calif.: Brooks/Cole Publishing Co., 1972.

55. Larson, L. E. "The Relative Influence of Parent-Adolescent Affect in Predicting the Salience Hierarchy among Youth." *Pacific Sociological Review* 15 (1972): 83–102.

56. ———. "The Influence of Parents and Peers during Adolescence: The Situation Hypothesis Revisited." *Journal of Marriage and the Family* 34 (1972): 67–84.

57. Leona, M. H. "An Examination of Adolescent Clique Language in a Suburban Secondary School." *Adolescence* 13 (Fall 1978): 495–502.

58. Lemer, R. M. et al. "Actual and Perceived Attitudes of Late Adolescents and Their Parents." *Journal of Genetic Psychology*, 1975.

59. ———. "Attitudes of High School Students and Their Parents toward Con-

temporary Issues." *Psychological Reports* 31 (1972): 255–258.

60. Littrell, M. B., and Eicher, J. B. "Clothing Opinions and the Social Acceptance Progress among Adolescents." *Adolescence* 8 (1973): 197–212.

61. Manaster, G. J., and Novak, D. "Post High School Adolescents: An Ecological Approach to Studying Group Differences." *Adolescence* 12 (Summer 1977): 269–275.

62. Manilow, B. "Sunday Father." Copyright 1979, Kamakazi Music Corp.

63. Mitchell, J. "Down to You." Copyright 1974, Crazy Crow Music. New York: Warner Brothers Publications.

64. ———. "Trouble Child." Copyright 1974, Crazy Crow Music. New York: Warner Brothers Publications.

65. ———. "Hissing of Summer Lawns." Copyright 1975 and 1976, Mad Man's Drum Music and Crazy Crow Music. New York: Warner Brothers Publications.

66. Munns, M., Jr. "The Values of Adolescents Compared with Parents and Peers." *Adolescence* 7 (1972): 519–524.

67. Musa, K. E., and Roach, M. E. "Adolescent Appearance and Self Concept." *Adolescence* 8 (1973): 385–394.

68. Newman, P. R. "Social Settings and Their Significance for Adolescent Development." *Adolescence* 11 (Fall 1976): 405–418.

69. Niemi, R. G. et al. "The Similarity of Political Values of Parents and College-Age Youths." *Public Opinion Quarterly* 42 (Winter 1978): 503–520.

70. Niles, F. S. "The Adolescent Girls' Perceptions of Parents and Peers." *Adolescence* 14 (Fall 1979): 591–597.

71. Offer, D. et al. "A Longitudinal Study of Normal Adolescent Boys." *American Journal of Psychiatry* 126 (1970): 917–924.

72. Orloff, H., and Weinstock, A. "A Comparison of Parent and Adolescent Attitude Factor Structures." *Adolescence* 10 (1975): 201–205.

73. Phillips, D. P. "Suicide, Motor Vehicle Fatalities, and the Mass Media: Evidence toward a Theory of Suggestion." *American Journal of Sociology* 84 (March 1979): 1150–1174.

74. Ramsey, Charles E. *Problems of Youth.* Belmont, Calif.: Dickenson Publishing Co., 1967.

75. Rice, B., and Cramer, J. "Comes the Counterrevolution." *Psychology Today* (September 1977): 56ff.

76. "Rock'n'Roll: The Sound of the Sixties." *Time*, 1965.

77. Rogers, D. *Adolescence: A Psychological Perspective.* Monterey, Calif.: Brooks/Cole Publishing Co., 1972.

78. Rutter, M. et al. "Adolescents and Their Parents: A Study of Attitudes." *Journal of Genetic Psychology* 130 (1977): 239–245.

79. Sack, A. L., and Thiel, R. "College Football and Social Mobility: A Case Study of Notre Dame Football Players." *Sociology of Education* 52 (January 1979): 60–66.

80. Seltzer, S. "Quo Vadis, Baby?: Changing Adolescent Values as Reflected in the Lyrics of Popular Music." *Adolescence* 11 (1976): 419–429.

81. Simmons, J. L., and Winograd, Barry. "Songs of the Hang-Loose Ethic." In *Adolescence for Adults* 22 (1970): 32–39.

82. Simon, P. "I Do It For Your Love." Copyright 1975, Paul Simon.

83. ———. "You're Kind." Copyright 1975, Paul Simon.

84. Smart, M. S., and Smart, R. C. *Adolescents: Development and Relationships.* New York: Macmillan Co., 1973.

85. Smith, Ernest A. *American Youth Culture.* New York: Free Press, 1962.

86. Spanier, G. B. "Measuring Social Class among College Students: A Research Note." *Adolescence* 11 (Winter 1976): 541–548.

87. Stone, L. H. et al. "Parent-Peer Influence as a Predictor of Marijuana Use." *Adolescence* 14 (Spring 1979): 115–122.

88. Streisand, B., and Summer, D. "Enough Is Enough—No More Tears." Copyright 1979, Olga Music/Fedora Music.

89. Thomas, I. E. "Clothing and Counterculture: An Empirical Study." *Adolescence* 8 (1973): 93–112.

90. Thurnher, M. et al. "Value Congruence and Behavioral Conflict in Intergenerational Relations." *Journal of Marriage and the Family* 36 (1974): 308–319.

91. U.S. Bureau of the Census, Department of Commerce. *Statistical Abstract of the United States, 1978.* Washington, D. C.: U.S. Government Printing Office, 1978.

92. Warwick, D. "I'll Never Love This Way Again." Copyright 1979, Irving Music, Inc.

93. Wattenberg, W. W. *The Adolescent Years,* 2d ed. New York: Harcourt Brace Jovanovich, 1973.

94. Weinstock, A., and Lerner, R. M. "Attitudes of Late Adolescents and Their Parents toward Contemporary Issues." *Psychological Reports* 30 (1972): 239–244.

95. Williams, Madelyn C., and Eicher,

Joanne B. "Teen-Ager's Appearance and Social Acceptance." *Journal of Home Economics* 58 (1966): 457–461.

96. Yankelovich, D. *The New Morality: A Profile of American Youth in the 70's.* New York: McGraw-Hill, 1974.

97. Young, J. W., and Ferguson, L. R. "Developmental Changes through Adolescence in the Spontaneous Nominations of Reference Groups as a Function of Decision Content." *Journal of Youth and Adolescence* 8 (June 1979): 239–252.

CHAPTER 11

Social Development, Relationships, and Dating

Outline

The developmental tasks of adolescence that relate only to social development and relationships should include at least six important needs of youths.

1. The need to establish caring, meaningful, satisfying relationships with individuals.
2. The need to broaden childhood friendships by getting acquainted with new people of differing backgrounds, experiences, and ideas.
3. The need to find acceptance, belonging, recognition, and status in social groups.
4. The need to pass from the homosexual interests and playmates of middle childhood to heterosexual concerns and friendships.
5. The need to learn about, adopt, and practice dating patterns and skills that contribute to personal and social development, intelligent mate selection, and successful marriage.
6. The need to find an acceptable masculine or feminine sex role and to learn sex-appropriate behavior.

The content of this chapter has been selected primarily with these social needs of the adolescent in mind. Discussion of masculine-feminine sex roles and appropriate sexual values and behavior is reserved for Chapters 12 and 13.

Companionship

NEED FOR FRIENDSHIPS

The need for close friends becomes crucial during adolescence. Up to this time, children's dependence upon peers has been rather loosely structured. They have sought out playmates of their own ages with whom they share common interests or activities. They have engaged them in friendly competition, and won or lost some measure of their respect and loyalty, but emotional involvement with them has not been intense. Children have not depended primarily upon one another for emotional satisfaction. They have looked to their parents for fulfillment of their emotional needs and have sought their praise, love, and tenderness. Only if they have been unloved, rejected, and adversely criticized by parents will they have turned to friends or parent substitutes for emotional fulfillment. (30)

During adolescence, the picture changes. Sexual maturation brings new feelings, the need for emotional fulfillment and for emotional independence and emancipation from parents. Adolescents now turn to their peers to find the support formerly provided by their families.

Adolescents' first needs are for relationships with others with whom they can share common interests. (22, p. 126) As they grow older they desire a closer, caring relationship that involves sharing mature affection, problems, and their most personal thoughts. They need close friends who stand beside them and for them in an understanding caring way. (30) Friends share more than secrets or plans; they share feelings and help each other resolve personal problems and interpersonal conflicts. As one boy said:

He is my best friend. We can tell each other things we can't tell anyone else; we understand each other's feelings. We can help each other when we are needed. (67, p. 72)

One of the reasons friendships are crucial is that adolescents are insecure and anxious about themselves. They lack personality definition and secure identities. Consequently, they gather friends around them from whom they gain strength, and who help establish the boundaries for their selves. From them they learn the necessary personal and social skills and societal definitions that help them to become a part of the larger adult world. They become emotionally bound to others who share their vulnerabilities and their deepest selves. They become comrades in a hostile world. (2, p. 60)

One of the greatest problems of adolescents is the problem of loneliness. Konopka, in her classic work, *The Adolescent Girl in Conflict*, quotes one of the girls she studied.

Have you ever been lonely? When I was in a foster home I could not see my sister or my brother. I felt so lonely. I wanted to hang around other kids. (41, p. 40)

One comment was from a girl who became pregnant out of wedlock.

I am just terribly lonesome. I don't think I was ever in love. I just wanted to get close because I was so lonesome.

Anne Frank's comment from *The Diary of a Young Girl* is appropriate: "For in its innermost depths, youth is lonelier than old age." (21, p. 278) A recent survey by *Psychology Today* magazine substantiates this contention: the younger the respondents, the greater the percentage who said they felt lonely "sometimes" or "often": 79 percent of those under age eighteen, compared to 37 percent of those over age fifty-five. (58, p. 54) In another study, a group of high school students, as well as a comparison group of adults, were supplied with beepers that went off at random intervals during the day, from 7:30 A.M. until midnight, to signal them to fill out activity and mood checklists. Adolescents were more volatile than adults in their reports on loneliness, swinging from one extreme to another, depending partly on the time and place. Not surprisingly, they reported being lonely most often on Friday and Saturday nights when they were home without dates. (65, p. 89) Part of this feeling was socially conditioned; youth culture emphasizes that if you're alone on Friday night you're going to be miserable, so adolescents end up feeling that way.

EARLY ADOLESCENT FRIENDSHIPS

The need for companionship causes young adolescents to pair off: to choose a best friend or chum or two, almost always of the same sex in the beginning. The adolescent will spend long hours conversing with this friend on the telephone, will attend school, club, and athletic events with him or her, and strive to dress alike, look alike, and act alike. Usually this best friend is from a similar socioeconomic, racial, and home background, from the same neighborhood, school, and school grade, of the same age, and with numerous interests, values, and friends in common. (10) Best friends usually get along well if they are well selected, because they are similar and thus compatible. Successful friendships, like successful marriages, are based on each person's meeting the needs of the other. If best friends meet each other's needs, the bonds of friendship may be drawn tightly.

These early adolescent friendships are intense, emotional, and sometimes stormy if needs are not meet. Adolescents may have made a bad choice. Instead of their best friends meeting their needs, they stimulate frustration and anger. The more intense and narcissistic the emotions that drove adolescents to seek companionship, the more likely it is that sustained friendships will be tenuous, difficult, and tempestuous. Once thwarted, immature, rejected, unstable adolescents react with excessive emotion, which may disrupt their friendships temporarily or permanently. (31, p. 182)

Therefore, friendships during early adolescence usually are unstable. Studies of the stability of friendships at this time indicate an increase in friendship fluctuations accompanying the onset of pubescence (at about age thirteen for girls and age fourteen for boys), followed by a decline in friendship fluctuations to age eighteen. (13) (See Figure 11–1.) After eighteen years of age, friendship fluctuations increase because students leave home for college, jobs, the armed services, or marriage. (69)

There seem to be some sex differences in the intimacy and stability of adolescent friendships. Between fourteen and sixteen years of age, girls' relationships have been found to be more intimate and more reciprocal than those of boys, (18) but they are often less enduring, for it is more demanding to maintain a close relationship than a casual one. Boys of this age make no demands for emotional

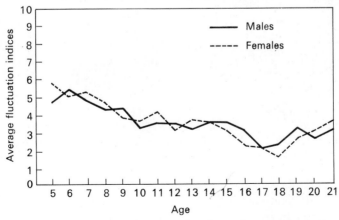

Figure 11–1.   Friendship fluctuations of 1,018 females and 775 males (503 were college students; the rest were urban children ages 5–18). (Adapted from C. A. Skorepa, J. E. Horrocks, and G. G. Thompson. "A Study of Friendship Fluctuations of College Students," *Journal of Genetic Psychology* 102[1963]: 151–157. Used by permission.)

closeness and support. Their early friendships involve emotional ties with those with whom they can share common interests in activities.

BROADENING EARLY FRIENDSHIPS

When young adolescents leave the confines of their neighborhood elementary schools and transfer to district or consolidated junior high schools, they are immediately exposed to much broader and more heterogeneous friendships. They now have an opportunity to meet youths from other neighborhoods, social classes, and from different ethnic and national origins. These youths may act, dress, speak, and think differently from those they have known before. One social task at this stage of development is to broaden their acquaintances, to learn how to relate to and get along with many different types of people. During this early period adolescents want many friends.

Group Acceptance and Popularity

As the number of acquaintances broadens, adolescents become increasingly aware of their needs to belong to a group. They want to be liked by their peers; therefore, by midadolescence the goal toward which they strive is acceptance by members of a clique or crowd they strongly admire. At this stage they are very sensitive to criticism or to others' negative reactions to them. They are concerned about what people think because their concepts of who they are and their degree of self-worth are partly a reflection of the opinions of others. (26)

The following questions are typically asked by adolescents in the seventh, eighth, or ninth grades who are worried about their social positions. (8, p. 73; 66, p. 32)

· How should a boy who is very shy go about overcoming the problem?
· How can you get other kids to like you?
· How can you become more sociable?
· Why do you feel left out when you're around a group of friends that don't even know you're there?
· What do you do when a person hates you?
· Why are some kids so popular and others not? How can you get popular?
· If you're a dud like me, how can you become graceful?

ACCEPTING NEWCOMERS

Adolescents whose families move to new communities are at a special disadvantage in making friends. They arrive in new communities only to find that various cliques, crowds, gangs, and other social groupings already exist. They are faced with the task of gaining acceptance in already established groups. One study of seventh- and eighth-graders showed considerable differences between males and females in reactions toward same-sex newcomers; (72) female friendship pairs displayed more negative, rejecting attitudes toward female newcomers than boys did toward male newcomers. The girls judged the newcomers less favorably, were less welcoming, and were more likely than the boys to ignore a newcomer's suggestions in a group.

The researchers offer several speculative explanations of these differences between the sexes. The differences may reflect: (1) differences in levels of hostility, (2) differences in degrees of shyness and social anxiety, or (3) differences in social cohesiveness between male and female groups. Also, because girls tend to develop a few close friends and boys tend to be more group oriented, the boys would be more likely to be friendly toward newcomers. Whatever the explanation, the results of this study suggest it is harder for female newcomers to be accepted by other girls than for male newcomers to be accepted by other boys. (72) In actual practice there are a number of ways youths try to find group acceptance and recognition.

CONFORMITY

Best friends are chosen partly on the basis of homogamy: the choice of someone like oneself. One researcher found that adolescents choose their friends so as to maximize the congruency (similarity) within the friendship pair. (36) If there is a state of unbalance such that the friend's attitude or behavior is incongruent, the adolescent will either break off the friendship and seek another friend, or keep the friend and modify her or his own behavior. (36, p. 435)

Cliques and groups operate in the same way. Each group takes on a personality of its own: members are characterized according to dress and appearance, scholastic standing, extracurricular participation, social skills, socioeconomic status, reputation, and personality qualifications. (See Chapter 10.) One way the individual has of being a part of a particular group is to be like other members of the group. This may include using special slang, wearing a certain type of pin, hair ribbon, or different-colored socks on each foot. When a fad is in fashion, every person in the group adopts it. Those who are different are excluded as "queer" or "gross."

One study of 538 boys and girls from nine to sixteen years of age substantiated this relationship between group acceptance and conformity. (19) Table 11–1 shows the strong positive correlation between group normative integration and the proportion of group members conforming to perceived peer-group expectations: the greater the proportion of conformers in a group, the higher the level of group integration. This is understandable, for those insisting on being different from other group members either voluntarily withdraw, are never admitted, or, if once admitted, are pressured out of the group.

Conformity can be a helpful, positive social influence, or a negative one, de-

Table 11–1. Level of group normative integration by percentage of conformers in group (N = 61).

Group Normative Integration	N	Percentage of Conformers
Low	20	37.6
Medium	20	39.4
High	21	44.6

From R. A. Feldman, "Normative Integration, Alienation, and Conformity in Adolescent Groups," *Adolescence* 12 (1972): 336. Used by permission.

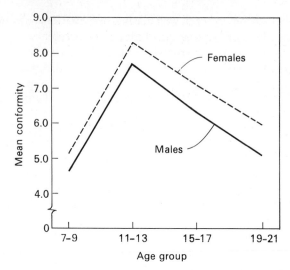

Figure 11–2.   Mean conformity as a function of age. (Adapted from Philip R.
Costanzo, and Marvin E. Shaw, "Conformity as a Function of Age Level," *Child
Development* 33[1966]:967–975. Copyright The Society for Research in Child
Development, Inc., 1966. Used by permission.)

pending on the group and its values. The adolescent boy who wants to belong
to a juvenile gang of delinquents and has to pull off a robbery to do so is obviously conforming, but to a peer code that may get him in trouble.

There has been a great deal of research to try to understand conformity during adolescence. (12, 13) A number of findings are significant. For one thing,
conformity changes with age, increasing through early adolescence (to eleven
to thirteen years of age) *and declining after that period.* (12, 13) (See Figure
11–2.) Some research indicates that the age of maximum conformity may be
somewhat later for boys than for girls, and later than shown on the graph, with
the greatest conformity for boys coming at around age fifteen. Apparently, the
later physical maturity of boys does not stimulate a need for social conformity as
early as for girls.

Conformity needs also depend upon adolescents' family adjustments. (77)
Youths with a good family adjustment who are fond of their parents have less
need to conform to peer demands, at least in some things, so that when confronted with decisions, parental rather than peer opinions are accepted. (7, p. 96;
20; 33; 82) There are certain areas of their culture over which adolescents resent
parental control, such as dress, selection of friends, and taste in music. (37, 43,
44) The significant point is that total adjustment to parents influences the degree to which adolescents conform to parents versus peers, (20, 33, 82)

Socioeconomic status also correlates with adolescent conformity. (62) Higher
status adolescents conform more than ones from low socioeconomic status families. They more often like school, plan to continue their education, attend church,
and make higher level vocational choices. (See Chapter 19.)

*Adolescent females show a greater degree of conformity than do adolescent
males.* This means that members of girls' groups are more concerned with har-

monious relations, social approval and acceptance, and living up to peer expectations than are members of boys' groups. (19, p. 330; 20)

ACHIEVEMENT

Another way of finding group acceptance and approval is through achievement: in sports, club membership, recreational activities, or academic subjects. But the recognition and acceptance the individual achieves depends upon the status accorded the activity by the peer group. Research indicates consistently that high school athletes are awarded higher social status (by several criteria of interpersonal popularity) than are scholars, but that athlete-scholars are the most popular of all, suggesting some positive status given to both academic and athletic achievements. (10) Because of the negative status awarded some activities, participation or achievement in these activities is a handicap to the adolescent seeking wider social acceptance.

PARTICIPATION

Joining in-school clubs and participating in a variety of out-of-school social activities are other ways the adolescent has of finding social acceptance. The most popular students are the joiners, usually in multiple activities in schools, but also as members of out-of-school, community-sponsored youth groups and as participants in every conceivable type of social and recreational activity among friends. (10) The group life of adolescents has been characterized as herd life. The herd assembles at the local hangout for refreshments and small talk; the herd goes joyriding in the car, to a drive-in movie or a dance, or to hear a rock group at the local community center. The herd may go on a hayride, skiing, or to the seashore. To be a part of the social scene, one has to join and be with the herd. When Coleman asked youths to rank the items that were most important in achieving popularity, the girls indicated that to be popular with one's own sex or with the opposite sex, one first had to be in the leading crowd and, second, had to be a leader in activities. (See Figure 11–3.) The boys felt that being an athlete was the most important activity and being in the leading crowd was next in importance. (10, pp. 43, 47)

Since Coleman's study in the 1960s, efforts have been made to see if these criteria for popularity have changed. Is there less emphasis now on sports and more on academics in United States high schools? Are adolescents today less concerned about being in the leading crowd? The overall answer is that the criteria for popularity have not changed. The most recent comprehensive study was by Eitzen, who distributed questionnaires among random samples of sophomores, juniors, and seniors in each of nine high schools. (16) The schools were located in Kansas, Illinois, and Indiana, and, like those in Coleman's study, were selected because they differed in certain ways. He found that the relative ranks of the criteria for status had remained stable since Coleman's study. Figure 11–4 shows the average ranks given by boys to five criteria for popularity with other boys and for five criteria for popularity with girls. (16, p. 271)

Eitzen's results did, however, show considerable variations according to the size and type of school and community and the socioeconomic status of people in

Criteria for popularity with other girls

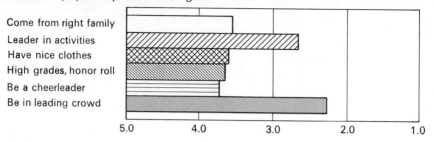

Criteria for popularity with boys

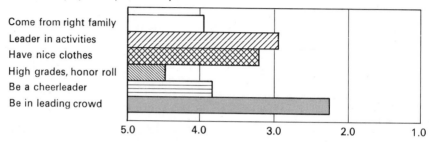

Figure 11–3.   Average ranks given by girls to six criteria for popularity with other girls and popularity with boys. (Redrawn with permission of Macmillan Publishing Co., Inc. from *The Adolescent Society*, p. 48, by J. S. Coleman. Copyright The Free Press, a Corporation, 1961.)

the communities. (16, p. 275) The strongest support for athletics existed in small rural communities, among sons of the undereducated, especially among students who were at the center of school activities, and in schools with a strict authority structure that encouraged sports. The weakest support for athletics was among affluent sons of college-educated fathers from large urban or suburban permissive schools. Even in these schools, however, athletics was still selected as the most important criterion for popularity, but to a lesser extent than in the other schools. As school unification and community growth continues, and if each generation becomes better educated, it is likely that the enthusiasm for sports as the dominant criterion for social status will diminish. (16, p. 275)

PERSONALITY AND SOCIAL SKILLS

The early studies by Coleman (10) and the more recent one by Eitzen (16) did not survey personal qualities and social skills as important criteria for popularity, yet these have been found to be very important in gaining social acceptance. (1, 3, 47, 53, 60, 71) Considerable evidence shows that personal qualities are the most important factors in popularity. One survey among 320 high school juniors from a midwestern community of 38,000 showed that personal qualities (including such factors as pleasing personality, good looks, and neatness) ranked first as the criterion for being a "big wheel" in the local high school. (71) Table 11–2 shows the results of the study. (71, p. 132)

Criteria for popularity with other boys

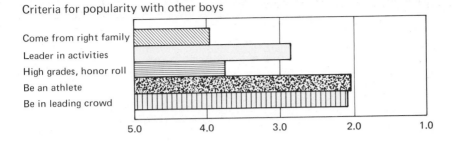

Criteria for popularity with girls

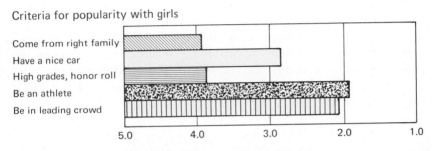

Figure 11–4.   Average ranks given by boys to five criteria for popularity with other boys and popularity with girls. (From D. S. Eitzen, "Athletics in the Status System of Male Adolescents: A Replication of Coleman's *The Adolescent Society*," *Adolescence* 10[1975]:267–276. Used by permission.)

As can be seen in the table, students felt that personal qualities and material possessions (money, car, clothes, parents have a nice house) ranked first and second in importance for prestige among peers. Significantly more girls than boys felt that personal qualities were very important for prestige. More boys than girls felt that activities-athletics was important. (71, p. 134) Other research also emphasizes the importance of personal qualities, including physical appearance, as a criterion of popularity. (1, 47) When a group of high school sophomore girls were asked to describe the characteristics of attractive boys, they listed the following characteristics (listed in decreasing order of importance): good personality, good looks, good physique, behavior of boy, sincerity and considerateness,

Table 11–2.   Percentage of students giving selected criteria as important for being a "big wheel" in their high school, by sex.

Criteria	Boys (N = 142)	Girls (N = 178)
Personal qualities	60.6	89.3
Material possessions	49.3	55.1
Activities-athletics	35.9	23.6
Academic achievement	21.8	25.8
"Right" friends	17.6	10.1

From E. E. Snyder, "High School Student Perceptions of Prestige Criteria," *Adolescence* 6 (1972): 132. Used by permission.

and dressing well. (60, p. 164) Commenting on the importance of physical appearance, one girl remarked:

Everybody says looks don't mean anything, but they do. I like dark hair because it seems more there. I like them taller than me—about six feet. An attractive boy has good looks. He can't be all scrawny. I like them taller than me and I like nice skin. (60, p. 163)

Other girls mentioned personality factors.

I used to go all by what their faces look like and their build. Now I notice personality. I know you have to know a guy to like him.

A person who is really nice, considerate—not rough and tough. One who is interested in what I am interested in—and caring. (60, p. 163)

Thus, one of the principal ways adolescents find group acceptance is by developing and exhibiting personal qualities that others admire and by learning social skills that assure acceptance. Table 11–3 gives a summary of personality traits youths like or dislike in one another. The summary is a composite of a number of studies. (1, 3, 10, 47, 60, 71)

In general, it can be seen that popular youths are accepted because of their personal appearance, sociability, and character. They are the neat, well-groomed, good-looking youths who are friendly, happy, fun-loving, outgoing, and energetic, have developed a high degree of social skills, and like to participate in many activities with others. They have a good reputation and exhibit qualities of moral character that most people admire. They are usually those with high self-esteem and positive self-concepts. (9)

Among the most unhappy adolescents are those who don't fit the stereotypes, especially in terms of physical appearance. Janis Ian sings about the dilemma of those who are not part of the social scene:

I learned the truth at seventeen
That love was meant for beauty queens
and high school girls with clear-skinned smiles
who married young, and then retired

The valentines I never knew
The Friday night charades of youth
were spent on one more beautiful
At seventeen I learned the truth

And those of us with ravaged faces
lacking in the social graces
desperately remained at home
inventing lovers on the 'phone
who called to say 'come dance with me'
and murmured vague obscenities
It isn't all it seems at seventeen.*

DEVIANCE

Until now, little has been said about achieving group acceptance through deviant behavior; that is, behavior different from that of the majority of youths (largely

* Janis Ian, "At Seventeen." Reprinted by permission of Mine Music Ltd. Copyright © 1974 by Mine Music.

Table 11–3. Personality traits liked or disliked.

Liked	Disliked
Personal Appearance	*Personal Appearance*
Good-looking	Homely, unattractive
Feminine, nice figure (girls)	Boyish figure, or too fat or skinny
Masculine, good build (boys)	(girls)
Neat, clean, well groomed	Sissy, skinny, fat (boys)
Appropriate clothes	Sloppy, dirty, unkempt
	Clothes out of style, don't fit, not
	appropriate, dirty
	Greaser (boys)
	Physical handicap
Social Behavior	*Social Behavior*
Outgoing, friendly	Shy, timid, withdrawn, quiet
Active, energetic	Lethargic, listless, passive
Participant in activities	Nonjoiner, recluse
Social skills: good manners,	Loud, boisterous, ill-mannered,
conversationalist, courteous,	disrespectful, braggart, show-off,
poised, natural, tactful, can dance,	not "cool," giggles, rude, crude,
play many games, sports	tongue-tied, doesn't know how to
Lots of fun, good sport	do or play anything
Acts age, mature	Real drip, poor sport
Good reputation	Childish, immature
	Bad reputation
Personal Qualities of Character	*Personal Qualities of Character*
Kind, sympathetic, understanding	Cruel, hostile, disinterested
Cooperative, gets along well, even	Quarrelsome, bully, bad-tempered,
tempered, stable	domineering, sorehead
Unselfish, generous, helpful	Inconsiderate, selfish, stingy
Cheerful, optimistic, happy	Pessimistic, complaining person
Responsible, dependable	Irresponsible, not reliable
Honest, truthful, fair	Liar, cheat, unfair
Good sense of humor	Can't take a joke, no sense of humor
High ideals	Dirty minded
Self-confident, self-accepting but	Conceited, vain
modest	

middle class) but considered acceptable in a particular group that itself deviates from the norms. Whereas overtly aggressive, hostile behavior may be unacceptable in society as a whole, it may be required in a ghetto gang as a condition of membership. Or what might be considered a bad reputation in the local high school (fighter, troublemaker, uncooperative, antisocial, sexually promiscuous, delinquent) might be a good reputation among a group of delinquents. One study of twelve- to sixteen-year-old boys who were overaggressive and bullies toward younger, weaker youths showed that the bullies enjoyed average popularity among other boys; (55) those who were the targets of aggression were far less popular than the bullies. These findings illustrate that standards of group behavior vary with different groups, so that popularity depends not so much on a fixed standard as on group conformity. Cleanliness, neatness, and smartness of dress is next to godliness in traditional middle class culture, but may be completely rejected by hippie society as "establishment" dress. There are those, therefore, who find acceptance by accepting deviance. But within the deviant group itself rigid standards of membership and acceptance may be enforced, which, if not upheld, automatically exclude one from that group.

One writer has suggested that sometimes peer groups are formed because of hostility to family authority and a desire to rebel against it. When this happens, the peer groups may become delinquent gangs, hostile to all established authority, yet supportive of the particular deviancy accepted by the group. (2, p. 60)

Heterosexuality

PSYCHOSEXUAL SOCIAL DEVELOPMENT

One of the most important social goals of midadolescence is to achieve heterosexuality. In the process of psychosexual social development, children pass through three stages.

Autosexuality—the early preschool period of development in which the child's chief pleasure and satisfaction is himself or herself. This is most typical of the two-year-old who wants to be in the company of others, but who plays alongside them, not with them. The adolescent who is still a "loner," who doesn't have any friends, is still in this preschool period of development.

Homosexuality—the primary school period of development in which the child's chief pleasure and satisfaction are in being with others of the same sex. Every normal child passes through this important stage of forming same-sex friendships. (54, p. 33) But adolescents who never get to know or feel comfortable with the opposite sex remain at this immature stage of psychosexual social development. From a psychoanalytic viewpoint, homosexuality before puberty is quite normal; after puberty it indicates arrested development. (18, p. 82)

It must be emphasized, however, that this is only one point of view, drawn from psychoanalytical, clinical experience. Even after puberty, some homosexual components remain in everyone (adults don't give up all same-sex friendships, for example). However, the majority of adolescents also develop heterosexual friendships.

Heterosexuality—the adolescent and adult stage of development in which the individual's pleasure and friendships are found with those of both sexes.

Getting acquainted and feeling at ease with the opposite sex is a painful process for some youths. Here are some typical questions which worry the adolescent becoming attracted to new relationships. (8; 66, pp. 28, 38)

• How do you go about talking to a girl?
• What do you do if you're chicken to ask a girl on a date?
• How can you attract the opposite sex?
• Does a girl wait for a boy to actually say he likes her? . . . . [my] trouble is that
    I feel I don't hit it off exactly right with them, I'm more a friend than a boy.
• Why are we so self-conscious when we meet new boys?
• Should you worry if you don't have dates right away?

• How can you get a boy to notice you and like you?
• Why is it that boys shy away from being introduced?

With sexual maturity comes a biological-emotional awareness of the opposite sex, a decline in hostile attitudes, and the beginning of emotional responses. The girl who was looked upon before as a sissy, giggly, pain-in-the-neck kid now takes on a new allure. On the one hand, the now-maturing male is fascinated and mystified by this young woman; on the other hand, he is awed, terrified, and bewildered. No wonder he ends up asking: "How do you go about talking to a girl?"

The boy's first effort is to tease by engaging in some sort of physical contact: swipe her books, pull her hair, hit her with a snowball. Her response is often a culturally conditioned, predictable one: scream, run (either away or after him), and pretend to be very upset. The boy is not very good at talking to girls, but he knows how to roughhouse, so he uses this time-honored method of making his first emotionally charged heterosexual contacts.

Gradually these initial contacts take on a more sophisticated form. Teasing is now kid stuff. To be "cool"—confident, poised, unemotional, a good conversationalist, comfortable and mannerly in social situations—is the order of the day. The group boy-girl relationships change into paired relationships, and these deepen into affectionate friendships and romance as the two sexes discover each other. Table 11–4 lists the usual stages of psychosexual development. (23, p. 26; 67)

EXPLORING HETEROSEXUAL ROLE ACCEPTANCE

Broderick and Rowe devised a scale for measuring preadolescént heterosexual development and tested it on a sample of 1,029 ten-, eleven-, and twelve-year-olds in Pennsylvania. (6) Retesting on a sample of 610 youths of the same age from Missouri showed the same results. (See Table 11–5.) Commenting on their study, Broderick and Rowe observe that recognition of the heterosexual nature of marriage is one of the most important concepts of the early years and that until this step is achieved, progress in relating to the opposite sex is inhibited. Once he or she has recognized the desirability of marriage someday, the indi-

Table 11–4.   Ages and stages in psychosexual social development.

Age	Stages
Infancy	Autosexual: Boy and girl interested only in themselves.
About ages 2–7	Seek companionship of other children regardless of sex.
About ages 8–12	Homosexual: Children prefer to play with others of same sex; some antagonism between sexes.
Ages 13–14	Girls and boys become interested in one another (heterosexual) with girls' interests developing first.
Ages 15–16	Some boys and girls pair off.
Ages 17–18	Majority of adolescents are dating; some, particularly girls, marry.

Table 11–5.   Guttman Scale analysis of five items on a social heterosexuality scale for Pennsylvania and Missouri boys and girls ten to twelve years of age.

Item	Positive Percentages			
	Penn. girls	*Mo. girls*	*Penn. boys*	*Mo. boys*
Want to marry	84	85	62	62
Have girlfriend/boyfriend	71	72	56	57
Have been in love	51	50	47	47
Prefer opposite sex for movies	39	35	39	34
Have had a date	22	11	24	19

Adapted from C. B. Broderick and G. P. Rowe, "A Scale Of Preadolescent Heterosexual Development," *Journal of Marriage and the Family* 30 (1968): 97–101. Used by permission.

vidual sooner or later begins to single out a member of the opposite sex and places him or her in the category of boyfriend or girlfriend. (6, p. 100)

Other studies have indicated that at an early age the boyfriend-girlfriend relationship may not be reciprocal and the object of affection may not be aware of the love affair. (4) (The author once knew a preadolescent boy who sold his girlfriend to another boy for 100 baseball cards, but the girl was never aware of the fact she had been a girlfriend in the first place.) With advancing age, however, expected and actual reciprocity begin to converge. Overall, the average age for choosing opposite-sex companionship has been declining, probably because of earlier sexual maturity as well as changing social customs.

ADOLESCENT LOVE AND CRUSHES

Along with the development of real or imagined reciprocal relationships comes the experience of "being in love." Falling in love serves a positive need in the lives of most people. College dating couples who report they are in love are also the ones who report the greatest happiness. (14) Young adolescents may have an intense crush on someone they really don't know and fantasize all sorts of romantic encounters with this person. The fewer actual romantic contacts, the more likely they are to develop an intense emotional crush and to fantasize the involvement. (5, p. 29) Often a crush is on an older person. It may even be a crush on an older person of the same sex. (49, p. 67) Therefore, imagining oneself in love with someone of the opposite sex serves a useful purpose: it motivates adolescents to seek heterosexual companionship. Finally, the desire for cross-sex companionship motivates them to the next big step: going out on a date. (6, p. 100)

Dating

Sociologists have been careful to emphasize that dating in American culture is not always equivalent to courtship, at least in the early and middle years of adolescence. In a recent study, a group of nondating eleven- and twelve-year-old boys and girls from a small city in the Midwest were asked: "What does dating

Table 11–6. What does dating mean to you?

Females	% Response	Males	% Response
To go out with opposite sex	58	To go out with opposite sex	35
To go out with special person (friend)	18	It's dumb, don't know	18
To go to a special place (party)	7	It's fun (recreation)	18
To go out for a special time span	6	To go out without parents	10
To get to know someone better	6	To go to a special place	9
It's "dumb," "gross," etc.; don't know	5	To get to know someone	9

Adapted from D. W. Jackson, "The Meaning of Dating from the Role Perspective of Non-Dating Pre-Adolescents," *Adolescence* 10 (1975): 124. Used by permission.

mean to you?" (35) The answers shown in Table 11–6 reflect the lack of maturity of the respondents. Only 6 percent of the girls and 9 percent of the boys thought dating was an opportunity for getting to know someone better; 10 percent of the boys thought of dating primarily as a means of going out without parents. (35, p. 124) Other studies with older adolescents reveal that most youths see dating primarily as a social experience rather than as a prelude to marriage. If dating isn't courtship, what are the primary purposes of dating in the eyes of adolescents? (32; 44, p. 52)

RECREATION. One major purpose is to have fun. Dating provides amusement; it is a form of recreation and source of enjoyment. It can be an end in itself. (48) One young woman commented:

It's the best. You just have more fun. You find more things to do. You have somebody to talk to. I love it. What would you do without boys? (60, p. 173)

COMPANIONSHIP WITHOUT THE RESPONSIBILITY OF MARRIAGE. Wanting to be with the opposite sex is a strong motive for dating. Wanting the friendship, acceptance, affection, and love of the opposite sex is a normal part of growing up. (60, p. 173) In one study, it was found that male college seniors preferred a female friend as their chief confidante and that one of the strong motivations for going together was to be able to share feelings and thoughts. (40) Another study emphasized that most students are able to develop closer social intimacy with someone of the opposite sex than they are with someone of their own sex. (59)

STATUS GRADING, SORTING, AND ACHIEVEMENT. (27, 76) Youths of higher socioeconomic levels date more frequently than do lower class youths, and they use dating partly to achieve, prove, or to maintain status. In his study of 739 adolescents, grades ten to twelve, Grinder pointed out that those who had the greatest number of friends were also most interested in dating and that membership in a clique was associated with the status-seeking aspects of dating. (24)

SOCIALIZATION. Dating is a means of personal and social growth. It is a way of learning to know, understand, and get along with many different types of people. Through dating, youths learn cooperation, consideration, responsibility, numerous social skills and matters of etiquette, and various techniques for interacting with other people. (48)

SEXUAL EXPERIMENTATION, SATISFACTION, OR EXPLOITATION. Recent studies have shown that dating has become more sex oriented as more adolescents have sexual intercourse. (50, 73, 78) Whether dating is used to have sex or sex develops out of dating depends upon the attitudes, feelings, motives, and values of the boy and girl. A boy who picks up a girl whom he does not know, especially if she is of a lower socioeconomic class than himself, may do so primarily for sexual exploitation. However, researchers are quick to point out that most dating is with those within one's social class, (29, 42) with sexual participation with such partners coming as an outgrowth of the total relationship. (50) In fact sexual intimacy is most likely to take place between dating partners who consider themselves social equals. Sexual behavior in this instance is usually not exploitative, although it depends upon how the boy and girl perceive and feel toward one another and on the sex values they have learned while growing up. Behavior varies tremendously from class to class and culture to culture. (63) Skipper and Nass did a study of the expectations of fifty college boys concerning the sexual permissiveness of college girls, working girls, and student nurses. (68) The results are shown in Table 11–7. The authors make it clear that the college boy's stereotype of the sexual permissiveness of student nurses creates a real dilemma for the nurse. If she is not cooperative, she does not meet expectations and is dropped by the boys. If she is cooperative, she builds a reputation and becomes fair game. Stereotyped expectations of her probably push her into being more permissive than she normally would be. (68) Other research suggests that both the male and female think that the other is more sexually permissive in expectations than he or she actually is and that this expectation results in more permissiveness. (11)

MATE SORTING AND SELECTION. Whether this is a conscious motive or not, it is eventually what happens, especially among older youths with prior dating experience.(48) The longer a couple dates, the less they tend to overidealize each other and the greater their chances of really knowing each other. (52, p. 621)

Table 11–7.   College boys' expectations of the sexual permissiveness of college girls, working girls, and student nurses during casual dating, in percentages.

Group	Very Permissive	Average Permissiveness	Not Very Permissive
College girls	8	40	52
Working girls	10	46	44
Student nurses	38	44	18

Adapted from J. F. Skipper and G. Nass, "Dating Behavior: A Framework for Analysis and an Illustration." *Journal of Marriage and the Family* 28 (1966): 412–420. Used by permission.

Also, dating provides an opportunity for two people to become a pair. (45, p. 16) If the boy and girl are similar in personality characteristics, they are more likely to develop a compatible relationship than if they are dissimilar in physical attractiveness and psychological and social characteristics. (75)

ACHIEVING INTIMACY. Erikson has suggested that the development of intimacy is the primary psychosocial task of the young adult. (17) By intimacy, Erikson meant the development of openness, sharing, mutual trust, respect, affection, and loyalty, so that a relationship with the opposite sex could be characterized as close, enduring, and involving love and commitment. (56, p. 74) A study of dating among Harvard males showed that "finding a female friend" was listed as the most important motive for dating and that "sitting around the room talking" was the preferred private activity on dates. (79) Interest in dating simply as a form of recreation had declined since a similar study in 1964. Dating as a means of enhancing reputation was listed as the least important motive; dating as a means of finding a wife was the next-to-last motive. These findings indicate an intense desire to develop close, intimate relationships through the dating experience. Consequently, being a good conversationalist (along with attractiveness) was listed as the number one requirement of a dating partner. (79)

The capacity to develop intimacy varies from person to person. Usually, females find it easier than males to talk about intimate things. One study of college students showed significant differences in the level of intimate disclosure. (39) The level of freshman males to males was low; of freshman males to females and senior males to males, moderate; and of senior males to females and females of either age to friends of either sex, high. (39, p. 815)

Some adolescents establish only superficial relationships with friends. (56, p. 85) Others remain isolated, withdrawn, and self-preoccupied, never developing close peer relationships. Others are self-aware, sensitive individuals who communicate openly and deeply with friends. They are sensitive to the innermost thoughts and feelings of their partner and are willing through self-disclosure to share personal information, private thoughts, and feelings. (64) Therefore, heterosexual relationships vary greatly in the depth of communication and intensity of feelings in the relationship. (56, p. 86) Dating can provide the opportunity for close relationships, but whether or not real intimacy develops varies with individuals and with different pairs. Dating can remain quite superficial. (32) Under such conditions, it is not as helpful a means of mate selection or of marriage preparation as it otherwise might be.

One helpful description of intimacy development was made by Orlofsky, who studied the intimacy statuses of junior and senior males at the State University of New York at Buffalo. (57) Orlofsky divides the men into five groups:

Isolates—withdraw from social situations and lack personal relationships with peers except for a few casual acquaintances. They participate in few extracurricular activities, are not very popular, and do not begin to date until two or more years later than students in other statuses. They rationalize by saying they prefer work and studies, which doesn't give them much time for interpersonal involvement.

Pseudointimates—enter into somewhat premature, security-motivated heterosexual love relationships that lack closeness and depth and are without much shared feeling.

Stereotyped Relationships—relationships with either male or female friends that are characterized by superficiality and by a low degree of personal communication and closeness. Relationships with girls are either formal and stiff or are characterized by sexual conquest. In neither case is the girl treated as a whole person. Like isolates, they begin dating late, but they maintain and enjoy relationships.

Preintimates—have not entered into an enduring love relationship, are ambivalent about commitment, and try to develop "pure" love relationships devoid of ties and obligations. Given time and maturity, they may form intimate relationships.

Intimates—form deep relationships with male and female friends and are involved in an enduring, committed love relationship with a girlfriend or wife.

AGE PATTERNS FOR DATING

The median age at which youths begin dating has decreased by almost three years since World War I. In 1924 the median age for girls beginning to date was sixteen years. (70) In 1958 it was 13.3 and in 1968, 13.2. (3) A recent study of dating practices among tenth-, eleventh-, and twelfth-grade black and white adolescents in a northeast Texas community showed that the mean age for the first date had remained relatively stable for whites for a decade: 13.59 years in 1964 and 13.88 years in 1974. However, the mean age of first date had decreased for blacks: from 14.91 years in 1964 to 13.93 in 1974. (15, p. 603) Socioeconomic status also has an influence on the age at which youths begin to date,

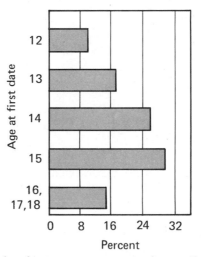

Figure 11–5. Frequency distribution in percentages of age at first date. (Adapted from S. L. Hansen, "Dating Choices of High School Students," *The Family Coordinator* 26[April 1977]:134. Copyrighted 1977 by the National Council on Family Relations. Used by permission.)

with those families of high education and socioeconomic status starting to date earlier. (68) Figure 11–5 shows the percentage of black and white youths who begin dating at each level according to a study of Florida high school youths, ages fifteen to nineteen. (25, p. 134)

NUMBER OF DATING PARTNERS

Usually the number of dating partners increases up to about the twelfth grade, after which the total number of partners declines. A recent Florida study (1977) at the high school level indicated that at any given time about one-third of the students were dating only one person (a little over one-fourth of all students were going steady with one person), about one-third were random dating or dating two or three people, and about one-third never or almost never dated. (25, p. 134)

DATING FREQUENCY

How often do youths date? As indicated, frequency varies with age, socioeconomic factors, sex, maturity level, and certainly with local customs. One study at the college level indicated that females dated considerably more than males: only 22 percent of males dated two or more times a week, compared with 62 percent of females. Most of the girls preferred dating older boys, whom they considered more sophisticated than younger ones. Those who dated most frequently also rated highest on dating adjustment and were most often involved in a committed relationship. (28) The study of high school students from a Florida community indicated that over half the youths dated at least once a week. (25, p. 134) (See Table 11–8.)

ACTIVITY ON DATES

The study in the northeast Texas community showed that going to the movies and driving around were the most popular activities on dates. (15, p. 605) Dancing was a popular activity among blacks, but not among whites. A greater percentage of whites than blacks went to parties and bowling. When asked if they

Table 11–8. Frequency distribution (in percentages) of dating among high school students in a Florida community, 1977.

Frequency of Dates	% of Students (N = 354)
Do not date	12.2
Date occasionally	36.1
One date a week	20.5
Two to three dates a week	20.2
Three or more dates a week	11.1

Adapted from S. L. Hansen, "Dating Choices of High School Students." *Family Coordinator* 26 (April 1977): 133–138. Copyrighted 1977 by the National Council on Family Relations. Reprinted by permission.

"parked" on dates, 78 percent of the whites and 76 percent of the blacks replied in the affirmative. (15, p. 605)

GOING STEADY

For many adults, particularly parents, going steady is equivalent to committing an unforgivable sin. As a result, steady dating probably receives more attention than any other aspect of dating, except perhaps sex and dating behavior. How widespread is going steady? Is it harmful or useful? Why do youths do it, often in spite of contrary pressures from their parents and leaders?

Because one of the worries of parents is that youths will make premature commitments, they urge their offspring to play the field and to date a large number of partners. Research indicates, however, that those who date the greatest number of partners also have the greatest number of different steady relationships; the larger the number of casual partners, the greater the chances of going steady with them. Because marital success is positively correlated with the number of friends of both sexes one has before marriage, youths ought to go with large numbers of partners even though their chances of going steady with any one are greater. Steady dating for a long period can limit the number of dating partners, and a community that accepts steady dating as the norm for the group makes it harder for youths to avoid the pattern. In some cases they either have to go steady or not date at all. (76, p. 96)

A study of going steady was conducted by Thomas Poffenberger among 1,232 eleventh- and twelfth-grade students from one Nevada and eight California schools. The schools were in large, medium, and small towns; the students were from a wide range of social classes. A summary of the most significant findings follows. (61)

1. Forty-two percent of the boys and 25 percent of the girls had never gone steady.
2. Twenty-seven percent of the boys and 30 percent of the girls were going steady at the time of the study.
3. Of those who had gone steady, 39 percent of the boys and 44 percent of the girls had gone steady with three or more different people.
4. Of those who had gone steady, 40 percent of the boys and 28 percent of the girls never went steady longer than six months, but 28 percent of the boys and 48 percent of the girls had gone steady for over a year.
5. While going steady, 65 percent of the boys and 60 percent of the girls went out with their steady three or more nights a week. Fifteen percent of the boys and 20 percent of the girls went out five to seven nights a week.
6. Parental attitudes had considerable influence on whether the adolescent went steady or not. Of those going steady at the time of the study, 84 percent of the boys' parents and 75 percent of the girls' parents approved, but of those not going steady, only 53 percent of the boys' parents and 33 percent of the girls' parents would have approved.
7. Of those going steady, over 40 percent of the boys and over 50 percent of the girls said they planned to marry their steady.

This study indicates that for those who are going steady, the relationship is an intense, sometimes marriage-oriented one. The younger the adolescents are, however, the less likely the relationship is to be marriage oriented. (51, p. 57) The primary motive seems to be able to enjoy the company of someone the individual enjoys.

Going steady has both advantages and disadvantages. (81, p. 65) Steady dating provides dating security for some adolescents, although this is not a primary motive for most. (81, p. 63) Low self-esteem youths who are not as socially popular more often go steady than do high self-esteem, popular youths. (38) Apparently they do so because they need to, emotionally and socially. They try to find someone to love and be loved by, who understands and sympathizes. This is a tremendous need of the low self-esteem adolescent. The bashful adolescent also finds it easier to continue with the same person than to meet new ones. Udry (76) feels that steady dating imposes more sexual controls and a greater responsibility on males than does random dating, and from this standpoint is an advantage. However, he does say that females are more likely to become sexually involved. (76, p. 97)

The disadvantages are many. Some youths feel "it's a drag," that they have more fun with different people. One girl said, "Instead of going steady, I wound up staying home steady. Ted didn't take me out." Some youths are not mature enough emotionally to handle such an intimate relationship and the problems that arise. And breaking up leads to hurt feelings. One boy asked: "How can I ditch Kathy without hurting her feelings?" This is a frequent remark from youths who are involved but who don't know how to get uninvolved. The problem of jealousy often arises. Boys tend to be jealous over sexual issues; girls complain of lack of time and attention. (74) The basic problem may be that neither person is ready for an intense, intimate relationship with one person over a long period of time. Most youths admit that steady dating becomes a license for increasing sexual intimacy. "You get to feeling married, and that's dangerous" is the way one adolescent expressed it. Others feel that going steady adds respectability to petting or even to intercourse, and that this is an advantage rather than a disadvantage. Research indicates that those within a particular socioeconomic class who date the most frequently, and who begin at the earliest ages, are more likely to get married early as well; therefore, whenever steady dating pushes youths prematurely into early marriage, it is a serious disadvantage. (61) (See Chapter 15 on early marriage.)

Conclusions

This chapter has discussed five important psychosocial tasks at adolescence that relate to social development:

1. The need to establish close, emotional attachments with a friend or friends as a replacement for attachments to parents. This is why best friends are needed with whom one can be really close.
2. The need to broaden friendships. Young adolescents need a lot of friends as symbols of popularity. The older adolescents get, the more selective they are in choosing friends. They don't need a large number, but they need good friends.

3. The need for group acceptance and membership. This is one reason for the large numbers of adolescent club and social groups. Some adolescents who are not accepted in socially approved groups seek out deviant groups, some of which are undesirable from an adult viewpoint. Yet, if adolescents are not accepted in approved groups, they need to find acceptance somewhere. The problem is how to help them find acceptance in socially approved ways.
4. The need to become heterosexual and learn to know and feel comfortable with the opposite sex.
5. The need to develop dating patterns and skills that contribute to personal enhancement, social development, and successful marriage. In spite of the fact that much dating among adolescents (especially younger adolescents) is not marriage oriented, dating is the principal system of mate-sorting in Western culture. The modern trend has been toward earlier dating, with fewer partners. This has led to earlier marriage because the sophistication process toward adulthood is speeded up. (See Chapter 15.) This does not mean that the two sexes ought to be kept segregated as long as possible (as some parents and other adults try to do), but that adolescents need to be encouraged to develop many friendships, to make early dating fun oriented rather than marriage oriented, and to discover the personal and social benefits of heterosexual social contacts that emphasize friendship rather than romance and early marriage. It is a real advantage for boys and girls to be brought up together, knowing one another as people, before they become love objects.

Adolescents who are social isolates, who haven't found group acceptance, ought to be of more concern to parents and youth leaders. Some parents are glad their children don't date; this seems unfair and unrealistic. Family, neighborhood, and school social events can be planned to help adolescents who are having difficulty with one of the most important adjustments in life: learning to know and relate to other human beings.

Panel Discussion

Invite a group of high school age youths to the class to form a panel. Local high school guidance counselors are usually willing to recruit the students. Try to get an equal number of males and females, representing different class levels, high school programs, and socioeconomic groups. Thus, a panel of six might include two students (a boy and a girl) from the college preparatory program, two from the vocational or commercial program, and two from the general high school program. Grades nine through twelve should be represented. Ask the guidance counselor to select two students from the "leading crowd" and others from other social groups and cliques. Different races and/or ethnic groups might also be represented if the school is multiracial or multiethnic.

The purpose of the panel is to allow class members an opportunity to learn about adolescents by asking them questions in front of the whole class. Announce to the class the discussion topic is "Social Relationships and Dating" and that all questions ought to be related to this subject. Other topics could be dealt with in subsequent discussions.

Class members should ask questions directly of the adolescent panel members, who need to respond so that all students can hear. (If the classroom is a large one, a microphone and amplifier system may be needed.) The instructor or a regular member of the class can act as moderator. After panel members leave, it is helpful if the instructor leads a class discussion to determine what the students have learned and to summarize some of the more important things that were said.

Bibliography

1. Allen, C. D., and Eicher, J. B. "Adolescent Girls' Acceptance and Rejection Based on Appearance." *Adolescence* 8 (1973): 125–138.

2. Bensman, J., and Liliesfield, R. "Friendship and Alienation." *Psychology Today* (October 1979): 56ff.

3. Berg, D. H. "Sexual Subcultures and Contemporary Heterosexual Interaction Patterns among Adolescents." *Adolescence* 10 (1975): 543–548.

4. Broderick, C. B. "Socio-Sexual Development in a Suburban Community." *Journal of Sex Research* 2 (1966): 1–24.

5. ———. "Normal Sociosexual Development." In *The Individual, Sex, and Society*. Edited by C. B. Bernard and J. Bernard. Baltimore: Johns Hopkins University Press, 1969, pp. 23–40.

6. Broderick, C. B., and Rowe, G. P. "A Scale of Preadolescent Heterosexual Development." *Journal of Marriage and the Family* 30 (1968): 97–101.

7. Bronfenbrenner, U. *Two Worlds of Childhood: U.S. and U.S.S.R.* New York: Russell Sage Foundation, 1970.

8. Byler, R. V., ed. *Teach Us What We Want to Know.* New York: Mental Health Materials Center, 1969.

9. Chambliss, J. et al. "Relationships between Self-Concept, Self-Esteem, Popularity, and Social Judgments of Junior High School Students." *Journal of Psychology* 98 (January 1978): 91–98.

10. Coleman, J. S. *The Adolescent Society.* New York: Free Press of Glencoe, 1961.

11. Collins, J. K. "Adolescent Dating Intimacy: Norms and Peer Expectations." *Journal of Youth and Adolescence* 3 (1974): 317–328.

12. Costanzo, P. R. "Conformity Development as a Function of Self-blame." *Journal of Personality and Social Psychology* 14 (1970): 366–374.

13. Costanzo, P. R., and Shaw, M. E. "Conformity as a Function of Age Level." *Child Development* 37 (1966): 967–975.

14. Critelli, J. W. "Romantic Attraction and Happiness." *Psychological Reports* 41 (December 1977): 721–722.

15. Dickinson, G. E. "Dating Behavior of Black and White Adolescents before and after Desegregation." *Journal of Marriage and the Family* 37 (1975): 602–608.

16. Eitzen, D. S. "Athletics in the Status System of Male Adolescents: A Replication of Coleman's *The Adolescent Society.*" *Adolescence* 10 (1975): 267–276.

17. Erikson, E. *Identity: Youth and Crisis.* New York: W. W. Norton & Co., 1968.

18. Feibleman, J. K. "The Philosophy of Adolescence." In *Adolescence: Studies in Development.* Edited by Z. M. Cantwell and P. N. Svajian. Itasca, Ill.: F. E. Peacock Publishers, 1974, pp. 75–98.

19. Feldman, R. A. "Normative Integration, Alienation, and Conformity in Adolescent Groups." *Adolescence* 12 (1972): 327–341.

20. Floyd, H. H., Jr., and South, D. R. "Dilemma of Youth: The Choice of Parents or Peers as a Frame of Reference for Behavior." *Journal of Marriage and the Family* 34 (1972): 627–634.

21. Frank, Anne. *The Diary of a Young Girl.* New York: Modern Library, 1952.

22. Gallatin, J. E. *Adolescence and Individuality.* New York: Harper and Row, 1975.

23. Gordon, C. "Social Characteristics of Early Adolescence." In *Twelve to Sixteen: Early Adolescence.* Edited by Jerome Kagan and Robert Coles. New York: W. W. Norton & Co., 1972, pp. 25–54.

24. Grinder, R. E. "Relations of Social Dating Attractions to Academic Orientation and Peer Relations." *Journal of Educational Psychology* 57 (1966): 27–34.

25. Hansen, S. L. "Dating Choices of High School Students." *Family Coordinator* 26 (April 1977): 133–138.

26. Hartup, W. "Peer Interaction and Social Organization." In *Carmichael's Manual of Child Psychology,* vol. 1. 3d ed. Edited by P. H. Mussen. New York: John Wiley and Sons, 1970, pp. 361–456.

27. Herold, E. S. "Stages of Date Selection: A Reconciliation of Divergent Findings on Campus Values in Dating." *Adolescence* 9 (1974): 113–120.

28. Herold, E. S. "Variables Influencing the Dating Adjustment of University Students." *Journal of Youth and Adolescence* 8 (March 1979): 73–79.

29. Hollingshead, A. B. *Elmtown's Youth and Elmtown Revisited.* New York: John Wiley and Sons, 1975.

30. Horrocks, J. E., and Weinberg, S. A. "Psychological Needs and Their Development during Adolescence." *Journal of Psychology* 74 (1970): 51–69.

31. Hurlock, E. B. *Developmental Psychology.* 4th ed. New York: McGraw-Hill, 1975.

32. Husbands, C. T. "Some Social and Psychological Consequences of the Amer-

ican Dating System." *Adolescence* 5 (1970): 451–462.

33. Iacovetta, R. G. "Adolescent-Adult Interaction and Peer-Group Involvement." *Adolescence* 10 (1975): 327–336.

34. Ian, J. "At Seventeen." Copyright © 1974 by Mine Musı .

35. Jackson, D. W. "The Meaning of Dating from the Role Perspective of Non-Dating Pre-Adolescents." *Adolescence* 10 (1975): 123–126.

36. Kandel, D. B. "Homophily, Selection, and Socialization in Adolescent Friendships." *American Journal of Sociology* 84 (September 1978): 427–436.

37. Kandel, D. B., and Lesser, G. S. *Youth in Two Worlds.* San Francisco: Jossey-Bass, 1972.

38. Klemer, R. H. "Self-Esteem and College Dating Experience as Factors in Mate Selection and Marital Happiness: A Longitudinal Study." *Journal of Marriage and the Family* 33 (1971): 183–187.

39. Klos, D. S., and Loomis, D. F. "A Rating Scale of Intimate Disclosure between Late Adolescents and Their Friends." *Psychological Reports* 42 (June 1978): 815–820.

40. Komarovsky, M. "Patterns of Self-Disclosure of Male Undergraduates." *Journal of Marriage and the Family* 36 (November 1974): 677–686.

41. Konopka, G. *The Adolescent Girl in Conflict.* Englewood Cliffs, N.J.: Prentice-Hall, 1966.

42. Krain, M. et al. "Rating-Dating or Simply Prestige Homogamy? Data on Dating in the Greek System on a Midwestern Campus." *Journal of Marriage and the Family* 39 (November 1977): 663–674.

43. Larson, L. E. "The Relative Influence of Parent-Adolescent Affect in Predicting the Salience Hierarchy among Youth." Paper presented at the annual meeting of the National Council on Family Relations, Chicago, October 1970.

44. ———. "The Influence of Parents and Peers during Adolescence: The Situation Hypothesis Revisited." *Journal of Marriage and the Family* 34 (1972): 67–74.

45. Lewis, R. A. "A Longitudinal Test of a Developmental Framework for Premarital Dyadic Formation." *Journal of Marriage and the Family* 35 (1973): 16–25.

46. Mahoney, E. R. "Subjective Physical Attractiveness and Self-Other Orientations." *Psychological Reports* 43 (August 1978): 277–278.

47. Mathes, E. W. "The Effects of Physical Attractiveness and Anxiety on Heterosexual Attraction over a Series of Five Encounters." *Journal of Marriage and the Family* 37 (1975): 769–773.

48. McDaniel, C. O. "Dating Roles and Reasons for Dating." *Journal of Marriage and the Family* 31 (1969): 97–107.

49. Miller, D. *Adolescence: Psychology, Psychopathology, and Psychotherapy.* New York: Jason Aronson, 1974.

50. Mirande, A. M., and Hammer, E. L. "Premarital Sexual Permissiveness: A Research Note." *Journal of Marriage and the Family* 36 (1974): 356–358.

51. Moss, J. J. et al. "The Premarital Dyad during the Sixties." *Journal of Marriage and the Family* 33 (1971): 50–69.

52. Murstein, B. I. "Person Perception and Courtship Progress among Premarital Couples." *Journal of Marriage and the Family* 34 (1972): 621–626.

53. Newman, P. R., and Newman, B. M. "Early Adolescence and Its Conflict: Group Identity versus Alienation." *Adolescence* 11 (1976): 261–274.

54. Offer, D., and Offer, J. "Four Issues in the Developmental Psychology of Adolescents." In *Modern Perspectives in Adolescent Psychiatry.* Edited by J. G. Howells. New York: Brunner/Mazel, 1971, pp. 28–44.

55. Olweus, D. "Aggression and Peer Acceptance in Adolescent Boys: Two Short-Term Longitudinal Studies of Ratings." *Child Development* 48 (December 1977): 1301–1313.

56. Orlofsky, J. L. "Intimacy Status: Relationship to Interpersonal Perception." *Journal of Youth and Adolescence* 5 (1976): 73–88.

57. ———. "The Relationship between Intimacy Status and Antecedent Personality Components." *Adolescence* 13 (Fall 1978): 419–441.

58. Parlee, M. B. "The Friendship Bond." *Psychology Today* (October 1979): 43ff.

59. Peretti, P. O. "Closest Friendships of Black College Students: Social Intimacy." *Adolescence* 11 (Fall 1976): 395–403.

60. Place, D. M. "The Dating Experience for Adolescent Girls." *Adolescence* 10 (1975): 157–174.

61. Poffenberger, T. "Three Papers on Going Steady." *Family Life Coordinator* 13 (1964): 7–13.

62. Purnell, R. F. "Socioeconomic Status and Sex Differences in Adolescent Reference-Group Orientation." *Journal of Genetic Psychology* 116 (1970): 233–239.

63. Reiss, Ira I. *The Family System in America.* New York: Holt, Rinehart and Winston, 1971, pp. 151–181.

64. Rivenbark, W. H. "Self-disclosure Patterns among Adolescents." *Psychological Reprints* 28 (1971): 35–42.

65. Rubin, Z. "Seeking a Cure for Loneliness." *Psychology Today* (October 1979).

66. Schultz, E. D., and Williams, S. R. *Family Life and Sex Education: Curriculum and Instruction.* New York: Harcourt, Brace and World, 1969.

67. Selman, R. L., and Selman, A. P. "Children's Ideas about Friendships: A New Theory." *Psychology Today* (October 1979): 71ff.

68. Skipper, J. K., and Nass, G. "Dating Behavior: A Framework for Analysis and an Illustration." *Journal of Marriage and the Family* 28 (1966): 412–420.

69. Skorepa, C. A.; Horrocks, J. E.; and Thompson, C. G. "A Study of Friendship Fluctuations of College Students." *Journal of Genetic Psychology* 102 (1963): 151–157.

70. Smith, G. F. "Certain Aspects of the Sex Life of the Adolescent Girl." *Journal of Applied Psychology* 8 (1924): 347–349.

71. Snyder, E. E. "High School Student Perceptions of Prestige Criteria." *Adolescence* 6 (1972): 129–136.

72. Sones, G., and Feshbach, N. "Sex Differences in Adolescent Reactions toward Newcomers." *Developmental Psychology* 4 (1971): 381–386.

73. Sorensen, R. C. *Adolescent Sexuality in Contemporary America: Personal Values and Sexual Behavior, Ages 13–19.* New York: World Publishing Co., 1973.

74. Teismann, M. W., and Mosher, D. L. "Jealous Conflict in Dating Couples." *Psychological Reports* 42 (June 1978): 1211–1216.

75. Till, A., and Freedman, E. M. "Complementarity versus Similarity of Traits Operating in the Choice of Marriage and Dating Partners." *Journal of Social Psychology* 105 (June 1978): 147–148.

76. Udry, J. R. *The Social Context of Marriage.* 2d ed. Philadelphia: J. B. Lippincott Co., 1971.

77. Van der Veen, F., and Haberland, H. W. "Family Satisfaction and the Consequence of Family Concepts among Adolescents and their Parents." *Proceedings,* 79th Annual Convention, American Psychological Association, 1971.

78. Vener, A. M., and Steward, C. S. "Adolescent and Sexual Behavior in Middle America Revisited: 1970–1973." *Journal of Marriage and the Family* 36 (1974): 728–735.

79. Vreeland, R. S. "Is It True What They Say about Harvard Boys?" *Psychology Today* 5 (1972): 65–68.

80. Walster, E. et al. "Equity and Premarital Sex." *Journal of Personality and Social Psychology* 36 (January 1978): 82–92.

81. Wittman, J. S. "Dating Patterns of Rural and Urban Kentucky Teenagers." *Family Coordinator* 20 (1971): 63–66.

82. Yost, E. D., and Adamek, R. J. "Parent-Child Interaction and Changing Family Values: A Multivariate Analysis." *Journal of Marriage and the Family* 36 (1974): 115–121.

Sexuality and Sex Roles

Outline

One of the most important considerations in any discussion of adolescent sexuality is the concept of masculinity and femininity. This chaper begins with a discussion of biological determinants of gender, and then goes on to discuss environmental influences. Theories of sex-role development are explained and changing concepts of masculinity and femininity examined.

Gender Determination

GENETIC BASES

The development of gender is both genetically and hormonally determined. (50, 54, 55, 56) This biological influence is well known. The fetus becomes a male or female depending upon whether it has XY or XX sex chromosomes and on the balance between the male and female sex hormones in the bloodstream. Occasionally nature makes a mistake: the male gets an extra X (female) chromosome (labeled XXY, Klinefelter's syndrome), so a "man" is produced with a distinctly feminine appearance and with small testicles that are incapable of producing sperm. (35, p. 265) Sometimes a female is born with one of the X choromosomes missing (labeled XO, Turner's syndrome), so that her external sex organs are poorly developed and infantile in size and her ovaries are missing. (51) To what extent then can she be labeled a woman? Genetically speaking she is only part woman. Until about six weeks of development, it is not possible to tell whether the growing fetus will be a boy or girl, for they have identical equipment prior to this time.

HORMONAL INFLUENCES

Hermaphroditism is the condition in which an individual has the gonads of both sexes: that is, has both testes and ovaries. True hermaphroditism is very rare, with only about one hundred cases reported worldwide. (35, p. 439) *Pseudohermaphroditism* is much more common, occuring in about 1 out of every 1,000 infants. In this disorder, the male may have rudimentary testes, but his external genitals are not fully developed or are feminine in appearance. This is caused by a deficiency of male hormones as the male child develops. The female hermaphrodite has ovaries, though usually incompletely developed, but her external genitals and other bodily characteristics are male to a greater or lesser degree. (35, p. 440) This condition results from an excess of male hormones in her bloodstream as she develops into womanhood.

It is obvious that hormones have a definite influence on physical characteristics. Male hormones can be administered to a woman, encouraging the growth of the beard, body hair, the clitoris, and the development of masculine muscles,

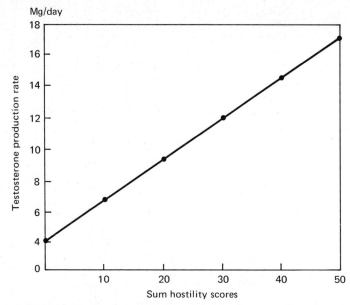

Figure 12–1. The relationship between the rate of production of testosterone and hostility scores in eighteen men between seventeen and twenty-eight years of age. (Adapted from H. Persky, K. D. Smith, and G. K. Basu, "Relation of Psychologic Measures of Aggression and Hostility to Testosterone Production in Man," *Psychosomatic Medicine* 33[1971]:265–277. Used by permission.)

build, and strength. Similarly, female hormones can be administered to a man, encouraging breast development and other female traits. Physical femaleness or maleness is thus somewhat tenuous and may be partially altered.

Hormones alter physical characteristics, but do they influence sex-typed behavior? The most that can be said is that *after birth, hormonal changes usually only accentuate or minimize certain masculine-feminine characteristics already in evidence. The hormones do not change the basic sexuality of the person. In adults, male hormones seem to exert more influence on males, and female hormones on females.* Thus, whereas administration of the male hormone, testosterone, will slightly increase the level of aggression in a younger adult male, it will not have the same effect on the female. (45) If testosterone is administered to adult females, their physical appearance changes but their behavior is affected very little. In fact, in some adult females, testosterone inhibits aggression and causes hyperfeminization. (45)

Recent studies have shown, however, a direct relationship between the rate of production of testosterone and measures of aggression and hostility among normal adult males. (See Figure 12–1.) Interestingly, this relationship did not hold true for men over thirty years of age. This means that some of the variance in adolescent behavior and some of the turbulence of this period may be accounted for by the effect of the rapid increase in the secretion of testosterone at puberty. However, changes in hormonal levels in older adult males do not have a marked effect on behavior.

Environmental Influences

MASCULINITY AND FEMININITY

But biological influence is only part of the picture; environment also plays an important role. Certain qualities of maleness are defined and become "masculine," not only because of heredity but also in the way society prescribes that a male ought to be a man. Society prescribes how a male ought to look and behave, what type of personality he ought to have, and the roles he should perform. Similarly, a female is created not only by genetic conception, but also by those psychosocial forces that mold and influence her personality. (28) Masculinity and femininity refer to those qualities of personality characteristic of man or woman. When one speaks of a masculine man, that person is expressing a value judgment based upon an assessment of the personality and behavior characteristics of the male according to culturally defined standards of "maleness." Similarly, a feminine woman is labeled according to culturally determined criteria for "femaleness." In this sense, the development of masculinity or femininity is education in human sexuality: in what it means to be a man or a woman, or in what it means to be sexual, within the context of the culture in which one lives. (15)

Concepts of masculinity and femininity vary with different human societies and cultures. Margaret Mead, in studying three primitive tribes, discovered some interesting differences. (61) Arapesh men and women both displayed "feminine" personality traits. Both male and female were trained to be cooperative, unaggressive, and responsive to the needs and demands of others. In contrast, both Mundugumor men and women developed "masculine" traits: ruthless, aggressive, positively sexed, with maternal cherishing aspects of personality at a minimum. In the third tribe, the Tchambuli, the sex attitudes and roles prescribed by American culture were reversed: the woman was dominant, impersonal; the man was less responsible and emotionally dependent. (38)

Concepts of masculinity and femininity have undergone considerable changes in the United States. In the days of George Washington, a "true man," especially a gentleman, could wear hose, a powdered wig, and a lace shirt without being considered unmanly; today he would be considered quite feminine or "gay." Thus, the judgments made about masculinity or the extent of "manliness" are subjective judgments based upon the accepted standards of "maleness" as defined by the culture. These standards vary from culture to culture, or with different periods of history in the same society.

THEORIES OF SEX-ROLE DEVELOPMENT

Because environment plays such an important role in the establishment of the criteria for masculinity and femininity and in development of maleness or femaleness, it is important to understand how this development takes place. There are three major theories explaining how sex-role behavior is learned: cognitive developmental theory, social learning theory, and parental identification theory. Each of these will be discussed in detail.

COGNITIVE DEVELOPMENTAL THEORY

The cognitive developmental theory suggests that sex-role identity has its beginning in the gender that is cognitively assigned to the child at birth and that is subsequently accepted by him or her while growing up. At the time of birth, gender assignment is made largely on the basis of genital examination. The child from that point on is considered a boy or a girl. As has been seen, if genital abnormalities are present, this gender assignment may prove to be erroneous if it is not in agreement with the sex chromosomes and gonads that are present. However, even if it is erroneous, Money has pointed out that sex identification usually follows the sex in which the child is reared. (41, p. 15) This is true despite ambiguities in physical sexual characteristics. If a hermaphrodite is assigned one sex at birth, he or she will grow up to be that sex even though it may later be discovered that the original assignment was wrong. If sex reassignment is to be successful, it should be done before age eighteen months. (41, p. 15) A child given sex reassignment after eighteen months of age may never differentiate the new gender identity sufficiently to completely accept it. (41, p. 16)

It is important that gender identity be consistent and unambiguous. Money reports an example of a hermaphrodite child, first registered as a boy, whose name was later changed to a girl's without the change's being recorded on the birth certificate and without the masculinized external genitalia's being surgically corrected. The parents were thus indicating that they had no real conviction that their child was a daughter instead of a son, and they were transmitting ambiguous gender expectancies to their child. Under such circumstances it was inevitable that the child grow up ambiguous as to gender. If the parents had been unequivocal in their rearing of the child as a girl, the chances are high that the child would have differentiated a girl's identity. (41, p. 16)

The cognitive assignment of gender influences everything that happens thereafter. Kohlberg, the chief exponent of this view, emphasized that the child's self-categorization (as a boy or girl) is the basic organizer of the sex-role attitudes that develop. (29) The child who recognizes that he is a male begins to value maleness and to act consistently with gender expectations. He begins to structure his own experience according to his accepted gender and to act out appropriate sex roles. (57, p. 171) He reflects sex-role differences if he fantasizes himself as a daddy with a wife and children, just as a girl does who pretends she is a grown-up woman with breasts, lipstick, a job, and children to take care of. Sex differentiation takes place gradually as children learn to be male or female according to culturally established sex-role expectations and their interpretations of them.

It is important to emphasize that according to this theory, girls do not become girls because they identify with or model themselves after their mothers; they model themselves after their mothers because they have realized that they are girls. (52, p. 102) They preferentially value their own sex and are motivated to appropriate sex-role behavior.

SOCIAL LEARNING THEORY

The social learning theorists such as Mischel, (40) Bandura, (3) and Walters (4) reason differently. In their view, *a child learns sex-typed behavior the same way*

*he or she learns any other type of behavior, through a combination of reward
and punishment, indoctrination, observation of others, and through modeling.*
From the very beginning boys and girls are socialized differently. (26, p. 467)
Boys are expected to be more active, hostile, and aggressive. They are expected
to fight when teased and to stand up to bullies. When they act according to expectations, they are praised; when they refuse to fight, they are criticized for
being "sissies." Girls are taught to be "little ladies": quiet, submissive, and well
mannered. They are condemned or punished for being too boisterous or aggressive and are rewarded when they are polite and submissive. As a consequence,
boys and girls grow up manifesting different behaviors. (30) Figure 12–2 shows
the difference in aggressive behavior of preschool boys and girls. The first pair
of histograms shows the proportion of all aggressive acts (including verbal aggression) committed by boys and girls respectively. Subsequent histograms show to
whom these acts were directed: boys to boys, girls to girls, boys to girls, girls to
boys, boys to teachers, girls to teachers, boys to objects (toys, furniture, etc.) and
girls to objects. (13) The boys were twice as aggressive as the girls, and their aggression was directed predominantly toward other boys. (Boys are taught never to
hit girls.) Girls who were aggressive were usually equally aggressive to boys

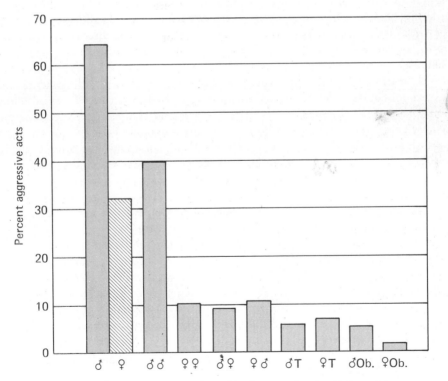

Figure 12–2. Aggressive behavior manifested by boys and girls. (Adapted from
C. Brindley et al., "Sex Differences in the Activities and Social Interactions of
Nursery School Children." In *Comparative Ecology and Behaviour of Primates*,
edited by R. P. Michael and J. H. Crook [London, New York, San Francisco:
Academic Press, 1972]. Used by permission.)

and girls, and only a little less so to the teacher. These findings were substantiated by another study of aggression in ten- and eleven-year-olds: boys more often than girls both initiated and evoked aggressive behavior. (53)

Traditional sex roles and concepts are taught in many ways as the child grows up. A study of sex-role socialization in nursery schools showed that even those schools that tried to minimize differential sex-role socialization of boys and girls still exerted subtle influence on sex-role expectations. (26, p. 470) For example, the girls received more compliments on wearing dresses than on wearing pants. The story books read to the children, the songs they learned, and the games they played all contained elements of traditional sex-role attitudes. In one song about a child who made noise on a bus were the words:

And the daddy went spank-spank and the mommy went "shh-shh." (26, p. 471)

One of the greatest influences on sex roles was the fact that all of the nursery school teachers were females. This alone would make it more difficult for children to understand that fathers, too, can share in child care responsibilities. (26, p. 471)

Sex-role stereotypes are still widely developed in many textbooks. (34, 59) A recent study of an annotated catalog of children's books (distributed by the National Council of Teachers of English to thousands of teachers and used for ordering books with federal funds) lists titles under the headings: "Especially for Girls" and "Especially for Boys." Boys "decipher and discover," "earn and train," or "foil someone." Girls "struggle," "overcome difficulties," "feel lost," "help solve," or "help out." One boy's story moves from "truancy to triumph." A girl "learns to face the real world" and to make "a difficult adjustment." (25)

School courses and programs also promote sex-typed roles. Physical education courses for boys emphasize contact sports and competition; those for girls usually promote grace, agility, and poise. Home economics is often offered only to girls, shop and auto mechanics only to boys. Guidance counselors often urge girls to become secretaries and nurses, boys to become business managers and doctors. (43, p. 253) Females are usually prepared for marriage and parenthood, boys for a vocation. (58, p. 30)

Sex role learning thus emphasizes that boys develop "maleness" and girls "femaleness" through exposure to scores of influences—parents, peers, school, the mass media—that indoctrinate them in what it means to be a man or a woman in the culture in which they are brought up. They are further encouraged to accept the so-called appropriate sex identity by being rewarded for one kind of behavior and being punished for another. Those who live up to societal expectations are accepted as normal; those who do not conform are criticized and pressured to comply. Society ostracizes nonconformers and forces them to seek those with similar concepts or identities.

PARENTAL IDENTIFICATION THEORY

Children also find appropriate sex roles through a process of identification, especially with parents. *Parental identification is the process by which the child adopts and internalizes parental values, attitudes, behavioral traits, and personality characteristics.* (31, p. 466; 32) This theory is sometimes discussed as one form of social learning; in other instances, it is considered psychoanalytic theory. It is listed separately here as parental identification to emphasize the importance of parents' influence in sex-role learning. When applied to sex-role development, parental identification theory suggests that children develop sex-role concepts, attitudes, values, characteristics, and behavior by identifying with their parents, especially with the parent of the same sex. Identification begins immediately after birth because of the child's early dependency upon parents. This dependency in turn normally leads to a close emotional attachment. Sex-role learning takes place almost unconsciously and indirectly in this close parent-child relationship. Children may learn that some mothers are soft, warm, and gentle, that they are affectionate, nurturing, and sensitive. Others may learn that fathers are muscular, sometimes rough or loud, or not as involved in day-by-day child care. On the other hand, it may happen that children learn that their mothers are rough or loud and not as involved in day-by-day child care, and that their fathers are warm, gentle, affectionate, nurturing, and sensitive. But the important point is that children listen and observe that each parent behaves, speaks, dresses, and acts differently in relation to the other parent, to other children, or to people outside the family. Thus, *children learn what a mother, a wife, a father, a husband, a woman, or a man is through example and through daily contacts and associations.*

Of course, *the extent to which identification takes place depends upon the amount of time parents spend with their children and the intimacy and intensity of the contact.* (31, p. 466; 36) Usually young boys and girls both identify more closely with the mother than with the father, primarily because they are more often with their mother. (31) As a result young boys often show more similarity to their mothers than to their fathers. This is one explanation of why males are often more anxious than females regarding their sex-role identification. On the one hand, they are more severely punished for being "sissies" than girls for being masculine, and, on the other hand, they have more difficulty breaking away from feminine influences and finding suitable male role models. (12, 32) When the father is absent from the home, the male child has the greater difficulty because of the lack of masculine influence. (10, 11, 63) One study showed that boys with absent fathers were found to be more dependent, less aggressive, and less competent in peer relationships than those whose fathers were present. (9)

The sex-role concepts the child learns depend not only upon the intensity of parental relationships, but also upon the patterns of role models exemplified. A girl who closely identified with a masculine mother becomes only weakly identified with a typically feminine personality. One brought up by a mother who is a professional career woman will get a less stereotyped concept of femininity than one whose mother is a housewife. Similarly, a boy brought up by a father who represents very traditional ideas of masculinity and the role of the husband and father in the family will likely develop quite different concepts from one brought up by an egalitarian parent. As a result, sex-role concepts are perpetuated from one generation to the next. They can be gradually changed, however, if each generation is able to analyze existing concepts in order to discard outmoded ideas and roles and to adopt improved ones.

Changing Concepts of Masculinity

TRADITIONAL CONCEPTS

Traditionally, masculinity has implied some specific characteristics: aggressiveness, dominance, strength, daring, courage, forcefulness, ruggedness, adventurousness, independence, confidence, and lack of emotion. (14, p. 141) Man's aggressiveness, strength, daring, and courage were needed in warfare, hunting, and protecting his family from harm. His dominance, forcefulness, and confidence were expected in his relationships with his wife and children. His aggressiveness, forcefulness, and confidence were expected in business; adventurousness, daring, ruggedness, and bravery were traits needed in exploring the unknown or in facing new challenges. And in times of crisis, or even in close associations with others, man was expected to be unexpressive and unemotional.

Although men needed many of these traits in primitive societies or on the frontier, where they were required to protect and provide with their bare hands or with primitive weapons, some of these traits are not necessary today. Some measure of aggressiveness may help in business or in furthering oneself and one's ideas in relationship to others, but the overaggressive male gets into trouble with friends, family, society, or the law. An earth full of aggressive males results in world wars and destruction. Thus, aggressiveness tends to be more and more outmoded in the contemporary United States. Cooperation is needed for economic, social, and physical survival.

Nor do men any longer have to be physically strong: machines can do the heavy work. William Whyte pointed out a number of years ago in *The Organization Man* that a man can live his whole life and never have a chance to find out if he is a coward or not. (64) Whereas the modern astronaut still needs daring, adventurousness, and cool emotions, these traits are not a prerequisite for getting along in civilized society. A man may have to be independent to smoke Camels ("they're not for everybody") or Tareytons ("I'd rather fight than switch"), but if he were truly independent, he wouldn't be persuaded one way or the other by Madison Avenue.

One of the unfortunate components of traditional masculinity has been the insistence that American males not show emotions. Italian, French, Russian, or Spanish males could embrace and kiss one another and their sons, or even weep, but not English or American males. Anglo-American males were cautioned not to show affection, grief, disappointment, appreciation of beauty, or even joy, else they would appear unmanly.

THE COWBOY TYPE. Balswick and Peek call the inexpressive male "a tragedy of American society." (2) They identify two types of inexpressive males: they call one the *cowboy type*: the two-fisted, strong, silent, 100 percent American he-man. He's rough and tough, doesn't talk much, but above all never shows any tenderness or affection toward women. He likes them but is very embarrassed by them and seldom kisses them. To do so would betray his manhood. He treats them with respect, but roughly and without affection. As Manville suggests:

The on-screen John Wayne doesn't feel comfortable around women. He does like them sometimes—God knows he's not *queer*. But at the right time, and in the right place —which he chooses. And always with his car/horse parked directly outside, in/on which he will ride away to his important business back in Marlboro country. (33)

This inexpressiveness and reserve of the American male toward women has been labeled the "cowboy syndrome." (1) The cowboy loved his horse and was intrigued by a girlfriend but usually chose the horse. The stereotype of today's rough adolescent male is of a he-man who loves his motorcycle, is "turned on" by his girlfriend, but who, if he's a real man, hesitates to express tender feelings toward his girl; paradoxically, such expression would conflict with his image of maleness. So when he hops on his bike and speeds away, he and his pals leave their "dolls" behind.

THE PLAYBOY TYPE.   The other type of inexpressive male described by Balswick and Peek is the *playboy type.* (2) His is the James Bond image, the Don Juan with dozens of sexy girl friends, all of whom he makes love to but with whom he is never to get emotionally involved. He wants a "playgirl" to sleep with in a nonfeeling way, and his measure of masculinity is judged by the degree to which he can make conquests without getting caught. (If he gets married, he's finished!) This type of male is incapable of showing deep, tender emotion; women and sex are purchasable commodities. Such a male would have difficulty in establishing a close, companionable, affectionate relationship with any woman. It is this type of male to whom women are objecting: "We don't want to be treated as sex objects."

The modern adolescent boy has been thoroughly indoctrinated in both the cowboy syndrome and the playboy philosophy. Both concepts have had a marked effect on his personality and his sexual behavior: he has learned to gauge his masculinity partly by his sexual prowess with women, by his ability to seduce, arouse, and satisfy numerous sexual partners without emotional involvement.

One research study (61) correlates the male's self-concept with his attitude toward females: whether the male sees a woman as a person, as a sex object, or as a stereotyped female. As seen in Table 12–1, those males with the lowest self-concept most often look upon women as sex objects. (61)

Finding an adequate self-concept and a satisfactory male image is a particular problem for the black adolescent male or for the white male adolescent

Table 12–1.   Males' self-concepts correlated with attitude toward females, in percentages.

Attitude toward Females	Self-Concept Rating		
	Good	*Fair*	*Poor*
Female is a person	39	10	0
Tends to stereotype female	55	62	15
Female is a sex object	6	28	85

Adapted from J. Vavrik and A. P. Jurick, "Self-Concept and Attitude toward Acceptance of Females: A Note," *Family Coordinator* 20 (1971): 151–152. Used by permission.

from a low socioeconomic status group, especially in a father-absent home. (5, 9, 23) One way such males have traditionally proven their masculinity is through the sexual exploitation of women.

Traditional concepts of masculinity are changing, especially among middle class, better educated youths. Some men no longer feel threatened by doing "women's" chores in the home, by wearing long hair, or even by open expression of feeling. (46) Elements of traditional concepts remain, however: the middle and upper class male likes to think of himself as a playboy, the lower class male as a rough, tough he-man. Both feel threatened by changing concepts of femininity with which they are confronted. What they haven't realized is that healthy nonexploitative relationships with women would not only free women from sex-role typing, but would eliminate the necessity for males to try constantly to prove their manhood. The result would be doubly liberating.

Changing Concepts of Femininity

Traditionally, females have been depicted as passive, dependent, quiet, meek, gentle, warm and affectionate, kind, sentimental, soft hearted, and sensitive. (6, 7) They have also been supposed to be more emotional and excitable, fickle, and frivolous than males. (20, 21) Numerous societies consider them man's inferior physically, intellectually, and socially. (27)

Most women are weaker in terms of physical strength and muscle power, but they are healthier, live longer, have fewer illnesses, and lack numerous sex-linked defects of the male such as color blindness, baldness, and hemophilia (bleeding disease). Women also have been given an inferior status in American society. (24) Table 12–2 shows that in the United States men continue to be paid higher wages than women. Data in Table 12–3 show that one of the reasons for women's lower wages is not only discrimination, but also the continued dominance of higher paid professions by men. A comparison of the 1960 and 1970 figures, however, indicates that male dominance is slowly declining.

A number of factors influence these earnings differentials. Men have higher status jobs than women. A greater percentage of men than women graduate from college and go on to earn higher degrees. Men have about twice as much work experience as women of comparable age. If all these factors are adjusted statistically so that women are assumed to have the same occupational status, edu-

Table 12–2.   Median annual income of full-time civilian workers by sex, age, and educational attainment, 1977.

Occupation Group	Male	Female
All workers 25 years old and over	$15,726	$ 9,257
Elementary education (8 years)	12,083	6,524
High school education (4 years)	15,434	8,894
College education (4 or more years)	20,625	12,656

From Statistical Abstract of the United States, 1978 (Washington, D.C.: U.S. Government Printing Office, 1978), p. 464.

Table 12–3.   Percentage of males in various professions, 1977.

Profession	Percent
Engineers	97.3
Lawyers and judges	90.5
Physicians and surgeons	88.8
Religious workers	87.0
College teachers	68.3
Authors, artists, and entertainers	64.5
Social and recreation workers	39.2
Teachers (except college and university)	29.1
Librarians, archivists, and curators	20.2
Nurses	3.3

From *Statistical Abstract of the United States, 1978* (Washington, D.C.: U.S. Government
 Printing Office, 1978), p. 420.

cation, working hours full time, and work experience as men, the income level of women is still only 62 percent of the male income level. The conclusion is inescapable: the primary reason for the lower income of women is discrimination; women are not receiving equal pay for equal work. Nationally, a female college graduate averages only slightly more income than a male with an elementary school education. Such sex discrimination is obviously unjust. Women are taught and pressured to assume an inferior position. (48)

A classic study by Wallin (62) illustrates this concept. His study was of a random sample of 163 unmarried undergraduate females from a western coeducational university where the ratio of men to women was about three to one. One of the most interesting aspects of the study was the extent to which women pretended inferiority to men: in artistic knowledge or taste, in intelligence, in "playing dumb" on dates, or in athletics. Almost half the women admitted pretending inferiority on one or more occasions. Whereas most women today would find such pretense demeaning, thousands learn to assume certain roles because they perceive that those roles are expected of them.

Flora (18) did an analysis of the female image, by class and culture, as depicted in women's magazine fiction.* The magazines selected were *True Story* and *Modern Romance,* as the two leading representatives of love story magazines for working class American women; and *Redbook* and *Cosmopolitan,* as the two leading representatives of magazines for middle class women. In particular, Flora examined evidence for the presentation of the female as dependent and ineffectual (incapable of completing a task); as one whose pride is dominated by a male; as one who reforms a male; and as one assuming a passive role. Forty-one percent of the stories showed female dependence as desirable and only 20 percent as undesirable. When broken down by class, 51 percent of the stories for middle class readers presented dependence as desirable compared to only 30 percent of the

---

* For an interesting commentary on the female image presented in European literature, see
 Williams. (65)

stories for working class readers. Working class fiction was less likely to present the traditional images of passive womanhood and more likely to emphasize an image of the woman as head of the household and working outside the home. Similarly, 33 percent of middle class fiction presented female ineffectuality as desirable compared to only 19 percent of working class fiction. Working class women were expected to take care of themselves; however, the women in working class fiction slightly more often reformed the male (10 percent for working class, 8 percent for middle class), not by forcing him to behave but by passive virtue, by being willing to stand by him.

The plot of the majority of stories centered on the female's achieving the proper dependent status, usually by marriage, and gaining the male's support. The female was generally placed in a position secondary to the male's, exchanging her sexuality for material and emotional support. Most activity carried on outside the home was a means of acquiring a husband. (18)

There have been significant changes in these traditional female concepts. (12, 42) Margaret Mead believes that the female role is becoming more masculinized and that the sex roles are now converging. (38) Feminists today (19, 37) are insisting on full employment rights and equality for women and on relieving women of the burden of child care by getting society to provide it free. (17) But whether or not the concept of the ideal female image and role will be changed by a shift in occupational roles and by being freer of child care roles remains to be seen. Some people have combined in their personalities autonomy (thought to be characteristic of the male) and sensitivity (attributed to the female). This fortunate combination of traits results in a very creative person. (8, 22)

Conclusions

Sex roles, values, and behaviors are changing. Whether people perceive these changes as good or bad, it seems evident to many observers that American women are becoming more "masculine" and American men more "feminine." Is this a good thing or a bad thing? Certainly, the effort to give women more independence and equal rights with men is a fair thing. The trend of men to become more sensitive and understanding is helpful in all of their interpersonal relationships. An overaggressive, uncaring, unsympathetic person is difficult to live with, whether male or female. Adolescents, male and female, need to look carefully at the changing sex roles of men and women and begin to sort out those personal qualities that they can't accept, whether traditionally masculine or feminine. This is not to suggest that men and women need to start dressing, talking, thinking, or acting alike, but that they need to rediscover what it means to be human men and human women.

Panel Discussion

Ask several female class members who are active in the women's movement to form a panel to discuss "Changing Concepts of Femininity and the Woman's Role Today: What Women Seek and Want."

Bibliography

1. Auerback, A. "The Cowboy Syndrome." Summary of research in a personal letter to Balswick and Peek (ref. 2), 1970.

2. Balswick, J. O., and Peek, C. W. "The Inexpressive Male: A Tragedy of American Society." *Family Coordinator* 20 (1971): 363–368. Used by permission of the publisher and author.

3. Bandura, A. "Social Learning Theory of Identificatory Processes." In *Handbook of Socialization Theory and Research.* Edited by D. A. Goslin. Chicago: Rand McNally, 1969, pp. 213–262.

4. Bandura, A., and Walters, R. H. *Social Learning and Personality Development.* New York: Holt, Rinehart and Winston, 1963.

5. Barclay, A. G., and Cusumano, D. "Father-Absence Cross-Sex Identity, and Field-Dependent Behavior in Male Adolescents." *Child Development* 38 (1967): 243–250.

6. Bardwick, J. *Psychology of Women: A Study of Bio-Cultural Conflicts.* New York: Harper and Row, 1971.

7. Bardwick, J. M. et al. *Feminine Personality and Conflict.* Monterey, Calif.: Brooks/Cole Publishing Co., 1970.

8. Barron, F. X. *Creative Person and Creative Process.* New York: Holt, Rinehart and Winston, 1969.

9. Biller, H. B. "A Note on Father-Absence and Masculine Development in Young Lower-Class Negro and White Boys." *Child Development* 39 (1968): 1003–1006.

10. ———. *Father, Child, and Sex Role: Paternal Determinants of Personality Development.* Lexington, Mass.: Heath Lexington Books, 1971.

11. Biller, H. B., and Bahm, R. M. "Father Absence, Perceived Maternal Behavior, and Masculinity of Self-Concept among Junior High School Boys." *Developmental Psychology* 4 (1971): 178–181.

12. Birnbaum, J. L. A. "Life Patterns, Personality Style, and Self-Esteem in Gifted Family Oriented and Career Committed Women." Ph.D. dissertation, University of Michigan, 1972.

13. Brindley, C. et al. "Sex Differences in the Activities and Social Interactions of Nursery School Children." In *Comparative Ecology and Behaviour of Primates.* Edited by R. P. Michael and J. H. Crook, New York: Academic Press, 1972.

14. Broderick, C., and Bernard, J. *The Individual, Sex, and Society.* Baltimore: Johns Hopkins University Press, 1969.

15. Calderone, M. S. "The Development of Healthy Sexuality." *Journal of Health, Physical Education, and Recreation* 35 (1964): 21–44.

16. Chodorow, N. "Being and Doing: A Cross-Cultural Examination of the Socialization of Males and Females." In *Women in Sexist Society.* Edited by V. Garnish and B. K. Moran. New York: Basic Books, 1971, pp. 173–197.

17. Clavan, S. "Women's Liberation and the Family." *Family Coordinator* 19 (1970): 317–323.

18. Flora, C. B. "The Passive Female: Her Comparative Image by Class and Culture in Women's Magazine Fiction." *Journal of Marriage and the Family* 33 (1971): 435–444.

19. Greer, G. *The Female Eunuch.* New York: Bantam Books, 1971.

20. Heilbrun, A. B., Jr. "An Empirical Test of the Modeling Theory of Sex-Role Learning." *Child Development* 36 (1965): 789–799.

21. ———. "Identification and Behavioral Ineffectiveness During Late Adolescence." In *Adolescents: Readings in Behavior and Development.* Edited by E. D. Evans. New York: Holt, Rinehart and Winston, 1970.

22. Helson, R. "Sex Differences in Creative Style." *Journal of Personality* 35 (1969): 214–233.

23. Hetherington, C. M. "Effects of Paternal Absence on Sex-typed Behaviors in Negro and White Preadolescent Males." *Journal of Personality and Social Psychology* 4 (1966): 87–91.

24. Horner, M. S. "Femininity and Successful Achievement: A Basic Inconsistency." In *Feminine Personality and Conflict.* Ed. by J. M. Bardwick. Monterey, Calif.: Brooks/Cole Publishing Co., 1970, pp. 45–73.

25. Howe, V. "Sexual Stereotypes Start Early." *Saturday Review,* 16 October 1971.

26. Joffee, C. "Sex Role Socialization and the Nursery School: As The Twig is Bent." *Journal of Marriage and the Family* 33 (1971): 467–475.

27. Kaplan, H. B., and Pokorny, A. D. "Sex-Related Correlates of Adult Self-Derogation: Reports of Childhood Experiences." *Developmental Psychology* 6 (1972): 536.

28. Kaye, H. E. "Lesbian Relationships." *Sexual Behavior* (April 1971): 80–87.

29. Kohlberg, L. "A Cognitive-Developmental Analysis of Children's Sex Role Concepts and Attitudes." In *The Development of Sex Differences.* Edited by E. Mac-

coby. Palo Alto, Calif.: Stanford University Press, 1966, pp. 82–98.

30. Linton, S. "Primate Studies and Sex Differences." *Women: A Journal of Liberation* (Summer 1970): pp. 43–44.

31. Lynn, D. B. "The Process of Learning Parental and Sex-Role Identification." *Journal of Marriage and the Family* 28 (1966): 466–470.

32. ———. *Parental and Sex-Role Identification: A Theoretical Formulation.* Berkeley: McCutchan, 1969.

33. Manville, W. H. "The Locker Room Boys." *Cosmopolitan* 166 (1969): 110–115.

34. Martin, W. "Seduced and Abandoned in the New World: The Image of Woman in American Fiction." In *Woman in Sexist Society.* Edited by V. Gornick and B. K. Moran. New York: Basic Books, 1971, 226–239.

35. McCary, J. L. *Human Sexuality.* 2d ed. New York: D. Van Nostrand Co., 1973.

36. McIntire, K. G.; Nass, G. D.; and Dreyer, A. S. "A Cross-Cultural Comparison of Adolescent Perception of Parental Roles." *Journal of Marriage and the Family* 28 (1972): 735–740.

37. McDonald, D. "The Liberation of Women." *Center Magazine* 5 (1972): 25–43.

38. Mead, M. *Sex and Temperament in Three Primitive Societies.* New York: Merton Books, 1950, pp. 279–288.

39. ———. Introduction to *Women: The Variety and Meaning of Their Sexual Experience.* Edited by A. M. Kirch. New York: Dell Publishing Co., 1953, pp. 9–24.

40. Mischel, W. "Sex-typing and Socialization." In *Carmichael's Manual of Child Psychology*, vol. 2. Edited by P. Mussen. New York: John Wiley and Sons, 1970.

41. Money, J., and Ehrhardt, A. A. *Man and Woman, Boy and Girl.* Baltimore: Johns Hopkins University Press, 1972.

42. Mussen, P. H. et al. *Child Development And Personality.* 3d ed. New York: Harper and Row, 1969.

43. Naffziger, C. C., and Naffziger, K. "Development of Sex Role Stereotypes." *Family Coordinator* 23 (1974): 251–258.

44. Negulici, E.; Christodirescu, D.; and Alexandru, S. "Psychological Aspects of the Testicular Feminization Syndrome." *Psychosomatic Medicine* 30 (1968): 45–50.

45. Neumann, F.; Steinbeck, H.; and Hahn, J. D. "Hormones and Brain Differentiation." In *The Hypothalamus.* Edited by L. Martini, M. Motta, and F. Fraschini. New York: Academic Press, 1970.

46. Ovesey, L. *Homosexuality and Pseudohomosexuality.* New York: Science House, 1969.

47. Persky, H.; Smith, K. D.; and Basu, G. K. "Relation of Psychologic Measures of Aggression and Hostility to Testosterone Production in Man." *Psychosomatic Medicine* 33 (1971): 265–277.

48. Poloma, M. M., and Garland, T. N. "The Married Professional Woman: A Study in the Tolerance of Domestication." *Journal of Marriage and the Family* 33 (1971): 531–540.

49. Rose, R. H.; Holaday, J. W.; and Bernstein, I. S. "Plasma Testosterone Dominance Rank and Aggressive Behavior in Male Rhesus Monkeys." *Nature* 231 (1971): 366–368.

50. Schaeffer, D. L. *Six Differences in Personality: Readings.* Monterey, Calif.: Brooks/Cole Publishing Co., 1971.

51. Shaffer, J. W. "Masculinity-Femininity and Other Personality Traits in Gonadal Aplasia (Turner's Syndrome)." In *Advances in Sex Research.* Edited by H. Beigel. New York: Harper and Row, 1963.

52. Sherman, J. A. *On the Psychology of Women.* Springfield, Ill.: Charles C Thomas, 1971.

53. Shortell, J. R., and Biller, H. B. "Aggression in Children as a Function of Sex of Subject and Sex of Opponent." *Developmental Psychology* 3 (1970): 143–144.

54. Simon, W., and Gagnon, J. H. "Psychosexual Development." In *The Sexual Scene.* Edited by W. Simon and J. H. Gagnon. New Brunswick, N.J.: Transaction Books, 1970, pp. 23–41.

55. ———. "The Creation of the Sexual in Early Adolescence." 1970.

56. ———., eds. *The Sexual Scene.* New Brunswick, N.J.: Transaction Books, 1970.

57. Skolnick, A. *The Intimate Environment.* Boston: Little, Brown and Co., 1973.

58. Steinmann, A., and Jurich, A. P. "The Effects of a Sex Education Course on the Sex Role Perceptions of Junior High School Students." *Family Coordinator* 24 (1975): 27–31.

59. U'ren, M. B. "The Image of Woman in Textbooks." In *Woman in Sexist Society.* Edited by V. Gornick and B. K. Moran. New York: Basic Books, 1971, pp. 218–225.

60. U. S. Bureau of the Census, Department of Commerce. *Statistical Abstract of the United States, 1978.* Washington, D.C.: U.S. Government Printing Office, 1978.

61. Vavrik, J., and Jurick, A.P. "Self-Concept and Attitude toward Acceptance of Females: A Note." *Family Coordinator* 20 (1971): 151–152.

62.   Wallin, P. "Cultural Contradictions and Sex Roles: A Repeat Study." *American Sociological Review* 15 (1950): 288–293.

63.   Walters, J., and Stinnett, N. "Parent-Child Relationships: A Decade Review of Research." *Journal of Marriage and the Family* 33 (1971): 81–82.

64.   Whyte, W. *The Organization Man.* New York: Simon and Schuster, 1956.

65.   Williams, B. "Molly Bloom: Archetype or Stereotype." *Journal of Marriage and the Family* 33 (1971): 545–546.

Sexual Values, Behavior, and Education

The onset of puberty is accompanied by an increasing interest in sex. At first this interest is self-centered, focusing on the adolescent's bodily changes and observable happenings. Most adolescents spend a lot of time looking in the mirror or examining various body parts in minute detail. This early concern is also centered on developing an acceptable body image rather than on erotic sensations or expression.

Gradually young adolescents become interested not only in their own development but also in that of others. More and more questions arise concerning development, changes, and sexual characteristics of the opposite sex. Junior high youths ask: Do boys have periods like girls? Do girls always grow faster than boys? How come some girls have bigger breasts than others? They also become fascinated with basic facts about human reproduction, asking: How does the sperm get into the egg? How can you know if you are going to have a boy or girl? Why do some people have twins? Both boys and girls also slowly become aware of their own developing sexual feelings and drives and how these are aroused and expressed. Most adolescents begin some experimentation: touching themselves, playing with their genitals, exploring holes and crevices. Often by accident they experience their first orgasm through self-manipulation. (61, p. 151) From that time their interest in sex as erotic feeling and expression increases. They ask: What is a wet dream? Is a fellow who masturbates a homo? How often do couples have sexual intercourse? What if the boy's penis is too big for a girl, or can it be? Adolescents begin to compare their ideas with those of others and spend a lot of time talking about sex, telling jokes, using sex slang, and exchanging sex-oriented literature. (105, p. 362) Adults are sometimes shocked at the language and jokes. Many parents have been horrified at finding "dirty" books hidden under the mattress. But these activities are motivated by a desire to understand human sexuality; they are a means of understanding, expressing, and gaining control over their sexual feelings. (63, p. 43)

Gradually also, adolescents become more interested in sexual experimentation with others. Some adolescents become involved in homosexual experimentation, (61, p. 154) although most seek experimentation with the opposite sex. Part of this is motivated by curiosity; (105, p. 360) part by a desire for sexual stimulation and release; part by a need for love, affection, intimacy, and acceptance from another person. In some adolescents, the need for emotional fulfillment and reassurance is a stronger motive for sexual participation than is physical fulfillment. (65) Along with experimentation, however, comes concern over their own behavior. How far should you go with a boy? If you're in love, is it all right to go all the way? How can you keep your feelings under control? How can you have sex without getting pregnant?

Much has been written in recent years about a sexual revolution. (61, p. 169;

94, p. 321) Most investigators now conclude that such a revolution does exist and that it includes marked societal changes and changes in individual sexual attitudes and behavior. One of the obvious manifestations of this revolution has been the release of masses of sex-oriented literature. Ever since the U.S. Supreme Court decisions that allowed much looser interpretations of obscenity laws, the market has been flooded with sex magazines, paperbacks, newspapers, and so-called adult movies. The flood of literature has stimulated a new openness in sexual matters. As one wife remarked: "When I was married, I didn't even know that men had pubic hair, since every nude male statue I ever saw was covered with a fig leaf. Now, my children go into any drug store and can see all the pubic hair they want in magazines."

This flood of literature has not been without its benefits. Most adolescents today are far more open and honest about sex and have little hesitancy in talking about any and all sexual matters. For a husband and a wife to be able to communicate and discuss sexual matters is an advantage in making satisfying sexual adjustments in marriage. Many have little hesitancy in nude bathing or in talking about any and all sexual matters. This matter-of-factness ought to contribute toward a more satisfying sexual adjustment in marriage.

The "new morality" has also included some definite changes in sexual attitudes and behavior. The most recent research documents the increasing sexual permissiveness of youths, especially of females, and the fact that our society now is pluralistic as far as sexual morality is concerned. We now tolerate and accept not one standard of sexual behavior, but many. In general, adolescents now accept an individual ethic—the fact that all people must decide on their own standards for themselves.

But these changes have not been without problems. There seems to be a growing tendency to separate sex from love, with the result that more and more youths accept sexual permissiveness without affection. Sex without any emotional involvement at all—recreational sex—has grown increasingly popular. Many psychiatrists are concerned because of the numbers of youths who afterward become very upset about their own behavior. (63, p. 401; 90; 105, p .359) Along with increased promiscuity has come a rise in venereal disease, illegitimacy, therapeutic abortions, and in the number of unwed mothers. The reason for the rise is that even though adolescents have become more sexually active, a majority still are not regularly and responsibly using effective means of birth control.

Today's adolescents, along with those of past generations, are confronted with the task of making sexual decisions. Youths today have the same sexual drives and urges that other generations have, but the difference is that these urges are being constantly stimulated and the guidelines for their control or expression are less clearly defined. Despite all the sex literature, many adolescents are still uninformed or misinformed about their sexuality, resulting in the need for positive programs of sex education, both to counteract the half-truths and distortions and to help adolescents wade through a jungle of moral confusion. This chapter seeks to examine additional facts about the sexual revolution, to increase insight into what is happening, and to offer some suggestions for the future.

Sexual Pluralism and the Individual Ethic

SOCIETY'S SEXUAL VALUES:
THE CATEGORIZATIONS OF I. RUBIN

One of the most influential and helpful formulations of cultural values relating to sexual attitudes was made by Isadore Rubin. (81) He emphasized the pluralistic nature of our society with respect to sexual values and outlined six value systems that compete side by side in American culture. (81, p. 86) He discussed these values on a continuum from the most repressive to the most liberal views. The six value systems are traditional repressive asceticism, enlightened asceticism, humanistic liberalism, humanistic radicalism, fun morality, and sexual anarchy. These systems are presented here to emphasize that the modern adolescent is confronted not with one value system, but many. The behavior of modern adolescents evidences the same wide variety of standards.

TRADITIONAL REPRESSIVE ASCETICISM. This view portrays sex as essentially wrong and dirty, even in marriage, where it is grudgingly acknowledged as necessary for procreation. This view is intolerant of any but very restrictive patterns of heterosexual behavior. It forbids any public and scientific discussion and study of sex and views sex morality in terms of the authoritarian "Thou shalt" and "Thou shalt not." Youths who have been brought up to feel that all sex is wrong and dirty, that they ought never to be interested in it, think about it, or express it, are reflecting this view. Because of this negative view, they often have difficulty in sexual adjustment in marriage. (6)

ENLIGHTENED ASCETICISM. This value system accepts the ascetic view as a safeguard against self-indulgence. It is best represented by David Mace, (58, 59) who emphasizes the need for self-control, discipline, and self-mastery. Mace accepts the Judeo-Christian ethic of premarital chastity, marital fidelity, and monogamy, and opposes any change in these codes, but he emphasizes the need for an open discussion of issues. The adolescent who has a fairly healthy attitude about sex but strong convictions reflecting traditional religious views and who is willing to let others disagree would fairly well reflect this view.

HUMANISTIC LIBERALISM. This value system is exemplified by the views of Lester Kirkendall, (52) who emphasizes the meaning and intent of sex in interpersonal relationships. According to this view, which is essentially situation ethics, the sex act itself is neither right nor wrong; it depends upon the consequences of the act upon the relationships of the people involved. Internalized controls are necessary to prevent sex from being cheap or hurtful. Premarital sex may be right for some mature persons who fulfill certain conditions: no guilt or anxiety, no unwanted pregnancy or venereal disease, no damage to individual integrity or the relationship. Youths who practice premarital sex and find it helps them and their relationship would reflect this view, as would those who have made a mature, well thought out choice not to indulge and are convinced it is the best thing for them.

HUMANISTIC RADICALISM. Walter Stokes (59, 91) holds this humanistic view, which emphasizes the effect of sex on people but holds that society ought to make it possible for youths to have complete sexual freedom, free from venereal disease, pregnancy, guilt, and fear. Those who advocate a restructuring of society to allow premarital sex would agree with Stokes.

FUN MORALITY. Albert Ellis (25) and Hugh Hefner (of *Playboy* magazine) uphold the view that sex is fun and the more fun the better. They believe in and urge premarital intercourse for well-informed and reasonably well-adjusted people and extramarital sex for consenting adults. Not to repress sex is to make one psychologically a sounder person. Youths who play the field and indulge promiscuously represent this view.

SEXUAL ANARCHY. This value system has been advocated by the French jurist René Guyon, (35, 58) who attacks virginity, chastity, monogamy, and any form of restriction except sex that may injure or do violence to other people.

In discussing these various values, Rubin emphasizes the need for *sex education* for youths, not *sex indoctrination*. He rejects rigid rules and ready-made formulas and urges a framework in which the values of a democratic society can become operative in sex education, namely: (1) faith in the free play of intelligence and respect for truth; (2) respect for the basic worth, equality, and dignity of individuals; (3) the right of self-determination of the individual; and (4) the recognition of a cooperative effort for the common good. (81, p. 188) He would urge a goal of equipping students for intelligent and mature sexual self-determination.

INDIVIDUAL ETHICS:
THE STANDARDS OF TODAY'S ADOLESCENTS

Since Rubin set forth his continuum of sexual values there have been other efforts to categorize standards of behavior. The work of Ira Reiss has been particularly noteworthy. (72, 73, 74, 75, 76, 77) He outlined four standards of sexual permissiveness in our culture: *abstinence, double standard, permissiveness with affection,* and *permissiveness without affection.* (72, 75) But the present situation among adolescents would seem to require an expansion of Reiss's categories to include the following:

- Abstinence
- The double standard
- Sex with affection, commitment, and responsibility
- Sex with affection and commitment but without responsibility
- Sex with affection
- Sex without affection
- Sex with ulterior motives

The exact meaning of *abstinence* may vary depending upon the point at which sexual activity ceases and abstaining begins. Some adolescents allow kissing only with affection; others kiss without affection. Kissing can be perfunctory, light kissing, heavy kissing, or French kissing. Some adolescents feel that necking is allowed (all forms of kissing and embracing), but disallow petting (body caresses below the neck). Others allow caressing of the female breasts, but not of the genitals. Others engage in genital stimulation, even mutual masturbation to orgasm, but stop short of actual coitus. Some adolescents are technical virgins—meaning they never allow the penis to enter the vagina, but engage in oral-genital, interfemoral stimulation (penis between the thighs), or other activity except intercourse itself. (8)

The *double standard* refers to one standard of behavior for males, another for females. As will be seen in a later discussion, any differences in standards between males and females is slowly being eliminated. (5, 26)

There are some adolescents who will engage in *sex only with affection, commitment, and responsibility.* They are in love; they are committed to each other and accept the responsibility and consequences of their actions. Responsibility in this case includes the use of dependable means of contraception to prevent unwanted pregnancies. In case of accidental pregnancy, they are willing to take full financial and other responsibility for whatever course of action they decide to pursue. But what does commitment mean? Interpretations vary. Some adolescents will have intercourse only if engaged, others only if they have an understanding to marry, others only if they are living together, others if they are committed to exclusive dating and going steady. "If you're in love and going steady, it's all right." But the distinguishing feature of this standard is that it includes love and responsibility as well as a defined degree of commitment.

Some adolescents want *sex with affection and commitment, but without responsibility.* They are in love, have committed themselves to one another, usually on a temporary basis only, but assume no real responsibility for their actions. Because they do not show real concern and care for one another, one wonders how they define love. They show evidence of immature sexual behavior.

Sex with affection has become the standard of many adolescents. They wouldn't think of making love unless they really loved (liked) and felt affection for each other. They may or may not show responsibility in the practice of birth control, but have made no promises or plans for the future. They are affectionate, are having intercourse, and that's it, at least for the time being.

Sex without affection characterizes people having sexual intercourse without emotional involvement, without the need for affection. They engage in sex for sex's sake because they like it, enjoy it, and do so without any strings attached. Some may be having sex for subconscious reasons and motives they do not recognize or understand. Some who practice this standard have already had sex with a large number of partners. Some of these people see nothing wrong with this and enjoy it. Others are promiscuous but feel conflict and guilt about it that they have difficulty controlling. Some people who have sex without affection are responsible in the use of contraceptives; others are irresponsible.

Sex with ulterior motives may include a number of different motives.

1. *To punish*—"She made me mad, so just for spite, I did it." In this case sex becomes an expression of hostility, anger, or revenge. Some adolescents have sex and strive for pregnancy to get even with parents or to punish a former lover.
2. *To win or return favors*—to get gifts or as an exchange for a pleasant evening. "I spent fifteen dollars on you tonight, now what do I get?" "I can't thank

you enough for the coat." This is really the prostitution of sex: giving sex as payment.

3. *To control behavior*—"If I sleep with you, will you marry me?" "Let's have a baby, then our parents will have to give us permission to marry."

4. *To build up the ego*—"Wait until the others find out whom I slept with last night." "I bet you five dollars I can score." "I'll show you who's irresistible."

5. *To exploit selfishly*—to use the other person for physical satisfaction without regard for that person's well-being or without regard for the consequences.

Most studies of adolescent sexual behavior today indicate that adolescents are not likely to use others sexually who they feel are their social equals. (104) One survey of university females, however, showed that one-half reported having been victims of sexual aggression in a dating situation. The types of aggression ranged from kissing to intercourse with violence, with one-fourth of the incidents involving forcible intercourse. (48) Another study of university females showed that 84 percent had experienced some type of sexual offense after age fourteen. (39) Figure 13–1 indicates the percentages who had been subject to various types of sexual offenses. (39)

All these standards of behavior are being practiced in our culture. Most adolescents feel that what the other person does sexually is his or her own business, that no one else has a right to interfere or judge. The only qualification they make is "as long as no one is hurt." Because intercourse involves two people, however, no ethic can be completely individualistic. At the very least it must take into account one's sex partner. One's actions may also affect many others: a child conceived out of wedlock, families and relatives, others in the community if one needs to turn to them for help or assistance. There is really no such thing as behavior that doesn't affect someone else.

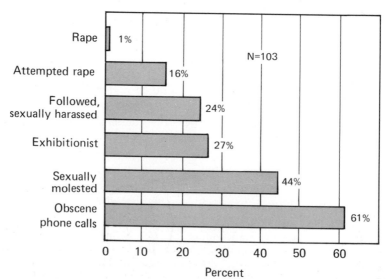

Figure 13–1.   Percentage of females, age 14 and over, experiencing sexual offenses. (Adapted from E. S. Herold et al., "A Study of Offenses against Females," *Adolescence* 14 [Spring 1979]: 65–72. Used by permission.)

It is obvious that not everyone who goes to bed with someone else does so out of love. Sex can mean "I love you," "I need you," "I don't care about you," or "I hate you and want to hurt you." Sex can therefore be either loving or hateful, helpful or harmful, satisfying or frustrating. The outcome will depend partially upon motives, meanings, and relationships, not just on whether one has it or does not. Sex is more than what one does; it also expresses what one is and feels. As Mary Calderone says, "Sex is not what you do, but what you are." (13) Morality "is a question of how one human being deals with another human being, responsibly, or irresponsibly." (10)

Changing Attitudes and Behavior

PREMARITAL SEXUAL INTERCOURSE

For a number of years, researchers indicated that the real revolution in sexual attitudes and behavior had occurred in the 1920s and had remained fairly constant since that time. In the late 1960s and early 1970s, however, researchers began to notice significant changes both in attitudes and behavior. Studies indicated a rapid rise in the percentage of youths approving of premarital sexual intercourse. Figure 13–2 compares the findings in 1975 with those in 1965 and

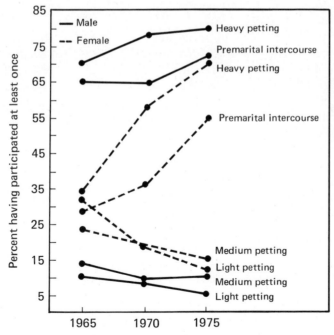

Figure 13–2. Percentage of college students petting and having premarital sexual intercourse, 1965, 1970, and 1975. (Adapted from K. King, J. O. Balswick, and I. E. Robinson, "The Continuing Premarital Sexual Revolution among College Females," *Journal of Marriage and the Family* 39 [August 1977]: 455–459. Copyrighted 1977 by the National Council on Family Relations. Used by permission.)

1970. (51) The student sample consisted of undergraduates attending a large, southern, state university (the University of Georgia). The students were representative of the university population in terms of class standing, major fields of study, and fraternity and sorority membership. (51, p. 456) It is obvious that standards for both men and women became more liberal over the ten-year period and that the changes for females were particularly large. As light petting and medium petting decreased, the percentage engaging in heavy petting and premarital sexual intercourse increased substantially. (51, p. 456)

The percentage of students at the University of Georgia engaging in various degrees of sexual intimacy cannot be generalized to apply to other schools, for there are substantial differences among different sections of the country. In general, students in the northeastern part of the United States are considered more liberal than those in the Midwest and South, but this varies from school to school. One might expect students in church-related colleges to be more conservative than those in state universities, and in fact, they are. Other significant correlates with premarital sexual behavior are:

Race: Other things being equal, blacks report a higher incidence of premarital coitus than whites. (14)

Religion: Religiosity and a lower level of sexual permissiveness go together, at least for whites. (3; 4; 19; 24, p. 708; 50; 89)

Young age at first intercourse: Those who are youngest at first sexual intercourse tend to be more permissive subsequently than do those who report older ages at first intercourse. (24, p. 709)

Liberality: A high level of social liberalism is correlated with a high level of sexual permissiveness, at least for whites. (89, p. 739) For example, those who favor careers for women, small families, and attach less importance to the family tend to be sexually more permissive than those who are less liberal. (49)

Sexual attractiveness: Those who feel they are the most sexually and socially attractive report the highest levels of sexual permissiveness. (49, 55)

Parental standards: Parents who are most liberal in their views of premarital sexual intercourse are those most likely to have adolescents whose views are also liberal. (53) Mothers' attitudes and standards of behavior are especially influential in forming adolescent attitudes.

Peer standards: Adolescents tend to form sexual standards close to peer standards. (19, 41, 53)

ACCEPTANCE OF NONVIRGINITY

Another way to measure premarital sexual permissiveness is to survey attitudes toward marrying a nonvirgin. In research on changing sex norms in the United States and Denmark, Christensen asked college samples to express agreement or disagreement with the statement: "I would prefer marrying a virgin, or in other words, someone who has not had previous coitus (sexual intercourse)." (13, p. 619) Those accepting nonvirginity were greatest among the Danish, fewest among the Mormons, with students from the Midwest somewhere in between. But in all three cultures, permissive attitudes of both sexes increased over the ten-year period studied (1958 to 1968). Interestingly enough, in all three cultures females were more permissive than males (with the exception of the 1968 Danish respondents, who were equal). This means that there were greater percentages of women who accepted nonvirginity in men than there were men who accepted nonvirginity in women. These findings are similar to those of a study at the University of Colorado in which fewer women than men said that "virginity in a prospective mate is important to me." (47, p. 394) The findings also agree with those in a study of college students in the United States, Canada, England, and Norway. In all these countries, fewer females than males were troubled at the thought of marrying a nonvirgin. (54, p. 308) Given that females are usually less permissive than males, why this attitude? Apparently, either the typical female realistically accepted the fact that more males had premarital intercourse, or she felt more sheltered and less experienced and therefore wanted an experienced male to teach her. (13, p. 620)

CHANGING MORALS

There have been other indications of changing attitudes toward premarital sexual permissiveness. (37) A 1978 Gallup poll showed that 54 percent of respondents eighteen to twenty-nine years of age would welcome more sexual freedom in our society. (31, p. 188) King investigated the attitudes of college students at a large, southern, state university toward the Judeo-Christian ethic as it relates to premarital sexual behavior. (51). The researchers found a radical change in student attitudes between 1965 and 1970. Table 13–1 shows the results.

In 1965, 33 percent of male students felt that premarital sexual intercourse was immoral, but in 1970 only 14 percent did. In 1965, 70 percent of female respondents felt that premarital intercourse was immoral, compared to only 34 percent in 1970. The results also indicated that far fewer males and females believed that having sexual intercourse with a great many people was either im-

Table 13–1.   Percentages of college students in 1965, 1970, and 1975 strongly agreeing with statements about the morality of premarital sexual relationships.

Statement	Males			Females		
	1965	*1970*	*1975*	*1965*	*1970*	*1975*
1. I feel that premarital sexual intercourse is immoral.	33	14	20	70	34	21
2. A man who has had sexual experience with a great many women is immoral.	35	15	20	56	22	30
3. A woman who has had sexual intercourse with a great many men is immoral.	42	33	29	91	54	41
4. A man who has had sexual intercourse with a great many women is sinful.	41	24	31	50	26	34
5. A woman who has had sexual intercourse with a great many men is sinful.	58	32	34	70	47	37

Adapted from K. King, J. O. Balswick, and I. E. Robinson, "The Continuing Premarital Sexual Revolution among College Females," *Journal of Marriage and the Family* 39 (1977): 455–459. Used by permission.

moral or sinful. The most significant findings, however, related to the changes in attitudes and behavior of women, and in the elimination of the double standard. Both males and females in 1975 were less likely than in 1970 to view a woman who had intercourse with a great many men as immoral, but were more likely than in 1970 to view a man who had intercourse with a great many women as immoral. These findings suggest that as the liberalization of premarital behavior and attitudes has taken place, especially in relation to females, the differences between male and female behavior and attitudes have diminished. (26, p. 458; 51)

In spite of the fact that youths have become more liberal in their views of sexual morality and immorality, guilt still plays a significant role in sexual behavior. Those who go to church most frequently are most likely to feel guilty about premarital sexual relations. (34) And not all those who indulge feel happy about it. Of those youths and young adults who used the services of the University of Chicago Student Mental Health Clinic, 20 percent said their current sexual experiences were making them feel guilty, 12 percent said they had had sexual intercourse with those they didn't want to, 12 percent were afraid they were promiscuous, 12 percent had sexual fantasies that disgusted them, 10 percent said they avoided sex because it made them feel guilty, 6 percent avoided it because they felt scared, and another 6 percent said they or their partner had had an abortion and then felt bad about it. (108, pp. 122, 123) Though in the minority, apparently some students are not able to accept their sexual behavior and feelings without negative reactions.

Changes in Premarital Sexual Behavior of Young Adolescents

VENER AND STEWART STUDY: 1970–1973

In a 1970 survey of three western shore Michigan communities, Vener and Stewart found no evidence of a major revolution in adolescent sexual behavior. (102) In fact their findings suggested a stability in reported coital rates since World War II. The communities studied were white and nonmetropolitan, ranging from upper working to upper middle levels. Over 4,000 boys and girls were involved in the study.

In 1973 community B, which included the widest range of socioeconomic status, was resurveyed. The community had a school district serving 25,000 residents. About 40 percent of the male wage earners held white-collar jobs. Seventy percent of the respondents' fathers were high school graduates, and 25 percent had completed four years of college. The respondents were all students present in school, grades eight through twelve, the day of the survey. They were asked to indicate their degree of experience at designated levels of heterosexual behavior. (103, p. 729) The results, shown in Figure 13–3, reveal some interesting traits.

1. Boys reported higher participation in each level of sexual activity (except light petting) at all ages.
2. The level of participation in each sexual activity increased with age.

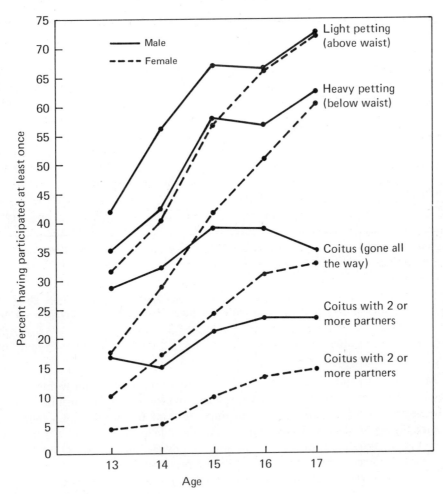

Figure 13–3.   Premarital sex activity in community "B" by sex and age, 1973. (Adapted from A. M. Vener and C. S. Stewart, "Adolescent Sexual Behavior in Middle America Revisited: 1970–1973," *Journal of Marriage and the Family* 36[1974]:728–735. Used by permission.)

3. The older the boys and girls, the more similar their participation in each sexual activity. There was no difference in the percentage of seventeen-year-old males and females engaging in light petting and very little difference in the percentage engaging in heavy petting or coitus. However, the percentage of seventeen-year-old males having coitus with two or more partners remained significantly higher than the percentage of seventeen-year-old females engaging in similar activity, indicating greater promiscuity among the males.

COMPARABLE STUDIES

How do the results of this survey compare with those from other studies? (23) Table 13–2 shows a comparison of the Vener and Stewart study with other studies by Zelnik (111) and Sorensen. (86)

Table 13-2.   Percentage of premarital sexual intercourse among young adolescents: a comparison of three studies.

Study and Sample	Age 15	Age 16	Age 17	Ages 13–15
Zelnik, Kim, and Kantner (111)				
Girls—1971	11%	22%	34%	—
Girls—1976	20%	33%	47%	—
Vener and Stewart (65)				
Girls—1970	13%	23%	27%	—
Girls—1973	24%	31%	35%	17%
Boys—1973	38%	38%	34%	33%
Sorensen (59)				
Girls—1973	—	—	—	30%
Boys—1973	—	—	—	44%

Data source: R. C. Sorensen, *Adolescent Sexuality in Contemporary America: Personal Values and Sexual Behavior: Ages 13—19* (New York: World Publishing Co., 1973); A. M. Vener and S. S. Stewart, "Adolescent Sexual Behavior in Middle America Revisited: 1970–1973," *Journal of Marriage and the Family* 36 (1974): 728–735; M. Zelnick, Y. J. Kim, and J. F. Kantner, "Probabilities of Intercourse and Conception among U. S. Teenage Women, 1971 and 1976," *Family Planning Perspectives* 11 (May/June 1979): 177ff.

In the Zelnik study, the sample was 2,000 never-married young women, ages fifteen to nineteen, including both whites and blacks. (111) The results of this study were similar in some respects to the results of the studies by Vener and Stewart. (103, p. 732) The results show a considerable increase from 1971 to 1976 in the percentage of youths having premarital sexual intercourse. (111) Sorensen's study showed even higher incidences of premarital sexual intercourse. His was a national sample, but included only 393 children whose parents were willing to allow them to be interviewed. Also, his sample did not include 115 children who were unwilling to be interviewed despite parental approval. It is probable that the parents and the children who participated in Sorensens' study were more permissive than those who refused to participate. (86, p. 733)

RELATIONSHIP TO OTHER BEHAVIOR

In the 1973 Vener and Stewart study, involvement in sexual behavior correlated significantly with delinquent behavior such as shoplifting, car theft, vandalism, assault, and reckless driving. In addition, involvement in sexual behavior showed a high correlation with the use of drugs such as marijuana, psychedelics, amphetamines, and sedatives; with smoking and alcohol consumption; and, to a lesser extent, with the use of narcotics. Sexually active youths showed less favorable attitudes toward the police, church, school, and teachers. Apparently, youths who were most sexually permissive were also most permissive in other forms of behavior. (103, p. 234)

The Use of Contraceptives

USE AMONG ADOLESCENTS

With approximately one-third of sixteen-year-olds and about two-thirds of nineteen-year-olds having premarital coitus, the rate of use of contraceptives becomes an important matter. (16, 27) What percentage of these young people are using some form of protection against pregnancy? Results from the 1976 Zelnik and Kantner study show that only 42 percent of fifteen- to nineteen-year-old unmarried girls *sometimes* used contraception; overall, only 27 percent of these teenage girls *always* used some method of contraception whenever they had intercourse; and 31 percent *never* used contraceptives. (110) These figures are in general agreement with other studies showing that nearly half of all teenagers used no method of contraception at most recent coitus. (100) A study of 16,000 female teenagers making initial visits to Illinois family planning clinics also showed that about half the girls (46 percent of whites and 55 percent of blacks) had never used contraception even though they were sexually active. (101)

A study of 421 male students enrolled in high schools in a large northeastern city showed that 55 percent were ineffective contraceptors; that is, they did not use a condom, nor did their female partners use an effective means of birth control. (27) Males of Hispanic and black origins were almost equally ineffective contraceptors (58 and 60 percent respectively); whites were the least inefficient (41 percent). (27, p. 446) The younger the males, the greater the percentage who were ineffective contraceptors. Ninety-four percent of black and 75 percent of Hispanic males aged fifteen or under were ineffective contraceptors. (27, p. 448) Males who did not use contraceptives were either unprepared or did not care if their partners became pregnant. (27, p. 450)

The biggest problem is getting sexually active teenagers to use effective contraceptives in the first place. Users have to have a knowledge of methods, be willing to admit that they are sexually active, and be able to obtain contraceptives as needed. Some students are misinformed about "safe" times and the likelihood of pregnancy. Because some have moral objections to intercourse, they deny the consequences: pregnancy; or they romanticize about the thrills of maternity; or they hesitate to obtain help for fear of parental disapproval. Once initial difficulties and objections are overcome, even young adolescents have been found to be efficient users. (66)

Figure 13–4 shows the types of contraceptives most frequently used, as indicated in the Zelnik and Kantner study. (110) The condom was the most popular birth control device used by both blacks and whites; 24 percent of whites used withdrawal, which is considered a very ineffective means of birth control. (62, p. 251) (The douche also is considered an ineffective birth control method.) Fifteen percent of girls had never used any method.

SHOULD ADOLESCENTS HAVE CONTRACEPTIVES?

On June 9, 1977, the U.S. Supreme Court affirmed that no state could legally restrict the distribution of contraceptives to minors, that nonprescription devices could be dispensed by those other than registered pharmacists, and that such

Method used most recently

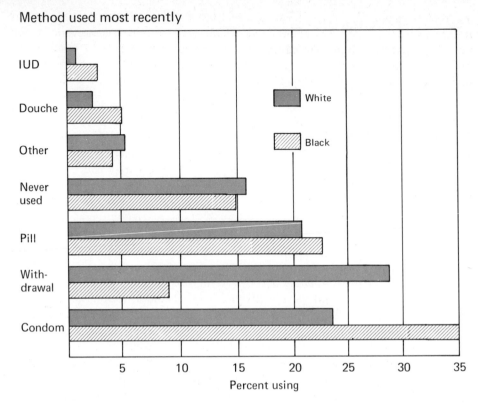

Figure 13–4. Percent of sexually experienced, never-married females, ages 15–19, using specific contraceptives, U.S.A., 1971. (Adapted from M. Zelnick and J. F. Kantner, "Sexual Experience of Young Unmarried Women in the United States," *Family Planning Perspectives* 4 [October 1972]: 9–18. Used by permission.)

devices could be openly displayed and advertised. (4, p. 191; 12) Whether adolescents should have access to contraceptives has been a controversial subject for the past few years. Some adults are worried that the ready availability of contraceptives will increase promiscuity; 70 percent of readers polled by *Better Homes and Gardens* magazine felt that people are having more sexual partners because of easy access to reliable contraceptives. Nevertheless, 80 percent of readers questioned agreed that contraceptive information should be made available to everyone, including teenagers. (97, p. 301) Evidence indicates that even if they do not have contraceptives, youths who are so inclined will have sexual intercourse anyhow. Youths usually seek contraceptive help after they have already been having intercourse. (32, 100, 101) Thus, their decision has already been made.

In one study of 217 young women between ages thirteen and seventeen who went to a Planned Parenthood center, only 17 had not experienced intercourse prior to their initial visit, but all expected to become sexually active. (65, p. 368) The number having only one sexual partner increased from 76 to 82 percent after a visit to the clinic, indicating that obtaining contraceptives decreased rather than increased promiscuity.

Access to contraceptives does not affect the decision to have intercourse, but it does affect the possibility of pregnancy. One study of girls ages seventeen and under showed that 55 percent of their parents knew they attended a family planning clinic. Forty-five percent reported their parents did not know. If the parents had to be told, 20 percent would have stopped going to the clinic and relied on nonmedical methods of contraception; 12 percent would have continued to have sex without using any method; only 4 percent said parental notification would cause them to stop having sex. (97, p. 281) Reiss writes:

There will be coitus regardless of what decision we make on the dissemination of contraceptive information. This decision will not be the major determinant of our coital rates although it may be a major determinant as to whether a particular girl becomes pregnant or not. (74, p. 56)

Reiss points out that research has shown that group membership rather than knowledge of contraception is predictive of sexual behavior; intercourse itself is not a function of contraceptive knowledge. (21, 74) As Siegel points out, "No girl ever became pregnant from knowing too much." (85, p. 373) Some of those who oppose sex education use the same argument: they are afraid if teenagers "know too much" they will use their knowledge to "get into trouble." Evidence indicates, however, that sexual knowledge has no influence on sexual behavior. (87, 106) What really influences behavior are the values and morals accepted by the individual and the groups to which he or she belongs. (15, 20, 47, 92) The fact remains that since the Zelnick and Kantner study in 1971, (110) contraceptives have become much more readily available to teenagers, but youths who have coitus use them only about half the time.

COLLEGE STUDENTS AND CONTRACEPTIVES

How do college students feel about contraception? Theoretically, they accept it. Ninety-six percent of undergraduate students in a study at Earlham College indicated they believed in limiting family size; over 90 percent said they were concerned about the population crisis. (83, p. 312) Only 2 percent of undergraduate students in three coeducational institutions in the Boston area said that they believed "it is wrong for a couple to use contraception." (17, p. 90)

According to data on actual behavior, however, not nearly as many believe in using contraceptives if unmarried. Many students who do have sexual intercourse still will not take the responsibility of providing contraception ahead of time. Some will not admit to themselves that they are going to have coitus, others feel that contraception interferes with the spontaneity of sex, other are misinformed or irresponsible. Table 13–3 shows the results of a 1970–1971 study of 582 undergraduates in health science classes at California State University in San Diego.(7)

Even though these students said that the male and female have equal responsibility for contraception, 45 percent of males and 21 percent of females expected their date to come equipped. If the male had not taken precautions, 71 percent of them would have asked the female if she had. If neither person had taken precautions, 60 percent of males and 34 percent of females would have had intercourse without any effective method. The figures indicate that men still put the burden

Table 13–3. Attitudes of undergraduate college students toward contraception, in percentages.

Response	Male	Female
Want first sex to be spontaneous and extemporaneous in nature.	78	72
Will possibly engage in premarital sex.	86	84
Male and female have equal responsibility for contraception.	80	83
Expect date to come equipped.	45	21
If haven't taken precautions, will ask date if he or she has.	71	96
If neither person has taken contraceptive precautions, will use withdrawal, rhythm method, or just go ahead and hope for the best.	60	34

Adapted from S. J. Bender, "Sex and the College Student," *The Journal of School Health* 43 (May 1973): 278–280. Used by permission. Copyright 1973 by the American School Health Association, Kent, Ohio 44240.

of responsibility upon the women, and that one-third of the females are still willing to have intercourse without any effective method. (82)

In a close relationship, when two students are very much involved, decisions about contraceptive use depend a lot on the attitude of one's partner. It has been found that the ability to discuss contraception and share their knowledge with each other fosters a much more effective use of birth control. (93, p. 490)

Unwed Pregnancy and Abortion

The net result of the increase in premarital sexual intercourse accompanied by a lack of efficient contraceptives has been an increase in the incidence of out-of-wedlock pregnancies—now estimated at 780,000 each year among young women fifteen to nineteen years of age. (110) Of this number, over 80,000 are miscarriages or stillbirths, over 270,000 (39 percent) are induced abortions, and the remaining 430,000 babies are born alive. About 250,000 expectant mothers marry hastily before their babies are born, leaving 225,000 babies born out of wedlock each year. (9, 28, 99, 110)

At the present time, about 80 percent of mothers decide to keep their babies. (78, p. 517) Some let their parents or other relatives adopt their babies, but the remainder want to raise their children themselves, assisted by whatever family or other help they can get.

From most points of view, unmarried motherhood of a young teenage girl is a tragedy. The single mother who decides to keep her baby may become entrapped in a self-destructive cycle consisting of failure to continue her education, repeated pregnancies, failure to establish a stable family life, and dependence on others for support. (78, p. 516) If she marries, the chances of her remaining married are only about one in five. Because few manage to complete their high school education, they are unable to get a good job to support themselves and their family and are likely to require welfare assistance for years. (78, p. 517)

Adolescent mothers have many motives for keeping their babies. One is to have someone to love. One mother said:

I planned on having this baby. She was no accident. I always wanted a baby so that I could have someone to care for. Now I can give her all the love that I never had myself. (78, p. 514)

Hoffman, director of the adolescent care unit of the New York University Care Center says she has never seen a girl from "a strong, loving family" actually have her baby. (29, p. 32) Such girls know they have important roles of their own to fulfill and so use birth control or get an abortion. The mother who has her baby and keeps it is trying to fulfill herself through the child. Hoffman comments:

They feel helpless and hopeless. They have no real sense of community or home. They have no sense of their role in life and they suspect nobody really cares about them. In their floundering they turn to a baby as a source of identity. That translates into instant role and instant femininity. (29, p. 32)

The desire to find fulfillment through a baby, but also some realization of the true situation is expressed by one pregnant teenager:

I'm going to live at home for a while. My baby's going to be in the room with me because the house is crowded and all. . . . As soon as I can I'm going to get welfare, to help out, and after I graduate from high school, I'm going to get a job and save lots of money and then I'll get an apartment of my own just for me and my baby. I want us to be close, so we can sit and talk about things and not be hush-hush about everything, the way me and my mom are. . . .
    Right now, though, I don't have a lot to give a baby really. All I got, I guess, is love. (29, p. 33)

Additional information on the adolescent mother may be found in Chapter 15.

Masturbation

How prevalent is the practice of masturbation? What place does it have, or should it have, in the lives of today's youths? Is it harmful? What effect does it have on sexual adjustment in marriage?

The term *masturbation* refers to any type of self-stimulation that produces erotic arousal, whether or not arousal proceeds to orgasm. It is commonly practiced among both males and females in premarital, marital, and postmarital states. The practice usually reaches its highest intensity in children between three and six years of age and again during adolescence. The reported incidence of masturbation varies somewhat among studies, but overall behavior has not changed very much, except that perhaps more girls are masturbating at early ages. (11) At least 36 percent of girls are masturbating by age fifteen and 42 percent by age nineteen. (86) Conger writes:

One might be tempted to conclude that masturbation would occur most commonly among adolescents lacking other outlets. Interestingly, however, current masturbation experience among contemporary adolescents seems about three times as frequent among those engaged in sexual intercourse or petting to orgasm as among the sexually inexperienced. (16, p. 223)

The latest study of eighteen-year-olds reveals that over 90 percent of males and at least 50 percent of females masturbate. (23, p. 55) The incidence of masturbation is higher among homosexuals than among heterosexuals, and is generally higher among whites than blacks.

Practically all competent health, medical, and psychiatric authorities now say that masturbation is a normal part of growing up and does not have any harmful physical and mental effects, nor does it in any way interfere with normal sexual adjustment in marriage. In fact, women who have never masturbated to orgasm before marriage have more difficulty reaching orgasm during coitus in the first year of marriage than do those who have masturbated to orgasm. The only ill effect from masturbation comes not from the act itself, but from guilt, fear, or anxiety when the adolescent believes the practice will do harm or create problems. These negative emotions can do a great deal of harm. A survey of students who reported to the University of Chicago Student Mental Health Clinic showed that 25 percent feared that they masturbated too frequently. (108, p. 122) If numbers of youths continue to believe that masturbation is unhealthy or harmful but continue to practice it, then various degrees of anxiety eventually result.

Apparently old myths die hard. Many youths still believe that masturbation causes mental illness, idiocy, pimples, impotency, or other ills ascribed to it in the past. Much of the literature directed to adolescents or their adult leaders, teachers, or parents takes the viewpoint that masturbation is not harmful if it is not excessive. But what is excessive? Dr. Benjamin Spock feels that the warning not to masturbate too often is a mistake. He points out that there is no medical reason for this limitation and that it only shifts the worry of the child to the question of what is too often. (88) Masturbation should be considered excessive only in the same sense that reading or watching television can be excessive: the activities themselves are not bad, but when they become all-consuming they suggest the presence of problems that the individual is unable to handle. An adolescent who masturbates to the exclusion of normal friendships and social activities has a problem, not with masturbation, but in social relationships. The term *excessive* is vague, undefined, and subjective. Are adolescents who masturbate daily doing it to excess, especially if they seem to have made a happy emotional and social adjustment? In *Sexual Hygiene and Pathology*, a standard manual for physicians, Dr. John Oliven suggests: "As a general rule, it is probably best to advise parents to disregard evidence of masturbation in juveniles, not to 'look for it' nor to try to prevent it." (68)

Sexual Promiscuity

INCIDENCE

The dictionary suggests that *promiscuity* is an indiscriminate mingling or association with others. In this context, sexual promiscuity would imply having sex indiscriminately, without using too much thought in the selection of a partner. Most adolescents are not sexually promiscuous. They have sex only with one or a few people, and then only with those they care about. Females more often tend to insist on being in love, going steady, or being engaged to marry than do males.

In Mirande's study of female sexual behavior at Virginia and North Dakota colleges, less than 10 percent of females indicated they would have coitus if they did not feel particular affection for their partner. (64) Greater percentages of males will have intercourse without affection, but most prefer a loving relationship. Many males and more females have sex only with the person whom they later marry.

A minority of adolescents, however, are promiscuous. In the study at the University of Chicago Student Health Clinic, 11.5 percent of patients reported having had intercourse reluctantly and another 11.5 percent felt they were promiscuous. (108, p. 122) A study of 411 female undergraduate students at West Virginia University revealed a high correlation between multiple drug use and sexual promiscuity. (56) Seventy-five percent of those who were drug users (defined as those who used two or more drugs) reported having sexual relations with four or more partners. Thirty-eight percent had engaged in full coitus with ten or more partners. (56, p. 195)

CAUSES

Promiscuity is usually a symptom of the disturbed, immature adolescent. Those who feel rejected by parents, who feel isolated, lonely, or empty, are likely to plunge into loveless sexual relationships. Sometimes they are seeking infantile love. Girls may seek cuddling and have to pay the price of intercourse. Boys also may seek to be cuddled, others have intercourse because of peer pressure, and still others play out their hostilities toward females by using their penis as a weapon. (63, p. 428) One boy commented:

She groaned and writhed as I made love to her as if I was hurting her. She made me so mad I thought, "Fuck you," and so I did it as hard and as long as I could. I didn't care whether she enjoyed it or not. (63, p. 429)

Some men who are promiscuous are not hostile. Rather, they have deep-seated feelings of inadequacy or inferiority that they are trying to hide by becoming Don Juans. There is no evidence that their sex drive is stronger than that of average males. In fact some may be quite fearful of their manhood, and therefore have to seek sexual experiences constantly to reassure themselves. (62, p. 396)

Some girls also collect penises without reflecting on their own feelings or those of the boys involved. Their promiscuity may be one way of trying to find love, or it may be their way of devaluing the worth of their male partner over whom they feel they have control. Some girls use sex to punish parents or themselves because they feel they are unloved anyway. (63, p. 429) In this case, promiscuity is not the result of a strong sex drive but an attempt to cope with other overpowering emotional problems. (62, p. 396)

Sex Knowledge and Sex Education

ADOLESCENT INTERESTS

One study of ninth-grade boys and girls from schools in the Boston area sought to discover the degree of interest in each of 112 topics listed on an interest checklist. (79) The words covered a wide variety of subjects. The top 13 topics are

Table 13–4.   Top thirteen sexual topics of interest to ninth-grade boys and girls, in order of interest.

Girls	Boys
Birth control	Venereal disease
Abortion	Enjoyment of sex
Birth control pill	Sexual intercourse
Venereal disease	Birth control
Pregnancy	Love
Love	*Oral intercourse
Fear of sex	Pregnancy
Guilt about sex	Abortion
*Rape	Guilt about sex
Enjoyment of sex	Birth control pill
Sexual intercourse	Fear of sex
Sex offenses	Sex offenses
Prostitution	Prostitution

* Not listed by the opposite sex among the top thirteen items.
Adapted from J. S. Rubenstein, "Young Adolescents' Sexual Interests," *Adolescence* 11 (Winter 1976) : 487–496. Used by permission.

listed in Table 13–4. Boys and girls selected 12 of the same topics, which is remarkable considering the total number on the list. Girls selected the topic "rape," which was not among the top 13 topics on the boys' list, and the boys selected "oral intercourse," which was not among the top 13 on the girls' list.

One surprising result was the adult level of concern of these fourteen-year-old adolescents. They were not interested in learning more about sexual anatomy, necking, petting, dating, masturbation, or menstruation. Their primary concerns were sexual intercourse, its consequences, and its context. Girls were interested in venereal disease, pregnancy, abortion, and whether they would enjoy intercourse, fear it, or feel guilty; whether it would be regulated by the birth control pill; and whether it would be associated with love, rape, prostitution, or sex offenses. (79, p. 494) Boys were more interested in the pleasure-punishment aspects of sex: enjoyment, oral-genital intercourse, penile-vaginal intercourse, and venereal disease, although they too were interested in love, guilt, fear, birth control, the pill, pregnancy, abortion, sex offenses, and prostitution. (79, p. 491) Any sex education curriculum should take these interests into consideration.

SOURCES OF SEX INFORMATION

The most complete and up-to-date information on adolescents' sources of sex information comes from Thornburg, who surveyed nearly a thousand students from twelve major universities in the United States. (95, p. 316; 96 p. 384) As seen in Table 13–5, adolescents gain the greatest amount of information from peers (37.8 percent), 20.9 percent from literature, 19.5 percent from school, 15.5 percent from parents (primarily from the mother), 5 percent from experience, and the remainder from physicians and ministers. (96, p. 386)

Table 13–5. Adolescent sex information sources, in percentages.

Source	Male	Female	Total
Peers	45.7	32.4	37.8
Literature	16.7	23.8	20.9
School	18.3	20.4	19.5
Mother	5.6	18.7	13.4
Father	4.1	.7	2.1
Experiences	8.0	2.8	5.0
Minister	1.0	.6	.7
Physician	.6	.6	.6
Number	392	566	958

From *Contemporary Adolescence: Readings*, 2nd ed. by Hershel D. Thornburg, Copyright 1975 by Wadsworth Publishing Company, Inc. Reprinted by permission of the publisher, Brooks/Cole Publishing Company, Monterey, California.

The table shows some differences between males and females. Boys were more dependent upon peers and experience; girls were more dependent upon literature and their mothers. Mothers, however, provided girls with information on menstruation and the origin of babies, but only limited information on other subjects. (96, p. 386) The fathers were an insignificant source of information for both boys and girls. Information obtained from literature and schools has been increasing. (95, p. 317)

Information on specific subjects was obtained from peers and school. Table 13–6 shows the percentage of students gaining information on specific subjects

Table 13–6. Percentage of peer and school contributions to adolescents' sex information.

Concept	Peers	School
Abortion	18.6	28.8
Contraception	41.7	20.9
Ejaculation	43.3	18.2
Homosexuality	52.0	13.1
Intercourse	54.5	9.6
Masturbation	45.9	13.5
Menstruation	21.8	21.2
Origin of babies	26.2	14.1
Petting	55.7	7.2
Prostitution	50.0	6.4
Seminal emissions	26.3	27.2
Venereal disease	17.5	48.3
Total	37.8	19.5

From Hershel D. Thornburg, *Development in Adolescence.* Copyright 1975 by Wadsworth Publishing Company, Inc. Reprinted by permission of the publisher, Brooks/Cole Publishing Company, Monterey, Calif.

from each of these sources. (95, p. 319) As can be seen, adolescents obtain their information on contraception, ejaculation, homosexuality, intercourse, masturbation, petting, and prostitution primarily from peers. The schools are a significant source of information on abortion and venereal disease, and also provide information on contraception, menstruation, and seminal emissions. The schools are a poor source of information on petting, intercourse, and prostitution, apparently emphasizing health and hygiene subjects rather than discussing sexual behavior.

LITERATURE AND PORNOGRAPHY

It is evident that at least 20 percent of the adolescent's sexual information comes from literature. The real question, of course, is what type of literature? An analysis of fourteen confession-type magazines revealed the following story titles. (43, p. 499)

"I'm Taking a Sex Farm Cure and —Wow"
"My Passions Made Me Feel Raped"
"My Mom's Cheating Drove Me Into a Teenage Sex Orgy"
"We Made Love in Front of Our Biology Class"
"New! Stop a Pregnancy without an Abortion"
"15 New Facts about Male Sexuality"
"How Swinging Singles Play the Strip Poker Question and Answer Game"
"My Husband Doesn't Trust Me with Our Baby"
"Am I a Woman or a Man?"
"Sex is Dirty"
"I Was Sold to the Highest Bidder"

The researchers found that 75 percent of the story titles dealt implicitly or explicitly with sex. An alternative to the flood of cheap literature is to make certain that adolescents have access to reliable, scientific, mature, and moral literature that presents the facts with a mature attitude and responsible point of view. (80)

Experts disagree about the effects of pornography and erotica on adolescents. (107) Several of the negative effects are listed below.

1. Some of the material is unscientific and untrue. One article, for example, described the evils of masturbation; another described the so-called safe period as "midway between two menstrual periods."
2. A lot of pornography portrays sex as dirty and cheap. It often leads to negative feelings—fear, disgust, shame, and revulsion—just the opposite of those that need to be developed. The story entitled "Sex is Dirty" contains the confessions of a thirteen-year-old girl who was raised in sexual ignorance by her grandmother, was raped, and lives in fear that she is either pregnant or has venereal disease. (43, p. 502) It is not difficult to see that this story, read by impressionable teenagers, would produce negative feelings about sex, anxiety, and perhaps later, sexual dysfunction.
3. Most pornography distorts sex by emphasizing only physical stimulation and response without portraying the love and care that are present in the most meaningful relationships. Sex is more than flesh rubbing on flesh, but one wouldn't know it by reading and seeing only pornographic literature.

4. Violence in any form, sexual or otherwise, has been found to contribute to aggression and violence in children. (107)
5. Morally objectionable behavior depicted in erotica sets immoral standards of conduct for those who are exposed to it. This does not mean that all adolescents go out and do likewise, but it does mean that they have been exposed, and the greater the exposure, the more likely it is the material will have some influence.
6. Erotica is, and is meant to be, sexually stimulating to both males and females. Observation in situations that afford a reasonable degree of privacy—such as a drive-in movie—can and do stimulate sexual activity. Even the government report of the U.S. Commission on Obscenity and Pornography, which tended to minimize the adverse effects of erotica, admitted that a minority of male college students reported increased sexual aggressiveness and tension after exposure to erotic films. (98)

THE PARENTS' ROLE

If, as some people maintain, the place of sex education is in the home, then parents aren't doing a very good job. (22)

Some parents are too embarrassed to discuss the subject. Many have been brought up to feel that all sex is wrong and dirty, and become intensely uncomfortable any time the subject is mentioned. Some have a pathological, irrational fear of sex, generated by years of repressive and negative teaching.

Parents have difficulty overcoming the incest barrier between themselves and their adolescents. That is to say, the taboo on parent-child sexual behavior may be so strong that any verbalization about sex in this relationship becomes almost symbolic incest. It has been found that even in families where there has been some communication about sex with young children, this communication drops as the children approach adolescence. Apparently, the parent's rejection of the child's sexual maturation and the adolescent's desire for independence and privacy make communication difficult. Some authorities feel that parents ought to play the primary role in sex education in the lives of young children, but that the emotional ties between parents and youths interfere with effective communication. David Mace writes:

The accepted view has been that sex education is primarily a parental responsibility. . . . I have recently come to question seriously the validity of this assumption. I have seen so many exemplary parents fall down on this job. Many of them admitted to a deep, apparently insurmountable emotional resistance which I could not reasonably attribute to immaturity or inhibition or neurotic anxiety.

Pondering this phenomenon one day, I was suddenly assailed by the question, "Is this barrier the incest taboo?" The more I considered this, the more feasible it seemed. . . .

If the emotional barrier that makes parents shrink from intimate communication about sex with their children is indeed the incest taboo, have we any right to put pressure on them to overcome it? . . . The real need of young people is to come to terms with their *emotional* attitudes about sex. I am coming to think that parents are the last people who can help them with this. (57)

Some parents are uninformed and do not know how to explain to their children. One mother remarked, "I don't understand menstruation myself, so how can I explain it to my daughter?" But parents need more than background knowledge and subject matter; they also have to have practice in putting ideas together in words in ways meaningful to their children. The author has found that when parents are given sample questions that children ask, the parents learn by having to struggle to put the answer into words. After some practice, parents are able to explain easily.

Some parents are afraid that knowledge will lead to sexual experimentation; they don't tell their children because they want to keep them innocent. The old argument is: Keep them ignorant and they won't get into trouble. In fact the reverse is true: youths who are uninformed are more likely to get into trouble. There is no evidence to show that sexual knowledge per se leads to sexual experimentation. There is a lot of evidence to show that ignorance leads to trouble. (44)

Other parents tell too little too late. Most parents are shocked to learn that the time to explain the basic physical facts about reproduction is *before* puberty. Most children ought to know about fertilization and how it takes place in humans by ages seven to nine. For some children, this is too late; they ask questions during the preschool period that demand a simple, honest explanation. The parent who says, "Wait until you are older" is running the risk of telling too little too late. The time to explain about menstruation is just before the girl starts her menses, not after. As one boy said, "All the way through my childhood, whenever I asked questions about sex, my parents would say: 'Wait until you're older.' Now that I'm eighteen and I ask them something, they remark, 'For Pete's sake, you're eighteen years old, you ought to know that!' "

Some parents set a negative example at home. It's not just the words parents use that are important; it is also the lives they lead and the example they set. Parents who treat sex as dirty by their actions are giving negative instruction. One adolescent remarked:

My parents never came out and actually told me the facts of life. . . . But indirectly they told me plenty. They made me feel that sex was dirty and something to be ashamed of or embarrassed about. Yet they joked about it and my father always had some 'girly' magazines lying around the house.

Parents can do a better job by becoming better informed, both to increase their own knowledge and to be more comfortable in talking about sexuality. Reading or attending classes in human sexuality will help parents tremendously. Also, parents can help start and support family life and sex education programs in the schools to supplement their own efforts.

THE ROLE OF PUBLIC SCHOOLS

In a 1977 Gallup poll, 77 percent of those polled approved of sex education in the schools; 90 percent of those aged eighteen to twenty-four approved. (30, p. 37) Because so many parents do an inadequate job and adolescents need more reliable sources of information than peers, the public schools have a responsibility. There are several reasons.

Family life and sex education are natural parts of numerous courses already offered to adolescents. Biology courses should cover the reproductive system when other bodily systems are discussed; not to do so is hypocritical. It is difficult to study sociology or social problems without including a study of the family as the basic social unit or of social problems such as illegitimacy, early marriage, or divorce. Health education usually includes such topics as menstrual hygiene, masturbation, acne, venereal disease, and body odor. Home economics deals with parent-teen relationships, preparation for marriage, and child care and development. Literature courses may stimulate discussion about youth in today's world, moral values, interpersonal relationships, or other topics properly belonging to family life and sex education. Discussions of sex or sex behavior are hard to avoid in a course in the modern novel or in poetry. Even the study of the Bible as literature contains a sexual aspect. Thus, if existing courses are taught honestly, family life and sex education will have a place in many of them.

Preparing youth for happy marriage and responsible parenthood is an important educational goal. It is certain that having a happy marriage and being good parents are among the most important personal goals of the average parent. If the school doesn't prepare youth for this goal, as well as for a vocation, is it really preparing them for living as well as for making a living?

The school is the only social institution that reaches all youth, and therefore has an unusual opportunity to reach those youth that need family life and sex education the most. Some parents do an excellent job, but the majority of parents do not. Are their children to be deprived of proper information, attitudes, examples, and guidance? One would hope not. Other community youth-service organizations such as churches and scouts have a responsibility also, for family life and sex education of youth is a community responsibility. (7) None of these groups reaches as many youths, especially those of low socioeconomic status, as does the school.

The school, as the professional educational institution, is or can be equipped to do a fine job. This does not mean that all teachers are qualified to teach, or that the individual school already has the expertise and resources to develop a program, but it does mean that the school is able to train teachers, develop curricula, and provide the necessary resources once priorities and needs are established. For more information on sex education in the schools, see references 1, 2, 33, 36, 38, 40, 45, 69, 80, 84.

Conclusions

The premarital sexual attitudes and behavior of younger adolescents and college students have been summarized and analyzed in some detail in this chapter. But such an analysis has focused on what others think, feel, and do about premarital sex and on the factors influencing their feelings, views, and behavior. There is a need now to shift the direction of attention from others to self, and to think about personal attitudes and feelings about premarital sexual intercourse. The important question now is: "What do you as a person think and feel about premarital sexual intercourse?" The purpose in raising this question is not to encourage premarital sexual indulgence or abstention, but to encourage thoughtful decision making. (2, 46) Here are ten considerations in making sexual decisions.

Sexual behavior reveals and expresses the character of the individual. The individual who is loving, kind, unselfish, and thoughtful expresses these qualities of character in his or her sexual relationships; the individual who is callous, unfeeling, cruel, and selfish reveals these traits sexually. It is impossible to separate one's sex life from all other aspects of living. For this reason, examining sexual behavior is one way of gaining insight into oneself and into the personality of another person.

Sexual intercourse in itself is neither right nor wrong; it depends upon its use. Sex can be used to help or to harm, to give pleasure or sorrow, to express love or hate. Sex can enhance personal worth and self-esteem or detract from them. It can build companionship and unity or destroy relationships. Sex certainly is intended as a good: to give and receive love and pleasure and, under the right circumstances, to conceive a child. But sex is also sometimes used to punish or to hurt another, such as when intercourse is forced or when premarital pregnancy is planned as a way of hurting parents. Sex is sometimes used as a way of controlling the behavior of another: to exact promises or to force marriage. Sex is sometimes used as a means of building up the ego: the individual makes a conquest without regard for the feelings of the other person. Sex may also be a means of exploiting or using another person selfishly. It can also become a means of payment for money, gifts, an expensive supper, or an evening's entertainment. Such use is the prostitution of sex.

Marital status is not the only important consideration in determining the morality of sexual intercourse. Because a person is married does not mean that all sex relations with one's spouse are automatically loving and right. Is the husband who forces intercourse on his wife in drunken anger having moral sex? Is the unmarried girl who is sleeping with her fiancé because she loves him having immoral sex? Which is moral or immoral? The answer will be determined partly by whether or not the individual accepts an absolute standard or a situational standard. However, even in those instances when an absolute standard is accepted and premarital sexual intercourse is always considered wrong, marital intercourse is not always thereby right.

Making sexual decisions involves selecting a standard or standards. The choice of standards involves at least five important choices: (1) Is the standard an individual one or a social one? That is, is what is right or wrong the individual's choice, or is it based upon the mores of society or of a group in the society? Who decides what is right and wrong: the individual, or his or her community, church, family, or peers? Once decided, is the standard absolute or variable with circumstances? (2) Is the standard one of abstention or of permissiveness? (3) Is the standard single or double? Is there to be one standard for both men and women, or is there to be one standard for males and another for females? (4) Is the standard sex with affection or sex without affection? Is it considered necessary to have real feeling for the other person for intercourse to take place? If the standard selected is sex without affection, is it possible to have intercourse over a long period with one person without affection? Or, does this mean that intercourse will have to be confined to a series of brief episodes with different individuals so that no feelings will develop? Can sexual intercourse be meaningful and satisfying through one-night stands? What happens if one person starts to fall in love with another? Is it possible to adopt a standard of sex without affection without hurting someone else? What can be done to avoid hurting or to avoid being hurt? (5) Is the standard sex with commitment or without commitment? Is it necessary to have any commitment at all, such as going steady or an understanding to marry, before intercourse takes place? Or is intercourse permitted with no strings attached? Is it possible to have intercourse over a long period with one person without any commitment or promises?

Because intercourse involves two persons, whatever decision is made should be mutual. If the decision is not mutual, intercourse involves some element of exploitation or duress, resulting in one person's feeling used or pushed into a relationship he or she does not want.

There is need for complete honesty and truth, and a great deal of mutual understanding and trust in making decisions. The fellow who feeds his girl an insincere line to gain sexual favors is acting immorally. One young adult known to the author carries a ring in his pocket on every date, tells every girl he loves her and wants to marry her, and offers her the ring. "Give her the ring," he said, "and over on her back she goes." Such an example is extreme, but it shows that there are some completely dishonest people who will stop at nothing to gain sexual favors. It takes a fairly experienced and sophisticated woman not to be taken in by dishonest promises. Similarly, there are some completely dishonest women who will confess their love insincerely and grant sexual privileges in exchange for marriage or for monetary or other rewards. Men, too, learn to be on their guard against insincere women.

The development of understanding and trust requires willingness to communicate. Sex usually becomes less of a problem if two people are able to discuss their views and feelings with each other. This requires a fairly close relationship; when one exists, considerable misunderstanding and hard feelings can be avoided by talking things over.

Having sexual intercourse involves responsibility for the prevention of pregnancy by using the safest, most effective means of contraception. Couples who use no contraceptives or unreliable methods show that they are not responsible enough to enter into an adult relationship. Couples who won't use birth control because "they don't want to spoil their love" are in for a rude awakening. There are other responsibilities involved in intercourse, such as preventing the spread of venereal disease, but the chief responsibility is for the total well-being of the other person.

Exploitative sex hurts not only the individual being exploited, but also the person doing the exploiting. The exploiting person is developing self-centeredness and disregard for the welfare and happiness of others as long as pleasure is achieved and desires satisfied. This attitude is not a good one on which to build happy marriages or mature human relationships. One cannot deliberately exploit others without injury to one's own integrity and mental health or without building a pattern of unfeeling and ruthless values that will severely limit the possibility of entering caring relationships. It has been found, for example, that prison guards who use cruel punishment on prisoners become even more cr   as a result. Their behavior causes changes in their personality.

Patterns of behavior and the attitudes and values that are established premaritally may be carried over into marriage and contribute either to marital success or failure. The research does not say that having premarital sexual intercourse builds a happy marriage or detracts from it, (24) but it does say that the kind of person the individual becomes has much to do with the type of marriage that evolves.

Biographical Exercise

Write a term paper on the subject: "My Background and How It Has Influenced My Attitudes, Feelings, and Behavior in Relation to Sex." Such a paper might include sources of sex knowledge as one grows up, such as parents, peers, school, and literature. Early childhood experiences and those during and after puberty can be recalled and analyzed to determine their influences on attitudes and behavior. Parent-child relationships, friendships and peer relationships, social adjustment, and dating experiences during adolescence are all important in molding attitudes and behavior. The paper may conclude with an analysis of present attitudes, feelings, and behavior: what you feel and do and why, and what you would like to feel and do in the future.

Bibliography

1. Ambrose, L. "Misinforming Pregnant Teenagers." *Family Planning Perspectives* 10 (January/February 1978): 51.

2. Baizerman, M. "Can the First Pregnancy of a Young Adolescent Be Prevented? A Question Which Must Be Answered." *Journal of Youth and Adolescence* 6 (1977): 343–351.

3. Bayer, A. E. "Sexual Permissiveness and Correlates as Determined through Interaction Analyses." *Journal of Marriage and the Family* 39 (1977): 29–40.

4. Beiswinger, G. L. "The High Court, Privacy, and Teenage Sexuality." *Family Coordinator* 28 (1979): 191–198.

5. Bell, R. R., and Chaskes, J. B. "Premarital Sexual Experience among Coeds, 1958 and 1968." *Journal of Marriage and the Family* 32 (1970): 81–84.

6. Belliveau, F., and Richter, L. *Understanding Human Sexual Inadequacy.* New York: Bantam Books, 1970.

7. Bender, S. J. "Sex and the College Student." *Journal of School Health* 43 (May 1973): 278–280.

8. Berger, D. G., and Wenger, M. G. "The Ideology of Virginity." *Journal of Marriage and the Family* 35 (1973): 666–676.

9. Byrne, D. "A Pregnant Pause in the Sexual Revolution." *Psychology Today* (July 1977): p. 67ff.

10. Calderone, M. S. "Planning for Sex Education: A Community-wide Responsibility." *NEA Journal* 56 (1967): 26–29.

11. Cannon, K. L., and Long, R. "Premarital Sexual Behavior in the Sixties." *Journal of Marriage and the Family* 33 (1971): 36–49.

12. *Carey* v. *Population Services International*, U. S. Supreme Court (1977): 75–443.

13. Christensen, H. T., and Gregg, C. F. "Changing Sex Norms in America and Scandinavia." *Journal of Marriage and the Family* 32 (1970): 616–627.

14. Christensen, H. T., and Johnson, L. B. "Premarital Coitus and the Southern Black: A Comparative View." *Journal of Marriage and the Family* 40 (1978): 721–732.

15. Clayton, R. R. "Premarital Sexual Intercourse: A Substantive Test of the Contingent Consistency Model." *Journal of Marriage and the Family* 34 (1972): 273–281.

16. Conger, J. J. "Sexual Attitudes and Behavior of Contemporary Adolescents." In *Contemporary Issues in Adolescent Development.* Edited by J. J. Conger. New York: Harper and Row, 1975.

17. Corman, L., and Schaefer, J. B. "Population Growth and Family Planning." *Journal of Marriage and the Family* 35 (1973): 89–92.

18. D'Augelli, J. F., and D'Augelli, A. R. "Moral Reasoning and Premarital Sexual Behavior: Toward Reasoning about Relationships." *Journal of Social Issues* 33 (1977): 46–66.

19. Davidson, J. K., and Leslie, G. R. "Premarital Sexual Intercourse: An Application of Axiomatic Theory Construction." *Journal of Marriage and the Family* 39 (1977): 15–25.

20. Davis, P. "Contextual Sex-Saliency and Sexual Activity: The Relative Effects of Family and Peer Group in the Sexual Socialization Process." *Journal of Marriage and the Family* 36 (1974): 196–202.

21. Delamater, J., and Maccorquodale, P. "Premarital Contraceptive Use: A Test of Two Models." *Journal of Marriage and the Family* 40 (1978): 235–247.

22. Dickinson, G. E. "Adolescent Sex Information Sources: 1964–1974." *Adolescence* 13 (1978): 653–658.

23. Diepold, J., Jr., and Young, R. D. "Empirical Studies of Adolescent Sexual Behavior: A Critical Review." *Adolescence* 14 (1979): 45–64.

24. Dignan, M., and Anspaugh, D. "Permissiveness and Premarital Sexual Activity: Behavioral Correlates of Attitudinal Differences." *Adolescence* 13 (1978): 703–711.

25. Ellis, A. *If This Be Sexual Heresy.* New York: Lyle Stuart, 1963.

26. Ferrell, M. Z. et al. "Motivational and Societal Changes in the Sexual Double Standard: A Panel Analysis (1967–1971; 1970–1974)." *Journal of Marriage and the Family* 39 (1977): 255–271.

27. Finkel, M. L., and Finkel, D. J. "Male Adolescent Contraceptive Utilization." *Adolescence* 13 (1958): 443–451.

28. Forrest, J. D. et al. "Abortion in the United States, 1976–1977." *Family Planning Perspectives* 10 (September/October 1978): 271–279.

29. Fosburgh, L. "The Make-Believe World of Teen-Age Maternity." *New York Times Magazines,* 7 August 1977, pp. 29ff.

30. Gallup, G. *The Gallup Poll: Public Opinion 1977.* Wilmington, Del.: Scholarly Resources, 1978.

31. ———. *The Gallup Poll: Public Opinion 1978.* Wilmington, Del.: Scholarly Resources, 1979.

32. Godenne, G. D. "Sex and Today's Youth." *Adolescence* 9 (1974): 67–72.

33. Goodman, B., and Goodman, N. "Effects of Parent Orientation Meetings on Parent-Child Communication about Sexuality and Family Life." *Family Coordinator* 25 (1976): 285–290.

34. Gunderson, M. P., and McCary, J. L. "Sexual Guilt and Religion." *Family Coordinator* 28 (1979): 353–357.

35. Guyon, R. *The Ethics of Sexual Acts.* New York: Alfred A. Knopf, 1934.

36. Hansson, R. O. et al. "Contraceptive Knowledge: Antecedents and Implications." *Family Coordinator* 28 (1979): 29–34.

37. Herold, E. S., and Foster, M. E. "Changing Sexual References in Mass Circulation Magazines." *Family Coordinator* 24 (1975): 21–25.

38. Herold, E. S., and Benson, R. M. "Problems of Teaching Sex Education: A Survey of Ontario Secondary Schools." *Family Coordinator* 28 (1979): 199–203.

39. Herold, E. S. et al. "A Study of Sexual Offenses against Females." *Adolescence* 14 (1979): 65–72.

40. Hoffman, A. D. "Adolescents, Sex, and Education." *New York University Education Quarterly* (Summer 1977): 7–14.

41. Hornick, J. P. "Premarital Sexual Attitudes and Behavior." *Sociology Quarterly* 19 (Autumn 1978): 534–544.

42. ———. "Premarital Contraceptives Usage among Male and Female Adolescents." *Family Coordinator* 28 (1979): 181–190.

43. Hurowitz, L., and Gaier, E. L. "Adolescent Erotica and Female Self-Concept Development." *Adolescence* 16 (1976): 497–508.

44. Imbiorski, the Rev. W. "Six Arguments Against Sex Education." In *Becoming A Person.* Edited by P. Belanger and the Rev. W. Imbiorski. New York: Benziger, 1971, pp. 174–178.

45. Joe, V. C., and Smith, J. S. "Conservatism and Inadequate Sex Information." *Psychological Reports* 42 (April 1978): 402.

46. Juhasz, A. M. "A Chain of Sexual Decision-Making." *Family Coordinator* 24 (1975): 43–49.

47. Kaats, G. R., and Davis, K. E. "The Dynamics of Sexual Behavior of College Students." *Journal of Marriage and the Family* 32 (1970): 390–399.

48. Kanin, E. J., and Parcell, S. R. "Sexual Aggression: A Second Look at the Offended Female." *Archives of Sexual Behavior* (1977): 67–76.

49. Kelley, J., "Sexual Permissiveness: Evidence for a Theory." *Journal of Marriage and the Family* 40 (1978): 455–468.

50. King, K. et al. "Religiosity and Sexual Attitudes and Behavior among College Students." *Adolescence* 11 (1976): 535–539.

51. King, K. et al. "The Continuing Premarital Sexual Revolution among College Females." *Journal of Marriage and the Family* 39 (1977): 455–459.

52. Kirkendall, L. A. *Premarital Intercourse and Interpersonal Relations.* New York: Julian Press, 1961.

53. Libby, R. W. et al. "A Test and Reformulation of Reference Group and Role Correlates of Premarital Sexual Permissiveness." *Journal of Marriage and the Family* 40 (1978): 79–92.

54. Luckey, E. B., and Nass, G. D. "A Comparison of Sexual Attitudes and Behavior in an International Sample." *Journal of Marriage and the Family* 31 (1969): 364–379.

55. MacCorquodale, P., and DeLamater, J. "Self-Image and Premarital Sexuality." *Journal of Marriage and the Family* 41 (1979): 327–339.

56. MacDonald, A. P. et al. "College Female Drug Users." *Adolescence* 8 (1973): 189–196.

57. Mace, D. R. "Some Reflections on the American Family." *Marriage and Family Living* 24 (1962): 109–112.

58. Mace, D. R., and Guyon, R. "Chastity and Virginity: The Case for and the Case Against." In *The Encyclopedia of Sex Behavior.* Edited by A. Ellis and A. Abarbanel. New York: Hawthorn Books, 1961, pp. 247–257.

59. Mace, D. R., and Stokes, W. R. "Sex Ethics, Sex Acts, and Human Needs: A Dialogue." *Pastoral Psychology* 12 (1961): 15–22, 34–43.

60. Mahoney, E. R. "Gender and Social Class Differences in Changes in Attitudes Toward Premarital Coitus." *Sociology and Social Research* 62 (January 1978): 279–286.

61. Matteson, D. R., *Adolescence Today: Sex Roles and the Search for Identity.* Homewood, Ill.: Dorsey Press, 1975.

62. McCary, J. *Human Sexuality.* 2d ed.

Princeton, N.J.: D. Van Nostrand Co., 1973.

63. Miller, D. *Adolescence: Psychology, Psychopathology, and Psychotherapy.* New York: Jason Aronson, 1974.

64. Mirande, A. M., and Hammer, E. L. "Premarital Sexual Permissiveness: A Research Note." *Journal of Marriage and the Family* 36 (1974): 356–358.

65. Mitchell, J. J. "Some Psychological Dimensions of Adolescent Sexuality." *Adolescence* 7 (1972): 447–458.

66. Mudd, E. H. et al. "Adolescent Health Services and Contraceptive Use." *American Journal of Orthopsychiatry* 48 (July 1978): 495–504.

67. "Number of Sex Partners Not Increased by Giving Contraception to Teens." *Family Planning Perspectives* 10 (November/December 1978): 368.

68. Oliven, John. *Sexual Hygiene and Pathology,* 2d ed. Philadelphia: J. B. Lippincott and Co., 1955.

69. "Parents and Teens Agree: Teenagers Should Get Birth Control Information—from Parents Primarily." *Family Planning Perspectives* 11 (May/June 1979): 200–201.

70. Peplau, L. A. et al. "Sexual Intimacy in Dating Relationships." *Journal of Social Issues* 33 (1977): 86–109.

71. Perlman, D. "Self-Esteem and Sexual Permissiveness." *Journal of Marriage and the Family* 36 (1974): 470–473.

72. Reiss, L. L. *Premarital Sexual Standards in America.* New York: Free Press, 1960.

73. ———. "Premarital Sexual Permissiveness among Negroes and Whites." *American Sociological Review* 29 (1964): 688–698.

74. ———. "Contraceptive Information and Sexual Morality." *Journal of Sex Research* 2 (April 1966): 51–59.

75. ———. *The Social Context of Premarital Sexual Permissiveness.* New York: Holt, Rinehart and Winston, 1967.

76. ———. *The Family System in America.* New York: Holt, Rinehart and Winston, 1971.

77. ———. "Standards of Sexual Behavior." In *Encyclopedia of Sexual Behavior.* Edited by A. Ellis and A. Abarbanel. New York: Hawthorn Books, 1961, pp. 996–1004.

78. Rice, F. P. *Marriage and Parenthood.* Boston: Allyn and Bacon, 1979.

79. Rubenstein, J. S. "Young Adolescents' Sexual Interests." *Adolescence* 11 (1976): 487–496.

80. Rubenstein, J. S. et al. "An Analysis of Sex Education Books for Adolescents by Means of Adolescents' Sexual Interests." *Adolescence* 12 (1977): 293–310.

81. Rubin, I. "Transition in Sex Values: Implications for the Education of Adolescents." *Journal of Marriage and the Family* 27 (1965): 185–189.

82. Scales, P. "Males and Morals: Teenage Contraceptive Behavior amid the Double Standard." *Family Coordinator* 26 (1977): 211–222.

83. Scarlett, J. A. "Undergraduate Attitudes towards Birth Control: New Perspectives." *Journal of Marriage and the Family* 34 (1972): 312–314.

84. Schinke, S. P. et al. "Preventing Unwanted Pregnancy: A Cognitive-Behavioral Approach." *American Journal of Orthopsychiatry* 49 (January 1979): 81–88.

85. Siegel, J. E. "Why Teach Family Planning?" *Family Coordinator* 18 (1969): 371–374.

86. Sorensen, R. C. *Adolescent Sexuality in Contemporary America: Personal Values and Sexual Behavior, Ages 13–19.* New York: World Publishing Co., 1973.

87. Spanier, G. B. "Sexualization and Premarital Sexual Behavior." *Family Coordinator* 24 (1975): 33–41.

88. Spock, B. *A Teen-Ager's Guide to Life and Love.* New York: Simon and Schuster, 1970.

89. Staples, R. "Race, Liberalism-Conservatism, and Premarital Sexual Permissiveness: A Bi-Racial Comparison." *Journal of Marriage and the Family* 40 (1978): 733–742.

90. Staton, T. F. "The Emotions and Sex Education." In *Understanding Adolescence.* 3d ed. Edited by J. F. Adams. Boston: Allyn and Bacon, 1976.

91. Stokes, W. W. "Guilt and Conflict in Relation to Sex." In *The Encyclopedia of Sex Behavior.* Edited by A. Ellis and A. Abarbanel. New York: Hawthorn Books, 1961, pp. 466–471.

92. Teevan, J. J., Jr. "Reference Groups and Premarital Sexual Behavior." *Journal of Marriage and the Family* 34 (1972): 283–291.

93. Thompson, L., and Spanier, G. B. "Influence of Parents, Peers, and Partners on the Contraceptive Use of College Men and Women." *Journal of Marriage and the Family* 40 (1978): 481–492.

94. Thornburg, H. D., ed. *Contemporary Adolescence: Readings.* 2d ed. Monterey. Calif.: Brooks/Cole Publishing Co., 1975.

95. ———. *Development in Adolescence.* Monterey, Calif.: Brooks/Cole Publishing Co., 1975.

96. ———. "Sources in Adolescence of Initial Sex Information." In *Contemporary Adolescence: Readings.* 2d ed. Edited by H. D. Thornburg. Monterey, Calif.: Brooks/Cole Publishing Co., 1975.

97. Torres, A. "Does Your Mother ·Know . . . ?" *Family Planning Perspectives* 10 (September/October 1978): 280–282.

98. U.S. Commission on Obscenity and Pornography. *Report of the Commission on Obscenity and Pornography.* Washington, D.C.: U.S. Government Printing Office, 1970.

99. U.S. Bureau of the Census, Department of Commerce. *Statistical Abstract of the United States, 1978.* Washington, D.C.: U.S. Government Printing Office, 1978.

100. U.S. Department of Health, Education and Welfare. Bureau of Community Health Services. *Family Planning Digest* 1 (May 1972): 6.

101. U.S. Department of Health, Education and Welfare. Bureau of Community Health Services. *Family Planning Digest* 3 (March 1974): 15.

102. Vener, A. M., and Stewart, C. S. "The Sexual Behavior of Adolescents in Middle America: Generational and American-British Comparisons." *Journal of Marriage and the Family* 34 (1972): 696–705.

103. ———. "Adolescent Sexual Behavior in Middle America Revisited: 1970–1973." *Journal of Marriage and the Family* 36 (1974): 728–735.

104. Walster, E. et al. "Equity and Premarital Sex." *Journal of Personality and Social Psychology* 36 (January 1978): 82–92.

105. Wattenberg, W. W. *The Adolescent Years.* 2d. ed. New York: Harcourt Brace Jovanovich, 1973.

106. Weichmann, G. H., and Ellis, A. L. "A Study of the Effect of 'Sex Education' on Premarital Petting and Coital Behavior." *Family Coordinator* 18 (1969): 231–234.

107. Wills, G. "Measuring the Impact of Erotica." *Psychology Today* (August 1977): 30ff.

108. Winer, J. A. et al. "Sexual Problems in Users of a Student Mental Health Clinic." *Journal of Youth and Adolescence* 6 (1977): 117–126.

109. Zelnik, M., and Kantner, J. F. "Sexual Experience of Young Unmarried Women in the United States." *Family Planning Perspectives* 4 (October 1972): 9–18.

110. ———. "Contraceptive Patterns and Premarital Pregnancy among Women Age 15–19 in 1976." *Family Planning Perspectives* 10 (May/June 1978): 135ff.

111. Zelnik, M.; Kim, Y. J.; and Kantner, J. F. "Probabilities of Intercourse and Conception among U.S. Teenage Women, 1971 and 1976." *Family Planning Perspectives* 11 (May/June 1979): 177ff.

PART 6

Familial

Adolescents in Their Families

Outline

In some ways parents and adolescents are alike: both are experiencing an identity crisis relating to sexual life, roles, authority, emotional adjustment, and values. In other ways they are different, especially in their basic personalities and orientations to life. This chapter compares the identity crisis at middle age with a similar crisis at adolescence, and then discusses some of the basic personality differences between parents and their adolescent children. The chapter discusses some of the difficulties parents have with adolescents and what youths expect of their parents in the way of interest and help, communication, love and acceptance, trust, autonomy, discipline, home life, and example. The chapter concludes with a discussion of adolescent-sibling relationships and the relationships of youths with other relatives in the family.

Middle Age and Adolescent Identity Crises

Practically every book on youth emphasizes the period of adolescence as a time of identity crisis. (See Chapter 8.) But it is important to emphasize also that middle age is a period of identity crisis for the adult. (3, 62) Adolescence arrives at a rather unhandy time for some parents. It comes at a time when middle-aged parents are asking: Who am I, what have I accomplished, where am I now, and what does the future hold for me? (17) In some ways the psychosocial tasks of adolescence parallel those of middle age. (See Chapter 3.) As Scherz expressed it, "The parents' and adolescents' tasks and problems interlock." (70) The assertion is not difficult to illustrate.

SEXUAL IDENTITY CRISIS

Both parents and children are questioning their sexual identity during middle age and adolescence. (14) The bodily changes at puberty require adolescents to readjust to their new sexuality. The reversal of these bodily changes for the female at menopause requires also that she readjust to her new, infertile sexual identity. (65) As menstruation ceases and the childbearing years end, the woman may have difficulty accepting physical changes. Along with the loss of child-bearing capacity may come a fear of decline in sexual attractiveness and responsiveness. (87) If a woman tends to gain weight easily or if she has been sloppy about her personal appearance, she may have lost some of her appeal and may be especially sensitive to this when she sees her teenage daughter with her beautiful figure, skin, and hair, at the full bloom of her youth. It takes a mature mother not to be envious and a little bit frightened, both for herself and for her daughter. The mother may react by pushing her daughter into popularity and intimate relationships to relive her own life through that of her daughter, or she may react by sheltering, protecting, repressing her daughter, by denying her full womanhood out of anxiety and panic. (4) A case in point is that of a mother who began to mistreat her daughter when the girl began her first menstrual period. (27, p. 61) In this situation, the daughter's menses coincided with the mother's menopause.

A father, too, has a crisis of sexual identity. He becomes supersensitive about his growing paunch, increasing baldness, and gray hairs. One author cites the example of one father who had a coronary attack while attempting to compete with his son in ten different athletic contests. (4, p. 307) The father had finished eight events before he was rushed to the hospital. Some men fear loss of potency and physical charm. Some men start chasing other women; others encourage their teenage sons to do so. Still others become hostile, defensive, and resentful whenever their sons reach for manhood and want increased contact with girls, an expanding social life, or adult sexual experiences. (17) Some fathers become fearful of their daughters when they start going out with boys. The author knows of one father who thinks that every boy who takes out one of his daughters is going to seduce her. His fear is a projection of his own guilt, because of his own promiscuous sexual conduct when he was younger.

CRISES OF ROLES

Both parents and adolescents start questioning their roles in life. (68) Adolescents have to face up to what they want out of life philosophically and vocationally. The father faces the fact that his life is half over and that he may not have accomplished nearly all the things he wanted to. He wonders where he's going from this point on, whether he should change jobs, and how he's going to find security for the future. (20, p. 219) The mother has to decide whether to continue her job or whether to go back to school to improve her job status. If she has been at home, she has to decide whether or not to take up her profession, or how else to fulfill herself during these years after the children are launched. Her role of motherhood is about over, and she wonders what role can she best fulfill now. (14)

This change in roles for both parents and adolescents has some real pitfalls. Will parents start pressuring their adolescents to assume roles they really wanted for themselves but never were able to fulfill? (77, p. 118) Will the adolescents be able to find fulfillment as independent adults, especially when the comfort and security of their homes seem so appealing? Or in their desire for independence, will they overreact, leave home and school prematurely, strike out on their own unprepared, and be unable to fulfill their own ambitions or dreams because they are too immature and unprepared to accomplish the task?

AUTHORITY CRISIS

Parents and adolescents are simultaneously facing an authority crisis. (7, p. 47) Parents hate to lose authority. (64) For years their children have depended upon them for everything: their physical and emotional needs and guidance and advice. Now the adolescents strive for independence, for the right to govern their own lives and to make their own decisions. (21) Parents have difficulties changing the pattern of child guidance that was developed over the years with a dependent child so that they can relate to their adolescents as growing adults. Adolescents have to fight for freedom, and sometimes the ensuing battle of wills is heated. (5, 19) Anthony writes: "With every artifice at their command, certain parents will attempt to close the doors and raise the drawbridges and dig deep moats to keep their burgeoning offspring in, for they cannot bring themselves to realize that the loss entailed is almost as inevitable as death and almost as irreversible." (4, p. 319)

EMOTIONAL READJUSTMENT

Middle age and puberty demand dramatic emotional readjustment. Adolescents strive to become emotionally independent and turn to their peers (especially a friend of the opposite sex) for emotional fulfillment. (86) Parents feel hurt and rejected and may deeply resent this transfer of affection to someone else. (27, p. 61) If the parents encourage dependency, their children cannot really grow up; if they overreact and reject their adolescents, the adolescents are hurt and resentful and may be pushed into the arms of another boy or girl. The dependency-independency crisis must be solved in such a way that parent and child remain friends, but now as adult to adult. One way parents can do this is to let their adolescents go and, if the parents are still married, to turn to their spouses to rebuild their sometimes fractured relationship by learning again to find emotional fulfillment with each other. (14, 68) One way adolescents can find emotional fulfillment is through the love of their peers. Even though parents and adolescents each need emotional satisfaction, they must find it apart from their relationships with each other.

REASSESSMENT OF VALUES

Parents and adolescents are facing a conflict of values. (47; 66, p. 103) Sometimes the conflict is between parental and adolescent values, but just as often the parents are experiencing value conflict within themselves, just as the adolescents are. The adults are aware of value changes around them that sometimes conflict with the traditional values with which they have grown up. They have lost some of the idealism of their own youth; usually they have become more cynical and realistic and less certain about many things. At the same time, adolescents are also questioning the values with which they have grown up; they are getting acquainted with new and different friends, some of whom have completely different values than they do. Adolescents start rethinking their values: sometimes the new thoughts are shocking to parents, and never reassuring, because they remind the parents of their own confusion. The result is that adolescents make the adults feel even more uncertain. Adults may react with dogmatism and authoritarianism to convince both their adolescents and themselves that they are right. At other times they capitulate at the slightest challenge, leaving the adolescents insecure, with some loss of respect for their parents, but still groping through their own moral confusion.

Sometimes the conflict is not so much over a difference in values as over the intensity and manner with which the values are expressed. (30, 41, 43) When

225 university students were given a questionnaire on contemporary issues, it was found that on many questions the students' beliefs were closer to perceived parental beliefs than to perceived peer beliefs. (48) One study of the beliefs of activists at the University of Chicago showed that students "were for the most part attempting to fulfill and extend an ideological and cultural tradition already present in their families, rather than rebelling against the values on which they had been raised." (31, p. 47) What this really means is that parents who were liberal tended to produce offspring who were liberal. (30) But in some cases the offspring were willing to become actively involved in protest or other expressions of their liberal values, whereas the parents were not. This suggests that the differences in values of college students and their parents are not so much a matter of actual discrepancy as a matter of intensity. (41, p. 120; 43)

RESULTS OF THE CONFLICTS

What are some results of the identity crises both parents and adolescents are facing? Generally, confusion sets in, at least for a while. As one author expressed it, "Families with adolescents can be described as living in a stage of transitional crisis characterized by confusion." (55, p. 209) The confusion usually continues until each generation resolves its own identity crisis.

Another result is that each generation is absorbed with its own problems and therefore tends to overlook, misinterpret, and misunderstand the problems of the other. Sometimes the feeling is expressed: "Don't bother me with your problems, I've got problems of my own." One of the chief complaints of both parents and youths about each other is: "They don't seem interested or try to understand my problems."

Research indicates that both mothers and fathers underestimate the attitude divisions between themselves and their adolescents. (42, p. 34) Adolescents, on the other hand, tend to magnify such discrepancies, assuming them to be greater than they are. (42, p. 351) Thus, one study of parent-adolescent political attitudes showed that youths perceived less consistency in these attitudes between themselves and their parents than really existed. (53)

If a permanent rift develops, parents and youths may never get back together, or are able to do so only years later. There are increasing numbers of youths wandering around the country, some runaways, many voluntarily or otherwise cut off from all contact with their parents. (10) Some of these are youths who have not been able to solve their own identity crisis and at the same time adjust to parents who are struggling with their own identities as well. (45)

Most families weather the crisis as the adolescent gets older and as parents learn how to deal with themselves and their adolescents. (80) One study of 1,278 high school boys from private Catholic schools in New York, Pennsylvania, New Jersey, and Maryland showed that 80 percent were satisfied with their home life and that 89 percent felt their home life was happy. However, a greater number had difficulties with fathers than with mothers. (49) Other research also points to boys' having more conflict with fathers, (52, p. 103) probably because fathers more often try to dominate their sons than mothers do.

Parent-Adolescent Personality Differences

Parent-adolescent misunderstanding arises also from the two different types of personalities of adults and youths. A comparison of two possible personality types is given in Table 14–1. Although not all adults or youths fit the types described, enough are similar to make personality differences a major source of conflict.

A careful look at Table 14–1 reveals some significant differences between middle-aged parents and adolescent children. From a vantage point reached after many years of experience, parents feel that youths are crazy, reckless, and naive, too inexperienced even to recognize that they are foolish to take chances. Parents worry that their youths will have accidents, get hurt, or get in trouble with the law. Youths feel their parents are overly cautious and worry too much.

Parents who are middle aged tend to compare today's youths and life styles to the way things were when they were growing up. (1) Dad remembers how he had to get up mornings to milk twenty cows and walk three miles to school and becomes critical of his teenager who gets up ten minutes before time for the school bus to take him to the consolidated school. Parents often suffer from a perennial "cultural lag" (8)—a situation Sebald says "renders them helpless, relatively poorly informed, and places them against 'experts' who have taken over a sizeable proportion of the socialization process" so that "children and teenagers show a tendency to generalize the inefficiency of parents as instructors and have started to question their reliability as educators in general." (74, p. 70)

Parents also become a little cynical about human character, somewhat disillusioned about trying to change the world and everybody in it; they realistically learn to accept some things as they are. Adolescents are still extremely idealistic and very impatient with adults who are part of the establishment and accept and

Table 14–1.   Middle-aged adult and adolescent personalities.

Middle-Aged Adult Generation	Adolescent Generation
1. Cautious, based upon experience	1. Daring, willing to try new things, but lacks judgment based upon experience
2. Oriented to past, compares present with way things used to be	2. Present is only reality. Past is irrelevant, future is dim, uncertain
3. Realistic, sometimes cynical about life, people	3. Idealistic, optimistic
4. Conservative in manners, morals, mores	4. Liberal, challenges traditional codes, ethics, experiments with new ideas, life styles
5. Generally contented, satisfied, resigned to status quo	5. Critical, restless, unhappy with things as they are
6. Wants to stay young, fears age	6. Wants to be grown-up, but never wants to become old. Contempt for aged

Adapted from W. J. Andersen, *Design for Family Living*, Minneapolis: T. S. Denison & Co., 1964, p. 256. Used by permission.

like things as they are. Adolescents want to reform the world overnight and become very annoyed when their parents do not agree with their crusade. (See Chapters 1 and 7.)

Adolescents also grow to be wary of adults, primarily because they feel most adults are too critical and won't understand them. Youths feel they have good ideas too and know more about some things than their parents do, and because they want to be grown-up, they may scoff at parental suggestions or ideas. Some youths become very arrogant and contemptuous of adults, usually if they are insecure and envious of the adult's status. Adults react to criticism and rejection with anger and hurt.

Finally, aging adults become oversensitive about growing old or being considered aged. Because they hate to think of growing old, they focus more and more attention on staying young. If parents carry this insecurity to extremes in their dress and behavior, they succeed only in attracting the embarrassed shame and icy glares of their own teenagers and the amused ridicule of other youths as well.

Parents and youths view each other from prejudiced positions that don't help them to understand how to live with the other generation. (19)

Parent-Adolescent Conflict

The particular focus of conflict of parents with their adolescents may be in any of five areas. (61)

SOCIAL LIFE AND CUSTOMS

Adolescents' social lives and the social customs they observe probably create more conflict with parents than any other area. The most common sources of friction are:

- choice of friends or dating partners
- how often they are allowed to go out, going out on school night, frequency of dating
- choice of clubs, activities, societies
- where they are allowed to go, type of activity attended
- curfew hours
- age allowed to date, ride in cars, participate in certain events
- going steady
- choice of clothes, hair styles

RESPONSIBILITY

Parents become the most critical of adolescents who do not evidence enough responsibility. Parents expect adolescents to show responsibility in:

- performance of family chores
- earning and spending money
- care of personal belongings, clothes, and room
- use of the family automobile

- use of the telephone
- doing work for others outside the house
- use of family property or belongings: furniture, tools, supplies, equipment

SCHOOL

School performance, behavior at school, and adolescents' attitudes toward school receive much attention from parents. Specifically, the parent is concerned about adolescents':

- grades and level of performance, whether or not they are performing according to their potential
- study habits and homework
- regularity of attendance
- general attitude toward school studies and teachers
- behavior in school

FAMILY RELATIONSHIPS

Conflict arises over several things:

- immature behavior (36, p. 195)
- general attitude and level of respect shown to parents
- quarreling with siblings
- relationships with relatives, especially aged grandparents in the home

VALUES AND MORALS

Parents are concerned especially with:

- drinking, smoking, and use of drugs
- language and speech
- basic honesty
- sexual behavior
- obeying the law, staying out of trouble
- going to church, Sunday school

SUMMARIES OF CONFLICTS AND APPROVAL

One investigation of university freshmen to determine the main sources of conflict between parents and youths revealed that the five most frequent causes in descending order were: eating with the family, arguing, church attendance, peer group, and being home enough. (39) Another study, of seventh-, eighth-, and ninth-grade Mormon students ranging from ages twelve through fifteen, showed that the three most common areas of conflict, from a list of ten, in descending order were performing home chores, use of time, and attitude toward studies. (73, p. 173) Table 14–2 summarizes the results. In this same study, parents indicated some of the reasons for approving of their adolescents. (73, p. 176) These reasons included such things as:

- good character
- growing up to be worthwhile, good children

Table 14–2.   Summary of conflicts between parents and youths.

Sources of Conflict	Frequency Mentioned
Performing home chores	134
Use of time	104
Attitude toward studies	76
Expenditures of money	72
Morals and manners	48
Choice of friends	43
Selection of clothes	42
Use of phone	36
Dating practices	33
Use of car	27
Total	615

Adapted from J. D. Schvaneveldt, "Mormon Adolescents' Likes and Dislikes Toward Parents and Home," *Adolescence* 8 (1973) : 171. Used by permission.

- trying to do what is right
- talking to parents freely
- being dependable
- being fun to have around
- forgiving parental shortcomings

Adolescents also indicated some of the reasons why they felt their parents approved of them. Some of these reasons were: (73, p. 176)

- I am responsible
- I am honest
- I'm active in church
- I help out
- I try hard
- I keep my word
- I can play basketball
- I am kind to others
- I'm lovable
- They like my personality
- I don't talk back
- I don't complain
- I don't get into any trouble

VARIABLES AFFECTING CONFLICT

The particular focus of conflict in any one family will depend upon a number of factors. The age of the adolescent is one factor. (32) Powell found that girls were increasingly in conflict with their parents about boyfriends from age twelve on, with the peak years being fourteen and fifteen. The same conflict for boys about girlfriends peaked at age sixteen. (60)

The sex of the adolescent is another factor influencing conflict. (32) A study of the personal problems of 4,000 adolescents revealed that family problems made up only 10 percent of the most pressing difficulties reported by boys, but 22 percent of those of girls, indicating sex differences in the extent of family difficulty. (2)

The total atmosphere within the home influences conflict. (28) Conflict of all types is more frequent in authoritarian homes than in democratic homes. In authoritarian homes there was more conflict over such things as spending money, friends, social life, activities outside the home, and home chores.

The socioeconomic status of the family also influences the forms of conflict. (62) Low socioeconomic status families are more often concerned about obedience, politeness, and respect, whereas middle income families are more concerned with developing independence and initiative. Low socioeconomic status

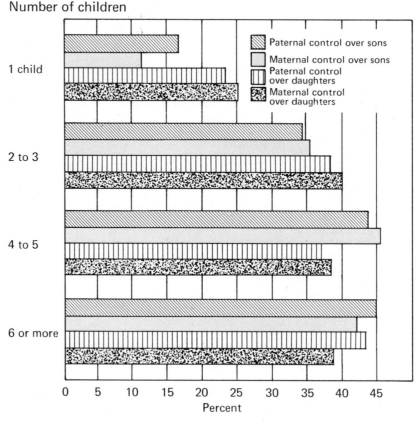

Figure 14–1.   Percent of middle class parents using high parental control, by family size and sex of child. (Adapted from E. T. Peterson and P. R. Kunz, "Parental Control over Adolescents According to Family Size," *Adolescence* 10[1975]: 423. Used by permission.)

families may worry more about keeping their children out of trouble at school; middle class parents are more concerned about grades and achievement. (9)

The total environment in which the child grows up will also determine what parents worry about. An adolescent growing up in an area where there is high delinquency or considerable drug abuse will find parents more concerned with these problems. (78)

Variations in parental reactions to adolescent behavior also influence the extent and focus of conflict. Some parents show little concern about only a few specific problems. Others are greatly and generally dissatisfied with the behavior of their adolescents. (15, 56)

Family size also has been found to be a significant variable, at least in middle class families. The larger the middle class family, the greater the degree of parent-youth conflict and the more often parents use physical force to control adolescents. (28, p. 105) A study of 6,725 adolescents from forty-six high schools across the United States showed that children from larger families perceived more parental control efforts than did children from smaller families. (59, p. 422) This finding held true, however, only for middle class families. It did not hold true for working class and lower class families, whose control efforts did not seem to vary among families of different sizes. Figure 14–1 shows the results for middle class families. (59, p. 423)

The variables influencing parent-adolescent conflict are almost countless, but the ones mentioned indicate how many factors may be involved. (71) Not all parents and adolescents quarrel about the same things, nor to the same extent.

Adolescent-Parent Expectations

What kind of parents do adolescents want and need? A compilation of research findings indicates that youths want and need parents who:

"Are interested in us and available to help us when needed."

"Listen to us and try to understand us."

"Talk with us, not at us."

"Love and accept us as we are, faults and all."

"Trust us and expect the best of us."

"Treat us like grown-ups."

"Discipline us fairly."

"Are happy people with good dispositions and a sense of humor, who create a happy home."

"Set a good example for us, and who will admit when they have made a mistake."

These qualities deserve a closer examination.

PARENTAL INTEREST AND HELP

One of the ways adolescents know their parents care about them is by the interest they show in them and by their willingness to stand beside them and help them as needed. (55; 66, p. 92) One girl, a drum majorette, was bitter because her parents never once came to a football or basketball game to see her perform. This same reaction is expressed by a high school basketball player.

I'm the star player on the school basketball team, but never once has either parent come to see me play. They're either too busy or too tired or can't get a baby sitter for my younger sister. The crowds cheer for me, the girls hang around my locker, some kids even ask me for my autograph. But it doesn't mean much if the two most important people in my life don't care. (24, p. 86)

Adolescents want attention from their parents. They especially resent parents who are away from home too much. (44)

Other parents overdo the companionship. Adolescents want to spend time with their own friends, to do their own thing, and don't want their parents to be pals. They need adult interest and help, not adults trying to act like adolescents.

I'm sixteen, my dad is forty-one. He keeps trying to be a "pal" to me, and it's driving me nuts! We used to have good times on hunting and fishing trips together, but he doesn't seem to realize that now I have a life of my own and don't always want to go off in the wilderness and act like a Big White Hunter. (24, p. 85)

LISTENING, UNDERSTANDING, AND TALKING

One of the most frequent complaints of adolescents is that their parents do not listen to their ideas, accept their opinions as relevant, or try to understand their feelings and points of view. Adolescents want parents who will talk with them, not at them, in a sympathetic way. (28)

We want parents we can take our troubles to and be sure they'll understand. Some parents won't listen or let their children explain. They should try to see things a little more from our point of view.

We wish our parents would lose an argument with us once in a while and listen to our side of problems. (64, p. 5)

Basically, adolescents are saying that they want sympathetic understanding, an attentive ear, and parents who indicate by their attitudes that they feel they have something worthwhile to say and therefore are willing to communicate with them. Research indicates that the respect parents show for adolescent opinions contributes greatly to the climate and happiness of the home.

Some parents feel threatened when their adolescent disagrees, doesn't accept their ideas, or tries to argue. Parents who refuse to talk and close the argument by saying "I don't want to discuss it; what I say goes" are closing the door to effective communication, just as are adolescents who get mad, stamp out of the room, refuse to discuss a matter reasonably, and who go into their rooms to pout. Blood and D'Angelo write:

It seems obvious . . . that the most important help a parent can give to a troubled adolescent is to listen. That is the beginning of communication. The least constructive action is to suppress expression by aggression or disengagement. Without it, the conflictual impulse is likely to engineer a crisis as a desperate venture to engage the adult in communication through shock treatment. (10, p. 490)

One key to harmonious parent-youth relationships is communication. Psychiatric social worker Virginia Satir reports that the average family dinner lasts ten to twenty minutes and that some families spend as little as ten minutes a week together. (11, p. 42) If families are to talk, they have to be together long enough to do so; they also have to develop an openness between the generations. (16) Many parents have no idea what their adolescents really think because they never give them a chance to explain.

LOVE AND ACCEPTANCE

One of the important components of love is *acceptance*. (63) One way love is shown is by knowing and then accepting adolescents exactly as they are, faults and all. There must be "a determined effort by parents both to give affection and to achieve enough objectivity to see the child as a human being, entitled to human attributes." (81, p. 164) Adolescents do not want to feel that their parents expect them to be perfect before they will love them, nor can they thrive in an atmosphere of constant criticism and displeasure. (23) Acceptance may also include *nurturance*, a parental attitude of warmth and helpful assistance toward the adolescent. (66, p. 99) *Rejection* is the opposite, reflecting indifference, nagging, or hostility. Adolescents may run away from homes where demonstration of love is lacking and affectional ties between parents and adolescents are weak; conflict intensifies to the point at which youths resort to flight. (10, p. 489) A high proportion of runaways report that they are not accepted at home by their parents. (10, p. 490) Adolescents who reject their parents do so as a defense against the hostility and rejection their parents have shown them. (67, p. 27)

The author once counseled a college girl whose course grades had fallen drastically. This girl had been a straight A student in high school and a superior student for the first few semesters of college. Then her grades plummeted. Subsequent conversation revealed that the girl's parents had always been perfectionists and overly critical. No matter what the girl did as a child her mother would say, "That's fine dear, but wouldn't it have been better if you had done this?" and would tell her all the things she should have done differently. No matter what the girl did, it was never good enough. The girl remarked, "I can never remember my parents being pleased about anything I did." Finally, the girl gave up trying, since she couldn't please her parents anyway. It was at this point that her grades dropped.

TRUST

Adolescents say:

Why are our parents always so afraid we are going to do the wrong thing? Why can't they trust us more? (64, p. 5)

Our parents could trust us more than they often do. They should tell us what we need to know about dating without being old-fashioned. Then they should put us on our own and expect the best of us so we have something to live up to. (22)

One of the most annoying evidences of distrust are parents' opening adolescents' mail, reading their diaries, or listening in on their telephone conversations. One girl complains:

My mother is forever going through my room under the pretense of "cleaning." I don't like to have my desk straightened up (it's where I keep my diary) or my bureau rummaged through. . . . Don't you think a sixteen-year-old girl needs privacy? (24, p. 95)

Some parents seem to have more difficulty trusting their adolescents than others do. Such parents tend to project their own fears, anxieties, and guilts onto the adolescent. The most fearful parents are usually those who are most insecure or who had personal difficulties themselves while growing up. The author has found, for example, that mothers who themselves have conceived or borne children out of wedlock are those most concerned about their own daughters' dating and sexual behavior. Basically, most adolescents feel that parents should trust them completely unless they have given the adults reason for distrust. (63)

AUTONOMY

One goal of every normal adolescent is to be accepted as an autonomous adult. (84, p. 111) A cross-cultural study comparing parent-adolescent relationships in the United States and Denmark revealed that American parents treat their adolescents as children longer than Danish parents do. (37, 38) American youths were not expected to be self-governing as Danish adolescents were. American youths were in school longer; they were not expected to make adult decisions as quickly as the Danes. American adolescents were found to be subject to delayed socialization in terms of both autonomy and discipline. Danish children were subject to stronger discipline than were Americans at an early age, but by adolescence Danish youths were more self-disciplined and could be given more freedom. (37, p. 358)

Another cross-cultural study presents American youths in a more favorable light than Indian adolescents. (82) This study of 100 ninth-grade boys and girls in an agricultural town in northern India and 100 ninth-graders from a rural town in the western United States showed that family cohesiveness was greater in India and that Indian adolescents were more subject to family authority. (82) Thus, any judgment as to whether or not American youths are given autonomy and opportunities for adult decision making and responsibility depends upon one's cultural reference.

The research does indicate, however, that behavioral autonomy increases sharply during adolescence. Table 14–3 summarizes changes in behavioral autonomy for girls at ages eleven and eighteen. (26) It has been suggested in other sections of this book (see Chapter 10 especially) that adolescents desire autonomy in some areas, such as clothing selection or choice of friends, but follow their parents' leads in other areas, such as formulating educational plans. (57, 83)

Evidence indicates that the shift to emotional autonomy during adolescence is not as dramatic as the shift to behavioral autonomy. Table 14–4 summarizes the trends toward emotional autonomy of girls at eleven and eighteen measured by selected indices in a study by Gold and Douvan. (26) In interpreting the results of this study, Douvan writes:

Overall, the differences reveal some growth in emotional autonomy. But the differences are in some cases small, and in many cases indicate that even at eighteen the model pattern among girls is family oriented and compliant. A majority of

Table 14–3.   Percentage of behavioral autonomy for girls at ages eleven and eighteen.

Item	Age 11 (N = 206)	Age 18 (N = 148)
Dates or goes steady	4	94
Has a job outside home	34	60
Has some independent funds	63	84
Spends most of free time with		
friends	22	46
family	68	44

Adapted from M. Gold and E. Douvan, *Adolescent Development*, Boston: Allyn and Bacon, 1969. Used by permission.

eighteen-year-olds choose their adult ideals within the family; (and) comply . . . with a parental request to give up a job and return home; . . . about a third of the girls indicate that the emotional bond to the parents remains preeminent. (33, p. 133)

Adolescents want and need parents who will grant them autonomy in slowly increasing amounts as they learn to use it, rather than all at once. (18, 85) Too much freedom too quickly granted may be interpreted as rejection. Youths want to be given the right to make choices, "to exert their own independence, to argue with adults and to assume responsibility, but they don't want complete freedom. Those who have it worry about it because they realize they don't know how to use it." (64, p. 9)

The opposite extreme from rejection is continued domination and the encouragement of overdependency. Parents who encourage dependency needs that become demanding and excessive, even into adulthood, are interfering with their child's ability to function as an effective adult. Some adolescents who have been

Table 14–4.   Percentage of emotional autonomy for girls at ages eleven and eighteen.

Item	Age 11 (N = 206)	Age 18 (N = 148)
Thinks friendship can be as close as family relationship	53	71
Chooses adult ideal		
a. outside the family	22	48
b. within the family	66	52
Projective: Response to request from lonely mother to give up good job and return to hometown		
a. reject request	8	26
b. comply, conditionally comply	78	59
Chooses as confidante		
a. a friend	5	33
b. one, both parents	67	36
Attitude toward parental rules		
a. right, good, fair	47	56

Adapted from M. Gold and E. Douvan, *Adolescent Development*, Boston: Allyn and Bacon, 1969. Used by permission.

dominated by their parents begin to accept and to prefer being dependent. The result is prolonged adolescence. (76, p. 114) Some adolescents, for example, may prefer to live with parents after marriage. (66) Others who are overly dependent on parents never achieve mature heterosexual relationships, establish a vocational identity of their own choosing, or develop a positive self-image as separate, independent people. (53) Horrocks writes:

> As in so many affairs of life, a golden mean appears to be the optimum situation. Parental behavior should lead to the inculcation of independent self-sufficiency and self-reliance that does not simultaneously obviate reasonable dependence upon parents in appropriate areas and acceptance of a healthy parent-child relationship. (30, p. 155)

There seem to be some sex differences in the dependent-independent behavior of adolescents. Mischel found that girls were generally more dependent than boys in middle and late adolescence. (51) Gradually, however, as concepts of femininity change, girls are becoming more concerned about the achievement of autonomy and do not as often see a conflict between their individual desires and feminine role identification. (27, p. 63)

DISCIPLINE

What kinds of family discipline and control best meet adolescents' needs? There are four basic patterns of family control: autocratic, democratic, permissive, and erratic.

Autocratic—the parent makes any decisions relevant to the adolescent. (50)

Democratic—decisions are made jointly by the parent and adolescent.

Permissive—the adolescent has more influence in making decisions than does the parent.

Erratic—control is inconsistent, sometimes authoritarian, sometimes democratic, sometimes permissive.

In a study of 2,327 American youths from three high schools (median age of the youths was sixteen), Kandel and Lesser found fathers were more often authoritarian than democratic, about an equal percentage of mothers were authoritarian and democratic, and both parents were infrequently permissive. (37) Table 14–5 records adolescents' perceptions of parental authority. The authors did not separately categorize those who were erratic.

Table 14–5.   Adolescents' perceptions of parental authority, in percentages.

Parental Authority	Mother N = 983	Father N = 955
Authoritarian	43	53
Democratic	40	29
Permissive	17	18

Adapted from D. Kandel and G. S. Lesser, "Parent-Adolescent Relationships and Adolescent Independence in the United States and Denmark," *Journal of Marriage and the Family* 31 (1969): 348–358. Used by permission.

What effect does each method of control have on the adolescent?

The usual effect of autocratic control is to produce a combination of rebellion and dependency. (6, 26, 69) Adolescents are taught to be submissive, to obey, and to be dependent upon their parents. They are expected to follow their parents' demands and decisions without question and not to try to decide things for themselves. They less often show initiative or autonomy as motivation for achievement, nor do they show adult independence. Parental overcontrol has been found to be related to low scholastic and educational performance. (69, p. 646) Adolescents in such environments usually are more hostile to their parents, often deeply resent their control and domination, and less often identify with them. (31) When they succeed in challenging parental authority, youths may become rebellious, sometimes overtly aggressive and hostile, especially if the parents' discipline has been harsh and unfair and administered without much love and affection. Thus, the effects on children growing up in autocratic homes differ. The meeker ones are cowed; the stronger ones are rebellious. Both usually show some emotional disturbances and have more problems. (86) Those who rebel often leave home as soon as they can; some become delinquent. (54)

The other extreme is a permissive home, in which adolescents receive very little guidance and direction, few restrictions from parents, and are expected to decide things for themselves. The effects vary. (29) If overindulged but not guided or properly socialized, spoiled, pampered adolescents will be ill prepared to accept frustrations or responsibility or show proper regard for others with whom they associate. They often become domineering, self-centered, and selfish, and get in trouble with those who won't pamper them the way their parents have. Without limits on their behavior, they often feel insecure, disoriented, and uncertain. (72, p. 88) If they interpret the parents' lack of control as disinterest or rejection, adolescents blame them because they did not warn or guide them. Lax discipline, rejection, and lack of parental affection also have been associated with delinquency. (46; 69, p. 646)

The democratic home has the most positive effect upon adolescents. (6, 25, 69) Parental concern expresses itself through guidance, but also encourages individual responsibility, decision making, initiative, and autonomy. Adolescents are involved in making their own decisions while listening to and discussing the reasoned explanations of parents. Adolescents are encouraged to detach themselves gradually from their family. As a result the home atmosphere is likely to be one of respect, appreciation, warmth, and acceptance. (69) This type of home, where there is warmth, fairness, and consistency of discipline, is associated with conforming, trouble-free, nondelinquent behavior for both boys and girls. (58)

Erratic, inconsistent parental control, like lack of control, has a negative effect upon adolescents. Lacking clear, definite guidelines, they become confused and insecure. Such youths often evidence antisocial, delinquent behavior. McCord and McCord found that consistent discipline, whether punitive or love-oriented, significantly reduced delinquency. (46) Nye found that 49 percent of both boys and girls who reported that their mothers "very often" failed to follow through on threatened punishment were in the "most delinquent" category, compared to 30 percent of boys and 22 percent of girls who reported that their mother "never" failed to follow through. (54) Balswick and Macrides found that when there is extreme inequality in parental authority (one parent exercising more authority than another), the result is confusion for adolescents. They react by evidencing a great amount of rebellion against their parents. (6, p. 263) Scheck reports that adolescents who receive inconsistent discipline and whose parents disagree in their expectations of them are more externally than internally oriented in their behavior, meaning that they show less self-control and therefore need more external control of their behavior. (69)

PARENTAL AND HOME HAPPINESS

One of the most important influences upon the adolescent is the emotional climate of the family. Some families evidence a prevailing mood of gaiety, joy, optimism, and happiness. Other families reflect a climate of fear, depression, cynicism, and hostility. The happier the parents and the more positive the home climate, the more beneficial the effect on the growing children. The best-adjusted children are those who grow up in the happiest homes. Table 14–6 shows the relationship between the happiness of the parents' marriage and adolescent rebellion. As can be seen, when youths see their parents' marriage as unhappy rather than happy, they are more likely to rebel. When the type of child-rearing practices are taken into account also, the effect is even more evident. Either very restrictive or very permissive child-rearing practices together with an unhappy marriage produce the most rebellion of all. There is also a tendency for parental happiness and rebellion to be more strongly related when the home is patriarchal. (6, p. 257) Numerous research studies (58,72) emphasize the positive relationship between marital adjustment, family happiness, family solidarity, family cohesiveness, family cooperation, and nondelinquent behavior. In other words, the quality of the interpersonal relationship between the husband and wife, and between the parent and child is crucial in its effect upon the children.

PARENTAL EXAMPLE

Youths say they want parents who:

"Practice what they preach"
"Set a good example for us to follow"
"Follow the same principles they try to teach us"
"Make us proud of them"

Table 14–6.   Percentage of adolescent rebellion in relation to parental happiness and child-rearing practices.

Parental Happiness	Total Sample	Very Restrictive or Very Permissive	Slightly Restrictive or Slightly Permissive	Average	Nonpatriarchal	Patriarchal
Unhappy	29%	49%	23%	22%	23%	31%
Happy	19%	23%	21%	10%	22%	17%

Adapted from J. O. Balswick and C. Macrides, "Parental Stimulus for Adolescent Rebellion," *Adolescence* 10 (1975): 256. Used by permission.

Adolescents want to feel proud of their parents, to feel they are the kind of people they can admire. Youths like adults who have a pleasant disposition, a good sense of humor, who don't get angry or upset all the time, who are fair, treat their children without favoritism, and who are truthful and honest as they want their teenagers to be. Youths object to adults who nag about things they themselves do all the time or who are hypocritical in their beliefs and actions. As one adolescent expressed it:

It's good to feel our parents have a religion they're sincerely trying to live right in the family and everywhere else. . . . It makes us feel we really belong and gives us something to build on. (22)

Youths also want to feel proud to be a part of their families. (79) In most communities, adolescents receive a part of their identity from their family. Youths who like their family name, are proud of the neighborhood and house they live in, are proud of the work that their parents do and of the status of their parents in the community, feel better about themselves. These adolescents are able to say proudly "I am a Jones" or "I am a Levy."

Some young people are ashamed of their families. They hate their surname, are ashamed of their national origin, their neighborhood, their house, or the way their parents look and act. This is especially true of first-generation American youths who feel ashamed of the old-country ways of their parents. Such rejection of their families leads to emotional problems or to difficulties in achieving an identity themselves. (79, p. 514)

Relationships with Other Family Members

ADOLESCENT-SIBLING RELATIONSHIPS

Research efforts have concentrated on exploring parent-adolescent relationships in the family, but little information is available, and some of it is contradictory, on adolescent-sibling relationships. Yet the relationships between brothers and sisters are vitally important, because they may have a lasting influence on development and on the individual's ultimate adult personality and roles. (40, p. 38) Sibling relationships are important in a number of ways.

Older siblings are likely to serve as role models for younger brothers and sisters. (27, p. 58) Older youths represent sex-role models—masculine or feminine personalities or behavior—to younger siblings. They set a character and behavior example, representing through appearance, personality traits, and overall behavior the type of person they are. This has a strong influence on the development of younger brothers and sisters. One adolescent commented:

Since I come from a family of eight, one of the biggest changes, for me, when I became a teenager was the increased responsibility. Because I am the oldest child, my actions now serve as an image for the younger children. My parents stressed this image early in adolescence, and this has had a great effect on me as well as the other children. (66, p. 93)

Older siblings often serve as surrogate parents, acting as caretakers, teachers, playmates, and confidantes. (40, p. 38) Pleasant relationships can contribute to younger children's sense of security, belonging, and acceptance. Hostile, rejecting relationships may create deep-seated feelings of anxiety, insecurity, resentment, or hostility. If older children feel they are displaced by younger siblings and lack attention and care formerly given to them, they may carry this feeling of displacement, jealousy, and competition into adulthood. If, however, older children feel useful, accepted, and admired because of the care they give younger children, this added appreciation and sense of usefulness contributes positively to their own sense of self-worth. Many adolescents learn adult roles and responsibilities by having to care for younger brothers and sisters while growing up.

Siblings often provide companionship, friendship, and meet one another's needs for affection and meaningful relationships. They act as confidants for one another, are able to help one another when there are problems, and share many experiences. Of course, the closer they are, the more likely also that conflict and tension will result, but this too has its positive aspects for it provides training opportunities in how to get along with others. Siblings of necessity have to learn to share, to consider one another's feelings and desires, and to deal with differences.

One study of over 8,000 junior and senior high adolescents in relationship to siblings revealed the following: (13)

Sixty-five percent reported they felt close to siblings.

Only a relatively few were hostile to siblings and living in a state of conflict.

Females were more likely than males to feel close to siblings.

Same-sex siblings were preferred.

Adolescents generally felt closer to older siblings than to younger.

Junior high youths generally felt closer to either older or younger siblings than did senior high youths.

There is a little more sibling closeness in two-child than in larger families. (13, p. 53)

If siblings are six or more years apart in age, they tend to grow up like single children. (40, p. 39) If there is less than six years' difference, however, they are often a threat to each other's power and command over their parents, rivalry is more pronounced, and conflicts tend to be more severe. (40, p. 39) Relationships with siblings tend to be more frictional during early adolescence than later on. As adolescents mature, they accept their siblings in a calmer, more rational manner, with the result that conflicting relationships subside and are replaced by friendlier, more cooperative ones. (36, p. 194)

RELATIONSHIPS WITH RELATIVES

One study of families in three generations revealed that 70 percent of married couples saw their parents weekly or more often. (34) One-third of the grandchildren and grandparents visited each other weekly. Another study, of 764 Pennsylvania State University students, showed that 47 percent had visited three out of four categories of secondary relatives—paternal grandparents, maternal grandparents, cousins, and aunts and uncles—within the prior three months. (88) Altogether, about 10 percent of married elderly parents and 17 percent of previously married elderly parents live with a married child. (75) This means that adolescents have frequent contacts with relatives; a large number live together in the same household.

During early adolescence, contact with older relatives may be frictional. Some grandparents assume an active role in the rearing and guidance of children in the family. Some interfere too much by nagging, ridiculing, or trying to control their grandchildren, often against the parents' wishes. Others take the adolescents' side against parents by pampering or overprotecting, thus undermining parental discipline. In either case, tension develops in the household, affecting all members negatively and stimulating adolescent rebellion and defiance. It is a rare grandparent who achieves the right degree of helping without interfering.

Gradually, as adolescents get older, they are able to accept grandparents and older relatives more graciously than before. Older relatives themselves usually are not as inclined to boss older adolescents as they are the younger adolescents. These two factors result in a gradual subsiding of tension between the generations. (36, p. 194)

Conclusions

The identity crisis adolescents face is more difficult if parents are experiencing a parallel crisis at the same time. Adolescents strive to come to terms with their newly developed sexuality; parents begin to fear the loss of theirs. Adolescents are working out their personal and vocational roles in life; parents are being forced to readjust their roles after the children are launched. Adolescents begin to challenge parental authority; parents hate to let go of it. Adolescents seek emotional emancipation from parents and fulfillment through peers; parents may seek emotional fulfillment through children and deeply resent peer competition. Adolescents are questioning adult values; many parents are also. Those parents who are not questioning values tend to hold more rigidly to those they have. These situations tend to put adolescents and parents in competition or opposition to one another. There can also be some basic personality differences between adolescents and parents: daring vs. cautious, idealistic vs. realistic, liberal vs. conservative, critical vs. satisfied, desirous of growing up vs. desirous of staying young, and oriented to present vs. oriented to past. These differences also create parent-adolescent conflict.

All parents have some difficulties with their adolescents. These problems usually are related to one or more of the following areas: social life, responsibility, school, attitudes and relationships in the family, or values and moral behavior. Adolescents want parents who show interest and concern, who will listen and talk to them and try to understand them and their problems, who love and accept them, who show they trust them, who are willing to grant autonomy and emotional independence, who discipline democratically and consistently, who strive to maintain a happy climate within the home, and who set a good example for them to follow.

Obviously, most parents are not as perfect as their adolescents would like them to be; nor do most young people live up to all the expectations of parents. This results in some tension and conflict, especially during early adolescence, when both parents and youths are making their first adjustments to the identity crisis with which each is confronted. Gradually, however, conflict and tension subside if parents are willing to change their relationship with their children from a parent–dependent child orientation to an adult–growing adult relationship.

Most adolescents report close relationships with siblings in the family. These relationships are important. Older siblings often act as models and surrogate parents, fulfilling important emotional and social needs of younger brothers and sisters. Whenever sibling rivalry and jealousy exist, quarreling and resentment are common; therefore, it is important for all children to come to feel that they are loved equally by the parents. Gradually, as they get older, adolescents learn to get along with siblings as well as with older relatives who live with them in their family.

Panel Discussion

Form a panel of parents and adolescents of different ages to discuss parent-teen relationships in the family. The purposes of the panel are:

1. To learn from parents what criticisms and expectations they have of adolescents.
2. To explore the most important sources of friction in parent-adolescent relationships.
3. To gain insight into these problems and what can be done about them.
4. To learn from adolescents the chief gripes and criticisms about parents.
5. To discover what adolescents expect of parents.
6. To learn how adolescents and parents can begin to communicate and solve their problems.
7. To gain insight into adolescent-sibling relationships and rivalry in the family and how situations can be improved.
8. To explore adolescent-grandparent (or other relative) relationships in the family: what they think of one another, what the chief sources of friction are, what they expect of one another, and how their relationships can be improved.

Bibliography

1. Adams, B. N. *The American Family: A Sociological Interpretation.* Chicago: Markham, 1971.

2. Adams, J. F. "Adolescent Personal Problems as a Function of Age and Sex." *Journal of Genetic Psychology* 104 (1964): 207–214.

3. Andersen, W. J. *Design for Family Living.* Minneapolis: T. S. Denison and Co., 1964.

4. Anthony, E. J. "The Reactions of Parents to Adolescents and Their Behavior." In *Parenthood: Its Psychology and Psychopathology.* Edited by E. J. Anthony and T. Benedek. Boston: Little, Brown and Co., 1970, pp. 307–324.

5. Anthony, E. J., and Benedek, T., eds. *Parenthood: Its Psychology and Psychopathology.* Boston: Little, Brown and Co., 1970.

6. Balswick, J. O., and Macrides, C. "Parental Stimulus for Adolescent Rebellion." *Adolescence* 10 (1975): 253–266.

7. Baumrind, D. "Authoritarian vs. Authoritative Control." *Adolescence* 3 (1968): 255–272.

8. Bengston, V. L. "The Generation Gap: A Review and Typology of Social-Psychological Perspectives." *Youth and Society* 2 (1970): 7–32.

9. Berkowitz, L. *The Development of Motives and Values in Children.* New York: Basic Books, 1964.

10. Blood, L., and D'Angelo, R. "A Progress Research Report on Value Issues in Conflict Between Runaways and Their Parents." *Journal of Marriage and the Family* 36 (1974): 486–491.

11. Blue Cross Association. "On Being an American Parent." *Blue Print for Health* 22 (1970): 89–96.

12. Bowerman, C. E., and Elder, G. H., Jr. "Variations in Adolescent Perception of Family Power Structure." *American Sociological Review* 29 (1964): 551–567.

13. Bowerman, C. E., and Dobash, R. M. "Structural Variations in Inter-Sibling Affect." *Journal of Marriage and Family* 36 (1974): 48–54.

14. Burr, W. R. "Satisfaction with Various Aspects of Marriage over the Life Cycle: A Random Middle Class Sample." *Journal of Marriage and the Family* 32 (1970): 29–37.

15. Campbell, M. M., and Cooper, K.

"Parents' Perception of Adolescent Behavior Problems." *Journal of Youth and Adolescence* 4 (1975): 309–320.

16. *Children and Parents: Together in the World.* Report of Forum 15, 1970, White House Conference on Children. Washington, D.C.: Superintendent of Documents, 1971.

17. Chilman, C. S. "Families in Development in Mid-Stage in the Family Life Cycle." *Family Coordinator* 17 (1968): 297–313.

18. Coleman, J. C. "The Study of Adolescent Development Using a Sentence-Completion Method." *British Journal of Educational Psychology* 40 (1970): 27–34.

19. Conger, J. J. "A World They Never Knew: The Family and Social Change." *Daedalus* (Fall 1971).

20. ———. *Adolescence and Youth.* New York: Harper and Row, 1973.

21. Cooper, D. *Death of the Family.* New York: Pantheon, 1970.

22. Cooperative Extension Service, Montana State College. "What Kind of Parents Do Teen-Agers Want?" Bozeman, Montana, 1963. Mimeographed.

23. Dahlem, N. W. "Young Americans' Reported Perceptions of their Parents." *Journal of Psychology* 74 (1970): 187–194.

24. Daly, S. J. *Questions Teen-Agers Ask.* New York: Dodd, Mead and Co., 1963.

25. Devereux, E. C. et al. "Child-Rearing in England and the United States: A Cross-National Comparison." *Journal of Marriage and the Family* 31 (1969): 257–270.

26. Douvan, E., and Adelson, J. *The Adolescent Experience.* New York: John Wiley and Sons, 1966.

27. Dreyfus, E. A. *Adolescence. Theory and Experience.* Columbus, Ohio: Charles E. Merrill Publishing Co., 1976.

28. Edwards, J. N., and Brauburger, M. B. "Exchange and Parent-Youth Conflict." *Journal of Marriage and the Family* 35 (1973): 101–107.

29. Elder, G. H., Jr. "Parent-Youth Relations in Cross-National Perspective." *Social Science Quarterly* 49 (1968): 216–228.

30. Fengler, A. P., and Wood, V. "Continuity between Generations: Differential Influences of Mothers." *Youth and Society* 4 (1973): 359–372.

31. Flacks, R. "Youth Intelligence in Revolt." *Trans-Action* (June 1970): 47–55.

32. Floyd, H. H., Jr., and South, D. R. "Dilemma of Youth: The Choice of Parents or Peers as a Frame of Reference for Behavior." *Journal of Marriage and the Family* 34 (1972): 627–634.

33. Gold, M., and Douvan, E. *Adoles-*

cent Development. Boston: Allyn and Bacon, 1969.

34. Hill, R. et al. *Family Development in Three Generations.* Cambridge, Mass.: Schenkman Publishing Co., 1970.

35. Horrocks, J. *The Psychology of Adolescence.* 3d. ed. Boston: Houghton Mifflin Co., 1962.

36. Hurlock, E. B. *Developmental Psychology.* 4th ed. New York: McGraw-Hill, 1975.

37. Kandel, D., and Lesser, G. S. "Parent-Adolescent Relationships and Adolescent Independence in the United States and Denmark." *Journal of Marriage and the Family* 31 (1969): 348–358.

38. ———. *Youth in Two Worlds.* San Francisco: Jossey-Bass Publishing Co., 1972.

39. Kinloch, G. C. "Parent-Youth Conflict at Home: An Investigation among University Freshmen." *American Journal of Orthopsychiatry* 40 (1970): 658–664.

40. Lambert, B. G. et al. *Adolescence: Transition from Childhood to Maturity.* Monterey, Calif.: Brooks/Cole Publishing Co., 1972.

41. Lerner, R. M. "Showdown at Generation Gap: Attitudes of Adolescents and Their Parents toward Contemporary Issues." In *Contemporary Adolescence: Readings.* 2d ed. Edited by H. D. Thornburg. Monterey, Calif.: Brooks/Cole Publishing Co., 1975, pp. 114–126.

42. Lerner, R. M., and Knapp, J. R. "Actual and Perceived Intra-familial Attitudes of Late Adolescents and Their Parents." *Journal of Youth and Adolescence* 4 (1975): 17–36.

43. Lerner, R. M. et al. "Attitudes of High School Students and Their Parents toward Contemporary Issues." *Psychological Reports* 31 (1972): 255–258.

44. Loeffler, D. et al. "Content and Process of Inter-Generation Communication." *Family Coordinator* 18 (1969): 345–352.

45. Lorenz, K. "The Enmity between Generations and Its Probable Ethological Causes." *Psychoanalytic Review* 57 (1970): 333–377.

46. McCord, J., and McCord, W. "The Effects of Parental Role Model on Criminality." In *Readings In Juvenile Delinquency.* Edited by R. Corvin. Philadelphia: J. B. Lippincott, 1964.

47. Mead, M. *Culture and Commitment: A Study of the Generation Gap.* New York: Doubleday and Co., 1970.

48. Meisels, M., and Canter, F. M. "A Note on the Generation Gap." *Adolescence* 6 (1971): 523–530.

49. Meissner, W. W. "Parental Inter-

action of the Adolescent Boy." *Journal of Genetic Psychology* 107 (1965): 225–233.

50. Mikesell, R. H., and Tessor, A. "Life History Antecedents of Authoritarianism: A Quasi-Longitudinal Approach." *Proceedings*, 79th Annual Convention, American Psychological Association, 1971.

51. Mischel, W. "Sex Typing and Socialization." In Mussen, P. H., ed. *Carmichael's Manual of Child Psychology*, vol. 2., 3d ed. New York: John Wiley and Sons, 1970.

52. Musgrove, F. *Youth and the Social Order*. Bloomington, Ind.: Indiana University Press, 1964.

53. Niemi, R. G. "Political Socialization." In *Handbook of Political Psychology*. Edited by J. N. Knutson. San Francisco: Jossey-Bass, 1973, pp. 117–138.

54. Nye, F. I. *Family Relationships and Delinquent Behavior*. New York: John Wiley and Sons, 1958.

55. Offer, D. *The Psychological World of the Teen-Ager: A Study of Normal Adolescent Boys*. New York: Basic Books, 1969.

56. Offer, D.; Marcus, D.; and Offer, J. L. "A Longitudinal Study of Normal Adolescent Boys." *American Journal of Psychiatry* 126 (1970): 917–924.

57. Orloff, H., and Weinstock, A. "A Comparison of Parent and Adolescent Attitude Factor Structures." *Adolescence* 10 (1975): 201–205.

58. Peterson, D. R., and Becker, W. C. "Family Interaction and Delinquency." In *Juvenile Delinquency: Research and Theory*. Edited by H. C. Quay. Princeton, N.J.: D. Van Nostrand Co., 1965, pp. 36–99.

59. Peterson, E. T., and Kunz, P. R. "Parental Control over Adolescents according to Family Size." *Adolescence* 10 (1975): 419–427.

60. Powell, M. "Age and Sex Differences in the Degree of Conflict within Certain Areas of Personal Adjustment." *Psychological Monographs* 69 (1955).

61. Propper, A. M. "The Relationship of Maternal Employment to Adolescent Roles, Activities, and Parental Relationships." *Journal of Marriage and the Family* 34 (1972): 417–421.

62. Renne, K. S. "Correlates of Dissatisfaction in Marriage." *Journal of Marriage and the Family* 32 (1970): 54–67.

63. Reuter, M. W. "The Father-Son Relationship and the Personality Adjustment of the Late Adolescent Male." *Dissertation Abstracts* 70 (1969): 5327.

64. Rice, F. P. "Getting Along With Your Teenager." Bulletin No. 511. Orono, Maine: Cooperative Extension Service, University of Maine, 1965.

65. ———. "The Change of Life." Bulletin No. 541. Orono, Maine: Cooperative Extension Service, University of Maine, 1967.

66. Rogers, D. *Adolescence: A Psychological Perspective*. Monterery, Calif.: Brooks/Cole Publishing Co., 1972.

67. Role, A. "Perceptions of Parental Behavior among Alienated Adolescents." *Adolescence* 6 (1971): 19–38.

68. Rollins, B. C., and Feldman, H. "Marital Satisfaction over the Family Life Cycle." *Journal of Marriage and the Family* 32 (1970): 20–28.

69. Scheck, D. et al. "Adolescents' Perceptions of Parent-Child Relations and the Development of Internal-External Control Orientation." *Journal of Marriage and the Family* 35 (1973): 643–654.

70. Scherz, F. H. "The Crisis of Adolescence in Family Life." *Social Casework* 48 (1967): 209–215.

71. Schiamberg, L. "Some Socio-Cultural Factors in Adolescent-Parent Conflict: A Cross-Cultural Comparison of Selected Cultures." *Adolescence* 4 (1969): 333–360.

72. Schneiders, A. *Adolescents and the Challenge of Maturity*. Milwaukee: Bruce Publishing Co., 1965.

73. Schvaneveldt, J. D. "Mormon Adolescents' Likes and Dislikes towards Parents and Home." *Adolescence* 8 (1973): 171–178.

74. Sebald, Hans. *Adolescence: A Sociological Analysis*: New York: Appleton-Century-Crofts, 1968.

75. Shanes, E. "Family Help Patterns and Social Class in Three Countries." *Journal of Marriage and the Family* 29 (1967): 257–266.

76. Shapiro, S. H. "Vicissitudes of Adolescence." In *Behavior Pathology of Childhood and Adolescence*. Edited by S. L. Copel. New York: Basic Books, pp. 93–117.

77. Smart, M. S., and Smart, R. C. *Adolescents*. New York: Macmillan Co., 1973.

78. Smith, T. E. "Foundations of Parental Influence upon Adolescents: An Application of Social Power Theory." *American Sociological Review* 35 (1970): 860–873.

79. Solomon, J. C. "Family Identity." *Adolescence* 7 (1972): 511–518.

80. Stinnett, N. et al. "Marital Need Satisfaction of Older Husbands and Wives." *Journal of Marriage and the Family* 32 (1970): 428–434.

81. Stokes, Walter R. "Intelligent Preparation of Children for Adolescence." *Journal of Marriage and the Family* 27 (1965): 163–165.

82. Sundberg, N. et al. "Family Co-

hesiveness and Autonomy of Adolescents in India and the United States." *Journal of Marriage and the Family* 31 (1969): 403–407.

83. Sutton-Smith, B. *Child Psychology.* New York: Appleton-Century-Crofts, 1973, pp. 462–483.

84. Thornburg, H. D. *Development in Adolescence.* Monterey, Calif.: Brooks/Cole Publishing Co., 1975.

85. Walters, J., and Stinnett, N. "Parent-Child Relationships: A Decade Review of Research." *Journal of Marriage and Family* 33 (1971): 70–111.

86. Weiner, I. B. *Psychological Disturbance in Adolescence.* New York: John Wiley and Sons, 1970.

87. Wilson, R. A. *Feminine Forever.* Philadelphia: J. B. Lippincott, 1966.

88. Winch, R. F., and Greer, S. A. "Urbanism, Ethnicity, and Extended Families." *Journal of Marriage and the Family* 30 (1968): 40–45.

Early Marriage

Outline

What is considered an early marriage? Is the incidence of early marriage increasing or decreasing? What are the prospects for the success of early marriages? What types of young people are marrying young and for what reasons? What adjustments and problems do they face after marriage? What policies do public schools follow concerning marriage or marital or premarital pregnancies of students? These are the major questions with which this chapter is concerned.

Defining Early Marriage

What constitutes an early marriage? Any specific answer to this question is relative to personal views of the term *early*. It is relative also to cultural framework: what is considered early in the United States might not be thought so in countries such as India or China with large peasant populations. The answer is also relative to the period of history: the median age of marriage changes over the years.

An extensive investigation of most of the research into early marriages in the United States reveals a lack of consistency of definition of what constitutes early marriage. Early marriage has been equated with teenage marriage (under age twenty for both male and female). Age twenty or under for one of the couple has also been used as the delineator. Early marriage has sometimes been defined as any age below the median age at first marriage (under twenty-three for males and under twenty-one for females). One of the most important researchers and writers in this field, Lee Burchinal, tends to equate early marriage with high school age marriage, focusing on those couples at least one of whom has not yet reached his or her nineteenth birthday. (9, 10, 11)

This lack of consistency in definition is perhaps not surprising because of the relativity of the word *early*, but the inconsistency creates difficulties when one attempts to analyze and compare data from different studies. One solution, suggested by Burchinal, is "to ignore the variations and definitions of marriage and to present findings of the available research." (10, p. 6) He goes on to emphasize that "this simple solution is not as disconcerting as it might appear, for virtually all data . . . are for brides who were 18 years or less." (10, p. 6)

This solution is satisfactory in discussing early marriages of girls, but not when applied to boys, for boys generally mature physically, emotionally, and socially about two years later than girls. With these maturational differences in mind, Bartz and Nye prefer extending the criteria for early marriage to age twenty or under for the groom and age eighteen or under for the bride. (4) This differentiation makes it possible to include most marriages involving high school students and the marriages of males two years after high school graduation. All factors considered, this definition seems balanced and reasonable and will be used in this chapter.

Trends and Incidence

Figure 15–1 gives a detailed picture of U.S. statistics on marriage ages between 1950 and 1976. The median age of first marriage for females stopped declining in 1956 and for males in 1972 and has been increasing slowly since. (68, 69) The median age of first marriage in 1976 was 22.9 for males and 21.0 for females. It appears that the steady drop in median age of marriage that was especially noticeable in the 1940s has been arrested. However, these are still high percentages of youth, especially girls, who are marrying young. Census figures for 1975 show that 22 percent of girls and 7 percent of boys age nineteen or under are (or have been) married. (69) Seventy percent of women and 40 percent of men aged twenty to twenty-five are or have been married.

Prospects and Prognosis

In order to evaluate whether early marriage is wise or unwise, desirable or undesirable, one must ask how successful early marriages are. If they are strong, happy, satisfying marriages, there is no cause for complaint or alarm; but if they are weak, unhappy, frustrating marriages, causing much personal suffering and numerous social problems, there is ample cause for concern.

Divorce statistics are an obvious means of measuring marriage success or failure. Using this measure, early marriages don't work out well, especially if

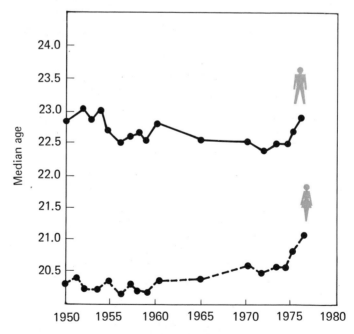

Figure 15–1.   Median age at first marriage in the United States, 1950–1976.
(Adapted from U.S. Bureau of the Census, Department of Commerce, *Current Population Reports.* Series P-20, No. 255 [Washington, D.C.: U.S. Government Printing Office, 1973]; and *Statistical Abstract of the United States, 1978,* p. 79.)

both the husband and wife are young. Numerous research studies indicate that the younger people are when married, the greater the chance of unhappy marriage and thus of divorce. (8, 21, 69) A 1972 study indicates that white women marrying at ages nineteen to twenty had 2¼ times the divorce rate and those from ages fourteen to seventeen had over 3½ times the divorce rate of those marrying at ages twenty-two to twenty-four. (8) See Figure 15–2 for comparative figures for different ages of whites and blacks. A government analysis of national statistics shows similar trends among males. (67) White males who marry at age twenty-one or under have 2½ times the divorce rate of those marrying at age twenty-eight or over. (67)

It is evident that the older the couple at marriage, the greater likelihood the marriage will succeed. But this direct correlation between age at first marriage and marital success diminishes for men at about age twenty-seven, when the decline in divorce rate slows down considerably. (66) For women, the divorce rate declines with each year they wait to marry until a gradual leveling off occurs at about age twenty-five. (66) Therefore, strictly from the standpoint of marital stability, men who wait to marry until at least age twenty-seven and women who wait until about age twenty-five have waited as long as practical to maximize their chances of success. (43, p. 240)

EXPRESSED DISSATISFACTION

Many couples marrying young may never get divorced, but some express deep dissatisfaction with their marriage. Of a sample of sixty Iowa girls who married before graduation from high school, Burchinal found that 55 percent would delay marriage if they had the same thing to do over again. (9) Here are some of their comments.

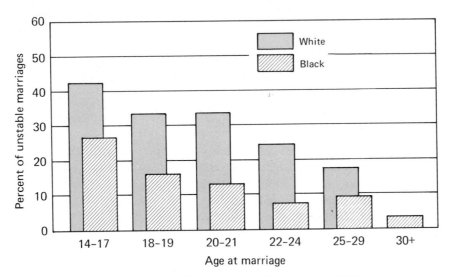

Figure 15–2.   Age at marriage and the experience of marital instability among ever-married women under age 45 in 1970. (Adapted from L. L. Bumpass and J. A. Sweet, "Differentials in Marital Instability: 1970," *American Sociological Review* 37[1972]:754–766. Used by permission.)

I don't think people should marry young. It's hard to get along when he is going to school. Our income is rather short. We probably should have waited.

We thought we were in love, we would get married and have good times. We had a very poor idea of what marriage was. We thought we could come and go, do as we pleased, do or not do the dishes, but it isn't that way.

I have missed several years of important living, the dating period, living with another girl, being away from home, working, maybe. I wouldn't get married so young again.

I would have waited to finish high school first. It has me tied down so. I've had no fun since I was married. I can't go to dances. I don't feel right there. . . . I guess I thought he was the only one in the world, I was badly mixed up.

I wanted to get away from home. My stepfather never showed any real interest in me. (9)

PREMARITAL COUNSELING

Realizing that very young couples have a poor chance of marital success, the state of California has pioneered a program requiring any persons under the age of eighteen to participate in premarital counseling if the court deems it necessary and if the court feels the partners are capable of paying for the counseling. (23) The purpose of the counseling is not to talk a couple out of marriage, but to assist them in assessing their emotional, economic, and social readiness for marriage, to help them evaluate their decision to marry and their motivation for marriage, to stimulate communication between them and with adults, to help them grow both as individuals and as a family, to create an awareness of potential strengths and weaknesses that would affect their marriage, to explore and clarify their role expectations, to provide sex information, and to explore any special circumstances surrounding the marriage such as racial, ethnic, or religious differences, pregnancy, physical or emotional handicaps, and parental attitudes. (23, p. 438) Each couple are counseled for at least four sessions. Most couples counseled feel the law is "an okay law." About 50 percent of the girls are already pregnant. One of the chief advantages of the program is that the couple become involved with the counselor in a meaningful way and thus are stimulated to want counseling help after marriage, if needed. (23, p. 439)

A Profile of the Young Married

AGE RELATIONSHIP

Early marriages primarily involve young wives and their older husbands. (11) Typically, a high school girl will marry a boy who is past high school age, usually from 3.5 to 5.5 years older. In fact the age difference between spouses is inversely related to the age of the bride. (11) For fifteen-year-old brides, the average groom is 5.5 years older; for eighteen-year-old brides, 3.6 years older. The age difference at age twenty-one is only 1.9 years. (10, 11)

INTELLIGENCE AND SOCIOECONOMIC STATUS

Early marriages disproportionately involve adolescents from lower socioeconomic backgrounds. (5, 10, 11, 20) Typically their parents have less education and are of a lower occupational status.

There are several good reasons why low socioeconomic status correlates with early marriage. As a group, these youths are less interested in high school and post–high school education, so they see no need to postpone marriage to finish their schooling, especially when marriage seems much more attractive than school. (4, p. 265) Less skilled occupations require only a minimal amount of education. In some communities marriage by age eighteen, especially for girls, is generally approved, because the youths have reached a dead end in school and marriage seems the only attractive course. (4) The parents are less often likely to object to early marriage. (4, p. 264) Furthermore, premarital pregnancy, one of the principal causes of early marriage, is much more common among youths from low socioeconomic status families. (10)

Similarly, adolescents who have lower intelligence and poorer grades in school more often marry early. (4, p. 263; 13) Furthermore, those who marry during school are more likely to drop out of school. (20) It becomes a vicious circle: the academically inferior marry earlier, and once married, are less likely to continue their education. This is especially true of those who have children soon after marriage. (73)

DEMOGRAPHIC AND ETHNIC FACTORS

Place of residence seems to have some influence on age at marriage. Rural residents tend to marry a year earlier than urban residents. (32, p. 162) Those from the South tend to marry earlier than others, those from the Northeast later, with those from the central and western states somewhere in between. Youths of foreign parentage usually marry later than those of native-born parents. (22) Foreign-born Irish males have the highest age at marriage (29.4 years), those with Spanish surnames the earliest (25.6 years). The age is variable, depending upon native customs. (32, p. 162)

EMOTIONAL AND SOCIAL MALADJUSTMENT

There is some evidence that the less emotionally adjusted a boy or girl is, the more likely early marriage is to occur. Also, the early married are more socially maladjusted at the time of marriage than are others. (72) However, a five-year follow-up by Vincent showed that young marrieds evidenced the most personality improvement during five years, more so than did the nonmarrieds, so that at the end of five years the personality differentials had virtually disappeared. (72) If the marriages can survive, marriage itself seems to be a contributing factor in developing personal and social maturity.

PARENTAL RELATIONSHIPS

First-born males tend to marry earlier than the later born, probably because of earlier parental socialization. (26) For some reason, the same does not hold true for women. Those youths who marry early tend to have less satisfactory relationships with their parents. They have more disagreement with parents before marriage and less attachment to their fathers. Furthermore, those wives who report problems with families in their childhood and adolescence report unhappiness, doubt, and conflict in early marriage. (29)

Reasons for Early Marriage

The most important causes or reasons for early marriage are:

Sexual stimulation, pregnancy
Early dating, acceleration of adult sophistication
Social pressure
Overly romantic, glamorous views of marriage
Escape; attempt to resolve personal, social problems
Affluence, prosperity

These reasons deserve a closer examination.

SEXUAL STIMULATION AND PREGNANCY

The number one reason for early marriage, particularly while still in school, is pregnancy. (20, 52) Pregnancy rates vary from study to study according to the age of the youths. The younger the adolescent at the time of marriage, the more likely pregnancy is to be involved. Pregnancy rates may be as high as 50 percent when at least one of the partners is still in high school.

Adolescents today are bombarded with sexual stimuli in magazines, newspapers, books, plays, movies, and on radio and television. Constant stimulation, greater privacy and freedom, lack of adult supervision, and dating patterns that very early push youths into paired relationships and sexual intimacy and that encourage permissiveness with affection have resulted in a great deal of sexual experimentation. (63, 71, 76) These factors plus a general lack of use of reliable birth control measures (12, 76) have increased the number of premarital pregnancies among adolescents. In spite of the widespread use of abortion as a means of terminating these pregnancies, many adolescents still get married because of pregnancy.

EARLY DATING

Research clearly indicates that within a social class, the earlier a boy or girl starts to date, the more likely early marriage is to occur. (4) It is important to emphasize the phrase *within a social class,* for adolescents from higher socioeconomic status groups start dating earlier than those from lower socioeconomic status groups, yet the latter marry earlier. Why? Although higher status youths start dating earlier, they proceed at a slower pace from dating to marriage. Lower status youths start dating a little later, but are more likely to become romantically involved, go steady, and proceed more rapidly from first date to marriage. (42) Age when dating starts is not itself the deciding factor. What is important is the length of the person's dating experience before marriage—generally speaking, the longer the better. (4; 6, p. 66)

There are other correlates to these statements. The more dates a girl has compared to others her age, the more likely early marriage is to occur. (47) Also, the earlier a girl begins to go steady and the more steady boyfriends she has in high school, the more likely is her early marriage. (4) But again the emphasis should be not just on how young dating begins, but how rapidly the young person advances to serious dating, going steady, engagement, and to other symbols of adult status.

SOCIAL PRESSURE

Social pressure from parents, friends, and society also pushes adolescents toward early marriage. (13) Educators report a chain reaction of early marriages in their schools. (10, p. 5) When one couple marries, there is increased pressure on others to do the same. No one wants to be left out. Pressure also comes from parents who don't want their daughters to be wallflowers or spinsters or their sons to be thought "queer."

ROMANTIC VIEWS OF MARRIAGE

A survey of couples who were dating indicated that being in love was related positively to the level of happiness. (18) Being in love in our culture is held to be so romantic and wonderful that many youths don't wait to enter this blissful state. The concept of marriage for love leads youths to feel that the goal of life is to find love, and that once found, one must hurry up and marry, at all costs, before it escapes. Girls who marry early often feel that marriage is their goal in life. Bartz and Nye put it this way: "The more optimistic a girl's expectations and attitudes toward marriage, the more likely early marriage will occur." (4, p. 261) For information on the aspirations of black versus white teenage girls regarding age at marriage, see the research by Kuvlesky. (39)

ESCAPE

Marriage also is sometimes used as a means of escape from an unhappy home situation, lack of school achievement, personal insecurities or inadequacies, or unsatisfactory social adjustment with one's peers. The less attractive one's present situation and the more attractive marriage seems, the more the emotionally insecure or socially maladjusted individual feels pushed toward marriage as an escape from an unhappy environment into something that promises to be better. (4, 42, 56) One recent study showed that high school youths from broken homes held more romantic and unrealistic conceptions of love than did those living with parents whose marriages were intact. (38)

AFFLUENCE AND PROSPERITY

More early marriages occur also in times of economic prosperity than in times of economic depression. The reason is obvious: getting married costs money; therefore, when employment is readily available, young couples feel they can afford to get married.

Adjustments and Problems in Early Marriage

IMMATURITY

Many of the adjustments young couples must make or the problems they must solve are no different from those of other couples, but they are aggravated by immaturity. It is essentially the problem of immaturity that is the great obstacle to successful teenage marriage.

Immaturity creates problems in many ways. *The less mature are less likely to make a wise choice of mate.* When the time span between first date and marriage is shortened, youths have less chance to gain experience in knowing and understanding the kind of person with whom they are compatible. The young adolescent girl or boy in the throes of a first love affair is at a distinct disadvantage in making an intelligent choice of mate.

The less mature are less likely to evidence the ultimate direction of their personality growth. Youths change as they mature, and may find they have nothing in common with their partners as they grow older. Two young people who might genuinely find a community of interest and a good reciprocal interaction at a particular point in their growth, could easily grow away from each other in the ensuing two or three years as their personalities unfold.

The most common example of this is the case of a young girl who dropped out of school to work to put her husband through college only to discover afterward that he has grown away from her intellectually, and they can no longer enjoy talking together. The same thing holds true of a boy who marries young. He may marry a girl who has not yet found herself in life, and runs the risk of living with a girl different from the woman she will be several years later. Many girls marry only to discover later that they resent having to give up a promising career.

The less mature are less likely to be able to handle the difficult and complex adjustments and problems of marriage. There is ample evidence to show that emotional maturity and good marital adjustment go together. (19, 57)

Many teenagers are still insecure, oversensitive, and somewhat tempestuous and unstable. Many are still rebelling against adult authority and seeking emotional emancipation from parents. If these youths marry, they carry their immaturities into marriage, making it difficult to adjust to living with their mate and making it harder to make decisions and solve conflicts as they arise.

Most youths have not yet become responsible enough for marriage. The average teenage boy is not really ready to settle down with one girl. He wants to go out, have fun, be with the gang, and be free to do as he pleases. He may resent being tied down and possibly having to support a wife and child. He may not yet evidence a "monogamous attitude." (8) Nor are many teenage girls ready to be wives and probably mothers, to manage a family budget, or to handle their share of the responsibility for the homemaking tasks.

EARLY PARENTHOOD

One of the real problems and disadvantages of early marriage is that it is often associated with early parenthood. (20, 73) A study of eighty-two married couples from Franklin County, Ohio, where the husband was age 19 or under (the median age of the husbands was 18.6 and of the wives was 17.9), showed that two-thirds of the couples were having a baby within one year after marriage. (24, p. 257)

A series of record-linking studies of the correlation between age at marriage and intervals to first birth, by Christensen, revealed that the younger the brides and grooms, the sooner they started having children. Also, the earlier the age at marriage, the greater the percentage of brides who were premaritally pregnant. (17) In the Ohio sample, for example, 55.8 percent of the brides under 20 years of age had a baby within the first year of marriage as compared with 31.4 percent of the brides aged 20 or older. In the Utah II sample, 43.5 percent of the brides under age 20 had a baby within the first year of marriage, compared to 38.5 percent for brides 20 and older. (17, p. 274) Because both premarital pregnancy and early postmarital pregnancy is followed by a higher than average divorce rate, large numbers of children of early marriages grow up without a secure, stable family life or without both a mother and a father. (17, p. 276) Apparently, many young marrieds are not mature enough to assume the responsibilities of both marriage and early parenthood, so the marriages often fail and the children suffer.

Not only do adolescent parents begin having children at an earlier age, but they also have more children. A study of a national sample of 1,000 thirty-year-olds indicated that those who first became parents as adolescents had an average of nearly three children, whereas for the remainder of those with children the average was two. (60, p. 177) Unfortunately, the young women who are the least happily married are also the ones who experience unplanned pregnancies. (14)

Physicians have emphasized the medical risks of early pregnancy. Children born to adolescent mothers are more likely to be born premature, with low birth weight and with physical and neurological defects than are infants born to mothers in their twenties. (48, p. 23) Low birth weight and prematurity have been found to be twice as high among children of adolescents as among young adults, and are usually considered to be primary medical risks. (2, 5, 6) Perinatal, neonatal, and infant mortality have been found to be higher for children of young mothers. (48, 49, 64) Babies born to adolescents under age sixteen are two to three times as likely to die in their first year. (48, p. 23) Besides increasing the natality risk of the child, prematurity is linked to such conditions as epilepsy, cerebral palsy, mental retardation, blindness, and deafness. (48, p. 23)

The higher incidence of physical defects in children born to adolescent mothers is not due solely to the age of the mother. It is related also to the fact that these mothers may be pregnant out of wedlock and of low socioeconomic status, and so receive inadequate nutrition and poor or inadequate prenatal care. (48, p. 24) Malnutrition in the pregnant mother may be a very serious factor for the infant, causing mental retardation. (64, p. 255) Follow-up studies of premature babies ten to fifteen years after birth reveal a high incidence of nervous system disorders, emotional disturbances, and mental and physical retardation.

Early pregnancy is also a medical risk for the young teenage girl. If she becomes pregnant while her own body is still growing and maturing, the growing fetus imposes an additional strain upon her system, and she is more prone to complications of pregnancy, such as toxemia or eclampsia. Other serious risks for pregnant adolescents include anemia, cephalopelvic disproportion (irregular size or position of the infant relative to the pelvic structure of the mother) and prolonged labor. (48, p. 23; 64, p. 254)

FINANCIAL PRESSURES

One of the major problems of early marriage is financial worry. (20, 54, 58) In a study of high school couples, de Lissovoy found that lack of adequate income and disagreement over how to spend what money was available was rated the number one problem by both husbands and wives. (20) Table 15–1 shows the ratings of problems by the husbands and wives in the third and thirtieth months of marriage. (20, pp. 246, 249) As can be seen, money was the primary problem at both times.

The primary difficulties are inadequate income and the fact that income has not reached the level expected. (44, p. 502; 60, p. 177) Little education, inexperience, and youth do not bring high wages. Some couples marry without any income.

With little or no income, couples receive part or all of their financial assistance from parents. (54) Forty-three percent of the couples in Burchinal's sample received financial help from parents at the beginning of marriage, but after several months only 29 percent reported doing so. (9) Families usually give some assistance to their children in the first year of marriage. Assistance in this study includes wedding gifts, clothing, home furnishings and equipment, food, loans of household equipment and car, baby-sitting services, money, and other gifts.

Not only low income but also inexperience in financial management and naively optimistic expectations get young marrieds into financial trouble. (58) A study of Texas high school juniors and seniors revealed that "teenagers expected to be able to purchase immediately for their projected family units many of the items that probably had taken their parents years to acquire." (15) In addition to a refrigerator and range, over three-fourths of the group expected to have a washer and air conditioning. Fifty-seven percent expected to have a dryer and 38 percent expected to have a dishwasher.

One of the expensive obsessions of adolescent males is to have a car. In spite of their low income, 86 percent of young heads of families (ages eighteen to

Table 15–1.   Mean ratings of problems by 37 couples in the third and thirtieth months of marriage.*

| | Husbands | | Wives | |
Area of Adjustment	3rd month	30th month	3rd month	30th month
1. Spending family income	2.50	2.01	2.12	1.91
2. Sex relations	2.90	2.10	3.51	3.05
3. In-law relationships	3.30	3.61	3.15	3.92
4. Mutual friends	4.05	3.80	3.10	2.91
5. Child training	4.10	3.11	4.20	3.02
6. Religious activities	4.10	3.51	4.10	4.02
7. Social activities	4.15	4.10	2.30	2.21

* The five-point scales were constructed so that a rating of 1 was an indication of low adjustment and 5 was a high rating.

Adapted from V. de Lissovoy, "High School Marriages: A Longitudinal Study," *Journal of Marriage and the Family* 35 (1973): 246, 249. Used by permission.

twenty-four) have cars. (69) This heavy outlay for cars and transportation is a major drag on the budgets of young families that need funds for current expenses or for household goods to begin marriage.

SEX RELATIONS

As can be seen in Table 15–1, husbands and wives both expressed a marked decrease in sexual satisfaction after thirty months of marriage. The husbands ranked sex relations the number two problem in both the third and thirtieth months of marriage. (20, p. 248) Wives rated it less of a problem. When couples were questioned about the frequency of sex relations, however, the wives expressed less satisfaction, indicating they wanted sex less frequently than their husbands. (20, p. 249)

SOCIAL ACTIVITIES AND MUTUAL FRIENDS

The problem ranked second by wives in de Lissovoy's study was social activities and the number three problem was mutual friends. (20, p. 248) De Lissovoy writes:

Essentially it was clear that the husbands remained "boys" in a number of ways. They went "out" with former "buddies," stayed after school to play basketball and other sports. . . . The wives on the other hand felt "dropped" by former friends and led rather lonely lives. While husbands' former friends and classmates dropped in often, very few of the wives reported callers. The wives did not welcome the husbands' friends and many reported that they felt they were "taken for granted" or "left out" when friends arrived. (20, p. 248)

CHILD TRAINING

Seven couples in de Lissovoy's study had children after three months of marriage. (20) Most of the other women were at various stages of pregnancy (forty-six out of forty-eight were premaritally pregnant). As a result, child training was not considered much of a problem in the beginning. After thirty months of marriage, however, the husbands ranked child training as the third biggest problem, and wives ranked it as a significantly greater problem than it had been. (20, p. 248)

IN-LAW RELATIONSHIPS

In de Lissovoy's study, husbands ranked in-law relationships as third and wives ranked it as the fourth most important problem after three months of marriage. (20, p. 248) After thirty months of marriage, husbands tended to rate this area higher, whereas the wives indicated a lower evaluation of in-law relationships. (20, p. 250) This problem is more likely if young couples live with parents or accept financial help from them. Burchinal found that 67 percent of his Iowa couples lived with one or the other parental family at the beginning of marriage and 20 percent were still doing so at the time of the study. (9) When parents give assistance to married children, they often expect continual affectional response, inclusion in some of their children's activities, personal service and attention, and compliance with parental wishes. The more immature the young marrieds, the more likely parents are to try to "help," to direct and interfere in their children's lives, and the more likely the young couple is to enact the residues of late adolescent conflicts over autonomy and dependence. (29)

Marriage and Public Schools

EDUCATIONAL ASPIRATIONS

Early marriage diminishes educational attainment among those attending high school. Not only do young marrieds make less educational progress during the four-year period, but they also tend to have lower educational aspirations for the future. (37, p. 105) The converse is also true: those with lower educational aspirations tend to marry earlier than those with higher aspirations. (47)

HIGH DROPOUT RATES

In a study of 2,070 Pennsylvania students who had married while still in high school, it was found that 80 percent dropped out of school after marriage. (21) However, the dropout rate was much lower for boys (37 percent) than for girls (90 percent). (21) A similar study of 2,000 married California high school students showed that 83 percent of girls and 48 percent of boys dropped out of school within six months. (41) A study of married high school couples in Pennsylvania revealed that 85 percent of girls and 73 percent of boys left school before graduating. (20) These high rates reflect the fact that 96 percent of the girls were pregnant before marriage and that school administrative policies and programs at that time either failed to keep the students in school or contributed directly to their leaving. Girls more frequently leave either by dropping out voluntarily or being forced out because of premarital pregnancy. Once she has dropped out, the chances of the adolescent mother's returning to continue her education are relatively small, especially if she keeps her baby and receives little encouragement or help in returning. (25, 60) Boys who drop out most often do so for economic reasons.

VOCATIONAL LIMITATIONS AND PLACEMENT

Adolescents who drop out of school to get married or because of marriage are limited in their educational attainment and are faced with a serious problem. (37) Subsequent lack of education seriously limits their economic potential. Marriage itself imposes greater economic necessity. Furthermore, without extensive parental or outside help, they have little opportunity to return to high school or to go on to higher education. (11) Thus, early marriage usually results in lower socioeconomic status. (4)

A related difficulty is that adolescents are often forced to accept and keep jobs they don't really like and are not free to explore, grow, develop, and prepare for a vocation for which they are more suited and in which they could better find fulfillment. By the time they find out who they are and what they want to do, they are already locked into a job they may hate. Early marriage has destroyed their freedom to be their best selves and to achieve their maximum potential.

LEGAL RIGHTS OF MARRIED AND/OR
PREGNANT STUDENTS

What are high schools legally permitted to do when a student marries? What are they permitted to do when they discover a student is pregnant out of wedlock? What are the student's constitutional rights? What are the rights of the school board? What does the law say?

With the implementation of the Regulations issued under Title IX of the Education Amendments of 1972, all married students and unmarried girls and young mothers are entitled to complete their education with full access to the resources and facilities provided by the public school system. Specifically, these regulations require that any school system receiving federal funds shall not (a) apply any rule concerning a student's actual or potential parental, family, or marital status that treats students differently on the basis of sex; and (b) discriminate against or exclude any student from its education program or activity on the basis of such student's pregnancy or pregnancy-related condition. Assignment of a student to a separate portion of the program or activity of the school can be made only if the student voluntarily requests such assignment or a physician certifies inability to continue in the normal program. Any separate instructional program for pregnant students must be comparable to that offered nonpregnant students. (28, p. 20)

There are legally defensible reasons for a board to remove a pregnant girl from school, but these defenses sometimes are so difficult to prove that a board may wonder if it is all worth the effort. A school district may be able to justify in court the removal of a pregnant girl from the regular school program if: (53, p. 24)

1. The girl refuses to place herself under medical care. A regular school program could pose a health hazard for some pregnant girls, and until the matter is decided by a physician, a school board probably is justified in keeping a pregnant girl away from activities that could be dangerous to her health.

2. The district is willing to claim and able to prove that the girl in question clearly is immoral. But pregnancy outside of marriage is not in itself proof of promiscuity or immorality. As one court ruled, "The court would like to make manifestly clear that lack of moral character is certainly a reason for excluding a child from public education. But the fact that a girl has one child out of wedlock does not forever brand her as a scarlet woman undeserving of any chance for rehabilitation or the opportunity for further education." (52)

3. The board is able to prove that a pregnant girl causes a substantial disruption in the operation of her school. Chances are that a pregnant girl will be the object of some whispering, giggling, and pointing, but a court may not rule that such attention adds up to a substantial disruption. Boards may want to think twice about admitting—much less trying to prove—that one pregnant girl can make a shambles of the educational program.

4. The board is able to prove that a pregnant girl presents a clear and present danger to the health, welfare, and safety of other students. Will other students run out and become pregnant because they see one of their classmates in that condition?

Generally, courts have said that the denial of regular academic education can be exercised in only the most severe cases, and that marriage and pregnancy are not in themselves acceptable reasons for dismissal. This reasoning forces boards to rely on defenses such as the four just mentioned, and those defenses (except in the case of the girl who refuses to place herself under the care of a doctor) can become difficult affairs.

If a school board is bent on restricting a pregnant student's activities, it may be able to keep her out of extracurricular activities. There is considerable legal evidence to support the contention that any educational restriction arbitrarily placed on pregnant students will be lifted by the judges.

Courts have ruled that married students and pregnant students (married or not) can participate in extracurricular activities in those instances when:

- School officials could not prove that "any inconvenience or damage was suffered." (75)
- No disruption of or interference with school activities or threat of harm to other students could be linked to the appearance of a pregnant, unmarried student at extracurricular activities. (51)
- Courts could not find a reasonable relationship between legitimate school purposes and rules that deny extracurricular activities to married and/or pregnant students.

The courts have also said that it is illegal for schools to punish offenders by denying them an education. When a married student sued her school board because of a board rule that prohibited married students from engaging in school activities, the court ruled that the board policy failed to promote a compelling state interest. (33)

Indeed, the board has failed to show that the regulation in question is even rationally related to—not to mention "necessary" to promote—any legitimate state interests at all. Instead, it is apparent that the sole purpose and effect of the regulation is to discourage, by actually punishing, marriages which are perfectly legal under the laws of Tennessee and which are thus fully consonant with the public policy of that state. It is the opinion of the court that such a regulation is repugnant to the Constitution of the United States in that it impermissibly infringes upon the rights to due process and equal protection of the law of those students who come within its ambit. (33)

SCHOOL POLICIES

It is evident from the Tennessee court ruling that the courts are now clearly on the side of married and/or unmarried pregnant students who want to continue their education. In spite of these judicial decisions, not all school boards have changed their policies to conform to the law. A variety of policies are still followed. (55, 74)

Some schools automatically dismiss married students, or retain them only after a full hearing where all factors are considered.

Some schools dismiss all pregnant students outright, married or not; in some cases they refuse to allow them ever to return to regular day classes. In only some instances are home tutors provided to allow them to continue their education. In some districts students are dismissed but allowed to reenter after a certain period following the birth of their child.

Some schools dismiss only unmarried pregnant students, refusing to allow them to return to regular day classes.

Some schools dismiss married and/or unmarried pregnant students at certain stages of the pregnancy: (1) immediately; (2) at the end of the week; (3) not later than the third month of pregnancy; (4) when the pregnancy becomes observable; (5) at the end of the semester; (6) if a second semester senior, only after all graduation requirements are met; or (7) only if a physician recommends their withdrawal.

Some schools require that admitted or court-proven fathers of unwed mothers drop out of school for a set period or that the fathers be excluded from athletics.

Some schools allow pregnant girls to remain in school but bar them from extracurricular activities, deny them the right to hold office, to work for honors, or to attend commencement. (40) Some segregate them during lunch time.

Some schools allow pregnant students to continue in regular school programs, but offer, in addition, counseling, health services, and courses designed exclusively for them.

Some districts place all pregnant students in special programs and segregated classes within the regular building, but more often removed geographically from the school. These special programs may include health services, family life education programs, and child-care courses in addition to or in lieu of regular academic programs.

When school policies are restrictive, the only way that students who are dismissed, barred from certain activities, or pushed into special programs can regain their full rights is to go to court. Many, especially the unmarried and the poor, are unable or unwilling to do so. (74)

It seems obvious that the motives of school policies are mixed. There is fear that pregnancies will become popular if condoned within the school. Most administrators feel that pregnancy will put them and the school in a bad light in the eyes of the community. Others believe that married students or unmarried pregnant students are a bad influence on others in the school. All too often the motive is punishment. Whenever special restrictions are imposed, the rule usually reflects official disapproval of in-school marriage; it is imposed partly as a disciplinary measure to discourage a mass movement toward marriage or pregnancy, and it is argued that it allows married students more time to devote to their mates and children. There is an effort too to protect the girl from embarrassment and to safeguard her health. Some schools make a real effort at rehabilitation. Others are relieved if she drops out of school voluntarily, and many of these schools make no effort to get her to return, even after the baby is born. (70)

SPECIAL PROGRAMS FOR PREGNANT STUDENTS

Probably the most successful approaches are those including special programs and services especially for expectant mothers. Some of these programs are based on the philosophy that it is better to keep pregnant girls in regular classrooms rather than segregating them, but to offer them special services and help in addition. One such program with a very liberal philosophy is offered in Azusa, California. (31, p. 480) The objective of the program is to build self-confidence to help the pregnant girls again feel equal to other teenagers. Staff members counsel the girls and encourage them to study and socialize with other girls. The girls work at their own pace. Because there is so much "spirit of incentive" at the school, many of the girls graduate early. (31; p. 480)

Another such program is offered cooperatively by the Emory University School of Medicine in cooperation with the Atlanta, Georgia, Board of Education. (70) Students are systematically contacted during pregnancy, informed of the special services offered through the program, encouraged to attend their regular classes and to return to school as quickly as possible after delivery. The special services provided include the following:

Individual treatment plans for the prenatal, obstetrical, and postnatal medical care are drawn up.

Social services include assignment of caseworkers to assist each girl. These caseworkers inform the girls of available services of existing agencies and encourage them to utilize these services. Girls receive employment assistance, educational and vocational counseling, public financial assistance, help with birth control, and assistance in finding housing.

Educational services include not only regular academic courses and assistance with these, but also courses in reproductive health. Most important, the girls are helped in every way possible to continue their education during and after pregnancy. It has been found that if students can continue day school the quarter of delivery, they are motivated to return after delivery and maintain the continuity of their schooling.

Table 15–2 shows the percentage of program students reporting some school attendance before and after delivery. This group is compared with a control group who were not part of the program. Subjects in the control group were similar in racial and socioeconomic composition to the program group, but they were either encouraged to withdraw or required to withdraw from school after pregnancy was discovered. (70, p. 223) Girls in the control group did not receive casework services except as they normally would through existing agencies. They were subject to the same counseling and recruitment services as any students in

Table 15–2.   Percentage of subjects reporting some school attendance during the quarter before delivery and returning to day school and to other educational programs after delivery.

Program Status	Attending before Delivery	Not Attending before Delivery	Returning to Day School	Returning to Other Educational Programs
Program group	38	62	51	24
Control group	9	91	25	37

Adapted from P. A. Ewer and J. O. Gibbs, "School Return among Pregnant Adolescents," *Journal of Youth and Adolescence* 5 (1976): 227. Used by permission.

the school, but no publicity was given to the possibility of day school following delivery, nor were they encouraged to return to school after delivery. As can be seen, the percent of students in the program group who stayed in school and who returned to regular day school was much higher than those in the second group. It is evident that school policies that discourage attendance during pregnancy and do not encourage return to school after delivery are responsible for the high dropout rates of pregnant students. (70, p. 229) It is also evident that high rates of regular day school continuation and of return after delivery were not achieved even by offering all the special services to pregnant students in regular class-rooms.

Even if pregnant students are allowed to attend their regular school and classes, they are often too embarrassed or uncomfortable to do so, so they drop out, never completing their education. For this reason many schools have found it advisable to offer special classes and programs, usually away from the regular school building, to get the girls away from the scrutiny of other students. (36, 50, 53) Often other community health or youth service agencies cooperate with the school in offering a full range of classes, programs, and services to expectant mothers. These programs are expensive, but they have succeeded in keeping many girls in school, in giving them proper prenatal, obstetrical, and postnatal health care, and in providing counseling and guidance for a wide range of aca-demic, vocational, family, social, and emotional problems with which they are confronted.

One such program is conducted in the Edgar Allan Poe Schools in Baltimore, Maryland. (36) In this program there are two separate schools, one housing pregnant junior high students and the other housing pregnant high school stu-dents. Students are referred from all over the city of Baltimore, and during the six years the program has been in operation, 65,000 students have been en-rolled and educated. A girl who does not demonstrate complications during preg-nancy may return to the special school two weeks after delivery. She does not return to her home school until after her postpartum checkup, and usually ar-rangements are made to transfer her back to her home school at the end of a quarter or semester. Students are offered the regular academic, special, and voca-tional classes available to other students throughout Baltimore. Those who do not desire to return to school after delivery are offered employment counseling and placement services. Thus, all girls either return to school or are encouraged to enter permanent employment. (36, p. 304) Guidance counseling is available to all, along with necessary health and social services. Every girl must be registered in a medical facility, given prenatal care, proper predelivery orientation, ob-stetrical service, and postpartum care. Every girl is also required to attend a special educational program that includes sex information and education, birth control information, prenatal care, child care and development, and family re-lationships. Special child care seminars are also conducted regularly throughout the school year and are open to all mothers. One result of this comprehensive program has been to increase the percentage of infants born with normal age and weight from 54 to 71 percent. (36, p. 305)

Different school systems offer some variations to the program. One program, called YMED (Young Mothers' Educational Development), in Syracuse, New

York, is conducted cooperatively by the State University of New York, the Up-state Medical Center of Syracuse, the Syracuse Board of Education, and the On-ondaga County Department of Health. It has been outstandingly successful in reducing the number of out-of-wedlock pregnancies. (32) Out of a total of 240 pregnant girls, with a mean age of 16.2 when referred to the program, only 16 became pregnant again out of wedlock. (31, p. 478) One reason for the low rate of repeat pregnancies is because sex education, contraceptive counseling, and birth control devices are made available on an optional basis to all girls who want them.

For a more complete discussion of the problems and adjustments of pregnant unwed mothers and of programs and services for them, see Chapter 22 of *Marriage and Parenthood* (57) and the following references: 1, 3, 7, 30, 34, 35, 45, 46, 48, 59, 60, 61, 62, 65, 73, 77.

Conclusions

Punitive measures have not been successful in preventing early marriages or premarital pregnancies. These events must themselves be considered consequences of a complicated series of personal, social, and familial conditions with which the student is confronted. There are, however, some positive steps that can be taken both to try to prevent premarital pregnancy and early marriage and to help unmarried pregnant girls and young couples once they are married.

A positive program of marriage and family life education is needed in the schools. (25) Instead of disciplining students for becoming pregnant or getting married, a more positive approach is for the school to assume responsibility in preparing youths for happy marriage and responsible parenthood as an important educational goal. If the school doesn't prepare adolescents for this goal as well as for college or for a vocation, is it really preparing them for living as well as for making a living? The school is the only institution that reaches all adolescents; therefore, it has an unusual opportunity to reach those who need marriage and family life education the most.

Because pregnancy is one of the primary reasons for early marriage, the problem needs to be looked at realistically to determine what can be done. Some adults advocate more birth control education and services for adolescents. Others advocate expanded adoptive services for children of unwed mothers. Still others emphasize offering abortion services to all those who wish to terminate their pregnancies.

School systems should strive to offer comprehensive educational, social, and medical programs and services to unmarried and married pregnant teenage girls. These programs and services ought to be modeled after some of the successful ones already described.

More adequate counseling and guidance services must be available to adolescents. Early marriage is partially the result of pregnancy, emotional maladjustments, difficulty in school and social relationships, and parent-adolescent problems. One way to prevent early marriage is to give adolescents more help with the problems that pushed them into early marriage in the first place. School and clinic guidance and counseling services for adolescents must be expanded if additional help is to be provided. (16, 27)

Parents and other adults can help by not pressuring adolescents into premature emotional involvements and commitments. Young people need to be encouraged to have many friends rather than steady boyfriends or girlfriends, and to delay serious involvement with one person until they are more mature. Overly romantic, unrealistic views of marriage can be offset by more realistic concepts taught by concerned adults.

Finally, communities need to face these problems and to plan cooperatively in solving them. Interagency cooperation will help make use of all available resources. Most problems can be solved or eased once communities see a real need and are willing to work together.

Learning Experiences

Field Trips

1. Visit a school or special class for pregnant teenagers and talk to the girls and/or teachers.
2. Visit a family planning clinic to talk to the staff about birth control use by adolescents.
3. Visit a residential home for expectant unwed mothers.
4. Visit an abortion clinic.
5. Visit an adoption agency.

Interviews

1. Interview school administrators and/or school board members concerning school policies on married students and married or unmarried pregnant adolescent girls and their boyfriends.
2. Interview married high school couples concerning the benefits, adjustments, and problems of early marriage.
3. Interview several clergymen from different churches or synagogues concerning their views on early marriage and the roles of the church and other community organizations in serving young couples.
4. Interview several obstetricians to discuss the causes of premarital pregnancy, the problems and adjustments of adolescent mothers, and the special health problems of bearing children when the mother is young.

Bibliography

1. Adams, B. N. "The Pregnant Adolescent: A Group Approach." *Adolescence* 11 (1976): 467–485.

2. Alan Guttmacher Institute. "11 Million Teenagers: What Can Be Done about the Epidemic of Adolescent Pregnancies in the United States." New York: Planned Parenthood Federation of America, 1976.

3. Ambrose, L. "Misinforming Pregnant Teenagers." *Family Planning Perspectives* 10 (January/February 1978): 51ff.

4. Bartz, K. W., and Nye, F. I. "Early Marriage: A Propositional Formulation." *Journal of Marriage and the Family* 32 (1970): 258–267.

5. Bayer, A. E. "College Impact on Marriage." *Journal of Marriage and the Family* 34 (1972): 600–609.

6. Benson, L. *The Family Bond: Marriage, Love, and Sex in America.* New York: Random House, 1971.

7. Bruce, J. A. "Adolescent Parents: A Special Case of the Unplanned Family." *Family Coordinator* 27 (1978): 75–78.

8. Bumpass, L. L., and Sweet, J. A. "Differentials in Marital Instability: 1970." *American Sociological Review* 37 (1972): 754–766.

9. Burchinal, Lee G. "How Successful Are School-Age Marriages?" *Iowa Farm Science* 13 (1959): 7–10.

10. ———. "Research on Young Marriage: Implications for Family Life Education." *Family Life Coordinator* 9 (1960): 6–24.

11. ———. "Trends and Prospects for

Young Marriages in the United States." *Journal of Marriage and the Family* 27 (1965): 243–254.

12. Burkart, J., and Whatley, A. E. "The Unwed Mother: Implications for Family Life Educators." *Journal of School Health* 43 (1973): 451–454.

13. Call, V. R. A., and Otto, L. B. "Age at Marriage as Mobility Contigency: Estimates for the Nye-Berardo Model." *Journal of Marriage and the Family* 39 (1977): 67–79.

14. Card, J. J. *Long-Term Consequences for Children Born to Adolescent Parents.* Palo Alto, Calif.: American Institute for Research in the Behavioral Sciences, 1978.

15. Cateora, R. R. "An Analysis of the Teenage Market." Studies in Marketing, no. 7. Austin, Tex.: Bureau of Business Research, University of Texas, 1963, pp. 64–69.

16. Cattanach, T. J. "Coping with Intentional Pregnancies among Unmarried Teenagers." *School Counselor* 23 (1976): 211–215.

17. Christensen, H. "Child Spacing Analysis Via Record-Linkage." *Marriage and Family Living* 25 (1963): 272–280.

18. Critelli, J. W. "Romantic Attraction and Happiness." *Psychological Reports* 41 (December 1977): 721–722.

19. Crosby, J. F. *Illusion and Disillusion: The Self in Love and Marriage.* Belmont. Calif.: Wadsworth Publishing Co., 1973.

20. De Lissovoy, V. "High School Marriage: A Longitudinal Study." *Journal of Marriage and the Family* 35 (1973): 245–255.

21. De Lissovoy, V., and Hitchcock, M. E. "High School Marriages in Pennsylvania." *Journal of Marriage and the Family* 27 (1965): 263–270.

22. Edington, E., and Hays, L. "Difference in Family Size and Marriage Age Expectation and Aspirations of Anglo, Mexican American, and Native American Rural Youth in New Mexico." *Adolescence* 13 (1978): 393–400.

23. Elkin, M. "Premarital Counseling for Minors: The Los Angeles Experience." *Family Coordinator* 26 (1977): 429–443.

24. Eshleman, J. R. "Mental Health and Integration in Young Marriages." *Journal of Marriage and the Family* 27 (1965): 255–262.

25. Ewer, P. A., and Gibbs, J. O. "School Return among Pregnant Adolescents." *Journal of Youth and Adolescence* 5 (1976): 221–229.

26. Friedman, J. H. "Birth Order and Age at Marriage in Females." *Psychological Reports* 42 (June 1978): 1193–1194.

27. Gallagher, U. M. "Changing Focus on Services to Teenagers." *Children Today* 2 (1973): 24–27.

28. Goldmeier, H. "School Age Parents and the Public Schools." *Children Today* 5 (1976): 19–20, 36.

29. Goodrich, W. et al. "Patterns of Newlywed Marriage." *Journal of Marriage and the Family* 30 (1968): 383–389.

30. Hansen, H. et al. "School Achievement: Risk Factor in Teenage Pregnancies." *American Journal of Public Health* 68 (August 1978): 753–759.

31. Heller, J., and Kiralry, J., Jr. "An Educational Program for Pregnant School Age Girls." *Clearing House* 47 (1973): 476–482.

32. Hogan, D. P. "The Effects of Demographic Factors, Family Background, and Early Job Achievement on Age at Marriage." *Demography* 15 (May 1978): 161–175.

33. *Holt* v. *Shelton,* U.S.D.C., M.D., 833 (Tenn., 1972).

34. Honig, A. S. "What We Need to Know to Help the Teenage Parent." *Family Coordinator* 27 (1978): 113–119.

35. Kaplan, H. B. "Psychosocial Antecedents of Unwed Motherhood among Indigent Adolescents." *Journal of Youth and Adolescence* 8 (1979): 181–207.

36. Kappelman, M. et al. "A Unique School Health Program in a School for Pregnant Teenagers." *Journal of School Health* 44 (1974): 303–306.

37. Kerckhoff, A. C., and Parrow, A. A. "The Effect of Early Marriage on the Educational Attainment of Young Men." *Journal of Marriage and the Family* 41 (1979): 97–107.

38. Knox, D. H., Jr. "Attitudes toward Love of High School Seniors." *Adolescence* 5 (1970): 89–100.

39. Kuvlesky, W. P., and Obordo, A. S. "A Racial Comparison of Teen-Age Girls' Projections for Marriage and Procreation." *Journal of Marriage and the Family* 34 (1972): 75–84.

40. Landis, J. T. "High School Student Marriages, School Policy, and Family Life Education in California." *Journal of Marriage and the Family* 27 (1965): 271–276.

41. ———. "A Study of High School Student Marriages, Pregnancies and School Policy, 1964. In "The Teenage Parent: Early Marriage and Child Bearing." Edited by E. Werner. Davis, Calif.: University of California, University Extension, 1965. Mimeographed.

42. Larson, D. L. et al. "Social Factors in the Frequency of Romantic Involvement

among Adolescents." *Adolescence* 11 (1976): 7–12.

43. Lasswell, M. E. "Is There a Best Age to Marry?: An Interpretation." *Family Coordinator* 23 (1974): 237–242.

44. Lee, G. R. "Age at Marriage and Marital Satisfaction: A Multivariate Analysis with Implications for Marital Stability." *Journal of Marriage and the Family* 39 (1977): 493–504.

45. Lorenzi, M. E. et al. "School-Age Parents: How Permanent a Relationship?" *Adolescence* 12 (1977): 13–22.

46. Magid, D. T. et al. "Preparing Pregnant Teenagers for Parenthood." *Family Coordinator* 28 (1979): 359–362.

47. Marini, M. M. "The Transition to Adulthood: Sex Differences in Educational Attainment and Age at Marriage." *American Sociological Review* 43 (August 1978): 483–507.

48. McKenry, P. et al. "Adolescent Pregnancy: A Review of the Literature." *Family Coordinator* 28 (1979): 17–28.

49. Mednick, B. R. et al. "Teenage Pregnancy and Perinatal Mortality." *Journal of Youth and Adolescence* 8 (1979): 343–357.

50. Milk, J. C. "Adolescent Parenthood." *Journal of Home Economics* 65 (1973): 31–35.

51. *Ordway* v. *Hargraves*, 323 F. Suppl. 1155 (1971).

52. *Perry* v. *Granada*. 300 F. Supp. 748. (Miss., 1969).

53. "Pregnant Schoolgirls and Pregnant Teachers. The Policy Problem School Districts Can Sidestep No Longer." *American School Board Journal* 160 (1973): 23–27.

54. Price-Bonham, S. "Student Husbands versus Student Couples." *Journal of Marriage and the Family* 35 (1973): 33–37.

55. Punke, H. H. "Restricting Educational Opportunity for Married Youth." *Family Law Quarterly* (March 1971): 11–31.

56. Reiss, I. L. *The Family System in America.* New York: Holt, Rinehart and Winston, 1971, p. 282.

57. Rice, F. P. *Marriage and Parenthood.* Boston: Allyn and Bacon, 1979.

58. Romino, I. "Financial Management Practice of 52 Couples with Teen-Age Wives in Baltimore County, Maryland." Master's thesis, College of Human Development, The Pennsylvania State University, 1970.

59. Rothstein, A. A. "Adolescent Males, Fatherhood, and Abortion." *Journal of Youth and Adolescence* 7 (1978): 203–214.

60. Russ-Eft, D. et al. "Antecedents of Adolescent Parenthood and Consequences

at Age 30." *Family Coordinator* 28 (1979): 177–179.

61. Schinke, S. P. et al. "Teenage Pregnancy: The Need for Multiple Casework Services." *Social Casework* 59 (July 1978): 406–410.

62. Schinke, S. P. et al. "Preventing Unwanted Adolescent Pregnancy: A Cognitive-Behavioral Approach." *American Journal of Orthopsychiatry* 49 (January 1979): 81–88.

63. Sorensen, R. C. *Adolescent Sexuality in Contemporary America: Personal Values and Sexual Behavior, Ages 13–19.* New York: World Publishing Co., 1973.

64. Sugar, M. "At-Risk Factors for the Adolescent Mother and Her Infant." *Journal of Youth and Adolescence* 5 (1976): 251–270.

65. Tatelbaum, R. "Management of Teenage Pregnancies in Three Different Health Care Settings." *Adolescence* 13 (1978): 713–728.

66. U.S. Bureau of the Census, Department of Commerce. *Current Population Reports.* Series P-23, No. 32. Washington, D.C.: U.S. Government Printing Office.

67. ———. *Current Population Reports.* Series P-20, No. 223.

68. ———. *Current Population Reports.* Series P-20, No. 255. Washington, D.C.: U.S. Government Printing Office.

69. ———. *Statistical Abstract of the United States. 1976.*

70. U.S. Department of Health, Education, and Welfare, Bureau of Community Health Services. *Family Planning Digest* 3 (1974): 15.

71. Vener, A. M., and Stewart, C. S. "Adolescent Sexual Behavior in Middle America Revisited: 1970–1973." *Journal of Marriage and the Family* 36 (1974): 728–735.

72. Vincent, C. E. "Socialization Data in Research on Young Marrieds." *Acta Sociologica* (1964): 118–127.

73. Waite, L. J., and Moore, K. A. "The Impact of an Early First Birth on Young Women's Educational Attainment." *Social Forces* 56 (March 1978): 845–865.

74. Warren, D. F. "Pregnant Students' Public Schools." *Phi Delta Kappan* 54 (1972): 111–114.

75. *Wellsand* v. *Valparaiso Community Schools Corporation et al.* U.S.C.C., N.D., 71 Hlss (2) (Indiana, 1971).

76. Zelnick, M., and Kantner, J. F. "The Probability of Premarital Intercourse." *Social Science Research* 1 (1972): 335–341.

77. Zongker, C. E. "The Self-Concept of Pregnant Adolescent Girls." *Adolescence* 12 (1977): 477–488.

CHAPTER 16

Experiments in Group Living: Cohabitation and Trial Marriage

Outline

Group life in the United States is changing along with other elements of society. Dating and courtship customs of the past are no longer considered adequate means of meeting, knowing, and selecting a marital partner. Life styles have become more intimate, more personal, more natural through coed living arrangements of many kinds. Formal engagements have been rejected by many youths and replaced by trial periods of living together. Even legal marriage itself has been rejected by some who favor voluntary, nonlegal, companionate marriage instead. Experiments with many forms of group life are taking place across the United States.

The purpose of this chapter is to take an honest look at some of the experiments in group living and to understand their rationales, natures, meanings, promises, and problems as viewed both by older adolescents and by researchers who are probing and trying to understand the phenomenon.

Collegiate Dormitory Arrangements

PARIETALS

Student demand that colleges and universities cease playing the role of absentee parent, called *in loco parentis*, has resulted in change and liberalization of many restrictions formerly imposed upon residents of college dormitories. (14, 16, 37) At most colleges all restrictions have been removed on both female and male students. Students may come and go as they please, at any hour, without signing out for the night or weekend and without signing in again upon return. In other instances doors are locked at a particular hour, primarily for security purposes, and unlocked early the following morning. In other colleges, women are unrestricted except for signing in and out. Freshmen may be restricted, but not upperclass women. The stricter schools still have various requirements: certain hours for women, limitations on days and evenings out, and signing in and out at particular times.

The word *parietal*, meaning "within a college," refers to limited visiting hours during which students may entertain those of the other sex in their rooms. Some schools strive to regulate an "open door" policy: doors must always be unlocked, open a book's width, or have a towel tied from handle to handle so the door cannot be tightly closed. Other schools no longer try to control student behavior by open doors. Responsible authorities hesitate to check when visiting hours are over. Controls of this nature, however, are becoming increasingly rare.

In many schools, particularly those that allow unlimited visiting hours between sexes, cohabitation within college dorms is common. For example, even though official policy at Cornell forbids "continuous residence" with someone of the opposite sex in a dorm room, such a policy is difficult to enforce and liberal parietal policies make almost continuous cohabitation possible. (30, p. 466)

In other instances, however, conservative students complain about the new freedoms. A girl can't study because her roommate wants to entertain her boyfriend for the evening. A boy with a devoutly religious background finds the behavior of his dorm neighbors unacceptable. "Sleep ins" have become the fashion for some students, but not for all. Some girls feel relieved when they lose their virginity. Others get deeply upset when they discover their best friend is behaving much more liberally than they do. Many students feel: "What they do is their own business, but why should I get locked out of my room in the process?" or "Why can't they find a motel?" Not every student who wants an apartment off campus wants to move in with a lover: some move even though they don't want to. Students today generally believe in freedom of choice for each person, but they are disturbed when their own rights are imposed upon by those with different views.

DIVIDED DORMS

Divided dorms house both men and women, but in different wings or sections. Some colleges have adopted the system to make maximum use of dormitory space. Why have half a woman's dorm empty when many men are without campus housing?

Such an arrangement is satisfactory to many administrators and students alike. Students whose chief problem is getting to know and feel comfortable with the opposite sex find that such living arrangements make it much easier to get to know others as friends and as people, without the overly romantic overtones and responsibilities of dating. Furthermore, they see one another in a natural setting and find it easier to be genuine and honest in their relationships. Many meaningful friendships have developed in such a setting. The advantage to the administration is an efficient use of space, without the dangers of public criticism of completely coed dorms.

In some instances doors between sections are locked at midnight, after all students have supposedly returned to their own sections. In other situations no artificial barriers are created at any time, allowing increased opportunities for cohabitation. (31, 55)

COED DORMS

The arrangement of men and women living in adjacent rooms represents what is, to adults, a fairly radical departure from tradition. In a few instances men and women are allowed to share university apartments. But from a student's point of view, coed living is desirable because it's natural. As one girl said:

When you're separated, it's so unnatural. Your friends are all girls. You walk into a boy's dorm and they all stare at you. When you're all living together, the boys look at girls less as sex objects.

Another girl remarked:

The point is that we want to know boys as friends and companions, as well as dating objects. . . . It used to be, a guy kept trying to get the girl to bed, and she kept trying to stay out. Now they both want a good, honest relationship first. . . . And I'm not talking about promiscuity. Sometimes I think parents think so much dirtier than we do. I'm talking about the total relationship, as opposed to sex roles.

The primary objection from an adult point of view is that coed dorms lead to promiscuity. However, students who want to sleep together find ways of doing so under any arrangement. Individual sexual behavior patterns are rapidly becoming more liberal, but men and women living in the same residence less frequently engage in sexual activity than do those from separate residences. Also, the smaller the residence is, the less sex seems to occur.

But more important, students form relationships other than those based exclusively on sex. (43, p. 209) They go beyond sexual attraction to a more encompassing relationship. They participate less in structured, one-to-one dating, and more in informal group activities. They plan more group activities and events. Administrators report that students spend as much time studying as those in single-sex residences, that the level of conversation is intellectually higher, and that there is less vandalism.

Not all students want or choose coed living when given the option. Some find it too much of a strain to "get dressed before walking down the hall" or "having to be on your best behavior all the time." Generally, the cautious or socially immature student (one who could benefit most from coed living) is most likely to choose a single-sex residence. When Lambda Nu, a fraternity at Stanford University, went coed, four men quit but ten joined. Forty-two girls applied and twenty were picked by lot. The men and women live in separate sections of the house, but there are few rules. Students admit there is little promiscuity.

Although coed living is not for everybody, it has many advantages in promoting natural heterosexual development and relationships without stimulating promiscuity. Evidence such as the fraternity experience at Stanford points to the fact that natural friendships develop without the arificial, sex-oriented relationships that arise when the sexes are kept segregated. Also, such naturalness ought to act as a deterrent to hastily conceived, ill-chosen marriages.

Living Together: Varieties of Cohabitation

INCIDENCE

A nationwide survey of students from fourteen state universities across the United States revealed that approximately 25 percent had ever lived with a person of the opposite sex in a cohabiting relationship. (4, p. 449) Altogether, more males (34 percent) than females (23 percent) had cohabited. Among those who had cohabited, 96 percent said they would like to get married at some time, so living together was not considered a substitute for marriage. (4, p. 451) There is a wide range of patterns and possibilities for living together. (64) They include:

1. Temporary arrangements.
2. Arrangements for fun and convenience without commitment.
3. Intimate involvements with emotional commitment.

4. Living together as a prelude to marriage.

5. Living together as a trial marriage.

6. Living together as an alternative to marriage.

TEMPORARY ARRANGEMENTS

These possibilities would include all short-term arrangements: staying together overnight, for the weekend, during spring break in Florida, or traveling cross-country.

Adolescents today feel far less bound by traditional and public disapproval of "staying overnight at your girl's house unless you're married." Young men and women often share the same room, trailer, or tent overnight or for several days. The boys are over at the girls' apartment for a party; the hour grows late; they all decide to stay overnight. They find it cheaper to travel across country and to share the same living quarters throughout a trip. Youths may share a coed hosteling trip across Europe for the summer. (25, p. 8) The chief characteristic of such arrangements is their transitory nature. Such arrangements may or may not involve sexual intimacy, but usually no personal commitment is involved.

ARRANGEMENTS FOR FUN OR CONVENIENCE WITHOUT COMMITMENT

These types of arrangements constitute a small minority of situations. (30, 50) Sometimes they are hastily or informally decided. After a weekend of fun and a short acquaintance, the fellow decides to move into his girl's apartment. He ends up staying the rest of the semester. Sometimes the arrangement is carefully worked out over a time as desirable for members of a group that want just to live and have fun together. They are very good friends, but want no permanent, intimate commitment. (47) Often it is an arrangement of convenience: five youths decide to share the rent of a large apartment. They figure it's cheaper and more fun. Their living together includes sharing expenses, doing the dishes and laundry, and sharing the other economic and material necessities that a married couple do.

Cooperative houses, as they are usually called on the East Coast, are most frequently organized by a group of girls who share the rent. Frequently their boy friends decide to move in and stay awhile. In urban areas where housing is scarce and rents high, this sort of arrangement is especially common among college youths. A variation is an arrangement such as eight fellows and one girl living together. The girl is not intimately involved with "any of my guys." She goes with another fellow who does not live with her. Her living arrangement is strictly to share expenses and because she prefers living with males rather than females.

These temporary arrangements for convenience would not be considered *cohabitation* by some researchers, because the term is more strictly applied to two persons of the opposite sex living together "under marriage-like conditions." (40) Researchers at California State add the phrase "living together in a relatively permanent manner." (31, p. 48) They found that 25 percent of the student body have cohabitated at some time according to this description. (23) Macklin, of Cornell, defined cohabitation as "having shared a bedroom and/or bed with someone of the opposite sex (to whom one was not married) for four or more nights a week for three or more consecutive months." (30, 31) According to this definition, 31 percent of students at Cornell had cohabited. (31, p. 55) Researchers at the University of Texas do not restrict the definition to any particular span of time, but found that 36 percent of the student body had cohabited for periods of three months or longer. (48)

INTIMATE INVOLVEMENTS WITH EMOTIONAL COMMITMENT

The majority of cohabiting college couples place themselves in this category. (30, 31, 48) Couples describe themselves as having a strong, affectionate relationship. (37, p. 354) Although some permit dating outside the relationship, monogamy is the rule, with the majority considering themselves "going steady" and dating others as "out of bounds." (20, 31, 48) Although there is a strong emotional commitment, there are no long-range plans for the future or for marriage. When asked if they have any plans for marriage, they usually reply, "Heavens, no!" (30, p. 467) They are content to "wait and see what happens" and do not consider themselves married in any sense. (31, p. 57)

Such couples intend to continue the relationship indefinitely, but most involvements are of fairly short duration. Three researchers found that 36 percent of cohabitors had dated less than one month. (9) Another reported that cohabitation was a purposeful act for only 25 percent of the sample. Most had simply drifted into sleeping together more and more often. (30) Studies at American University showed that a third of the relationships lasted less than one month; only one-third had endured six months or longer. (18) At Penn State, half the men and one-third of the women said their longest experience had been less than one month. (37, p. 348) In contrast, most couples at the University of Texas had established cohabitation for more than six months, some for two years or longer. (48, p. 4)

LIVING TOGETHER AS A PRELUDE TO MARRIAGE

In this type of relationship, the couple have already committed themselves to legal marriage. (50) They are therefore engaged, formally or informally, but find no reason to live apart while they are waiting to be married or while they are making arrangements for their marriage. Many times, their living arrangements just develop over a time, without conscious intent. Here is one student's story.

My boy friend and I never really *decided* we were going to live together before marriage. It just happened. He would come over to my apartment weekends. It would be late, so I'd put him up for the night. Then several weekends he stayed the whole time; it was easier than driving all that distance back home. After a while, we got thinking: "Isn't this silly, why should we be separated, why can't he just move in with me?" So he did. Finally, he gave up his own place, because it was cheaper for us to maintain only one apartment. Six months later we got married. If someone would ask: "What made you decide to live together before marriage?," my answer would be: "I don't know. It just happened."

Under these circumstances there is never an intention that cohabitation will replace marriage or even be a trial period before marriage. It is just something the couple decide to do before they get married.

To what extent do today's youths feel it is all right to live together before marriage? One 1974 study showed that the percentages who weren't cohabiting but would like to ranged from a low of 43 to 57 percent of females to a high of 63 to 71 percent of males. (14, p. 723) Fifty-six percent of all students surveyed at Florida State University indicated that, given the right conditions, they would sometime be living with a person of the opposite sex without being married. (20) Large numbers of youths, however, indicate they would live together only if they are in love. The implication is that the couple should have a serious relationship.

LIVING TOGETHER AS A TRIAL MARRIAGE

In this type of arrangement, the couple decide to live together to test their relationship: to discover if they are compatible and want to enter into legal marriage. This arrangement is "the little marriage before the big marriage that will last." (16) Studies at the University of Georgia showed that one-fourth to one-third of cohabiting couples considered their relationship a testing ground for marriage. (50) A complete discussion of this type of arrangement is included in a later section of this chapter.

LIVING TOGETHER AS AN ALTERNATIVE TO MARRIAGE

This arrangement has been called *companionate marriage, a covenant of intimacy,* or a *nonlegal voluntary association*. It is intended not as a prelude to marriage but as a substitute for it. (29) A full discussion of this type of arrangement may be found in a later section of this chapter.

LIVING ARRANGEMENTS YOUTHS PREFER

What type of living arrangement would youths prefer? One study of 400 single undergraduate students at the University of Connecticut showed that egalitarian marriage was still the preferred life style. (51) Table 16–1 shows student preferences for each of twelve marital arrangements in descending order of preference. As can be seen, the alternatives that received the four highest ratings, though in varying order for males and females, were egalitarian marriage, long-term cohabitation, traditional sex-role-segregated marriage, and the five-year evaluation and renewal of marriage. (51, p. 496) Two of these, egalitarian marriage and traditional marriage are the dominant forms in our culture, but significant interest in long-term cohabitation and in the five-year renewable marriage lends support to the view that permanence is becoming a less salient aspect of marriage. (51, p. 496) There seemed to be little interest in spouse swapping, group marriage, or serial monogamy. Males were slightly more interested than females in rural communes with shared sex and in consensual extramarital sex, but neither was very popular. Remaining single or childfree in marriage seemed almost equally unattractive to males and females, all of which proves that students today are still fairly conservative in their views. (51, p. 495)

Table 16–1.   Ratings of willingness to participate in alternative marital and family forms, by sex of respondent.*

Male Ratings (N = 185)		Female Ratings (N = 168)	
Egalitarian marriage	2.46	Egalitarian marriage	1.74
Long-term cohabitation	3.25	Five-year evaluation and renewal of marriage	4.10
Traditional marriage	3.38	Long-term cohabitation	4.19
Five-year evaluation and renewal of marriage	4.01	Traditional marriage	4.36
Rural commune, shared sex	4.20	Childfree marriage	4.49
Childfree marriage	4.22	Remain unmarried	4.71
Remain single	4.51	Role reversal	4.72
Consensual extramarital sex	4.91	Rural commune, shared sex	4.92
Spouse swapping	5.05	Consensual extramarital sex	5.40
Group marriage	5.18	Serial monogamy	5.50
Serial monogamy	5.23	Spouse swapping	5.65
Role reversal	5.36	Group marriage	5.67

* Ratings given were from 1 to 6, with 1 defined as "very willing to participate" and 6 defined as "very unwilling to participate."

Adapted from L. D. Strong, "Alternative Marital and Family Forms: Their Relative Attractiveness to College Students and Correlates of Willingness to Participate in Nontraditional Forms," *Journal of Marriage and the Family* 40 (1978): 495. Used by permission.

PROBLEMS WITH COHABITATION

The author has talked to a number of couples who were living together out of wedlock. Some had a close emotional involvement without commitment to marriage of any kind; others intended their relationship to be a period of testing; others originally had no intention of marrying, but saw their relationship as a substitute for legal marriage; others were waiting to get married and were living together in the meantime. Most seemed to have problems in common.

One problem that couples face is where to live. The majority of women who cohabit also maintain their own separate room in a dorm, sorority, or an apartment with other women. This is done to keep parents from finding out about the arrangement and to serve as a place to live if the relationship doesn't work out. Most go to their rooms to see friends, to study, or to pick up belongings or mail. (30, p. 465) At Cornell the most common pattern was for the woman to move into the man's room in an apartment or house that was also shared with other men or another couple. Usually each heterosexual couple had their own bedroom. Living arrangements were usually not jointly arranged until the couple had lived together over one year. The older they were, the more likely the couples were to live alone in an apartment or house. (30, p. 465) Studies in other universities indicate that over half of all couples share their living quarters with other people. (18, 37) As a result, lack of space and privacy is a concern. (48)

In some communities, landlords won't rent to unmarried couples, either because they don't approve personally or because such couples usually don't stay very long. If a lease is required, will only one person be responsible or will both sign? One girl reported to the author that she and her boyfriend moved into their apartment, posing as husband and wife, with only the man signing the lease. However, the landlady found out about their unmarried status. After that, the landlady was constantly snooping, interfering, and pressuring them to leave until they finally did so.

The primary problem couples face is the attitude of parents. The majority of undergraduate college couples away from home never tell their parents of their coed living arrangements. Some parents approve of the actions of their children, but others completely disapprove. In fact it is not unusual for parents to be dumbfounded by the actions of their children. Students report that their parents were so upset that they disowned them, withdrew all financial support, or took disciplinary action to force a change in living arrangements. Some parents urge marriage: "If you want to live together, then get married." As a result couples live in fear that parents will find out. They feel guilty about deceiving parents and regret they are not able to talk to parents about their experiences. Some couples develop elaborate schemes to prevent discovery. (34, p. 57; 37, p. 348)

The social stigma of living together unmarried is diminishing as the trend becomes more accepted. A minority of adults do not accept the trend. One woman reported that every time she went to the post office to pick up her mail the postmaster treated her "like the biggest slut in town." She said she hadn't intended to get married, but social pressure forced her into deciding to do so. One college male said that he and his girlfriend weren't planning on being married, but that his girl began to feel more and more uncomfortable in an unmarried state, so, because he loved her, he got married to please her. These attitudes were more prevalent in small rural communities than in large urban centers, where people enjoy greater anonymity. (11)

Another major category of problems relates to the emotional involvement and feelings of the individuals concerned. (30, 48) A minority complain about overinvolvement, feeling trapped, a loss of identity, the overpermissiveness of their partner, or the lack of opportunity to participate in activities with others. (30, 48) Without realizing it, these people became enmeshed in relationships for which they were not emotionally prepared. Once in, they did not know how to escape without hurt. (52) Others report being exploited or used by another person who didn't really care about them. Jealousy of others' involvements is common. (30, 48) One major worry is concern and uncertainty about the future. (22, p. 65) This uncertainty pressures some into marriage, others into breaking off the relationship.

Cohabitation is not always a problem, however; the majority of couples indicate few or no emotional problems. Sixty-four percent at the University of Texas said their relationship was very happy. (48, p. 6) A few, however, are devastated by relationships that don't work out.

There is some indication that a few people enter cohabitation as a means of trying to solve their own emotional problems or as a means of finding identity. (15) For some who have trouble establishing heterosexual friendships, cohabitation becomes a substitute for dating, much as steady dating is a means of gaining security and recognition in high school. (21) As a group, cohabiters more often come from broken homes, (14, 28, 37) have disturbed relationships with parents, and have had unhappier childhoods than noncohabiters. (23, 28, 57) The academic performance of cohabiters and noncohabiters is similar. (31, 37)

The other problems youths face while living together unmarried are similar to those of any people sharing the same quarters. Arranging to do the house-keeping chores is a challenge to unmarried as well as married couples. One study of college couples who were cohabiting without being married showed that the women were still taking primary responsibility for performing most household tasks. (49) Traditional sex-role concepts and role specialization in the division of labor were quite evident among these couples. Table 16–2 shows the comparison of cohabiting males and females on actual performance of household tasks.

Far greater percentages of females than males reported cooking, dusting, dishwashing, vacuuming, doing laundry, scrubbing, feeding pets, and planning menus—traditionally feminine chores. Males reported major responsibility for cutting the lawn, washing the car, doing repairs, cleaning the garage, and shovel-

Table 16–2.   Comparison of cohabiting unmarried males and females on the actual performance of household tasks, in percentages.

Task	Male Reports of Performance		Female Reports of Performance	
	Perform task always or more than females	Share task equally	Perform task always or more than males	Share task equally
Cook	12	36	85	11
Dust	0	48	63	22
Wash dishes	8	52	48	33
Vacuum	4	52	56	19
Laundry	4	44	48	41
Scrub	8	32	59	15
Cut lawn	40	12	4	48
Feed pets	12	36	33	19
Pull weeds	20	16	4	26
Wash car	66	36	15	33
Wash pets	20	28	4	33
Finances	40	44	26	41
Repairs	60	20	4	30
Garbage, trash	40	44	7	30
Clean garage	28	8	0	22
Wash windows	12	20	19	19
Plan menus	12	40	52	37
Shovel snow	44	16	0	30

Adapted from R. Stafford, E. Backman, and P. Dibona, "The Division of Labor among Cohabiting and Married Couples," *Journal of Marriage and the Family* 39 (1977): 43–57. Used by permission.

ing snow—traditionally masculine chores. More males than females reported an equal sharing of traditionally feminine chores, indicating that men reported they helped with these tasks more often than women felt they did. (49, p. 51) It is obvious that nonmarital cohabitation is not a cure-all for sex-role inequality. Some tasks are shared, but generally the female partners do women's work and the male partners men's work (as defined by traditional standards). This division leaves the women with most of the household duties regardless of whether they are going to school and are employed as well. The more studies that are done of cohabitation, the more evidence there is that the couples involved behave like ordinary married couples. (49, p. 55) Learning to know and understand each other's moods, temperaments, and personalities, and adjusting to schedules, personal habits, and idiosyncrasies arise in unmarried relationships as well as in marriage unions. Couples who have sexual problems experience some of the same difficulties as married couples: different degrees or periods of sexual interest, orgasmic dysfunction, fear of pregnancy, vaginal irritations or discharge after intercourse, discomfort during intercourse, or impotency. (30, 42) The majority of cohabiting couples, however, report that their sex life is satisfying. (18, 31) Many problems arise also from the fact that the couple are immature: emotionally, socially, financially, and in other ways. They have to face most of the same problems that young marrieds face as a result of their immaturities and insecurities.

CONSEQUENCES

What are the likely or possible consequences of nonmarital cohabitation on couples, on marriage, and on society? (35)

The majority of those who have cohabited indicate positive feelings about the experience. Students report the experience as "pleasant," "successful," "highly productive." Many students indicate that it fostered personal growth and maturity, resulting in a deeper understanding of themselves or of what marriage requires. (35, p. 469; 40, p. 157; 48, p. 7)

A minority of students have regretted the experience. (40, p. 158) Some were very unhappy living together, experiencing much tension and frequent conflict. Others were hurt, either because the relationship didn't work out or because of the expectation that it would result in marriage and did not. Several studies have shown that men and women have somewhat different reasons for cohabitation. Males most often cite the need for sexual gratification as the reason, whereas females state that marriage is the most important motive. (35, p. 599) When the relationship doesn't lead to marriage, some women feel used and exploited. The men expect them to pay half the expenses, do many of the household chores, and provide regular bed privileges, without a commitment of any kind. Then there is always the anxiety about pregnancy, in spite of contraception. (30, 48) If pregnancy occurs, some say they would marry, yet marriage because of pregnancy is one of the worst possible motives in terms of subsequent chances for marital success. *All that can be said with certainty now is that cohabitation has been helpful to some and harmful to others.* The effect depends upon the individuals involved, on how they feel, and on what happens. (40, p. 160)

Will cohabitation result in more successful marriages? Given the information presently available, it appears that cohabitation has the potential either to help or to harm marriage. (41, p. 134; 17) The effect depends upon the needs, motivations, and competence of the persons involved. (41, p. 134) In a comparison of married couples with and without prior cohabitation experience, few differences were found in role expectations and fulfillment, closeness to ideal partner, (38) communication, fulfillment of emotional needs, sexual attractiveness and satisfaction, and relationship stability. The researchers concluded that premarital cohabitation did not provide learning experiences that significantly altered—positively or negatively—an individual's preparation for marriage. (17, p. 38) At the present time, there is not enough scientifically valid evidence to show either positive or negative effects upon marriage of living together beforehand. (3)

There are a number of important "ifs" to be answered before individual effects can be known. If after living together couples feel pushed into marriages for which they are not ready, the effect is detrimental. Sometimes parents force a decision once they find out what is going on. At other times the couples themselves feel obligated, for various reasons. One question being asked is: Will cohabitation limit individual growth and the development of identity? Do youths need to become persons in their own right before they develop identity as couples? If couples enter into "heavy" relationships to fulfill dependency needs, and are thereby stifled in developing their individual identities and autonomy, the experience may keep them from maturing as adults. (31) Some authorities feel that the more insecure, unhappy cohabitors are the very ones most likely to marry early. (28) If so, the result would be less stable marriages.

Some people wonder if cohabitation will replace conventional marriage. If the example in Sweden (54) or France is any indication, the effect is not to replace conventional marriage but to delay it. (5) This is helpful because the older couples are (up to about age twenty-six or twenty-seven), the greater the chances of marital success. Another positive potential of cohabitation is expressed in the following:

The essence of marriage is commitment, the contract and the concern shared by the couple. If they express these mutual responsibilities as living together without formal marriage, it is likely that when the formal promises are made the marriage will have greater endurance. (24, p. 41)

The authors go on to caution, however: "If living together is undertaken as a trial of compatibility motivated by curiosity rather than by commitment, the results are likely to be as whimsical and unpredictable as the curiosity of the participants." (24, p. 41)

LEGALITIES

Most young people do not think much about the legal implications of cohabitation, but those who intend to remain unmarried for a long time or those who own property or have children ought to give some thought to legal problems. Some cohabiting couples end up in financial and legal entanglements they had not anticipated. For example, if a wealthy man goes on a weekend trip with a poor woman, goes jogging, and is killed by a car, and she testifies that they posed as husband and wife to the hotel clerk and, therefore, had agreed to marry, could they be considered to have a common law marriage, and would she be entitled to an intestate share of his estate? (2, p. 361) A jury could decide either way.

Or, a man and woman purchase a house for $30,000 after cohabiting three months. He has a terrible credit rating so it is purchased in her name. They occasionally pose as husband and wife to avoid embarrassment. They separate. Can the husband "get a divorce" and share the equity in the house? A jury could decide either way. (2, p. 362)

If couples buy any kind of property for which there is a title—a house, car, stocks and bonds—the title spells out who is the recorded owner. If they are to be legally entitled to an equal share if they break up, they will have to be certain both their names are on the title as joint owners. Sharing personal property for which there is no clear title requires a sense of fair play, but if one runs off with the stereo or television, the other has no legal recourse, unless bills of sale can be submitted. Similarly, if charge accounts are set up, in whose name will they be? The person whose name is on the account is legally responsible. (8, p. 363)

The most difficult problem arises when a child is born to an unmarried couple. The father may voluntarily legitimate a child or adopt it and become legally responsible for its support. But if the man leaves behind a pregnant woman and/or a child and does not admit paternity and agree to assume legal responsibility, the woman must establish paternity before child support can be enforced. Even then, absentee fathers are sometimes hard to locate so that the law can be carried out. (8, p. 364)

Nonmarital cohabitation is still a criminal offense in approximately half the states in this country. A divorced person with custody who cohabits may jeopardize his or her right to keep the child. Children of unmarried persons are often severely penalized; they may be deprived of all claim to their biological parent's estate. Unwed fathers may not be given custody of their own children even if the mother dies. Workmen's compensation, Social Security, and other benefits may be withheld from unmarried survivors. (34, p. 359)

Trial Marriage

BERTRAND RUSSELL ON TRIAL MARRIAGE

The concept of a testing period before marriage is not new. It was first proposed by Judge Ben Lindsay in 1927. (26, 27) In *Marriage and Morals* (1929) Bertrand Russell approved of Lindsay's concept and asserted that marriage should not be final when there are no children, so that if the relationship proved sterile it could be easily dissolved. (44) In outlining his view of a "new kind of marriage," Russell reiterated the views of Lindsay, who said there are three ways in which the new kind of marriage, companionate marriage, can be distinguished from ordinary marriage.

First, that there should be for the time being no intention of having children, and that accordingly the best available birth control information should be given to the young couple. Second, that so long as there are no children and the wife is not pregnant, divorce should be possible by mutual consent. And third, that in the event of divorce, the wife would not be entitled to alimony. (44)

In defending Lindsay's position, Russell espoused several arguments. He felt that companionate marriage would do a great deal of good because it would eliminate incompatible couples, particularly sexually incompatible couples. He wrote: "It seems absurd to ask people to enter upon a relation intended to be lifelong, without any previous knowledge as to their sexual compatibility. It is just as absurd as it would be if a man intending to buy a house were not allowed to view it until he had completed the purchase." (44) He argued also that marriage should never be considered consummated until the wife's first pregnancy, because children rather than intercourse are the true purpose of marriage.

MARGARET MEAD ON TWO-STEP MARRIAGE

Anthropologist Margaret Mead caused a stir in 1966 with a proposal for marriage in two steps. (32) Mead outlined two forms of marriage. The first was *individual marriage,* which was a business union between two individuals who would be committed to each other for as long as they wanted to remain together, but not as parents. This first step would be marriage without children and would give two young people a chance to know each other more intimately than would be possible through a brief love affair. If their relationship deepened and was compatible, they could agree to move onto the second step, *parental marriage.* If they decided to separate, however, the husband would not be responsible for the continued financial support of his wife, so there would be no alimony.

Mead emphasized the seriousness of both steps. Individual marriage should be considered a serious commitment, entered into in public, validated and protected by law and religion, in which each partner would be looking toward a lifetime relationship (though not yet bound to it) and concerned deeply for the happiness and well-being of the other. (32) Parental marriage would be allowed only after a good individual marriage; it would be difficult to contract and would be entered after a period of preparation. The couple would have to demonstrate their economic ability and, perhaps, their emotional capacities to raise a child. If parental marriage did end, divorce would be arranged to offer maximum protection for the children. (32)

In the rationale for marriage in two steps, Mead emphasized several important points. One, marriage is the necessary prelude to responsible parenthood, and all children born of a marriage should be wanted and properly cared for. Two, under the present system of dating, courtship, and mate selection, young couples enter early marriage and become parents before they know each other as husband and wife. Three, Americans have finally come to accept the notions that sex is a natural activity and that young Americans cannot be expected to postpone sex until their middle twenties. Society has encouraged early marriage as a way of providing a sex life for adolescents; but in doing so, it has generated new difficulties. The young couple, being inexperienced, are apt to bungle their first sex relationships. They are faced with the problems of adjustment of early marriage, such as finances and making friends. Using early marriage as a means of solving the sex problems of youths raises the possibility these adolescents will be irrevocably trapped. They ought to be committed to each other when they marry, but such commitments should not be irrevocable. Individual marriage would provide the first step without the final commitment. (32)

MICHAEL SCRIVEN'S THREE-STEP PLAN

Philosophy professor Michael Scriven has elaborated on Margaret Mead's two-step plan. (46) He proposes three types of marriage: *Preliminary marriage,* which would be legitimized cohabitation, entered into contractually for one year without the need for subsequent commitment; *personal marriage,* similar to Margaret Mead's idea of individual marriage, which could be entered into only after a year's trial of preliminary marriage; and *parental marriage,* the last step to be taken, and only after successful personal marriage. (46)

OTHER WRITERS ON TRIAL MARRIAGE

In recent years, other writers have presented variations of the basic suggestions already made. In *The Sexual Wilderness,* Vance Packard suggests a two-year confirmation period, after which marriage would become final or be dissolved. (36) He feels that because the first two years of marriage are the most difficult, two years of confirmation would be adequate. Packard does not refer to "trial marriage," which he regards as little more than unstructured cohabitation; rather, a period of confirmation with no expectation of permanency would contribute to the success of the plan. (36)

Family therapist Virginia Satir introduced a plan to make marriage a statutory five-year renewable contract. (45) Like other writers, Satir felt there needs to be "an apprentice period . . .in which potential partners have a chance to explore deeply and experiment with their relationship, experience the other and find out whether his fantasy matched the reality." (45)

Whether one agrees with any of these proposals or not, it has become evident that without the benefits of legal sanction, and in some cases, of social sanction, increasing numbers of youths are using cohabitation as trial marriage. Berger would like to see the trend harnessed constructively by providing a counseling and legal service for young people who venture into trial marriage. Thus, when students were ready to marry their current partner or someone else, their selection of mate would have sophistication and insight. If they have had repeated adjustment problems with roommates, they might be motivated to seek counseling. (19)

Companionate Marriage:
A Nonlegal Voluntary Alternative

Companionate marriage described in this section differs from trial marriage in that it is not here considered a period of preparation for marriage, but rather a substitute for or alternative to it. (7, 39) This view is based on the feeling that legal marriage itself, as it exists in our society, is all wrong, and that instead of bending all one's efforts to helping the individual adjust to marriage, the form of marriage itself should be changed to be more in harmony with human experience and need. (12) As of now, such relationships only involve a small minority of couples. (50)

The arguments for a nonlegal voluntary association are as follows.

1. If state registrations were eliminated, people would stay together for the only reason that would make marriage viable: because they wanted to. (33) Why stay together against one's wishes, because of legal requirements? To do so is to make marriage a nonfulfilling, unrewarding, sometimes even a brutal experience. Marriage should imply a deep personal commitment, but legal papers do not guarantee the commitment. The only real commitment is a voluntary one, and this may change over the years; therefore, the relationship ought to be allowed to change if necessary. (53)

2. Legal bonds do not now insure continuity of marriage. It can be broken by annulment or divorce, but at considerable cost, often with great difficulty, upset, and hypocrisy. During the years when New Yorkers were allowed to divorce only on grounds of adultery, mates would either have to spy and catch their mates in the act or arrange the evidence through prying or collusion. Such tactics are unnecessary when marriage is not a legal contract in the first place. (15)

3. Making marriage a nonlegal, voluntary association would provide more freedom for developing alternative forms. Perhaps polygamy, polyandry, or group marriage would be more desirable forms under some circumstances. (12)

4. Marriage as a lifelong contract between two people is unnatural. A student writes:

   The inventors of marriage did not anticipate a life span of seventy years or more and would certainly have made other arrangements if the possibility of spending as much as fifty years with the same person had been feasible (52)

   This same student goes on to point out that when marriage is contracted primarily for financial reasons, it is marriage in name only and ought to be broken when the financial reasons are no longer valid. When marriage is for love, what happens to the marriage when love passes and the couple learn that love is not just listening to "our song" or eating candlelight suppers? Many marriages are a direct result of sex, compelling couples to enter into "shotgun weddings" to avoid social stigma. Should they be forced into a lifetime of misery, however socially acceptable or legal? Given that many of the reasons for legal marriage are not valid, why have to enter into legal marriage anyhow?

5. Nonlegal voluntary marriage allows more opportunity for individual as well as mutual growth. The emphasis here is on individuality; when individuality is lost, individual growth is stymied. Nonpermanence is a part of this growth concept. The individuals are free to get and to give as long as they can. When they can no longer make it together, "they can split." One student writes:

   In the non-marriage union, if either individual no longer feels needed and an important part of the union, he or she now leaves this self-debasing situation, and replaces it with one in which both individuals again mutually fulfill their needs. They search for a person who is at their same developmental stage of growth. (52)

EFFECTS ON CHILDREN

The chief criticism of this kind of arrangement is that it does not provide any permanent relationship in which children can grow. Several answers have been given. One, having children should be out of the question. Two, children should be considered a possibility only when the couple have become integrated and desirous of a lasting relationship. Three, if children are born to a nonmarriage union and the two parents eventually go their own ways, the results are less harmful to the child than are the effects of a bitterly fought, upsetting divorce or of staying together in an unhappy marriage just for the sake of the children. When children are used to save a marriage, the marriage sometimes destroys the children. Four, a woman who is used to caring for herself, supporting herself, and at least sharing expenses has less trouble adjusting to being alone than a woman who has been taken care of, supported, and coddled. Because she is less upset, the child is less affected by maternal trauma than in the case of legal divorce.

However valid the arguments, the fact remains that nonlegal, voluntary marriage does not provide any certain answers to the problem of raising children in a secure, happy environment, unless the voluntary marriage is permanent and secure enough to fulfill the needs of children during their dependent years.

Conclusions

Undoubtedly, new forms of group life will develop in the future. Youths are seeking community because of an inner need to belong to someone or to something bigger than themselves, because of a desire for love and companionship in their lives. For some, cohabitation has been a substitute family; for others it is a means of self-expression, self-fulfillment, or sexual expression. At the very least, it is—for some —a convenience. Adolescents who have not found love, acceptance, and understanding within their nuclear families may decide that other living arrangements hold more promise for them than the way their parents lived, or that they don't want to commit themselves to permanent relationships.

This does not mean that traditional marriage or the nuclear family will soon become obsolete. The majority of youths still marry in traditional ways and raise children as society always has. (8) But it does mean that new life must be breathed into old structures if they are to meet human needs, or today's generation will turn increasingly to new forms to meet their desires.

Interviews of Cohabiting Couples

One of the best ways of finding out about cohabitation is to interview those who are involved. Class members can seek out couples to interview, tape the conversations, and use the information as a basis for writing papers or for playing to the class to stimulate class discussion. The following questions are only suggestive of those that might be asked couples.

1. How long have you lived together? Is it temporary? For a set period of time? Indefinite?
2. Why are you living together? What factors made you decide to enter into this arrangement? How did you get started?
3. Where do you live? Tell me about your living arrangements. Did you have any trouble finding or renting a place? Does your landlord know you're not married? Did you sign a lease? Whose name is it in? Have you also kept a room in a dorm or another place? Why? Are there others living with you? How does this work out? Who pays the rent?
4. What sort of financial arrangements do you have with each other and with other occupants in your living quarters?
5. How do you divide housework, cooking, laundering, food buying, and other chores in and around your living quarters?
6. What do you have in the way of furniture? Who owns it? What would you do with it if you broke up? Do you drive a car? Who owns it? Who drives it? Who would get it if you broke up?
7. How would you describe your relationship? Are you in love? How do you feel about each other? What sort of commitment do you have? Engaged? Intend to get married? Any special plans for the future? Do you consider living together a trial marriage?
8. Do you go out with or date others? Can you? Do you want to while you're living together? How do you feel about this? Any jealousy problems?
9. Do you have sex together? Any special problems with your sexual relationship? Do you use birth control? What method(s)? What would you do if you (your partner) got pregnant?
10. What would you say are your biggest problems in cohabiting?
11. What about your parents? Do they know? Why or why not? How do you think they feel about your cohabiting? What would happen if they knew? How do you keep them from finding out?
12. Does cohabiting help you in any way to select a mate? Prepare for marriage? Do you think you have a better chance of having a happy marriage because you have cohabited?
13. How do your friends feel about your living together? How do you feel about it? Do you ever feel guilty?
14. What worries you the most about cohabiting?
15. Would you advise other young people to cohabit? How old should you be?

Bibliography

1. Berger, M. "Trial Marriage: Harnessing the Trend Constructively." *Family Coordinator* 20 (1971): 38–43.

2. Bernstein, F. E. "Legal Problems of Cohabitation." *Family Coordinator* 26 (1977): 361–366.

3. Blaine, G. B. "Does Living Together before Marriage Make for a Better Marriage?" *Medical Aspects of Human Sexuality* 9 (1975): 32–39.

4. Bower, D. W., and Christopherson, V. A. "University Student Cohabitation: A Regional Comparison of Selected Attitudes and Behavior." *Journal of Marriage and the Family* 39 (1977): 447–452.

5. Cherlin, A. "Cohabitation: How the French and Swedes Do It." *Psychology Today* (October 1979): 18ff.

6. Clayton, R. R., and Voss, N. L. "Shacking Up: Cohabitation in the 1970s." *Journal of Marriage and the Family* 39 (1977): 273–283.

7. Coffin, P. "The Young Unmarrieds." *Look* 35 (1971): 63–67.

8. Coffin, P., ed. "The Marriage Experiments." *Life*, 28 April 1972, p. 41.

9. Croake, J. W. et al. *Unmarried Living Together: It's Not All Gravy*. Dubuque, Iowa: Kendall/Hunt, 1974.

10. Fonzi, G. "The New Arrangement." *Philadelphia Magazine* (January 1970): 98–104, 126–135.

11. Glick, P. C., and Norton, A. J. "Marrying, Divorcing, and Living Together in the U.S. Today." *Population Bulletin* Washington, D.C.: Population Reference Bureau, 1977.

12. Greenwald, H. "Marriage as a Non-Legal Voluntary Association." In *The Family in Search of a Future*. Edited by H. A. Otto. New York: Appleton-Century-Crofts, 1970, pp. 51–56.

13. Hassett, J. "A New Look at Living Together." *Psychology Today* (December 1977): 82ff.

14. Henze, L. F., and Hudson, J. W. "Personal and Family Characteristics of Cohabiting and Noncohabiting College Students." *Journal of Marriage and the Family* 36 (1974): 722–727.

15. Huang, L. J. "Research with Unmarried Cohabiting Couples: Including Non-Exclusive Sexual Relations." Illinois State University, 1975. Unpublished manuscript.

16. Jackson, R., and Jackson, J. "Living Together: A Guide for Unmarried Couples." 1973. Unpublished manuscript.

17. Jacques, J. M., and Chason, K. J. "Cohabitation: Its Impact on Marital Success." *Family Coordinator* 28 (1979): 35–39.

18. Kahn, L. et al. "Cohabitation: Marriage License?" American University, 1972. Unpublished manuscript.

19. Kardiner, S. H. "Convergent Internal Security Systems: A Rationale for Marital Therapy." *Family Process* 9 (1970): 83–91.

20. Kieffer, C. "Consensual Cohabitation: A Descriptive Study of the Relationships and Sociocultural Characteristics of Eighty Couples in Two Florida Universities." Florida State University, 1972. Unpublished manuscript.

21. Klemer, R. H. "Self-Esteem and College Dating Experience as Factors in Mate Selection and Marital Happiness: A Longitudinal Study." *Journal of Marriage and the Family* 33 (1971): 183–187.

22. Knox, D. *Marriage: Who? When? Why?* Englewood Cliffs, N.J.: Prentice-Hall, 1975.

23. Lautenschlager, S.Y. "A Descriptive Study of Consensual Union among College Students." Master's thesis, California State University, 1972.

24. Lee, R. V. "Does Living Together before Marriage Make for a Better Marriage?" *Medical Aspects of Human Sexuality* 9 (1975): 41–44.

25. LeShan, E. J. "Mates and Roommates: New Styles in Young Marriages." Public Affairs Pamphlet, No. 468. New York: Public Affairs Committee, 1971.

26. Lindsay, B. "The Companionate Marriage." *Redbook* (October 1926): (March 1927).

27. Lindsay, B., and Evans, W. *The Companionate Marriage*. New York: Liveright, 1927.

28. Lyness, J. F. "Aspects of Long Term Effects of Nonmarital Cohabitation." Reports on two studies: #1–Univ. of Colorado, NIMH Research Grant 1969–1970. #2–Ft. Wayne, Indiana, 1973–1974. Unpublished manuscript, 1975.

29. Lyness, J. F. "Happily Ever After? Follow-up Living Together Couples." *Alternative Lifestyles* 1 (February 1978): 55–70.

30. Macklin, E. D. "Heterosexual Cohabitation among Unmarried College Students." *Family Coordinator* 21 (1972): 463–472.

31. ———. "Cohabitation in College. Going Very Steady." *Psychology Today* 8 (1974): 53–59.

32. Mead, M. "Marriage in Two Steps." *Redbook* 127 (1966): 48–49.

33. "Miss McCann and Mr. Estridge, Unmarried, Have a New Baby Girl." *Life*, 28 April 1972, pp. 62–65.

34. Myricks, N., and Rubin, R. H. "Sex Laws and Alternative Life Styles." *Family Coordinator* 26 (1977): 257–360.

35. Newcomb, P. R. "Cohabitation in America: An Assessment of Consequences." *Journal of Marriage and the Family* 41 (1979): 597–602.

36. Packard, V. *The Sexual Wilderness*. New York: David McKay Co., 1968, pp. 466–468.

37. Peterman, D. J.; Ridley, C. A.; and Anderson, S. M. "A Comparison of Cohabiting and Noncohabiting College Students." *Journal of Marriage and the Family* 36 (1974): 344–354.

38. Polansky, L. W. et al. "A Comparison of Marriage and Cohabitation on Three Interpersonal Variables: Affective Support, Mutual Knowledge, and Relationship Satisfaction." *Western Sociological Review* 9 (Summer 1978): 49–59.

39. Ramey, J. W. "Emerging Patterns of Innovative Behavior in Marriage." *Family Coordinator* 21 (1972): 435–456.

40. Rice, F. P. *Marriage and Parenthood*. Boston: Allyn and Bacon, 1979.

41. Ridley, C. A. et al. "Cohabitation: Does It Make for Better Marriage?" *Family Coordinator* 27 (1978): 129–136.

42. Rogers, C. *Becoming Partners: Marriage and Its Alternatives*. New York: Dell Publishing Co., 1972.

43. Rosenfeld, A. " 'The Arrangement' at College: Part II." In *Love, Marriage, Fam-*

ily. Edited by M. E. Lasswell and T. E. Lasswell. Glenview, Ill.: Scott, Foresman and Co., 1973, pp. 208–209.

44. Russell, B. *Marriage and Morals.* 1929. Reprint. New York: Bantam Books, 1961, pp. 106–113.

45. Stair, V. "Marriage as a Statutory Five Year Renewable Contract." Paper presented at the American Psychological Association 75th Annual Convention. Washington, D.C., Sept. 1, 1967. Mimeographed.

46. Scriven, M. "Putting the Sex Back into Sex Education!" *Phi Delta* 49 (1967).

47. "Sharing Room with Man Working Out Fine for Her." *Portland* (Me.) *Press Herald,* 26 March 1975.

48. Shuttleworth, G., and Thorman, G. "Living Together: Unmarried Relationships." University of Texas, 1975.

49. Stafford, R. et al. "The Division of Labor among Cohabiting and Married Couples." *Journal of Marriage and the Family* 39 (1977): 43–57.

50. Storm, V. "Contemporary Cohabitation and the Dating-Marital Continuum." Master's thesis, University of Georgia, 1973.

51. Strong, L. D. "Alternative Marital and Family Forms: Their Relative Attractiveness to College Students and Correlates of Willingness to Participate in Nontraditional Forms." *Journal of Marriage and the Family* 40 (1978): 493–503.

52. Taylor, L. "Marriage: A Changing Concept." Term paper, University of Maine, 1972.

53. Trost, J. "Married and Unmarried Cohabitation in Sweden." 1975. Unpublished manuscript.

54. Trost, J. "A Renewed Social Institution: Nonmarital Cohabitation." *Acta Sociologica* 21 (1978): 303–315.

55. Whitehurst, R. N. "Living Together Unmarried: Some Trends and Speculations." University of Windsor (Ontario), 1974. Unpublished manuscript.

56. Yllo, K. A. "Nonmarital Cohabitation: Beyond the College Campus." *Alternative Lifestyles* 1 (February 1978): 37–54.

57. Yost, E. D., and Adamek, R. J. "Parent-Child Interaction and Changing Family Values: A Multivariate Analysis." *Journal of Marriage and the Family* 36 (1974): 115–121.

PART 7

Moral

CHAPTER 17

The Adolescent and Religion

Outline

Types of Religious Experience
Dimensions of Religion
Religion and the Contemporary College Student
Conclusions
Case Studies
Bibliography

An examination of numerous writings on the psychology of religion during adolescence reveals several different views of what happens to the faith and practices of youths. One view depicts adolescence as a religious conversion crisis; others says it is a religious identity crisis. Another view describes it as a time of religious awakening; a fourth view emphasizes adolescents' partial or even complete repudiations of religion. This chapter examines these views and goes on to describe the religious life of adolescents in the United States. The adolescent's religion is analyzed in five dimensions: the ritualistic, experimental, ideological, intellectual, and consequential. Religious life is analyzed according to practices, personal experiences, ideas, knowledge, and the consequences religion has for the adolescent's life. The chapter concludes with a discussion of the changes in religious beliefs and practices that have taken place in the life of the contemporary college student and the implications of these events for the future.

Types of Religious Experience

ADOLESCENCE AS A CONVERSION CRISIS

This view emphasizes adolescence as a time of religious storm and stress, during which the young person finds a spiritual rebirth (68, p. 214; 84, p. 145) and is converted to "the faith." Father Babin writes:

> The central point toward which the faith of adolescents is evolving is a crisis, a conversion, which normally takes place between 17 and 25 years. It is important to be aware of this privileged moment, of this climax toward which adolescence is tending. . . . (5, p. 128)

Father Babin goes on to emphasize that this conversion is not always highly dramatic, but that it nearly always constitutes a crisis, because the young person passes from a received faith to a personal faith. The faith that has been taught (received) must now become personally one's own. This requires commitment. Some youths will never come to this crisis of commitment; others will come to it late in life. "But in every case, the faith of adolescence takes on meaning only in relation to this point of crisis and resolution. . . ." (5, p. 129)

Other writers emphasize the varieties of religious experience of adolescents and stress that the type of conversion experienced (if at all) is influenced by the nature and views of particular religious institutions. (55, p. 229) Evangelical groups emphasize the need to be saved, to be reborn, to be converted; therefore their efforts are bent on involving the young in a dramatic, sometimes stressful, emotional, religious experience. Churches believing in crisis theology tend to produce experiences of crisis. (42, p. 158) Many adolescents (13, p. 117) experience intense religious feelings accompanied by a conversion experience. The following is one student's account of his conversion.

While I was home, my brother, who had been a Christian for about six months, occasionally took me to some meetings conducted by a group called Young Life. I went basically because I felt close to my brother and wanted to see what he was into.

...They started talking about a relationship with Jesus ... and afterward they gave an invitation for anybody to come up and rap with them. Even though I normally would have passed it up because my mind was made up about God, something took me up there to talk to Phil the drummer. ...

"Ask Jesus into your life," he said, "and be willing to follow Him. He will let you know that He is there."

... Finally that night in bed I said, "Jesus, come into my life. I'll believe you if you show me that you are there and that you are real. ..."

... He had to show me if He was real. And He did. All those things I had been into before vanished and suddenly seemed absurd. ...

Now love is something that can be lived and not just talked about. Where all the philosophy, drugs, and revolutionary doctrine had been, Jesus now lives and works and protects and guides my living. Now I know that He has planned and is enacting the greatest possible life I could have. (26)

ADOLESCENCE AS A GRADUAL RELIGIOUS AWAKENING

The more liberal churches emphasize that religious consciousness during adolescence ought to be a continuation of the gradual religious awakening begun during childhood. (47; 55, p. 228) It is a period during which the adolescent examines, questions, and searches for answers; during which faith is examined, refined, and strengthened but not radically changed. (29; 56, p. 189)

Nearly a century ago, Horace Bushnell (19), writing during a time of religious revivalism in which the churches were emphasizing the sinfulness of children and the necessity of miraculous conversion, revolutionized Protestant concepts of Christian education by suggesting that children ought to be reared in such a way that they grow up never knowing the time when they weren't Christian. Children reared with love and faith, taught over a period of years, don't need to be converted in a sudden, dramatic way, because they are already Christians. Only those reared apart from the faith with different values and separated from the love of God need be saved. Conversion implies change, but why wait until adolescence to accomplish the change? Why not nurture children as Christians from the time of their births? Then change will not be necessary. Bushnell was especially critical of parents who prayed for the sudden salvation of their children but in the meantime reared them in an atmosphere of unchristian love. (19)

Hurlock and others (42, 55) emphasize that whether conversion is catalytic or gradual is dependent on a number of factors. The lower socioeconomic status groups, with less education and located in particular geographic areas (such as the Bible Belt of the rural South) are more likely to be identified with denominational groups emphasizing catalytic religious conversion. (11, 72) The adolescent with an unstable, emotional temperament, (15) plagued by guilt and conflict, is more predisposed to a dramatic type of religious experience. The higher socioeconomic status adolescents, particularly college-educated youths belonging to more formal churches, are more likely to experience a gradual awakening rather than a sudden conversion. (55, p. 230)

RELIGION AND IDENTITY CRISIS

In describing adolescence as a period of religious crisis, other writers show the relationship between the religious crisis and the total identity crisis of young people. (53, 54, 75) Engel writes:

... The major questions raised by ... adolescents have to do with identity. They have [a] component ... which asks, "Who am I?" Insofar as such questions raise matters of ultimate concern for the individual, they are religious. (29)

Engel emphasizes that the major function of religious education is not to answer questions for adolescents, but to ask them, thus confronting them with the task of finding their religious identities. He says:

The fundamental issue of identity is posed in the form of a question. The question drives us forth on a quest. The quest is education. . . .
    This is really what religious education is all about—understanding the basic questions and seeing that they are asked. (29)

The basic questions that confront adolescents in their quest for religious identity are questions such as: Who am I? Why am I here? What is the purpose of life? What can I believe? What can I value? How should I live? Adolescents' questions also now have a social dimension. (2) Instead of asking: What must we do to be saved? they are asking: What can we do to save the world? (17) What can we do with this mess? (29) The crisis of modern adolescents hinges partly on finding their identities or losing them in diffusion, self-doubt, and uncertainty about their roles in society. They are searching for something or somebody to be true to and for a cause to which they can devote themselves. (76, p. 55; 88, p. 171)

Father Babin insists that the *quest for identity* expresses itself in the need to be recognized, accepted, and affirmed by others. With this desire comes a need for fulfillment, a *quest for participation* that

means placing one's own tiny block into the building of the world or into the highway of history, a stone that is small but nonetheless necessary and important. Any expression—belonging to a union, supporting a family, working in a political campaign, participation in a movement—can be seen as a contribution to the improvement of society. It is clear that through this expression of self, through this creation and this sharing, man finds an inherent meaning in life. (6, p. 33)

PSYCHOANALYSIS AND RELIGION

The psychoanalyst would describe the religious experience of adolescence differently. (39) The crisis stems from the fact that a personal God is described as a father; in S. Freud's words: "The personal God is psychologically nothing other than a magnified father." (40) When adolescents begin to rebel against their fathers' authority, their religious faith also begins to collapse. Sudden eruptions of religiosity in the adolescent are explained as a reawakening of their oedipal wishes for a father. Religiously, adolescence is characterized by conflict between dependence and independence of a father image, between love and hate, between obedience and rebellion, between faith and disbelief. If adolescents are rebelling against their parents, (91) they may use religion as a means of striking against them. (35) They reject religion as a way of emancipating themselves from parents who are not giving them the freedom they seek. (46) Adolescents' rebellion against going to synagogue or Sunday school is one expression of this rebellion against parental authority. They can't react against the parents to whom their anger is directed, so they react against the religion their parents want them to have.

WHICH VIEW?

Any one view cannot be applied to all adolescents. Youths react differently to their religion or lack of it. There are many adolescents who begin to examine critically, for the first time, the faith in which they were brought up. Until this time, many have accepted at face value the beliefs and practices in which they were reared. Gradually they are exposed to many new and different ideas and philosophies. Their courses in school, their broadening contacts with an increasing circle of friends and acquaintances, their exposure to many other religions and cultures through television and other forms of mass media stimulate their thinking about their own faith. The more adolescents mature intellectually and the more intellectual stimulation to which they are exposed, the more likely they are to begin to question, to doubt, and to challenge the beliefs in which they were reared. (See Chapter 1.) Research seems to indicate that broadening social and educational experiences result in a more reasoned, more abstract, less literal interpretation of religion. (3) The adolescent's views become more liberal, more tolerant, less dogmatic in relation to orthodox teachings.

This is what happens to many adolescents, but it does not happen to all. Some children who have been very strictly and narrowly reared, whose religious commitment was made years before the identity crisis of adolescence, never really chose their faith and may never dare examine or question it, even as adults. They simply accept and defend it against any and all attacks. Their reaction is defensive, holding on to what has been given, because of unwillingness to question dogma (doubting is considered sinful) and because of fear of losing faith.

Other adolescents repudiate their religion in search of other beliefs and values. (14) Many eventually return to their original faith; others never do. Still other adolescents, some brought up outside the bounds of formal churches, find a deep religious commitment during this period, a commitment they carry with them throughout adulthood.

Adolescents manifest a wide variety of religious experiences and reactions. No one pattern may be applied to all. In succeeding sections, the religion of American adolescents, their beliefs and practice of religion, will be examined in more detail.

Dimensions of Religion

There are several different elements of religion, among which are faith, morals, and rituals. One of the most helpful descriptions has been given by Glock and Stark in *Religion and Society in Tension*. (45) They distinguish five dimensions of religion.

1. *The ritualistic dimension:* religious practices such as worship, prayer, sacraments, and fasting.
2. *The experiential dimension:* subjective religious experiences and emotions.
3. *The intellectual dimension:* the knowledge and information people have about the basic tenets of their faith and its sacred scriptures.
4. *The ideological dimension:* religious beliefs.
5. *The consequential dimension:* the effects and influence of religion upon the individual.

These five dimensions will be considered in discussion of the religion of American adolescents.

THE RITUALISTIC DIMENSION

This aspect of religion focuses on the extent to which youths attend church, pray, and participate in other rituals of the church. Research indicates that by these criteria less than one-third of American youths are religious. Statistics for 1973 indicate that only 28 percent of young people between eighteen and twenty-nine years of age attended church during an average week. (58) The figure is considerably lower than that for adults, which showed 40 percent in attendance during an average week. (58, p. 262) The figure for adults represents a decline of 9 percent since 1958. Figure 17–1 shows the overall decline in churchgoing since 1955. (58, p. 262) This decline since 1955 can be attributed almost entirely to a drop in Catholic attendance. In 1973, 55 percent of Catholics attended in a typical week, compared to 71 percent in 1964. In contrast, Protestant churchgoing remained fairly stable for the decade, with 37 percent attending church in an average week. Jewish attendance at synagogue increased from 17 percent per week in 1964 to 19 percent in 1973. (58, p. 262) Women attended church more frequently than men. Both male and female residents in the South and Midwest attended more frequently than did those residing in the West or East. (58, p. 263) Table 17–1 shows the findings by population groups. (58, p. 263)

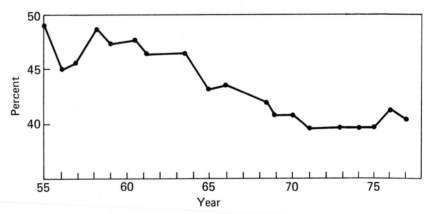

Figure 17–1. Churchgoing since 1955. (From *Yearbook of American and Canadian Churches, 1979,* edited by Constant Jacquet. Copyright © 1979 by the National Council of the Churches of Christ in the United States of America. Used by permission of Abingdon.)

Table 17–1.   Percentage of church attendance by population groups, 1973.

Group	Percent Attending during an Average Week
All adults	40
Catholics	55
Protestant	37
Jewish	19
Men	35
Women	43
White	40
Non-white	41
College educated	40
High school educated	38
Grade school educated	43
18–29 years	28
30–49 years	41
50 and over	46
East	38
Midwest	43
South	44
West	29

From Constant Jacquet, ed., *Yearbook of American and Canadian Churches, 1975.* Copyright 1975 by the National Council of the Churches of Christ in the United States of America. Used by permission of Abingdon.

These studies do not bring out clearly enough, however, that there are significant differences among various groups of adolescents. Adolescent girls have a higher frequency of church attendance than do boys. (27, 59) There also are significant differences according to age: attendance decreases slightly during later adolescence (high school seniors and especially college youth). (27, 59)

Adolescent participation also depends on parental involvement. Young people are more likely to attend if their parents do. (88, p. 116) DeBord found that adolescents more often attend church when their denominational affiliation is similar rather than dissimilar to that of their mothers. (27, p. 564) Research indicates also that when the father's participation is less than the mother's, girls tend to keep up the same level of interest as the mother, but boys tend to follow the father's example of less participation. (85, p. 116) Furthermore, in homes of interfaith marriages, there is a tendency to place less emphasis on religious observances and less parental pressure to attend church. Because the parents may disagree on religion, the net effect seems to be to discourage the youths from attending regularly. (88, p. 117)

There are some variations according to denominational preferences. (44) The stricter, more authoritarian Protestant groups, which place a high social prestige value upon regular church attendance, and the Orthodox Jewish and Catholic groups encourage and get more regular attendance from their members than do the more liberal groups. (44, 59) Figure 17–2 shows the relationship between orthodoxy and church attendance among Catholics and Protestants of all ages. (44) Table 17–2 shows the percentage of the 9 million members of the three largest Lutheran denominations (American Lutheran Church, Lutheran Church

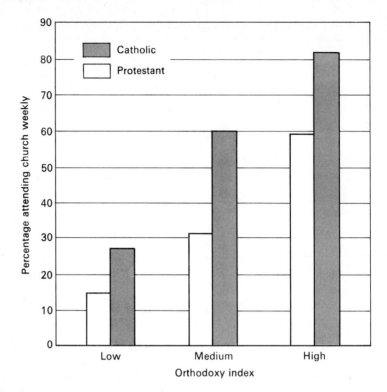

Figure 17–2.   Orthodoxy and church attendance. (Adapted from C. Y. Glock and
R. Stark, "Will Ethics Be the Death of Christianity?" *transaction* 7[1968]:7–14.
Used by permission.)

in America, and Lutheran Church—Missouri Synod) who engage in various
religious rituals. (59, p. 53) This study is cited because these three groups constitute about 90 percent of all Lutherans, because Lutherans are the third largest
Protestant denomination, and because this group represents a fairly conservative
Protestant group. (59, p. 48) As can be seen, the percentage in attendance each
week is considerably higher than the overall national figure for all Protestant
members. Like other denominations, Lutherans show the greatest decline in religious participation in the nineteen- to twenty-three-year-old age group. After
this age the percentage of participation in all forms of religious activity increases
gradually to age sixty-five. (59, p. 53)

THE EXPERIENTIAL DIMENSION

Statistics on church attendance among adolescents indicate what they do, but the
figures don't give the motives or indicate the significance of the actions. To reach
meanings and feelings one must look at the experiential dimension of religion.
How do youths feel about religion? Is religion a vital personal experience for
today's youths? In a nationwide survey among 3,522 youths ages sixteen to
twenty-five, Yankelovich showed a marked decline from 1969 to 1973 in the
percentage who said that religion was a very important value. (95)

Table 17-2.   Percentage of participation by Lutherans in religious rituals, by age.

Activity	Response Category	15–18	19–23	24–29	30–41	42–49	50–65
Bible reading	At least weekly	12	12	16	21	25	32
Reading about faith	Frequently	10	11	15	22	30	41
Prayer	Regularly	41	40	46	52	57	66
Worship attendance	At least weekly	60	41	49	59	61	65
Holy communion	Regularly	47	32	38	49	49	59
Congregational activity	Active	40	23	31	41	44	44

Adapted from A. L. Johnson et al., "Age Differences and Dimensions of Religious Behavior," *Journal of Social Issues* 30 (1974): 53. Used by permission.

A thirty-seven-year study of college freshmen at Harvard and Clark Universities showed that attitudes toward the church became far less favorable over the thirty-seven years prior to 1970. (60) For example, 78 percent of the early group and 17 percent of the latest group agreed with the item: "I think the church is a divine institution and it commands the highest loyalty and respect." This increase in disaffection with the church was only partially accompanied by a less favorable attitude toward religion in general, however. The percentage who said that religion had little or no influence on their ethical conduct increased only from 25 to 30 percent. (60) The students were disillusioned with the established church's teachings and practices in relation to current social, civic, and economic problems, but at the same time many expressed marked interest in a variety of religions and religious experiences. (60) Interest in mystical and Far Eastern religions especially has grown. Many youths have become Vendantists, Zen Buddhists, Mahayana Buddhists, Hindus, Bahais, and Muslims. A growing number of adolescents have joined the Jesus People, who offer a contemporary expression of fundamentalist Christianity. Therefore, while many American adolescents are rejecting traditional American forms of religion, many are also accepting other forms. Their religious views and values are in a state of flux and change, but this does not mean all have become irreligious. (87, p. 206)

Many youths still express religious concerns. One of the most widely used instruments for surveying these concerns has been the Mooney Problem Check List. (70) The Check List identifies eleven problem areas, each with thirty specific problems, making it possible to delineate clusters of problems as well as specific difficulties. This check list was administered to 583 male and female freshmen and sophomores at Michigan State University. (10) Seventeen out of thirty items on the Moral and Religion scale covered religious concerns and conflicts. The percentage of students checking each of these concerns is given in Table 17–3. As can be seen, five of seventeen concerns were checked by at least 25 percent of the respondents. Four of these deal with belief crises; the fifth relates to decline

Table 17–3.   Percentage of 583 students checking each of the religion items on the
Mooney Problem Check List.

Item	Percentage
Confused in some of my religious beliefs	29.8
Not going to church often enough	29.5
Doubting the value of worship and prayer	26.4
Don't know what to believe about God	26.4
Wanting to feel close to God	25.1
Losing my earlier religious faith	24.0
Dissatisfied with church services	22.7
Having beliefs that differ from my church	19.0
Wanting to understand more about the Bible	14.7
Differing from my family in religious beliefs	8.7
Affected by racial or religious prejudice	8.5
Missing spiritual elements in college life	8.3
Troubled by lack of religion in others	8.2
Science conflicting with my religion	7.7
In love with somebody of a different race or religion	7.2
Failing to see the relation of religion to life	7.0
Wanting more chances for religious worship	6.2

Adapted from B. Beit-Hallahmi, "Self-Reported Religious Concerns of University
Underclassmen," *Adolescence* 9 (1974) : 335. Used by permission.

in church attendance. All reflect confusion and change involved in the loss of
faith. (10, p. 337)

Any measurement of adolescent concern over religion depends on what is
included under religion: specific beliefs, dogma, philosophy of life, values, personal ethics, morals, or behavior. Adolescents are concerned about their personal
morality and about a philosophy of life; thus, they are interested in religion.

THE IDEOLOGICAL DIMENSION

This dimension of religion deals with individuals' beliefs and their acceptance
or rejection of church dogma. What do today's adolescents believe? One survey
of doctrinal beliefs of adolescent boys and girls between the ages of thirteen
and seventeen in the same community spanned a three-year period (1970–1973).
The survey showed a slight increase in the percentage of youths holding orthodox religious views. (97) That is, any one age group in 1973 held a greater percentage of people expressing orthodox religious beliefs than did the comparable
age group in 1970. (97) The one exception to this was the decline in belief in God
as "a Heavenly Father who watches over and protects us." (97, p. 56) This study
also showed some general decline in religious orthodoxy with increasing age.
(97, p. 57) That is, seventeen-year-olds were less likely to hold orthodox religious
views than were thirteen-year-olds and younger. There were, however, two
exceptions: the percentage of youths who believed in the second coming of Christ

showed no decline with age, and the percentage believing in life after death showed an increase. (97, p. 58)

There is no indication, therefore, that early adolescence is a time of widespread repudiation of traditional beliefs. There may be some discarding of specific beliefs, increased wondering about death, heaven, God, and life's purposes, but no general discarding of the faith of the fathers. As youths get older, however, the trend is from belief to skepticism. By age eighteen the issues of faith are far from settled, but there is more wondering about belief than actual disbelief.

One of the needs of the adolescent is to doubt and to begin to question. Doubting can be a good thing; it indicates thinking and a desire to grow in understanding. The adolescent who never questions may never mature or move beyond childish concepts. (55, p. 233) Adolescents who believe God is "like an old man with a beard who lives up in the clouds" or that "hell is a hot place underneath the earth" may be said to believe, but their beliefs are naive. They need to be stimulated to think, to make their beliefs more acceptable and meaningful to them. One of the tasks of church leaders is not just to indoctrinate, but to explain and to help youths think through their faith, for a shallow, naive concept of religion will not often survive attack and trial. Adolescents need a faith that is meaningful to them, that gives them real trust and reasons for living.

THE INTELLECTUAL DIMENSION

The intellectual dimension measures the extent to which the individual has knowledge and understanding of his religion. There are some indications that today's youths are woefully uninformed. A study of the biblical knowledge of Protestant and Jewish university sophomore students revealed real ignorance of the Old and New Testaments. On a test of a hundred items, fifty on the Old Testament and fifty on the New, scores ranged between zero and eighty, with a median of only seventeen. (73)

THE CONSEQUENTIAL DIMENSION

This aspect of religion measures the extent to which individuals' religions have consequences for them; that is, whether religion influences their behavior or changes their lives. There is some indication that religion has a significant influence over some aspects of behavior, such as the incidence of premarital sexual intercourse or the use of alcohol and marijuana. It has been found, for example, that premarital permissiveness is negatively and significantly related to many different measures of religiosity, (22, 24, 69) but especially to the intellectual and ideological dimensions. (81) Similarly, use of alcohol and marijuana is negatively related to religious participation: people who go to church frequently are less likely to use either. (18) In some instances, however, it is hard to establish cause and effect. "By definition, an act can be a religious effect only if it flows from religiosity." (45, p. 35) Because two factors are related does not necessarily mean they are causally linked, nor is the direction of cause and effect always certain. If a study shows that those who attend church have more religious and ethnic prejudices, does this mean that church attendance causes prejudice? It could also mean that prejudiced people are more likely to attend church. Similarly, some studies have found a neutral or even negative association between church participation and/or religious beliefs and delinquency. (18, 85) Are religious practices or beliefs the causal agent for less delinquency? Religiosity and delinquency could both be linked to other causal factors, such as social class or family relationships.

Another factor that may have significance here is the often found discrepancy between belief and practice, between one's ideals and one's actual conduct. This was brought out very clearly in a study by Gannon on the relationships between religious control and delinquent behavior. (41) The study was conducted with a random sample of Catholic boys who had been processed through a juvenile detention home in Cook County, Illinois. Only a small fraction of this group felt that stealing was all right. But of the 86.7 percent who generally disapproved of stealing, almost one-third had several times stolen items worth up to fifty dollars, and over one-third had several times stolen items worth over fifty dollars. Over half said they would not hesitate to "borrow" a car, and had done so with some regularity. (41, p. 425) Similarly, although almost three-fourths stated they would always or usually refuse if their gang wanted them to go along with something they knew was wrong or sinful, almost half had always or usually gone along when the group stole, fought, or caused general disorder. (41, p. 425) Over half the total group attended church, some more often than their parents. Most felt they ought to go to church every Sunday. In addition, the study showed little difference between delinquents and nondelinquents in the attitude toward God. On tests of religious and moral orthodoxy, the delinquent group revealed a basic theoretical knowledge of the doctrines of their faith, except for a lack of awareness of God as a person who is interested in them individually. (41, p. 427) What caused the marked inconsistency between the boys' religious values and their related behaviors?

One answer may be that the boys' religious commitment was marginal. All were born Catholics; their initial commitment was made for them by their parents. Their religion was not their own; it was something received as desirable, but impersonal. There may have been no personal relationship between the individual and his God. Parental influence was ambiguous (many parents did not attend church); thus, the adolescents were surrounded by ineffectual adult models. At the same time, the youths were often under the direct influence of their own peer groups, and the influence was often negative. (37) Therefore, religion was not a crucial factor in influencing behavior, because it was impersonal and not supported by other influences immediately crucial to the delinquent. (41, p. 426) The author concludes:

The effectiveness of religion depends upon the internalization of standards during the critical formative years of childhood and is developed through close identification with parents, family members, and other significant primary groups. Much of this control is exercised unconsciously and depends largely upon behavioral examples and religious experience rather than on precept. Only later does it reach the level of conscious decision and personal commitment.

If other supporting controlling agencies are missing, this simply means that the church has encountered a difficulty in coping with factors in modern life that tend to neutralize the fundamental tenets of religious teaching. (41, p. 429)

Religion and the Contemporary College Student

DECLINE OF INSTITUTIONALISM

It has been suggested that college students today are turning away from institutionalized religion and that campuses are becoming more secularized. (51) This is indicated by the decline in church attendance and participation and by the decrease in orthodox beliefs as adolescents get older. This trend is fairly recent, having occurred primarily since the late 1950s. (4, 51)

ORTHODOXY DURING THE 1930s TO THE MIDDLE 1950s

The evidence seems clear that between the 1930s and 1950s there was a marked increase in religious interests, values, orthodoxy, and traditional religious practices among college students. A study at Northwestern University showed increases in traditional beliefs between the middle 1930s and 1949. (43) A study of religious values at Dartmouth College showed an increase of similar values between 1940 and 1956. (12)

Just why there was increased attention and interest in orthodox religion is not certain. It may be that the years of the Great Depression and of World War II had considerable influence, causing many youths to think about life's goals, purposes, and values in a new light. It is certain that during and after World War II there was a mass return to traditional religion, with large numbers of veterans going into the ministry and other forms of social service, partly as a reaction to the horrors and injustices of war. The silent generation returned to the church to try to find personal faith and social salvation.

THE SOCIAL GOSPEL

From the late 1950s to the present, interest in traditional religion has waned. There has been a decrease of religious orthodoxy, a turning away from traditional institutional religion to political and social activism and protest. (20, 23, 25, 34, 51, 82) The rapid decline in traditional religious commitment during the 1950s and 1960s accounts for much recent discussion of campus secularization. (19, 22, 48, 77)

But whereas there has been a decline in religious orthodoxy, there has been renewed interest in the religious ethic, so much so that Glock and Stark have suggested that "ethics will be the death of Christianity." (44) There has been a shift in emphasis from personal salvation and holiness to love of neighbor as the central obligation. "The long Christian quest to save the world through individual salvation has shifted to the quest to reform society." (44, 86) The new theology places less emphasis upon what one believes about God and more upon what one believes about goodness, justice, and compassion. (7, 32, 80, 95) Glock and Stark are quick to point out that ethicalism is most prevalent in the least orthodox denominations, and that individuals whose religious beliefs are the least orthodox score higher on ethicalism than the most orthodox. (44)

Lipset has shown the inverse relationship between religious orthodoxy and student protest. (67) During the 1930s and in the middle and late 1960s and early 1970s, students became politically active. These were the same years that religious orthodoxy and traditionalism were on the decline. But the years from 1940 to the middle 1950s saw an increase in traditional beliefs with such a decline in student activism that the youths of these years were labeled "the silent generation." (51, 67) As Flacks and others have pointed out, student activists of today may hold intense political, ethical, or social commitments but are generally not traditionally religious. (29, 61, 62, 63, 64) At the same time, the religious traditionalists, especially those emphasizing personal salvation, are not interested in political and social reform. (44)

EMOTIONALISM AND RELIGIOUS CULTS

One of the phenomena of the 1970s has been an increase in religious revivalism, emotionalism, and mysticism among the young. The churches experiencing the greatest growth have been those that emphasize religious conversion and personal salvation. These emotional appeals have reached increasing numbers of young people, who have become "born again" Christians.

Another phenomenon has been an increase in the popularity of groups such as the Moonies and Hare Krishnas. Parental legal attacks against the Moonies for brainwashing youths into joining have resulted in a leveling off of membership, but not before the group had recruited thousands of members and millions of dollars in assets. Similarly, the Hare Krishnas appeal to some college youths, who have been wooed into joining the ranks and come regularly to the sect's forty-five *ashrams* to savor Indian food, hear lectures, and meditate. Other oriental religions, such as Zen Buddhism, various yoga groups, and others that offer transcendental meditation, have also been popular.

Young people who join such groups do so partly out of emotional and social need: the need to be a part of a group larger than themselves. Such membership gives them identity and an opportunity to share in religious experiences that they find real and rewarding. Also, youths seem to be looking for authority and certainty in a world of changing ideologies and values. Then too, membership gives them a cause to which to commit themselves that adds meaning to life. Membership in such groups may be short-lived, often for less than a year, but in the meantime youths find a faith, a sense of belonging, and a cause.

THE JESUS MOVEMENT

One of the largest and most lasting groups has been the modern Jesus movement. Its members are called the Jesus people. The Jesus people (24, p. 108) are one example of young evangelicals who emphasize personal salvation rather than social reform. The Jesus movement began in California around 1968 and since that time has become an international movement, so that today there are over 600,000 members worldwide. (8, p. 24) It is now possible to find groups of Jesus people and Jesus communes in England, France, Holland, Germany, Italy, Belgium, and Switzerland, and in Latin America, Australia, and Southeast and Central Asia. (94, p. 38) The largest groups are in the United States, but membership is rapidly growing elsewhere. Known variously as *Jesus people, street*

Christians, Jesus freaks, God's Forever Family, Children of God, or *Jesus boppers,* the movement contains very diverse, loosely organized groups. (8, p. 23) One radical fringe group, the Children of God, claims to have 250 communes in over eighty countries, and is still growing. (94, p. 38)

The Jesus movement is made up mostly of youths in their late teens or early twenties who have dropped out of school and are from middle to upper middle class families. (8, p. 24) Interviews of members in the Seattle area revealed that they come from all types of religious and nonreligious backgrounds and that there were "perhaps disproportionate representations of Catholics and Jews." (74, p. 264) Regardless of their religious backgrounds, they have one thing in common: they are disillusioned hippies who have now become double dropouts at variance both with the basic values of straight society and with many of the values of the youth counterculture. (8, p. 25) Many were formerly heavily involved with drug abuse, others in anarchistic communities seeking love, peace, and happiness for all by everyone "doing their own thing." Others were political activists, spending long hours campaigning for McCarthy or McGovern, or joining protest marches, ecology groups, and antiwar demonstrations. Some were jailed in their fight for racial equality; others joined violent revolutions on campus or in the ghettoes. (94, p. 37) Then, becoming discouraged with the success of the counterculture activities and seeking another way to express their alienation and rejection of society, they became Jesus people, a movement that allows them means of radical protest without "copping out" to the establishment. (79, p. 59) Thus, "conversion to the Jesus movement has allowed these youth to return to the 'system' with a minimum of 'culture shock' by providing a kind of asylum or haven from both the system and the counterculture . . ." (79, p. 51) The movement has enabled them to continue their protests, but to give up drugs, free love, and the radical social activism with which they became disillusioned. "Converts are viewed as really 'wanting' to be socially integrated." (79, p. 59) They are depicted as young ex-hippies who "have lived for the moment, but in the process have found that although man does not live by bread alone, he does need bread." (8, p. 36) The more sophisticated the movement becomes, the more it appeals to relatively "straight" types, (79, p. 55) but its membership is made up largely of two apparently contradictory impulses: the fundamentalist Christian leading a hippie style of life. (8, p. 27)

Jesus people may be characterized as young, radical, antiestablishment, fundamentalist, fanatical, dedicated, communal, narrow and bigoted, joyful, and apocalyptic. (94, p. 39) They are similar to other fundamentalist Christians in their emphasis on negative ethics: don't use drugs, don't drink, don't gamble, don't fight, don't fornicate. (38; 79, p. 49) There are very strong prohibitions against drug use. (1, 50) Members are urged instead to become "high on Jesus," or to "turn on with Jesus," or to "take a trip with Jesus." (8, p. 34) They are also very puritanical in their views on sex. (79, p. 50) Like other fundamentalist Christians, they emphasize the sinfulness of the world and the need to separate oneself from society. In their desire to escape worldliness and to live a separated life, members of the Texas-based Children of God retreat to rural communities. Numerous writers have noticed their depoliticization and diminished interest in radical social protest and their tendency to criticize strongly the radical and peace groups. (1, 30, 50)

One expression of the desire to escape worldliness is the emphasis on the second coming of Jesus. Members are taught that the world is in its last days. They point to many signs: the reestablishment of the State of Israel according to biblical prophecy, the population explosion, the food shortage, pollution, depletion of natural resources, changes in the earth's climate, the threat of nuclear holocaust, and indications that the world can't continue much longer on its present course. (94, p. 39) Richardson writes: "The overt rejection of society is evidenced by the fact that an overwhelming majority of the persons we interviewed expected the 'end of the world' during their generation, and they wanted this to happen." (78) "This apocalyptic feature of the movement dissuades young people from rejoining society." (1, p. 56)

Like other fundamentalist groups, the Jesus people are anti-intellectual in their religious emphasis and suspicious of any rational approach to the Bible and to religion. They attempt to preserve "historic" Christianity by emphasizing such tenets as the virgin birth, miracles, the bodily resurrection of Jesus, a literal heaven and hell, and the Bible as the verbally inspired word of God. Jesus people rely on subjective feelings (16, p. 260) and the guidance of the Holy Spirit in interpreting the Bible. A common practice is to cite Bible verses as proof to support points they are trying to make. (8, p. 29) Above all, they emphasize a personal encounter and relationship with Jesus, who has "come to dwell in my heart." The believers emphasize experiential feelings and getting "high on Jesus" to the extent that they yield their lives to His guidance and that of the Holy Spirit. One manifestation of the Spirit's presence is the ability to "speak in tongues" as on the day of Pentecost. (8, p. 35) This practice of "speaking in tongues" meshes well with the counterculture emphasis on spontaneity, yielding to impulse without intellectual control, and doing one's own thing. (79, p. 51)

Another characteristic of the Jesus movement is its use of gospel rock concerts and festivals. (8, p. 26) Members gather in city parks and other places for worship services that include gospel rock music accompanied by the same guitars and other instruments used by conventional rock groups. In the fall of 1975, some 30,000 Jesus people gathered for a three-day festival on a potato farm near Morgantown, Pennsylvania. Gospel rock, preaching, and shouting were mixed with long periods of Bible study and instruction. (96)

Like most highly evangelical groups, the longer the Jesus movement continues, the more likely it will evolve into more conservative expressions. Some groups are already encouraging their members "to get jobs, return to school, and make amends with parents and the law." (30, p. 228) Others have joined forces with other Pentecostal churches, have abandoned street preaching, and are recruiting less stigmatized and alienated young people. (57) Some members have married, have joined regular churches, and are spreading their evangelical spirit throughout these denominations. New converts continue to stream in through evangelical youth organizations such as the Crusade for Christ, Intervarsity Christian Fellowship, the Navigators, and the Campus Ambassadors. (96) Some observers feel that Jesus people will lose their special identity as they become more involved with these organizations and institutional churches. Others feel it will evolve into another sect as so many other have. (96) In the meantime, thousands of young people have been influenced by this phenomenon.

Conclusions

For the majority of older students religious beliefs have become more liberal, and traditional religious practices have diminished. (51) But many of these students are also more aware of and interested in the political and social problems of society and people, (92) and much of this ethical concern of modern youths is expressed outside the organized church. The church has lost some of its authority with these adolescents, but youths are holding onto its social ethics, giving them new meanings and applications in their lives. (71) Thus, although the modern generation is antichurch, it is not unconcerned, nor is it unreligious.

What the future holds is hard to say. Churches are experimenting with new forms of worship, new types of ministries, new ways of reaching youth and providing them with an instrument of social action. Some clergy have vacated their pulpits and taken to the streets with their young people following along. Others have become political organizers or social reformers, encouraging youths by precept and example to work in and through the established system. Still others and their youths have reacted against the social gospel and turned back to personal salvation as the answer to the world's problems. Jesus movements have sprung up in college campuses across the land. (49, 89) It does not appear likely in the immediate future, however, that large numbers of youth are going to return to the organized church for their answers. What does appear likely is that they will struggle, with the church's encouragement, to save the world.

Case Studies

Locate several members of the Jesus movement and talk to them to learn as much as possible about their personal and family backgrounds, religious history, activities, and beliefs before joining the Jesus movement; their conversion, why and how they joined the movement; its effect on their thinking, behavior, and lives; and their beliefs and plans for the future. Write each person's story as a case study, comparing and analyzing differences, similarities, philosophies, and so forth.

Bibliography

1. Adams, R., and Fox, R. "Mainlining Jesus: The New Trip." *Society* 9 (1972): 50–56.

2. Adelson, J. "The Political Imagination of the Young Adolescent." *Daedalus* (Fall 1971): 1013–1050.

3. Adelson, J. et al. "The Growth of the Idea of Law in Adolescence." *Developmental Psychology* 1 (1969): 327–332.

4. Aldridge, J. W. *In the Country of the Young.* New York: Harper and Row, 1971.

5. Babin, P. "The Faith of Adolescents toward the End of School." *Religious Education* 57 (1962): 128–131.

6. ———. *Adolescents in Search of a New Church.* New York: Herder and Herder, 1969.

7. Bachman, J. G. *Youth Looks at National Problems: A Special Report from the Youth in Transition Project.* Ann Arbor: Institute for Social Research, University of Michigan, 1971.

8. Balswick, J. "The Jesus People Movement: A Generational Interpretation." *Journal of Social Issues* 30 (1974): 23–67.

9. Barbour, I. G. "Science, Religion, and the Counterculture." *Journal of Religion and Science* 10 (1975): 380–397.

10. Beit-Hallahmi, B. "Self-Reported Religious Concerns of University Underclassmen." *Adolescence* 9 (1974): 333–338.

11. Bellah, R. N. "Religious Evolution." *American Sociological Review* 29 (1964): 358–374.

12. Bender, I. E. "Changes in Religious Interest: A Retest after 15 Years." *Journal of Abnormal and Social Psychology* 57 (1958): 41–46.

13. Blaine, G. B. *Youth and the Hazards of Affluence.* New York: Harper and Row, 1966.

14. Block, J. H. et al. "Socialization Correlates of Student Activism." *Journal of Social Issues* 25 (1969): 143–177.

15. Blos, P. *The Young Adolescent: Clinical Studies.* New York: Free Press, 1970.

16. Bressler, L., and Bressler, M. *Youth in American Life.* Boston: Houghton Mifflin Co., 1972.

17. Bryant, B. E. *High School Students Look at Their World.* Columbus, Ohio: Goettler, 1970.

18. Burkett, S. R., and White, M. "Hellfire and Delinquency: Another Look." *Journal for the Scientific Study of Religion* 13 (1974): 455–462.

19. Bushnell, H. *Christian Nurture.* 1888. Reprint. New Haven, Conn.: York University Press, 1947.

20. Cirese, S., and Koon, J. "College Seniors View Campus Unrest and National Issues, Spring, 1970." Berkeley, Calif.: Center for Research and Development in Higher Education, 1970, Mimeographed.

21. Clark, E. T., and Propper, M. M. "Alienation Syndrome among Catholic Male Undergraduates." *Psychological Reports* 25 (1969): 167–172.

22. Clayton, R. R. "Premarital Sexual Intercourse: A Substantive Test of the Contingent Consistency Model." *Journal of Marriage and the Family* 34 (1972): 273–281.

23. Converse, P. E., and Schuman, H. " 'Silent Majorities' and the Vietnam War." *Scientific American* 222 (1970): 17–25.

24. Cordwell, J. D. "The Relationship between Religious Commitment and Premarital Sexual Permissiveness: A Five Dimensional Analysis." *Sociological Analysis* 30 (1969): 72–81.

25. Cottle, T. J. *Time's Children: Impressions of Youth.* Boston: Little, Brown and Co., 1971.

26. Curtis, D. "The Re-making of a Revolutionary." *Student Action* 5 (1971): 2, 7.

27. DeBord, L. W. "Adolescent Religious Participation: An Examination of Sub-Structure and Church Attendance." *Adolescence* 4 (1969): 557–570.

28. Drane, J. F. *A New American Revolution.* New York: Philosophical Library, 1973.

29. Engel, D. E. "Education and Identity: The Functions of Questions in Religious Education." *Religious Education* 63 (1968): 371–375.

30. Enroth, R. et al. *The Jesus People.* Grand Rapids, Mich.: Erdmans, 1972.

31. Erikson, E. H. "Reflections on the Dissent of Contemporary Youth." *International Journal of Psychoanalysis* 51 (1970): 11–22.

32. Erlick, A. C. *People Problems: Population, Pollution, Prejudice, Poverty, Peace.* Report of the Purdue Opinion Panel, June, 1970. Lafayette, Ind.: Purdue University, 1970.

33. Faulkner, J. E., and DeJong, G. F. "Religiosity in 5-D: An Empirical Analysis." *Social Forces* 45 (1966): 246–254.

34. Feigelson, N. *The Underground Revolution.* New York: Funk and Wagnalls, 1970.

35. Feuer, L. S. *The Conflict of Generations.* New York: Basic Books, 1969.

36. Flacks, R. "The Liberated Generation: An Exploration of the Roots of Student Protest." *Journal of Social Issues* 23 (1967): 52–75.

37. Fodor, E. M. "Resistance to Social Influence among Adolescents as a Function of Level of Moral Development." *Journal of Social Psychology* 85 (1971): 121–126.

38. Freemesser, G. F., and Kaplan, H. B. "Self-Attitudes and Deviant Behavior: The Case of the Charismatic Religious Movement." *Journal of Youth and Adolescence* 5 (1976): 1–9.

39. Freud, A. "Adolescence as a Developmental Disturbance." In *Adolescence: Psychosocial Perspectives.* Edited by G. Caplan and S. Lebovici. New York: Basic Books, 1969.

40. Freud, S. *The Future of an Illusion.* London: Hogarth Press, 1943.

41. Gannon, T. M. "Religious Control and Delinquent Behavior." *Sociology and Social Research* 51 (1967): 418–431.

42. Garrison, K. C. *Psychology of Adolescence,* 6th ed. Englewood Cliffs, N.J.: Prentice-Hall, 1965.

43. Gilliland, A. R. "Changes in Religious Beliefs of College Students." *Journal of Social Psychology* 37 (1953): 113–116.

44. Glock, C., and Stark, R. "Will Ethics Be the Death of Christianity?" *Transaction* 7 (1968): 7–14.

45. ———. *Religion and Society in Tension.* Chicago: Rand McNally and Co., 1965.

46. Goethals, G. W., and Klos, D. S. *Experiencing Youth: First-Person Accounts.* Boston: Little, Brown and Co., 1970.

47. Gordon, C. "Social Characteristics of Early Adolescence." *Daedalus* (Fall 1971): 931–960.

48. Grant, P. K. "Religious Attitudes of Young American Catholics." *Critic* 33 (1974): 68–73.

49. Greeley, A. "Jesus Freaks and Other Devouts." *New York Times Book Review*, Part 2, 13 February 1972, pp. 4ff.

50. Harder, M. W., and Richardson, J. T. "The Jesus People." *Psychology Today* 6 (1972): 45–50, 110–113.

51. Hastings, P. K., and Hoge, D. R. "Religious Change among College Students over Two Decades." *Social Forces* 49 (1970): 16–28.

52. Havighurst, R. J. *Growing Up in River City.* New York: John Wiley and Sons, 1962.

53. Hoffman, M. L. "Conscience, Personality, and Socialization Techniques." *Human Development* 13 (1970): 90–126.

54. ———. "Identification and Conscience Development." *Child Development* 42 (1971): 1071–1082.

55. Hurlock, E. *Adolescent Development.* 3d ed. New York: McGraw-Hill, 1967.

56. ———. *Developmental Psychology.* 4th ed. New York: McGraw-Hill, 1975.

57. Jacobsen, C. K., and Pilarzyk, T. "Faith Freaks and Fanaticism: The Growth, Development, and Demise of the Milwaukee Jesus People." *Social Compass* 21 (1974): 2.

58. Jacquet, C. H., Jr., ed. *Yearbook of American and Canadian Churches, 1975.* New York: Abingdon Press, 1975.

59. Johnson, A. L. et al. "Age Differences and Dimensions of Religious Behavior." *Journal of Social Issues* 30 (1974): 43–67.

60. Jones, V. "Attitudes of College Students and Their Charges: A 37-Year Study." *Journal of Genetic Psychology* 3 (1970): 80.

61. Keniston, K. *Young Radicals: Notes on Committed Youth.* New York: Harcourt Brace Jovanovich, 1968.

62. ———. "The Agony of the Counter-Culture." *Yale Alumni Magazine* (October 1971): 10–13.

63. ———. *Youth and Dissent.* New York: Harcourt Brace Jovanovich, 1971.

64. Kerpelman, L. C. *Activists and Nonactivists: A Psychological Study of American College Students.* New York: Behavioral Publications, 1972.

65. Kiell, N. "God, Father, and the Adolescent." In *The Universal Experience of Adolescence.* Edited by N. Kiell. New York: International Universities Press, 1964, pp. 609–655.

66. Lenski, G. *The Religious Factor: A Sociological Study of Religion's Impact on Politics, Economics, and Family Life.* rev. ed. Garden City, N.Y.: Doubleday Anchor, 1963.

67. Lipset, S. M. "Student Opposition in the United States." *Government and Opposition* 1 (1966): 351–374.

68. Matteson, D. R. *Adolescence Today: Sex Roles and the Search for Identity.* Homewood, Ill.: Dorsey Press, 1975.

69. Middendorp, C. P. et al. "Determinants of Premarital Permissiveness: A Secondary Analysis." *Journal of Marriage and the Family* 32 (1970): 369–379.

70. Mooney, R. L., and Gordon, L. V. *Manual for Mooney Problems Check List.* New York: Psychological Corporation, 1950.

71. Mussen, P. H. et al. *Child Development and Personality.* 3d ed. New York: Harper and Row, 1969.

72. Parsons, H. L. "Religious Beliefs of Students at Six Colleges and Universities." *Religious Education* 58 (1963): 538–544.

73. Payne, R. "Knowledge of the Bible among Protestant and Jewish University Students: An Exploratory Study." *Religious Education* 58 (1963): 289–294.

74. Petersen, W., and Mauss, A. L. "The Cross and the Commune: An Interpretation of the Jesus People." In *Religion in Sociological Perspective.* Edited by C. Y. Glock. Belmont, Calif.: Wadsworth Publishing Co., 1973.

75. Podd, M. H. "Ego Identity Status and Morality: The Relationship between Two Constructs." *Developmental Psychology* 6 (1972): 497–507.

76. Powell, M. *Youth: Critical Issues.* Columbus, Ohio: Charles E. Merrill Publishing Co., 1972.

77. Propper, M. M. et al. "Alienation Syndrome among Male Adolescents in Prestige Catholic and Public High Schools." *Psychological Reports* 27 (1970): 311–315.

78. Richardson, J. T. et al. "Thought Reform and the Jesus Movement." *Youth and Society* (December 1972): 185–202.

79. Robbins, T.; Anthony, D.; and Curtis, T. "Youth Culture Religious Movements: Evaluating the Integrative Hypothesis." *Sociological Quarterly* 16 (1975): 48–64.

80. Roszak, T. *The Making of a Counter Culture: Reflections on the Technocratic Society and Its Youthful Opposition.* Garden City, N.Y.: Doubleday Anchor, 1968.

81. Ruppel, H. J., Jr. "Religiosity and Premarital Sexual Permissiveness: A Response to the Reiss-Heltsley and Broderick Debate." *Journal of Marriage and the Family* 32 (1970): 647–655.

82. Sampson, E. E., and Korn, H. A., eds. *Student Activism and Dissent: Alternatives for Social Change.* San Francisco: Jossey-Bass Publishing Co., 1970.

83. Scammon, R., and Wattenberg, B. J. *The Real Majority.* New York: Coward, McCann & Geoghegan, 1970.

84. Schneiders, A. A. *Adolescents and the Challenge of Maturity.* Milwaukee: Bruce Publishing Co., 1965.

85. Scholl, M. E., and Beker, J. "A Comparison of the Religious Beliefs of Delinquent and Non-Delinquent Protestant Adolescent Boys." *Religious Education* 59 (1964): 250–253.

86. Settlage, C. F. "Adolescence and Social Change." *Journal of the American Academy of Child Psychiatry* 92 (1970): 203–215.

87. Smart, M. S., and Smart, R. C. *Adolescents: Development and Relationships.* New York: Macmillan Co., 1973.

88. Stewart, C. W. *Adolescent Religion.* New York: Abingdon Press, 1967.

89. Streiker, L. D. *The Jesus Trip: Advent of the Jesus Freaks.* New York: Abingdon Press, 1971.

90. *New York Times* 1 June 1969.

91. Troll, L. E. et al. "Similarity in Values and Other Personality Characteristics in College Students and Their Parents." *Merrill-Palmer Quarterly* 15 (1969): 323–336.

92. Whiteleather, M. K. "Seven Polarizing Issues in America Today." *Annals of the American Academy of Political and Social Science* 397 (1971): 1–139.

93. Whitman, L. B. et al. *The Presbyterian National Education Survey,* vol. 3. New York: Board of Christian Education of the United Presbyterian Church in the United States of America, 1965.

94. Wormus, J. W. "The Jesus Movement." *Risk* 11 (1975): 35–39.

95. Yankelovich, D. *The New Morality: A Profile of American Youth in the 70's.* New York: McGraw-Hill, 1974.

96. "Young 'Jesus People': Coming of Age." *U.S. News & World Report,* 29 March 1976.

97. Zaenglein, M. M.; Vener, A. M.; and Stewart, C. S. "The Adolescent and His Religion: Beliefs in Transition, 1970–1973." *Review of Religious Research* 17 (1975): 51–60.

CHAPTER 18

The Development of Moral Judgment, Character, Values, and Behavior

Outline

The process by which children and youths develop moral judgment is extremely interesting. A number of major theories, based upon sound research findings, have been developed and will be discussed in this chapter. The work of Jean Piaget and Lawrence Kohlberg represents theories that emphasize the development of moral judgment as a gradual cognitive process, stimulated by increasing, changing social relationships of children as they get older. Other theories relating to moral development emphasize personality and ego-superego development and their relationship to the development of moral character and behavior. The work of Robert Havighurst and R. H. Peck will be discussed as most representative of this viewpoint. Other researchers have concentrated on an examination of various family correlates that influence moral development. Such factors as parental warmth, parent-teen interaction, discipline, parental role models, and independence opportunities outside the home are discussed in relation to their influence on moral learning. Finally, other social influences such as peer and reference groups, television, and schools will be examined. The effects of these influences on the development of values and behavior are important and need to be understood.

Cognitive-Socialization Theories of Development

JEAN PIAGET

The most important early research on the development of moral judgment of children is that of Piaget. (76, 77) Although some details of his findings have not been substantiated by subsequent research, (13, 98) Piaget's ideas have formed the theoretical basis for later research. And even though his work was with children, the theoretical framework that outlines his stages of development may be applied to adolescents and adults as well as children. It is important, therefore, to understand Piaget's discoveries.

Piaget's work is reported in four sections. (76) The first section discusses the attitudes of children to the rules of the game when playing marbles. The second and third sections report the results of telling children stories that require them to make moral judgments on the basis of the information given. The last section reviews his findings in relation to social psychology, particularly to the work of Durkheim, (18) who argues that the sanctions of society are the only source of morality.

In studying children's attitudes to the rules of the game, Piaget concluded that there is first of all a *morality of constraint* and, second, a *morality of cooperation*. In the early stages of moral development children are constrained by the rules of the game. These rules are coercive because children regard them as inviolable and because they reflect parental authority. (76, p. 104) Rules constitute a given order of existence and, like parents, must be obeyed without question. (1, 2) Later, as a result of social interaction, children learn that rules are not absolute; they learn that they can alter them by social consensus. (22) Rules are no longer external laws to be considered sacred because they are laid down by adults, but social creations arrived at through a process of free decision, and thus deserving of mutual respect and consent. (21) Children move from *heteronomy* to *autonomy* in making moral judgments. (76, p. 57)

Piaget also discusses the motives or reasons for judgments. He says there are, first, judgments based solely upon the consequences of wrongdoing (*objective judgments*) and, second, judgments that take into account intention or motive (*subjective judgments*). Piaget claims there is a growing pattern of operational thinking, with children moving from *objective* to *subjective responsibility* as they grow older. He writes:

These two attitudes may coexist at the same age and even in the same child, but broadly speaking they do not synchronize. Objective responsibility diminishes on the average as the child grows older, and subjective responsibility gains correlatively in importance. (76, p. 129)

Piaget would insist that although the two processes overlap, the second gradually supersedes the first. (76, p. 129) The first stage is superseded when children deem motive or intention more important than consequences.

The child finds in his brothers and sisters or in his playmates a form of society which develops his desire for cooperation. Then a new type of morality will be created in him, a *morality of reciprocity* and not of *obedience*. This is the true morality of intention. (76, p. 133)

Piaget is careful to note that obedience and cooperation are not always successive stages, but nevertheless are formative processes that broadly follow one another. "The first of these processes is the moral constraint of the adult, a constraint which leads to heteronomy and consequently to moral realism. The second is co-operation which leads to autonomy." (76, p. 193) (By moral realism Piaget means submitting meekly to the demands of law.)

Before moral judgment moves from the *heteronomous* to the *autonomous* stage, the self-accepted rules must be internalized. This happens when, in a reciprocal relationship, and out of mutual respect, people begin to feel from within the desire to treat others as they themselves would wish to be treated. They pass from *preoperational* to *operational thinking,* from premoral to moral judgment as they internalize the rules they want to follow. (52)

In the third section of his report, Piaget discusses the child's concept of justice as the child moves from moral restraint to moral cooperation. Two concepts of punishment emerge. The first results from the transgression of an externally imposed regulation; this Piaget calls *expiatory punishment*, which goes hand in hand with constraint and the rules of authority. The second is self-imposed punishment, which comes into operation when the individual, in violation of his or her own conscience, is denied normal social relations and is isolated from the group by his or her own actions. Piaget calls this the *punishment of reciprocity,* which accompanies cooperation. (76, p. 193) An ethic of mutual respect, of good as opposed to duty, leads to improved social relationships that are basic to any concept of real equality and reciprocity.

In the last section of his work, Piaget, following Durkheim, asserts that "society is the only source of morality." (76, p. 326) Morality, to Piaget, consists of a system of rules, but such rules require a sociological context for their development. Thus, "whether the child's moral judgments are heteronomous or autonomous, accepted under pressure or worked out in freedom, this morality is social, and on this point, Durkheim was unquestionably right." (76, p. 344)

One of the important implications of Piaget's view is that the changes in moral judgments of children are related to their cognitive growth and to the changes in their social relationships. At first children judge the severity of transgressions by their visible damage or harm. They also develop the concept of *imminent justice:* that punishment is impersonally ordered in the performance of transgression: "If you do wrong, you will certainly be punished." Furthermore, they judge the appropriateness of this punishment by its severity rather than by its relevance to the transgression. Only as children get older are they likely to recommend that the transgressor make restitution or that punishment be tailored to fit the wrong done. Gradually, also, they come to see that the application of rules must be relative to people and situations, and that rules are established and maintained through reciprocal social agreements. (96, p. 513)

As an example, if six-year-olds are told the story of a little boy who has accidentally dropped a sweet roll in the lake, they are likely to respond: "That's too bad. But it's his own fault for being so clumsy. He shouldn't get another." For them, a punishment implies a crime, and losing a roll in the lake is clearly a punishment in their eyes. They are incapable of taking extenuating circumstances into account. Adolescents, however, make moral judgments on the basis of what Piaget calls *equity,* assigning punishments in accordance with the transgressors' abilities to take responsibility for their crimes. Adolescents are able to employ the same sort of reasoning in relation to moral dilemmas as they are in solving intellectual puzzles. Rather than being tied to concrete facts and a narrow range of possibilities (there is punishment, therefore there must be a crime), they are able to imagine a wide range of possibilities. (The roll is lost, someone may or may not be to blame.) As a result they are able to take into account the youthfulness of the child, many of the possible reasons why the roll was lost, and to show more compassion: "It may not have been his fault; he should get another treat." (24, p. 116)

Another important implication of Piaget's view is that the changes in judgments of children must be related to the changes in their social relationships. As peer-group activity and cooperation increase and as adult constraint decreases, the child becomes more truly an autonomous, cooperative, moral person.

One of the best summaries of Piaget's conclusions has been given by Kay (38, p. 157) in a series of simple propositions about the moral lives of children.

1. Human beings develop an intelligent and informed respect for law by experiencing genuine social relationships.

2. Such social relationships are found in two basic forms. They are first characterized by child subordination and adult supremacy and then slowly change until the relationship is reciprocal. In this case it can either be based on equality or equity.

3. These social relationships are functionally linked with a system of moral judgment. When the relationship is one of subordination and supremacy then the moral judgment exercised is based on authoritarian considerations which are objective and heteronomous. And equally when the relationship is reciprocal moral judgments are autonomous and reflect the subjective system of morality which now activates the child from within.

4. Judgment and conduct at the final stage of moral development are based not on subscription to an external code of law nor even in the regulation of rigid reciprocity in human relationships. It consists of the recognition of the rights and needs of all individuals with due regard to the situational circumstances and the moral principles expressed in them.

Although Piaget's conclusions were deduced from research with children up to age twelve, they have some relationship to the moral life of adolescents. It has been emphasized that Piaget said that children move from a morality of constraint (or obedience) to a morality of cooperation (or reciprocity); children pass from heteronomy to autonomy in making moral judgments; and they move from objective to subjective responsibility. Piaget has said that this second stage of moral development gradually supersedes the first as children grow older.

Some subsequent research questions this view. For example, it has been found that adolescents, as well as children, tend to seek justice in an authority person. There are adolescents, and even adults, who obey certain laws and rules only because of coercion and the threat of external punishment. They are constrained by authority, not by an inner conscience. If they break the rules, their concern is not remorse at doing wrong, but at having been caught. In other words, they never move from heteronomy to autonomy, from objective judgment to subjective judgment, from a morality of constraint to a morality of cooperation. They remain, like young children, at a preoperational, premoral stage of development, for the rules have never been internalized, and they never desire to do the right thing from mutual respect and concern for the feelings and welfare of others.

It is unreasonable, therefore, always to attach age categories to the stages of moral development. There are children, adolescents, and adults at any one stage of moral growth. This is one reason why Piaget's findings may be applied to adolescents as well as children. Researchers like Brennan, (11) Johnson, (37) Kohlberg, (42–51) and Loughran (64) have each confirmed some aspect of Piaget's conclusions, but they would not assign each stage of development to a particular age group.

LAWRENCE KOHLBERG

One of the principal deficiencies of Piaget's work was his exclusive concern with children under the age of twelve. Kohlberg compensated for this deficiency by using adolescents in a series of studies; (42–51) he confirmed Piaget's conclusions and showed their validity when applied to adolescents.

Kohlberg's initial study included seventy-two boys aged ten, thirteen, and sixteen. (42) All groups were similar in IQ; half of each group was upper middle class. Data were collected through taped interviews in which ten moral dilemmas were presented to each subject. In each dilemma, acts of disobedience to legal-social rules or the commands of authority figures conflicted with the human needs or welfare of others. Each subject was asked to select one of two acts as the more desired solution and was then questioned about the reasons for his choice. Kohlberg's material and technique were both Piagetian in form. (42, p. 12) In this study Kohlberg was concerned not with moral behavior, but with moral judgment and the process of thought by which the individual made his judgment. There were no right or wrong answers expected; the individual was scored according to his mode of reasoning, regardless of the direction of the given response.

From his analysis of the interviews, Kohlberg identified three major levels of moral development, each level with two types of moral orientation or judgment. (47, 49) The levels and subtypes are listed in Table 18–1. Kohlberg found that premoral thinking declined sharply from the younger to the older age groups. Level II increased until age thirteen, then stabilized. Level III also increased markedly between ten and thirteen years of age, with some additional increase between ages thirteen and sixteen. (44)

In outlining his stages, however, Kohlberg is careful not to equate each type with a particular age. Within any one age group, individuals are at different levels of development in their moral thinking: some are retarded, others advanced. No person fits neatly into any one of the six types. Kohlberg indicates that the development of moral thought is a gradual and continuous process as the individual passes through a sequence of increasingly sophisticated moral stages. (49)

Thus, type 1 obeys rules to avoid punishment. Type 2 conforms in order to

Table 18–1.   Kohlberg's levels of development of moral thought.

Level I. Premoral Level
Type 1: Punishment and obedience orientation
             (Motivation: To avoid punishment by others)
Type 2: Naive instrumental hedonism
             (Motivation: To gain rewards from others)

Level II. Morality of Conventional Role Conformity
Type 3: Good-person morality of maintaining good relations with, and approval of
             others
             (Motivation: To avoid disapproval of others)
Type 4: Authority-maintaining morality
             (Motivation: To maintain law and order and because of concern for the
             community)

Level III. Morality of Self-Accepted Moral Principles
Type 5: Morality of democratically accepted laws
             (Motivation: To gain the respect of an individual or community)
Type 6: Morality of individual principles of conduct
             (Motivation: To avoid self-condemnation for lapses)

From Lawrence Kohlberg, "The Development of Children's Orientations toward a Moral
    Order. 1: Sequence in the Development of Moral Thought," *Vita Humana* 6 (1963): 11–33.
    Used by permission.

obtain rewards or have favors returned. At Level I, which comprises these two types then, children are responsive to the defiinitions of good and bad provided by parental authority figures. Moral decisions are egocentric, based on self-interest; children interpret acts as good or bad in terms of physical consequences. (72) Type 3 is the good boy–nice girl orientation in which the child conforms to avoid disapproval and dislike by others, whereas type 4 conforms because of a desire to maintain law and order or because of concern for the larger community. Thus, Level II, comprising types 3 and 4, is less egocentric and more sociocentric in orientation, developing a conformity to social conventions that is based on a desire to maintain, support, and justify the existing social structure. (72) Type 5 conforms in order to maintain the respect of an impartial spectator or to maintain a relation of mutual respect. At this stage, the individual defines morality in terms of general principles such as individual rights, human dignity, equality, contractual agreement, and mutual obligations. Because moral principles have been accepted by society as a whole, the individual is motivated to accept them because of a concern for human well-being and public welfare. This is the social-contract, legalistic orientation in which justice flows from a contract between the governors and the governed. (71, p. 53) Unjust laws must be changed, and individuals flexible in their approach to these laws seek to improve them through consensus. This type is represented by those who accept the official morality of the United States Constitution, which recognizes important moral principles. Only one-third of Americans have reached this level of moral development. (72, p. 215) Finally, type 6 conforms to avoid self-condemnation. (38) The approach to moral issues is based not on egocentric needs or conformity to the existing social order, but on autonomous, universal principles of justice that are valid beyond existing laws, social conditions, or peer mores. Thus, individuals governed by universal ethical principles may break unjust civil laws because they recognize a morality higher than existing law. Americans who avoided the draft and accepted the penalty, as a protest against the Vietnam war, practiced civil disobedience in the interest of what they felt was a higher moral good. They felt there were universal moral principles that should be followed even though these challenged the existing official morality of their own government. (72, p. 216) Martin Luther King wrote from a Birmingham jail:

I do not advocate evading or defying the law. . . . That would lead to anarchy. One who breaks an unjust law must do so openly, lovingly, and with a willingness to accept the penalty. An individual who breaks the law that conscience tells him is unjust, and willingly accepts the penalty of imprisonment in order to arouse the conscience of the community over its injustice is, in reality, expressing the highest respect for the law. (40, p. 86)

Thus, Level III is made up of individuals who accept democratically recognized principles or universal truths, not because they have to but because they believe in the principles or truths.

Kohlberg emphasized that a stage concept such as this implies sequence: that each child must go through each successive level of moral judgment before passing on to the next. (44) The data seemed to support this conclusion. (19, p. 58) Kohlberg also emphasized that a stage concept implies universality of sequence under varying cultural conditions. That is, the development of moral judgment is not merely a matter of learning the rules of a particular culture; it reflects a universal process of development. In order to test this hypothesis, Kohlberg used his technique with boys ten, thirteen, and sixteen in a Taiwanese city, in a Malaysian (Atayal) aboriginal tribal village, and in a Turkish village, as well as in Great Britain, Canada, and the United States. (44) The results for Taiwan and the United States are compared in Figure 18–1 and indicate similar age trends in boys of both nationalities.

Kohlberg says that although his findings show a similar sequence of development in all cultures, the last two stages of moral thought do not develop clearly in preliterate village or tribal communities. It seems evident from the United States data also, however, that the great majority of American adults never reach Level III either, even by age twenty-four. Only 10 percent of his middle class urban male population had reached Level III, with another 26 percent at Level II. (44) Although Kohlberg studied ten- to sixteen-year-olds, studies of students at Berkeley, California, showed that 72 percent were still at Level II (32 percent at stage three, 40 percent at stage four). Those who had arrived at the sixth stage were active protestors on campus. (27) This correlation has led some writers to question the whole philosophical concept of moral maturity. (75)

Kohlberg tested his hypothesis with children of both middle and working classes, Protestants and Catholics, popular and socially isolated children, and

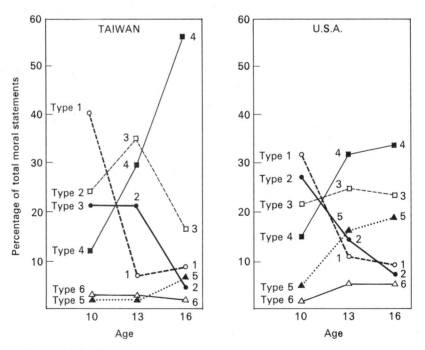

Figure 18–1.   Mean percentage of use of each of six stages of moral judgment at three ages in Taiwan and the United States. (Adapted from L. Kohlberg, "Moral Education in the School, A Developmental View," *The School Review* 74 [1966]:1–30. Copyright 1966, The University of Chicago Press. Used by permission.)

girls as well as boys. He found the same general stages of development among all groups, but some differences in the *level* of moral development of middle and working class children, with the middle class children, at all ages, in advance of the working class children. Kohlberg emphasized that these differences were cognitive and developmental in nature, with middle class children moving faster and farther. (44) The explanation is not that lower class children favor a different type of thought or hold values different from those of the middle class, but that working class children have less understanding of the broader social order and less participation in it; thus, their moral development is retarded. This explanation is further substantiated by the fact that children with extensive peer-group participation advance considerably more quickly through the successive stages of development of moral thinking. (44)

One other variable should be mentioned at this time. Moral judgment also correlates highly with IQ, indicating that it is more cognitive in nature than either the "good habits" or "early emotions" views. (44) As children participate more and more in social groups, they lose some of their cognitive naiveté and adopt a more sophisticated view of authority and social relationships. (56) This does not necessarily mean that they become better persons; they acquire a greater capacity for moral thinking, but whether such knowledge leads to better behavior depends upon emotional and social influence in their backgrounds and relationships.

Kohlberg's theories have been tested by researchers. Weinreich (103, 104) has shown that the rapidity and extent of progression through the sequence of stages are related to intelligence and, to some extent, to social class. Johnson (37) showed that moral judgment was significantly and positively associated with chronological age and with IQ; older, brighter youngsters evidenced greater maturity of moral judgment than did younger, less intelligent children. Tomlinson-Deasey (97) has produced some evidence that achieving a particular moral stage is dependent on reaching certain Piagetian levels and that the ability to perform certain logical operations seems to be a prerequisite to performing certain moral operations. Johnson found that parental attitudes toward their children also were significant. (37) The findings were similar to Kohlberg's conclusions that children's moral judgment is enhanced by parental warmth in the parent-child relationship. (44) Hoffman (31) also has shown that the stage at which the individual finally arrives in adulthood is related to family environment.

In one final research study, Turiel (98) showed that Kohlberg's stages form an invariant sequence, in which each individual passes through the stages in the manner described. Turiel's subjects learned more by exposure to the stage directly above their level than to stages farther above or to stages below, indicating the manner by which they learned new modes of thought. The fact that they assimilated the higher stage more readily than the lower one, even though they could understand the concepts of the lower stage as well as if not better than those of the higher one, indicated that the attainment of a higher stage involved a reorganization of the preceding modes of thought rather than an addition of new elements of the later stages. (98) Turiel has also suggested that exposure to diversity of individual and cultural values that gives an awareness of moral differences may act as the stimulus for growth from one stage to the next. (99)

LATER DEVELOPMENTS AND CRITIQUE OF KOHLBERG

One of the problems researchers have had in testing Kohlberg's theory has been the difficulty of determining at what stage an individual is. In one study of 957 individuals, more than 45 percent could not be placed in one stage or another; most of the groups were in transition between two stages, and some gave responses that straddled three stages. (71, p. 54) Moreover, Kohlberg and his associate Kramer found that many who had been in stage four in previous interviews had regressed to stage two, indicating that stage change was not always just upwards. Individuals may make moral judgments at one stage in one situation and at another stage in another situation. One circumstance may require a stage four response; another, a more universally applicable response. Also, Kohlberg's scale evaluates the motivation for making judgments, which can vary under different circumstances.

Furthermore, Kohlberg's original scale for measuring stages lacked standardization in administration and scoring. In response, Kohlberg and colleagues have completed a five-part manual that he promises will provide the consistency and reliability critics are looking for. (71, p. 54) Stage six (or type 6) has been dropped from the new manual entirely, for Kohlberg has estimated that only about 7 percent of sixteen-year-olds in the United States and Mexico and less than 1 percent of the same age group in Taiwan used stage six reasoning. None of those studied in Turkey or Yucatán had ever reached stage five. (71, p. 57)

Critics have also argued that it is really not true or fair to say that the higher the stage, the greater the level of morality. For example, more women ended up in stage three, and more men in stage four. Women were more desirous of pleasing others, which enabled them to smooth tensions and bring people together. Men were more concerned about maintaining law and order. Why should stage four be considered superior to stage three? This criticism has led Kohlberg to emphasize stage four more as concern for the larger community rather than the concern for law and order. More and more, Kohlberg has suggested that an important goal of moral education should not be to reach stage five, but rather "a solid attainment of the fourth stage commitment to being a good member of a community or a good citizen." (71, p. 57)

No evaluation of levels of moral judgment can be used to predict moral behavior; to know doesn't mean to do. Two people at the same level of reasoning might act differently under the pressure of circumstances. In fact, investigation of students at the University of California who participated in the Free Speech Movement revealed large numbers of persons in stages five or six, but also a large percentage of students who were in the relatively primitive stage two. (71, p. 54)

Personality Types, Ego Theory, and Moral Character

PERSONALITY TYPE AS THE KEY TO MOTIVATION AND BEHAVIOR

A number of writers and researchers, particularly Robert Havighurst and his colleagues, (74) have sought to show the relationship between personality types and morality, between moral character and behavior, between the ego-superego balance and moral maturity. From this point of view, developing moral character is not so much a matter of learning fixed moral virtues such as honesty, but of developing emotional maturity and balance: love instead of hate for others, guilt instead of fear, self-esteem and trust instead of inadequacy and distrust. (79) This point of view seeks to define and describe personality types and their characteristic affective responses as they might be revealed by projective personality tests or described by people's judgments of the child's moral character. This viewpoint emphasizes that personality type controls moral behavior. Thus, personal traits are *the* motivational factor in behavior.

PECK AND HAVIGHURST

Peck and Havighurst (74) have been the most influential contemporary exponents of this point of view. Early in their study, they decided to place their emphasis upon the predictability of moral conduct as revealed by persistent attitudes and traits the individuals manifested in their relationships with other people. The researchers' chief source of information about individual subjects, ages ten to seventeen, was the opinions others held about them. The authors defended their method when, after reviewing previous research, they concluded "that 'popular opinion' about the generality of moral character [was] . . . not so far wrong at all." (74, p. vi) To assure continuity in their research, they also studied the adolescents who had been surveyed earlier by Havighurst and Taba in order to draw upon earlier findings to supplement their own research.

They ask the all-important question "What is moral character?" and go on to describe it not only according to five character types, but also in terms of the various environmental influences that affect its development. By paying particular attention to the family, the peer group, and the social environment, they show how each makes its contribution to the moral development of the individuals studied.

The five character types they identify are: *amoral, expedient, conforming, irrational-conscientious,* and *rational-altruistic.* The authors emphasized that their categories were descriptive devices only, and no one character fits exactly the description for one type. (74, p. 166) These types are similar to Loevinger's six stages on her ego-development scale: *impulse ridden, opportunist, conformist, conscientious, autonomous,* and *integrated.* (61)

Peck and Havighurst emphasize two very important secondary hypotheses. First, the different personality types constitute five primary types of moral motivation. (74, p. 4)

This set of character types was intended to: (1) be defined and labeled in terms of the control system the individual uses to adapt his search for satisfaction to the requirements of the social world: (2) include all the possible modes of adaptation: (3) be defined in terms of motivation (so long as it achieves behavioral expression).

Second, each of these types not only is a component of character and a motivational factor but also represents a definite stage in a developmental scheme. "This serves the additional purpose in thinking about the motivational patterns as an ascending developmental sequence, from childlike reasons to mature reasons for behaving morally." (74, p. 4) The writers even go further and suggest that these developmental stages may be located from infancy to adulthood as follows: (74, p. 3)

- Amoral type: infancy
- Expedient type: early childhood
- Conforming type: later childhood
- Irrational-conscientious: later childhood
- Rational-altruistic: adolescence to adulthood

It must be recognized that there are some adolescents and adults at each of these stages of development; not everyone shows the same degree of moral growth.

Amoral persons are those who are completely egocentric. Their goal is self-gratification. They have little ego strength, cannot define their own personal goals, and are disorganized and unhappy. They have weak superegos and cannot control their impulses, lacking an integrated system of internalized moral principles. As a result they have trouble in interpersonal relationships, are hostile to themselves and others, and are antisocial persons.

Expedient persons are still egocentric because they are self-centered and selfish, but they seek to mask their socially unethical conduct and to appear moral. They have a weak ego, conscience, and superego. The only internalized principle of control is self-gratification, but by taking the easy way out. They fit into the social world by subscribing to authoritative sanctions. They suppress spontaneity, which leads to personal unhappiness, for they receive few rewards in return. Their expedient adaptations to society are self-defeating. (74, p. 93) They are not actively moral but merely lack immorality. They lead a drifting, fear-ridden, conscienceless life. In public life they are the persons whose greed corrupts and exploits the community about them. (74, p. 97)

Conforming persons are controlled by a single internalized principle: desire to conform to the norms of the group. Their actions are based on the rules of the group so that they can do what others do, and their only worry is that they may attract public disapproval for some action. (74, p. 97) Such persons display moral stability, but it is produced more by the superego than by the reasoning power of a developed ego. This stability results from conformity to the conventions of society. Behavior is influenced by what others expect. Society views them as "good children" because they are submissive. Their behavior is "other-directed." Such persons are uncomfortable when they break rules. They have strong superegos and are unable to control the harsh punitive effect of their consciences. Such people are usually depressed and unhappy, for they live under the strain of self-depreciation. Peck and Havighurst indicate that most people become fixated at this stage of development. "The unthinking conformer, who often does not want to think for himself, probably makes up the largest single group of Americans and perhaps of humanity everywhere." (74, p. 196)

Irrational-conscientious persons are distinguished from conforming persons by degree. They too have weak egos and strong superegos, but they are distinguished from conformers by an even more powerfully developed superego. They do not want to violate the moral conventions incorporated in the process by their own superego development.

Both the conforming and irrational-conscientious levels of conduct are characteristic of later childhood. The dividing line between the two is the transition from heteronomy to autonomy, when the criterion of moral conduct changes from conformity to the group code to conformity to internalized standards of right and wrong. Irrational-conscientious persons are literal-minded and rigid and therefore difficult to live with, particularly because they demand that others abide by their codes. They are ruled by the dictates of conscience, firmly established as a body of rules, but their motivations for morality are not human welfare, but a compulsion to follow the rules. Life's only pleasure seems to be the cold satisfaction of living an impeccable life. Such persons possess little warmth, are unattractive to others, and have missed the joys of living.

Rational-altruistic persons are at the highest level of moral behavior; they are motivated by consideration for the welfare of others. Their behavior is rational because they consider each situation on its own merit. The essential element in the motivation of the conduct of these persons is an altruistic impulse. They have a high regard for others. They cannot enjoy themselves at the expense of others, and are unhappy at the prospect of harming others. Their integrated personalities leave them free to use their emotional energy in socially constructive, moral activities. The rational element is not clearly defined in the life of these persons. But it seems clear that they have developed control in consideration of others' feelings and needs. (74, p. 17)

One interesting result of the research of Peck and Havighurst was their conclusion that basic personality structure, or character type, tends to persist, to remain fairly stable between the ages of ten and seventeen. The conduct of the individual is, therefore, relatively predictable.

As the children were studied from age ten to seventeen, each individual tended to show a stable predictable pattern of moral character. Many of their overt actions changed, of course, as they grew older, learned new social and intellectual skills, and developed through puberty. However, each child appeared to maintain very persistently his deeply held feelings and attitudes toward life, and the modes of reacting which we call his character structures. (74, p. 155)

The evidence of these researchers supports the view that there is an enduring basic pattern of moral character, which means that any effort to modify antisocial attitudes is a difficult educational task, as many moral educators have discovered. These difficulties can be partly overcome by attacking the developmental tasks appropriate to each stage of development (29) with the awareness that, when successful, moral education can create socially desirable attitudes that are equally enduring.

Some research efforts have shown the relationship between ego development and the various stages of moral development. Sullivan and associates (91) administered Loevinger's (61) scale of ego development to twelve-, fourteen-, and seventeen-year-olds and found a significant correlation that increased with the age of the subjects. Podd (79) interviewed undergraduate college students and found that those with an "ego identity" were at more mature levels of moral judgment. Those undergoing an identity crisis were unstable and inconsistent in their moral reasoning. Lambert (53) found a correlation between the level of ego development and moral judgment, and concluded that ego development at any stage *precedes* development to the equivalent moral stage. Overall, the studies indicate that both moral judgment and moral behavior are influenced by ego development. (106, p. 188)

Family Factors and Moral Learning

All the important research in the moral development of children and adolescents emphasizes the importance of parents and the family in the total process. A number of family factors correlate significantly with moral learning.

1. The degree of parental warmth, acceptance, mutual esteem, and trust shown the child.
2. The frequency and intensity of parent-teen interaction and communication.
3. The type and degree of discipline used.
4. The role model parents offer the child.
5. The independence opportunities the parents provide.

Each of these factors needs elaboration, clarification, and substantiation. (For additional information on parent-adolescent relationships, see Chapter 14.)

PARENTAL ACCEPTANCE AND TRUST

One important aid to moral learning is a warm, accepting relationship of mutual trust and esteem between parent and child. Young children who are emotionally dependent upon their parents and have a strong emotional attachment to them develop strong consciences, whereas nondependent children grow up more lacking in conscience. Studies by Bandura and Walters (5) of delinquent fifteen- and sixteen-year-old boys on parole showed that their violence and destruction was indicative of a lack of conscience, a low capacity to resist temptation, and little evidence of guilt. When young, these boys showed an almost pathological degree of nondependence, having been punished often for dependency supplications, such as a request for attention and affection. (5) Cross-cultural studies of father-son relationships of Italian and American boys 11.5 to 17.5 years of age showed that those whose fathers were not sufficiently affectionate were less socially oriented, less concerned about their relationships with peers, and less well adjusted socially than their peers who received adequate paternal affection. (55) Furthermore, the boys whose fathers gave them less than adequate affection were less secure or self-confident, less calm and relaxed, and more unhappy: all important emotional factors in moral development.

There are a number of explanations for the correlation between parental warmth and moral learning. In a warm, emotional context, respected parents are likely to be admired and imitated by youths, resulting in similar positive traits in the adolescents. Youths learn consideration for others by being cared for, loved, and trusted by their parents. (96, p. 515) In an atmosphere of hostility and rejection, youths tend to "identify with the aggressor," taking on the antisocial traits of a feared parent. In Sutherland's (93) theory of *differential association*, which outlines conditions that facilitate both moral and criminal learning, the impact of a relationship varies according to its *priority, duration, intensity,* and *frequency.* The all-important parent-child relationship (high priority) over many years (long duration), which is characterized by close emotional attachment (high intensity) and a maximum amount of contact and communication (high frequency), has the maximum positive effect on the moral development of children. Similarly, a negative parent-child relationship existing for many years in an intense, repetitive way will have a disastrous and negative effect.

FREQUENCY AND INTENSITY
OF PARENT-TEEN INTERACTION

Role-modeling theory maintains that the degree of identification of the child with the parent varies with the amount of the child's interaction with the parent. Sons who have more frequent and intensive interactions wtih their fathers are more likely to be influenced by them. Similarly, daughters with frequent, close relationships with their mothers are more likely to identify with them. Frequent interaction offers opportunities for the communication of meaningful values and norms, especially if the exchange is democratic and mutual. A one-sided form of autocratic interaction results in poor communication and less learning for the adolescent. It is important, therefore, for the channels of communication betwen parents and youths to be kept open.

One study of father-absent homes, where there could be absolutely no interaction with a male parent, showed that paternal absence had an adverse effect on the moral development of adolescent boys especially. (30) Father-absent boys scored relatively low on all indexes of moral development, especially those measured by conscience development. They scored lower even than boys who were brought up in father-present homes where there was only minimal identification with the fathers. The conscience development of girls was not adversely affected by father absence, presumably because the girls identified primarily with their mothers. (30)

TYPE OF DISCIPLINE

Research on the influence of parental discipline on the moral learning of youth indicates that discipline has the most positive effect when it is consistent rather than erratic; (5, 74) when it is accomplished primarily through clear, verbal, explanations to develop internal controls rather than through external, physical means of control; (5, 9) when it is just and fair and avoids harsh, punitive measures; (5, 9, 84) and when it is democratic rather than permissive or autocratic. (6) Each of these factors needs to be examined.

One of the most important requirements is that discipline be consistent, both *intraparent* (within one parent) and *interparent* (between two parents). Erratic parental expectations lead to an ambiguous environment, and so to poor moral learning, anxiety, confusion, instability, restlessness, disobedience, and sometimes hostility and delinquency in the adolescent. (5, 74) Peck and Havighurst found that lack of consistency was most common in the families of "amoral" children. (74) Youths at this immature level of moral development seldom experienced consistency in moral standards, were unlikely to be rewarded for moral behavior, and were not consistently punished for not obeying. (74, p. 10) Other studies of factors associated with delinquency show that inconsistent discipline is significantly more common among parents of aggressive, hostile youths. (6) The combination of a harsh, restrictive father and an overindulgent, lenient mother is especially damaging. (5, 16)

Inconsistency alone is not the sole determinant. If accompanied by family cohesiveness and parental warmth, it is less likely to produce antisocial behavior than if the parents are also rejecting. If parents are inconsistent, harsh, and rejecting, the effect is most damaging. (See Chapter 14.)

Parents who rely on clear, rational, verbal explanations to influence and control behavior have a more positive effect than those who use external controls, (5, 9) primarily because cognitive methods result in the internalization of values and standards, especially if explanations are combined with affection so that the adolescent is inclined to listen and to accept them. (33) Reasoning or praise used to correct or reinforce behavior enhances learning, (96, p. 515) whereas physical means of discipline, negative verbal techniques such as belittling and nagging, or infrequent explanations are more often associated with antisocial behavior and delinquency.

The evidence is convincing that the types of disciplinary methods used are partly class oriented. Middle class parents are more likely than lower class parents to offer explanations, and this in turn better enables the middle class adolescent to know what is expected, to respect parents, value their advice, and obey them. Lower class parents make more frequent use of physical punishment and other nonverbal techniques. Their effort seems to be to teach unreasoned obedience and to keep their children out of trouble rather than to internalize controls through cognitive means. (107) (See Chapter 22.)

Parents who rely on harsh, punitive methods are defeating the true purpose of discipline: to develop a sensitive conscience, socialization, and cooperation. (65, p. 211) Cruel punishment, especially when accompanied by parental rejection, develops an insensitive, uncaring, hostile, rebellious, cruel person. (13, 77, 103) Instead of teaching children to care about others, it deadens their sensitivities, so that they learn to fear and hate others and no longer care about them or want to please them. They may obey, but when the threat of external punishment is removed, they are antisocial. Many criminal types fit this description. (13, 77, 103).

Parents who are overly permissive also retard the socialization process and the moral development of their children, for they give the children no help in developing inner controls. Without external authority the child will remain amoral. Adolescents want and need some parental guidance. Without it they may grow up as "spoiled brats," disliked by their peers because of their lack of consideration for others and lacking self-discipline, persistence, and direction. (74)

PARENTAL ROLE MODELS

It is important for parents to be moral people themselves if they are to offer positive role models for their children to follow. (31, 32) A thirty-year follow-up study of adults, mostly from lower class homes, who as children were referred to a clinic because of antisocial behavior, found that antisocial behavior of the father correlated significantly with deviance of the subjects in adolescence and adulthood. Furthermore, the father's antisocial behavior was the most significant factor in predicting the consistent antisocial behavior of the individual between adolescence and the mid-forties. (84) A study of eighty-six eleventh- and twelfth-grade males from a working class community showed that those who identified with and strongly valued the esteem of parents and teachers were less likely either to cheat or to have police records than were nondependent boys who did not esteem parental and teacher models. (78)

INDEPENDENCE OPPORTUNITIES

Peer influences are also important to the child's development, particularly in the lives of those youths who are given maximum opportunity for varied social experiences outside the home. Social contacts with those from different cultural and socioeconomic backgrounds facilitate moral development. (17, 44)

Numerous research studies show that the development of moral autonomy and judgment is faster among boys than among girls, (17) apparently because boys are less dependent on parental controls: parents give them more freedom than girls, and so they have greater opportunities for social experiences outside the home. Kohlberg found adolescent boys significantly more mature than girls in moral judgment. Boys, however, tend to be more preoccupied with problems of self-control, especially controls over aggression. (17, p. 115) They are more willing than girls to confront authority directly, and therefore worry more about their uncontrollable impulses. Douvan and Adelson found that

girls are in general more compliant to authority than boys are. They show a greater degree of reliance on authority not only in relation to the parents but to other adults as well.

. . . Adolescent boys are actively engaged in establishing their independence from parental control; they are acutely aware of personal control as a problem, as a goal, as an issue.

. . . "Autonomous morality"—in which personal standards are based on a differentiation from parental standards—is more commonly a masculine pattern. (17, p. 115; 118)

More discussion of some of the social influences outside the home is in the next section.

Social Reinforcement, Influences, Values, and Behavior

SOCIAL REINFORCEMENT

One of the important ingredients of moral development is to acquire knowledge and respect for the existing values and rules of one's social milieu. (34, p. 7) Once known, these values and rules must be internalized. According to Piaget, (76) this internalization brings about a qualitative transformation in character structure and a sense of "moral realism"; as a result individuals follow the rules regardless of the difficulty in doing so. According to psychoanalytic theory, parents who are nurturant and responsive to children encourage identification and conscience development. As a result of this total "introjection" or "incorporation" of the parent, the child's superego becomes the internal construct that governs morality. (13, p. 196)

According to Bandura (4) and other social learning theorists, internalization of values and rules comes through identification and modeling: children observe a relevant adult model acting according to a social norm and discover that the adult is praised or otherwise rewarded. Being natural imitators, the children strive to do likewise, particularly because the parents are the chief source of love or hate, physical gratification or deprivation, comfort or pain, and security or anxiety, and the children desire rewards and satisfaction. Gradually they become socialized to adopt the expected behavior themselves, even when the external rewards stop; compliance becomes a reward in itself. (34, p. 7)

Thus, social learning theory (see Chapter 3) emphasizes the acquisition of values through a process of *identification, internalization,* and *reinforcement.* (89) Much has already been said about identification and internalization, but reinforcement needs to be discussed in more detail. *Reinforcement* is used in a particular context here to mean those social influences that parallel parental influences and further enhance the learning and acceptance of particular values. (39) When the peer group, school, church, or mass media emphasize values similar to those found in the family, learning of those values is enhanced. (12) However, when the school, church, and other community agencies teach values different from those of parents, the inconsistency of influence creates conflict. This is often the case with lower class youths: the community teaches middle class values, and the parents incompletely accept or cannot afford to accept these values and substitute their own. (96, p. 516) One outcome of this inconsistency is moral confusion. Another outcome may be rigidity or authoritarianism. Values must be adhered to rigidly if they are to be maintained at all.

It is important to recognize the pluralism—or inconsistency—of values in the culture in which youths are reared today. (25)

Example 1: "All men are created equal."
But: "Women are given an inferior status to men."

Example 2: "Honesty is the best policy."
But: "Everyone is entitled to cheat sometime."

Example 3: "The kind of person you are is the most important thing in winning the respect of others."
But: "Having a lot of money certainly helps."

These few examples are enough to illustrate that there are many contradictions of values in our culture. (50, 51) These discrepancies between value statements and behavior patterns trouble adolescents; because in their search for moral values, for rights and wrongs by which to live, they find it difficult to discover consistent standards. (68; 81, p. 115)

REFERENCE GROUPS

Studies of parent versus peer influence show that most parents still exert a tremendous influence over the moral development of their children. (15, 105) However, these studies also show that peer influence has increased, particularly in the last ten years, and especially in those families in which parental influence has declined. (55) As described in Chapter 10, adolescents turn primarily to peers as a reaction against parental neglect and rejection. (14, 54) In such cases, the values of the peer group are particularly important in influencing adolescent behavior.

Youths may be members of many formal organizations, each of which has an influence, (28) but they are just as likely to be influenced by neighborhood gangs or by the general cultural environment around them. Adolescents who are surrounded by deviant moral values may become delinquent because of their environment. Such delinquency has its origin in the values represented by the surrounding subculture. In a study of individual values, peer values, and sub-cultural deliquency, Lerman (59) identified six deviant value items that are common among male delinquents.

1. The ability to keep one's mouth shut to the cops.
2. The ability to be hard and tough.
3. The ability to find kicks.
4. The ability to make a fast buck.
5. The ability to outsmart others.
6. The ability to make connections with a racket.

Lerman went on to say that these values were basic elements of the delinquent subculture in which the boys grew up. Boys who scored high on these six values were more likely to engage in illegal behavior. Furthermore, these values were shared values; 50 percent of boys who chose a deviant value were associated with peers who also were high in deviant values. Attraction to these deviant values began early, increased especially at age twelve to thirteen, and persisted as a counter-attraction to school and work. But on an individual level, without the support of a delinquent peer group, deviant values were unstable and were likely to shift to a conforming value. (59) Without the support of a peer group, individuals rarely held deviant values. If they were to maintain their values, they generally sought out those who could share and support their values. (23) It has been shown also that boys who associate with greatest frequency, duration, and intensity with delinquent peers are more likely than other youths to report delinquent behavior. Also, a high rate of delinquency in a neighborhood provides numerous opportunities for youths to learn deviant skills and values and offers support for deviant activities.

TELEVISION

Present surveys indicate that the average American family views television some 6.12 hours per day, representing over one-third of all waking hours. (86, p. 73) By age eighteen, children will have watched television approximately 22,000 hours, compared to 11,000 hours in the classroom. During 5,000 of these hours they will have been exposed to about 35,000 commercials. (26, 58, 62) One researcher reports that some adolescents spend as much as 51 hours per week watching television. (7, p. 370)

Public concern over the content of television shows has focused on the effect on children and youths of watching so much violence. By the time adolescents are fourteen and in the eighth grade, they will have watched 18,000 human beings killed on TV and violent assaults on thousands more. (58, 62) A Michigan State University study during 1975–1976 showed that children are more likely to see violence on television on Saturday morning than during the weeknight "family hour," and that violence was almost twice as high on Saturday morning as on prime time. (100) This study also said that the 8–9 P.M. family hour had about the same number of violent acts as the next two hours, which had been designated adult-program hours. The programs were also analyzed for "prosocial" and "antisocial" acts. Prosocial acts included altruism, showing affection and self-control; antisocial acts included physical and verbal violence as well as deceit and hostility. Cartoon shows contained about two antisocial acts for each positive act; situation comedies and family dramas had three prosocial acts for every two negative acts. Overall, the three commercial networks showed an average of forty-two antisocial and forty-three prosocial acts per hour. (100)

The real question is: What effect does TV violence have on the moral behavior of children and youths? A report of the United States Surgeon General's Advisory Committee on Television and Children's Aggression indicates that there is no *causal* relationship between television programs that depict violence and aggressive behavior in children. (101) However, not all committee members agreed with the conclusion. Social scientists Robert Liebert and John Neale, members of the committee writing in *Psychology Today* in 1972, (60) indicate that the data were distorted and in some cases misinterpreted in the process of arriving at compromises during the writing of the report. They cite the following extracts as examples.

As matters now stand, the weight of the experimental evidence from the present series of studies, as well as from prior research, suggests that viewing filmed violence has an observable effect on some children in the direction of increasing their aggressive behavior (101, p. 109)

. . . On the basis of these findings, and taking into account their variety and their inconsistencies, we can tentatively conclude that there is a modest relationship between exposure to television violence and aggressive behavior or tendencies, as the latter are defined in the studies at hand. (101, p. 178)

According to Liebert and Neale, the data, which were extensive, came from a wide range of socioeconomic status groups and showed that any child from a normal background may respond to television violence by behaving somewhat more aggressively. (60) They quote further from two other studies:

Our research shows that among boys and girls at two grade levels (junior high and senior high) the more the child watches violent television fare, the more aggressive he is likely to be . . . [After partialing a number of variables] the basic result is the same as for the raw correlations. . . . A substantial component [of aggressive behavior at age 19] can be predicted better by the amount of television violence which the child watched in the third grade than by any other causal variable measured, and reenforces the contention that there is a cause-and-effect relation between the violence content of television and overt aggressive behavior. (60, p. 39)

Most of the classic studies on the relationship between television violence and aggression in children and adolescents support this definite correlation. (For more complete information see the discussion of the research of Bandura and Walters in Chapter 3.)

Television violence not only increases aggressiveness in children, but also influences moral values and behavior. LeMasters (58) lists six predominant values portrayed by the media that are in conflict with those of most parents attempting to prepare their children for the future.

Sex: Usually presented in movies and TV on a physical level, both visually and verbally, yet is presented to the viewers as "love."

Violence: By age 14 the average American child has seen 18,000 human beings killed on TV.

The idealization of immaturity: Idols are not Abraham Lincolns, but are often as juvenile and immature as is the viewer, and seem to have gained "early wealth and fame . . . with a little talent and beauty and a hard-driving agent."

Materialism: The implication is that happiness comes with success, and success comes with houses, cars, and rugs . . . and it all seems free—on the easy credit plan.

Hedonism: Exposure to an unreal world to which one can quickly escape . . . and be entertained.

Commercialism of the media. (58)

The corresponding parental values on these issues are, of course, sexual restraint (and association of sex with love), lifetime monogamy, avoidance of violence, developing responsibility, industry, and maturity, and planning for the future as opposed to enjoyment now. (26, p. 202)

One immediate criticism of LeMasters's analysis is that he presents television values as all negative and parental values as all positive, when the lines cannot be so neatly drawn. Many parents, by their behavior and example, portray many of the negative values of which LeMasters speaks. There are some positive social values taught on television along with the negative. Nevertheless, the analysis is partly true, even though its findings cannot be applied to all television programs or to all parents.

Television advertising has also been criticized for portraying superficial views of social and personal problems and their solution. Problems of romance, engagement, marriage, child rearing, employment, and neighborhood relations can all be solved by chemical means: use this headache remedy, nasal spray, deodorant, or toothpaste, and find happiness. (26, p. 202) Gunter (26) asked ten students in a social problems course to watch for such claims on television. The students listed forty-two such claims from the commercials in a two-hour period. (26, p. 202)

Although the daytime serial soap operas are programmed for housewives, they are watched also by thousands of adolescents during after school hours. One analysis of 600 hours of eight soap operas revealed the following: (80)

1. The families portrayed are all upper middle class with expensive tastes, comfortable or lavish homes, housekeepers and nurses for the children, expensive wardrobes and vacations. No primary male characters have working class occupations. Fifty percent are either physicians or lawyers.

2. The women are primarily affluent housewives who do their own housework because they "love it." Only eight out of fifty-seven female characters are

professional. Nineteen are either clericals, domestics, or shopowners. Thus, female roles are stereotyped.

3. The characters are constantly confronted with problems: rape (often by relatives), whether or not to have an abortion, infertility and whether or not to employ artificial insemination, genetic defects, illegitimacy, divorce, death, extramarital lovers, drug addiction, juvenile delinquency, social drinking and alcoholism, illnesses and operations, and mental illness. Certainly, the social value of these images that are presented to millions of viewers must be questioned. (94)

Others have pointed to the fact that television puts children in an extremely passive position. (69; 90, p. 133) They experience constant stimulation from the outside with little activity themselves. (70) This may lead to the expectation that their needs will be met without effort and to a passive approach to life. (69, p. 133) Some evidence has shown that watching television reduces the time that children spend reading and doing homework. (87) Studies also show that television watching decreases family interaction and communication. (102) Family members also are able to avoid one another and tense family interactions by watching television. This may sometimes reduce overt conflict, but it does nothing to help solve family problems through personal communication. (85, p. 110; 94)

Some television programs have positive influences upon youths awakening social consciousness and encouraging social concern and reform. (See Chapter 2.) Television can be an important social influence for evil or for good.

MORAL EDUCATION

Discussion has been going on for years about whether schools should or can teach moral values. Authors like Allport (3) advocate the deliberate inculcation of ideas and values as a goal of education.

If the school does not teach values, it will have the effect of denying them. If the child at school never hears a mention of honesty, modesty, charity, or reverence, he will be persuaded that, like many of his parents' ideas, they are simply old hat. . . . If the school, which to the child represents the larger outside world, is silent on values, the child will repudiate more quickly the lessons learned at home. He will also be thrown into peer values more completely, with their emphasis on the hedonism of teen-age parties or the destructiveness of gangs. He will also be more at the mercy of the sensate values peddled by movies, TV, and disk jockeys. (3, p. 215)

Allport feels that teachers should select those values from the whole of our American ethics, particularly those based on the "American creed" and Judeo-Christian ethics. Allport feels that teachers ought to teach what they themselves stand for, so that the teacher's enthusiasm and interest are ensured and so that "the teacher's self-disclosure leads the student to self-discovery." (3, p. 216)

One of the problems of moral education is that inculcating values does not necessarily result in moral behavior: there is a difference between *knowing* what is right and *doing* it. Traditional moral and religious education emphasized memorization of Bible verses, proverbs, and principles of conduct. (28, p. 13; 34) This version of moral education constitutes what Kohlberg calls a "bag of virtues"—honesty, service, self-control, friendliness, and other moral virtues.

Aristotle proposed a list that included temperance, liberality, pride, good temper, truthfulness, and justice. (72, p. 226) The Boy Scouts added that a scout should be honest, reverent, clean, and brave. Muuss writes:

Traditionally, children were encouraged to practice virtuous behavior—they were told about the advantages of good behavior and were warned of the harm that could befall them if they were not virtuous. Reward and punishment were used as well. . . . The problems with the bag-of-virtues approach to moral education is that . . . participation in the character-education program as provided in schools, Sunday schools, and Boy Scouts does not contribute to improved moral behavior as measured by a test involving honesty, self-control, and service. . . . More recent follow-up studies have supported these earlier findings, and moral knowledge and moral behavior showed only low correlations. (72, p. 226)

As a result, some writers, including Kohlberg, (44) face the issue more flexibly. Kohlberg feels the proper role of the teacher is neither to moralize individual, personal principles nor to indoctrinate state-defined values, but to stimulate development of the individual's moral judgment by encouraging free discussion, participation, and thought about real-life issues. (63) Kohlberg feels the teacher ought to be able to evaluate the maturity of the child's moral judgment, and, regardless of whether the child's values agree with his or her (or society's) own moral values, stimulate the child to develop to a higher stage of moral judgment. (Kohlberg suggests his own stages of moral judgment as a basis for evaluation.) The effort would be made to help the child judge the rightness or wrongness of moral action based upon "universal, consistent, objective, impersonal, ideal grounds." Kohlberg admits that it is not certain that advanced moral judgment will automatically produce more moral action (the child may know what is right but not want to do it), so the teacher also has to get the children to examine the pros and cons of their conduct in their own terms.

In this type of teaching the primary method used is to present case studies, or moral dilemmas for the students to solve.* Here is one dilemma that is used to promote thinking and discussion. (83, p. 158)

Joe is a 14-year-old boy who wanted to go to camp very much. His father promised him he could go if he saved up the money for it himself. So Joe worked hard at his paper route and saved up the $40 it cost to go to camp and a little more besides. But just before camp was going to start, his father changed his mind. Some of his friends decided to go on a special fishing trip, and Joe's father was short of the money it would cost, so he told Joe to give him the money he had saved from the paper route. Joe didn't want to give up going to camp, so he thought of refusing to give his father the money. (73, p. 126)

The students are then presented with several questions:

Should Joe refuse to give his father the money? Why? Why not?
What do you think of the father asking Joe for the money?
Does giving the money have anything to do with being a good son?
Should promises always be kept?

The students might also be asked to respond to the following: (83, p. 159)

* Much of the material in this section is from my book *Morality and Youth* (Philadelphia: Westminster Press, 1980). Used by permission.

Joe wanted to go to camp but he was afraid to refuse to give his father the money. So he gave his father $10 and told him that was all he made. He took the other $40 and paid for camp with it. He told his father the head of the camp said he could pay later. So he went off to camp, and the father didn't go on the fishing trip. Before Joe went to camp, he told his older brother, Alexander, that he really made $50 and that he lied to his father and said he'd made $10. Alexander wonders whether he should tell his father or not. (73, p. 128)

This dilemma raises a number of important issues: whether lying, withholding the truth, or tattling is justified; whether it is more important for Alex to be a loyal son or a loyal brother. (83, p.159)

Should Joe have lied?

Should Alex tell his father?

What should the father do if he finds out? (83, p. 160)

Teachers need to invent other situations that relate to students' own lives and thus are meaningful to them. (83, p. 160)

There is considerable evidence to support the conclusion that public schools are not having much effect on the values of youth, at least during high school. (10) A study (95) of personal and occupational values of high school students from ten schools in central California was undertaken to show changes in values from the freshman to the senior years of high school, and to discover significant correlates to values. The study involved 2,287 freshmen; by the senior year the sample had decreased to 1,365. Some of the more interesting findings included the following:

1. Personal values of the students, particularly boys, changed very little from the freshman to the senior year.
2. Little evidence was found to confirm that there was any relationship between personal values and the ability of teachers and students to communicate with each other.
3. There was a significant relationship between personal values and peer acceptance. The most popular students were hedonistic, whereas the socially rejected scored higher on orientation to the future.
4. The high achievers, college bound, and regular church attenders held what were defined as traditional values, emphasizing planning for the future, work success, and individual initiative.

As a result of the failure of moralizing as a method of teaching values, schools are now using an approach called *values clarification*. (8, 88) The values clarification approach of Raths (82) is not concerned with the *content* of values, but with the *process* of valuing. It does not aim to instill any particular set of values; rather, the goal is to help students become aware of the beliefs and behaviors they prize and would be willing to stand up for, to learn to weigh the pros and cons and consequences of various alternatives, to choose freely after considerations of consequences, and to learn to match their actions with their beliefs in a consistent way. A limited amount of research and a lot of experience with this approach indicate that students who have been exposed to it become less apathetic, less flighty, less conforming, less over-dissenting, more energetic, more critical in their thinking, and more likely to follow through on their decisions. (88, p. 20)

A number of authors have developed numerous exercises and strategies that may be used in the classroom to facilitate the process of values clarification.* Here are a few of the strategies that have been used. (83, p. 154)

Either-or forced choice. The teacher asks: Are you

———— more of a saver or a spender?
———— more of a loner or a grouper?
———— more physical or mental? etc.

Values continuum. Students are asked to arrange themselves in relation to an entire group of students to indicate their values position along a continuum. They might be asked, for example: How far would you go to be popular with your group? The students would place themselves anywhere along a continuum ranging from "Do anything, including risking safety" to "Do nothing at all."

Write down twenty things you would like to do, and indicate beside each the cost (in dollars and cents) of doing it, whether you like to do it alone or with other people, whether or not planning is required, and when you did it last. Then from the twenty items, list the five most important. Discuss with the class your selections and the reasons you made them.

Rank order. Students are asked to rank various items in order of preference; for example:

Where would you rather be on a Saturday afternoon?
———— at the beach
———— in the woods
———— in a discount store

What would you give the lowest priority to today?
———— space
———— poverty
———— defense
———— ecology

In *Advanced Value Clarification,* Kirschenbaum (41) describes the value clarification process in terms of five important dimensions.

Thinking about value decisions.
Feeling: becoming aware of one's feelings so as to enable one to achieve goals more readily.
Choosing: considering alternatives and doing achievement planning.
Communicating: listening and talking with others and resolving conflicts, which helps in establishing goals and values.
Acting repeatedly, consistently, and skillfully in achieving one's goals. (41)

Values clarification has not been without critics. For example, can anyone really be objective about what he or she values? Psychologists would say it is difficult. Does the act of clarifying one's values improve morality? Not if the values held are unworthy or superficial, and not if they remain unchanged.

* From *Morality and Youth* (Philadelphia: Westminster Press, 1980). Used by permission.

What are the real objectives of the program? Sharing one's personal values with others may bring a person into open conflict with parents or teachers. (83, p. 156)

In spite of weaknesses, "the values clarification approach to moral education is being widely used and with some success in stimulating thinking. Students are reported to be less apathetic, less conforming, and more energetic and critical in their thinking." (83, p. 156) Studies conducted at the college level in the late 1950s showed little change in the value orientation of students from their freshman to senior years. (36) More recent research, however, emphasizes that modern college students improve significantly in their ability to think critically, and become less dogmatic, less traditional in their morals and more willing to accept new ideas over the four-year college span. (35, 59) For example, in previous generations, college students tended to favor the same political parties as their parents. Today, however, according to a study in sixteen U.S. colleges, nearly as many students deviate from their parents' political views as conform to them. (67) This is some indication that influences outside the home are influencing the value orientation of modern college students, so that these youths no longer automatically adopt the values of their parents.

Conclusions

This chapter has discussed four major aspects of moral development.

1. Theories of development of moral judgment, represented by Piaget and Kohlberg.
2. The relationship of the development of personality types to moral character and behavior as discussed by Peck and Havighurst.
3. Family correlates to moral development.
4. The social influence of peers, television, and education on moral values and behavior.

In conclusion, several important factors need to be emphasized. First, there are marked similarities among the theories of Piaget, Kohlberg, and Peck and Havighurst. Kohlberg's research and theory is actually Piagetian in method and content and a substantiation of part of what Piaget said, even though the number and titles of the stages of development of moral judgment are different. Piaget outlined only two stages of moral development: a morality of constraint (or obedience) and a morality of cooperation (or reciprocity). In between is a transitional stage during which rules become internalized as the individual moves from heteronomy to autonomy. Kohlberg outlined three major levels of moral development: a premoral level, a morality of conventional role conformity, and a morality of self-accepted moral principles. Like Piaget, Kohlberg emphasized that the level of morality at which individuals operate depends upon their *motives* for doing right. Piaget says that as children become more moral, they depend less upon outside authority to constrain them and more upon an inner, subjective desire to cooperate and to consider the rights and feelings of others. Essentially, Kohlberg says the same thing: children's motives change gradually from a desire to avoid punishment, gain the reward of others, or avoid disapproval or censure, to a more positive motive of desire for individual and community respect and a desire to avoid self-condemnation. Amoral people do what is expected only if they have to avoid punishment or gain rewards. The most moral people depend upon inner controls because certain principles and values have been incorporated into their cognitive structures through socialization with others. In between are people who maintain a morality of convention to avoid disapproval or censure. They are not immoral, because they do conform, but they are not moral either, for their motives are selfish and their control is external.

Peck and Havighurst's view concerns the relation among personality type, character, and moral behavior. They were not concerned about the cognitive development of moral judgment as were Piaget and Kohlberg. However, there is some similarity between their views. Peck and Havighurst say that people behave the way they do because they are certain types of people. Because amoral people are completely egocentric and selfish with a weak ego and superego, their whole goal is self-gratification. At the opposite extreme are the rational-altruistic people whose motivation is the welfare of others. These types of people are similar to those at Piaget's and Kohlberg's highest level of moral development. Thus, the moral progression is similar in all three theories: from amorality to outer control to inner control; from negative, selfish motivations to positive, altruistic motivations; from a desire to escape external punishment to a desire to escape self-condemnation. Also according to all three theories, there are individuals of a particular age group in each of the stages of moral growth and development, although children tend to move to more advanced stages of development as they get older. All the theories emphasize also the importance of the socialization process, peer-group participation, and the parent-child relationship in moral development.

A second important conclusion needs to be emphasized: moral growth and development cannot be isolated from other aspects of the adolescent's life. They have many correlates in the parent-child relationship especially, and to a lesser extent in the childhood peer relationship. What happens to children at home, with peers, and in the neighborhood will affect their moral development.

Third, moral growth and development begin in early childhood and are not as amenable during adolescence to outside influences and change as is sometimes thought. Such socializing influences as TV, which can have a measurable effect upon youths, begin very early, and these early influences can still be measured during adolescence. The public senior high school seems to exert little measurable influence on morals; values change little during four years. At college age the situation is similar but not quite as static. The greater independence and autonomy of college students, especially of those away from home, makes them more amenable to school and peer influences; as a result some of their basic values and moral principles are changed during the years they are away from parents. Essentially, however, even this stage of their moral growth and development is the culmination of years of socialization rather than the result of the influences of a few years of college.

Topics for Term Papers

1. The Relationship between Moral Judgment and Moral Behavior
2. Differences between Lower Class and Middle Class Adolescents in Moral Development
3. Parent-Adolescent Relationships and the Development of Conscience
4. Parental Discipline as a Factor in Moral Development
5. Male-Female Differences in Autonomy and Moral Judgment
6. Parents versus Peers as Determinative Influences over Adolescent Values
7. Violence in Television Cartoons
8. Television Violence and Child and Adolescent Aggression

9. Values Taught through Television Commercials
10. The Role of the Public School in Moral Education
11. Moral Education through Memorization of Catechism and Bible Verses
12. Value Clarification in Public School Teaching
13. What Public Opinion Surveys Say about Adolescent Values Today
14. An Analysis of Modern Research on Kohlberg's Theory of Development of Moral Judgment
15. A Psychoanalytic View of Moral Development

Bibliography

1. Adelson, J. "The Political Imagination of the Young Adolescent." *Daedalus* (Fall 1971): 1013–1050.

2. Adelson, J. et al. "The Growth of the Idea of Law in Adolescence." *Developmental Psychology* 1 (1969): 327–332.

3. Allport, G. W. "Values and Our Youth." *Teachers College Record* 63 (1961): 211–219.

4. Bandura, A. *Social Learning Theory.* Morristown, N.J.: General Learning Press, 1971.

5. Bandura, A., and Walters, R. H. *Adolescent Aggression.* New York: Ronald Press Co., 1959.

6. ———. *Social Learning and Personality Development.* New York: Holt, Rinehart and Winston, 1963.

7. Baranowski, M. D. "Television and the Adolescent." *Adolescence* 6 (1971): 369–396.

8. Barr, R. D., ed. *Values and Youth.* Teaching Social Studies in an Age of Crisis, No. 2. Washington, D.C.: National Council for the Social Studies, 1971.

9. Becker, W. D. "Consequences of Different Kinds of Parental Discipline." In *Review of Child Development Research.* Edited by M. L. Hoffman and L. W. Hoffman. New York: Russell Sage Foundation, 1964, pp. 169–208.

10. Boyd, R. E. et al. *Values Clarification.* New York: Hart Publishing Co., 1972.

11. Brennan, W. K. "The Foundations for Moral Development." *Special Education* 54 (Spring 1965).

12. Bronfenbrenner, U. *Two Worlds of Childhood: U.S. and U.S.S.R.* New York: Russell Sage Foundation, 1970.

13. Cantwell, Z. M., and Svajian, P. N. *Adolescence: Studies in Development.* Itasca, Ill.: F. E. Peacock Publishers, 1974.

14. Condry, J., and Siman, M. L. "Characteristics of Peer- and Adult-Oriented Children." *Journal of Marriage and the Family* 36 (1974): 543–554.

15. Curtis, R. L., Jr. "Adolescent Orientations toward Parents and Peers: Variations by Sex, Age, and Socioeconomic Status." *Adolescence* 10 (1975): 483–494.

16. Dinitz, S.; Scarpitti, F. R.; and Reckless, W. C. "Delinquency Vulnerability: A Cross Group and Longitudinal Analysis." *American Sociological Review* 27 (1962): 517–522.

17. Douvan, E., and Adelson, J. *The Adolescent Experience.* New York: John Wiley and Sons, 1966.

18. Durkheim, E. *Moral Education.* New York: Free Press, 1960.

19. Elder, G. *Adolescent Socialization and Personality Development.* Chicago: Rand McNally & Co., 1968.

20. Elder, G. H., Jr. "Family Structure and the Transmission of Values and Norms in the Process of Child Rearing." Ph.D. dissertation, University of North Carolina, 1961.

21. Elkind, D. *Children and Adolescents: Interpretative Essays on Jean Piaget.* New York: Oxford University Press, 1970.

22. ———. "Cognitive Development in Adolescence." In *Understanding Adolescence.* Edited by J. F. Adams. Boston: Allyn and Bacon, 1968, pp. 128–158.

23. Fodor, E. M. "Resistance to Social Influence among Adolescents as a Function of Level of Moral Development." *Journal of Social Psychology* 85 (1971): 121–126.

24. Gallatin, J. E., *Adolescence and Individuality.* New York: Harper and Row, 1975.

25. Gilligan, C. et al. "Moral Reasoning about Sexual Dilemmas: A Developmental Approach." In *Recent Research in Moral Development.* Edited by L. Kohlberg and E. Turiel. New York: Holt, Rinehart and Winston, 1972.

26. Gunter, B. G., and Moore, H. A. "Youth, Leisure, and Post-Industrial Society: Implications for the Family." *Family Coordinator* 24 (1975): 199–207.

27. Haan, N. et al. "Moral Reasoning in Young Adults: Political-Social Behavior, Family Background, and Personality Cor-

relates." *Journal of Personality and Social Psychology* 10 (1968) : 183–201.

28. Hanson, R. E., and Carlson, R. E. *Organizations for Children and Youth.* Englewood Cliffs, N.J.: Prentice-Hall, 1972.

29. Havighurst, R. J. *Developmental Tasks and Education.* 3d ed. New York: David McKay Co., 1972.

30. Hoffman, M. L. "Father Absence and Conscience Development." *Developmental Psychology* 4 (1971) : 400–406.

31. ———. "Identification and Conscience Development." *Child Development* 42 (1971) : 1071–1082.

32. ———. "Conscience, Personality, and Socialization Techniques." *Human Development* 13 (1970) : 90–126.

33. ———. "Moral Development." In *Carmichael's Manual of Child Psychology.* Edited by P. H. Mussen. New York: John Wiley and Sons, 1970.

34. Hogan, R. "The Structure of Moral Character and the Explanation of Moral Action." *Journal of Youth and Adolescence* 4 (1975) : 1–15.

35. Huntley, C. C. "Changes in Value Scores during the Four Years of College." *General Psychology Monographs* 71 (1965) : 349–383.

36. Jacob, P. E. *Changing Values in College.* New York: Harper and Row, 1957.

37. Johnson, R. C. "A Study of Children's Moral Judgments." *Child Development* 33 (June 1962).

38. Kay, A. W. *Moral Development.* New York: Schocken Books, 1969.

39. Keller, F. S. *Learning: Reinforcement Theory.* 2d ed. New York: Random House, 1969.

40. King, M. L. *Why We Can't Wait.* New York: Harper and Row, 1964.

41. Kirschenbaum, H. *Advanced Value Clarification.* LaJolla, Calif.: University Associates, 1977.

42. Kohlberg, L. "The Development of Children's Orientations Toward a Moral Order." *Vita Humana* 6 (1963) : 11–33.

43. ———. "Moral Development and Identification." *Child Psychology* (1963).

44. ———. "Moral Education in the Schools, A Developmental View." *School Review* 74 (1966) : 1–30.

45. ———. *Stages in the Development of Moral Thought and Action.* New York: Holt, Rinehart and Winston, 1969.

46. ———. "Education for Justice: A Modern Statement of the Platonic View." In *Moral Education.* Edited by N. F. Sizer and T. R. Sizer. Cambridge, Mass.: Harvard University Press, 1970.

47. ———. "Moral Development and the Education of Adolescents." In *Adolescents and the American High School.* Edited by R. F. Purnell. New York: Holt, Rinehart and Winston, 1970.

48. Kohlberg, L., and DeVries, R. "Relations between Piaget and Psychometric Assessments of Intelligence." In *The Natural Curriculum.* Edited by C. Lavatelli. Urbana, Ill.: University of Illinois Press, 1971.

49. Kohlberg, L., and Gilligan, C. "The Adolescent as a Philosopher: The Discovery of the Self in a Postconventional World." *Daedalus* (Fall 1971) : 1051–1086.

50. Kohlberg, L., and Kramer, R. "Continuities and Discontinuities in Childhood and Adult Development." *Human Development* 12 (1969) : 93–120.

51. Kohlberg, L., and Turiel, E., eds. *Recent Research in Moral Development.* New York: Holt, Rinehart and Winston, 1972.

52. Kuhn, D. et al. "The Development of Formal Operational Thought: Its Relation to Moral Judgment." Harvard University, 1971. Unpublished paper.

53. Lambert, H. J. "A Comparison of Jane Loevinger's Theory of Ego Development and Kohlberg's Theory of Moral Development." Ph.D. thesis, University of Chicago, 1971.

54. Larson, L. E. "An Examination of the Salience Hierarchy during Adolescence: The Influence of the Family." *Adolescence* 9 (1974) : 317–332.

55. Lasseigne, M. W. "A Study of Peer and Adult Influence on Moral Beliefs of Adolescents." *Adolescence* 10 (1975) : 227–230.

56. Lavatelli, C. C., and Stendler, F. *Readings in Child Behavior and Development.* 3d ed. New York: Harcourt Brace Jovanovich, 1972, pp. 313–314.

57. Lehmann, O. J. "Changes in Critical Thinking, Attitudes, and Values from Freshman to Senior Years." *Journal of Educational Psychology* 54 (1965) : 304–315.

58. LeMasters, E. E. *Parents in Modern America.* rev. ed. Homewood, Ill.: Dorsey Press, 1974.

59. Lerman, P. "Individual Values, Peer Values, and Subcultural Delinquency." *American Sociological Review* 33 (1968) : 219–235.

60. Liebert, R. M., and Neale, J. M. "TV Violence and Child Aggression: Snow on the Screen." *Psychology Today* 5 (1972) : 38–40.

61. Loevinger, J. "The Meaning and Measurement of Ego Development." *American Psychologist* 21 (1966) : 195–206.

62. Looney, G. "The Ecology of Childhood." In *Action for Children's Television*. New York: Avon Press, 1971.

63. Lorimer, R. "Change in the Development of Moral Judgments in Adolescence: The Effect of Structural Exposition vs. a Film and Discussion." *Canadian Journal of Behavior Science* 3 (1971): 1–10.

64. Loughran, R. "A Pattern of Development in Moral Judgments Made by Adolescents Derived from Piaget's Schema of its Development in Childhood." *Educational Review* (February 1967).

65. Matteson, D. R. *Adolescence Today: Sex Roles and the Search for Identity*. Homewood, Ill.: Dorsey Press, 1975.

66. McKinley, D. G. *Social Class and Family Life*. New York: Free Press, 1964.

67. Middleton, R., and Putney, S. "Student Rebellion against Parental Political Beliefs." *Social Forces* 41 (1963): 377–383.

68. Mitchell, J. J. "Moral Dilemmas of Early Adolescence." *Adolescence* 10 (1975): 442–446.

69. Miller, D. *Adolescence: Psychology, Psychopathology, and Psychotherapy*. New York: Jason Aronson, 1974.

70. Murray, J. P. "Television in Inner City Homes: Viewing Behavior in Young Boys." In *Television in Day to Day Life Patterns of Use*. Edited by E. A. Rubenstein. *Television and Social Behavior*, vol. 4. Washington, D.C.: U.S. Government Printing Office, 1971.

71. Muson, H. "Moral Thinking: Can It Be Taught?" *Psychology Today* (February 1979): p. 48ff.

72. Muuss, R. E., *Theories of Adolescence*. 3d. ed. New York: Random House, 1975.

73. Pagliuso, S. *Understanding Stages of Moral Development: A Programmed Learning Workbook*. New York: Paulist Press, 1976.

74. Peck, R. H., and Havighurst, R. J. *The Psychology of Character Development*. New York: John Wiley and Sons, 1960.

75. Peters, R. S. "Moral Development: A Plea for Pluralism." In *Cognitive Development and Epistemology*. Edited by T. Mischel. New York: Academic Press, 1971.

76. Piaget, J. *The Moral Judgment of the Child*. 1932. Reprint. Glencoe, Ill.: Free Press, 1948.

77. Piaget, J., and Inhelder, B. *The Psychology of the Child*. Translated by Helen Weaver. New York: Basic Books, 1969.

78. Piliavin, I. M. et al. "Constraining Effects of Personal Costs on the Transgressions of Juveniles." *Journal of Personality and Social Psychology* 10 (1968): 227–231.

79. Podd, M. H. "Ego Identity Status and Morality: The Relationship between Two Constructs." *Developmental Psychology* 6 (1972): 497–507.

80. Ramsdell, M. L. "The Trauma of TV's Troubled Soap Families." *Family Coordinator* 22 (1973): 299–304.

81. Ramsey, C. E. *Problems of Youth*. Belmont, Calif.: Dickenson Publishing Co., 1967.

82. Raths, L. et al. *Values and Teaching*. Columbus, Ohio: Charles E. Merrill, 1966.

83. Rice, F. P. *Morality and Youth*. Philadelphia: Westminster Press, 1980.

84. Robins, L. N. *Deviant Children Grown Up*. Baltimore: Williams & Wilkins, 1966.

85. Rosenblatt, P. C., and Cunningham, M. R. "Television Watching and Family Tensions." *Journal of Marriage and the Family* 38 (1976): 105–111.

86. Rue, V. M. "Television and the Family: The Question of Control." *Family Coordinator* 23 (1974): 73–81.

87. Scheflen, A. E. "Living Space in an Urban Ghetto." *Family Process* 10 (1971): 429–450.

88. Simon, S. B. et al. *Values Clarification*. New York: Hart Publishing Co., 1972.

89. Skinner, B. F. *Contingencies of Reinforcement*. New York: Appleton-Century-Crofts, 1969.

90. Stein, A. H., and Frederick, L. K. "Television and Content and Young Children's Behavior." In *Television and Social Learning*. Edited by J. P. Murray. *Television and Social Behavior*, vol. 2. Washington, D.C.: U.S. Government Printing Office, 1971.

91. Sullivan, E. et al. "A Developmental Study of the Relationship between Conceptual, Ego, and Moral Development." *Child Development* 4 (1970): 399–412.

92. Survey by the *Christian Science Monitor*. Reported in the *Wisconsin State Journal*. Madison, Wis., 27 August 1968.

93. Sutherland, E. H., and Cressey, D. R. *Principles of Criminology*. 7th ed. New York: J. B. Lippincott, 1966.

94. *Television and Social Behavior*. 5 vols. Washington, D.C.: U.S. Government Printing Office, 1972.

95. Thompson, O. E. "Student Values in Transition," *California Journal of Educational Research* 19 (1968): 77–86.

96. Thornburg, H. D. "Behavior and Values: Consistency or Inconsistency." *Adolescence* 8 (1973): 513–520.

97. Tomlinson-Keasey, C., and Keasey, C. B. "Formal Operations and Moral Development: What is the Relationship?" Paper presented to American Psychological Association meeting, Honolulu, Hawaii, September 1972.

98. Turiel, E. "An Experimental Test of the Sequentiality of Developmental Stages in the Child's Moral Judgments." *Journal of Personality and Social Psychology* (1966): 611–618.

99. ———. "Conflict and Transition in Adolescent Moral Development." *Child Development* 45 (1974): 14–29.

100. "TV Study Shows Violence High Saturday A.M.S." *Portland (Me.) Press Herald*, 17 February 1977.

101. U.S. Surgeon General. Advisory Committee on Television and Children's Aggression. *Television and Growing Up: The Impact of Televised Violence*. Washington, D.C.: U.S. Government Printing Office, 1972.

102. Walters, J. K., and Stone, V. A. "Television and Family Communication." *Journal of Broadcasting* 15 (1971): 409–414.

103. Weinreich, H. E. "A Replication and Evaluation of a Study by Lawrence Kohlberg of the Development of Moral Judgment in the Adolescent." Master's thesis, University of Sussex, 1970.

104. ———. "The Structure of Moral Reason." *Journal of Youth and Adolescence* 3 (1974): 135–143.

105. Wortis, H. et al. "Child-Rearing Practices in a Low Socioeconomic Group." *Pediatrics* 32 (1963): 298–307.

106. Windmiller, M. "Moral Development." In *Understanding Adolescence*. 3d ed. Edited by J. F. Adams. Boston: Allyn and Bacon, 1976, pp. 176–198.

PART 8

Educational and Vocational

CHAPTER 19

Education and School

Outline

Adolescents View the Schools
Dropouts and Underachievement versus School Success
The Secondary School Teacher
Curriculum Considerations
Conclusions
Discussion Questions
Bibliography

Because the subject of adolescents and the schools is so broad, this chapter discusses only selected topics. First, what do adolescents like and dislike about school? What are their major complaints about school? Second, what factors can be correlated with school failure and dropping out of school, and what factors are correlated positively with school achievement and success? Third, what are the characteristics of a good teacher of adolescents? And fourth, what are the general characteristics, the criticisms, and strengths of the curricula in the modern comprehensive high school? What are the major suggestions for improvement?

Adolescents View the Schools

ATTITUDES TOWARD SCHOOLS

One cannot say that the majority of adolescents dislike or are very dissatisfied with school. Nationwide surveys show a positive attitude and a fairly high degree of satisfaction with school. (68; 16, p. 324; 74) Interviews in 1973 of a national, cross-sectional sample of 3,522 youths aged sixteen to twenty-five revealed that less than one-third felt they had had a poor education for the kind of life they wanted to live. (74, p. 85) Almost 75 percent wanted more education. In another survey, students from three suburban junior and senior high schools denied disliking school, but did not express a positive, active liking for it. (9) Figure 19–1 shows their attitudes in two of the schools surveyed. School A is located in a lower to middle class suburban community. School C is located in a high socioeconomic suburb of a medium-sized city. (9, pp. 53–54) These data indicate a slight decline in positive attitudes toward school between the junior high grades and the middle years of high school and a definite increase in positive attitudes between eleventh and twelfth grades. Moreover, some of those who were negative in their feelings or who were not doing well would have dropped out before the senior year, leaving more positive results in the remainder. Even so, the findings do not indicate any widespread disappointment. Rather, they indicate a high degree of indifference. A 1974–1975 poll of 22,300 students who were listed in *Who's Who among High School Students* revealed the following in answer to the question: "What do you think of the twelve years of education you have received?" (45)

39 percent said it was challenging.
50 percent said it was routine.
84 percent said it was important.
 8 percent said it was useless.
73 percent said the subjects were relevant.

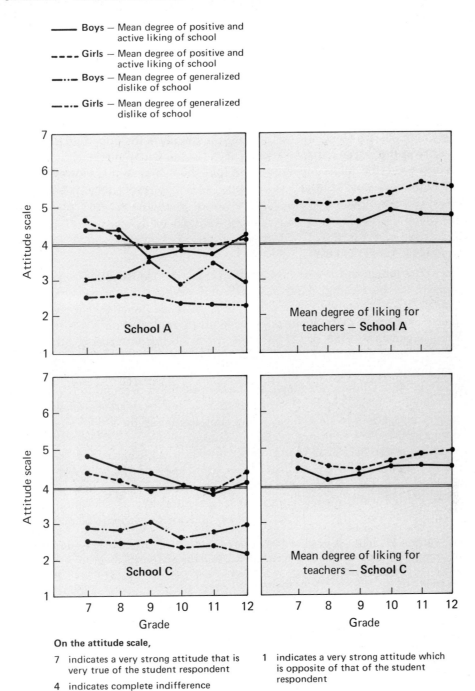

Figure 19–1. Intensity and direction of attitudes toward school and teachers in two communities. (Adapted from C. F. Buxton, *Adolescents in School* [New Haven, Conn.: Yale University Press, 1973], pp. 59, 63, 73. Used by permission.)

20 percent said the subjects were irrelevant.

55 percent said the teachers were good.

38 percent said the teachers were just adequate.

  3 percent said the teachers were poor.

54 percent said the school was stimulating.

37 percent said it was boring.

These opinions are from superior students and indicate the importance the great majority of them attach to education. They also show that over half thought the teachers good, the subjects relevant, and the school stimulating. However, many also felt school was "routine" or "boring." (45) The result, then, is some positive attitudes, combined with a high degree of indifference or acceptance, with only a minority expressing negative attitudes or feelings.

WHAT YOUTHS LIKE

When 700 junior and senior high pupils across the United States were asked: "What's the best thing about school?" and "What's the worst thing about school?" approximately 20 percent of the pupils cited "relationships with other pupils" as the best thing about school. No other single response was offered by such a large number. (58, p. 12) Such answers as "being with peers," "the friends I have," "seing everyone I know" were typical. Few youths indicated that anything involving the learning process was the best thing about school. Teachers and other adults did not identify pupil need to establish peer-group relationships as a school problem. The few teachers who indicated an awareness of the importance of peer-group relationships among adolescents felt the school ought not to become involved except through extracurricular activities.

Other researchers have found similar responses. Coleman's study of approximately 8,000 high school students from ten schools in the Midwest revealed nonchalance and even a negative attitude toward academic matters. (14) Adolescent culture was antieducation, or at least neutral toward education, emphasizing instead cars, dates, clubs, activities, and social events. Coleman writes:

Such student attitudes are not the direct consequences of class-room experience, but they are nevertheless the product of the school and the responsibility of the school. They stem from what might be called the "social organization" of the school, in contrast to its curriculum organization. This social organization has its values and norms; the standards are slanted either toward or away from intellectual endeavor. (14, p. 33)

Generally, the evidence indicates that as children move up through the grades, many become decreasingly interested in the academic program, more inclined to complain, and more interested in social activities, clubs, and sports. With increasing age, enthusiasm is replaced by boredom and indifference, with school becoming a chore and a burden, punctuated by interest in sports events and holidays. Thus, the adolescent who refers to a school "activity" usually means an extracurricular activity, not a school subject. This does not mean that the majority of adolescents dislike school. They like it, but because of the extracurricular program and opportunities for socialization, not the academic program.

Of course, students are individuals. One may become very involved with science, another with literature, music, or drama. Still another may never like anything about school and never get involved even in the extracurricular activities. Therefore, the research can only point to general conclusions drawn from studying numerous student populations.

WHAT YOUTHS DISLIKE

It is easier to find things that adolescents don't like about school. In the study of 700 junior and senior high students cited previously, a number of responses indicated anxieties about grades, class rank, getting into college, and other manifestations of competition. (58) In answer to the question "What's the worst thing about school?" students reply:

- "When I have to take a test."
- "The fierce competition that is building up for grades, college entrance, scholarships, etc."
- "As one gets older, the pressures of school grow stronger."
- "Grades are emphasized too much, and this creates competition and tension." (58, p. 9)

Students today feel tremendous pressure to earn good grades because college entrance is competitive. Thus, they are caught up in a competitive maze that emphasizes grades and class rank rather than learning.

Students are also concerned about the rigidity of requirements and the irrelevance of courses. (70, p. 260) Youths fail to see the need for certain required courses that seem to bear no relationship to their own personal needs. A student in the college prep program is forbidden to take a typing course he or she really wants, because it is offered in the sequence for commercial students. Or, a boy wants to take a course in family life and sex education, but it is offered only for girls in home economics. One thirteen-year-old girl writes:

I "learn" stuff, how to write morpheme strings, how to conjugate Spanish verbs, but will I ever use these when I'm older? There is a pattern: I learn morpheme strings, not necessarily because they'll help later in life, but because how else could I pass to eighth grade? In eighth grade I'll "learn" equally useless stuff so I'll pass to ninth grade, tenth grade, eleventh grade—if I can just make it to college! (73)

Thus, irrelevance is of particular concern to students. They ask: "Why should I study this stuff? How is it ever going to help me in my life?" One student remarked: "Yeah, I cut school a lot and I get into trouble when I'm there because I just don't regard any part of it as relevant." (19, p. 113)

The content of individual courses is often rigid and uninspiring. The teacher is required to cover the material in the text, whether or not it is of interest to the students. The same thirteen-year-old girl quoted previously writes:

Another thing I think is wrong with my (the?) school(s) is the textbooks. We have to cover the material, we have to cover the material, we have to cover the material! I carry a mental picture around of one of my teachers pulling, pulling my class through a waist-deep ocean of mud—which in reality is pp. 327–331, nos. 1–50— saying "Onward, children! We must make it by Tuesday!"
Another example of this: One of my teachers saying to us, "C'mon, if we can

just get through these last two pages, I'll let you do something fun for the rest of the period." (73)

A common criticism is the failure of a particular school, program, course, or teacher sufficiently to challenge the brighter students. (16) Such students often say their high school work was much too easy, so that they never learned how to study. (37)

Students who are more interested in vocational training complain that the average comprehensive high school is too exclusively oriented to serve the needs of the college-bound students. The total emphasis seems to be on getting as many students into college as possible. This often leads to neglect of the vocational program, which may include only a minimum number of courses, and these often poorly equipped. Students want to have more time to operate the various kinds of machines and equipment they will be using on the job. Such equipment is often inadequate.

Although the majority of students really like their teachers, one of the favorite pastimes is also criticizing them. (29, 61) Teachers are "unfair, play favorites, won't allow anyone to disagree or to discuss, are not interested in their subject or the kids, are boring and dull, not prepared to teach their subject or to answer questions (they don't know what they are talking about), are too strict, or have no control over the class at all." (22, 36) A more complete discussion of the teacher is given in a subsequent section.

One of the frequent criticisms of classroom methods is the lack of discussion. The same thirteen-year-old girl writes:

I mentioned before the lack of discussions. I never had one discussion in which I was really involved. There is no free exchange, no real communicating. It's just to have the teacher say, "And what do you think?" We all obediently raise our hands. "Johnnie?" And the kid meekly states his answer which is always right or wrong, never just an opinion. (73)

Tests often become the subject of student wrath. They are a potent source of student anxiety and are sometimes used as weapons by the teacher. (9, 61) Students often consider teacher-constructed tests, which are often poorly designed, to be unfair, ambiguous, or stupid. Another criticism is of various standardized tests that all students are required to take. The criticism is not necessarily of the tests themselves, but of the fact that the results are not made known to the students. Exceptions include the scores of the SAT test which are always revealed to the student; IQ scores, achievement test results, or even aptitude scores, however, are often kept secret.

This brief look at some of the more common student criticisms presents a rather pessimistic view. A more comprehensive view will be presented in later sections.

Dropouts and Underachievement versus School Success

ENROLLMENT FIGURES

Education for all youths has not always been the philosophy of the American people. The famous Kalamazoo decision in 1874 established the now-accepted principle that public education need not be restricted to the elementary schools. Prior to that, in 1870, American youths could choose from among only 800 public high schools. (28, p. 5) Most youths who were preparing for college attended private secondary schools, then called preparatory schools. In 1900 only 11 percent of high school aged youth were in school; by 1977 the number was 94 percent. Figure 19–2 (14, 66) shows the rise since 1900. Figure 19–3 shows the percentage of dropouts from school by age and race during 1977. (66) As can be seen, until age seventeen attendance figures are almost perfect, with little difference between whites and blacks. The dropouts occur during the high school years, especially after age seventeen, with a greater percentage of blacks than whites leaving school. (66, p. 147) The total number of dropouts is considerable, even though the rate has been decreasing over the years. During the decade 1960–1970, it is estimated that 7.5 million youths dropped out of high school before getting a diploma, and that 2.5 million acquired less than an eighth-grade education. (67) The overall dropout rate in 1977 was 11.7 percent. (66, p. 147)

WHO DROPS OUT AND WHY

There is a constellation of causes for youths' dropping out of school or underachieving. Socioeconomic factors, racial and ethnic prejudice and discrimination, family background, parental influence and relationships, personality problems, social adjustments, activities and associations, financial problems, health problems, intellectual difficulties or retardation, reading disability, school failure, misconduct, low marks, and lack of interest in school are all important factors. (42,

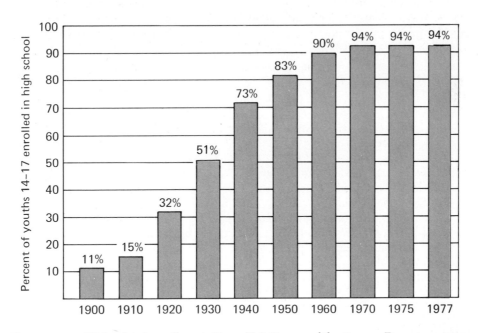

Figure 19–2.   High school enrollment. (From U.S. Bureau of the Census, Department of Commerce, *Statistical Abstract of the United States, 1978* [Washington, D.C.: U.S. Government Printing Office, 1978].)

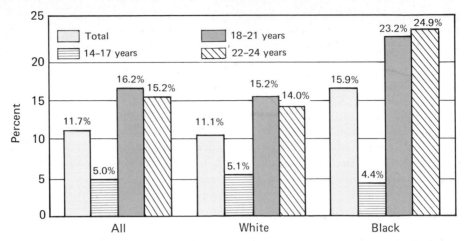

Figure 19–3. High school dropouts 14 to 24 years old, by race and age, 1977. (Adapted from U.S. Bureau of the Census, Department of Commerce, *Statistical Abstract of the United States, 1978* [Washington, D.C.: U.S. Government Printing Office, 1978], p. 147.)

48) Usually problems accumulate over the years until withdrawal occurs, often only after the legal requirements of age or number of years of schooling have been met. The actual event or circumstance that precipitates withdrawal may be minor: a misunderstanding with a teacher, a disciplinary action, difficulty with peers, misunderstanding at home, or other reasons. One boy withdrew in the last semester of his senior year because his foster parents would not buy him a suit for graduation. Another boy was refused admittance to a class until a late excuse was obtained from his gym teacher in the prior period. The gym teacher wouldn't give an excuse; the boy got angry, quit school, and never came back. In each incident like this, a whole series of prior events led to the final withdrawal: poor marks, grade retardation, conduct problems at school, strained family relationships, social maladjustment or isolation, and others. The State of Michigan Department of Public Instruction has listed twenty signs of possible early school withdrawal.

1. consistent failure to achieve in regular school work
2. grade level placement 2 or more years below average age for grade
3. irregular attendance
4. active antagonism to teachers and principals
5. marked disinterest in school with feeling of not belonging
6. low scholastic aptitude
7. low reading ability
8. frequent changes of schools
9. nonacceptance by school staff
10. nonacceptance by schoolmates
11. friends much younger or older
12. unhappy family situation
13. marked differences from school mates with regard to size
14. inability to afford the normal expenditures of schoolmates

15. nonparticipation in extracurricular activities
16. inability to compete with or ashamed of brothers and sisters
17. performance consistently lower than potential
18. serious physical or emotional handicap
19. being a disciplinary case
20. a record of delinquency (44)

These signs must be interpreted cautiously; the presence of one or more of these symptoms of early school withdrawal may be a false alarm. But at other times only one symptom may be present yet be a real indication of possible withdrawal. When as many as eight of these symptoms appear together, a prognosis of school withdrawal is more reliable. (12, p. 28)

SOCIOECONOMIC FACTORS

Research overwhelmingly indicates that low socioeconomic status correlates positively with early withdrawal from school. (43, p. 198) Why is the dropout rate higher among students from low socioeconomic families? There are a number of considerations.

Students from these families more often lack positive parental influences and examples. (4, 28) Many low socioeconomic parents want their children to have more education than they did. But if parents finished only fifth grade, they may consider graduating from junior high school sufficient. Thus, dropout parents produce dropout children. Sometimes parents completely discourage their children from attending school. Older daughters are urged to stay home to babysit or keep house; sons are expected to go out and get a job to help support the family. (69) In general, however, sons still receive more encouragement to finish school than daughters do. (60) In his study *Growing Up In River City*, Havighurst (32) found that among dropouts only 13 percent of parents opposed their dropping out, compared to 68 percent of parents of the nondropouts. (32, p. 60) This last group insisted their children remain in school. Thirty-four percent of dropouts reported their parents to be indifferent about school; only 7 percent of the controls indicated parental indifference. (32, p. 60)

Teachers are often prejudiced against youth from low socioeconomic families, showing preferential treatment to students from higher status families. (43, p. 197) Students of higher social class backgrounds are chosen more often for little favors—running errands, monitoring, chairing, committees—whereas students from lower status groups receive more than their share of discipline. Teachers are usually from middle class backgrounds and therefore often find it difficult to understand and accept the goals, values, and behavior of pupils from other social backgrounds. Thus, ethnic and social bias prevents them from treating pupils equitably. One effect is that teachers expect less of lower class students, an attitude that tends to be self-fulfilling. (17, p. 122) The lower class students themselves recognize and bitterly resent such differential treatment; they feel inferior, unappreciated, and unwanted. As one youth observed: "All of my teachers felt I was stupid." (71)

Low socioeconomic students receive fewer rewards for doing well and for staying in school than do students from higher status families. (43, p. 200) Rewards may take the form of academic grades, favors by teachers, social acceptance by peers, offices in school government, participation in extracurricular activities, or school prizes and awards. Lower status students less often receive any of these rewards than do higher status students. They do not get as good grades or enjoy as much social acceptance and prestige by peers; they seldom are elected to positions of leadership, are nonjoiners in extracurricular activities, and are not often given special prizes and awards by the school.

Lower socioeconomic students do not as often possess the verbal skills of their middle class peers. This in itself presents a handicap in learning to read or in almost all academic work. Insofar as lack of verbal skills are associated with low socioeconomic status, lower status youths do not do as well in school and are therefore more prone to drop out. (1; 15, p. 354)

Peer influences on low socioeconomic youth are often antischool and delinquency prone, emphasizing early marriage for the girls and gang activities for the boys. (15, p. 349; 31) Low socioeconomic youths often have severed their ties with adult institutions and values, becoming involved instead with groups composed of jobless dropouts. The gang commands the dropout's loyalty, and he or she obtains from it security, a sense of belonging, and excitement. Too often, the gang discourages academic achievement and participation. (2; 28, p. 428; 57)

ETHNIC CONSIDERATIONS

Black and other minority group students have a much higher dropout rate than whites do. (41, 66) The highest rates are among nonwhites from inner-city high schools. The value orientation and the trying economic, social, and familial conditions are not conducive to continuing education. Youths from such neighborhoods are frequently truant and tend to drop out as soon as they reach age sixteen.

FAMILY RELATIONSHIPS

The quality of interaction among members of the adolescent's family has a marked influence on school success. Studies of the family relationships of bright, high-achieving versus underachieving high school students show that the high achievers more often than underachievers describe their parents as typically sharing recreation and ideas, as understanding, approving, trusting, affectionate, encouraging (but not pressuring) with respect to achievement, and not overly restrictive or severe in discipline. (6; 15, p. 347; 64, p. 195)

One study (10) of the families of twenty-five matched pairs of white youths revealed interesting differences in the family life of the dropouts versus that of the successful students. The overwhelming majority of dropouts saw family members as failing to accept each other and failing to accept and understand them, whereas the majority of graduates saw family members as accepting and understanding each other as complete persons. The dropouts received less encouragement from their families in their educational and occupational plans than did the graduates; there were marked differences also in verbal family communication patterns. Eighty-one percent of the dropouts felt intercommunication in their families was inadequate, whereas 80 percent of the graduates felt it was at least adequate. Four out of five of the dropouts' families participated in leisure activities together "very infrequently" or "infrequently," whereas three out of four of the graduates' families were accustomed to participation in such family activities. Overall, the typical home of the dropout was reported as "very unhappy" (35 percent) or "unhappy" (27 percent); the typical home of the graduate was "very happy" (48 percent) or "happy" (16 percent). From this study the authors conclude that "the dropout is generally the product of a family deficient in primary relations." (10, p. 223)

The broken home is also strongly associated with dropping out of school. Youths whose parents are divorced or separated are twice as likely to drop out of school as those whose homes are intact. More than one-third of adolescents from broken families drop out of school. (31, pp. 93, 181)

PERSONALITY CHARACTERISTICS

Dropouts are more likely to be emotionally immature and less well adjusted than high school graduates. (40, 56, 62) They may manifest various symptoms of defective ego functioning: rebellion, negativism and alienation, deep-seated feelings of hostility and resentment, low self-esteem, feelings of inferiority, excessive fear and anxiety, or emotional instability. (63) What is so often described as laziness or a lack of willpower may actually be sullen resentment toward punitive parents, social rejection, or unfair treatment at school, which cause such feelings of rebellion that the adolescent refuses to do anything demanded by authority. (5, p. 6)

Five traits have been identified as common among underachievers: (1) negativism, (2) inferiority feelings, (3) high anxiety, (4) boredom, and (5) overprotectedness. (38) In one study of high school males, Propper and Clark (54) linked underachievement with alienation. They describe this alienation as characterized by pessimism, distrust, anxiety, egocentricity, and resentment.

SOCIAL ADJUSTMENT, PEER ASSOCIATIONS

Peer influences often are a major factor in influencing a particular student to stay in school or not. Most adolescents want to do what their friends are doing. If friends are dropping out of school to get jobs earning "big money" or to get married, the individual may be persuaded to do likewise. Similarly, the student who becomes acculturated into a lower class pattern of life that rejects education or into a delinquent group that is rebelling against the established system of education is strongly influenced by his or her peers to drop out of school. (63)

It is also important that the adolescent make friends, find social acceptance, and participate fully in the extracurricular activities at school. Poor social acceptance, social isolation, or other manifestations of social maladjustment are an important contributing cause of dropping out. Adolescents cannot remain happy in a school where they feel no sense of identity with any individuals or social groups. Havighurst (32) found dropouts to be quite unsuccessful in extracurricular affairs, seldom holding school offices or participating in clubs and outside activities. This life style led 67 percent of dropouts to express strong dislike for school, in contrast to only 12 percent of those staying in school. (32, p. 62)

EMPLOYMENT, MONEY

Financial considerations are also important in individual decisions about whether or not to stay in school. Even high school is expensive. This factor plus financial pressures at home force some adolescents to leave school to go to work. Sometimes parents pressure youths to go to work to help support the family. At other times there is the lure of being financially independent, having spending money for social activities or to buy a car. The desire for clothes, a car, or other symbols of status in an affluent society lures many youths to accept early employment. (5)

The desire to go to work is a much stronger factor in leaving school than is actual financial necessity. Nienstedt (49) reported that 67 percent of dropouts in Connecticut leave to enter employment, but only 7 percent leave because of financial necessity. Havighurst (32) found that only 5 percent of dropouts gave clear evidence of having to leave school for financial reasons.

SCHOOL FAILURE, APATHY, DISSATISFACTION

Many school factors have been associated with dropping out of school. Among these are poor reading ability, (1; 23, p. 137) grade retardation, repetition, misplacement, (33) low or failing marks, inability to get along with teachers, (8) misconduct, and low IQ or mental retardation. (31, 32) There is also a general, vague category that might be labeled apathy, lack of motivation, or a feeling that school is irrelevant. (24, 39, 65) Some students are not necessarily emotionally or socially maladjusted, but simply lack interest in school work, feel it is a waste of time, and would therefore rather get married or go to work. Such youths may be capable of doing acceptable work but have no interest in doing so. (27) Sometimes such a student has been placed in the wrong type of program. (23, p. 137) A switch to a vocational course that the student finds appealing is of help to the adolescent wrongly placed in the college prep program. Students who have had to repeat grades and who thus miss friends and feel themselves to be social misfits may develop an intense dislike for school and lose all interest and desire to learn. Similarly, students who have a history of low marks and failure find school only an unrewarding, painful experience and can't wait to get out. (27, 62)

Many students don't drop out but are thrown out or are given a temporary suspension, which they turn into a permanent absence. Students who are disciplined by temporary suspension are tempted not to return if they have experienced much long-term dissatisfaction or difficulty at school. Administrators and teachers often breathe a sigh of relief when the student doesn't come back. At other times a student is expelled and not allowed to return, so he or she has no choice in the matter.

PREGNANCY, MARRIAGE

Leaving high school to get married is seldom a reason boys drop out of school, but pregnancy and marriage are among the most common reasons for girls. One survey showed that the majority of female dropouts (53 percent) were the result of marriage or illegitimate pregnancy. (31) As many as 5 percent of all high school girls drop out because of pregnancy in any one year. (11, p. 153)

The Secondary School Teacher

WHAT MAKES A GOOD TEACHER?

One of the important keys to fruitful secondary school education is having good teachers in the school system. But what constitutes a "good" teacher? There is little agreement on the answer. Are good teachers those who are selected according to certain personality traits characteristic of mature, mentally healthy people? Are good teachers best defined by the degree of understanding, rapport, and warmth of the relationships they are able to establish with pupils, colleagues, and administrators? Or are they best defined by their professional backgrounds, qualifications, and abilities to use appropriate materials and methods in motivating learning in students? (13, p. 578) Even though various educators emphasize one category or another, there is sufficient evidence to justify emphasizing all three categories: (1) personality, (2) relationships, and (3) professional qualifications and performance.

PERSONALITY TRAITS AND CHARACTER

Teachers who are emotionally secure people free from excessive fears, worries, and anxieties, with an adequate self-concept, don't have to overcompensate for their failures or rationalize them or have to protect their own egos by projecting their inadequacies on others or blaming them for their own failures. (71) They can be confident, accepting, trusting people who feel and act secure and mature. In one study of what high school dropouts thought of their teachers, the students listed self-confidence as the most important attribute of an effective instructor, because such teachers would not need to belittle others in order to feel secure themselves. (71, p. 702)

It is also beneficial to students' emotional development if teachers are emotionally stable people with high frustration tolerances and fairly even, pleasant dispositions and temperaments, free of excessive emotionalism or extremes of mood. They are not always patient, but are usually so, and behave in a controlled manner.

One can think also of highly creative, intelligent people who are quite unstable, but who make imaginative teachers. Provided their instability is not so great as to harm students emotionally, some may do a superior job in stimulating cognitive understanding, problem-solving abilities, and creativity. However, some of these people also do a great deal of harm to students' feelings of security, emotional stability, and self-images. At the worst, highly emotional and insecure teachers can be detrimental to already oversensitive adolescents who are themselves groping for some degree of self-confidence and emotional stability.

Emotional security enables teachers to keep an open mind on various questions and issues, to be willing to entertain different points of view, to let students air their opinions and not pressure them to come up with the "right" answer (the teacher's answer). They can be flexible in scheduling, administrating, and teaching their classes and do not mind innovation or change if it makes a contribution to the learning process. (20) They are relatively free of racial, ethnocentric, religious, political, and other prejudices and biases, so that they can present issues honestly from different points of view. Thus, they can be as tolerant, impartial, and fair as possible.

Emotional maturity also enables teachers to show kindness, love, and genuine warmth and regard for other people. This enables them to find close personal attachments in their own lives and to build rapport with adolescents. Thus, they can communicate that they like adolescents, understand them, and enjoy being with them. Students also like teachers who are generally happy, pleasant, cheerful people.

Although there are "successful" teachers who are fairly self-centered, the better ones are unselfish and altruistic to the point of being pupil-centered, with a genuine concern for them and their welfare. Basically, teachers need to be honest, sincere, caring, socially responsible people who strive to set a good example of personal conduct in their own lives, and who are aware and sensitive to the social and ethical mores of the culture in which they live. This requires not only concern about individual ethics but also social morality.

Teaching is an exhausting profession, often requiring almost unlimited reservoirs of physical, emotional, and mental energy. It is not a profession for the sickly. Therefore, teachers need much drive and energy, backed up by a healthy constitution. Lethargic, phlegmatic, apathetic, bored people in poor health can neither inspire students nor meet the vigorous demands of their profession.

TEACHERS' RELATIONSHIPS WITH OTHERS

It is helpful if teachers enjoy satisfying social relationships outside school, so that there is no need to work off negative feelings on their pupils or to use students to fulfill their own emotional and social needs. Teachers who get along well with their colleagues, who have satisfactory personal lives as individuals or members of a family, who are accepted and liked by others and have found social acceptance in adult society make better teachers.

Furthermore, teachers need to like adolescents, to be able to relate to them as growing people who are becoming adults, and to treat them with admiration and respect as individuals. The teacher who basically hates youths, who is supercritical and rejecting of them, has no business in the classroom. Schmuck writes:

Some teachers unknowingly deprive youth of their self-respect, confidence, and esteem. The more an adolescent is treated as incompetent, the more he will come to exhibit this prophecy; and, of course, conversely when he is given support and respect, he develops a more positive view of himself. The adolescent's concept of himself, especially in the areas of expertness and personal efficacy, is built up through the accumulated reflected appraisals of teachers with whom he comes in contact. (59, p. 23)

Also, teachers who show preferential treatment, who can accept only those middle class pupils like themselves, and who reject those who are different can never fulfill the needs of all students. Too many teachers love only bright, attractive, well-adjusted, socially acceptable students but reject dull, rebellious, different adolescents who may present problems or who are sources of annoyance primarily because they are different. (35)

Furthermore, the best teachers evidence real understanding of youths, of the developmental tasks of adolescence, and of the particular problems, adjustments, and interests of young people. Thus, the basic teacher-pupil relationship is one of adult to growing adult, with genuine concern, tolerance, friendliness, and respect evident in their relationship, with the teacher manifesting real understanding of adolescents' lives and needs and an ability to relate and communicate with them.

PROFESSIONAL QUALIFICATIONS

One of the major criticisms of teacher candidates is that they are intellectually the poorest in the universities. This impression is commonly held among students outside colleges of education, but can also be found among faculty members in universities across the nation. (7) There is some research to substantiate this impression. One study at the University of Maine showed that the mean SAT scores of students in the College of Education were significantly lower than those of Arts and Science students. (3) However, the range of test scores overlaps among all college majors, so that there are some education majors scoring very high and Arts and Science majors scoring low in comparison. Also, test scores vary greatly from institution to institution.

Another criticism of teachers has been that they are too middle class and thus are not able to relate to lower socioeconomic class students. However, an increasing number of secondary school teachers now come from lower socio-economic classes. (7, 21) This does create problems, however; one study at the University of Maine revealed that (1) the fathers of College of Education students were generally of lower socioeconomic level, earned less money, and had less education than fathers of Arts and Science students; and (2) there were fewer books in the homes of Education students than in the homes of Arts and Science students. (21) It would seem, therefore, that although it is desirable from one point of view to employ more teachers from lower socioeconomic families, the likelihood of hiring teachers with lower scholastic ability thereby becomes greater, for there is a positive correlation between performance on scholastic aptitude tests and the socioeconomic status of the family. However, because a large number of those growing up in poor families are also of superior intelligence, it is sometimes possible to find both brains and ability to relate to all students in the same teacher.

It is important also that teachers, once trained, keep abreast of the times in attitude, instructional knowledge, and skills. (42) This means that teachers need to take advantage of numerous opportunities for professional improvement, participate in learned societies, attend workshops and conferences, take graduate courses, and keep up in their field by reading professional journals, new books, and research literature—not just in teaching methods, but in subject matter as well. (72)

A good teacher is willing to spend necessary time in preparation, plans carefully, and understands and uses sound principles of learning through a variety of appropriate teaching methods and techniques. Students are highly critical of teachers who are "never prepared," are "lazy," "aren't interested in teaching," who "don't care if we learn," or who "use films as a substitute for a good lesson." (59)

Hamachek (30) lists characteristics of teachers who are superior in "encouraging motivation and learning in students":

(1) willingness to be flexible, to be direct or indirect as the situation demands; (2) capacity to perceive the world from the student's point of view; (3) ability to "personalize" their teaching; (4) willingness to experiment, to try out new things; (5) skill in asking questions (as opposed to seeing self as a kind of answering service); (6) knowledge of subject matter and related areas; (7) skill in establishing definite examination procedures; (8) willingness to provide definite study help; (9) capacity to reflect an appreciative attitude (evidenced by nods, comments, smiles, etc.); (10) conversational manner in teaching—informal, easy style. (30, p. 237)

Curriculum Considerations

HISTORICAL PERSPECTIVE

High schools at the beginning of the twentieth century were for an elite minority of youths who wanted to go on to college. Although only 11 percent of youths were in high school, fully two-thirds of that 11 percent went on to higher education. Since then, the proportion of high school graduates attending college dropped to about half in 1920, then to about one-third from 1940 to the present time. (14)

The high school curriculum was designed to emphasize preparation for college. Thus, it became efficient in preparing students for more school, but less efficient in meeting their other needs. (53, p. 190) One good example of the way the high schools were influenced to design their curricula for college preparation can be seen in the work done on history curricula in 1897 by the National Education Association. The NEA appointed a special committee to determine history curricula for the high schools, but six of the seven committee members were college history professors. The committee report dictated four specific years of history, a fact that had a powerful impact on textbooks and curricula for years afterward. The net effect was that the college dictated the form of high school education. (14)

Gradually, however, the percentage of youths attending high school increased, and as the percentage of high school graduates attending college decreased, the emphasis began to change. High school graduates were no longer destined for college, but largely for industry and business. The majority now went directly into jobs. Industry needed practical courses such as industrial arts, typing, bookkeeping, drafting, and mechanics. Thus, the function, emphasis, and curriculum of the high school were changed to meet different needs.

In 1918 an NEA committee listed seven cardinal purposes of secondary education as: health, command of fundamental processes, worthy home membership, vocation, civic education, worthy use of leisure, and ethical character. (14) Thus, the content of the high school shifted in a nonacademic direction, from college preparation to life adjustment. The typical high school teacher also changed from an austere academician, emphasizing subject-centered teaching, to a more sympathetic, flexible teacher, trained in methods, educational psychology, and guidance as well as in subject matter.

This situation continued until the years immediately following World War

II, when the trend was reversed. Many returning veterans went to college on the GI Bill. Postwar industry began to demand and get highly educated employees; the number of high school graduates going on to college began to increase. Then, in the decade from 1952 to 1962, after the Soviets shocked the United States by orbiting the first Sputnik around the earth, the demand for college oriented, highly academic, technological education swelled to a roar. High school was considered too easy; there were too many frills such as industrial arts, home economics, physical education, driver education, and family life education. The federal government aided these changes by proposing the elimination of federal funds for vocational education and by carefully excluding all "extra" subjects from the National Defense Education Act. (Social sciences, music, art, and Latin were also casualties, for no one felt them useful in training scientists to catch up with the Russians.) Middle class parents, who were paying the taxes, got on the bandwagon to eliminate the frills of education and were pleased because the high schools were now preparing their children for college. Educators were happy because they were again preparing students for what they knew best—further schooling. (53, p. 190)

As the reader has guessed, the situation continued to change. The business recession of 1970 and after and cutbacks in business spending resulted in a rapidly declining need for so many college graduates. During 1976 over half of some college graduation classes went begging for jobs, especially those graduates who were not trained for specific jobs that were in demand. This is the major reason why enrollment in liberal arts courses declined so rapidly and participation in practical courses has boomed. (52) Also, as the wages of the American working people have skyrocketed, and the need for vocational services they supply has grown, there is again a renewed demand for vocational training in the high school program. Fewer students are seeing the economic advantages of four years of college when they can earn as much with two years of vocational training. State educational systems are now taking tax dollars out of state universities and putting them into vocational training institutes. Thus, the cycle of curriculum changes continues.

THREE CURRICULA

The average comprehensive high school today offers three basic curricula.

COLLEGE PREPARATORY. The most prestigious is still the college preparatory curriculum, enrolling about half the students. It has one goal: to prepare the student for success in the type of college that leads to graduate school. Some high schools, particularly in middle and upper middle class suburban communities, are particularly successful, boasting 80 to 90 percent of their students going on to college. Other schools, though enrolling large numbers of students in the college prep program, are particularly unsuccessful, because the majority of these students do not get into college. In such cases the college prep program does not meet the needs of the majority of students; even if they graduate they don't go to college, yet they are not employable without additional training.

VOCATIONAL. The vocational curriculum is the one curriculum designed for preparing students for gainful employment. Students spend about one-half of their time in general education, the rest in specialized courses and, in some cases, on-the-job training. (50, p. 157) Vocational teachers usually have work experience in the vocation they are teaching. The quality of the program varies from superb to mediocre. Some of the best programs are found in exclusively vocational high schools. (55, p. 429) However, the number of exclusively vocational high schools is limited, and because vocational enrollments in comprehensive high schools are typically limited to 20 percent of the student body, only the ablest students are accepted. The program therefore rejects many of those who need help the most.

GENERAL. The third and most inefficient curriculum is the general curriculum. Its students are the castoffs from the other two curricula plus those not committed either to college or to one of the vocations taught in the vocational curriculum. It has no goals other than to provide a general education for those who may be able to go on to some type of job or some type of vocational, post–high school education. Most dropouts and unemployed youths come from the general curriculum. More of these youths might have stayed in high school and been employable if they had had more specific vocational training. (A student bulletin, put out by a large, well-known guidance firm, describes a general program as one teaching "what everybody should know." This, according to the bulletin, includes English, math, science, social studies, and a foreign language. No wonder this program doesn't meet all students' needs.)

CURRICULUM IMPROVEMENT

Efforts over the years at curriculum reform have consistently confronted two major problems. One is the rigidity of course requirements, grade demands, scheduling, and the lockstep structure of schools. When certain subjects are required, when carefully chosen subject-oriented content is obligatory in any one course, and when these subjects must be taught at particular grade levels for prescribed periods of time, with the student earning certain minimum ranks, any curriculum reform has been difficult. To change would mean to overthrow the whole rigid system.

The second problem in instituting curriculum reform is the teacher and his or her methods. When teachers are required to cover so much material in a subject-centered course, when classes are overcrowded and budgets for hiring additional personnel are limited, teachers become conditioned to "coverage" and to "telling." If a new course or new topics in an old course are introduced, the temptation is to teach the new courses like the old. (25)

In an effort to overcome these obstacles, considerable effort has gone into making some sweeping changes in curricular approaches. (48) The new approaches emphasize student responsibility; individual study and growth at individual rates; and flexibility of content, scheduling, and methods of teaching for each course. (18, 26) In an article entitled "Developing Student Responsibility for Learning," Eugene Howard has suggested four concepts that, if implemented in a school, "would be making positive headway in translating some of the basic psychological principles of learning into a functioning organization" and would "foster student growth toward assuming an increasing greater share of the responsibility for his own education." (34) These four concepts may be summarized as follows.

THE CONCEPT OF STUDENT OPTIONS. This concept states that students should have progressively more to say about what they will learn; where and for how long they will learn it; and what materials, methods, and personnel they will utilize. (51, p. 52) In other words, the students are given options of pace, curriculum content, time, materials, and personnel. A team of teachers is needed to build the options into a multiple curriculum to present the student with choices.

CONTENT OPTIONS. This may include offering reading in a variety of books without requiring the same content of all students, and offering various methods (such as a variety of individual projects) for learning.

TIME OPTIONS. This allows students to progress at their own rates, to have something to say about how fast they will learn. (46) Thus, students are given individual pace options as well as content options. Students may select an accelerated, a decelerated, or a normal pace. Deceleration needn't mean learning less; students may select a depth option, in which they learn much but move to new subjects slowly. This option can be a fine means of combating superficiality by allowing students to probe in depth those subjects in which they are most interested.

FACILITY AND PERSONNEL OPTIONS. Students are allowed to have something to say about where they will work, what materials will be needed, and what faculty assistance they require. The new modular schedules allow this flexibility, by providing students with large blocks of unscheduled time that they may use in the places, studying the subjects, and getting the selected help they need. The students become the inquirers; the teachers provide the structure, the setting, and the guidance needed. (34)

Conclusions

On the whole, high school students like school because it involves them with their friends in a variety of activities, but the majority are neutral or indifferent to the educational process. Adolescents recognize the importance of education in their futures, but they seem to look upon grades, tests, and studies as necessary parts of a competitive system to succeed, even though at times they find the whole process boring and irrelevant. Students desire more voice in selecting and planning curricula and programs, believing that they know better what they need than school administrators and teachers do. The concepts of student options, nongraded classrooms, and student participation in policy making are some of the current efforts to make school programs more flexible and responsive to the needs of individual students.

The high school teacher continues to be the key to superior education. In spite of complaints, students like most of their teachers, especially those who are keenly interested in them and their problems and who take the job of teaching seriously. With the teaching profession overcrowded, schools now have their choice of graduates, and therefore no longer have the excuse that they can't find good teachers.

Schools and colleges of education can also be more selective in choosing their candidates for educational degrees. There is no reason why the poorest college students should be channeled into teaching. The teaching profession demands the highest cognitive and intellectual skills. Perhaps if only the brightest and most highly motivated are chosen and paid salaries commensurate with their abilities and financial requirements, this superiority in teaching faculties would begin to be reflected in products more worthy of high school diplomas. During the past several decades, educators have concentrated on providing secondary education to American's growing millions of adolescents. Now that mass education has been implemented, the future emphasis can be on quality and not on numbers alone.

Discussion Questions

The subject of school lends itself to animated and provocative classroom discussion. The following major subjects and some questions under each are only suggestive; the instructor may want to add others or ask members of the class to write out some questions they would like to see discussed.

Personal Experiences with School

1. Describe the type of high school you attended, evaluating the good and bad things about it.
2. What curriculum options were available in your school? Did these meet the needs of the students?
3. What courses were offered that you feel were unnecessary? What courses were not offered that you feel should have been?
4. What types of vocational education were offered in your school? Did these programs prepare students for jobs? What other types of vocational courses and programs should be offered?
5. In what ways did your high school program prepare you for college. In what ways was it deficient in preparing you for college?
6. What do you think of the guidance program and counselors in your school? How could the guidance program have been improved?
7. What place do you feel extracurricular activities have in the school program? How are they beneficial? How are they harmful? Was there too much emphasis on competitive athletics in your school? What benefits are derived from school athletics? Did the clubs and activities meet the needs of students from lower class families?
8. What did you think of your teachers? What qualities did you most admire? What qualities did you like least? What are the most important attributes of a good teacher? What characteristics do you admire least in teachers? What training or preparation should be given to teachers to enhance their abilities and qualifications to teach?
9. Did your school have many dropouts? Why did these students leave school? What kept you in school sometimes when you felt you would rather leave and go to work?

Grading and Evaluation

1. What are the purposes of grading and evaluation? Does the present system serve these functions? Should grades be given at all? Why? Why not?
2. What do you think of standardized tests such as the SAT as a means of evaluating ability to do college work? What changes would you make in college selection criteria?

3. What factors encourage cheating? What can be done to minimize cheating?

Student Options

1. Do you think students should have a voice in the organization and selection of high school curricula? How can the program become more relevant to student needs?
2. How much say should students have in deciding the specific subjects to be studied as a part of any one course?
3. What subjects do you feel are most unnecessary in the average high school curriculum?
4. What should be the role of the student council in high school? What role does it usually perform?
5. What are the advantages and disadvantages of vocational education in high school? Should there be separate vocational schools? Comment on vocational education as it now exists. How could it be improved?
6. Do you think high schools cater to college prep students while neglecting those in other programs?
7. Should students have any freedom in selecting their teachers? What do you think of team teaching versus teaching by one person for such courses as English, science, math, and history? What are the advantages of each method?

Discipline

1. Are high schools today too strict or too lax in discipline?
2. What forms of discipline should schools use?
3. What should schools do about such problems as drinking, smoking (cigarettes or pot), cheating, or vandalism in school?
4. Who should do the disciplining in school? Should parents be involved in school discipline?
5. For what reasons should students be expelled from school?

Teaching Methods

1. In what ways should the school library be used as a multimedia center to contribute to the learning process?
2. What are learning packages and how do they contribute to individualized instruction?
3. How can the computer contribute to the educational process?
4. What are dial-access and push-button learning systems? What is programmed instruction and how does it work?
5. What sort of teaching machines can be used in the high school?
6. How are electronic learning laboratories used in teaching foreign languages?
7. In what ways can commercial, public, and closed-circuit television contribute to the learning process?

Building and Design

1. What types of building designs facilitate learning?
2. What do you think of architecturally open classrooms?
3. What different types of spaces are needed in the most up-to-date high school building?
4. How do interior decor, acoustics, soundproofing, furnishings, carpets, and other design features influence the learning process?
5. How can the high school building best serve adolescents after school hours?

Bibliography

1. Ahrendt, K. M. "Reading Ability and the Potential Dropout." *Education Canada* 10 (1970): 13–15.

2. Alexander, C. N., Jr., and Campbell, E. Q. "Peer Influences on Adolescent Educational Aspirations and Attainments." In *Adolescents and the American High School.* Edited by R. F. Purnell. New York: Holt, Rinehart and Winston, 1970, pp. 220–231.

3. Apostal, R. "College Board Score Analysis of University of Maine Students in the Class of 1970. Testing And Counseling Service Report, No. 29." Orono: University of Maine, Summer, 1967.

4. Bachman, J. et al. *Dropping Out: Problem or Symptom? Youth in Transition.* Ann Arbor, Mich.: Survey Research Center, Institute for Social Research, 1971.

5. Blaine, G. B. *Youth And the Hazards Of Affluence.* New York: Harper and Row, 1966.

6. Bledsoe, J. C., and Wiggins, R. G. "Self-Concepts and Academic Aspirations of 'Understood' and 'Misunderstood' Boys and Girls in Ninth Grade." *Psychological Reports* 35 (1974): 57–58.

7. Brookover, W., and Gottlieb, D. *A Sociology Of Education.* New York: American Book Co., 1964.

8. Bureau of Guidance. "Reducing the School Drop-Out Rate." Albany: University of the State of New York, 1963.

9. Buxton, C. E. *Adolescents in School.* New Haven, Conn.: Yale University Press, 1973.

10. Cervantes, L. F. "Family Background, Primary Relationships and the High School Dropout." *Journal of Marirage and the Family* 27 (1965): 218–223.

11. ———. *The Dropout.* Ann Arbor: University of Michigan Press, 1965.

12. Chansky, N. M. *Untapped Good: The Rehabilitation of School Dropouts.* Springfield, Ill.: Charles C. Thomas, 1966.

13. Cole, L., and Hall, I. N. *Psychology Of Adolescence.* 7th ed. New York: Holt, Rinehart and Winston, 1970.

14. Coleman, J. S. *Adolescents And the Schools.* New York: Basic Books, 1965.

15. Conger, J. J. *Adolescence and Youth.* New York: Harper and Row, 1973.

16. Eisenman, R., and Platt, J. J. "Underachievement and Creativity in High School Students." *Psychology* 7 (1972): 52–55.

17. Elkin, F., and Handel, G. *The Child and Society: The Process of Socialization.* 2d ed. New York: Random House, 1972.

18. Fantini, M. "Alternatives within Public Schools." *Phi Delta Kappan* 54 (1973): 444–449.

19. Fish, K. L. *Conflict and Dissent in the High School.* New York: Bruce Publishing Co., 1970.

20. Fisher, R. J. "A Discussion Project on High School Adolescents' Perceptions of the Relationship between Students and Teachers." *Adolescence* 11 (1976): 87–95.

21. Folson, C. H., and Lucy, W. "A Comparison of Students in the Colleges of Education and Arts and Sciences on Variables of Family Background and Perceptions of Secondary School Experiences. Testing and Counseling Service Report No. 42." Orono: University of Maine, 1969.

22. Freese, G. T., and West, C. K. "Congruence, Empathy, and Regard: A Comparison of Adolescent Ratings with Teacher Self-Ratings." *Adolescence* 7 (1972): 525–529.

23. Gallagher, J. R., and Harris, H. I. *Emotional Problems Of Adolescents.* rev. ed. New York: Oxford University Press, 1964, p. 139.

24. Gillingham, J. "A Study of Dropouts." Miami: Dade County, Florida, Public Schools, 1964.

25. Goodlad, J. I. "The Education Program to 1980 and Beyond." In *Readings In Adolescent Development.* Edited by H. W. Bernard. Scranton, Pa.: International Textbook Co., 1969, pp. 306–320.

26. Gorman, B. W. "Change in the Secondary School: Why and How." *Phi Delta Kappan* 53 (1972): 565–568.

27. Green, D. A. "A Study of Talented High-School Drop-Outs." *Vocational Guidance Quarterly* 10 (1962): 171–172.

28. Grinder, R. E. *Adolescence.* New York: John Wiley and Sons, 1973.

29. Gross, R., and Osterman, P. *High School.* New York: Simon and Schuster, 1971.

30. Hamachek, D. E., ed. *Human Dynamics in Psychology and Education.* Boston: Allyn and Bacon, 1972.

31. Hathaway, S. R., and Monachesi, E. D. *Adolescent Personality and Behavior.* Minneapolis: University of Minnesota Press, 1963, pp. 177–178.

32. Havighurst, R. J. et al. *Growing Up In River City.* New York: John Wiley and Sons, 1962.

33. Herriott, R. E. "Some Social Determinants of Educational Aspiration." *Harvard Educational Review* 33 (1963): 157–177.

34. Howard, E. R. "Developing Student

Responsibility for Learning." *The National Association of Secondary-School Principals Bulletin* 50 (1966): 235–246.

35. Hurlock , E. *Adolescent Development.* 3d ed. New York: McGraw-Hill, 1967.

36. Jensen, R. E. "Cooperative Relations between Secondary Teachers and Students: Some Behavioral Strategies." *Adolescence* 10 (1975): 469–482.

37. Kipms, D., and Resnick, J. H. "Experimental Prevention of Underachievement among Intelligent, Impulsive College Students." *Journal of Consulting Clinical Psychology* 36 (1971): 53–60.

38. Kraft, A. "A Class for Academic Underachievers in High School." *Adolescence* 4 (1969): 295–318.

39. Lichter, S. O. et al. *The Drop-Outs.* New York: Free Press, 1962.

40. Liddle, G. P. "Psychological Factors Involved in Dropping Out of School." *High School Journal* 45 (1962): 276–280.

41. Lyda, W. J., and Copenny, V. P. "Some Selected Factors Associated with Rural and Urban Dropouts in Laurens County, Ga." *Journal of Negro Education* 34 (1965): 96–98.

42. Mahan, T. W. "The Teacher as a Provocative Adventurer." *Teachers College Record* 67 (1966): 330–337.

43. Manaster, G. J. *Adolescent Development and the Life Tasks.* Boston: Allyn and Bacon, 1977.

44. Michigan State Department of Public Instruction. "Quickie Kit on School Holding Power." Lansing, Mich., 1963.

45. Miller, D. D. "What Do High School Students Think of Their Schools?" *Phi Delta Kappan* 57 (1976): 700–702.

46. Muro, J. J. *Youth: New Perspectives on Old Dimensions.* Columbus, Ohio: Charles E. Merrill Publishing Co., 1973.

47. Namenwirth, J. Z. "Failing in New Haven: An Analysis of High School Graduates and Dropouts." *Social Forces* 48 (1969): 23–36.

48. National Task Force for High School Reform. *The Adolescent, Other Citizens and Their High Schools.* New York: McGraw-Hill, 1974.

49. Nienstedt, C. "A Report to the Council on Higher Education." Connecticut State Department of Education, 1963. Mimeographed.

50. Panel on Youth, President's Science Advisory Committee. *Youth: Transition to Adulthood.* Chicago: University of Chicago Press, 1974.

51. Powell, M. *Youth: Critical Issues.* Columbus, Ohio: Charles E. Merrill Publishing Co., 1972.

52. "Practical Courses Boom While Economy Quakes." *Maine Sunday Telegram,* 9 November 1975.

53. The Princeton Manpower Symposium. *The Transition From School To Work.* Princeton, N. J.: Princeton University Press, 1968.

54. Propper, M. M., and Clark, E. T. "Alienation: Another Dimension of Underachievement." *Journal of Psychology* 75 (1970): 13–18.

55. Purnell, R. F., and Lesser, G. S. "Examining Stereotypes about Youth in Vocational and Comprehensive High Schools." In *Adolescents and the American High School.* Edited by R. F. Purnell. New York: Holt, Rinehart and Winston, 1970.

56. Rich, V. N. "Dropouts and the Emotionally Disturbed." *Journal of Secondary Education* 41 (1966): 316–320.

57. Rigsby, L. C., and McDill, E. L. "Adolescent Peer Influence Processes: Conceptualization and Measurement." *Social Science Research* 1 (1972): 305–321.

58. Rollins, S. P. "Youth Education: Problems." In *Youth Education: Problems/Perspectives/Promises.* Edited by R. H. Muessig. Washington, D. C.: Association for Supervision and Curriculum Development, National Education Association, 1968, pp. 2–19.

59. Schmuck, R. "Concerns of Contemporary Adolescents." *National Association of Secondary-School Principals Bulletin* 29 (1965): 19–28.

60. Schwarzweller, H. K., and Lyson, T. A. "Social Class, Parental Interest, and the Educational Plans of American and Norwegian Rural Youth." *Sociology of Education* 47 (1974): 443–465.

61. Silberman, C. E. *Crisis in the Classroom.* New York: Random House, 1970.

62. Silver, R. R. "Immaturity Held Key to Dropouts." *New York Times,* 3 May 1964.

63. Stinchcombe, A. L. *Rebellion in A High School.* Chicago: Quadrangle Books, 1964.

64. Thornburg, H. D. *Development in Adolescence.* Monterey, Calif.: Brooks/Cole Publishing Co., 1975.

65. "Transfers, Entrants, and Dropouts in Los Angeles Secondary Schools, 1962–1963." Research Report No. 258. Los Angeles: Los Angeles City School Districts, Evaluation and Research Section, 1964.

66. U.S. Bureau of the Census, Department of Commerce. *Statistical Abstract of the United States, 1976.* Washington, D.C.: U.S. Government Printing Office, 1976.

67. U.S. Senate, 89th Congress, 2d Session. *Profile On Youth, 1966.* Senate Document No. 124, Part I. Washington, D.C.: U.S.

Government Printing Office, 1966, pp. 2, 30.

68. "The Unradical Young." *Life*, 8 January 1971, pp. 22–30.

69. Unruh, G. G., and Alexander, W. M. *Innovations in Secondary Education.* New York: Holt, Rinehart and Winston, 1970.

70. Wattenberg, W. W. *The Adolescent Years*, 2d ed. New York: Harcourt Brace Jovanovich, 1973.

71. Whiteside, M., and Merriman, G. "Dropouts Look at Their Teachers." *Phi Delta Kappan* 57 (1976): 700–702.

72. Wilcox, T. R. "Teacher Attitudes and Student Achievement." *Teachers College Record* 48 (1967): 371–374.

73. Wirth, P. "My Ideal School Wouldn't Be a School." *Teachers College Record* 72 (1970): 57–59.

74. Yankelovich, D. *The New Morality: A Profile of American Youth in the 70's.* New York: McGraw-Hill, 1974.

CHAPTER 20

Vocational Choice, Aspirations, and Guidance

Outline

The choice of a vocation is one of the most important choices that the adolescent has to make. This chapter examines the process of that choice: factors that influence choice and other factors that should. It discusses the major theories of vocational choice that have grown out of research discoveries and goes on to discuss the influence of parents, peers, school personnel, sex-role concepts, intelligence, aptitudes, interest, job opportunities, job rewards and satisfactions, socioeconomic status, and prestige factors.

The Importance of Vocational Choice

PRESSURES TO CHOOSE

Adolescents today are constantly pressured by other people to choose a vocation. Dad has asked for years: "What do you want to be when you grow up?" Peers inquire: "What are you going to do after you graduate?" School personnel want to know: "Which program do you want to enroll in?" The TV announcer proclaims: "Stay in school if you want to get a good job." "But which job, which vocation?" is the question the adolescent asks.

There are also societal pressures stemming from work values inherent in Western culture. (89) The puritan work ethic is geared to four principles: (1) it is a person's duty under God to work and to work hard (industry is blessed, idleness is sinful); (2) success in work is evidence of God's favor and of a person's worth; (3) the measure of success is money and property; and (4) the way to success is through industry and thrift. This ethic permeates the culture in which adolescents are brought up (some youths reject the ethic and are criticized); it is inevitable that they be influenced by these values. (48) Recent studies have indicated that a general repudiation of the work ethic among youth is not as widespread as was once supposed, and that today's students have work attitudes much like those of the college generation of the early 1960s. (9; 10, p. 510; 32)

Additional pressures arise from within adolescents themselves. Indecision and uncertainty regarding the future create anxiety, and they must face the decision if they are to find relief. (19, p. 141) Failure to do so results in turmoil, instability, and a sense of personal failure. Most adolescents are extremely confused and unhappy until future plans begin to take shape. (40) (See the section on Erikson in Chapter 3.)

Part of the pressure to choose arises from environmental circumstances. Once adolescents stop going to school, they are expected to start supporting themselves and in some cases a whole family. Parental financial support, even if offered during college, is now usually withdrawn. Marriage plans provide additional motivation to get jobs. The longer adolescents are out of school and unemployed, the more they are criticized by parents and acquaintances for not going to work.

VOCATIONAL CHOICE AS A DEVELOPMENTAL TASK

Robert Havighurst (49) defines a developmental task as "a task which arises at or about a certain period in the life of the individual, successful achievement of which leads to his happiness and to success with later tasks, while failure leads to unhappiness in the individual, disapproval by the society, and difficulty with later tasks." (49, p. 2) One of the tasks of adolescence, according to Havighurst, is "to organize one's plans and energies in such a way as to begin an orderly career; to feel able to make a living." (49, p. 62) Actually, accomplishing this task during adolescence is only one stage in the process of vocational development. Havighurst emphasizes that the process occurs in six stages, the first two of which occur before adolescence. (33, p. 235) The outline in Table 20–1 includes only the first four stages in Havighurst's six-stage version of vocational development. (10, p. 498) In Havighurst's plan, preparation for vocational choice begins early, when children first start identifying with adult workers, when they acquire their concepts of work and vocations and are developing habits of industry. Without adequate ego ideals these things may never happen.

There are sound psychological reasons why this task of vocational choice is an important one. All people need to meet their emotional needs for recognition, praise, acceptance, approval, love, and independence. One way individuals do this is by taking on a vocational identity, by becoming "somebodies" whom others can recognize and by which others grant them emotional fulfillment. (79) Through identifying with a particular vocation, they find selfhood, self-realization, and self-fulfillment. To the extent that they succeed in their own and others' eyes, they gain self-satisfaction and recognition. In their search for identity and self-satisfaction they are strongly motivated to make a vocational choice that will contribute to their fulfillment. (68) (See Chapter 8.)

Table 20–1. Havighurst's stages of vocational development.

Age	Stage of Vocational Development
5–10	Identification with a worker: father, mother, other significant people Concept of working becomes an essential part of the ego ideal
10–15	Acquiring the basic habits of industry Learning to organize one's time and energy to get chores and school work done Learning to put work ahead of play in appropriate situations
15–25	Acquiring identity as a worker in the occupational structure Choosing and preparing for an occupation Getting work experience as a basis for occupational choice and for assurance of economic independence
25–40	Becoming a productive person Mastering the skills of one's occupation Moving up the ladder within one's occupation

Adapted from H. Borow, "Career Development," in *Understanding Adolescence*, 3d ed. Edited by J. F. Adams (Boston: Allyn and Bacon, 1976), p. 498.

For adolescents who are of a philosophical frame of mind, their vocation is one channel through which their life goals and purposes might be fulfilled. It is the reason for their existence, the particular niche they feel compelled to fill in the world. If they believe life has meaning and purpose, they strive to find and to live out that meaning and purpose by the way they spend their time, talents, and energy. One way is through the work they perform. Vocational choice not only involves "How can I make a living?"; it also implies "What am I going to do with my life?"

For adolescents whose concern is one of service—for meeting the needs of people or bettering the society in which they live—the choice of vocation will depend upon the needs they recognize as most important and can best satisfy through their work. So they seek a vocation in which they can be of service. For adolescents who try to be "practical," the choice involves discovering the types of work in which there are the most vacant positions, which pay the best money, in which they are most interested, and for which they are best qualified. Such choices are based primarily on economic motives, practical considerations, and personal interests and qualifications. For other youths, seeking a vocation becomes a means by which they show they are grown up, financially independent, emancipated from parents, and able to make it on their own. For them, going to work becomes a means of gaining entrance into the adult world.

Sometimes, however, no rational choice of vocation is made at all. (63, p. 270) Adolescents just go out and get the first job they can find that pays well; or they accept a job because a friend has recommended them for it or because it happens to be the only one that opens up and that they hear about. Under such circumstances vocational choice is happenstance rather than a thoughtful process. (112, p. 400) Adolescents may temporarily enjoy economic and other benefits such employment brings. Only later do they discover they are unhappy, ill suited to the tasks, and sacrificing their freedom and lives for doubtful benefits. They need to back up, reassess their goals, talents, and opportunities, and discover the ways these might be combined in meaningful and rewarding work. Elder feels that

vocational choice and commitment might be premature if they are made without self-appraisals, experience, and learning gained from exploration and trial. In some cases, early formation of a vocational identity may precede the crystallization of other identities and thus require considerable adjustment in subsequent years. (25, p. 108)

A minority of adolescents choose not to work at all, at least no more than they can help. Their rebellion against the values exemplified in the lives of adults the values of their society have convinced them that they should reduce their need for money as much as possible and lead simple but impoverished lives to give them the freedom to do as they please. Sometimes this means doing absolutely nothing; at other times it means engaging in what they feel are self-fulfilling activities, even though not remunerative. (112, p. 400) This kind of "dropping out" became almost epidemic during the 1960s, when adolescents from New York to California, Maine to Florida, Oregon to Arizona began packing their bags and drifting throughout the country. This trend slowly abated during the 1970s. (22, p. 282)

Under the best of circumstances choosing a vocation is an increasingly difficult task as society becomes more complex. *The Dictionary of Occupational Titles*
now lists more than 47,000 different occupations, most of which are unfamiliar.
(17, p. 379) But if at all possible adolescents need to make rational, considered
choices of vocations. If they fail to identify themselves with the kind of work for
which they are suited and in which they can find satisfaction and fulfillment, their
vocational nonidentity reflects their larger failure to discover their own identity.
In a sense they will have failed to discover what their own lives are all about.

Theories of Vocational Choice

A number of theorists have sought to describe the process of vocational development. The particular theories that will be discussed are those of Ginzberg,
(34, 35) Super, (101, 102, 103) and Holland. (54, 55)

GINZBERG'S COMPROMISE WITH REALITY THEORY

Eli Ginzberg and associates (34, 35) emphasize that making a vocational choice is
a developmental process that occurs not at a single moment but over a long
period. It involves a series of "subdecisions" that together add up to a vocational
choice. (35, p. 27) Each subdecision is important because each limits individuals'
subsequent freedom of choice and their abilities to achieve their original goals.
(70, p. 23) For example, a decision not to go to college and to take a commercial
course in high school makes it difficult later to decide to go to college. Extra
time, effort, and sometimes money must be expended to make up for deficiencies.
As children mature they gain knowledge and exposure to alternatives; they learn
to understand themselves and their environment, and are better able to make
rational choices. (35, p. 29) Ginzberg divides the process of occupational choice
into three stages. (108, p. 409)

FANTASY STAGE. The fantasy stage occurs up to age eleven. During this time
children imagine things they want to be without regard to needs, ability, training, employment opportunities, or any realistic considerations. They want to be
airplane pilots, teachers, doctors, nurses, and so forth.

TENTATIVE STAGE. The tentative stage spans ages eleven through eighteen
years and is further subdivided into four periods or substages. During the *interest period*, from eleven to twelve, children make their choices primarily in the
light of their likes and interests. This stage represents a transition between fantasy choice and tentative choice. The second period, the *capacities period* occurs
between about thirteen to fourteen years of age. During this period adolescents
become aware of role requirements, occupational rewards, and different means
of preparation. However, they are primarily thinking of their own abilities in
relationship to requirements. During the third period, the *value period*, from ages
fifteen to sixteen, adolescents attempt to relate occupational roles to their own
interests and values, to synthesize job requirements with their own values and
capacities. They consider both the occupation and their own interests. (76, p. 103)
The fourth and last stage, between ages seventeen and eighteen, is a *transition*

period, in which adolescents make transitions from tentative to realistic choices in response to pressures from school, peers, parents, colleges, and the circumstance of graduating from high school.

Realistic stage. During the realistic stage, from age eighteen on, adolescents seek further resolution of their problems of vocational choice. (107) This stage is further subdivided into a period of *exploration*, during which they make an intensive search to gain greater knowledge and understanding; a period of *crystallization*, in which they narrowly define a single set of choices and commit themselves; and a period of *specification*, in which a general choice, such as physicist, is further limited to a particular type of physicist.

Ginzberg's interviews were conducted primarily with adolescents from upper income families, who no doubt had a considerably greater range of choices. The process would take longer for these youths than for others because their education is extended. Lower income youths often have an earlier crystallization of occupational choice, even though their choices still seem to parallel those of the theoretical model. (35, chapter 11) Also, Ginzberg's observations were primarily of boys, although he concluded that girls parallel the first two stages, fantasy and tentative. Other research indicates that the transition to realism applies to both boys and girls, but that girls tend to keep their vocational plans more tentative and flexible than boys do. (47; 66, p. 179)

Ginzberg's theory suffers from rigidity with respect to the exact sequence, nature, and timing of the stages; thus, it may be too artificial and contrived. Other research, however, generally supports the broad outlines of the hypothesis, althogh it does not always support the chronological ages associated with Ginzberg's different stages. For example, a study of ninety-one adolescent boys in a "potential scientist pool" showed that after eleventh grade, thirty-four moved out of the program and seventeen moved in, but only five of those who moved in after grade eleven stayed in. One boy moved in after graduation and stayed in. (112, p. 398) This finding indicates that some boys made relatively stable vocational choices before grade eleven, whereas others had not made up their minds even after high school. It is difficult, therefore, to apply exact chronological ages to the periods Ginzberg outlines. Some relatively young adolescents show a high degree of maturity in making vocational choices; others evidence emerging maturity; while still others never seem to show the maturity necessary to match interests with capacities and training with job opportunities. (112, p. 398) Some people continue to change vocations throughout adulthood.

Ginzberg has made some recent reformulations of his theory to take these factors into account. He now acknowledges that career choices do not necessarily end with the first job and that some people remain occupationally mobile throughout their work histories. He also now emphasizes that some people—the economically disadvantaged and minority races especially—do not have as many choices as the upper classes do. (34, p. 175)

SUPER'S SELF-CONCEPT THEORY

Donald Super and associates (101, 102, 103) emphasize vocational choice and development as a continuing ongoing dynamic process. In this process individuals explore and establish vocational roles that give them the greatest opportunities for the expression of concepts of self that have been developed over the years.

Adolescence is a critical period for revising and building a new self-image and self-concept and for finding and assuming an occupational role in which individuals can express themselves in manners consistent with their concepts of self. Self-concepts may begin to take shape earlier, but they are focused and channeled into occupational choices during adolescence. (46, p. 63) The role of vocational guidance is to help adolescents develop appropriate images of themselves in the work world, and then to test this self-concept by choosing a vocation that will both make them happy and successful and contribute to society. (102) This view assumes that before wise vocational choices can be made, individuals must have realistic views of themselves in order to evaluate their own strengths and weaknesses. (52) Super postulates five major vocational tasks through which each individual must pass.

Crystallization: Formulation of ideas about work that are in accord with the individual's self-concept. 14–18 years.

Specification of a vocational preference by narrowing one's choice and taking the first steps to be able to enter an occupation. 18–20 years.

Implementation of vocational preference by finishing training and entering employment. 21–24 years.

Stabilization: Settling down to the appropriate career choice. 25–35 years.

Consolidation: Advancement and attainment of status. After age 35.

In achieving these vocational tasks, the individual's development, environment, and available opportunities are limiting factors in attaining self-realization. Super believes however, that individuals may be able to succeed in a wide variety of occupations consistent with their abilities. There are constellations of interests and abilities, and numerous occupations within these constellations. Through a process of reality testing individuals need to relate their interests and abilities to occupations. As they encounter new experiences they may have to readjust their self-concepts and implement this process again as a result of their changing career choices and performance.

Super's research with ninth-grade boys (101) indicates a great deal of instability, uncertainty, and immaturity of vocational choice at this age; therefore, most of the process of vocational development must take place after the individual enters high school. In some cases this process is not completed for ten or more years. One study with disadvantaged high school students revealed no change in the accuracy of work-value estimates and interest self-estimates from grades ten to twelve. (109) One wonders whether retesting after five more years would show much improvement.

Subsequent to his original research, Super tried to develop a means of ascertaining the vocational maturity of individuals of different age levels. He decided on three major indices of maturity: *planning orientation, resources for exploration,* and *information and decision making.* These criteria are now included in his *Career Development Inventory,* which counselors and others can use in the vocational guidance of young people. (103)

HOLLAND'S OCCUPATIONAL ENVIRONMENT THEORY

According to Holland's theory of vocational choice, (54, 55) people select occupations that afford environments consistent with their personality types; they are more apt to choose and remain in a field when personal and environmental characteristics are similar. (55)

Holland outlined six personality types: *realistic, intellectual, social, conventional, enterprising*, and *artistic*, and occupational environments compatible with these types. Holland measures personality types with a *self-directed search system*. (54) This system has six scales, each corresponding to one of Holland's personality types. Holland believes that responses to the lengthy inventory of items on each scale reveal individuals' vocational environmental preferences. Thus, individuals striving for a suitable career seek out those environments compatible with their patterns of personal orientations and exhibit these inclinations through their responses to the personality test items. According to Holland, then, it is possible to ascertain occupational orientations by the scores on the personality scales. (54, 55)

Before Holland's theory can be considered useful and valid in vocational counseling, more research needs to be conducted to test and refine it. Some confirmatory research evidence already offers partial support. (75, 99)

People Influencing Choice

PARENTS

Parents influence their adolescent's choice of vocation in a number of ways. (12, 98, 114) *One way is through direct inheritance:* a son or daughter inherits the parents' business, and it seems easier and wiser to continue the family business than to go off on their own. (53, 56) One study showed that 95 percent of boys who chose farming as a career were sons of farmers. (39, p. 149)

Parents exert influence by providing apprenticeship training. A father who is a carpenter teaches his trade to his son by taking him with him on the job or by asking a carpenter friend to let him serve an apprenticeship under him. In the case of low socioeconomic status families, the adolescent may not have any other choices. Many mothers or fathers of such families have taught their skills to their children.

Parents influence their children's interests and activities from the time they are young, by the play materials provided, by the encouragement or discouragement of hobbies and interests, by the activities they encourage their children to participate in, and by the total experiences they provide in the family. Sibling influence also is important in stimulating masculine or feminine interests. (103) A mother who is a musician exerts an influence on her child to take music lessons and to like music in a way that a nonmusician mother can never do. A father who is a professional football player usually wants his son to be exposed to football from the time the boy is little. An estimated 44 percent of physicians' sons choose medicine and 28 percent of lawyers' sons choose law, a far greater percentage than mere chance would allow for. (17, p. 391)

Parents provide role models for their children to follow. Even though the parent may not try to exert any conscious, direct influence, the influence by example is there, especially when the child identifies closely with the parent. Bell (7) and other researchers, (32, 45) have found that fathers who serve as the most positive occupational and overall role models exert the strongest and most positive influence on their sons' future occupations. Mortimer found that the combination of a prestigious paternal role model and a close father-son relationship engendered the most effective transmission of vocational values and the clearest impact on sons' occupational decisions. (72, p. 253) This means that fathers of low socioeconomic status do not exert as positive an influence because (1) they are not as close to their adolescents nor as actively involved in their care, and (2) their occupations are less prestigious. (93) They do not have the high occupational prestige that engenders great admiration from the children and encourages emulation. (13) Although there has been no research on the influence of fathers on the vocational choices of females, (65) some findings have emphasized the importance of the mother's occupational role in influencing a daughter's vocational decisions. (3, 105)

Parents sometimes direct, order, or limit the choices of their children by insisting they go to a certain school, enroll in a particular major, or start out on a predetermined career. Parents who do so without regard for the talents, interests, and desires of their adolescent may be condemning the youth to a life of work to which she or he is unsuited. Often an adolescent has no strong objections and accedes to parental wishes from a desire to please them and from not knowing what else to do. One of the motives of parents for taking such a course of action is try to get the child to take up the occupation that the parents were always interested in but never got to do: the parents live vicariously through the child. (112, p. 408) Or, because the parents have a vocation and have found satisfaction, they urge the adolescent to share their goals because they are sure she or he would like it too. Stories are legion of the father who insists his son attend his alma mater, join the same fraternity, play football as he did, and become a professional man like himself. The father can exert a lot of pressure by offering or withholding money or by getting his son into his school and fraternity.

Sometimes parental influence is less direct. *Parents influence adolescents to follow an occupation in the same status category or in a status category immediately above that which they occupy.* For example, a physician mother influences a daughter to be a physician or to choose another profession offering similar prestige and rewards. A mother who is a skilled worker may urge the girl to choose either the same or another skilled occupation. A father who is a clerical worker may urge a son to seek a position in the next higher category, managerial work. "It has been estimated that 67 percent of all boys choose an occupation in either their father's status category or the next higher one." (39, p. 149)

It is also true, however, that of the one-third who do not choose an occupation in their father's status category, a number circumvent the entire status structure through extensive education in order to rise far above their parents. In this way they move from blue collar positions into professions. Others become socially mobile downward, never aspiring or able to succeed like their parents.

PEERS

Studies of the relative influence of parents and peers on the educational plans of adolescents (relating to the level of vocation rather than to the particular job) reveal somewhat contradictory findings. Using adolescent perceptions of the educational expectations held by eleven different types of people as sources of data on parental and peer influences, Herriott (51) found the highest correlation between the adolescent's educational aspirations and perceived expectations of a same-age friend. In a study of occupational aspirations of high school students, however, Simpson (97) found that for both middle class and lower class boys "parental influence was more strongly related to aspirations than peer influences." (97, p. 521) Kandel and Lesser found a synthesis of these. (61) They found that mothers of both boys and girls have a higher level of agreement with their adolescents' educational plans than do best school friends. (The influence of the mother is approximately twice as high as that of the best school friend.) They also found that girls have higher levels of agreement with their mothers than do boys. *The majority of adolescents (57 percent) hold plans in agreement with those of their mothers and their friends.* Of adolescents who agree with parents, 76 percent also agree with peers. Of adolescents who disagree with parents, only 59 percent agree with peers. Kandel and Lesser conclude that friends reinforce parental aspirations because adolescents associate with peers whose goals are consistent with parental goals. This is substantiated by the fact that when parents have college aspirations for their children, 65 percent of their children's best school friends also have college plans; when parents have high school plans, 66 percent of their children's best school friends also have high school plans. The adolescents' interactions with peers support the values of parents as far as educational aspirations are concerned. (61, 76)

It has been found that the extent of upward mobility of working class adolescents depends upon the influences of both parents and peers. Working class adolescents are most likely to aspire to high-ranking occupations if they are influenced in this direction by both parents and peers, and least likely to be high aspirers if they are subjected to neither of these influences. (97)

SCHOOL PERSONNEL

To what extent do school personnel influence adolescents' vocational plans? A great deal, according to a study of college freshmen at the University of Maine. (59) In this study, students were requested to indicate from a list of nine individuals or group of individuals the ones they felt were most influential in their decision to select a particular field of study. Thirty-nine percent indicated that their high school teachers had been most influential in helping them make their decision. This represented the highest percentage of any of the alternative choices, with "other adult acquaintances," next in rank order of influence, accounting for 19 percent of the responses. The other 42 percent of responses were variously distributed in lesser amounts among the following seven alternatives: father; mother; elementary school teacher or principal; high school counselor, dean, or principal; college teacher; college counselor, dean or other nonteachers; and close friends. *Teachers exerted a major influence on the plans of college bound students during the later part of their high school career:* 75 percent of the University of Maine entering freshmen made vital decisions regarding their future after they started the eleventh grade in high school; 55 percent made their decision regarding a major field of study during the last year of high school. This study was of entering college freshmen only; studies among the general high school population reveal much greater parental influence and less influence by both counselors and teachers. (78; 11, p. 399) The college bound have a much closer rapport with teachers than do other students. Forty-one percent of the entering freshmen said they knew one or two high school teachers well enough to be personally friendly with them and to be able to talk over matters other than school affairs. Twenty-six percent of the students felt they knew three or four teachers this well. Twenty-four percent indicated they knew five or more high school teachers on this basis. (59)

Sex Roles and Vocational Choice

CULTURAL EXPECTATIONS

Adolescents are strongly influenced by societal expectations as to the type of work that males and females should do. Traditionally, women have been far more limited than men in the number and categories of jobs available to them. (92) In spite of gains, women still outnumber men 1.7 to 1 in the service occupations, 3 to 1 in clerical jobs, and 5 to 1 in elementary level teaching. Ninety-seven percent of nurses, 80 percent of librarians, and 61 percent of social and recreation workers are women. Only 10 percent of lawyers and judges and 12 percent of physicians and surgeons are women. (110) (See Figure 20–1, Table 12–3, and the discussion of masculine-feminine roles in Chapter 12.)

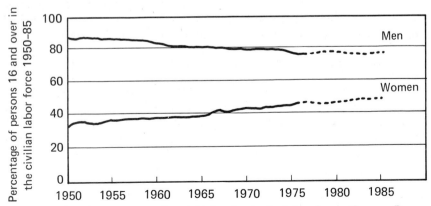

Figure 20–1.   Percentage of females and of males in the labor force. (Source: Bureau of Labor Statistics.)

This picture is being modified. Strict government enforcement of equal employment opportunity laws is at least assuring women opportunities in hitherto restricted fields. Any woman who strives for a particular position is legally entitled to it if she is qualified. Jobs that women are now occupying that before were restricted to men include commercial airplane pilots, subway train operators, baseball umpires, and jockeys. During the past decade the percent of women in all jobs in the United States has increased. (16, p. 57) However, there are still some professions that have a long way to go before they give full equality to women.

FEMALE MOTIVATIONS

Some women, especially the less educated, are not highly motivated to succeed in a full-time, long-term career. (16) Some want only to prepare for an occupation before and for a time after marriage, and as financial insurance in case anything should happen to their husband. (30) However, there is a rapidly increasing trend for females to work full-time throughout much of their lives; therefore, an increasing percentage of adolescent girls choose occupations that indicate a permanent, major interest in a career. (1, 29, 39)

One intensive study over four years of one class in the women's college of a private coeducational university showed that about 40 percent were career oriented by the time of graduation, 46 percent were noncareerists, and the other 14 percent were still confused about their goals. (3) Figure 20–2 shows the percentage in each of five categories at the time of graduation. (3, p. 466) As can be seen, only 18 percent of the women were careerists when they entered college but an additional 22 percent were converts who developed career aspirations during college. Thirty-three percent of the women were noncareerists from the

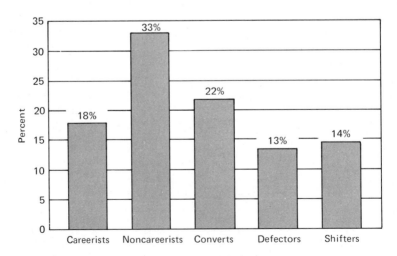

Figure 20–2.   Career aspirations of female students by the time of graduation (N = 87). (Adapted from S. S. Angrist, "Variations in Women's Adult Aspirations during College," *Journal of Marriage and the Family* 34[1972]: 466. Used by permission.)

beginning, with their interests totally centered on selecting a mate and raising a family. This group was joined by 13 percent who became defectors and moved away from career interests by their senior year. The 14 percent classified as shifters oscillated between career and noncareer throughout college. (3, p. 466) It is evident that college exerted a strong influence to enter careers. Although few women began college career oriented, many became so by their senior year. The result was a fairly equal distribution of careerists (40 percent) and non-careerists (46 percent) by the end of college.

What about these women after graduation? To what extent were they able to fulfill their aspirations or did they have to change them? To what extent were they frustrated in their achievement? A follow-up study seven years after graduation revealed the following: 41 percent showed a distinct correlation between aspirations and actual life styles; 32 percent showed a definite inconsistency; that is, they were career aspirants with family styles or family aspirants with career styles; 28 percent of the class exhibited the working pattern over the seven years. These were women workers who fit their work periods around family exigencies and found that geographic location hampered their opportunity to find agreeable employment. Some of these women aspired to careers, whereas others were primarily family aspirers. (1, p. 10) As to preferences and plans for the future, 48 percent were careerists with definite plans for specific careers; 31 percent were oriented mainly toward rearing children, having leisure activities and working only occasionally; and 22 percent envisioned keeping their partial work commitments or returning to the labor force soon, but without definite career goals. (1, p. 10) It is evident from these figures that seven years after graduation an increasing number of women saw themselves as careerists and wanted to work despite having young children. It is significant that almost half of these alumnae exhibited clear career patterns at this stage in the life cycle. (1, p. 13)

Many highly intelligent, capable women are still willing to settle for secretarial and other positions below their levels of ability because they don't want to spend the rest of their lives working. (5) Research indicates that some are afraid of career success because it is considered unfeminine. (57, 86, 94) This fear that having a career is masculine has led Margaret Mead to remark that in our culture "boys are unsexed by failure and girls by success." (69) Gradually, however, as sex role stereotypes are being overcome, more females are able to work for career success without fear of being considered unfeminine.

Other research on women who became wives, mothers, and career people in one indicates that these women more often come from higher social class backgrounds than do their conventional counterparts. (6, 87, 88) Their parents are often ambitious for them. (6, p. 532) They also tend to be only children or first-born children or are separated from siblings by a large age gap, so that they manifest what has been termed the *only-lonely child* syndrome. (6; 87, p. 25) There is often greater separation from parents or greater overall tension in their family backgrounds. (87) The resulting picture is of highly capable, creative women who are able to find personal fulfillment through both careers and family, in response to the way they were influenced and socialized while growing up.

Other Crucial Determinants of Vocational Choice

INTELLIGENCE

Mental ability has been shown to be important to vocational choice in several ways. (24, 26) *First, intelligence has been shown to be related to the decision-making ability of the individual.* (20) Bright adolescents are more likely to make vocational choices in keeping with their intellectual abilities, interests, capacities, and opportunities to receive training. The less bright are more likely to make unrealistic choices. They more often choose glamorous or high-prestige occupations for which they are not qualified or even interested, solely because of the prestige involved. They more often choose what they think parents want them to do or what peers consider desirable, rather than what they are capable of doing. (41; 58, p. 194)

In one study, 111 students were interviewed during the eighth, tenth, and twelfth grades and asked to write three occupational preferences. They were then classified by ability to do college work as indicated on the Otis Mental Ability Test. The results showed that a high percentage preferred professional and administrative work and that some, particularly those in the lowest aptitude levels, stated unrealistically high aspiration levels. (41)

Second, intelligence has been shown to relate to the level of aspiration. Students who show superior academic ability and performance tend to aspire to higher occupational choices than those with lesser ability. (80)

Third, intelligence is related to the ability of the individual to succeed or fail in a given occupation. For this reason, the vocational counselor usually measures level of intelligence as a beginning in assessing the vocational qualifications of a given student, because some occupations require a higher ability than others. But a high IQ is no absolute guarantee of vocational success, nor is a low IQ a prediction of failure. For one thing, the measurement may be in error. (See Chapter 19.) For another thing, interest, motivation, other abilities, and various personality traits determine success as much as intelligence does. A high IQ shows only that the individual has the capacity to succeed as far as intelligence is concerned. But actual achievement must also be taken into account. Research demonstrates that bright high-achieving students are generally superior to bright, underachieving students in study habits, aspiration levels, and in professionally oriented career expectations. (91) A bright individual who is poorly motivated and indifferent may fail in an occupation, whereas an individual of average mental ability who is highly motivated, industrious, and conscientious may overachieve and far surpass the brighter person.

Furthermore, where do the IQ requirements for different occupations begin? There is actually a great deal of overlap in tested intelligence among workers in various jobs. (8, p. 427) How "smart" do you have to be to be a miner, an accountant, a physician? Some people who become physicians, teachers, engineers, or business executives show on tests that their intelligence is much below average for their professions.

Educational institutions are faced with a dilemma in deciding on the cutoff point below which they will not admit students. Whereas SAT scores are helpful in predicting possibilities of success or failure for groups of students, they are no sure indicator of the individual. Counselors must be extremely cautious in interpreting test results, particularly in predicting success or failure based upon mental ability alone. Many individuals who are now successful in professional fields would not even be admitted to the training programs if they had to pass the entrance exams today. (82, p. 440)

APTITUDES AND SPECIAL ABILITIES

Different occupations require different aptitudes and special abilities. For example, mechanical ability tests may cover information required of mechanics: types of gears, kinds of wrenches, gauges, strengths of materials, sizes of fasteners, or certain aptitudes such as manual and finger dexterity. Some occupations require strength, others speed, others good eye-hand coordination, or good spatial visualization. Some require special talent such as artistic, musical, or verbal skills. Some fields require creativity, originality, autonomy; others require conformity, cooperation, ability to take direction. Possession or lack of certain aptitudes may be crucial in immediate job success or in the possibility of success with training and experience. (70, p. 141)

The exact measurement of some aptitudes, however, is not an exact science; therefore, it cannot always be determined which people are most likely to succeed in particular occupations. (50) The fault lies generally with the tests used. Droege (23) gave the widely used General Aptitude Test battery to more than 35,000 students in grades nine through twelve. Two years after graduation he obtained ratings on job or college success. The predictive ability of the test proved low. For such occupations as clerk, teller, cosmetologist, and service station attendant it was insignificant. (23) Before relying too much on aptitude tests, therefore, both counselors and students should be certain that the instruments used are valid measurements of the aptitudes tested.

INTERESTS

Interest is another factor considered important to vocational success. The theory is—and it is valid—that the more interested people are in their work, the more likely they will succeed. To put it another way, the more their interests parallel those who are already successful in a field, the more likely they are to be successful too, all other things being equal. Vocational interest tests are based upon this last principle: they measure clusters of interests similar to those of successful people in the field to predict the possibilities of success. The individual is counseled to consider vocations in the fields of greatest interest.

Intelligence, ability, opportunities, and other factors must be related to interests for success in a field. An individual may be interested in medicine but not have the ability or opportunity to become an M.D.; this person may then have to choose a career as a laboratory technician, physical therapist, or some related occupation. Whereas interests point to the field of inquiry, ability, opportunity, and other factors may have to point to the particular job choice within that field. Factor analysis of the Strong Vocational Interest Blank (100) indicates that interests may be subdivided and grouped to some degree by level. There are professional-scientific, professional-technical, and subprofessional-technical groups, as well as others. Interests are related to both the field and level of occupational choice. Interests that are based on abilities are stronger and more realistic than those influenced primarily by such things as prestige factors and group values.

Research substantiates the finding that there is no general correlation between interests and aptitudes. (31) About one-fourth of all high school students show from a fair to a high relationship between interests and aptitudes. Other students show little or negative correlation between the two factors. This means that both interests and aptitudes must be considered in making wise vocational choices. (31)

JOB OPPORTUNITIES

Being interested does not mean that jobs are available. Some employment fields, such as agricultural workers, are becoming smaller; others, such as clerical workers, are becoming larger. (21) This means youths need to control interests as well as be controlled by them, for interests and job availability are not synonymous. (88; 112, p. 55) Figure 20–3 shows the projected growth from 1976 to 1985 in the number of workers needed in various types of occupations. (111) As can be seen, the maximum growth will be in clerical and white collar occupations. Figure 20–4 shows the continued shift toward white collar occupations.

What are the employment opportunities in the professions? Table 20–2 shows projected needs to 1990. (111) The number one employment opportunity in terms of total job openings per year is in kindergarten and elementary education; registered nurses are second, accountants are third, practical nurses are fourth, and lawyers are fifth. (111) It is obvious that the greatest opportunities are in the health fields.

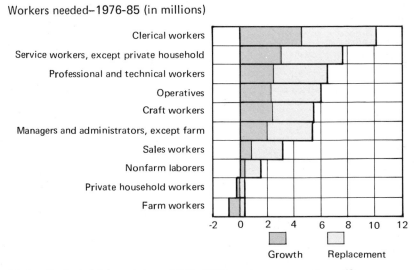

Figure 20–3.   Projected job openings, 1976–1985, various occupations. (Source: Bureau of Labor Statistics.)

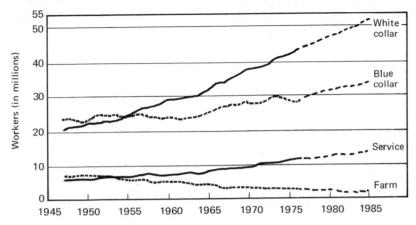

Figure 20–4. The shift toward white collar occupations through 1985. Fourteen- and fifteen-year-olds are included prior to 1958 only. (Source: Bureau of Labor Statistics.)

Table 20–2. Projected growth, various professions, 1978–1990.

	Latest Employment (1978 Estimate)	Average Annual Openings to 1990		Latest Employment (1978 Estimate)	Average Annual Openings to 1990
Administration			**Teachers**		
Accountants[3]	985,000	61,000	College	673,000	11,000
Bank officers,			Kindergarten, ele-		
managers[6]	330,000	28,000	mentary school[1]	1,322,000	86,000
Buyers	115,000	7,400	School counselors	45,000	1,700
City managers	3,300	350	Secondary school	1,087,000	7,200
Credit managers	49,000	2,200			
Health admin-			**Mathematics**		
istrators[10]	180,000	18,000	Actuaries	9,000	500
Hotel managers,			Mathematicians	33,500	1,000
assistants	168,000	8,900	Statisticians	23,000	1,500
Public-relations			**Scientists**		
workers	131,000	7,500	Astronomers	2,000	40
Purchasing agents	185,000	13,400	Biochemists	20,000	900
Urban planners	17,000	800	Chemists	143,000	6,100
			Geologists	31,000	1,700
Computer Specialists			Geophysicists	11,000	600
Computer			Life scientists	215,000	11,200
operators	666,000	12,500	Meteorologists	7,300	300
Computer repairers	63,000	5,400	Oceanographers	3,600	150
Programers	247,000	9,200	Physicists	44,000	1,000
Systems analysts	182,000	7,900	Soil scientists	3,500	180
Engineers			**Health Services**		
Aerospace	60,000	1,800	Chiropractors	18,000	1,500
Chemical	50,000	1,800	Dental assistants	150,000	11,000
Civil	155,000	7,800	Dental hygienists	35,000	6,000
Electrical	300,000	10,500	Dental lab		
Industrial	185,000	8,000	technicians	47,000	2,800
Mechanical	200,000	7,500	Dentists	120,000	5,500
Petroleum	17,000	900	Dietitians	35,000	3,300

Table 20–2 (cont.)

	Latest Employment (1978 Estimate)	Average Annual Openings to 1990		Latest Employment (1978 Estimate)	Average Annual Openings to 1990
Health Services (cont.)			Food technologists	15,000	500
Licensed practical			Forestry technicians	13,700	700
nurses[4]	518,000	60,000	Range managers	3,700	200
Medical-lab			Soil		
workers	210,000	14,800	conservationists	9,300	450
Operating room			Surveyors,		
technicians	35,000	2,600	technicians	62,000	2,300
Optometrists	21,000	1,600	Other Professions		
Pharmacists	135,000	7,800	Actors	13,400	850
Physical thera-			Airplane pilots	76,000	3,800
pists, aides	42,500	3,100	Air-traffic		
Physicians,			controllers	21,000	700
osteopaths[9]	405,000	19,000	Architects	54,000	4,000
Podiatrists	8,000	600	Dancers	8,000	550
Registered			Floral designers	56,000	4,200
nurses[2]	1,060,000	85,000	Foresters	31,200	1,400
Veterinarians	33,500	1,700	Funeral directors,		
X-ray			embalmers	45,000	2,200
technologists	100,000	9,000	Industrial		
			designers	13,000	550
Merchant Marine			Interior designers	79,000	3,600
Officers	13,500	700	Landscape		
Sailors	24,800	250	architects	14,000	1,100
			Lawyers[5]	487,000	37,000
Social Sciences			Librarians	142,000	8,000
Anthropologists	7,000	350	Musicians	127,000	8,900
Economists	130,000	7,800	Newspaper		
Geographers	10,000	500	reporters	45,000	2,400
Historians	23,000	700	Personnel, labor		
Political scientists	14,000	500	relations	405,000	17,000
Psychologists	130,000	6,700	Photographers	93,000	3,800
Sociologists	19,000	600	Radio, TV		
			announcers	27,000	850
Technicians			Singers	22,000	1,600
Drafters	296,000	11,000	Social workers[8]	385,000	22,000
Engineering, sci-					
ence technicians[7]	600,000	23,400			

Note. Superscripts indicate rank order. Adapted from Bureau of Labor Statistics, Department of Labor, *Occupational Outlook Handbook, 1980–1981.* Washington, D.C.: U.S. Government Printing Office, 1980.

JOB REWARDS AND SATISFACTIONS

One factor to consider in selecting a vocation is the financial reward. (27, 73) Table 20–3 shows an estimated starting pay for 1980 graduates with bachelor's degrees in different fields. Actual salaries vary in different parts of the country.

Today's young people are interested in job satisfactions other than money, however. Yankelovich has listed the top ten job criteria for young working people according to a nationwide survey. (115, p. 102)

- Friendly, helpful co-workers (70 percent)
- Work that is interesting (70 percent)
- Opportunity to use your mind (65 percent)

Table 20–3.   Starting monthly pay for graduates of 1980 with bachelor's degrees.

Field	Average Salary 1980
Engineering	$1,421
Accounting	1,260
Sales, marketing	1,150
Business administration	1,039
Liberal arts	1,018
Chemistry	1,259
Mathematics, statistics	1,212
Economics, finance	1,082
Other fields	1,201

Adapted from U.S. Department of Labor statistics.

- Work results that you can see (62 percent)
- Pay that is good (61 percent)
- Opportunities to develop skills/abilities (61 percent)
- Participation in decisions regarding job (58 percent)
- Getting help needed to do the job well (55 percent)
- Respect for organization you work for (55 percent)
- Recognition for a job well done (54 percent)

Many of the job criteria above cannot be ascertained before a vocation or a particular job is selected, but become important once the individual is on the job.

Socioeconomic Status and Prestige Factors

CHOOSING THE FAMILIAR

A study of the occupations chosen by over 1,000 boys and girls in a rural county in New York State and about 250 boys and girls from a school in Brooklyn showed that only 150 occupations were chosen by boys and even fewer by girls. (84) The occupations chosen could be grouped into two categories: those that were familiar to the rural community and those that were glamorous and prestigious.

Socioeconomic status tends to influence the knowledge and understanding youths have of different occupations. Middle class parents are more able than working class parents to develop broad vocational interests and awareness of opportunities beyond the local community. Socially disadvantaged adolescents have seen less, read less, heard less about, and experienced less variety in their environments in general and have fewer opportunities than the socially privileged. (8) As a result low socioeconomic status males and females are inclined to take the only job they know about at the time they enter the labor market. (19, 71)

The socioeconomic and cultural background of youths influences their job knowledge and their job preference. (43) Furthermore, local variations in occupational choice tend to correspond with variations in the economic structure: the larger the proportion of people employed in a particular kind of job in a city, the larger the proportion of youths who desire to go into that occupation. (25, p. 109) Whether an adolescent lives in a rural or urban environment is also a factor in vocational choice. Urban boys have higher occupational expectations than do rural boys. One reason is that youths in rural areas lack immediate contact with persons holding high status positions. (95)

PRESTIGE AND VALUE

Adolescents may also say they want to go into an occupation simply because it sounds glamorous or has high prestige. (10, p. 514; 70, p. 26) There are at least five commonly accepted assumptions about occupational values in our culture: (1) white collar work is superior; (2) self-employment is superior; (3) clean occupations are superior; (4) the importance of a business occupation depends upon the size of the business; and (5) personal service is degrading: it is better to be employed by an enterprise than to do the same work for an individual. (58, p. 216)

There have been other attempts at classifying values. One method has been to group values into three major value clusters: people oriented, extrinsic reward oriented, and self-expression oriented. One longitudinal study of youths in eighth, tenth, and twelfth grades showed that both boys and girls ranked self-expressive values first, followed by people-oriented values for girls and reward-oriented values for boys (people-oriented values were in last place for boys). (42) A survey of 1,800 pupils in ninth and again in tenth grade showed self-expression important to nearly all pupils. (106) Another study compared the occupational values held by pupils in junior high school and their parents and the values they held two years later. The parents consistently ranked self-expression first. In junior high school, girls placed helping others first, whereas boys placed the greatest emphasis on extrinsic rewards; but two years later both boys and girls agreed with the self-expression preference of their parents. (77) Apparently the parents' values determined what the adolescents ended up valuing.

Another study shows the influence of community values on children and youths. One researcher had twenty boys in each grade rank eleven jobs from 1 through 20 in order of their standing in the community. Boys in first and second grade equated the dangerous job of being a police officer with prestige, but lacked a well-defined status hierarchy. By third grade a highly individual status hierarchy began to emerge. In grades four to six, students used service to the community as the criterion for ranking from top to bottom. In seventh grade, service to the community was still the most frequently used criterion, but by eighth and ninth grades money, job attributes, psychological rewards, amount of education needed to enter the job, and power were also selected criteria. By tenth grade the boys assigned low rankings to jobs employing inferior quality people. In the last three years of high school the boys' rankings were similar to the rankings of the adult population in general. Apparently the social status ascribed to various occupations in our culture is crystallized in the minds of youths by grade ten. (44)

SOCIAL CLASS AND ASPIRATIONS

Research over the years has shown that middle class youths tend to choose occupations with higher status than do lower class youths. (15, 62) In evaluating status, the father's occupational level is of particular importance to both sons' and daughters' occupational preferences, whereas the position of the working mother is significant only for the occupational preferences of daughters. (62) Furthermore, when academic ability is held constant, class differences in occupational aspirations remain. For comparable levels of ability, those from higher social class backgrounds continue to show a greater orientation toward high-prestige occupations. (15)

There are a number of considerations in determining why this is so. For one thing, to aspire to a position is one thing; really to expect to achieve it is another. Lower class youths more often than middle class youths aspire to jobs they do not expect to achieve, but the fact that lower class youths realize the remoteness of reaching their goal makes them lower their level of aspirations. (7, 96) The greatest downward revision between aspiration and expected achievement is among sons of manual workers and farmers. (14)

The individual's preference hierarchy may also be at odds with the general consensus. This is another way of saying that some lower class youths do not ascribe the same status to job success and work as do middle class Americans. (83) Also, people with a lower class background sometimes consider certain kinds of blue collar work more desirable than white collar. (14)

Still another factor enters in. There is a correlation between academic ability and socioeconomic status. The higher the status, the higher the academic performance; and, as already discussed, the better the students' academic performances, the more prestigious the occupations to which they aspire. (24, 26) Apparently students see their high academic ability as providing them access to high prestige occupations. Table 20–4 shows the relationships among occupational aspiration, social class, and academic aptitude as revealed in one study. (14) Occupational aspiration is related to both social class and academic aptitude.

RACE AND ASPIRATIONS

When race is considered apart from social class, there is no conclusive evidence that race alone is the determinative factor in occupational aspirations. Goldstein

Table 20–4.   Mean occupational aspiration by social class and academic aptitude.*

Social Class	Academic Aptitude		
	High	Medium	Low
High	7.96	7.96	5.73
Middle	6.86	5.88	5.09
Low	6.75	5.17	4.91

* 9 = highest prestige; 1 = lowest prestige

Adapted from F. G. Caro and C. T. Pihlblad, "Aspirations and Expectations: A Reexamination of the Bases for Social Class Differences in the Occupational Orientations of Male High School Students," *Sociology and Social Research* 49 (1965): 465–475. Used by permission.

(36) summarized the findings of four studies and found that two studies showed that black males had lower aspirations than white males, and two studies showed that they did not. Two studies found that black girls had lower aspirations than did white girls, and one study showed they had higher aspirations. Thus, the hypothesis that black youths have lower aspirations than white youths is not proven. (36, p. 70) However, black youths of lower socioeconomic status have lower aspirations just as do white youths of lower status. (8, 11) Regardless of aspirations, there are fewer employment opportunities for youths than for adults, and fewer opportunities for blacks than for whites. (2, 74) In his study of low class delinquent and nondelinquent black adolescent males, Picou and staff (81) found that both the delinquent and nondelinquent respondents had rather high prestige occupational goals, but the majority of both groups felt that lack of financial resources for higher education was a major impediment to the attainment of their goals. More delinquents than nondelinquents felt that their race, their lack of intellectual capability, and poor job opportunities would have a deleterious effect on the attainment of their occupational aspirations. (See Chapter 21 for additional information.) The researchers emphasize that the occupational aspirations of many of these black youths were unrealistic. They conclude:

> This finding may reflect the vicious circle of poverty of all racial and ethnic categories. It can be summarized as follows: the lower class youngster is reared in an environment that emphasizes occupational and economic success. Being inculcated with these cultural values, he develops goals and values that imply future social mobility and achievement. However, because his parents lack the financial resources to insure the most important prerequisite for attainment—higher educational training —the youngster fails to realize his goals and plans for his future. Thus, he is forced to seek employment in low-paying unskilled occupations and once again the vicious circle of poverty begins with his children. (81, p. 296)

Conclusions

Choosing and preparing for a vocation is one of the most important developmental tasks of adolescence. Done wisely and realistically, it enables individuals to enter vocations for which they are well suited, in which they find satisfaction and fulfillment, and which are needed by society. Done haphazardly and foolishly, it leads to frustration, discontent, unhappiness, and social disapproval.

The process is often a complicated one. Ginzberg (34, 35) shows insight in emphasizing that it is a long-term process comprising many small decisions, each of which affects the next decision and further limits subsequent choices. Choices made early in high school affect the availability of later options. Thus, there is a fatalistic element to the process: individuals do not have complete freedom, but are limited by what they have already done and are also subject to many influences in the present. This is more true of low socioeconomic status adolescents, who are caught in a series of circumstances, some of which they are powerless to control. Adolescents from higher socioeconomic status groups are more fortunate because they have more options open to them and more resources to use in taking advantage of options.

Super (101, 102, 103) has made an important contribution in showing the relationship between the development of a self-concept and finding a suitable vocational role.

It is doubtful that a male in our work-oriented, career-conscious culture can find an acceptable identity apart from a successful occupation. It is highly important, therefore, that every effort be made to assist the adolescent boy in choosing a vocation, preparing for it, and becoming established in it.

What about girls? It is becoming more and more vital also for the adolescent girl to find a vocational identity apart from her marital and parenthood roles, first, because many women desire such identities apart from marriage and motherhood and are unhappy if they don't have them; and second, because it is more and more an economic necessity prior to marriage, during marriage, after parenthood, or during widowhood. Research tends to show, however, that many girls are motivated to enter only temporary, part-time careers, occupations often below the level of their abilities. Because they hope to get married they do not aspire to the higher professions. It would seem logical to assume, therefore, that such women never find maximum satisfaction from their occupations. In fact many find them extremely tiring, frustrating, and unrelated to their real interests or capacities. If a woman, in making marriage her career, neglects to prepare herself for an economic career consistent with her interests and capabilities, she will find little fulfillment in work pursuits at whatever stage of life she goes to work. It would seem wiser to prepare for both marriage and an occupation, recognizing that if she chooses or is forced to do both, she ought to strive for maximum fulfillment in both, just as the man is able to do.

Because parents apparently still play a major role in influencing the vocational choices of their adolescents, it seems obvious that vocational guidance ought to be directed to parents as well as their young people. Informational, educational, guidance, and counseling services for parents provided as part of the regular services of the schools would better enable parents to fulfill their guidance function. Some schools are already conducting meetings, conferences, workshops, and short courses for parents; more schools need to assume similar responsibilities.

School teachers often exert a more important influence over pupils than do school guidance personnel. This means that one approach to better guidance is to give all teachers maximum training in vocational guidance. This way, professional counselors will be relieved of assuming the total burden. Many teachers already do a superb job, but, unfortunately, the total effort of others is to persuade the better pupils to enter the teacher's field, whether or not this would be a wise thing.

Too many young people unrealistically choose prestige professions or those with which they are most familiar, without enough regard for their real interests and abilities or the social need for such occupations. Public school teaching is one best example. Thousands of girls, particularly, prepare to teach because it is a fairly prestigious profession open to women and has acceptable financial rewards. The fact that it is now an overcrowded profession also needs to be taken into account. (111) Many highly skilled occupations and trades, not as prestigious but more remunerative, remain open to both sexes. Such occupations do not require college training but intensive vocational training; therefore, schools need to put greater emphasis upon vocational preparation and less on preparing the majority of students to enter college. Furthermore, because so many adolescents are unfamiliar with many of the skills required in a rapidly growing technological culture, major efforts need to be made in acquainting them with these possibilities. This way, more youths will be led to prepare for positions that are needed and in which they can find employment. One of the frustrations of modern college students is to spend four years in college only to have difficulty in finding employment once they graduate. More will be said about the employment of adolescents in the following chapter.

Panel Discussion

Invite several local school guidance counselors to class to discuss the subject of vocational guidance of adolescents. The panel might include also a representative from the college student guidance and/or counseling center. Several student representatives from the class may want to meet with the instructor to decide on how the panel discussions are to be handled. There are several procedures from which to choose.

1. Give the panel a free hand to discuss the subject in any way they see fit.
2. Assign specific subtopics to the panel.
3. Give panel members carefully prepared questions ahead of time.
4. Let members of the class ask questions of the panel as a basis for discussion.
5. Use a combination of the methods above.

Bibliography

1. Almquist, E. M., and Angrist, S. S. "Women's Career Aspirations and Achievements: College and Seven Years After." Paper presented at the American Sociological Association Meetings, Chicago, September 1977.

2. *The American Almanac* (The Statistical Abstract of the United States), 2d ed. New York: Grosset and Dunlap, 1972.

3. Angrist, S. S. "Variations in Women's Adult Aspirations during College." *Journal of Marriage and the Family* 34 (1972): 465–468.

4. Bardwick, J. M. *The Psychology of Women: A Study of Bio-Cultural Conflicts.* New York: Harper and Row, 1971.

5. Bardwick, J. M. et al. *Feminine Personality and Conflict.* Monterey, Calif.: Brooks/Cole Publishing Co., 1970.

6. Bebbington, A. C. "The Function of Stress in the Establishment of the Dual-Career Family." *Journal of Marriage and the Family* 35 (1973): 530–537.

7. Bell, A. P. "Role Modeling of Fathers in Adolescence and Young Adulthood." *Journal of Counseling Psychology* 16 (1969): 3–35.

8. Bernard, H. W. *Adolescent Development.* Scranton, Pa.: Intext Educational Publishers, 1971.

9. Borow, H. "Apathy, Unrest and Change: the Psychology of the 1960's." In *Vocational Guidance and Human Development.* Edited by E. L. Herr. Boston: Houghton Mifflin, 1974.

10. ———. "Career Development." *Understanding Adolescence.* 3d ed. Edited by J. F. Adams. Boston: Allyn and Bacon, 1976, pp. 489–523.

11. Brody, E. B. *Minority Group Ado-* lescents in the United States. Baltimore: Williams & Wilkins, 1968.

12. Brunkan, R. J. "Perceived Parental Attitudes and Parental Identification in Relation to Field of Vocational Choice." *Journal of Counseling Psychology* 12 (1965): 39–47.

13. Buehler, C. J. et al. "A Cross National Application of a Model of Adolescent Self-Evaluation." Paper presented at the American Sociological Association Meeting, August 1974.

14. Caro, F. G., and Pihlblad, C. T. "Social Class, Formal Education, and Social Mobility." *Sociology and Social Research* 48 (1964): 428–439.

15. ———. "Aspirations and Expectations: A Reexamination of the Bases for Social Class Differences in the Occupational Orientations of Male High School Students." *Sociology and Social Research* 49 (1965): 465–475.

16. "A Close-Up of Women in U.S. . . . and Ways Their Status is Changing." *U.S. News & World Report,* 8 December 1975.

17. Conger, J. J. *Adolescence and Youth.* New York: Harper and Row, 1973.

18. Cosby, A. G., and Picou, J. S. "Place, Residence, Class, and the Vocational Expectations of Adolescents in Four Deep-South States." *Vocational Guidance Quarterly* (March 1971).

19. Davis, E. "Careers as Concerns of Blue-Collar Girls." In *Blue-Collar World.* Edited by A. B. Shostak and W. Gomberg. Englewood Cliffs, N.J.: Prentice-Hall, 1964, pp. 154–164.

20. Dilley, J. S. "Decision-Making Ability and Vocational Maturity." *Personnel and Guidance Journal* 44 (1965): 423–427.

21. Donovan, J. "Job Requirements and Growth, 1968–1980." *Time*, 1971.

22. Dreyfus, E. A. *Adolescence: Theory and Experience*. Columbus, Ohio: Charles E. Merrill Publishing Co., 1976.

23. Droege, R. C. "GATB Longitudinal Validation Study." *Journal of Counseling Psychology* 15 (1968): 41–47.

24. Elder, G. H. *Adolescent Socialization and Personality Development*. Chicago: Rand McNally & Co., 1968.

25. ———. "Achievement Motivation and Intelligence in Occupational Mobility: A Longitudinal Analysis." *Sociometry* 31 (1968): 327–354.

26. ———. "Occupational Level, Motivation, and Mobility: A Longitudinal Analysis." *Journal of Counseling Psychology* 15 (1968): 1–7.

27. ———. "Occupational Mobility, Life Patterns, and Personality." *Journal of Health and Social Behavior* 10 (1969): 308–323.

28. ———. "Socialization and Ascent in a Racial Minority." *Youth Society* (September 1970): 74–109.

29. Epstein, G. F. *Woman's Place: Options and Limits in Professional Careers*. Berkeley: University of California Press, 1970.

30. Epstein, G. F., and Bronzadt, A. L. "Female Freshmen View Their Roles as Women." *Journal of Marriage and the Family* 34 (1972): 671–672.

31. Ewens, W. P. "Relationship of Interest to Aptitude by Profiles and by Interest Areas." In *Adolescents and the American High School*. Edited by R. F. Purnell. New York: Holt, Rinehart and Winston, 1970, pp. 444–451.

32. Freidson, E., ed. *The Professions and Their Prospects*. Beverly Hills, Calif.: Sage Publications, 1973.

33. Gallatin, J. E. *Adolescence and Individuality*. New York: Harper and Row, 1975.

34. Ginzberg, E. "Toward a Theory of Occupational Choice: A Restatement." *Vocational Guidance Quarterly* 20 (1972): 169–176.

35. Ginzberg, E. et al. *Occupational Choice: An Approach to a General Theory*. New York: Columbia University Press, 1951.

36. Goldstein, B. *Low Income Youth in Urban Areas*. New York: Holt, Rinehart and Winston, 1967.

37. "Good News for '77 Graduates: More Openings, at Better Pay." *U.S. News & World Report*, 21 February 1977.

38. Gottlieb, D. *Youth and the Meaning of Work*. University Park, Pa.: Institute for the Study of Human Development, Center for Youth Studies and Social Policy, Pennsylvania State University, 1973.

39. Gottlieb, D., and Ramsey, C. E. *The American Adolescent*. Homewood, Ill.: Dorsey Press, 1964.

40. "Graduates and Jobs: A Grave New World." *Time*, 24 May 1971, pp. 49–59.

41. Gribbons, W. D., and Lohnes, P. "Occupational Preferences and Measured Intelligence." *Vocational Guidance Quarterly* 14 (1966): 211–214.

42. ———. *Emerging Careers*. New York: Teachers College Press, 1968.

43. Grigg, C. M., and Middleton, R. "Community of Orientation and Occupational Aspirations of Ninth Grade Students." *Social Forces* 38 (1968): 303–308.

44. Gunn, B. "Children's Conceptions of Occupational Prestige." *Personnel and Guidance Journal* 42 (1964): 558–563.

45. Hall, R. *Occupations and the Social Structure*. 2d ed. Englewood Cliffs, N.J.: Prentice-Hall, 1975.

46. Hansen, J. C., and Maynard, P. E. *Youth: Self-Concept and Behavior*. Columbus, Ohio: Charles E. Merrill Publishing Co., 1973.

47. Harmon, L. W. "Anatomy of Career Commitment in Women." *Journal of Counseling Psychology* 17 (1970): 77–80.

48. Harris, L. "Change, Yes—Upheaval, No." *Life*, 8 January 1971, pp. 22–27.

49. Havighurst, R. J. *Developmental Tasks and Education*. 3d ed. New York: Daniel McKay Co., 1972.

50. Graham, R. "Youth and Experiential Learning." In *Youth: The Seventy-fourth Yearbook of the National Society for the Study of Education*. Part I. Edited by R. J. Havighurst and P. H. Dreyer. Chicago: University of Chicago Press, 1975.

51. Herriott, R. E. "Some Social Determinants of Educational Aspiration." *Harvard Educational Review* 33 (1963): 157–177.

52. Hershenson, D. B., and Langbauer, W. R. "Sequencing of Intra-psychic Stages of Vocational Development." *Journal of Counseling Psychology* 20 (1973): 519–521.

53. Hill, R. et al. *Family Development in Three Generations*. Cambridge, Mass.: Schenkman Publishing Co., 1971.

54. Holland, J. L. *Professional Manual for the Self-Directed Search*. Palo Alto, Calif.: Consulting Psychologists Press, 1972.

55. ———. *Making Vocational Choices: A Theory of Careers*. Englewood Cliffs, N.J.: Prentice-Hall, 1973.

56. Horan, P. M. "The Structure of Occupational Mobility: Conceptualization

and Analysis." *Social Forces* 53 (1974):33–45.

57. Homer, M. S. "Femininity and Successful Achievement: A Basic Inconsistency." In *Feminine Personality and Conflict*. Edited by J. M. Bardwick; Monterey, Calif.: Brooks/Cole Publishing Co., 1970.

58. Hurlock, E. B. *Adolescent Development*. 4th ed. New York: McGraw-Hill, 1973.

59. Johnson, E. G. "The Impact of High School Teachers on the Educational Plans of College Freshmen." Testing and Counseling Service Report No. 32. Orono: University of Maine, 1967. Mimeographed.

60. Jorgensen, C. E. "Trends in Job Preferences Over a 15-Year Period." Paper presented at the American Psychological Association Convention, New York, 1961.

61. Kandel, D. B., and Lesser, G. S. "Parental and Peer Influences on Educational Plans of Adolescents." *American Sociological Review* 34 (1969): 213–223.

62. Krippner, S. "Junior High School Students' Vocational Preference and Their Parents' Occupational Levels." *Personnel and Guidance Journal* 41 (1963): 590–595.

63. Lambert, B. G. et al. *Adolescence: Transition from Childhood to Maturity*. Monterey, Calif.: Brooks/Cole Publishing Co., 1972.

64. Levine, S. "Occupation and Personality: Relationship between the Social Factors of the Job and Human Orientation." *Personnel and Guidance Journal* 41 (1963): 602–605.

65. Lipman-Blumen, J., and Tickameyer, A. "Sex Roles in Transition: Ten-Year Perspective." *Annual Review of Sociology* 1 (1975).

66. Matteson, D. R. *Adolescence Today: Sex Roles and the Search for Identity*. Homewood, Ill.: Dorsey Press, 1975.

67. Mayer, L. A. "New Questions about the U.S. Population." *Fortune* (February 1971): 82–85.

68. McCandless, B. *Adolescents: Behavior and Development*. New York: Holt, Rinehart and Winston, 1970.

69. Mead, M. *Male and Female*. New York: Dell, 1968.

70. Mihalka, J. A. *Youth and Work*. Columbus, Ohio: Charles E. Merrill Publishing Co., 1974.

71. Morland, J. K. "Kent Revisited: Blue-Collar Aspirations and Achievements." In *Blue-Collar World*. Edited by A. B. Shostak and W. Gomberg. Englewood Cliffs, N.J.: Prentice-Hall, 1964, pp. 134–143.

72. Mortimer, J. T. "Social Class, Work, and the Family: Some Implications of the Father's Occupation for Familial Relationships and Sons' Career Decisions." *Journal of Marriage and the Family* 38 (1976): 241–256.

73. Muro, J. J. *Youth: New Perspectives on Old Dimensions*. Columbus, Ohio: Charles E. Merrill Publishing Co., 1973.

74. NAACP Legal Defense Fund. *Jobs for Blacks*. New York, 1971.

75. Osipow, S. H. et al. "Personality Types and Vocational Choice: A Test of Holland's Theory." *Personnel and Guidance Journal* 45 (1966): 37–42.

76. Panel on Youth, President's Science Advisory Committee. *Youth: Transition to Adulthood*. Chicago: University of Chicago Press, 1974.

77. Perrone, P. A. "Stability of Values of Junior High School Pupils and Their Parents over Two Years." *Personnel and Guidance Journal* 46 (1967): 268–274.

78. ———. "A National Evaluation of Occupational Information by School Counselors." Research Report. University of Wisconsin Center for Studies in Vocational and Technical Education, 1968. Mimeographed.

79. Perrone, P. A. et al. *Guidance and the Emerging Adolescent*. Scranton, Pa.: International Textbook Co., 1970.

80. Picou, J. S., and Curry, E. W. "Structural, Interpersonal, and Behavioral Correlates of Female Adolescents' Occupational Choices." *Adolescence* 8 (1973): 421–432.

81. Picou, J. S. et al. "Occupational Choice and Perception of Attainment Blockage: A Study of Lower-Class Delinquent and Non-Delinquent Black Males." *Adolescence* 9 (1974): 289–298.

82. Powell, M. *The Psychology of Adolescence*. 2d ed. Indianapolis: Bobbs-Merrill Co., 1971.

83. Preble, E. "The Puerto Rican-American Teenager in New York City." In *Minority Group Adolescents in the United States*. Edited by E. B. Brody. Baltimore: Williams & Wilkins, 1968.

84. Ramsey, C. E. "A Study of Decision-Making of Adolescence." Unpublished data.

85. ———. *Problems of Youth*. Belmont, Calif.: Dickenson Publishing Co., 1967.

86. Rand, L. "Masculinity or Femininity? Differentiating Career-oriented and Homemaking-oriented College Freshmen Women." *Journal of Counseling Psychology* 15 (1968): 444–450.

87. Rapoport, R., and Rapoport, R. N. *Dual-Career Families*. Baltimore: Penguin Books, 1971.

88. Rapoport, R., Rapoport, R. N., and Fogarty, M. *Sex, Career, and Family*. Beverly Hills, Calif.: Sage Publications, 1971.

89. Reich, C. A. *The Greening of America.* New York: Random House, 1970.

90. Russo, M. "14 Million Vocational Students by 1975." *American Education* 5 (1969): 10–11.

91. Sanborn, M. P. "Vocational Choice, College Choice, and Scholastic Success of Superior Students." *Vocational Guidance Quarterly* 13 (1965): 161–168.

92. Sanders, E. B. "What Do Young Women Want?" In *Youth in Contemporary Society.* Edited by D. Gottlieb. Beverly Hills, Calif.: Sage Publications, 1973, pp. 113–136.

93. Scanzoni, J. H. *Opportunity and the Family.* New York: Free Press, 1970.

94. Schaeffer, D. L. ed. *Sex Differences in Personality.* Monterey, Calif.: Brooks/Cole Publishing Co., 1971.

95. Sewell, W. H., and Orenstein, A. M. "Community of Residence and Occupational Choice." *American Journal of Sociology* 70 (1965): 551–563.

96. Silberman, C. E. *Crisis in the Classroom: The Remaking of American Education.* New York: Random House, 1970.

97. Simpson, R. L. "Parental Influence, Anticipatory Socialization, and Social Mobility." *American Sociological Review* 27 (1962): 517–522.

98. Slocum, W. L. *Occupational Careers: A Sociological Perspective.* Chicago: Aldine, 1974.

99. Stockin, B. S. "A Test of Holland's Occupational Level Formulations." *Personnel and Guidance Journal* 42 (1964): 599–602.

100. Strong, E. K. *Vocational Interests of Men and Women.* Palo Alto, Calif.: Stanford University Press, 1943.

101. Super, D. E., and Overstreet, P. L. *The Vocational Maturity of Ninth-Grade Boys.* New York: Teachers College, Columbia University, Bureau of Publications, 1960.

102. Super, D. E. et al. *Career Development: Self-Concept Theory.* Princeton, N.J.: College Entrance Examination Board, 1963.

103. Super, D. E. et al. *Career Development Inventory, Form 1.* New York: Teachers College, Columbia University, 1971.

104. Sutton-Smith, B., and Rosenberg, B. G. *The Sibling.* New York: Holt, Rinehart and Winston, 1971.

105. Tangri, S. S. "Determinants of Occupational Role Innovation among College Women." *Journal of Social Issues* 28 (1972): 177–199.

106. Thompson, E. E. "Occupational Values of High School Students." *Personnel and Guidance Journal* 44 (1966): 850–853.

107. Thornburg, H. D. *Contemporary Adolescence: Readings.* Monterey, Calif.: Brooks/Cole Publishing Co., 1975.

108. ———. *Development in Adolescence.* Monterey, Calif.: Brooks/Cole Publishing Co., 1975.

109. Tierney, R. J., and Herman, A. "Self-Estimate Ability in Adolescence." *Journal of Counseling Psychology* 20 (1973): 298–302.

110. U.S. Bureau of Census, Department of Commerce. *Statistical Abstract of the United States, 1978.* Washington, D.C.: U.S. Government Printing Office, 1978.

111. U.S. Department of Labor. Bureau of Labor Statistics. *Occupational Outlook Handbook, 1980–1981.* Washington, D.C.: U.S. Government Printing Office, 1980.

112. Wattenberg, W. W. *The Adolescent Years.* 2d ed. New York: Harcourt Brace Jovanovich, 1973.

113. Webb, E. J. *The Teen-Ager and His Family.* West Haven, Conn.: Pendulum Press, 1973.

114. Werts, C. E. "Paternal Influence on Career Choice." *Journal of Counseling Psychology* 15 (1968): 48–52.

115. Yankelovich, D. *The New Morality: A Profile of American Youth in the 70's.* New York: McGraw-Hill, 1974.

CHAPTER 21

Employment and Money during Adolescence

Outline

What is the value of part-time work in the life of the adolescent? What percentage of youths work part-time? What type of work do they do? What jobs do they find in the summer? Where do adolescents get their money? How much do they receive? On what do they spend their money? How many youths who want to work are unemployed? Is youthful unemployment increasing or decreasing? What are the causes for the higher unemployment rate among youths? What is the duration of the unemployment? What is the relationship between education and employment? These are the major questions discussed in this chapter.

The Importance of Gainful Employment

Some adolescents reach the threshold of adulthood with a long history of summer camps, family vacations, or sojourns to the cottage or seashore, but with little or no experience in the world of work. They were never encouraged to work part-time or summers during high school and lived on the dole of indulgent parents. Some then go on to college and sometimes to graduate school, never having to work for money or hold a responsible job. As a result, when the educational process is over, they are prepared academically for a vocation, but unprepared experientially, and they sometimes have difficulty adjusting. They discover that the boss is not as understanding or indulgent as parents, that fellow workers expect them to do their share and not to goof off, that any job requires doing a number of unpleasant tasks they would rather not do, and that working eight hours a day, five days a week can get tiresome, burdensome, and boring.

Most youths, regardless of their parents' financial position, need to learn to work, to seek part-time employment during high school and college and full-time employment in the summers. There are a number of reasons why this experience is helpful.

THE VALUE OF WORK

By working, adolescents learn that work is an important and necessary part of life. (28) A family needs members to share the workload. A community or a society has functions that need be performed, and these activities require people to do the work. Even individuals cannot exist without working; to maintain their own person, their possessions, their home requires a certain amount of work. Work is as necessary to life as breathing. It is not an unnecessary hardship that adults try to impose upon youths; it is a necessary part of everyone's life. Youths need to learn to accept it as such. (28)

Working teaches adolescents responsibility, cooperation, punctuality, and industry. They learn to be able to accept responsibility for performing a task and to do it with a minimum of supervision. They learn to cooperate with other people in a social effort. They learn to get up in the morning, to get to work on time, and the importance of promptness in modern society. They learn to acquire the disciplines that apply to all employment—responsibility for conscientious effort, taking direction from a superior, promptness, proper handling of money, and learning to work with others. (8)

Working enables adolescents to use their spare time productively. Idleness is particularly demoralizing to young people. They become bored and are more likely to get into mischief just to have something to do, as indicated by the fact that crime rates are significantly higher among unemployed youths than among those who are working. (26)

Working helps adolescents learn social skills with many different types of people in a variety of situations. (8) They meet all kinds of people at work: young and old, pleasant and unpleasant, industrious and lazy, bright and dull. In their associations with co-workers, adolescents learn the need to talk and be-have differently with each type of person. They get to know human character and different aspects of their own character. They discover the kinds of people they like and those they dislike, and how to deal with each when thrown to-gether with them in a work situation. One of the chief requirements for success in any type of employment is the ability to get along with people. This can be learned only through experience.

Through working adolescents develop autonomy. (25, p. 66) They are bet-ter able to break away from parents, learn to make their own decisions, earn and manage their own money, and learn to depend upon others outside the family for friendship and emotional support.

Working helps adolescents develop self-assurance, a feeling of self-worth, and their own concepts of self. Adolescents learn they *can* do things, that their services are wanted, that they are important to somebody. Successful work ex-perience helps them gain confidence in themselves and in their ability to per-form necessary tasks. Adolescents who have been rejected at home or whose school experience has not been successful need ego fulfillment to feel right about themselves. The right kind of successful work experience can help them do this. (18)

Work enables adolescents to earn money for things they need now and in the future. (8) Most youths never have enough money from parents to afford things they need: clothes, hobbies, school lunches, grooming aids and cosmetics, snacks, records, dates, and movies. Low income youths especially need to work. If they didn't work, many wouldn't have any money for things they needed. By working they are able to buy some of the things other youths have, an im-portant consideration in achieving status and a sense of belonging with others. Working also enables youths to save money for future purchases, education, mar-riage, or other worthwhile goals.

Properly selected work can provide relevant training for adolescents for a future career. (25, p. 66) The best job is one that may be related directly to the vocation the adolescent plans to enter. Adolescents gain necessary knowledge and understanding of the vocation under consideration. Work-study programs are good ways of combining work with vocation preparation. (2, 14, 20) In some cases youths may change their minds as a result of their work experience; this is an important lesson also, for they eliminate undesirable possibilities before they spend much money and time in years of preparation for a job, only to discover later on they don't like it or aren't suited to it. (15)

Another approach is to become acquainted with a wide variety of occupations and work settings through different types of part-time work. Thus, by the time adolescents focus on particular vocations they are better able to make decisions based on a realistic understanding of what the work requires. (3, p. 14) What youths need is a chance to experiment, to acquire skills and experiences, so they can develop "vocational maturity." (5, 17)

In one study, 240 male and 181 female high school students who worked part-time were asked to name their most important personal reasons for working. The results are shown in Table 21–1. Males and females agreed on the first three most important reasons for working. Males were more interested than females in having money to buy and operate a car. A much higher percentage of females than males were interested in learning to get along in the adult world of work and in getting training and experience in a vocation. Fairly large percentages of males and females worked because it was an enjoyable activity and because it was something to do to fill their time. (8)

Part-Time and Summer Employment

PERCENTAGE WHO WORK

According to projections of the U.S. Bureau of Labor Statistics, 53 percent of sixteen- to nineteen-year-old males and 46 percent of sixteen- to nineteen-year-old females are expected to be in the civilian labor force in 1980. (31) These figures

Table 21–1. Reasons for part-time employment checked by male and female high school students, in percentages.

Reason	Males	Females
Money for current expenses	94.2	89.0
Savings account	74.2	75.7
Money for future education	68.7	66.3
Money for buying and operating automobile	60.0	33.7
Learning to get along in adult world of work	37.9	63.5
Enjoyable activity	37.5	44.2
Education not related to future vocation	28.7	29.3
Something to fill time	27.5	21.5
Training and experience in a vocation	19.2	38.1
Help support family	16.2	19.3
Family-owned business	7.1	7.7

Adapted from W. Hammond, "Part-time Employment," *National Association of Secondary School Principals Bulletin* 55 (1971): 67. Used by permission.

Table 21–2. Percentage of age group 16–19 and 20–24 in civilian labor force, 1975–1985.

Group	1975	1980	1985
Ages 16–19			
Males	54	53	53
Females	47	46	47
Ages 20–24			
Males	74	74	73
Females	63	63	65

Adapted from U.S. Department of Labor, Bureau of Labor Statistics, "Projections of the Labor Force," *Employment and Earnings,* vol. 20, no. 5 (Washington, D.C.: U.S. Superintendent of Documents, 1973).

did not include those in the armed forces, but did include those who worked either part-time or full-time sometime during the year. Table 21–2 shows comparable figures for twenty- to twenty-four-year-olds and the projections to 1985. The percentage of youths who work is expected to remain fairly steady, although periods of high unemployment decrease totals. (31) When these figures are broken down by race, age, and sex, some inequalities become obvious. Figure 21–1 shows the percentages. (32) As can be seen, white male youths have the highest rates of employment, black female youths the lowest. The lower the age group, the greater the differential between whites and blacks, indicating that adolescent blacks have a much harder time getting jobs than do whites of comparable ages. (12)

One interesting study was conducted with youths in a small community in rural Maine. (13) The youths were the entire junior class of Gardiner Area High School, a consolidated school serving three small rural communities. The median level of education of the parents in two of the communities was 11.2 years, and in the other community, 9.8 years. Average family incomes in 1970 were almost

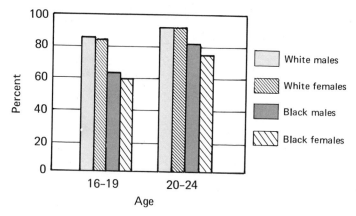

Figure 21–1. Civilian labor force employment, by sex, race, and age. (Adapted from U.S. Bureau of the Census, Department of Commerce, *Statistical Abstract of the United States, 1978* [Washington, D.C.: U.S. Government Printing Office, 1978].)

$1,000 less than the average for the United States. Only 12 percent of parents had college training or a degree; 54 percent had some high school education or a high school diploma; 34 percent had an eighth-grade education or less. (13) Over-all, the results showed that about an equal percentage of low and middle socioeco-nomic students worked during the school year (57 percent of the low versus 53 percent of the middle socioeconomic students), but that a considerably greater percentage of the low socioeconomic status students (84 percent) worked during the summer compared to the middle socioeconomic status students (74 percent). More of the middle socioeconomic students went away on vacations with parents, spent time at summer camps, or were engaged in summer activities other than gainful employment.

HOURS WORKED

National statistics reveal some interesting facts about the part-time working hours of adolescents. According to the information in Figure 21–2, 60 percent of all sixteen- to nineteen-year-old males and 50 percent of all sixteen- to nineteen-year-old females who work part-time do so for fifteen or more hours a week. (21) This represents a lot of work considering the fact that the majority are also in school. (21) In the twenty- to twenty-four-year-old group, 75 percent of males and 73 percent of females who work part-time do so for fifteen or more hours a week. (21)

SUMMER EMPLOYMENT

During the summer months many youths are employed full- or part-time in sea-sonal jobs that are available during only these months. (13) Farm work and yard work are very popular with younger adolescent boys. As they get older many get jobs as service station attendants or on construction projects or with highway, park, or recreational departments. Employment in summer camps is extremely popular with boys and girls. Many girls find work as waitresses, counter girls, or carhops, especially in summer restaurants, drive-ins, and resort hotels. Others are employed as store clerks. Many continue to be employed as babysitters or governesses during the summer. (11, 13)

Earning while Learning

NUMBERS INVOLVED

More than half the 10 million students enrolled in college are working to help pay their way. (6) At some institutions, such as the University of Colorado in Denver, 90 percent of students have jobs. One-third of these work forty hours a week. (6, p. 18)

PROGRAMS AND WAGES

Two well-established programs provide a large number of jobs for young men and women in college. One is the college work-study program, enrolling over half a million needy students who earn an average of $580 per year. (6, p. 28) The

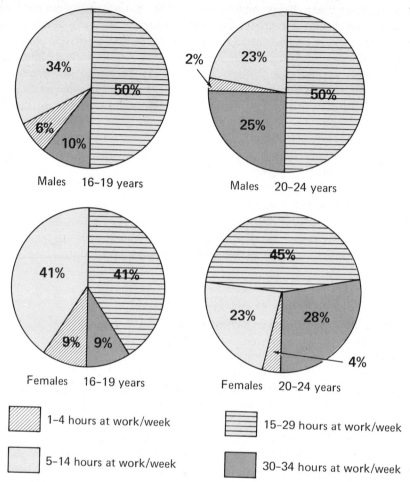

Figure 21–2.   Percent distribution of part-time hours worked, by sex and age, May
1970. (Adapted from G. H. Moore, and J. N. Hedges, "Trends in Labor and
Leisure," *Monthly Labor Review Reader*. U.S. Department of Labor, Bureau of
Labor Statistics, Bulletin No. 1868 [Washington, D.C.: U.S. Superintendent of
Documents, 1975], p. 476.)

typical student earns minimum wages; some jobs pay higher. Tutoring pays $3
to $4 per hour on most campuses. Research work may go as high as $5 per
hour. (6, p. 29) Another 120,000 students are employed in cooperative education
at 600 colleges and universities. This program enables students to rotate between
full-time study and full-time work. Students in this program are able to earn good
money and to be economically almost self-sufficient. At Northeastern University
in Boston the average co-op student is able to earn $3,267 during the 26 weeks he
or she is on the job each academic year.

TYPES OF JOBS

Students in work-study programs on campus usually are employed in service or
clerical positions. (6, p. 28) Work in offices, the library, or eating places is typical.

Most students working off-campus have to find jobs on their own through employment agencies. Some of them earn their money in unusual ways: as firemen, go-go dancers, nude models, bartenders, hospital orderlies, fiction writers, auto mechanics, zoo keepers, pallbearers, or as guinea pigs in scientifically conducted experiments. One student at Georgia State University worked as a tennis teacher, yard man, computer programmer, and pie taster. (6, p. 28) Students in Las Vegas earn big money running gaming tables or working as musicians or dancers.

NEED FOR MODERATION

Most college authorities advise against heavy work loads because of their effects on health and grades. The limit under the college work-study program is fifteen hours a week during the school year. Twenty hours a week is considered the maximum that any full-time students should work, although many work far longer. If students are able to budget their time, most can work ten to fifteen hours a week without hurting their grades. (6, p. 29)

Adolescent Money Management

SOURCES AND AMOUNT OF INCOME

Where do adolescents get their money and how much do they receive? In a study done by Gilbert Youth Research, it was found that 49 percent of the income of high school boys was from regular or part-time jobs, 22 percent from allowances and gifts, and 29 percent from summer employment. Forty-one percent of the income of high school girls was from regular or part-time work, 40 percent from allowances and gifts, and 19 percent from summer jobs. (24) The amount of money received from parents varies with the economic position of the family, the area of the country, the age of the adolescent, and what he has to use his money for. Youths in the suburbs receive substantially more than rural or inner-city adolescents. Older youths receive more than younger.

A study in rural Maine (13) found that for both low and middle socioeconomic status students, the most prevalent method of receiving money from parents was by direct handout. Forty-six percent of the students from the lower classes and 35 percent of those from the middle classes received money by this method during the week prior to the study. The next most popular method was an allowance. More lower class students (46 percent) received allowances than did middle class students (35 percent) during the week prior to the study. (It may be that more middle class students received monthly incomes so that the amount received during the week prior to the study was lower.) Table 21–3 shows the method of receiving income from family members during the week prior to the study. Few received money by working for parents.

HOW MONEY IS SPENT

What do youths spend their money on? A survey was conducted by the Rand Youth Poll to evaluate where the money goes every week. (33) Figures 21–3 and 21–4 show the breakdown of expenditures. There was a large difference between boys and girls on the nature of expenditures. Boys spent twice as much as girls

Table 21–3.   Method of receiving income from family members during the week prior to the study, by socioeconomic status, in percentages.

Source	Lower Class	Middle Class
Regular allowance	30	25
Direct handout from parents	46	35
Working for parents	14	12
Gift	7	4
Other	4	3
None	10	3

From R. Kontio, "Practices and Attitudes of High School Students Concerning Money," Master's thesis, University of Maine, 1970. Mimeographed.

on gasoline and cars (20 percent versus 10 percent), over twice as much on movies, dates, and entertainment (29 percent versus 13 percent), and twice as much on candy, ice cream, and soda (10 percent versus 5 percent). Boys also spent 6 percent of their income on hobbies; girls spent none. Girls spent enormous amounts on grooming: 12 percent for beauty and hair products, 15 percent for cosmetics and fragrances, and 8 percent for jewelry, trinkets, and notions. This was a total of 35 percent, over one-third of the girls' total income. Boys spent only 4 percent of their income on grooming. In addition, girls spent 23 percent

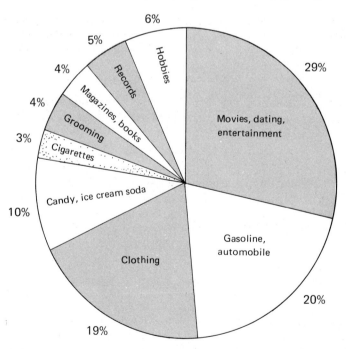

Figure 21–3.   How male youths, aged 16–19, spend their money. (Adapted from "Youth Spends Its Money," *Penney's Forum* [Fall/Winter, 1967]. New York: J. C. Penney Company, Inc. Educational & Consumer Relations, pp. 12, 13. Used by permission.)

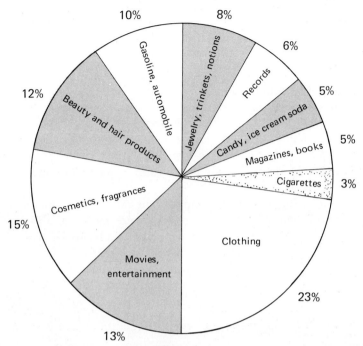

Figure 21–4.   How female youths, aged 16–19, spend their money. (Adapted from "Youth Spends Its Money," *Penney's Forum* [Fall/Winter, 1967]. New York: J. C. Penney Company, Inc. Educational & Consumer Relations, pp. 12, 13. Used by permission.)

of their income on clothing; boys spent 19 percent. Thus, a total of 57 percent of the girls' money went for grooming and clothing, compared to 27 percent for boys.

In the study of eleventh-grade youths in rural Maine, 59 percent owned a camera, 22 percent an auto, 85 percent a radio, 58 percent a record player, 31 percent their own TV set, and 76 percent owned a watch. (13)

Adolescents and Unemployment

NUMBERS

One of the major social problems in the United States is unemployed youths. (7) At the present time, nearly 17 percent of sixteen- to nineteen-year-olds and 10 percent of twenty- to twenty-four-year-olds are not enrolled in school and are jobless. This represents 12 percent of all teenagers and 28 percent of black ones. (10, p. 55; 29) This means that 1.9 million youths are out of work, a number that doubles in the summer. Almost half of all unemployed people in the United States are under age twenty-five.

These statistics probably underestimate the extent of the problem, for many adolescents who get discouraged and stop looking for work are therefore not counted as unemployed. (34) This high rate of joblessness means more crime, more drug addiction, more social unrest, and less income for many poor families. (26)

CAUSES OF UNEMPLOYMENT

Why is the rate of unemployment among youths so high? One major reason is the massive increase in the adolescent population as a result of the high birthrate of the 1940s and 1950s. The 1970 teenage labor force was 52 percent larger than in 1960, in contrast to a 15 to 20 percent increase in jobs. (25, p. 50; 29) Thus, there was a larger supply of workers than the market needed. Competition has been increased also by the increasing numbers of women entering the labor force for the first time. (10, p. 54)

Another reason for the high unemployment rate among youths is that they have little training and skill, little experience, and many are able to take only part-time jobs while in school. They are confined to a narrower range of the less skilled occupations, at which many can work only part-time. Youths with high school diplomas have better chances on the labor market than do dropouts, as is reflected by lower unemployment rates among graduates. Many employers require educational degrees that have little relationship to job skills; dropouts are often denied work, not because they cannot do the job but because they do not have the necessary pieces of paper. (34)

State licensing boards often operate to restrict entry into business. The Colorado Board of Cosmetology, for example, requires that a prospective hairdresser take 1,650 hours of instruction, including 100 hours of supervised practice at shampooing. (34) Such requirements hit hardest at the young, especially those who seek to combine work with schooling. Union requirements also limit participation of the young. It takes time and experience to acquire membership in a union; therefore, adolescents are not able to accept jobs in the construction industry, for example, which could be an important source of part-time and summer employment. (34) Many unions also limit the number of apprentices that can be trained. (10, p. 54) In cases of layoffs, seniority rules work in favor of the older, more experienced workers; youths are the first to lose their jobs.

Minimum wage legislation may also sometimes affect unemployment. (1) When the minimum wage goes up relative to the low productivity of inexperienced youths, employers hesitate to hire them, often preferring older people if they are available. (12) Furthermore, job turnover among youths is higher than among older, more stable workers. Some employers won't hire anybody under twenty-one for a regular job; they want those who have a greater degree of maturity. (34)

Many jobs in transportation, construction, manufacturing, and agriculture are closed even to youths available for full-time year-round work because of the legal minimum ages for hazardous work. (9, p. 46) Although state laws differ, the general standard is that all wage employment is barred to those under fourteen, all employment during school hours is barred to those under sixteen, and certain hazardous jobs and industries are barred to youths under eighteen. (34)

On the other hand, the average period of unemployment among youths is shorter than among older workers. Females average somewhat shorter periods of unemployment than males, and whites shorter periods than nonwhites. The fact that half of all unemployed youths have no more than four weeks without work reflects the seasonal and intermittent nature of their unemployment.

Education and Employment

The educational background of youths continues to improve. By 1982, 86 percent of seventeen-year-olds will be graduating from high school. (30, p. 130) Thirty-seven percent of all high school graduates will be graduating from college. Figure 21–5 shows the increases in the percentages of high school and college graduates from 1900 to 1982. (30, p. 130)

Despite this improvement, however, there are still many dropouts not able to get jobs as good as those of high school graduates. Many male graduates find their way into professional, technical, or sales occupations, and somewhat more are employed as craftsmen. (27) The dropouts are more heavily concentrated in operative service, labor, and farm occupations. (16) Among females, the disparities are even greater. The largest percentage of dropouts work as operatives, private household workers, or other service workers. It is obvious that those who do not continue their education are closing the doors to opportunity. Studies of dropouts consistently show that the high school graduate is superior to the early dropout in each of the following: (1) number of promotions and raises, (2) holding onto one job, (3) fewer and shorter periods of unemployment, (4)

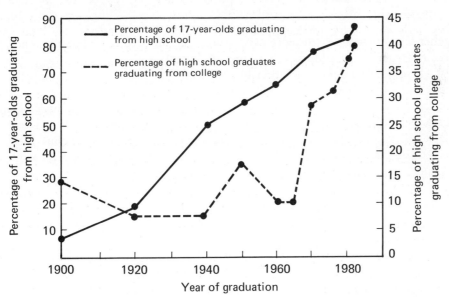

Figure 21–5. High school and college graduates, 1900 to 1982. (Adapted from U.S. Bureau of Census, Department of Commerce. *Statistical Abstract of the United States, 1973, 1978* [Washington, D.C.: U.S. Government Printing Office, 1973, 1978].)

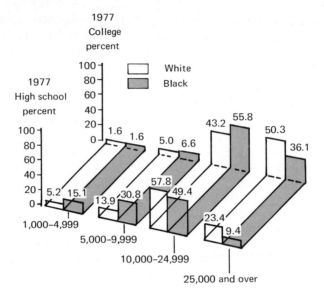

Figure 21–6.   Income of blacks and whites 25 years old and over with four years of high school or college, U.S.A., 1977. (Adapted from U.S. Bureau of the Census, Department of Commerce, *Statistical Abstract of the United States, 1978* [Washington, D.C.: U.S. Government Printing Office, 1978].)

higher job satisfaction, (5) more recreational pursuits, (6) more hobbies, and (7) greater frequency of additional training. (4, p. 439)

There is also a definite relationship between the degree of educational attainment and annual income. Figure 21–6 shows the percentages of high school and college graduates over twenty-five years of age in each of the annual income brackets. (30) As can be seen, in 1977, 50 percent of white and 36 percent of black college graduates had annual incomes over $25,000 per year, but only 23 percent of white and 9 percent of black high school graduates had incomes as high. (9)

Conclusions

The prevailing notion that the majority of modern adolescents have adopted an anti-work ethic does not seem to agree with the facts. Rates of employment vary with different ages of youths, racial and economic groups, and regions of the country, but in the United States in 1980 about half of all sixteen- to nineteen-year-olds and about 69 percent of all twenty- to twenty-four-year-olds are employed at any one time. (31) Many of those unemployed will look for either part-time or full-time jobs but will not be able to find them. This indicates at least that most adolescents want to work. It does not reflect an antiwork ethic. In the study in rural

Maine, a smaller percentage of middle class and upper middle class youths worked during the summer months than did lower class youths. This would indicate that where the antiwork ethic exists, it is more prevalent among comparatively affluent young people.

The jobs youths hold, particularly while in junior high school or high school, are not very pleasant. For the most part they involve manual labor and are often menial, uninspiring, and unrewarding. The percentage of youths in better jobs increases with age and education. Even while in school, middle class adolescents are at an advantage, earning more money in better jobs. Youths who drop out of school early remain severely handicapped with respect to the type of job they are able to hold and the amount of money they earn. It is encouraging that the percentage of all youths who graduate from high school continues to increase and that the percentage of high school graduates who graduate from college has been increasing since 1960 after ten years of decline.

Despite improved education, however, unemployment among youths increased during the 1970s. The unemployment rate among sixteen- to nineteen-year-olds remains about three times the adult rate. This fact should cause considerable concern. How can more jobs be made available to the young people who need them?

Not surprising is the fact that today's adolescents are quite affluent. Many are able to earn over $25 per week. (33) No wonder so many adolescents have their own car, record player, and camera. More surprising, perhaps, is the fact that a study in rural Maine showed that more adolescents received money from parents through direct handouts than from an allowance or by working for the parents. (13) Whether this is true of adolescents in other parts of the United States is not certain, but it is probably similar. If so, many youths have no set amount that they can expect from parents; whenever they need money they just ask for it. However, the fact that the average amount received from parents is still less than the average amount earned (24) indicates that the majority of youths assume the major responsibility for earning their income, rather than depending exclusively on parents.

All of this adds up to the fact that many adolescents take far more responsibility in earning their own money than many adults give them credit for. Learning to spend this money wisely takes more time, but some major beginnings have been made during the adolescent period.

Learning Experiences

There are a variety of ways of gaining more insight into this subject.

1. Invite one or more speakers to class to discuss youth employment and unemployment. The speakers might include one or more of the following:

    A representative from the youth division of the State Employment Security Commission.

    A representative from the Civil Service Commission.

    A representative from the local office of the U.S. Bureau of Apprenticeship, Dept. of Labor.

    A representative from CETA (Comprehensive Employment and Training Act). This person may be under the local mayor's office or another local human resources agency. The purpose of this act was to operate projects or cooperate with other groups to provide on-the-job and classroom training, basic education, work experience, and supportive services.

    A representative from Job Corps.

    A representative from a local labor union.

A representative from the employment or personnel office of a local industry or business.

A representative from special offices set up to provide summer employment for teenagers. Miami, for example, has a co-ordinator of the Summer Teen Employment Program.

A representative from the college placement office.

2. Keep a record of receipts and expenditures for one or more months to discover how you as a college student budget your money.

3. Write a term paper. The following subjects are only suggestive.

Where to Get a Summer Job
What Employers Look for in Prospective Employees
The Job Interview
How to Get a Job after Graduation
Youth Unemployment and Social Problems
Child Labor Laws and the Problem of Youth Unemployment
Unemployment among Minority Adolescents
How Youths Spend Their Money
Education, Employment, and Income
Adolescent Money Management
Alienated Youth and the Antiwork Ethic
The Protestant Ethic of Work
Work as Vocation and Fulfillment
Women and Employment Inequalities
Working Wives and Mothers
Dual-Career Wives

Bibliography

1. Adie, D. K. "Teen-Age Unemployment and Real Federal Minimum Wages." *Journal of Political Economy* 81 (March 1973): 435–441.

2. "All in a Day's Work-Study." *American Education* 6 (1970): 12–13.

3. Baizerman, M., and Cooper, N. C. "Working Youths: Select Findings from an Exploratory Study." *Journal of Youth and Adolescence* 3 (1974): 7–16.

4. Bernard, H. *Adolescent Development.* Scranton, Pa.: Intext Educational Publishers, 1971.

5. Center for Youth Development and Research. *Youth Encounters the World of Work.* Minneapolis: University of Minnesota, 1973.

6. "Earning While Learning: On the Upswing Everywhere." *U.S. News & World Report,* 13 January 1975, pp. 28–29.

7. *Encyclopedic Almanac.* New York: New York Times Company, 1970.

8. Hammond, W. "Part-time Employment." *National Association of Secondary School Principals Bulletin* 55 (1971): 67.

9. Horn, W. A., ed. "Income by Years of School Completed." *American Education* 13 (1977), back cover.

10. "Jobs: A Look at the Nation's Most Nagging Problem." *U.S. News & World Report,* 21 February 1977, pp. 54–55.

11. "Jobs and the Young: Chances of Finding Work This Summer." *U.S. News & World Report,* 17 May 1976, pp. 72–73.

12. "Jobs: The Story That Figures Don't Tell." *U.S. News & World Report,* 1 November 1976, pp. 83–86.

13. Kontio, R. "Practices and Attitudes of High School Students Concerning Money." Master's thesis, University of Maine, 1970. Mimeographed.

14. Kruger, W. S. "They Don't Have to Drop Out." *American Education* 5 (1969): 6–8.

15. Litzinger, W., and Visser, C. "Closing the Vocational Counseling Realities Gap." *Personnel and Guidance Journal* 46 (1968): 650–654.

16. Mayer, L. A. "New Questions about the U.S. Population." *Fortune* (February 1971): 82–85.

17. Measurement and Research Center. *Vocational Plans and Preferences of Adolescents.* Report of Poll No. 94 of the Purdue Opinion Panel. Lafayette, Ind.: Purdue University, 1972.

18. Meyer, J. A. "Suburbia: A Wasteland of Disadvantaged Youth and Negligent Schools?" *Phi Delta Kappan* 50 (1969): 575–578.

19. Miller, D. *Adolescence: Psychology, Psychopathology, and Psychotherapy.* New York: Jason Aronson, 1974.

20. Minear, L. P. "A Piece of the Action." *American Education* 5 (1969): 4–6.

21. Moore, G. H., and Hedges, J. N. "Trends in Labor and Leisure." *Monthly Labor Review Reader.* U.S. Department of Labor, Bureau of Labor Statistics Bulletin No. 1868 (1975): 471–479.

22. Morse, N. C., and Weiss, R. S. "The Function and Meaning of Work and the Job." In *Vocational Behavior.* Edited by D. G. Zytowski. New York: Holt, Rinehart and Winston, 1968, pp. 7–16.

23. NAACP Legal Defense Fund. *Jobs for Blacks.* New York: 1971.

24. *Notes on the Youth Market.* 3d ed. New York: Fairchild Publications, 1964.

25. Panel on Youth, President's Science Advisory Committee. *Youth: Transition to Adulthood.* Chicago: University of Chicago Press, 1974.

26. Phillips, L., and Votey, H. L., Jr. "Crime, Youth, and the Labor Market." *Journal of Political Economy* 80 (May 1972): 491–504.

27. Russo, M. "14 Million Vocational Students by 1975." *American Education* 5 (1969): 10–11.

28. Task Force to the Secretary of Health, Education and Welfare. *Work in America.* Cambridge, Mass.: MIT Press, 1973.

29. U.S. Bureau of the Census, Department of Commerce. "Projections of the Population of the United States, by Age and Sex: 1970 to 2020." *Current Population Reports,* Series P-25, No. 470. Washington, D.C.: U.S. Government Printing Office, 1971.

30. ———. *Statistical Abstract of the United States, 1978.* Washington, D.C.: U.S. Government Printing Office, 1978.

31. U.S. Department of Labor. Bureau of Labor Statistics. "Projections of the Labor Force." *Employment and Earnings.* Vol. 20, No. 5. Washington, D.C.: U.S. Supt. of Documents, November 1973.

32. ———. *Handbook of Labor Statistics, 1976.* Bulletin No. 1905. Washington, D.C.: U.S. Supt. of Documents, 1976, Table 4, pp. 31–32.

33. "Youth Spends Its Money." *Penney's Forum* (Fall/Winter 1967): 12, 13.

34. "Why It's Hard to Cut Teen-Age Unemployment." *U.S. News & World Report,* 17 May 1976.

Ethnic

The Culturally Different

Outline

Many chapters of this book have referred to cultural differences among adolescents. Differences between low socioeconomic status and middle class adolescents have been highlighted, as have some differences between black and white adolescents. This concluding chapter elaborates by gathering together some important information. The discussion concerns four major groups: (1) low socioeconomic status adolescents of whatever race or national origin, (2) black adolescents, (3) Mexican American adolescents, and (4) American Indian adolescents. The chapter begins with a definition and explanation of low socioeconomic status. Who are the low socioeconomic status young people? What are the special limitations imposed upon their lives? How is the cycle of poverty and deprivation perpetuated from generation to generation? The chapter goes on to discuss some of the characteristics and problems of low socioeconomic status adolescents: the instability in the families from which they come, the effect of living in female-based households or in homes where the mother works, the effect of parental child-rearing philosophies, the relationship of these young people to their peers and to the larger society, and poor mental health.

Following this general discussion of low socioeconomic status adolescents, the chapter discusses in detail, black, Mexican American, and American Indian adolescents. Such factors as discrimination, segregation, housing, education, employment, and income are explored. Some of the parental values of Mexican Americans and American Indians are highlighted to show the difficulties in socialization and the cultural conflicts that beset youths of these two minority groups.

The low socioeconomic status category cuts across many national and ethnic boundaries, reaching into one out of every ten American homes. These particular groups have been selected for discussion of the culturally different because black adolescents constitute the largest single minority group; Mexican Americans comprise the second largest minority group. Puerto Rican Americans, the third largest minority, are not included in this discussion. (73, 96) Instead American Indian adolescents have been selected because they constitute the most deprived minority group and because, as the only native Americans, they too need to be better understood.

Low Socioeconomic Status Adolescents

Various terms have been applied to youths who are of lower social classes and also poor: disadvantaged, culturally deprived, (79) educationally deprived, (44) low socioeconomic status, and working class. (53) The term *low socioeconomic status* has been selected here because it refers to two important aspects of the living condition: low social class and status, including cultural deprivation, and low income. Obviously, not all "lower class" youths are poor, nor are all low income youths culturally deprived, even though the two aspects frequently go together. However, this chapter emphasizes both lower social class and low income.

Low socioeconomic status adolescents grow up in the one out of ten American families classified as poor (with 1977 incomes of $6,191 per year for a nonfarm family of four). (104) In comparison with the general population they are more often from nonwhite families; have less education, fewer wage earners, and more female heads; and are from larger than average families. They reside more often in the South, in farm areas or in cities, and less often in rural nonfarm or suburban areas. (45, 47) By definition, they are also culturally deprived with only limited access to leisure facilities, educational advantages, work opportunities, health and medical care, proper living conditions, and many of the values, attitudes, customs, institutions, and organizations characteristic of the large masses of middle class Americans.

LIMITATIONS OF LOW SOCIOECONOMIC STATUS

These circumstances impose four important limitations upon the lives of low socioeconomic status adolescents. (32; 47, p. 2)

LIMITED ALTERNATIVES. These youths have not been exposed to a variety of social and cultural settings; they have experienced only a narrow range of situations and demands. Vocationally they have fewer opportunities, confront less complex situations on the job, and have fewer, less diverse standards to meet. Socially they are the nonjoiners, seldom going beyond the borders of kinship and neighborhood groups. Their limited experience and knowledge make it difficult to get out of or go beyond the narrow world in which they were brought up. Limited vision and experience limit the possibilities and opportunities in their lives.

HELPLESSNESS, POWERLESSNESS. In the working world their skills are limited, they can exercise little autonomy or influence in improving their conditions, they have little opportunity or knowledge to receive additional training, and they are the most easily replaced workers. They have little political or social influence in their communities and, sometimes, inadequate legal protection of their rights as citizens.

DEPRIVATION. They are aware of the affluence around them, of the achievements of and benefits received by others, but their situation makes them constantly aware of their own abject status and "failure," resulting in bitterness, embarrassed withdrawal and isolation, or to social deviation and rebellion.

INSECURITY. They are at the mercy of life's unpredictable events: sickness, loss of work, injury, legal problems, school difficulties, family difficulties, and others. Because poor adolescents have few resources, they are unable to protect themselves against these events. Any minor crisis can become an emergency: a slight illness turns into a major medical emergency; a missed rent payment by parents ends in eviction; a problem with the police winds up in juvenile court. The poor strive to "stay out of trouble"; they strive for security because they

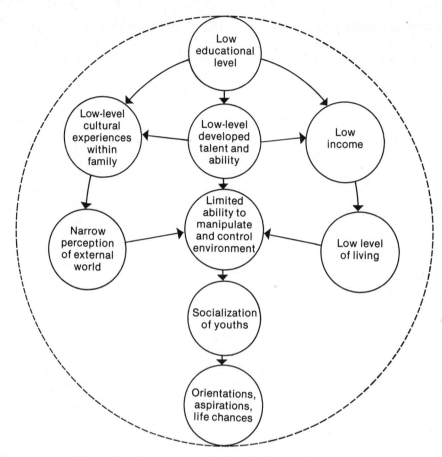

Figure 22–1. The cycle of poverty and cultural deprivation.

never feel certain about their own lives. They strive just to provide themselves with the basic necessities of life. (6)

THE CYCLE OF POVERTY AND DEPRIVATION

The net effect of the limitations imposed upon the lives of low socioeconomic status youths is to perpetuate poverty and cultural deprivation. Figure 22–1 illustrates this cycle of poverty and cultural deprivation.

The cycle begins at the top with the low level of education. Moving clockwise, little education results in a low income, which results in a low level of living, which results in limited ability to manage or control the external environment (the limited alternatives and powerlessness already mentioned). In turn the adolescents are socialized to expect low education, income, level of living, and powerlessness; their whole orientation serves to perpetuate the life style to which they have become accustomed.

Starting at the top again and moving counterclockwise, the low level of education results in a low level of developed talent and ability and a low level of cultural experiences in the family. This in turn results in a narrow perception of the external world, which, along with the low level of living, contributes to limited ability to manage and control their environment. Because of the limitations imposed upon them, parents in turn teach their children not to expect a very high income, level of living, or much education. Low socioeconomic status adolescents tend to be caught in a self-perpetuating cycle of poverty and cultural deprivation.

FAMILY INSTABILITY

Partly as a result of hasty early marriages, economic struggles, and a long list of other factors, low socioeconomic status families are much more unstable than higher class ones. The rates of divorce and separation increase as one goes down the socioeconomic scale. (34) One study shows that divorce and separation rates are three times higher in the lower socioeconomic levels than in the higher levels, and that couples in the lower levels who do remain together seem less happily married. (58)

Illegitimacy rates also are higher among those of lower socioeconomic status groups, particularly among nonwhites. (77) This is due partly to the fact that lower status groups have different values toward illegitimacy, (80) less often marry when pregnancy is involved, less often have abortions, and less often use contraceptives to prevent pregnancy. (77, p. 354) Again, this is especially true among nonwhites. Table 22–1 shows the estimated number of illegitimate births in the United States per thousand unmarried white and nonwhite females ages fifteen to forty-four, from 1940 to 1976. The greatest increase in illegitimacy rates came after World War II until 1960. Since then the rates for whites have gone up while the rates for nonwhites have declined. During the past several years the rates among whites have also declined slightly. These figures are of concern because they represent a large number of youths growing up without the benefit of a stable, two-parent family. Because illegitimacy is more common among low socioeconomic status families, adolescents of these families are especially affected.

THE FEMALE-HEADED HOUSEHOLD

Female-headed households are prevalent and persistent among the poor. (4) Research indicates that even though a single-parent family may not be entirely disadvantageous (a father may be a financial burden or a source of friction), the overall effects of the absence or only occasional presence of a father are detrimental to the emotional and social development of adolescents. (40) The difficul-

Table 22–1.   Estimated number of illegitimate births per thousand U.S. unmarried females, ages 15–44, by color of mother: 1940, 1950, 1960, 1965, 1970, and 1976.

Group	1976	1970	1965	1960	1950	1940
All unmarried females	24.7	26.4	23.5	21.6	14.1	7.1
Whites	12.7	13.8	11.6	9.2	6.1	3.6
Nonwhites	78.1	89.9	97.6	98.3	71.2	35.6

From U.S. Bureau of the Census, Department of Commerce, *Statistical Abstract of the United States, 1978* (Washington, D.C.: U.S. Government Printing Office, 1978), p. 65.

ties appear in oedipal conflict, overdependence on the mother, and lack of models in the development of masculine and feminine roles. (57) There are also more unsatisfactory peer-group relations than among other youths and more feelings of inferiority and insecurity. (38) There is evidence that these adolescents react as if it is their fault that their father is absent. Often they feel unlovable and self-derogating. These young people may see the love relationship between sexes as irregular and unstable.

WORKING MOTHERS

Large numbers of low socioeconomic status mothers must work, even in intact families. A part-time work commitment apparently has a relatively stable and positive effect upon girls from intact working class families. The daughters are usually highly active, engaging in many leisure-time activities but achieving a balance between family and friends. They are usually independent and responsible, showing an independence of thought and values generally rare among girls. They tend to develop autonomy, self-assertion, and other signs of independence. They often choose their mother as an adult model and show love and respect for their parents. Douvan and Adelson write:

> The girls have warm and close ties to families which provide them a feminine model of unusual energy, independence, and responsibility. In modeling themselves after their mothers, they develop an autonomy which . . . grows out of an identification with an independent mother and is encouraged by the parents. It implies not a rejection of the parents, but rather an internalization of their values. (22, p. 300)

What about mothers who work full-time? Girls from these low socioeconomic status families often show strong affection for and strong dependency on the mother. They may show premature seriousness, somewhat more responsibility for housekeeping tasks than do adolescents of nonworking mothers, and show intense loyalty and strong emotional ties to the family. (74) However, they do not spend their leisure time with their family. Many times they find a boyfriend and emotional satisfaction outside the family by going steady. (22, p. 304)

What is the effect of maternal employment on adolescent boys? The boys of part-time working mothers of the working class group exhibit patterns that resemble those of the girls in this group: they are often active, responsible, and mature. But the sons of full-time working mothers become more concerned with financial problems and may feel that their mother's working implies something is wrong with the father as provider. The father does not serve as an effective ideal, and the son less often chooses the father as a model. (74) These boys seem to have a low level of activity, are rebellious toward adult authority, and show signs of poor ego integration. They usually date heavily, which may reflect a lack of emotional security derived from the family. They do not have part-time jobs as often as other boys, nor do they have many organizational ties or leisure engagements. (22, p. 309)

CHILD-REARING GOALS AND PHILOSOPHIES

Lower socioeconomic status families tend to be hierarchical, evidencing rigid parental relationships with adolescents. The parents are repeatedly seen as closed or inaccessible to the adolescent's communication. The atmosphere is one of imperatives and absolutes, physical violence, and psychological distance, if not rejection, by the adults. (51) Parent-child interaction patterns are rigid and oriented toward maintaining order, obedience, and discipline. The discipline seems to be impulsive, harsh, inconsistent, and to emphasize physical punishment (even of adolescents) rather than verbal explanations and requests. (33) As a group, adolescents from low socioeconomic status families report more problems with parents than do those from more privileged families. (39)

It is certain that such parents mean well. They usually want to bring up their children to live decent, obedient, honest lives as "good Christians." They want their children to rise above them economically, and a good report card from school seems to promise upward movement. There is a great deal of concern over obedience, respect for adults, conformity to externally imposed standards, and staying out of trouble. The lower class parent is concerned with overt behavior, with the immediate situation, and not with what behavior means in terms of future development. (14, 53, 88) There is little concern for personality growth or for desirable child-rearing goals such as the development of creativity, curiosity, independence, or self-direction. (47, 53) Greater family control is exercised over adolescent daughters than sons, which is why many girls use marriage as an escape from home.

In large families especially, parents seem to lack the time and will to control and give attention to their children as they get older. (81) The mother is preoccupied with a new baby, leaving the adolescents feeling left out and rejected. When problems arise with the adolescents, the parents feel hurt, bewildered, and powerless to remedy the situation. Frequently the attitude of parents is "We've done the best we could, you've made your bed, now you'll have to lie in it. There is nothing I can do." Their fatalistic attitude of accepting what comes is evident in the child-rearing task. (14)

Among lower socioeconomic status youths, physical, social, and emotional emancipation from the family comes early and is often abrupt and psychologically premature. Adolescents don't yet feel ready or prepared to take their place in an adult world. Their social and emotional needs foster excessively dependent relationships with peers during the transition period from youth to adulthood. (97)

PEER ORIENTATION

Because adolescents from low socioeconomic status families tend to maintain weaker ties with parents than do youths from middle class families, they form stronger, more lasting peer relationships. Those who report a low evaluation of parents tend to be more peer oriented than those who have a high evaluation of parents. (97) This may be for at least two reasons.

One, adolescents do not gain status through their familial identifications. Their fathers may be "nobodies"; they don't feel important because their fathers are professors, doctors, and businessmen. They feel keenly their father's lack of status in the community, and, therefore, their own lack of status. If their mother has a bad reputation in the adult society, the adolescents' status is likewise threatened. Thus, the adolescents can establish status only in relationship to their friends, by being tougher, wilder, sexier, funnier, or more daring than others. It has been found that adolescent boys with inadequate fathers have a special need to find peer approval as good guys or tough guys. Juvenile gangs evolve partly out of a need for status, identity, and recognition. (18, 35, 49, 107) Particular groups are formed on the basis of ethnic identity, a neighborhood locale, or a common purpose. When a group in an achievement-oriented society cannot gain status in socially acceptable ways, theft, extortion, narcotics, assault, sex, vandalism, or other antisocial expressions may become the means of gaining status and recognition. (58)

Thus the adolescent peer group takes on an identity of its own, with its own characteristics and functions; it tends to incorporate subcultural influences at variance with adult culture. (4) The peer group replaces the family as the adolescent's primary reference group.

The importance of the peer group apparently carries into adulthood. The tendency to seek friendships with those outside the family continues as part of the leisure pattern of the low socioeconomic status male, who prefers going "out with the boys." (58, p. 203) Such associations give him the same feelings of status, security, and virility that he needed in his youth. The more he is criticized by his wife, rejected by his children, or in other ways loses status at home, the more he turns to his buddies for recognition.

The second reason why low socioeconomic status adolescents become more peer oriented than parent oriented is their need for security. Physically, and perhaps psychologically, adults have left them. They feel a lack of communication and contact with adults and turn to their peers to find physical protection, mutual security, and emotional satisfaction. In the ghetto they need their gangs to protect lives; outside of crime neighborhoods, they need their gangs for companionship, direction, and fulfillment.

SOCIAL OUTCASTS

Low socioeconomic status adolescents are inadequately socialized to assume a place in adult middle class society. (9) They lack social skills in matters of dress, speech and manners. Often they have only a slight awareness of the subtleties of interpersonal relationships, and lack tact or sensitivity to the feelings and reactions of others. The typical loud, ill-mannered, vulgar toughs are scorned by polite society. Poor impulse control, along with a tendency to be aggressive, (54) hostile, fearful, and distrustful, gets them into trouble and alienates them from those who otherwise would be willing to be their friends. Low self-esteem and sometimes shyness and withdrawal keep them away from many social functions and groups. Inappropriate clothing and inadequate neatness and cleanliness label him as a tough or her as a tramp. (53)

Ordinarily, school is an important part of the social world of the adolescent. But academic failure and prejudicial treatment by middle class adults and students make the low socioeconomic status adolescents social outcasts. (84) They are apt to find themselves more and more socially isolated as they proceed through the grades, and as a result tend to seek friendships with out-of-school youths. (15)

Sometimes the association with other out-of-school youths influences adolescents to drop out of school. By associating with those who have already failed and dislike school they are pressured by the same attitudes and motives that caused those youths to leave. Once they leave school, they spend nearly all their leisure time away from home with their clique of friends. Many hours are spent in wandering from one place to another and lounging on street corners. Out-of-school activities such as reading, music lessons, hobbies (except perhaps for cars), and membership in various middle class youth groups do not figure in the social life of out-of-school adolescents. Sometimes special centers or clubs are established for these youths, attracting some through programs of organized sports and other recreational activities.

Low socioeconomic status youths generally become involved in social activities of a physical nature in an effort to get a kick out of life. Drinking, driving or riding in cars for pleasure, attending drive-in theaters, playing cards, attending sports events, dancing, seeing exciting movies, becoming involved in sexual adventures, engaging in physical conflict, and, in rural areas, going hunting, fishing, or snowmobiling are all a part of their life style. The favorite indoor activity is watching television by the hour.

MENTAL HEALTH

The lack of emotional security and stability in lower class homes and particular patterns of child-rearing give rise to a high rate of psychological problems and mental illness among adolescents. (5, 58) The incidence of schizophrenia, the most common psychosis of adolescents as well as adults, is significantly associated with social class. Furthermore, once hospitalized, low socioeconomic status adolescents are less likely to receive adequate treatment; are less often accepted for psychotherapy (partly due to a lower IQ level); are assigned less skilled staff members; are treated for shorter periods with less intensive techniques; and are less likely to improve in psychotherapy. (78)

The higher rates of mental illness among lower class males have very complicated causes. (There are twice as many boys as girls under age fifteen admitted to public mental hospitals.) (85) The reasons lie in the multiple factors in the family and social experiences of male children that create greater anxiety and pressures and the higher visibility of male deviant behavior. These factors are not as present in the lives of girls. Genetic factors may also play a role, but to what extent is unknown. (15)

Black Adolescents

THE LEGACY OF DISCRIMINATION

For generations, black families, especially those of lower class, were forced to assume an inferior role in order to get along in white society. Getting along in those days meant sitting in the back of the bus, avoiding all "white only" restaurants, rest rooms, recreational facilities, theaters, playgrounds. Black parents had to teach their children the black role. As one mother bluntly put it, "You have to let them know before they get out of their own backyard." Black children left their homes for school at their peril if they had not learned where they could sit and what they could or could not do if they got hungry or thirsty. At five, just as surely as at fifteen or twenty-five, they had to know their place. Also one of the important lessons to learn was that no matter how unjustly they were treated they must control anger and conceal hostility. They must be subservient, polite in the face of provocation, and walk with eyes straight ahead, unmoved by taunts and jeers. Above all, they must ignore insults and never argue or get in a fight with a white person. Black parents felt they must use severe measures to inculcate fear in their children as their best protection, or else white society would punish them more severely.

Richard Wright wrote of his "first lesson in how to live as a Negro." He had become involved in a fight with white boys who threw bottles at him and his friends; he was badly cut.

I sat brooding on my front steps, nursing my wound and waiting for my mother to come home from work. . . . I could just feel in my bones that she would understand. . . . I grabbed her hand and babbled out the whole story. She examined my wound, then slapped me.

"How come yuh didn't hide?" she asked me. "How come yuh always fightin?"

I was outraged and bawled. Between sobs I told her that I didn't have any trees or hedges to hide behind. . . .

She grabbed a barrel stave, dragged me home, stripped me naked, and beat me till I had a fever of one hundred and two. She would smack my rump with the stave, and, while the skin was still smarting, impart to me gems of Jim Crow wisdom. I was never to throw cinders any more. . . . I was never, never under any conditions to fight white folks again. And they were absolutely right in clouting me with the broken milk bottle. (115)

Not all black families used these means to protect their children from the wrath of whites. Upper class families told their children to avoid fights or brawls with whites, not because it was dangerous but because it was beneath their social status. (32, p. 176) These families tried to isolate their children from racial discrimination as much as possible by outsegregating the white segregationists. They tried to hide from children the fact that they could not go into certain places and taught them that whites were rejecting the lower class blacks, not them. Such efforts were only partly successful for eventually children learned that they too were outsiders. As a result they often developed ambivalent attitudes toward themselves as blacks. (32, p. 176)

THE NEW IMAGE

The image of blacks has been changing. (3) A series of sweeping judicial decisions that promised to desegregate their lives; the emergence of a significant black middle class; the rise of political leadership among the blacks themselves; enfranchisement; the legalization and regulation of fair employment practices; and determined efforts to discover their uniqueness, their heritage, and their culture, and to teach that "black is beautiful" have all contributed to the formation of a new image of black people in the minds of white and black alike. (46) Lewis Jones writes: "The one clear feature of the new self-image of Negro youth, of whatever status, is a sense of security expressed by assuming positive and sometimes aggressive attitudes and postures." (32, p. 77) With a newly gained confidence and sense of security, young blacks no longer give the impression that they feel inferior or that they are a helpless minority. (20) They have a new sense of power and know that now they can be leaders rather than meek followers. Some black youths strive to hide feelings of inferiority by overcompensation through delinquent behavior. Others have become extremely aggressive, militant, and openly hostile. (25, 26) However, most black youths now consider segregationists to be the minority, themselves the majority that includes the federal government and white people of considerable influence. The black person no longer has to apologize for living or constantly prove his or her worth. (50, p. 78) More and more, black adolescents are accepting the fact that they are human beings of worth, with a positive identity, united with other soul brothers in proclaiming their admission into the human race and into middle class culture. (7, 41, 75)

CONTEMPORARY SEGREGATION

On May 17, 1954, the U.S. Supreme Court overruled the principle of "separate but equal" opportunity in education. In 1956 Dr. Martin Luther King, Jr., launched his passive resistance movement against the segregated bus system of Montgomery, Alabama. Although the court battles have been fought and won, there is still a considerable differential between white and black income, education, and other standards of living, and segregation continues to be a fact of life. (91) The percentage of blacks living in segregated neighborhoods has actually increased since 1960, according to a special census in fifteen cities. (109, p. 15) This is due partly to the fact that blacks continue to migrate to urban areas, especially to cities of the Northeast, where they are forced to settle in segregated slum areas.

UNEQUAL EDUCATION

In spite of the legal efforts to insure equal education for all citizens, black adolescents still do not enjoy that privilege. In terms of the total number of years of schooling, young blacks have almost caught up with whites. If only those in the twenty-five- to twenty-nine-year-old age group are considered, the educational attainment of these young nonwhites almost equals the attainment of all races together. Figure 22–2 shows the improvement between 1960 and 1977.

If quality of education is considered, however, blacks still lag far behind whites.

UNEMPLOYMENT RATES

When the unemployment rates of nonwhite and white teenagers are compared, the differences are striking. As can be seen in Figure 22–3, nonwhite teenagers have a far greater unemployment rate than their white contemporaries: 40 percent of nonwhite teenagers seeking employment in 1977 could not find jobs. Many jobless youths were wandering the streets with nothing to do.

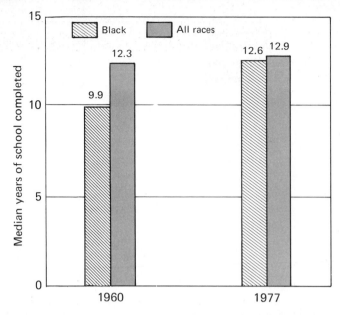

Figure 22–2. Educational attainment, blacks and all races combined, ages 25–29, 1960–1977. (From U.S. Bureau of the Census, Department of Commerce, *Statistical Abstract of the United States, 1978* [Washington, D.C.: U.S. Government Printing Office, 1978].)

INCOME

In spite of the fact that the income of both whites and blacks has been increasing, the income gap between whites and nonwhites has widened, not closed. (64) In 1947 the dollar gap between white and black income was $2,534; in 1977 it was $6,598. (104) The dollar gap continues to widen. In every occupational category, blacks are paid less than whites for the same work. Unequal income, un-

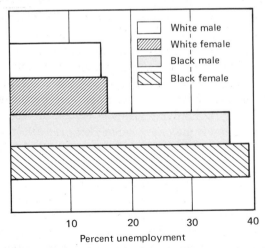

Figure 22–3. Nonwhite and white unemployment rates, ages 16–19, 1977. (From U.S. Bureau of Census, Department of Commerce, *Statistical Abstract of the United States, 1978* [Washington, D.C.: U.S. Government Printing Office, 1978].)

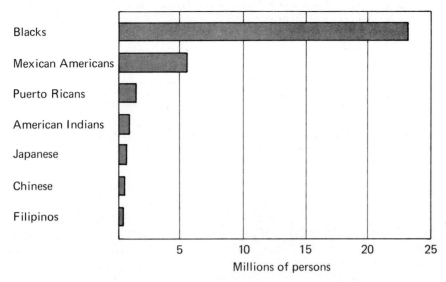

Figure 22–4.   Size of selected disadvantaged minority groups in the United States, 1973. (From U.S. Bureau of the Census, Department of Commerce, *Statistical Abstract of the United States, 1976* [Washington, D.C.: U.S. Government Printing Office, 1976].)

equal education, segregation, and discrimination are still a reality. Legally, black adolescents should have equal rights with white youths; in actuality, complete equality is still a goal to be attained. (86)

Mexican American Adolescents

Mexican Americans constitute the second largest minority group in the United States. Figure 22–4 shows the relative population of different minority groups. Adolescents fifteen to nineteen years of age constitute about 9 percent of the total Mexican American population, or over 450,000. (107) In spite of the fact that thousands of Mexicans enter the United States illegally each year, (9, 56) 90 percent of Mexican American youths (ages fifteen to nineteen) are native born; in six out of ten families both parents were born in the United States; thus, the majority of these adolescents are at least second-generation American. About 87 percent reside in the five states of Arizona, California, Colorado, New Mexico, and Texas; the vast majority live in California and Texas. (37, p. 15)

NOMENCLATURE

Various terms are used to describe Mexican Americans. The preferences vary by region, ranging from *Latin American* in Texas, *Spanish American* in New Mexico, and *Mexican* in Arizona and eastern Colorado, to *Mexican American* and *Chicano* in California. (68) A survey of Mexican American high school sophomores in border towns of southern Texas revealed a decided preference for the term *Mexican American;* about one-fourth of respondents preferred *Chicano*, especially low socioeconomic status males. (60, p. 242) One reason for this preference may be the political association of "Chicano" with working class males who have been struggling for fair economic treatment. "Chicano power" has been the slogan of this group. (101)

SEGREGATION AND HOUSING

Mexican American youths, like white youths, are primarily urbanized: 79 percent live in urban areas. (37, p. 16) Many adults and youths live in cities and go to work as migrant workers on farms. Those living in cities live in relatively segregated areas. An examination of segregation in thirty-five cities of the Southwest revealed highly segregated populations of Mexican Americans, but in no instance were they as segregated as blacks were in those cities. (59) If the degree of segregation could be represented by an index number, with 0 representing no segregation and 100 complete segregation, the index of Mexican American segregation from Anglo Americans ranges from a low of 30 in Sacramento, California, to a high of 76 in Odessa, Texas, with a nationwide mean of 54. By comparison, the mean of black segregation is 80. (59) About 75 percent of all Mexican Americans are segregated in residential ghettos called *colonias* or *barrios* (neighborhoods). (37)

Mexican Americans show unusual deprivation in their level of housing. Nearly one-third of their housing is dilapidated; the rate of overcrowding is about four times the Anglo rate. (37) In recent years Mexican Americans in such cities as Los Angeles have been able to move to areas outside the central city. (91) Increases in real income, available housing, and a decrease in discrimination practices have all contributed to the suburban migration. Nevertheless, most who have moved out live in segregated suburban neighborhoods, and the central city has become even blacker, browner, and poorer. The attainment of an integrated society is still distant. (91)

LACK OF ACCULTURATION

One result of physical segregation is social isolation, making acculturation, or the process of adopting the cultural patterns or traits of majority groups, difficult. One study of the participation of Mexican Americans in politics showed that they do not participate to any significant extent. Chicano youths have a poor record of registering to vote, more so than either Anglos or blacks. (95)

EDUCATION

Mexican American children enter school without the kind of cognitive experiences on which successful school life depends. There is a language problem for some children whose parents do not speak English at home. The restricted, authoritarian environment discourages conversational facility in English, free thinking, autonomy, and curiosity. Children are taught to be respectful but are not encouraged to show intellectual curiosity and initiative or freely to express their own ideas. Finally, little parental emphasis is placed on intellectual effort and on schooling, so children do not have much positive influence or help from home when they do go to school. Under these circumstances it is not surprising that their scholastic performance is poorer than that of Anglo American children.

Table 22–2.   Percentage of people age 25 or older with designated years of schooling.

Age	Mexican Americans	Anglo Americans
Less than five years of school	23.3	3.0
Four years of high school or more	33.6	67.0

From U.S. Bureau of the Census, Department of Commerce, *Statistical Abstract of the United States, 1978* (Washington, D.C.: U.S. Government Printing Office, 1978).

The longer Mexican Americans stay in school, the more they fall behind in scholastic achievement. The Civil Rights Commission found that almost 50 percent of Mexican American students were three years below their grade level. (105) Research in California found that 64 percent were below average in reading, compared to 27 percent of Anglos. (105) In Arizona, the average grade in reading among Mexican American students entering high school was 5.2. Seventy-two percent of ninth-grade students placed below the twenty-fifth percentile on the Academic Promise Test, which measures math and language abilities. (100)

One important factor that results in poor school work is the fact that many Mexican American children enter school bilingual. Forty-seven percent of first-graders do not speak English as well as Anglos do. (101, p. 359) As a result the overall educational level of Mexican Americans is very low. Table 22–2 shows the percentage of Mexican and Anglo Americans age twenty-five and older with less than five years of school or with four years of high school.

Another factor in the poor scholastic performance of Mexican American adolescents is the school teacher. Many Anglo teachers are hostile to Mexican American children, especially if they persist in speaking Spanish or if they speak with a considerable accent. (48) The teachers often do not understand Spanish or Mexican American culture and the sociocultural factors affecting the classroom behavior of the children.

MEXICAN AMERICAN FAMILIES

Mexican American families tend to be larger than Anglo American ones, averaging one more child per family than Anglos. (17) It has been shown that students with more siblings have less chance of realizing their occupational aspirations than do those from smaller families. Mexican American boys with four or more siblings show as much as ten points lower IQ than those with no sibling or only one.

Favoring Mexican American families is the fact that the marriages are much more stable than either those of Anglos or blacks. Figure 22–5 shows the marital stability of blacks, Anglos, and Mexican Americans. The greater stability of Mexican American families holds true even when statistical allowances are made for differences in age, age at first marriage, education, and place of residence. (24, p. 618) Apparently the traditional, paternalistic Mexican American family is highly cohesive. (62) There is some evidence, however, that the traditional emphasis on the family is beginning to decline. (17) Whereas Mexican American women formerly found their major role to be that of wives and mothers, more are now going to work outside the home. This is particularly true among many

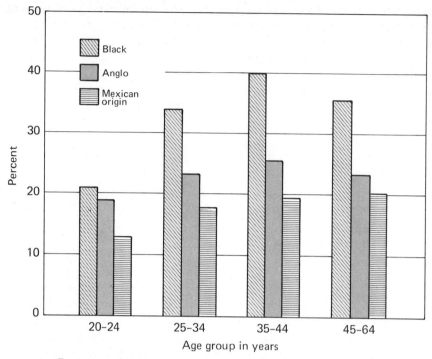

Figure 22–5.   Percentage distribution of ever-married women in the Southwest whose marriages are or have been unstable, by ethnicity and age, 1970. (Marital instability refers to women married more than once, with the first marriage terminated other than by the death of spouse, and those divorced or separated.) (Adapted from U.S. Bureau of the Census, Department of Commerce, *Public Use Sample of Basic Records from the 1970 Census, Description and Technical Documentation* [Washington, D.C.: U.S. Government Printing Office, 1972].)

college-educated wives and among those with preschool-age children. (17, p. 261) What effect these changes will have on marital stability remains to be seen.

SOCIALIZATION OF ADOLESCENTS

Mexican American parents emphasize some values that hinder the advancement of adolescents in an individualistic, highly competitive, materialistic society. (8) An emphasis on family ties and dependency, authority, honor, masculinity, living in the present, and politeness are not conducive to independence, achievement, deferred gratification, and success. For example, the older son's role is an extension of that of the father: protector, orderer, and guardian of the younger children. Excessive family dependency hinders the development of initiative and autonomy, particularly when sons are overindulged, given much social freedom but little motivation to succeed educationally and occupationally. Girls are closely supervised and taught primarily to take their place in the home. The emphasis on honor and respectful conduct leads to extraordinary courtesy and politeness. Young people are taught to show respect, obedience, and humility. (In traditional homes the answer to the parent's call is *mande usted*—"at your command.") Therefore, in school or work, adolescents are not prodded to take risks but to be careful not to bring shame upon themselves or their families. This is one reason why comparisons between Mexican American and Anglo American adolescents show that the latter are much more competitive. Mexican Americans are less concerned with personal gain and more often avoid competitive behavior. (2) Furthermore, children are not expected to defer gratification but to live in the present. Such an orientation is not conducive to upward mobility.

There is also a lack of emphasis on getting ahead by getting an education. In one study, when asked how much schooling they wanted their children to have, only 25 percent of Mexican Americans (in contrast to 50 percent of blacks and 67 percent of Anglo Americans) mentioned college. Thirty-seven percent of Mexican Americans, compared to 6 percent of the Anglo Americans, said they would be satisfied if their children received only a junior high school education. (87) The lack of independence training in the family, (1) the negative self-identity of many Mexican American youths, (107) and prejudicial treatment in the schools (98) also interfere with academic achievement.

HETEROSEXUAL RELATIONSHIPS

When the male reaches adolescence, he is expected to take an interest in females and talk and act in the sexual sphere to demonstrate his virility. There are "bad" girls whom he can exploit for sexual purposes to prove his *machismo* (manhood), and "good" girls whom he can idealize, and one of whom he can eventually marry. (71) In Mexico, every effort is made to protect girls from male advances. Chaperones are employed during the courtship process, which is formal and elaborate. (71) Dating is frowned upon, but once the family moves to America suppression of the practice is difficult. However, a matchmaker or *portador* is still called into service when male selection reaches a serious stage. Some youths in America prefer to bypass the elaborate ritual of courtship and the expenses of the wedding by eloping. (82)

The adolescent female is protected by her father and older brother; nowhere in the Western world is female chastity more venerated. At the same time, she becomes the object of attention; romantic suitors elevate her to a pedestal and submit to her "as slave to queen," as Mexican rhetoric puts it. She is adulated, sought after, and no doubt develops an overly romantic view of love and marriage. (71)

SEX EDUCATION

The importance of modesty is highly emphasized, especially for girls, who are not supposed to learn about sexual relations by either conversation or experience. Mothers do not discuss sex with daughters, nor usually even menstruation. The daughter is left to cope with the traumas of menstruation and of sex in marriage. As a result the honeymoon period and early days of marriage are upsetting, often painful experiences for them. Because of the negative, repressive attitudes they learn, wives neither care much about sex nor enjoy it as much as their husbands. (76)

Sex education for males is learned primarily from other male friends and from experience. Boys tell one another about and seek experiences with "bad" girls and prostitutes who help them learn about the physical aspects of sex. Such education is also negative and exploitative, for males learn to use females rather than to share companionship, love, and sex with them.

American Indian Adolescents

POPULATION, DISTRIBUTION, AND RELOCATION

The number of American Indians of all ages in the United States is dependent upon the definition of what constitutes an Indian. At the present time the Bureau of Indian Affairs (BIA) defines Indians as those with one-fourth or more Indian blood. The latest census figures (1970) indicate that 792,730 persons identify themselves as Indians. (73, 99) No one knows with certainty how many of these have at least one-fourth Indian ancestry. The bureau is concerned primarily with those Indians living on or near land under some form of federal supervision. In 1970 this included approximately 425,000 persons. (94) In addition to those living on or near reservations, over 300,000 have migrated off reservations. (67, p. 16) In spite of this large outflow, the number living on reservations continues to increase.

American Indians live in every state, but those under the Bureau of Indian Affairs are distributed on 52 million acres of land on reservations in twenty-six states. (103) Of the total population of Indians, 45 percent live in the West and Southwest: Arizona, New Mexico, California, and Oklahoma. Thirty-seven percent live in the northern tier: Alaska, Washington, Oregon, Utah, Nevada, Idaho, Montana, North and South Dakota, Minnesota, Wisconsin, Michigan, Illinois, and New York. Six percent live in North Carolina.

The two states with the largest Indian populations, Arizona and Oklahoma, represent two extremes in tribal representation. Arizona has the largest number of Indians, and the largest single tribe, the Navaho (estimated at 120,000 in 1973), live on the largest reservation in the United States, most of which lies within Arizona. (114, p. 138) Oklahoma, in contrast, has the largest number of tribes, about sixty. (108) This land was once the Indian Territory, to which Indians from all over the country were moved when their tribal lands were coveted by whites. Because the Indians were newcomers, living on land next to their white neighbors (who had also recently immigrated), most Oklahoma Indians lived among the general population, although there are some remote reservations in the state. In states such as New Mexico and the Dakotas the majority of the Indian population is still confined to original reservations. In other states, such as North Carolina, California, and New York, the majority either resisted movement to reservations or now live on land where government control has terminated. (67, p. 23)

Since the beginning of World War II there has been a rapid migration of Indians to urban areas. (110) In 1940 only 7.2 percent of the total Indian population was urban; in 1975, 45 percent was urban. (12) This rapid migration was partly the result of youths' leaving reservations during World War II to join the armed services or of adults' going to work in wartime factories. The government encouraged migration and offered assistance through a relocation program that sought to promote rapid integration into American life. But this relocation created many problems. Jack Forbes wrote in 1964:

To move from a rural to a highly urban environment creates tension enough—to move from a tribal society into the center of a great city must be, for many, a traumatic experience. . . . Perhaps to be truly "assimilated" every minority group must become urban slum-dwellers, sinking into the whirlpool of a great city and becoming absorbed in the mass of humanity around them. But how many private tragedies occur in the whirlpool, and how many useful lives are lost along the way? (30, p. 123)

There is considerable evidence that government efforts to relocate Indians in urban areas and to assimilate them into white society has not been successful: Indians in cities are not integrated, but are an alienated, invisible minority group. (12, p. 361) Urbanization has increased their level of income, rate of employment, quality of housing, and "perceived quality of life," (16) but it has not been a panacea for poverty, discrimination, and alienation. (12, p. 318) For example, for those Indians who already had problems with alcoholism or crime, moving to the city only increased these problems. (16) Many Indians go to the city with the promise of better job opportunities, income, medical care, housing, environment, and more recreational opportunities. (52) Sometimes friends or relatives already in the city urge them to move. It has been estimated, however, that if comparable job opportunities could be found in and around reservations, 75 percent of urban Indians would return to the reservations. (16, p. 121) The problem is twofold: lack of assimilation into the white culture, and active discrimination against Indians in both economic affairs and interpersonal relationships. (36, 112) Whites and Indians say they support assimilation, but whites will not tolerate cultural differences, and Indians want to preserve Indian ways. (12, p. 366) Indians demand equal opportunities but do not want to adopt values that might assure their ability to take advantage of such opportunities. (12, p. 368)

The federal relocation program and its effects on the Indians highlights one of the major problems of contemporary Indian youths: the problem of cultural conflict between the way of life on reservations and the way of life in urban America. This conflict will be examined in greater detail in a later section.

BIRTHRATES AND HEALTH

American Indians have the highest birthrate, the highest death rate, and the shortest life expectancy of any group in the United States. Although Indian birthrates of 32.9 per 1,000 population are almost double the 1972 national average of 17.3, (103, p. 52; 11) the infant mortality rate (32.2 deaths per 1,000 live births) is twice as high among Indians as it is for other Americans. After the first twenty-seven days of life, the death rate for Indian infants is four times that among whites. (29, p. 386) Indians are afflicted with all major diseases to a much greater degree than other Americans. Leading causes of death among American Indian infants include respiratory, digestive, infectious and parasitic diseases. (29, p. 387) Deaths from influenza and pneumonia are double the national average; the tuberculosis death rate is five times the national rate. (106) Ear infections, some of which result in loss of hearing, are the leading illnesses among Indian children, affecting 80 percent of those in Alaska; as many as one-fourth of Eskimos in some areas suffer hearing impediments. In 1968 trachoma and other eye infections afflicted over 3,600 Indians on reservations; more than half of these were under fourteen years of age. (10, p. 58)

Dental problems also are significant in the poor health of the Indian child. One recent study showed that periodontal disease was a major reason for the high rate of tooth loss among Indian children. (61) Many of these illnesses are directly related to inadequate nutrition and poor sanitary conditions in homes and communities.

Indians suffer more from hunger and malnutrition than does any other group in the United States. This is reflected in congenital malformations and stunted growth. Each year, many Indian children are admitted to hospitals as a result of severe protein deficiency from subsisting largely on maize. The clinical effects of the disease are muscular atrophy, poor appetite, diarrhea, and sometimes death. Malnutrition also results in poor concentration and attention span and a general inability to compete with other children in school. (29, p. 387) Accidents, cirrhosis of the liver (attributable to poor nutrition and excessive drinking), and homicide among Indians are nearly triple the national rate.

SUICIDE AND DELINQUENCY

Suicide is the leading cause of death among Indian youths fifteen to nineteen years old, with a rate five times the national average. (28, 65) There are, however, significant differences among different tribes, ranging from a low of 8 per 100,000 to a high of 120 per 100,000. (21, 89)

One 1972 comparison of Anglo and Indian delinquency among ninth- through twelfth-grade students attending two schools in the Wind River Reservation area in Wyoming revealed that a higher proportion of Indian youths committed a variety of offenses. (31) This was especially true of Indian females compared to their Anglo counterparts. (31, p. 196)

EMPLOYMENT AND INCOME

American Indians have a lower standard of living than any other minority group in the United States, with unemployment high and income low. It is estimated that in the general population 10 percent of families are at or below the poverty level; but approximately 75 percent of Indian families fall into this category. (23, p. 500) The average family income for the American Indian is frequently under $2,000 a year. (29) In 1970 the per capita income among Navaho was $900 per year in contrast to $3,935 among the general population. (83, 104) The unemployment rate among Navaho was 60 percent and the average level of education was five years. (66) In 1970 over half the Indian labor force was unemployed, with unemployment on some reservations running as high as 80 to 90 percent. In most Indian communities the pattern is one of bare subsistence, with the result that some of the worst slums in the United States are on Indian reservations.

EDUCATION

The record of Indian education is one of broken promises, inadequate resources, the poorest teachers, and worst yet, the use of education as a tool to destroy Indians' culture and way of life to try to make them into white people. (10, p. 27) The Bureau of Indian Affairs operates seventy-seven boarding schools (10, p. 28) because there is no public or federal school near some homes, or because some youths are "social referrals," which describes anyone from a youth with bilingual difficulties to one with emotional or delinquency problems. (42, p. 105) Altogether, over two-thirds of Indian children not in public schools attend boarding schools, living away from their homes and families. (29) In addition, the BIA operates a number of day schools located on or near the reservations. The day schools serve about 14 percent of Indians in school. In 1977, 94 percent of Indian children of school age were attending school. The BIA has sought to transfer much of the responsibility for educating Indian children to local school districts, through contracts with the states, with the result that in 1977, 72 percent of Indians in school were attending public schools with non-Indians. (10, p. 28; 104, p. 150)

Each type of school creates problems. In Alaska there are only two federal high schools; therefore, many Alaskan Indians are sent to a boarding school in Oregon; others go to school in Chilocco, Oklahoma, 6,000 miles away. Ninety-two percent of Navaho children attend boarding schools. The schools have a dropout rate of 60 percent, compared to a national average of 23 percent. (42, p. 105)

From the beginning, education was viewed as a means of waging cultural war against Indians. It was the Indians' great misfortune to be conquered by people intolerant of cultural diversity. Indians spoke a different language, looked different, had their own customs and religion. So Indian education policies were formulated to make Indians conform to "civilization," to assimilate them into white culture: in the words of a Commissioner of Indian Affairs, "to prepare him for the abolishment of tribal relations, to take his land in severalty and in the sweat of his brow and by the toil of his hands to carve out, as his white brother has done, a home for himself and his family." (10, p. 32) The efforts of whites to take Indian lands and to force white culture upon Indians is described in a modern folk ballad by Michael Murphey. (63)

People people don't you know
The Indians have got no place to go
They took old Geronimo by storm
And ripped the feathers from his uniform
Now Jesus told me and I believe it's true
The Redmen are in the sunset too
Took their land and didn't give it back
And they sent Geronimo a Cadillac.* (61)

BOARDING SCHOOLS. Once in a boarding school, many Indian children are effectively cut off from their families. Parents cannot visit often because of

* Michael Murphey, "Waking Up." Copyright © 1972 by Mystery Music, Inc. BMI. Used by permission.

great distances or impassable roads. Even when children are close, parents are discouraged from visiting; visitation is used as a reward for good behavior or denied as punishment. School officials report that parental visits are discouraged because the children often become hard to manage and run away after parents leave. From the Indians' point of view education is a forced journey to alien institutions. The Navaho refer to BIA schools as "Washingdoon bi oltka," meaning "Washington's schools." (10, p. 32, 33)

Life at boarding schools is regimented. Each hour of the day is planned according to strict schedules. Classes, meals, study periods, chores, free time, bed—the routine never varies. Frequent headcounts are taken to identify runaways. Demerits, handed out for rule breaking, are removed by performing chores or sacrificing privileges such as TV, a movie, or snacks. At the boarding high schools adolescent have few ways of developing normal heterosexual friendships for the sexes are separated most of the time. Students become rebellious and hostile, and sneak out to drink and make love. (42, p. 107) Many students seek to escape the boring life by glue, paint, and gasoline sniffing, or by chronic drunkenness. In a Northern Cheyenne boarding school of 250 students, there were twelve attempted suicides in eighteen months. (42, p. 109)

Estranged from family, regimented by an alien culture, and unable to talk to teachers (who do not know Indian dialects), Indians' academic performance is poor. For the first few years Indian children keep up with white children, then slowly fall behind between the sixth and ninth grades, and, if they don't drop out, finish high school with a 9.5 grade-level education. (42, p. 106) The average educational level for all Indians under federal supervision is five school years. One out of five Indian males has less than five years of schooling. One-third of the entire Navaho tribe are functional illiterates in English. (10, p. 27) The Cherokee of Oklahoma have an educational level 2.2 school years lower than that of the state's black population. (10, p. 27)

DAY SCHOOLS. Traditional day schools on or "near" reservations present problems also. In Utah, Indian children wake up at 4:30 A.M, walk three to four miles to the school bus, then ride sixty-five miles to school. Physical facilities in day schools are notoriously inadequate, texts and supplies are scarce and outdated, and little money is available to hire competent staff. Many teachers who come to the reservations to teach know little about the children they teach or about Indian culture (only 1 percent of reservation elementary teachers are Indian). Traditional teacher orientation and training take little account of Indian culture or of the problems a teacher encounters in teaching children who speak little or no English. (10, p. 30) Yet BIA schools conduct all classes in English.

At the secondary level the school curriculum is the standard white one: ancient history, European history, American history, geography, arithmetic. A report on education in Indian schools in Alaska says that "education which gives the Indian, Eskimo, and Aleut knowledge of—and therefore pride in—their historic and cultural heritage is nonexistent." (42, p. 106)

RECENT IMPROVEMENTS

The Indian Education Act of 1972 (known as Title IV) has resulted in some improvements in the educational situation. (13, p. 45) One study of Indian boarding schools revealed that more than half the teachers had taken one or more courses relating to Indian tribes, cultures, and history. (13) Most teachers who had done so had taken the courses since 1970. As a result several schools have started courses in Indian history, tribal governments, and Indian art and craftwork. (13, p. 44) In addition, many tribes are trying to gain control over their schools, with school boards made up of tribal Indian appointees. According to Title IV, parent committees have to be legally appointed and involved in assessing needs, program development, and evaluation. In addition, the school district is supposed to hire people from the Indian community whenever possible and to use funds only for the benefit of Indian children. (13, p. 45)

Many problems remain. School administrators want federal funds under Title IV, but many find it difficult to let Indian parent committee members participate in policy making. (19) Sometimes committee members aren't even given copies of the regulations outlining their duties. (13, p. 45) In many cases Indian youngsters are still transported great distances from home. (13, p. 44) Some tribes want to keep the boarding schools open, to enable them to send the problem students to boarding schools and keep the others on the reservations. Some students are given a choice between reform school or boarding school. Offenses run the gamut from creating disturbances to murder. (13, p. 44) In other cases children are taken out of the homes of alcoholic parents and sent to boarding schools to be taken care of. (90) These circumstances create havoc with the educational process in boarding schools.

One hopeful sign is the rise in the number of Indian young people going to college. Just a few years ago there were only 3,000 Indians in college; today there are 38,000. (104, p. 163) In 1968 the Sacramento, California, area office had higher-education scholarship funds for only 20 students; now it has enough for 8,000. Previously, Indians were given only vocational education; now many are receiving higher education in the professions. (13, p. 45) Nationwide, increasing numbers of Indians have acquired Master's degrees and a few have earned their doctorates. (70, p. 31)

CULTURAL CONFLICT

One of the most difficult problems Indian youths face is the problem of cultural conflict, created largely by attitudes toward Indians taught in the schools and reflected in the larger society. Most Indian children are not only deliberately kept ignorant of their culture, history, and heritage, but are also taught to be ashamed of it. School texts that deal with Indian history are appallingly inadequate. A history text used in California gives this description of Indians:

The Indians who lived in the Stanislaus area were known as the "Diggers," although they were the Walla tribe. They were stupid and lazy and it is said they were given their name because of their habit of digging in the earth. (93)

The late Senator Robert F. Kennedy related this experience:

We were in Idaho the other day and I was asking the superintendent of schools, where they had 80 percent Indian children, whether they taught anything about Indian history or Indian culture. The tribe was a very famous tribe, the Shoshone, which had a considerable history, and he said, "There isn't any history to this tribe. . . ." So I asked him if there were any books in the library where all these children could go and read about Indian history, and he said, "Yes," and we went to the library. There was only one book and the book was entitled, "Captive of the Delawares." It showed a white child being scalped by an Indian. (10, p. 35)

A recent study compared the image of Indians in novels of the 1960s and novels of the 1930s to ascertain whether there had been any change in Indian stereotypes. (102) Most of the more recent novels as well as the older ones presented Indian life as it existed in the past; Indian characters wore traditional dress and body decoration, lived in primitive dwellings, and used weapons of an earlier period. The Indian economy was presented as basically hunting and fishing. Five of the thirteen recent novels presented the Indians as "dirty" or "smelly." Most of the recent and old novels presented the contradictory image of the Indian as both the dirty, drunken, cruel and warring savage and the glorified, noble, but naive savage. (102, p. 34) The points were made that whites disrupted the group life patterns of Indians, who had to make difficult adjustments, and that many Indians were never given the opportunity to adjust because they were exterminated. (102, p. 34) The novels of the earlier period said nothing about contemporary problems of Indian adjustment. Indian leaders of today demand that their people be accurately described. Most Indian males are pictured as cruel and savage, and the beautiful Indian princess is all that white men desire. (102, p. 35) Stereotypes are being overcome slowly.

Indians are making a determined effort to retain and to teach their cultural values to their young people. Most clothing styles have changed until an almost pan-Indian costume has evolved. Indian women of the Southwest have retained the brightly colored Spanish and Mexican shawls. The men wear standard cowboy costumes. But there has been an effort to retain native garb, and in recent years modern fashion has been influenced greatly by Indian apparel, especially among youths who have adopted Indian headbands, fringed jackets, long dresses, beads, and moccasins. Indian crafts are still being practiced, partly as a source of income. Split basketry is popular in the North, as are weaving, pottery, and jewelry making in the Southwest. (23, p. 500) In areas where large numbers of Indians are concentrated, Indian dances are still performed to native music.

Religion has always been very important to American Indians, although its practice has clashed with white ways for a long time and has partly blocked Indian assimilation into American society. Many practices were banned when the federal government conducted its sixty-year (1870–1930) program of enforced enculturation. (99) However, some traditional religious practices are still found in more remote areas of large concentrations of Indians. The peyote religion, known as the Native American Church, with a membership of 500,000, blends equal parts of Christian and Indian elements. This group has government permission to use peyote, a mild hallucinogen, as part of their religious practice.

Puberty rites or equivalent rites of passage are still practiced by some tribes and form a part of religious rituals. When the federal government banned all Indian assemblies during the years 1870–1930, except between July 1 and July 4, the Apache changed the individual rite that marked a girl's first menstruation to a group rite in which all girls who had come of age during the year participated. The mandatory rite marks a transition in status from childhood to adulthood and makes her eligible for marriage. Navaho boys and girls go through a religious ceremony at about the time of appearance of secondary sex characteristics. Through this ceremony they are introduced to full participation in ceremonial life. In addition, females go through a four-day ritual at the time of first and second menstruation, after which they attain the status of women. (23)

Indian values are at variance with the larger American culture. (85) The Indian is present oriented, concerned with decisions about the concrete present and not concerned about the future or with time; white people are future oriented, concerned about time and planning ahead. Indians see human life as being in harmony with nature; whites seek conquest over nature. Indian life is group oriented, emphasizing cooperation. White people emphasize individualism and competition, which is one reason Indians are not competitive in white society and do not easily assume positions of leadership. Family life, especially the extended family, is still important to Indians, which is why many youths prefer going back home to the reservation to be with the family, even after receiving their education in white schools. Most Indians teach their children not to show emotions, but to maintain a rather severe reserve. The ability to endure pain, hardship, hunger, and frustration without external discomfort is emphasized, as are bravery and courage. Many Indians have a fear of the world as dangerous; some even fear witchcraft. Many are fatalists and feel powerless over their situation. There also seems to be an emphasis on practical jokes that is nearly everywhere highly channelized institutionally. (85) (The author remembers spending July 4 on a Mescalero Indian reservation in New Mexico, where Indian boys set off large firecrackers under his feet; the boys thought it was quite a joke.) The tendency may be a throwback to the days when white men treated the Indians as buffoons.

As a result of conflicting cultures, Indian youths today are faced with a dilemma: whether to accommodate themselves to the white world and learn to compete in it or to retain traditional customs and values and live apart from the white world. Over 150 years of determined government effort has not succeeded in destroying Indian culture and society. Yet the longer Indian youths are isolated, the greater their chances are of remaining America's most deprived minority. Certainly one answer is to help both Indians and whites to appreciate and understand the values of Indian culture and the importance of preserving a rich heritage. The Indian adolescent who is proud of being Indian, as many are, and who is respected by white society, can contribute richly to a Western world that prides itself on being the world's melting pot. America's original inhabitants have never been accepted as an important segment of American life. As a consequence, most contemporary Indian youths suffer psychological strain under the impact of cultural change. Progress has been slow because they are caught between two cultures and immobilized from going in either direction easily. (85) The following poem was written by Marie Ann Begay, a Navaho, while completing her senior year at Del Norte High School in Albuquerque, New Mexico.

THOUGHTS TO PONDER

Sitting here
A thought came into my mind:
Living in two worlds—

That seems hard sometimes,
Especially if you are an Indian.
You feel like two persons
Trying to struggle for something
That you don't care about at times.

I ask myself what I am doing here,
But all odds add up to my own benefits
And a look at the new side.
Even though I should be
Riding or running in the open countryside
With the fresh clean air racing along with me,
Seeing the rain fall in the distance
And thunder that shakes the earth—

But here I am sitting trying to get
What I think is good for an Indian
Who's trying to make it
In the White Men's world and his own.

Conclusions

One must conclude from the personal, social, economic, and political injustices described in this chapter that the problems of ethnic minorities in the United States
are enormous and lend themselves to no easy solution or quick answers.

This chapter has described four groups of adolescents: (1) those who are of low socioeconomic status, whose distinctive characteristic is that they are both poor and
culturally deprived (this includes a wide variety of ethnic groups); (2) those who
are black, whose identity lies in the color of their skin; (3) those who are of
Mexican American origin; and (4) those who are American Indians. The last two
groups may be distinguished by their national origins. These four groups have
much in common as well as many differences.

All four groups are culturally different, meaning different from middle class Americans.
Of the four groups, the black adolescents are less different than any of the others.
Many blacks are middle class and have adopted middle class values, mores, customs, habits, and ways of living. Blacks also have adopted and assimilated white
culture more than most minority groups in the United States. Unfortunately, when
black people were wrenched from their tribal settings, when their family life and
structure were consciously destroyed, when they were forced to work and live in
close proximity to whites, they lost much of the culture that gave them their identities and came to be regarded as different only on the basis of skin color. Because
of this difference, which led to discrimination, they were forced to accept the lower
class status that is the important key to cultural differences. Poor people, black
or white, have not necessarily rejected middle class values; they just cannot afford
them, and therefore remain different and isolated.

Blacks have made far more social and economic advances than any of the other groups,
partly because they are not as culturally segregated. Blacks are more segregated
in housing than Mexican Americans (though not as much as Indians on the reservations), but even in their own neighborhoods, white culture has largely filled the
vacuum left when black culture was destroyed. Those blacks who remain culturally
different do so largely because of poverty or the desire to regain their cultural
identity.

Groups like the Mexican Americans and American Indians have not been assimilated into the culture around them. These groups more often strive to maintain their cultural identity, which is more intact than blacks' and which is treasured even when their lot improves economically. All minority groups are gradually assimilated into the cultural milieu about them, but some, like American Indians, resist the trend more than others.

The four groups are distinguishable by the fact that they occupy a lower socioeconomic status than members of the general population. They have less formal education, lower incomes, poorer health and medical care, less adequate housing, larger families, and higher birth and death rates than does the general population. Of the three ethnic groups, American Indians are the most neglected, followed by Mexican Americans, with blacks far better off than either of these.

The adolescents of all of these groups have many special problems because they are culturally deprived and culturally different. Most of their problems stem from the fact that the dominant culture in which they live will not tolerate cultural differences and diversity. White, middle class society penalizes those who are different by discriminating against them, ostracizing, rejecting, and segregating them. Under such circumstances it becomes difficult for the culturally different adolescent to find an acceptable identity, apart from a negative one or one that is subcultural. The society that hates the adolescents who are different perpetuates those differences by rejecting the efforts of the different people to become a part of the larger world in which they live.

Panel Discussion

Ask several students from minority groups to be on a panel to discuss some of the problems with which they have been confronted while growing up. Emphasize several or more of the following categories: relationships with those of other races or ethnic origins, evidences of prejudices and discrimination, educational opportunities, employment opportunities for parents, family relationships, parental philosophies, economic problems and opportunities, advantages and disadvantages of being a member of that minority group, dating and courtship customs, sex education, ideas about marriage, or religious views and practices. Invite class members to ask questions of the panel to bring out other topics of interest.

Bibliography

1. Anderson, J. G. "Family Socialization and Educational Achievement in Two Cultures: Mexican-American and Anglo-American." *Sociometry* 39 (1976): 209–222.

2. Avellar, J., and Kagan, S. "Development of Competitive Behaviors in Anglo-American and Mexican-American Children." *Psychological Reports* 39 (1976): 191–198.

3. Baughman, E. E. *Black Americans: A Psychological Analysis.* New York: Academic Press, 1971.

4. Bell, R. R. "The One-Parent Mother in the Negro Lower Class." Paper presented at the meeting of the Eastern Sociological Society, New York, 1965.

5. Birch, H. G., and Gussow, J. D. *Disadvantaged Children: Health, Nutrition, and School Failure.* New York: Grune and Stratton, 1970.

6. Blackbourn, J. M., and Summerlin, C. G. "Need Occurrence in Disadvantaged and Non-Disadvantaged." *Adolescence* 9 (1974): 233–236.

7. Bridgete, R. E. *Self-Esteem in Negro and White Southern Adolescents.* Ph.D. dissertation, University of North Carolina, 1970.

8. Brody, E. B. *Minority Group Adolescents in the United States.* Baltimore: Williams & Wilkins, 1968.

9. Bustamante, J. "Structural and Ideological Conditions of the Mexican Undocumented Immigration to the United States." *American Behavioral Scientist* 19 (1976): 364–376.

10. Cahn, E. S., ed. *Our Brother's Keeper: The Indian in White America.* New York: World Publishing Co., 1969.

11. Campbell, E. Q., and Coleman, J. S. "Inequalities in Educational Opportunities in the United States." Paper presented to the American Sociological Association, August 31, 1966.

12. Chadwick, B. A., and Stauss, J. H. "The Assimilation of American Indians into Urban Society: The Seattle Case." *Human Organization* 34 (1975): 359–369.

13. Chavers, D. "New Directions in Indian Education." *Indian Historian* 4 (1975): 43–46.

14. Chilman, C. S. "Child Rearing and Family Relationship Patterns of the Very Poor." *Welfare Review* (1965): 3, 9–19.

15. ———. *Growing Up Poor.* U.S. Department of Health, Education, and Welfare. Social and Rehabilitation Service. Publication No. 109. Washington, D.C.: U.S. Government Printing Office, 1969.

16. Clinton, L. et al. "Urban Relocation Reconsidered: Antecedents of Employment among Indian Males." *Rural Sociology* 40 (1975): 117–133.

17. Cooney, R. S. "Changing Labor Force Participation of Mexican American Wives: A Comparison with Anglos and Blacks." *Social Science Quarterly* 56 (1975): 252–261.

18. Cressey, D. R., and Ward, D. A. *Delinquency, Crime, and Social Process.* New York: Harper and Row, 1969.

19. DeMontigny, L. H. "The Bureaucratic Game and a Proposed Indian Play." *Indian Historian* 8 (1975): 25–30.

20. Deutsch, M. et al., eds. *Social Class, Race, and Psychological Development.* New York: Holt, Rinehart and Winston, 1968.

21. Dizmang, L. H. et al. "Adolescent Suicide at an Indian Reservation." *American Journal of Orthopsychiatry* 44 (1974): 43–49.

22. Douvan, E., and Adelson, J. *The Adolescent Experience.* New York: John Wiley and Sons, 1966.

23. Driver, H. E. *Indians of North America.* 2d ed. Chicago: University of Chicago Press, 1970.

24. Eberstein, I. W., and Frisbie, W. P. "Differences in Marital Instability among Mexican Americans, Blacks, and Anglos: 1960 and 1970." *Social Problems* 23 (1976): 609–621.

25. Elder, G. H., Jr. "Socialization and Ascent in a Racial Minority." *Youth Society* (1970): 74–109.

26. ———. "Intergroup Attitudes and Social Ascent among Negro Boys." *American Journal of Sociology* 76 (1971): 673–697.

27. *Equality of Educational Opportunity.* Catalog No. FS 5.238:38001. Washington, D.C.: U.S. Government Printing Office, 1966.

28. Farris, C. E. "A White House Conference on the American Indian." *Social Work* 18 (1973): 80–86.

29. Farris, C. E., and Farris, L. S. "Indian Children: The Struggle for Survival." *Social Work* 21 (1976): 386–389.

30. Forbes, J. D., ed. *The Indian in America's Past.* Englewood Cliffs, N.J.: Prentice-Hall, 1964.

31. Forslund, M. A., and Cranston, V. A. "A Self-Report Comparison of Indian and Anglo Delinquency in Wyoming." *Criminology* 13 (1975): 193–198.

32. Frazier, E. F. *Black Bourgeoisie.* New York: Crowell-Collier Publishing Co., 1962.

33. Gecas, V., and Nye, F. I. "Sex and Class Differences in Parent-Child Interaction: A Test of Kahn's Hypothesis." *Journal of Marriage and the Family* 36 (1974): 742–749.

34. Glick, P. C., and Norton, A. J. "Frequency, Duration, and Probability of Marriage and Divorce." *Journal of Marriage and the Family* 33 (1971): 307–317.

35. Gold, M. *Delinquent Behavior in an American City.* Monterey, Calif.: Brooks/Cole Publishing Co., 1970.

36. Graves, T. D. "The Personal Adjustment of Navaho Indian Migrants to Denver, Colorado." *American Anthropologist* 72 (1970): 35–54.

37. Grebler, L. et al. *The Mexican-American People.* New York: Free Press, 1970.

38. Green, M., and Beall, P. "Paternal Deprivation: A Disturbance in Fathering." *Pediatrics* 30 (1962): 91–99.

39. Harper, J., and Collins, J. K. "A Different Survey of the Problems of Privileged and Underprivileged Adolescents." *Journal of Youth and Adolescence* 4 (1975): 349–358.

40. Hauser, S. T. *Black and White Identity Formation: Studies in the Psychosocial Development of Lower Socioeconomic Class Adolescent Boys.* New York: John Wiley and Sons, 1971.

41. Healey, G. W., and BeBlassie, R. R. "A Comparison of Negro, Anglo, and Spanish-American Adolescents' Self Concepts." *Adolescence* 9 (1974): 15–24.

42. Henninger, D., and Esposito, N. "Indian Schools." In *America's Other Youth: Growing Up Poor.* Edited by D. Gottlieb and A. L. Heinsohn. Englewood Cliffs, N.J.: Prentice-Hall, 1971, pp. 105–110.

43. Herzog, E. *About the Poor.* U.S. Department of Health, Education and Welfare. Children's Bureau. Publication No. 14. Washington, D.C.: U.S. Government Printing Office, 1966.

44. Hill, C., and Spector, M. "Natality and Mortality of American Indians Compared with U.S. Whites and Non-Whites." *Health Services and Mental Health Administration Reports* 68 (1974).

45. "How Many Live in Real Want? Official Answers under Fire." *U.S. News & World Report,* 8 November 1976, pp. 55–58.

46. Hraba, J., and Grant, G. "Black Is Beautiful: A Reexamination of Racial Preference and Identification." *Journal of Personal and Social Psychology* 16 (1970): 398–402.

47. Irelan, L. M., ed. *Low-Income Life Styles.* U.S. Department of Health, Education and Welfare. Publication No. 14. Washington D.C.: U.S. Government Printing Office, 1966.

48. Jackson, R. M., and Cosca, L. R. "Methods and Results of an Every-Child Program for the Early Identification of Developmental Defects." *Psychology in the Schools* 10 (1973): 421–426.

49. James, H. *Children in Trouble: A National Scandal.* New York: Pocket Books, 1971.

50. Jones, L. W. "The New World View of Negro Youth." In *Problems of Youth: Transition to Adulthood in a Changing World.* Edited by M. Sherif and C. W. Sherif. Chicago: Aldine, 1965, pp. 65–88.

51. Kamii, K. C., and Radin, N. L. "Class Differences in the Socialization Practices of Negro Mothers." *Journal of Marriage and the Family* 29 (1967): 302–310.

52. Kerri, J. N. "Brief Communications." *Human Organization* 35 (1976): 215–220.

53. Komarovsky, M. *Blue-Collar Marriage.* New York: Random House, 1964.

54. Luchterhand, E., and Weller, L. "Effects of Class, Race, and Educational Status on Patterns of Aggression of Lower-Class Youth." *Journal of Youth and Adolescence* 5 (1976): 59–71.

55. Maldonado, D., Jr. "Ethnic Self-Identity and Self-Understanding." *Social Casework* 56 (1975): 618–622.

56. Martinez, V. S. "Illegal Immigration and the Labor Force." *American Behavioral Scientist* 19 (1976): 335–350.

57. McCord, J. et al. "Some Effects of Paternal Absence on Male Children." *Journal of Abnormal and Social Psychology* 64 (1962): 361–367.

58. McKinley, D. *Social Class and Family Life.* London: Collier-McMillan, 1964.

59. Mexican-American Study Project. Progress Report No. 1. Los Angeles: University of California, Graduate School of Business Administration, 1965, p. 3.

60. Miller, M. V. "Mexican Americans, Chicanos, and Others: Ethnic Self-Identification and Selected Social Attributes, Rural Texas Youth." *Rural Sociology* 41 (1976): 234–247.

61. Moore, W. et al. *Nutrition, Growth and Development of North American Indian Children.* Washington, D.C.: U.S. Government Printing Office, 1972.

62. Murillo, N. "The Mexican American Family." In Wagner, N. W., and Hand, M. J., eds. *Chicanos: Social and Psychological Perspectives.* St. Louis, Missouri: C. V. Mosby Co., 1971.

63. Murphey, Michael. "Geronimo's Cadillac." Copyright 1972 by Mystery Music, Inc. BMI.

64. NAACP Legal Defense Fund. *Jobs for Blacks.* New York, 1971.

65. National Institute of Mental Health. *Suicide, Homicide, and Alcoholism among American Indians: Guidelines for Help.* Washington, D.C.: U.S. Government Printing Office, 1973.

66. Navaho Tribe. *The Navaho 10 Year Plan.* McCleod Printing Co., 1972.

67. Neils, E. M. *Reservation to City.* Chicago: University of Chicago, Department of Geography Research Paper No. 131, 1971.

68. Nostrand, R. L. " 'Mexican American' and 'Chicano': Emerging Terms for a People Coming of Age." *Pacific Historical Review* (1973): 389–406.

69. Passel, J. S. "Provisional Evaluation of the 1970 Census Count of American Indians." *Demography* 12 (1976): 397–409.

70. Patterson, A. "Among Arizona Indians . . . Fewer Red Apples." *Indian Historian* 8 (1975): 26–31.

71. Penalosa, F. "Mexican Family Roles." *Journal of Marriage and the Family* 30 (1968): 680–689.

72. "Poverty-Level Children Show Drop from 1970." *Portland* (Me.) *Press Herald,* 1 March 1977.

73. Preble, E. "The Puerto Rican-American Teenager in New York City." In *Minority Group Adolescents in The United States.* Edited by E. B. Brody. Baltimore: Williams & Wilkins, 1968.

74. Propper, A. M. "The Relationship

of Maternal Employment to Adolescent Roles, Activities, and Parental Relationships." *Journal of Marriage and the Family* 34 (1972): 417–421.

75. Proshansky, H., and Newton, P. "The Nature and Meaning of Negro Self-Identity." In *Social Class, Race, and Psychological Development.* Edited by M. Deutsch et al. New York: Holt, Rinehart and Winston, 1968.

76. Rainwater, L. "Marital Sexuality in Four Cultures of Poverty." *Journal of Marriage and the Family* 26 (1964): 457–466.

77. Reiss, I. *The Family System in America.* New York: Holt, Rinehart and Winston, 1971.

78. Riesman, F. et al., eds. *Mental Health of the Poor.* London: Free Press of Glencoe, 1964, pp. 16–36.

79. Riessman, F. *The Culturally Deprived Child.* New York: Harper and Row, 1962.

80. Rodman, H. et al. "Lower-Class Attitudes toward 'Deviant' Family Patterns: A Cross-Cultural Study." *Journal of Marriage and the Family* 31 (1969): 315–321.

81. Rosen, B. C. "Social Class and the Child's Perception of the Parent." *Child Development* 25 (1964): 1147–1153.

82. Rubel, A. J. *Across The Tracks: Mexican-Americans in a Texas City.* Austin: University of Texas Press, 1966, pp. 72ff.

83. Ruffing, L. T. "Navajo Economic Development Subject to Cultural Constraints." *Economic Development and Cultural Change* 24 (1976): 611–621.

84. Schneider, J. "Treatment of the Socially Deprived Adolescent." *Adolescence* 7 (1972): 211–220.

85. Sebald, H. *Adolescence: A Sociological Analysis.* New York: Appleton-Century-Crofts, 1968.

86. Shannon, L. W. "False Assumptions about the Determinants of Mexican-American and Negro Economic Absorption." *Sociological Quarterly* 16 (1975): 3–15.

87. Shannon, L. W., and Krass, E. M. "The Economic Absorption and Cultural Integration of Immigrant Mexican-American and Negro Workers." Iowa City: State University of Iowa, Department of Sociology and Anthropology, 1964, pp. 240–244.

88. Shoemaker, L. P. *Parent and Family Life Education for Low-Income Families.* U.S. Department of Health, Education and Welfare. Children's Bureau. Washington, D.C.: U.S. Government Printing Office, 1965.

89. Shore, J. H. "American Indian Suicide: Fact and Fantasy." *Psychiatry* 38 (1975): 86–91.

90. Shore, J. H., and Nicholls, W. M. "Indian Children and Tribal Group Homes: New Interpretations of the Whipper Man." *American Journal of Psychiatry* 132 (1975): 454–456.

91. Siembieda, W. J. "Suburbanization of Ethnics of Color." *Annals of the American Academy of Political and Social Science* 422 (1975): 118–128.

92. Staples, R. "Black Policy and the Changing Status of Black Families." *Family Coordinator* 22 (1973): 345–351.

93. Statement by Rupert Costo. "Indian Education Subcommittee Hearings." 90th Congress, 1st and 2d sess. 4 January 1968, p. 242.

94. Steiner, Stan. *The New Indians.* New York: Harper and Row, 1968.

95. Stevens, A. J. "The Acquisition of Participatory Norms: The Case of Japanese and Mexican American Children in a Suburban Environment." *Western Political Quarterly* 28 (1975): 281–295.

96. Stevens, S. "The 'Rat Packs' of New York," *New York Times,* 28 November 1971, pp. 29ff.

97. Stinette, N., and Walters, J. "Parent-Peer Orientation of Adolescents from Low-Income Families." *Journal of Home Economics* 59 (1967): 37–40.

98. Teske, R. H. C., Jr., and Nelson, B. H. "An Analysis of Different Assimilation Rates among Middle-Class Mexican Americans." *Sociological Quarterly* 17 (1976): 218–235.

99. "The Denial of Indian Civil and Religious Rights." *Indian Historian* 8 (1975): 43–46.

100. Thornburg, H. D. *An Investigation of Attitudes among Potential Dropouts from Minority Groups During Their Freshman Year in High School: Final Report.* San Francisco: U.S. Office of Education, 1971.

101. Thornburg, H. D., and Grinder, R. E. "Children of Aztlan: The Mexican-American Experiment." In *Youth: The Seventy-fourth Yearbook of the National Society for the Study of Education* Part I. Edited by R. J. Havighurst and P. H. Dreyer. Chicago: University of Chicago Press, 1975.

102. Troy, A. "The Indian in Adolescent Novels." *Indian Historian* 8 (1975): 32–35.

103. U.S. Bureau of the Census, Department of Commerce. *Census of Population, 1970: American Indians.* Washington, D.C.: U.S. Government Printing Office, 1973.

104. ———. *Statistical Abstract of the United States, 1976.* Washington, D.C.: U.S. Government Printing Office, 1976.

105. U.S. Commission on Civil Rights. *The Excluded Student: Educational Practices*

Affecting Mexican Americans in the Southwest. Report 3. Washington, D.C.

106. U.S. Department of Health, Education and Welfare. *Justification of Appropriation Estimates for Committee on Appropriations, Fiscal Year 1970.* Washington, D.C.: U.S. Government Printing Office, p. 3.

107. *Juvenile Court Statistics 1970.* Washington, D.C.: National Center for Social Statistics, U.S. Department of Health, Education and Welfare, 1972.

108. U.S. Department of the Interior. Bureau of Indian Affairs. *Indians of Oklahoma.* Washington, D.C.: U.S. Government Printing Office, 1965.

109. U.S. Department of Labor. Bureau of Labor Statistics. *Black Americans: A Chartbook.* Bulletin No. 1699. Washington, D.C.: U.S. Government Printing Office, 1971.

110. Waddell, J. O., and Watson, O. M., eds. *The American Indian in Urban Society.* Boston: Little, Brown and Co., 1971.

111. Wagner, H. "Attitudes toward and of Disadvantaged Students." *Adolescence* 7 (1972): 435–446.

112. Walker, D. E., Jr. *The Emergent Native Americans.* Boston: Little, Brown and Co., 1972.

113. *World Book Encyclopedia.* Vol. 1. s.v. "Alaska/Education." 1974.

114. *World Book Encyclopedia.* Vol. 10. s.v. "Indian American." 1973.

115. Wright, R. "The Ethics of Living Jim Crow." *American Stuff.* New York: Harper and Row, 1937.

Author Index

Subject Index